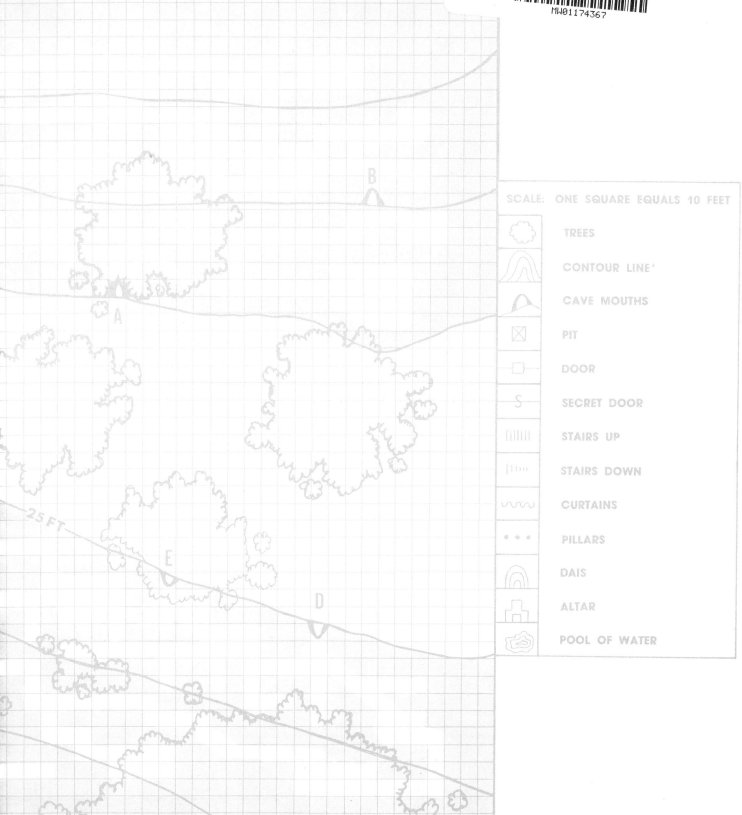

SCALE: ONE SQUARE EQUALS 10 FEET

🌲	TREES
⌒	CONTOUR LINE·
⌂	CAVE MOUTHS
⊠	PIT
☐	DOOR
S	SECRET DOOR
⦚⦚⦚	STAIRS UP
⦚⦚⦚	STAIRS DOWN
∿∿∿	CURTAINS
· · ·	PILLARS
⌂	DAIS
⛪	ALTAR
🌀	POOL OF WATER

25 FT

D&D®
INTO THE BORDERLANDS

A FIFTH EDITION CONVERSION & CLASSIC HOMAGE

B1: IN SEARCH OF THE UNKNOWN
B2: THE KEEP ON THE BORDERLANDS

Conversion by Chris Doyle and Tim Wadzinski

INTO THE BORDERLANDS

Full credits for the original editions of B1: In Search of the Unknown and B2: The Keep on the Borderlands can be found in their respective sections of this book, where they are scanned verbatim from prior printings. The credits that follow are for the 5E portion of this work.

Original Writers	Gary Gygax and Mike Carr
5E Conversion Design and Writing	Chris Doyle
5E Edition Editing and Additional Support	Tim Wadzinski
Additional Writing	Luke Gygax, Michael Curtis, Mike Mearls, Alex Kammer, Brendan J. LaSalle, Harley Stroh, Jim Wampler
5E Edition Playtesters	Alec Doyle, Lisa Doyle, Devin McCullen
Additional Research	David Friant
Cover Design	Lester B. Portly
Cover Art	Jim Roslof (front), Darlene (back)
Interior Layout	Jamie Wallis
Interior Art Direction	Jeremy Mohler
Interior Art	Ger Curti, Dean Kotz, Aaron Palsmeier, Chris Yarbrough
Cartography	Keith Curtis
Scans and Restoration	Steve Crompton
Publisher	Joseph Goodman

VISIT US ONLINE AT: WWW.GOODMAN-GAMES.COM

TABLE OF CONTENTS

Foreword

The Adventure that Thousands of Gamers Shared... Including Me

by Luke Gygax

You, bold reader, hold in your hands a seminal work that shaped the way Dungeons & Dragons was played in its heyday. *The Keep on the Borderlands* was included in the Basic D&D boxed set in the early 1980s and was the beginning module for the vast majority of new DMs and players at that time. Perhaps you were one of those young people back then and holding this module evokes many fond memories of your nascence as a gamer. However, if this is your first exposure to *The Keep on the Borderlands*, you are in for some old school flavored fun. It is one of those few modules, along with the "G" (*Against the Giants*), "A" (Slave Lords), and "D" (Drow) series, that was part of the common fabric of D&D players throughout the 1980s. Even amongst those classic modules I see *The Keep on the Borderlands* in a league of its own. *The Keep on the Borderlands* was designed as a how-to manual for the newly initiated D&D player who had only played (or perhaps just read the rules) and wanted to start their own campaign. It was the cipher that translated the myriad of rules, charts, and tables into a clear example of what an actual game of D&D entailed. This module fashioned the beginnings of tens of thousands of campaigns and set the mold for the classic D&D gaming experience. As a matter of fact, B2 was the module that I used to run my first campaign at the tender age of 9 years old.

My family lived in a large colonial style house on Foxhollow Road not too far from the village of Clinton, Wisconsin, back then. There were several families with children ranging from elementary to high school and I had a good group of friends with whom to ride dirt bikes, swim, fight BB gun wars, play cops and robbers, have giant army men battles (with fire crackers around the 4th of July), and other typical activities for boys in rural Mid-America in the '80s. In the summer we had ample time on our hands, like tens of thousands of other kids at that time, and we decided to play D&D.

It was the summer of 1980 when I gathered together a group of boys and my older sister, Cindy, to play Dungeons & Dragons. I wasn't too clear on all the rules since I was using my AD&D rule books, but that wasn't a hindrance. We rolled up characters and I read the background to them about the forces of Chaos pressing in on the valiant defenders of The Realm, and how the Keep is a bulwark between the forces of weal and the vile creatures that wish to destroy civilization. I recall rolling on the "Rumors" table for information as they talked to the barkeep after buying him a honey mead. They found out that "Bree-yark" is goblin for "we surrender," which led to great fun in the Caves of Chaos. I remember my excitement as they walked into the Orc Lair with the watcher cleverly spying on them before alerting his brethren to the intruders.

I loved the unpredictable and fantastic, especially as a child. So I gave the party a *wand of wonder* since there were only four in the group. That was a source of many outlandish and funny situations.

From stinking clouds billowing forth to engulf the entire battle to a shower of gems pummeling kobolds to death, the wand rarely failed to add to the adventure. The look of surprise on their faces when a rhinoceros appeared in a 10-foot-wide hallway facing their direction was priceless... "Run away!" There are many memories that I could share and I imagine that they are similar to those experienced by others fortunate enough to have delved into the Caves of Chaos in the 1980s.

Being the son of Gary Gygax, you would think that my experience as a gamer was atypical from that of almost anyone else, to the point of being unique. However, I believe that it was largely the same as that of every other boy picking up B2 and trying their hand at DMing. You are probably thinking to yourself, "How can that possibly be, Luke? Your Dad created the game and wrote that module! How can you have shared a similar experience?"

Before writing this foreword I reviewed the original. Holding it in my hands summoned old memories to the forefront of my mind. The colorful slipcover art by Jim Roslof with the baboon-faced hobgoblins battling a band of adventurers, the black and white drawing on the front of the booklet with the owl bear, the cramped text made even more efficient with the use of abbreviations for stats, and of course the light blue and white map on the inside of the cover. I realized as I read through the text it was like listening to my Dad talking about D&D or even DMing. This module feels very familiar to me because this is essentially how we played together. The tips on being an effective DM, the importance of mapping (and how the DM shouldn't correct mistakes!), bartering for goods, lots of pole arms, talking to the barkeep and patrons to gather information, and of course the wolf in sheep's clothing which I won't elaborate on lest I give too much away. What I learned by observation and play, my father communicated to so many others in writing through this module. At the time he wrote this material it was fresh and new. However, as it became the template for so many campaigns, the once-new concepts became trope. Decades have passed and what was old is new again! And I take great pleasure at the thought of novice and veteran gamers alike experiencing *The Keep on the Borderlands* anew. So pack up your leather backpack with iron rations, flasks of oil, and a tinderbox, secure your longsword about your waist and grab your 10-foot pole. Adventure awaits!

Luke Gygax is one of Gary Gygax's children and was raised at the gaming table. He is the author of several fantasy adventure modules and the primary force behind Gary Con, an annual convention that honors the life and works of his father, Gary Gygax. Luke is currently a major in the California Army National Guard, proud father, and husband.

Of Keeps, Borderlands, and Searches of the Unknown

by Mike Mearls

I have a long and complex relationship with *The Keep on the Borderlands*. It was the first D&D adventure I read, though it would be years before I ran it. Its presence in every Basic Set at the time meant every D&D fan in the area had access to it.

The Keep and its little slice of a world set my mind on fire. I had never thought to give such structure and organization to the imaginary people, places, and things in my young mind. The world it revealed hinted at great evils clashing with dauntless heroes. The Caves of Chaos crawled with strange monsters. The ogre was a mercenary who could be bought off. The minotaur was so ferocious that the other monsters feared it. Looming above them all was a sinister temple of evil, filled with undead and foul villains.

The Keep and its environs were no less captivating to my young eyes. It was an entire world captured within the tight walls of a small fortress. The seemingly friendly priest who would betray the party showed that the forces of evil were active in seeking to undermine the realm. The castellan would sponsor those adventurers who earned his trust, a sensible position given that chaos could lurk in the unlikeliest places. The myriad accounting of its defenders, supplies, and tactics showed that invasion from the Caves was a constant threat.

The Keep on the Borderlands has its flaws. The Keep's inhabitants lack names. Having so many hostile monster groups live in close proximity strains credibility. The Caves of Chaos are presented as a mysterious location, yet they are a short stroll from the Keep. As I grew older, the sense of wonder the Keep evoked faded into a jaded realization that the adventure was at best a thin, mindless dungeon crawl. At worst, it might have turned away people who otherwise would have taken up the RPG hobby.

Put down your pitchforks. There's a reason that statement comes in the middle of this essay, rather than the end. We're about to hit the inevitable change of heart in this tale.

What I've since learned goes back to the original nature of the adventure. Go back to the third paragraph. Notice how often the word "show" appears. That's the key to the Keep, and the thing that has turned my opinion on it. Despite its thin narrative and lack of proper names, the Keep does a tremendous job of showing off the key elements of the implied setting of Dungeons & Dragons. It hits on a tremendous number of key concepts that have echoed through the years. The list includes:

- The world is marked by a constant conflict between civilization and the wild.
- The gods are in conflict in the world, squaring off between good and evil.
- Evil is splintered into a multitude of factions that can fight among themselves.
- Evil infiltrates civilization, seeking to corrupt it from within.
- Dungeons are dangerous, distant places that are hard to find, and hold strange magic.
- Since evil is splintered, you can bargain with monsters if you make a good offer.
- Adventure occurs in civilized towns, the wilderness, and dungeons.
- Direct assaults only get you so far. Clever play is required for the best success.
- The world is open, and the players have a lot of freedom to determine their path.
- Choosing the best path requires smart planning, roleplay, and information gathering.

The fun thing about this list is that it makes *The Keep on the Borderlands* an intriguing litmus test for any D&D setting. Since *Keep* establishes so many key elements, it is a great model to use for getting across what makes a setting interesting. Imagine adapting it to a setting like Dark Sun. You might end up with an adventure that features:

- An isolated village, founded by slaves and far from the sorcerer-kings.
- Nearby ruins from a bygone age, infested with monsters and marauders.
- A terrible evil is active in the ruins, perhaps a templar dispatched by a sorcerer-king to infiltrate and destroy the village.
- The characters must explore the nearby wilderness in order to find the ruins. This being Athas, the characters must carefully manage food and water if they want to survive in the wilds.
- With success against the monsters of the ruins, the characters can slowly win the village's trust and eventually become its sponsored champions.

It's not hard to see why Dark Sun is such an eminently gameable setting. Worlds like the Forgotten Realms and Greyhawk pass this test with ease. Other settings snap into a clearer focus when given this treatment. Imagine transporting the Keep to Spelljammer. Give the characters a small vessel, transform the Keep into a friendly port, the wilds become points of interest in space, and the Caves of Chaos become a strange, wandering comet studded with a dozen or more dungeons to visit. It's a fun exercise, and a great way to consider how

B2: The Keep on the Borderlands was shared by thousands of gamers, including Luke Gygax, son of D&D co-creator Gary Gygax. You can read more of Luke's experience on page 4.

Gary Gygax and his son Luke as a baby

Luke and family around the kitchen table

Luke and his family on Halloween of the year 1984.

a setting you are working on or want to use in your campaign might play out. In my opinion, the Keep provides the best model for starting a campaign.

The Keep on the Borderlands stands out not in what it did, though those details have provided countless hours of gaming, but instead for how Gary Gygax approached its design. In its 32 pages, *Keep* provides the clearest, most concise definition of D&D that you can find. It compacts the entire concept of the game into one adventure.

In Search of the Unknown came to me a bit later in my gaming career, when late in middle school I read a friend's copy. I came to D&D too late to see it as the original adventure included with the Basic Set. Instead, it was an interesting curio. *In Search of the Unknown* was interesting because it had to be. Lacking a preset roster of monsters, it had to entertain and captivate by offering interesting locations and hints of a much larger story hidden within its room descriptions. As a friend of mine once observed, the dungeon in the adventure had to have stuff like a mushroom forest and a room of bizarre, magical pools, because that was all the designer had to work with.

That material has served me well many times across the years. I've run it as a traditional dungeon crawl, monsters spread through its halls almost at random. I've used it as the headquarters of a sinister cult. I've transformed it into a minotaur's labyrinth. I've made it a battleground between a berserker tribe and a loathsome clan of troglodytes. Once, I even ran it as a dungeon overrun with amateur treasure seekers, eager to find hidden loot and prone to unleashing unspeakable horrors sealed away in the place.

If *Keep* shows you how to present a world, *In Search of the Unknown* suggests you make your dungeons interesting by making them filled with odd elements even if they are deserted. The next time you try building a dungeon, take on that challenge. Create your map and describe the rooms with elements that will keep your players busy and engaged even if there are no monsters present. Entire books have been written on dungeon design, seeking to capture the elements that *In Search of the Unknown* shows us how to use.

Once again, there's that word: show. Constrained by 32 pages of space, and further forced to spend precious word count laying out advice for beginners, the early D&D designers had no choice but to show rather than tell. There's a useful lesson for today's RPG designers. It's easy to tell DMs how the game is supposed to work. It's much harder to just show them. I like to think that the D&D team of today has learned the lessons of the past and that we're applying them to make today's adventures as interesting and fun as ever. But I have to admit, that even 40 or so years later and hundreds if not thousands of adventures that have since published, I return to these two again and again. This is pure, unadulterated D&D, the stuff that planted the seeds for decades of gaming and invented our modern concept of what a game can be.

Mike Mearls manages the D&D creative team at Wizards of the Coast. He was the co-lead designer on D&D 5th edition. His work includes Xanathar's Guide to Everything *and* Volo's Guide to Monsters *for D&D, and the board games* Castle Ravenloft *and* Betrayal at Baldur's Gate.

Discovering the Caves of Chaos

by Harley Stroh

B2 was my introduction to Dungeons & Dragons. I was the pale, asthmatic second grader, deemed too weak by doctors to spend my summers outdoors. *The Keep on the Borderlands* was the remedy.

A babysitter ran the first session for me and my little brother. Excited at the promise of adventure I took the lead and boldly marched into the kobold warren . . . only to pitch down the pit trap and be promptly devoured by diseased giant rats. (My brother's character survived, but likely retired from adventuring to settle down with the tavern keeper's daughter.)

That first session proved to be our last. Our babysitter's parents discovered that D&D was a satanic, corrupting influence, and demanded he throw away all his books. And in retrospect, perhaps there was some corrupting element: Instead of throwing the books away, he gave them to me.

Standing in the abandoned lot behind his house, receiving the box of contraband, it all seemed very important: B2, with its stand-alone cover to conceal secrets; the brilliant colors of the Moldvay rulebook; the strange off-blue dice; hand-written character sheets. Relics that had been forbidden by adults and now I was their keeper.

I ran my first game the next week, DMing *The Keep on the Borderlands* for my mother, father, and little brother (his character fresh out of retirement). I recall my father's PC died from a spear as they fled the goblins and their ogre enforcer. From my read of the example play in the rulebook, I knew that you weren't supposed to leave a body behind, so I insisted the PCs carry off his corpse in a backpack. Whether it was the joy of judging, or fear of losing another PC to a pit trap, I continued to run games for my brother and our friends all through elementary school, high school, and into college.

Being eight years old and living an hour from the nearest city, finding new modules was a challenge. (I did manage to score *The Isle of Dread* and two of the Slavers adventures at a junk store.) However, B2—with its overland map and scattered encounters—hinted at a larger story, providing enough adventure for dozens of sessions. We robbed the keep's moneylender, spent our ill-gotten gains on honey mead at the tavern, and crossed swords with the mad hermit on more than one occasion. As our characters approached name level, we built our assassin's guild on the swampy island in the river south of the keep (recruiting the raiders to aid us against the lizard men), and rode against the forces of Law and the Castellan. (Mostly because we wanted to own the ballistae and catapults.)

While an introductory adventure, B2 didn't dumb down the game. Rather it provided the means necessary for children to step into a mature undertaking. The glossary of arcane words, the succinct design tips for urban and dungeon complexes, the tables of NPCs; in each instance the reader is exhorted (expected!) to rise to the challenge of becoming an active co-author. This facet of RPGs (and especially the OSR) might seem obvious to us now, but as a child it was a remarkable invitation. The reader, young or old, was regarded as intelligent and creative enough to make a dungeon on par with the Caves of Chaos; all we needed were the tools.

What child discovered the sheet of blank graph paper on page 27 and didn't begin drawing his or her first dungeon? What fledgling DM didn't roll up NPCs (usually picking one or two of the best to serve as DM PCs) to seed the tavern with hirelings? In a decade when children's imaginations were increasingly boxed and branded, B2 offered a world of freedom, and did so by treating children with respect.

Looking back from nearly 40 years of game design, it's easy enough to find critiques of B2—often characterized as a densely populated "monster hotel." (Though the case could be made that the wicked humanoids were drawn to, or even created by, the font of Evil Chaos.) But you would be hard-pressed to name a more effective or succinct introduction to open world gaming—the heart of fantasy RPGs.

Even today, Gygax's call to adventure rings true, bidding us to loosen our swords in their scabbards and cinch our shields a little tighter. Unsullied by the passage of time or editions, the Caves remain, awaiting the next band of adventurers foolish enough to plumb their depths:

> *A flock of ravens rise croaking from the ground, the beat of their wings and their cries magnified by the terrain to sound loud and horrible. Amongst the litter of rubble, boulders, and dead wood scattered about on the ravine floor, you can see bits of gleaming ivory and white—closer inspection reveals that these are bones and skulls of men, animals, and other things...*
>
> *You know that you have certainly discovered the Caves Of Chaos.*

Harley Stroh has designed dozens of adventure modules for the Dungeon Crawl Classics series, including several with nefarious traps inspired by a longtime appreciation of Grimtooth's work. The DCC series has more than 90 adventures in print as of this writing, and Harley's fearsome traps have been hard at work killing characters since Dungeon Crawl Classics #12.5: The Iron Crypt of the Heretics. *Harley lives in Colorado with his wife, his dog, his children, and far too many gaming books.*

My Journey to the Keep: Or, Greyhawk on One Evil Amulet a Day

by Brendan J. LaSalle

I had been playing D&D for several years before I explored *The Keep on the Borderlands*. My friend Don modified it for AD&D and ran it for our tiny group. Don was an excellent DM with a unique, laid back style, the first DM I played with who had a real poker face. He would nod, thoughtfully, while you described what your characters were doing and then casually add, "Yeah, um, go ahead and roll for surprise . . ." He got us again and again and again.

I remember my character—Andrew Vendi, a half-elf fighter/magic-user. He and his two companions—my buddy's thief and an NPC cleric we brought along—arrived at the keep and the very next day set out for the Caves of Chaos! Glory would be ours . . .

. . . or so we thought.

We passed under a tree on our way up to the first cave and were ambushed by kobolds, who dropped down on us and slew us all. I didn't even get a chance to cast my *sleep* spell!

I remember being both bummed out—who wants to die in the first five minutes? —and a little elated that we would get to make up new characters, a part of the game I love dearly.

We decided that we would make up a new group with the specific purpose of finding out what happened to our first crew. I created Andrew's cousin Jackeel Vendi—a FULL magic-user and a full elf, who was determined to get to the bottom of what happened. He assembled a team of worthies—a fighter, a cleric, a ranger, AND a thief—and we headed back out to the Caves of Chaos with a new mission—revenge!

We crawled through the Caves of Chaos all summer and finally walked away victorious, flush with gold and nearly third level! This was more than 30 years ago at this point but I still remember looking over our carefully drawn map, and the long list we had of our conquests: dead monsters in the left-hand column, treasure on the right. Sure felt good.

One of my fondest memories of that campaign was visiting a sage after the adventure. Remember visiting the sage? Old guy with a beard who knew absolutely everything about absolutely everything? Happy to discuss any topic at length if you could pay his price? Lived alone in a house full of ancient books and, presumably, all the gold he had extracted from dingbat adventurers who couldn't read draconic or figure out how to use their newly liberated *Apparatus of Kwalish*? Good times.

Our band of stalwart adventurers had collected dozens of identical amulets from the Shrine of Evil Chaos (just typing that gives me a frisson of sunny nostalgia), taken from the corpses of evil clerics and their skeleton and zombie minions. It had to mean something!

So we head off to ask the sage. Two hundred gold pieces later, the sage let us know exactly what we had on our hands: more than two dozen amulets of *protection from good*. That bit of our haul led to one of the funniest game discussions I ever took part of. Who had made

all of those magical amulets? Was there some wholesale anti-good amulet maker going from dungeon to dungeon, medicine-show style, hawking his anti-good charms like Tom Fury in "Something Wicked This Way Comes?" ("Adventurers are going to come to this dungeon—I can smell them!")

And most importantly—how were we going to turn the stupid things into cash? Could we, as heroes of the realm, ethically hang out in front of an evil temple with the amulets all hung on the inside of our cloaks like a guy pedaling hot watches and try to pawn them off on anybody who looked like they could be a potential henchman?

"Say buddy—you have a dishonest face. Are the good guys getting you down? Need a little something to keep those paladins and ki-rin at bay? Well today is your lucky day!"

We laughed our fool heads off, 14 years old and tapped into a magical word of infinite possibility. Don was the author, we were the characters, and Gary Gygax was the architect. The world he created felt like home, a home we would defend against evil with our swords held high.

That group of characters became known to us as the Old School Game Crew. We took turns DMing and had a system to keep it fair, since we would be running our own characters through as NPCs when it was our turn behind the screen. We only ran published adventures, never made any changes to monsters or treasure, and we let the dice fall where they fell.

The Old School Game Crew became the longest running adventuring party that I ever participated in. I went off to college, and when I would come home for the summer we would get together and pull out the Old School Game Crew and explore and conquer. Always switching off DMs between dungeons, we took that crew through *The Secret of Bone Hill*, *Expedition to the Barrier Peaks*, and *Against The Giants*. When we last pulled these characters out we were in the halls of King Snurre of the fire giants, trying to discover who was behind their diabolical attacks.

I haven't spoken with any of those guys in years—the real world, and a real-world falling out, split us up. But we shared a story, a story that lived and breathed, a story that only we ever saw to the heart of, and it's a shared thing that we had all to ourselves. Some of the greatest stories the world has ever seen have been told exactly once by people with dice in their hands, and our expedition to *The Keep on the Borderlands* kicked off one of the defining stories of my life.

Brendan J. LaSalle is a writer, game designer, and odd-job man who had the good fortune to discover his true calling in 1977 when he was introduced to AD&D. He is the author of several DCC adventures and supplements for Goodman Games, Fat Dragon, Savage Mojo, Hand Made Games, Pandahead Publishing, Troll Lords Games, and others. He is best known as the creator of Xcrawl, the dungeon-adventure-cum-alternative-modern-death-sport he has published since 2012. He lives in Salem, Massachusetts, with his wife, cat, and

How B2 Started my Adventure Module Collection

by Alex Kammer

All these years later, I still distinctly remember seeing the Dungeons & Dragons end cap display at Value Village in Portage, WI. It was 1982 and I was 12 years old. And, I had never seen anything as singularly awesome as this.

It was a four-section cardboard stand-up display showing copies of the *Players Handbook, Dungeon Masters Guide, Monster Manual,* and *Deities & Demigods.* I can still recall the feeling of wonder and excitement as I saw those tomes for the first time. I could not believe that such beautiful books existed. And, I could buy them. . . . Me.

Sure, I had previously glanced at a friend's copy of the Basic Set sometime earlier that year,[1] but this was different. The Basic Set in its boxed form looked more like a typical board game to my completely novice eye. For me at least, these hardbounds were a whole different ballgame. And all that I had to do was mow a ton of lawns to be able to buy them.

And mow I did. After hoping for rain to grow more grass followed by some furious mowing, I soon had my very own copy of the *Players Handbook* (8th printing).[2] I remember taking it home and eagerly poring over it. I was only 12 at the time. I remember thinking that I generally got what it was saying, but it seemed like an impossibly complicated game to me—mind-blowingly awesome, but complicated.

Soon thereafter, I remember being in the 7th grade library with my friend who had the *Basic Set.* He had brought it to school and we were actually going to play for the first time. That was when he pulled out the module from the set: *B2: The Keep on the Borderlands.* First, I saw the bright colors of the cover and the incredible artwork (bright pink with heroes fighting orcs!), and then the maps. I could not believe it. This is where adventurers actually fought fell monsters. This was where amazing treasures were found. This was where heroes were born. This was D&D!

You see, I was only four years old when D&D came out in 1974. In the very early days of OD&D, there were no published adventures. And, at that time, TSR had no plans on publishing any. The company's ethos was nicely summed up in the Afterwards at the very end of the OD&D rules: ". . . why have us do any more of your imagining for you?"[3] The first modules were produced by third-party publishers: *Palace of the Vampire Queen* (1976) by Wee Warriors being the first, followed by several Judges Guild products and *The Lost Caverns of Tsojconth* in 1977.

The first official modules released by TSR were the now iconic *Against the Giants* series: *G1: Steading of the Hill Giant Chief, G2: The Glacial Rift of the Frost Giant Jarl,* and *G3: Hall of the Fire Giant King* in 1978. These were followed by the equally hallowed *S1: Tomb of Horrors* and *B1: In Search of the Unknown.*

Despite the fact that published adventures in module form were never part of the original TSR plan, selling a lot of something has a way of changing plans quickly. In just a few short years, TSR was producing dozens of modules per year and they were selling like crazy. Consider that in 1983 alone, TSR sold more than 126,000 copies of *M1: Blizzard Pass;* more than 117,000 copies of *I4: Oasis of the White Palm;* more than 112,000 copies of *I3: Pharaoh;* and more than 107,000 copies of each *EX1: The Land Beyond the Magic Mirror* and *EX2: Dungeonland.*[4] With sales numbers like that, it is easy to understand why modules quickly become big business for TSR.

So, just as modules were becoming huge sellers for TSR, I, along with thousands of others, entered this transcendent hobby.

Ever since playing B2 with my 7th grade buddy, splashing around in the Caves of Chaos and subsequently reading B1 which was an unbelievably good "how-to" guide for the beginning DM, I have been in love with TSR modules. While I did eventually pick up all of the hardbounds, I always bought the most recently released modules first.

I still remember the feeling of sublime excitement and keen anticipation from seeing a new module title, complete with bright and ornate art, sitting there on the game store shelf. There just was nothing like tearing off the shrink-wrap and seeing what sort of devilish surprises the author had cooked up for the players. I still vividly remember seeing *I2: Tomb of the Lizard King* for the first time and excitedly tearing it open. It was my adoration of these products that led me to not only buy them and keep them, but also to carefully preserve them and eventually collect them.

Because the modules were always my favorite D&D product, I took care of my copies before collecting really became popular in D&D. I wanted all the modules, every single one of them. Even at points in life where I was not actively playing D&D, I always made sure that my collection was safe and secure.

I have become an avid collector of all things TSR, but the focus of my collection is the modules. I have a complete set of all the BECMI modules, all the AD&D modules, and all of the 2E modules. In fact, I have multiple copies of each and nearly have a complete set of BECMI and AD&D modules in original shrink-wrap (I am only three modules away from being complete!). My collection features rares like *ST1: Up the Garden Path;* multiple copies of *Palace of the Vampire Queen; The Dwarven Glory; Lost Tomoachan; The Lost Caverns of Tsojconth; B3: Palace of the Silver Princess* (orange) (one NM and one in original shrink-wrap); all of the original Daystar West modules (*Rahasia, Pharaoh, Eye of the Dragon,* and *Brimstone*); and, finally, multiple copies of all the "R" series and the "RPGA" series modules. Many of these are signed by the authors. I even have a couple of copies of modules that were originally part of the TSR library. In total, I have nearly 1,000 copies of pre-1998 TSR modules.

If you are interested in collecting modules, I have one piece of advice for you: do your research. Many TSR modules have multiple printings. A given module can vary tremendously in value depending on the printing. For example, B1 has six distinct printings and B2 has eight. Beyond the printings, condition is everything. When you are considering buying a module and given that most of these sales are done virtually these days, if a seller gives their module a high grade, make sure that the seller is not only reputable, but is also competent to give that grade in the first place. Auction sites like eBay have a feedback system and if you have not purchased something from that seller before, do your research.

And while auction sites like eBay are fine, Facebook has an excellent RPG auction[5] group not surprisingly called RPG Auctions. Unlike the typical auction site, the Facebook group is an actual community. You can post questions and comments in order to really understand exactly what you are bidding on. This first-rate group is growing quickly. It is a very useful service if you are a collector.

Finally, an excellent resource is the collector's site The Acaeum.[6] I am a member and have found it to be an invaluable resource when it comes to researching TSR products and for connecting with other collectors. It is a great community and it gets my highest recommendation.

So, cheers to the TSR modules! Thank you for providing me so much joy over the years and thank you for being such a rewarding and inspiring collectible!

Alex Kammer is a D&D addict, an avid TSR collector, a lawyer, a freelance writer, owner of two pubs, and the Director of Gamehole Con.

[1] In retrospect, probably a 9th or 10th printing Basic Set.

[2] Of course, I had no idea that separate printings of books were even a thing at that time.

[3] Thanks to Jon Peterson for referencing this excellent quote in his Introduction to *The Habitition of the Stone Giant Lord.*

[4] Thanks to William Meinhardt for sharing this sales data with me directly from a TSR sales memo dated 2/27/84.

[5] www.facebook.com/groups/RPGAuctions

[6] www.acaeum.com

Goodman Games Interviews
Mike Carr

by Jim Wampler

To say that TSR alumnus Mike Carr has been gaming since the birth of the hobby, at least in its modern form, is not an understatement. As a teenager, Mike Carr was at the very first official Gen Con held in 1968 at the legendary Lake Geneva Horticultural Hall. He has been attending and running games at every single Gen Con since. Also in 1968, Mike wrote, designed, and published the seminal World War I aerial combat game Fight in the Skies (known as Dawn Patrol in later editions).

In 1976, Mike Carr was hired on by Gary Gygax at TSR. Mike began his career at TSR as a general production person, then graduated to writing and editing for the games division—in effect becoming the TSR Games counterpart to TSR Publications editor Tim Kask. It was in this capacity that Mike edited the entirety of the core AD&D manuals, and wrote the first adventure module to be bundled inside the D&D Basic Set—*B1: In Search of the Unknown*.

Mike Carr recently sat down with us to discuss his early contributions to gaming in general, and to D&D and B1 specifically.

Goodman Games: Let's start with everyone's favorite question, how did you first get into gaming?

Mike Carr: Like so many children of the 1950s and 1960s, I enjoyed playing a variety of games published by Parker Brothers and Milton Bradley, which were often played with family and friends. As I got a little older, I developed an interest in history, including military history. Just as I was becoming a teenager, the Civil War Centennial was going on, so that further piqued my interest in historical topics. Historical board games were also starting to appear at that time with the advent of the Avalon Hill Game Company and its ground-breaking titles. The first wargame I purchased was U-Boat, and it wasn't long before my teenage friends and I were enjoying an assortment of AH games.

GG: You must have gotten bitten by the wargaming bug hard, because you were also only a teenager when you had your first game published. What was the inspiration behind Fight In The Skies?

MC: The game Fight in the Skies (later retitled and trademarked as Dawn Patrol) was literally inspired by the 1966 movie "The Blue Max", which tells the story of the fictional Bruno Stachel, a German fighter pilot on a quest to win Germany's highest award, the Orden Pour le Merite, or Blue Max. It's an adaptation of the novel by Jack D. Hunter, which was the first in a trilogy. Interestingly, the book and movie endings are completely different, but the aerial scenes are astounding and that's what inspired me to create the game. I thought, "Wouldn't it be cool if a game could reflect the nature of World War I aerial combat with the planes zooming around in a dogfight, with you as the pilot?" That was the impetus for the idea, allowing players to get a feel for the elegant flight of those historic planes and the thrill of a life-or-death fight in the skies.

GG: So this would all be around the time that you first met Dave Arneson and Gary Gygax. Living in Saint Paul, Minnesota, I'm going to guess that you met Dave first.

MC: As a teenager, my growing interest in Avalon Hill board games led me to subscribe to that company's gaming magazine *The General*, where gamers could place ads seeking others to play with, either locally or by mail. I placed one of those ads and Dave Arneson–who, like me, lived in Saint Paul, Minnesota–responded to it and invited me to come across town to meet him and his friends, who were all several years older than I was. They were heavily involved in tabletop miniatures gaming as well as board games like Diplomacy, and that broadened my gaming horizons somewhat, as well.

Avalon Hill's *The General* brought together enthusiasts from across the country, allowing them to get in touch with each other as a true gaming community began to form. Not long after the appearance of *The General*, informal gaming clubs sprung up like tribes (with fanciful names like Aggressor Homeland) who challenged each other to imaginary turf battles, matching wits by playing a variety of Avalon Hill games to prove their dominance. Through Aggressor Homeland, I met Bill Hoyer of West Allis, Wisconsin, the first gamer I got to know outside of Saint Paul and Minneapolis. Before too long, Bill was one of the officers in the International Federation of Wargaming (IFW), a national club that grew in prominence just as clubs like Aggressor Homeland were fading away.

The IFW brought together like-minded enthusiasts and promoted gaming activities through its magazine, including "societies" that formed around particular games such as Avalon Hill's Stalingrad. Along with Bill Hoyer and Len Lakofka of Chicago, Gary Gygax of Lake Geneva, Wisconsin, was one of the IFW's movers and shakers, enthusiastically advocating a wide variety of gaming activities–among those, the first Gen Con game convention and the Wargame Inventors Guild (WGIG). It was through the IFW that I met Gary, who learned that I had been inspired to create a World War I aviation game and urged me to self-publish it through the WGIG, which I did in its first three editions (of 25, 50, and 100 copies each). Gary later suggested to Don Lowry that he publish the 4th Edition of Fight in the Skies under his Guidon Games label, which Don did in 1974.

Of course, Tactical Studies Rules (later TSR) was starting out during that time and began to obtain momentum after the publication of Dungeons & Dragons in 1974. As TSR began to expand its line, Gary and his business partner Brian Blume agreed to publish the 5th Edition of Fight in the Skies as the company's second boxed game, which appeared in the Spring of 1976 just as I was joining the company as its seventh employee. Subsequently, TSR published the 6th Edition several years later and the 7th Edition as Dawn Patrol.

GG: Speaking of Dawn Patrol, you have the distinction of being the only person known to have attended every single Gen Con since its inception in 1968, and that Dawn Patrol is also the only game that has been run at every single Gen Con. Is that correct?

MC: Yes. In August of 1968, I was just shy of my 17th birthday. Through the IFW newsletter, I learned of the proposed Lake Geneva

MIKE MEARLS, MIKE CARR, AND JOSEPH GOODMAN ANNOUNCE THIS PROJECT AT GARY CON 2017

convention being organized by Gary Gygax and was eager to attend, so I asked my parents if we might go to Lake Geneva (300 miles from Saint Paul) for a weekend vacation–and they agreed, bless their hearts! That allowed me to participate in the first Gen Con on August 24, 1968, and I've attended every one since.

Fight in the Skies/Dawn Patrol is the only game that has been featured every year at Gen Con. In fact, after Gary Gygax's welcoming remarks at Gen Con I in 1968, I ran the very first event, a Fight in the Skies game using 1/72 scale models on a square tiled floor–a game that was documented in a subsequent issue of the IFW magazine. We've run Fight in the Skies and Dawn Patrol events every year since then, making it the only game played every year at Gen Con since 1968. That's a pretty minor claim to fame, but considering the history and scope of Gen Con, I'm proud to enjoy that honor.

GG: Let's shift the topic to D&D. Tell us about your personal introduction to Dungeons & Dragons.

MC: I was privileged to be one of the original players of Dungeons & Dragons as part of the fledgling Blackmoor campaign. I'm proud to say that I was the very first cleric character ever, and participated in a number of dungeon adventures in that role. It was a modest beginning, but it was all new so that made it more than just interesting.

GG: Since you first played in the famous Blackmoor campaign, tell us what Dave Arneson was like as a Dungeon Master? Before their later falling out, Gary referred to Dave in the introduction to the Blackmoor supplement with high praise, saying that, "I cannot recommend him more highly than simply saying that I would rather play in his campaign than any other..."

MC: Dave Arneson was the original Dungeon Master and really set the standard for all who followed, although it should be noted that he

in turn drew inspiration from the earlier Braunstein roleplaying games that Dave Wesely created and ran several times in Saint Paul. Quite simply, as a game master, Dave Arneson was superb in every respect–creatively, organizationally, and operationally. It was a genuine pleasure to participate in his games because he was so good at challenging players in a variety of ways, with the occasional surprise twist to delight or confound them.

Besides developing and running the Blackmoor world, he also single-handedly created the massive multi-player Twin Cities Napoleonic Simulation Campaign that included more than 20 players throughout Minneapolis and Saint Paul (plus Gary Gygax as one of several American players, suitably remote in Lake Geneva). Each Napoleonic campaign–which he did twice–ran for several years and encompassed an amazing amount of detail, which he managed extremely well considering that this was all before personal computers existed. He did everything by hand, using index cards, notebooks, and plenty of paper. It was an amazing feat considering the scope of the whole campaign, which encompassed diplomatic activities, army and navy budgets, operational movements of armies and fleets, large and small battles on land and sea, and a copious amount of bookwork to keep it all straight. In essence, strategic movements by opposing players resulted in encounters that were resolved as tabletop battles using miniatures. For one person to do the bulk of this–and handle it so well–was astounding.

Compared to that grand undertaking, running the Blackmoor world was a relative breeze, I would imagine, because of its lesser scope, but he handled that equally well from both an organizational and a game mastering standpoint. Playing in his campaigns was a real pleasure and I have many fond memories of it.

GG: So how did you end up going from playing D&D in college with Dave Arneson to moving to Lake Geneva to work for TSR in March 1976?

MC: I graduated from Macalester College in Saint Paul in 1973 with a degree in History, hoping to become a high school Social Studies teacher. But there were virtually no openings at the time in Minnesota, so my options in the field of education were limited. For some months I continued working at my college job, which was as the night cook at The Ground Round restaurant in Roseville, Minnesota. That store was one of the busiest in the entire chain, so it was a training ground for aspiring managers–and with few other options, I asked the regional manager if I might be considered as a management trainee. My expectation was that, if accepted, I would be training there in Roseville, but when the offer was made to me it was for a position in Cedar Rapids, Iowa–take it or leave it. I had no desire to leave the Twin Cities, but this was a genuine opportunity and the only one I had, so I took it.

I enjoyed the restaurant business, but working six days a week and having only Tuesdays off took most of the fun out of it. I really disliked living in Cedar Rapids, so after spending 1974 and 1975 there as a trainee and assistant manager, I was more than delighted when Gary Gygax offered me a position with TSR in early 1976. He felt that with my gaming background and now my management experience, I would be of value to the growing enterprise as an editor and potential manager.

At The Ground Round I had worked my way up from $150 a week to $205 a week, but Gary's offer was for just $110 a week, with the promise of some corporate stock in lieu of salary and the opportunity to buy more shares at a discount. Since I had developed an interest in the stock market as a teen, I was well aware of what that could mean for the founders and early investors if the business became a solid success–and that's exactly what transpired over the next seven years. Besides, I was single and loved gaming, so taking a pay cut of that magnitude, although significant, was something I was more than willing to do. So in mid-March of 1976, I happily pulled up stakes in Iowa and moved to Lake Geneva. I've been a Wisconsinite ever since. To this day, I live outside of Oconomowoc, which is about 40 miles north and 45 minutes away from Lake Geneva, so I'm able to visit there any time I like.

GG: So initially at least, your job duties at TSR were informal and more managerial, before becoming the games and rules editor?

MC: Yes. As with any small company, we all performed a variety of tasks, creative and otherwise, including unloading boxes of newly printed products being delivered. Among other duties, I did some editing and proofreading on several projects along with Brian Blume which led to more editorial work and a change in my title from general manager to games and rules editor.

GG: It seems that an entire mythology has arisen around what life was like back at TSR in its earliest days. Can you describe the TSR environment when you first came on with the company, as well as how you saw it change over the time you were there? What do you think the catalyst was for those changes?

MC: I came to work at TSR in mid-March of 1976, and was there until July of 1983. I had attended Gen Con every year, so I was somewhat familiar with Lake Geneva and knew I'd enjoy living there. I arrived just a couple of weeks after artist Dave Sutherland III had hired on and it was suggested that we share an apartment, which was one unit of a two-story fourplex. Although Dave was from Minneapolis and I was from Saint Paul, we had somehow never met. But we got along just fine as roommates and co-workers. After some time, Dave left to get married and I ended up staying in that apartment for the duration of my time in Lake Geneva, enjoying the company of several other roommates like Tim Jones, Harold Johnson, John Danovich, and Jim Quinn.

When I arrived in Lake Geneva, TSR was headquartered in a two-story home on Williams Street, across from the Pizza Hut (which is still there, by the way). I was given one of the upstairs rooms as my personal office, which was next to the artists' room where Dave Sutherland (and later Dave Trampier, as well) did his work. Anyone going to or from the artists' room had to pass through my office, so I had a steady stream of traffic going by my desk all day long.

With the company growing so rapidly, it was a very dynamic time and it was exciting to be a part of such a bustling enterprise. I really enjoyed my ever-growing number of co-workers. I got to work on a wide variety of projects and was able to do plenty of gaming, both developing and playtesting potential products, as well as enjoying other games during evening hours and weekends.

GG: How about later? How did things change at TSR as it grew and moved into larger facilities after the house on Williams Street?

MC: When TSR purchased the three-story Hotel Clair downtown, we moved the operation there and I was given a nice third-story office, one of the few that had a window that looked toward the lake. I spent one weekend with a couple of my co-workers painting the walls mustard yellow. I loved that office and working in this larger building was a joy. There was so much going on with lots of products in the pipeline and a continually expanding staff. Playtesting games of different kinds was a pleasure and the mix of personalities made it interesting and fun–so yes, the work environment was truly something special in those days. Even though there were certainly problems, conflicts, disagreements, and disappointments at the time, I loved it and look back fondly on those times.

When the company expanded to the property on Sheridan Springs Road, things began to change again and so did the atmosphere. It was essential that the whole enterprise become more business-like and less informal, which meant the creation of formal job descriptions, organizational charts, and all the other trappings of a growing corporation. Much of the early ambiance disappeared, but it was still a very dynamic situation for all of us, and still enjoyable.

Eventually, when TSR management decided to form their own manufacturing division, I was asked to become the Vice President of Manufacturing. I initially turned down that position because I loved working on the creative side and didn't feel qualified to oversee a manufacturing effort (which I also knew would be a lot less fun), but Gary Gygax insisted, so I felt I had little choice and took the job for the good of the company. When the business started to go south and the staff was being downsized, I changed positions and ended up writing three children's books. One of those was *Robbers & Robots* which ended up selling a quarter of a million copies, so that was a fitting cap to my TSR career. I was one of the dozens let go during the third wave of layoffs, thus ending that chapter of my life.

That being said, I really enjoyed working at TSR, especially in the first five years of my seven-year stint. I knew that working with games would be much more fun than doing anything else–and it was!

GG: Well going back to the earliest days, at a fairly early point TSR divided itself into two separate entities—TSR Games and TSR Periodicals. It sounds like back then you filled a similar role for the games division to that performed by Tim Kask on the periodicals side. Do I have that right?

MC: Yes. TSR was growing exponentially, so there were a number of organizational changes and reorganizations over the following years as staff were added and the number of products increased. Before long, I was in charge of the creative group and working as the lead editor, overseeing a growing staff and numerous product development projects.

GG: In an earlier interview with Allen Hammack, Allen described the role of editor at TSR back in the late '70s and early '80s as involving a good deal of project management. Assuming this was so, to what extent did you have to coordinate projects with the various departments and how easy was it to do so?

MC: I would agree with his assessment–and we were colleagues who worked in concert. Like most publishing companies, TSR had a pipeline of projects in different stages of development, starting with proposed concepts or outside submissions that required evaluation and consideration. We had weekly production meetings to evaluate the status of every project in the pipeline and compare that to the master schedule, which was updated at least that often, depending upon the dictates of upper management and development delays that occurred from time to time.

As it moved from concept to finished product, each project required coordination between the editing, artistic, marketing, advertising, purchasing, and finance groups. The two greatest constraints–as in any production environment–were limited time and resources. That was a challenge, but what made it even more so (and very frustrating at times) were the occasional dictates of senior management, which could arrive unexpectedly and wreak havoc with what was going on or already scheduled–like a wild card that couldn't be ignored. After this happened a few times, we decided with some amusement that the letters TSR actually stood for "That's So Ridiculous." Nonetheless, things did function fairly well and we were gamers, so we enjoyed the challenge, even if that meant having to burn the midnight oil at times.

GG: "That's So Ridiculous!" That's hilarious. As an editor, one can assume there must have been a range of styles between the writers. How easy it was to edit for them, were there easier as well as harder writers to edit? How would you compare editing a Gary Gygax manuscript versus anybody else's work?

MC: Writing styles certainly differ widely from author to author, but that's something that an editor learns to handle as he or she gains experience. In the case of gaming products, editors need to assess the content not only in how it is presented (is it well organized, fairly complete and relatively free of errors, as submitted?), but also in terms of its content (does the gaming system work smoothly and is everything understandable?).

Because of the staff's knowledge and experience, the material developed in-house was usually easier to edit than it was for outside submissions, which could vary widely in quality and presentation. The solution, of course, was to reject or send back for reworking any manuscript that was deemed to be of poor quality.

Gary Gygax was not only a prolific writer, he was a very good one, in my opinion. His material was always well-organized and his manuscripts didn't require a lot of corrections or revisions. This was in the era just before computer word processing, so it's remarkable that he did so well using just a typewriter. There were always a few typos to correct and occasionally we'd have to ask him for a clarification, but overall his material was easy to edit compared to others.

Working as an editor also helped me become a better and more conscientious writer, which has served me well ever since. My goal is to make the editor's job as easy as possible and I'm not shy about telling them that every time I start to work with someone new. And as a freelance writer, I've written material for quite a few different editors.

GG: You were the editor of the first three AD&D books. Given the page counts, that must have been a monumental task. As a gamer more interested in historical simulations, would it be fair to say that you sometimes brought a voice of reason to a fantasy rules set that was quickly becoming quite dense and increasingly arcane?

MC: The three AD&D books were a testament to Gary's expanded vision for the game, as well as his desire to provide a comprehensive platform for players and Dungeon Masters. Presenting this vast material in the form of hardbound books was a totally new approach that had an immediate impact, both in the minds of the purchasers and in the gaming market as well. It was my privilege to be the editor for those volumes, and it was quite exciting to be so intimately involved in the production of such seminal products.

But no question–editing each of the books was a monumental task, although the extent of my efforts paled in comparison to what Gary Gygax put into each of those projects. His original manuscripts, if I recall, each ran well over 300 typed pages in double-spaced format, which was a hefty pile of paper to tackle. And although "quite dense and increasingly arcane" is a fair description of what was presented, he had done a really excellent job overall, which made my editing task quite manageable, although the time required for editing was prodigious, as you can imagine.

When I first began to spend long hours editing TSR material, I purchased–at my own expense–a nice La-Z-Boy reclining chair as my personal work space for editing. I spent a lot of hours in that chair with my red pen in hand, working through those manuscripts for many months. Believe it or not, I still have that chair today and use it almost daily, so perhaps it has some historical value. It's been re-upholstered once and is overdue to be re-covered again if I ever get around to it!

The fact that I was well familiar with D&D, but not an avid player, did help me to be an effective editor, because I was not too close to the material or overly knowledgeable about the intricacies of the game. That allowed me to look at everything as someone new to the game would see it, so the value I added was to make sure that things were clearly explained and understandable in that light. My goal was to be true to the author and his material, while making it all accessible for the players and game masters. Gary was pleased with the end results and those books sold like hotcakes, so that was especially gratifying.

GG: Well this has been a great interview so far, but we better focus at some point on the module *B1: In Search of the Unknown*. How did you get tapped to write an introductory adventure for the Basic Set? Were you given the direction to write a module that intentionally taught fledgling Dungeon Masters how to populate a dungeon (i.e. had fill-in-the-blank monster entries for rooms, along with monster population lists)—or was that primarily your invention?

MC: When the decision was made to include an introductory module with the Basic Set, I raised my hand and said I'd like to write it, which I ended up doing largely on my own time. After outlining my plan and getting the approval of Gary Gygax and Brian Blume, I set to work with very little input from anyone–I was really given carte blanche to bring my own vision to life, which I did. I was well aware that this was going to be an important product that would serve as a model for countless players to use and enjoy, so I really gave it a lot of thought and tried to make it not only illustrative of good design, but also interesting and challenging.

GG: What were your initial design goals then?

MC: In creating this module, I had several goals. First and foremost was to present it as a true introductory work suitable for first-time Dungeon Masters and players. That meant explaining to the Dungeon Master what was being presented, as well as the rationale behind it. For the players, it was giving them a background sheet that outlined the reason and motivation for their adventure, to get them thinking like roleplayers.

Second, I wanted to show what a good dungeon design looks like, starting with architectural aspects (like including all the necessary rooms for housing dozens of people in a functional way, considering aspects such as basic drainage, the location of cooking, eating, and sleeping areas, etc.). I also included aspects that might confuse the adventurers or make the place difficult to map, including some angled or irregular walls.

Third, I wanted to give an example of a solid "back story" that would provide a reason for the adventure and inspire the players' imaginations. To give the Dungeon Master an example of how to tailor certain details to individual players, I included a random roll for rumors or legends that each player's character might have heard, which could be true or false.

Fourth, I wracked my brain to come up with as many interesting and mysterious features as I could think of for what could be discovered within the place, particularly the garden of giant fungi and the room of pools. That had to be done considering that the adventurers were going to be low-level characters, so nothing could be too deadly or too challenging to overcome–and that meant that there were limited options on the design side.

Fifth, I wanted each Dungeon Master to be able to provide some of their own input through the placement of various monsters and treasures in different locations–with the suggestion that some rooms have one or the other, or none at all. That was my idea, but it reflected what was done in Dave Megarry's Dungeon! board game, where level-appropriate monsters and treasures are placed in each room, albeit randomly.

Lastly, I included advice for both the Dungeon Master and the players, hopefully to keep them on track while emphasizing that flexibility and the ability to adapt on the fly are key elements to achieve success in any roleplaying endeavor.

GG: We recognize B1 now as a seminal adventure, but there was a lot in it for neophyte DMs that we take for granted today and that you just spoke about—how to create a plausible storyline to explain why the player characters are in the dungeon to begin with, how to correctly and architecturally fit dungeon levels on top of each other, how to populate dungeons by level, how to set up basic risk versus reward scenarios. That's pretty good for a guy who didn't consider himself a hardcore D&D player.

MC: Even though I created this project decades ago, I still get occasional compliments on it, which is somewhat amazing considering that it seems a lifetime ago when it was published. I think what I am most proud of is that I had a vision for this, gave it a lot of thought, then was able to carry it out effectively. I really wanted to do it right and the comments I received were quite positive, so that's very gratifying–even today.

With the advent of the Internet since then, it's been fun to read some of the independent analyses of B1, which are often quite detailed and mostly positive. It's been especially fun to see someone deconstruct what I've written and make surmises about my sources, inspirations, or intent–sometimes right on the money, other times not even close.

GG: Since you were also the games editor when you wrote B1, how involved were you with the layout and art direction?

MC: As games and rules editor, I was very involved with the layout of many booklets, as well as obtaining and evaluating price quotes from printing companies for varying quantities of each product. Layout of pages was always a challenge because many of the products, including the hardbound books and B1, were very text-heavy. That was simply the nature of the material–we were trying to get as much as we could within the pages available. Page layout today is way easier and much more adaptable because of computer software capabilities, but in the 1970s it was still quite rudimentary. Long "galleys" of type were created electronically by typesetters who retyped the original manuscript into the new form. After proofreading and correcting those, we had to cut and paste the corrected galleys onto each page in the desired locations, which the production department at the printer would do likewise before creating the negative film that would be used to make the lithographic press plates. During the layout process, the editor's main concern was working around charts and diagrams within the body copy and then using filler art to add some interest and fill any white space.

During layout is when I would ask the artists for fillers, depending upon where the space was that we needed to fill (or where the text was lengthy and we simply wanted to break it up with an illustration). As you'd expect, most of the time I'd ask for a certain-sized drawing that tied in with the nearby copy.

For most of the covers, each editor would suggest that the artist depict something significant within the game or module, then give the artist license to create some sketches for consideration by the editor and senior management, who would choose the one they preferred. After that, the artist would create the finished drawing or painting.

For instance, for the box cover of the original Dungeons & Dragons Basic Set, it was decided to depict a dragon–as you'd expect–and I specifically asked Dave Sutherland to show a fighter aiming a tautly drawn bow and arrow, which would convey imminent action.

GG: Is there any particular reason that B1 was added to the Basic Set, and similarly, why was it replaced in relatively short order with B2? Apart from the fact that it'd be nice to have a module in the Basic Set to help people figure out how to play, was there any business reason? Do you recall how your compensation (if any) was structured for that work–lump sum, royalties, shares, or what have you?

MC: The Basic Set was created specifically for the mainstream audience in hopes that D&D would become much more than a niche product. Prior to the release of the Basic Set, D&D was becoming increasingly popular, but mostly within the gaming community. The

Basic Set was aimed at the mass market, so that it could be sold far more widely–and it really did take off. However, it was soon obvious that most buyers–who had grown up on traditional board games and to whom roleplaying and dungeon creation were alien concepts–wanted and needed something to allow them to more easily get started. TSR management was aware of that and I believe that they wanted to enhance the product for solid business reasons–to make it easier to grasp and play, thus increasing sales and removing an obstacle to getting started.

When I was given the go-ahead to start working up the module, Gary Gygax suggested a bonus royalty of 2% of the cover price, which he and Brian Blume signed off on in an agreement dated January 1, 1979. With a cover price of $5.50, the royalty was 11 cents per copy. That was certainly nice, but the fact that every Basic Set included a copy of B1 meant that the module I wrote was riding the coattails of TSR's flagship product, which was selling like crazy. I knew that would result in a financial windfall for me, and it certainly did, even though I also realized it might not last.

By the end of September, at the impetus of Kevin Blume on the financial side of the business, Brian Blume asked me to accept a lower percentage prior to them paying me anything, ostensibly to preserve the profitability of the product. I was able to refute that contention with solid production cost data and pointed out that the 2% number had come from Gary himself and that Brian had agreed to it. So I stuck to my guns and asked them to make good on what they had promised. After some hemming and hawing, they paid the rather significant amount that was due to me, but that large payout no doubt prompted their decision to replace B1 with B2. That didn't surprise me at all–and unfortunately, it was not the first or last time that I had to compel Brian Blume to deliver on a previous promise or agreement.

GG: Well I think that about wraps up this interview. Thank you so much for sharing your memories of the early days and history of TSR and the creation of so many fine gaming products—not to mention the genesis of *B1: In Search of the Unknown*.

MC: It was my pleasure.

AT GARY CON 2017, THIS PROJECT WAS ANNOUNCED AT THE WHAT'S NEW WITH GOODMAN GAMES SEMINAR. LEFT TO RIGHT: MIKE CARR, JOSEPH GOODMAN, MIKE MEARLS, AND CHRIS DOYLE.

The Mystery of the Alternate B1 Cover Art

As a few astute gaming historians and fans may have noticed, the cover art used on the first monochrome edition of *B1: In Search of the Unknown* has a few notable peculiarities. It appears at first glance to be art done by TSR's then-art director David Sutherland III, but carries the mysterious signature "DIS & DAT." It also features a background quite unlike the typical Sutherland style. Then, in a later 1982 edition of *Polyhedron* magazine (an RPGA newsletter), a piece of Dave Trampier art that almost exactly mirrors the B1 cover art appeared.

Surely there is a story behind these two extremely similar drawings, and while interviewing Mike Carr, I decided to ask him about it.

According to Mike, "For B1, I asked for an illustration depicting the room of giant mushrooms, which I felt would be striking as well as exotic." Regarding the two separate but similar drawings by Trampier and Sutherland, Mike told me, "I don't recall specifically, but I suspect that TSR management deemed the Trampier drawing too cartoony, and the end result was the Sutherland version that was used instead."

Mike also added that, "Despite that change, which I think made sense, I do like the Trampier depiction and I'm glad it survived and was used in the *Polyhedron* magazine later, I believe."

The original David Trampier version of the B1 cover art was, in fact, later published in *Polyhedron* magazine #5 in 1982. I then decided to talk to Frank Mentzer, founder of the RPGA and Editor-in-Chief of *Polyhedron* magazine at the time, to see what he recalled about this particular choice of art.

Frank explained that during the initial run of *Polyhedron* magazine, which was considered as more of a newsletter at first, he was not given an art budget. Instead, Frank was asked by TSR management to mine the art archive for unused pieces of art to illustrate his new publication. It may shock us now that a lot of the art that was produced for early TSR products was tossed casually into a file folder and sometimes even thrown out. Frank reminded me that at the time, this was not an unusual procedure. He told me that, "In fairness, we didn't know this was a ground-breaking, 40 years later, 'my God, look back at all of this' situation. We had no idea at the time that this was more than a passing fad, or in modern parlance, the next 'pet rock.'" So the attitude at the time, according to Frank, while certainly full of a passion for the games, was also one of "making hay while the sun shined."

And although Frank was not on staff at the time when B1 was produced, he did share his personal insights into how art direction decisions were probably made at the time, like the rejection of Trampier's initial B1 cover art.

"Dave (Trampier) represented, of course, a conundrum. He always did it his way," Frank shared. "So we see a lot of works of his that are just careless toss-offs of a cartoonist's style, and then we see absolutely world class pointillism in other expressions of his. He had an innate, incredible talent."

Frank also speculated that at that time, TSR was in the very beginning throes of deciding how best to mass market D&D. According to Frank, the decision to reject the more cartoony David Trampier art in favor of the conglomerate Sutherland/Trampier piece that was eventually used was probably based on a discussion of which version would sell best at a Sears-Roebuck. Even though Frank was not at TSR at the time, the decision makes perfect sense to him. He noted that in redoing the Trampier art, David Sutherland basically kept Trampier's magnificent mushroom garden while excising the figures. Frank points out that Sutherland substituted figures that echoed the same adventuring party used in the D&D Basic Set rulebook.

The rest of the story, Frank well-knows first-hand. While laying out issue #5 of *Polyhedron* magazine, he saw a wonderful unused piece of David Trampier art, and placed it in a layout hole he had on page 11 of that issue, thereby sharing with the world an unearthed historical gem that we would otherwise know nothing about. - Jim Wampler.

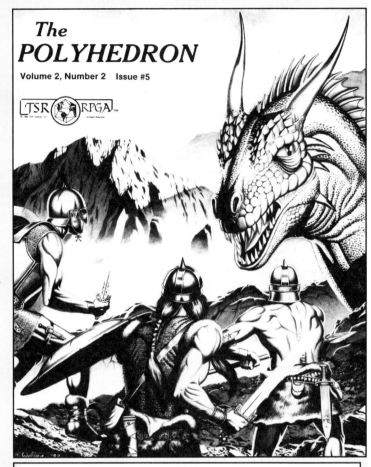

The POLYHEDRON

Volume 2, Number 2   Issue #5

Issue #5   The POLYHEDRON

SPELLING BEE

There are a few Official AD&D™ spells that are NOT covered in the hard-cover books. Two appeared in Gary Gygax's module G3 (*Hall of the Fire Giant King*), and are now included in the revision of the G series, G 1-2-3 (*Against the Giants*). These spells are the rare 9th level magic-user spells, **crystalbrittle** and **energy drain**.

(*The spell descriptions hereafter are from Module G 1-2-3 "Against the Giants," ©1978, 1981 TSR Hobbies, Inc.*)

Crystalbrittle *(Alteration)*

Level: 9
Range: *Touch*
Duration: *Permanent*
Area of Effect: *2 cubic feet per level*
Components: *V, S*
Casting Time: *9 segments*
Saving Throw: *Special*

Explanation/Description: The dweomer of this spell causes metal, whether as soft as gold or as hard as adamantite, to turn to a crystalline substance as brittle and fragile as crystal. Thus a sword, shield of metal, metal armor, or even an iron golem can be changed to a delicate, glass-like material easily shattered by any forceful blow. Furthermore, this change is unalterable short of a **wish** spell; i.e., **dispel magic** will not reverse the spell effect. The caster must physically touch the target item — equal to a hit in combat if the item is worn, wielded, or a monster.

Any single metal item can be affected by the spell. Thus, a suit of armor can be changed to crystal, but the shield would not be affected, or vice versa. All items gain a saving throw equal to their magical bonus value or protection. A sword +1/+3 would get a 10% chance to save (the average of the two pluses), magic armor +5 a 25% chance to be unaffected, and an iron golem a 15% chance to save (for it is hit only by magic weapons of +3 or better quality). Artifacts and relics of metal have a 95% chance to be unaffected by the spell. Affected items not immediately protected will be shattered and permanently destroyed if struck by a normal blow from a metal tool or any weighty weapon, including a staff.

Comments: Well, first of all I don't like to cast a spell of the highest rank possible and have it blown because of that percentage roll. There are numerous ways to help it, though; a *luckstone* for example, can alter the roll in your favor. But this is a specialty spell; you won't be running around with it ready "just in case." A *shape change* or *prismatic sphere* would be much more generally useful. Once your mage is over 21st level, and has multiple 9th level spells to toss around, this is one to consider as an extra.

When a character adds this spell to his or her repertoire, the DM should design a

climactic finale to an adventure in which a *crystalbrittle* spell is vital: a powerful guardian untouchable as long as a magic metal device it has is used; metal shielding around the final goal; there are many possibilities. Remember to plan uses for plenty of the party's other capabilities, along with this central idea for the end.

Energy Drain *(Evocation)*

Level: *9*
Range: *Touch*
Duration: *Permanent*
Area of Effect: *1 creature*
Components: *V, S, M*
Casting Time: *3 segments*
Saving Throw: *None*

Explanation/Description: By casting this spell, the magic-user opens a channel between the plane he or she is on and the Negative Material Plane; the caster becomes the conductor between the two planes. As soon as he or she touches any living creature (equal to a hit if melee is involved); the victim loses two energy levels (cf spectre in *Monster Manual*). A monster loses two hit dice permanently, both for hit points and attack ability. A character permanently loses levels, hit dice and points, and abilities (unless regained through adventuring, if applicable). The material component of the spell is essence of spectre or vampire dust. Preparation requires three segments, the material component is cast forth, and upon touching the victim the magic-user speaks the triggering word ("entropy," "nihil est," or whatever), and the dweomer takes effect instantly. There is always a 1 in 20 chance that the caster will also be affected by the *energy drain* and lose 1 energy level also when the victim is drained of two. Humans or humanoids brought to zero energy levels by this spell become zombies.

Comments: This is a nice example of

Gary's writing style, and includes a rare detailed description of the play-by-play action in the casting.

It's clear enough: a mage can knock two levels off of an opponent if a hit can be scored. This can be tough for a mage, but the spell would be a bit too powerful if it had a range. Note that *restoration* doesn't work on this effect; more experience points are necessary to regain the levels.

The last sentence deals with a procedure that was revised a bit: a human or humanoid brought to zero energy levels is a Level Zero character, i.e. typical townie wimp. One more level drain kills, with the victim rising as an undead (zombie, in this case) a day or so later. The "first published" rule applies here; the G modules came out after the PH, but before the DMG, where that revision occurred.

There were 26 new clerical spells published in DRAGON™ magazine #58 in Len Lakofka's column *Leomund's Tiny Hut*. Most are good, some are okay, one or two are not; TSR's Design department should be reviewing them soon, rephrasing and cross checking the details so they fit nicely into the AD&D system.

I'll put off detailed comments until they're in better shape, and also because we're nearly out of space. Briefly, though: several *ceremonies* are included, for campaign use (logical ones like marriage, burial, etc.); some holes in the system have been filled, by spells like the 3rd level *remove paralysis* and *water walking*. *Magic stone*, a first level, gives clerics another magical missile weapon, but the spell description still has many problems. DON'T use it as given.

When we get the Final Official versions, we'll print them, complete with comments.

Next column, the eternally disputed **phantasmal force**, with ramifications.

CHAPTER TWO
B1: In Search of the Unknown Original Publication

B1: *In Search of the Unknown* was first published by TSR in November 1978. It went through six printings and was included in the D&D Basic Set for a period of time (specifically the fourth and fifth printings of that set). The cover design for the first, second, and third printings of B1 was a yellow monochrome featuring a dual-signed illustration. Beginning in the fourth printing, the cover becomes a full-color piece by Darlene.

In this volume we present complete scans of the second and sixth printings. The contents of the various printings are not appreciably different, though if you look carefully at pages 6-7 you will see one of the more noticeable differences.

DUNGEONS & DRAGONS®

Dungeon Module B1
In Search of the Unknown

by Mike Carr

This package (a cover folder with maps and descriptive booklet within) forms a complete module for use with BASIC DUNGEONS & DRAGONS®. It is especially designed as an instructional aid for beginning Dungeon Masters and players, specifically created to enable new Dungeon Masters to initiate play with a minimum of preparation. With only minor modifications, this module is also eminently suitable for use with ADVANCED DUNGEONS & DRAGONS® as well.

In addition to descriptive and situational material, this module also includes special informational sections giving: background history and legends, listings of possible monsters and treasures and how to place them, a list of adventuring characters, tips on various aspects of play for the Dungeon Master, and helpful advice for starting players.

If you enjoy this module, look for more releases in the D & D® family from TSR, The Game Wizards!

© 1979, TSR Games

TSR Games
POB 756
Lake Geneva, WI 53147

Special Instructional Module

9023

ENTRANCE

DOOR

SECRET DOOR

FALSE DOOR

STAIRS, UP

STAIRS, DOWN

STATUE

PITS, COVERED

DUNGEONS & DRAGONS®

Dungeon Module B1
In Search of the Unknown

by Mike Carr

This package (a cover folder with maps and descriptive booklet within) forms a complete module for use with BASIC DUNGEONS & DRAGONS®. It is especially designed as an instructional aid for beginning Dungeon Masters and players, specifically created to enable new Dungeon Masters to initiate play with a minimum of preparation. With only minor modifications, this module is also eminently suitable for use with ADVANCED DUNGEONS & DRAGONS® as well.

In addition to descriptive and situational material, this module also includes special informational sections giving: background history and legends, listings of possible monsters and treasures and how to place them, a list of adventuring characters, tips on various aspects of play for the Dungeon Master, and helpful advice for starting players.

If you enjoy this module, look for more releases in the D & D® family from TSR, The Game Wizards!

Distributed to the book trade in the United States by Random House, Inc. and in Canada by Random House of Canada, Ltd.

© 1979, TSR Games

TSR Games
POB 756
Lake Geneva, WI 53147

Special Instructional Module

9023

Basic DUNGEONS & DRAGONS®
Special Instructional Dungeon Module #B1
IN SEARCH OF THE UNKNOWN
by Mike Carr

INTRODUCTION: This package forms the special instructional module for play of Basic DUNGEONS & DRAGONS®, and as such, is specifically designed for beginning players and Dungeon Masters. Due to its special design, it has numerous applications and serves a multiplicity of purposes.

Most material within this module is that contained in the D & D Basic Set game booklet. In some instances, new material (such as additional monsters, magic items, etc.) is included, and when this is so, every effort has been made to provide a pertinent explanation of important aspects and effects.

Those who intend to be beginning players using this module would be well advised to stop reading this now and to avoid further examination of the module details or game map. The reason for this is that enjoyment of the module will be much more enhanced when the challenge of the unknown and unexpected confronts the participants, who will not be able to benefit from any familiarity with the game situation other than the background provided by the referee. This element of the unknown and the resultant exploration in search of unknown treasures (with hostile monsters and unexpected dangers to outwit and overcome) is precisely what DUNGEONS & DRAGONS is all about, and "knowing too much" can greatly spoil the fun of the gaming experience that makes D & D so special. So, if you're going to be a player in this module, stop reading here, resist the temptation (which will be considerable) to go further in examining the contents, put the module aside, and wait for your Dungeon Master to get ready to use this package for gaming. You won't be sorry!

NOTES FOR THE DUNGEON MASTER

As a beginning Dungeon Master, you will find this module helpful in many ways. First of all, it serves as a graphic example of a beginning dungeon. For this reason, it should prove illustrative to fledgling Dungeon Masters who will benefit from a look at what another dungeon design "looks like". Those designing their own dungeons will want to note various aspects of this dungeon which will give them valuable insights into the creative process which allows them to formulate their own unique dungeon and game setting. Those going on to design their own dungeons and campaigns should be advised of the various playing aids available from TSR as official DUNGEONS & DRAGONS accessories — most notably the various sets of geomorphs (see the products list within the Basic D & D booklet for details on subjects and prices) which allow preparation of large map areas with a minimum of time and effort.

Second, this package provides an almost "ready-made" game situation which can be utilized for one or more playings. Some initial preparation is necessary in addition to reading the material through one or more times before using it in a game. The preparation, however, is interesting and fun as well as instructional, for it shows how a Dungeon Master (or DM) "stocks" the dungeon with assorted treasures and monsters before any adventuring begins. Separate lists of monsters and treasures to key with the various locations inside the dungeon insure that no two similar modules will be the same when set up by different DM's, and will also guarantee that players will not know what to expect in any given room or location. As for player characters, participants can use their own characters rolled up according to

the guidelines within the Basic DUNGEONS & DRAGONS rulebook or choose from a list of pre-generated characters supplied here (including possible hirelings and/or henchmen to accompany the player characters in their adventuring).

Thirdly, there are several salient points of good dungeon design illustrated in this module which new DM's would be wise to note. Likewise, they should keep these factors in mind when they start to design their own game maps and situations:

1) Since it is important to offer a challenge commensurate to the players' level, this two-level dungeon design is made specifically for Basic D & D for exploration by beginning players in a party of 3 to 6 adventurers (player and non-player characters combined). This is reflected in various ways:

  a) In general, this dungeon is less deadly and more forgiving than one designed to test experienced players. It is designed to be fairly challenging, however, and is by no means "easy". Careless adventurers will pay the penalty for a lack of caution — only one of the many lessons to be learned within the dungeon!

  b) The dungeon is designed to be instructive for new players. Most of it should be relatively easy to map, although there are difficult sections — especially on the lower level where irregular rock caverns and passageways will prove a real challenge.

  c) The monsters encountered will generally be commensurate with the adventurers' ability to defeat them. For the few that are too formidable, the adventurers will have to learn the necessary art of fleeing or else employ more powerful means against them.

  d) The treasures to be found will generally be small, although a couple of more lucrative finds are possible if the adventurers are clever or lucky.

2) The dungeon includes a good assortment of typical features which players can learn to expect, including some interesting tricks and traps:

  a) Several one-way secret doors
  b) Illusions and magic mouths
  c) A wind corridor which may extinguish torches and open flames
  d) A room of mysterious pools
  e) A room of doors
  f) A water pit trap which suddenly drops adventurers to the lower level
  g) A portcullis trap where vertical bars drop behind the party in a dead end corridor
  h) A pair of teleport rooms to confuse explorers
  i) Several magical treasures — most beneficial, some cursed
  j) Mysterious containers with a variety of contents for examination

3) There is a legend or story explaining some details of the setting and providing a background (i.e., why it exists, its background, how the characters became involved with it, etc.). Of course, players/adventurers will probably only know bits of this information — or perhaps only rumors of dubious reliability. Most good dungeons (and indeed, entire game campaigns) rest upon a firm basis of interesting background and "history" as set for the players by the game moderator, or Dungeon Master.

2

4) The setting is neither too simple nor too difficult. Adventurers can exit by either returning to the entrance or locating the other secret exit. Two ways down to the lower level are available for discovery, and a trap may also bring adventurers unexpectedly there.

PREPARATION FOR THE USE OF THE MODULE

The use of this module by the Dungeon Master first requires a working familiarity with its layout and various design features. Therefore, the first step is to completely read the module, doing so with care and with reference to the two maps provided to learn the basic layout and location of the various parts described in the written commentary. A second and third reading will also prove beneficial in preparing for a game employing the module.

Once the DM has obtained a background knowledge of the situation and the various features of the area to be explored, he must **key** the two maps by placing various monsters and treasures within the dungeon complex. To do so, he utilizes the two lists provided which follow within this booklet, taking advantage of the special system to allow easy setup and reference.

Upon examination of the two game maps, it will be noticed that each prominent room or chamber has a Roman numeral for designation purposes. Each Roman numeral corresponds to a written description within the body commentary which accompanies the maps and which is contained in this booklet. Thus, a description of each such area of the dungeon is easily referenced by locating the written material within the booklet, and these are arranged in numerical order. The basic descriptions are standard, but in most cases there is no mention of either monsters inhabiting a particular area or specific treasures to be found within (except for occasional items which are part of the furnishings and which may have some unusual value). A space exists after each description with a brief area for listing either a monster or a treasure (or both) which may be within that room; exactly what will appear in each room, however, is up to the Dungeon Master, who will fill in some of the spaces to denote their presence. This is done easily through the use of the number and letter-coded lists provided for monsters and treasures, respectively. It is important to note, however, that not every room will contain a monster, a treasure, or both — in fact, a fair number of rooms will contain neither, and in some cases the treasure will be hidden or concealed in some manner. Further details on the use of the two lists is contained in the description which precedes them in the section entitled KEYING THE DUNGEON.

Once the dungeon has been keyed and the Dungeon Master's preparation is complete, he must assist the players in getting ready for the adventure. The first step is in providing them with the background outline which sets the stage for the game. This "Player's Background Sheet" (which differs in some ways from the more detailed description/background for the referee) is on a perforated sheet at the end of this booklet. It is designed to be removed and handed to the players prior to the adventure (or simply read aloud to them if you do not wish to remove it from the booklet).

Once the players know the background, they can prepare their characters for the adventure. If new characters are needed (as they will be if the players are just starting their first game), they can be rolled up by using the dice and following the prescribed procedure within the Basic DUNGEONS & DRAGONS rule booklet. Each player also determines his amount of starting money (the number of gold pieces he has to begin with), and this amount is available for the purchase of arms and equipment for adventur-ing. Once the players have decided upon the equipment they will be carrying, as well as their own arms and armor, they are ready to start play. A written record of abilities, wealth, and equipment owned and carried is kept by each player.

As an alternative to spending time rolling the characters up, a list of assorted adventuring characters is included on the reverse side of the "Player's Background Sheet". If the Dungeon Master decides to do so, the players can choose one of the characters listed there as their player character. In such a case, the DM then provides the pertinent specifications and ability ratings of the character to the player, who makes a note of it on the side. The DM's master list of character abilities for these characters is within this booklet.

If there are only two or three players, or if a party wishes additional assistance, one or more hirelings or henchmen (non-player characters who will be a part of the party but who will not be under the total control of the players) can be added to the group of adventurers at the Dungeon Master's discretion. These characters can also be from the list, and their specifications and ability ratings are also on the master list for the Dungeon Master.

When players have hirelings (characters who serve for pay) or henchmen (characters who serve out of admiration or loyalty), the Dungeon Master must use common sense in their employment within the game. Obviously, allowing players to assemble large bands of armed assistants at this stage of the game would be unfair and unbalancing, so it will be unusual to see more than one or two non-player characters appearing in the first games. Only after players have survived to earn some repute and wealth to attract (and afford) them will they be able to locate additional adventurers to aid their exploration.

Seeking hirelings and henchmen is a matter to be handled by the Dungeon Master. A player's success in attracting either will depend upon the financial rewards offered (in the case of hirelings) or the charisma of the seeker (in the case of henchmen). Once a henchman or hireling has decided to join a group (this usually being determined by a secret dice roll by the Dungeon Master), the non-player character will generally function according to the directions of the player character being served. However, in some situations — most notably, those involving great risk or danger — the Dungeon Master serves as the "conscience" of the henchman or hireling, and may cause him to balk at ordered action or perhaps even desert in the face of danger or as a result of unrewarded courage or accomplishment. For example, if a party is facing a hazardous situation and a player tells his henchmen to do something which would seem more dangerous than the actions pursued by the other player adventurers, the henchmen may hesitate to act upon the order — or in some cases might simply run away if the chance of death is great (this being determined by the DM's secret die roll at the chances of his choosing, depending upon the situation). Likewise, if a henchman successfully executes a hazardous action (slaying a dragon without much help, for instance) and does not get a proportional reward, then he will understandably consider deserting the player character who ill-treated him. In such cases, the DM will determine the outcome, and, as always, his decisions (often the result of die rolls at appropriate chances which he determines) are final.

An alternative to having either hirelings or henchmen under player control is simply to have non-player adventurers available for single-game participation. In this case, an additional character accompanies the group and participates, but is independent of player control other than to be

3

helpful and generally cooperative. The Dungeon Master runs the character in essence, although his actions will generally follow the desires and suggestions of the players (unless an unduly hazardous action is demanded). The independent character participates in return for a share of the treasure gained, and this share (which will at least be proportional, or even greater than proportional if the character is better than the player characters) must be agreed upon before the adventure starts. If your players are trying to attract such help, roll a die to see how hard a bargain the extra character drives in order to be convinced that participating is worthwhile . . . After the adventure has been completed, the extra character might simply take his treasure share and disappear from further use, or if the DM desires, be available for similar service in future quests. The section entitled THE CHARACTER LISTS gives additional suggestions for the employment of non-player hirelings and henchmen.

Once the players have completed their preparations for the game, the referee finishes "setting the stage" by bringing the player characters from the background story to the place where the game adventure will begin. This is usually simply a matter of providing a brief narrative (such as, "Your group, after purchasing supplies and getting organized, left their town and went cross country till a deserted pathway was found which led into the hills, and finally to a craggy outcropping of rock . . . "). Use of the LEGEND TABLE (described elsewhere in this booklet) is also made at this time.

To start the adventure, the players must decide on an order of march for all of the characters in their group — who will be in front, who in the middle, who at the rear, and so on. This should be diagrammed on a sheet of paper and given to the Dungeon Master for reference, and any change in the order of march during the adventure should be noted. In a standard 10' wide corridor, the most common arrangement is two adventurers side by side in each rank, although three characters could operate together in a single rank if all of their weapons were short and easily wielded (daggers or small hand axes, for instance).

One player in the group should be designated as the leader, or "caller" for the party, while another one or two players can be selected as mappers (at least one is a must!). Although individual players have the right to decide their own actions and relay them to the Dungeon Master as play progresses, the caller will be the one who gives the DM the details on the group's course of action as they move around and explore (such instructions as "We'll move slowly down this corridor to the east . . . " or "We'll break down this door while so-and-so covers our rear . . . " are typical directions given by a caller to the DM). In the course of the adventure, the caller will naturally discuss the options available to the party with the rest of the adventurers, but it is he who the DM relies upon for the official instructions (although individual players can still pursue alternate courses of action at appropriate times, if they insist, by telling the Dungeon Master). Once a caller (or any player) speaks and indicates an action is being taken, it is begun — even if he quickly changes his mind (especially if he realizes he's made a mistake or an error in judgment). Use your discretion in such cases.

The player or players mapping the explored area should use graph paper. Orient them according to the same directions on the referee's map (with the top being north in almost all cases). After that, allow them to draw their maps from your descriptions as they wish — but make certain that your verbal descriptions of the areas they explore are accurate (although you can say such things as "approximately sixty feet", especially in large or open areas, or places where

there are irregular rock surfaces). Above all, avoid the considerable temptation to correct their maps once they have drawn them. It will not be uncommon for players to show you their map (especially if they're confused) and ask you, "Is this right?". In most such instances, you should avoid correcting any mistakes there, unless it would be obvious through the eyes of the adventuring characters. Encourage good mapping skills and an attention to detail rather than falling into the rut of continual player map questions.

Exploration of the entire area comprising the module may well take more than one game session. It is also quite possible that adventurers (especially if wounded or reduced in number) may want to pull out of the stronghold and prepare for a return visit when refreshed or reinforced. If this is done, they must work their way to an exit and discuss with you the pertinent details and time passage until their return. In such cases, the exact status of areas already explored will depend upon your judgment — whether areas cleared of monsters might in some cases be re-occupied by new ones, doors left open closed again and locked, or whatever.

If the exploring adventurers wish to suspend the game temporarily during a rest period (when the adventuring characters stop to sleep, as they must do every 24 hours), appropriate notes should be made of each adventurer's status so that resumption of the game can begin at the same point on the next meeting of the players. Their choice of where to camp is a factor to consider, as well, since a check for wandering monsters must be made up to three times for any 8-hour period they remain there (these checks are made at a normal 1 in 6 chance). It is customary to have one or more adventurers in the party standing guard at any one time, as the party members sleep in shifts in order to always have continual protection (although the devious DM may give a slight chance of a guard being asleep if a monster comes . . .). Just as with march order, it is important that players provide the DM with the sleeping location of each member and the placement of the guard or guards, since this may be crucial if and when a monster approaches from a given direction.

Experience points earned and any benefits gained will only be applicable if and when the adventurers successfully exit the dungeon; experience gained in an adventure is only credited after the adventure is complete. However, successfully exiting the dungeon and then returning later would allow the characters to use experience gained on the previous foray, if applicable.

TIME

As adventures go on, the Dungeon Master is responsible for keeping track of time elapsed.

In normal movement and exploration, each turn is considered to be ten minutes (see page 9 of the Basic D & D booklet for details). If an encounter or melee occurs, the Dungeon Master immediately (but temporarily, for the duration of the encounter) adjusts the time frame to melee turns consisting of ten 10-second melee rounds (see page 20 of the Basic D & D booklet).

Every third turn of adventuring, the DM should take a die roll for the possible appearance of wandering monsters at the indicated chances (which are normally 1 in 6, but which may vary depending upon location and dungeon level). Some occurrences (such as noise and commotion caused by adventurers) may necessitate additional checks.

Paper and pencil can be used to tally time, and the DM

4

should monitor its passage as he sees fit, but keeping in mind that exploring, mapping, and examining various features takes up considerable time — with the larger the area and the greater the care taken in examining, the more time consumed. Wasted time is also a factor which should be noted, as players may waste time arguing or needlessly discussing unimportant manners or by simply blundering around aimlessly. On the other hand, time can pass quickly if adventurers move rapidly through areas which have been previously explored and mapped. In all cases the DM should use his good judgment and common sense.

Generally, eight hours of each twenty-four must be spent resting and sleeping, and prudent adventurers will sleep in shifts with a guard always awake. As a general rule, three checks will be made each "night" for possible wandering monsters.

The passage of a day — or 24 hours — will mean the healing of 1 hit point of damage for each character.

COMPUTING EXPERIENCE

At the conclusion of an adventure (the party's emergence from the dungeon), the surviving characters divide the treasure (with equal shares generally awarded to each and magical or special items diced for by eligible characters) and experience is computed. Henchmen and hirelings usually get an equal share of any treasure, although their experience point award may vary at the Dungeon Master's discretion from half to the full amount awarded to player characters, depending upon their accomplishments.

As an example, let us assume that two first level player characters (a magic-user and a fighter) and a first level hireling (a fighter) survive an adventure and return to the outside world from a dungeon which has claimed several of their comrades. The treasure they carry out with them amounts to the following: 630 g.p., 9 50 g.p. gems, a scroll of 2 magic-user spells, a +1 sword, and a +1 **ring of protection**. In the course of their adventure, their party caused the following monsters to be slain: 8 kobolds, 5 orcs, and a giant tick.

In this instance, the treasure is rather easily divided: the gold pieces are split into 210 apiece, 3 gems are awarded to each character, the scroll goes to the magic-user (since he is the only one who can use it), and the two fighters roll dice for the sword and the ring, with one going to each (in some instances, a non-player character may end up with the best treasure this way, but such is the luck of the dice . . .). This gives each adventurer the equivalent of 210 g.p. cash, plus 150 g.p. in gems (if traded or sold for gold pieces), plus one other item which can be retained and used.

The monsters slain are considered for experience point values as follows (see page 11 of the Basic D & D booklet): the 8 kobolds are worth 5 points apiece as creatures under 1 hit die, the 5 orcs are worth 10 points each as 1 hit die monsters, and the giant tick is worth 50 points (35 points as a 3 hit dice creature plus 15 points for its special ability to cause disease). The total value of all monsters killed is thus 140 experience points — 40 for the kobolds, 50 for the orcs, and 50 for the giant tick. This divides to 46 experience points per surviving adventurer for monsters slain.

Total experience points for each adventurer, assuming they were of first level (a higher level of experience would dictate a fractional adjustment), would be 360 (the g.p. equivalent of coins and gems) plus 46 (for the monsters killed), or 406 points each. No additional points are awarded for the special or magical items.

Once enough points are accumulated, a character can rise to the next higher level of experience, and gain the benefits of the new level. Wealth obtained, besides counting initially for experience, can be used to purchase equipment or supplies, defray everyday expenses, attract hirelings, sponsor various enterprises, or can be spent in any manner (including payments of tithes to the church, especially for clerics!).

HOW TO BE AN EFFECTIVE DUNGEON MASTER

The Dungeon Master, as referee, is the pivotal figure in any game of DUNGEONS & DRAGONS. Accordingly, his ability and expertise — as well as fairness — will be important factors in whether or not the game will be enjoyable for all of the participants, as well as for himself.

D & D is a role-playing game, and is unlike traditional games which have a firm basis of regulated activity and repetitious action. D & D is free-flowing, and often goes in unknown and unpredictable directions — and that is precisely the reason it is so different and challenging. The Dungeon Master is best described as the moderator of the action, for he oversees the whole process, keeps the game moving, resolves the action based upon events occurring and player choices made, and monitors the actions and events outside the player group (i.e. handles monsters encountered, determines the actions of non-player characters encountered, etc.). His responsibilities are considerable, but his foremost concern should be to provide an enjoyable game which is challenging to the players. This means that risk should be balanced with reward, and that game situations are neither too "easy" nor too deadly. Above all, he must be fair, reasonable (without kowtowing to the unreasonable demands of the players), and worthy of the respect of all the participants.

Beginning Dungeon Masters who are not familiar with the game often ask the most common first question, "Exactly how do you referee the game?". The answer is that there is no single best way — different DM's have different styles, just as individual players do. However, there are certain guidelines which are important to follow . . .

First of all, it is crucial to keep in mind that D & D is a game based on player interaction and player choice. The game generally follows the course of the player's actions — if not always their plans! As moderator, you present an ever-changing situation as it occurs (sort of like an unfolding story, or even a movie, if you like to think in those terms), and the players respond pretty much as they desire. As the game goes on, you are presenting them with a hundred different opportunities and choices — exactly how the game goes will depend upon their response to those opportunities and choices. For instance, if players decide to walk down a corridor and find a dead end with three doors, they have a number of choices — simply turn around and ignore the doors, listen at one or more before proceeding elsewhere, try to open one or more (either normally, by forcing them, or even by simply bashing them in), or whatever. You describe the situation, then await their decision as to a course of action. Of course, some decisions will be more difficult, or quick, or crucial to survival — and as always, imagination and resourcefulness, as well as quick thinking, will usually be rewarded.

Second of all, a good DM remains "above the battle" and does not attempt to influence player actions or channel the activity in a particular direction. The Dungeon Master should do all he can to assist players in their quest without actually providing important information unless the players themselves discover it or put the pieces of a puzzling problem to-

5

gether through deduction or questioning, or a combination of the two. A large part of the game consists of player questions, many of which are "what do we see?". Your job as gamemaster is to answer those questions without giving too much away. You need not hint to players any information that they do not ask for on their own, except in unusual instances. Allow them to ask the questions, and allow them to make the choices.

In the same vein, as Dungeon Master you will enjoy watching players wrestle with the problems you present them with. Although you may set up situations to challenge them, you must understand that you are not their adversary, nor are you necessarily out to "defeat" them. You will enjoy moderating a well-played game where players respond to the challenges encountered much more than one where the adventurers foolishly meet their demise in quick time. However, if your players abandon caution or make stupid mistakes, let them pay the price — but be fair. In many cases, a danger due to lack of caution can be overcome, or a mistake in judgment countered by quick thinking and resourcefulness, but *let your players do the thinking and the doing.*

As Dungeon Master, you are the game moderator. This means you set the tempo of the game and are responsible for keeping it moving. Above all, *you* remain in control of the situation, although with reasonable players your game should always be in control. If players are unusually slow or dilly-dally unnecessarily, remind them that time is wasting. If they persist, allow additional chances for wandering monsters to appear — or at least start rolling the dice to make the players think that you are doing so. If players are argumentative with each other, remind them their noise also serves to attract unwelcome monsters; if they persist, show them that this is true.

Lastly, it is important to remember that the Dungeon Master is the final arbiter in his or her game. If players disagree with you, hear them out and reasonably consider their complaint. However, **you** are the final judge — and they should understand that, as well as the fact that not everything will go their way, or as they expect. Be fair, but be firm. With human nature as it is, players will undoubtedly attempt to try to talk you into (or out of) all sorts of things; part of the fun of being a DM is this verbal interplay. But in the end, what you say is what goes.

USING THIS MODULE WITH ADVANCED DUNGEONS & DRAGONS

Although this module is specifically designed for use with Basic D & D, experienced players will have no difficulty in using this package with the rules for ADVANCED D & D.

Dungeon Masters who wish to employ the module with A D & D will have no problem utilizing the two level maps and the descriptive copy to form the basic outline. In a similar manner, the Legend Table will be used as described. The DM, however, can disregard the various lists of monsters, treasures, and non-player characters and make appropriate substitutions using the greater and more challenging ideas of his A D & D players. Likewise, more formidable and deadly tricks and traps will be called for in order to fully challenge the mettle of the more sophisticated players.

BACKGROUND

Many years ago, rumor has it, two noted personages in the area, Rogahn the Fearless (a fighter of renown) and Zelligar

the Unknown (a magic-user of mystery and power) pooled their resources and expertise to construct a home and stronghold for the two of them to use as a base of operations. The location of this hidden complex was chosen with care, since both men disliked visitors and intruders. Far from the nearest settlement, away from traveled routes, and high upon a craggy hill, the new construction took shape. Carved out of the rock protrusion which crested the heavily forested hill, this mystical hideaway was well hidden, and its rumored existence was never common knowledge. Even less well known was its name, the Caverns of Quasqueton.

Construction of the complex, it is said, took over a decade, even with the aid of magic and the work of hundreds of slaves and laborers. Vast amounts of rock were removed and tumbled off the rough cliffs into large piles now overgrown with vegetation. A single tower was constructed above ground for lookout purposes, even though there was little to see other than a hilly, forested wilderness for miles around.

Rogahn and Zelligar lived in their joint sanctuary for quite some time, conducting their affairs from within except for occasional adventures in the outside world where both men attempted to add to their reputations as foremost practitioners of their respective arts.

The deeds and adventures of these two characters were never well known, since they both kept their distance from civilization. Some say, and perhaps rightly so, that their motives were based on greed and some kind of vague (or chaotic) evil. No one knows for sure.

What is known more widely is the reputation of each. Despite their questionable alignment of suspected evil, both Rogahn and Zelligar capped their reputation of power when they joined forces to stop a barbarian invasion threatening the great valley below. In a crucial battle at a narrow pass in the hills, the two combined powerful forces and decisively turned back the invasion. Rogahn slew a horde of barbarians single-handedly and Zelligar's powerful magic put their army to flight. A grateful populace rewarded the pair and their henchmen with considerable treasure, after which the two retired to their hideaway. Most of the reward treasure was apparently used to finance the further construction of Quasqueton, although some of it may yet be hidden somewhere. In any case, the hill stronghold was not completed in its entirety when, years later, the intrepid pair apparently embarked on their last adventure.

Some years ago, Rogahn and Zelligar apparently decided upon a joint foray into the lands of the hated barbarians. Taking most of their henchmen and associates along in a great armed band, the two personages disappeared into the forbidding alien lands to the north, far from the hills and forests surrounding Quasqueton.

Word just reaching civilization tells of some great battle in the barbarian lands where Rogahn and Zelligar have met their demise. This rumored clash must have occurred some years ago, and there are few details — and no substantiation of the story. The only thing certain is that Rogahn and Zelligar have been gone far too long. If only one had the knowledge and wherewithal to find their hideaway, he would have great things to explore! And who knows what riches of wealth and magic might be there for the taking???

Note: In the mythical WORLD OF GREYHAWK (available from TSR) the stronghold can be considered within any one of the following lands — the Barony of Ratik, the Duchy of Tenh, or the Theocracy of the Pale.

LEGEND TABLE

Prior to the first adventure into the stronghold, the Dungeon Master will utilize this table to impart "background knowledge" (from rumors or legends known) to the adventurers. The table itself includes bits and scraps of information regarding the place to be explored — most of it accurate; however, legends and rumors being what they are, some of the information is false and misleading. It will be up to the players to act upon the information they "know"; the Dungeon Master will tell them that these are legends or rumors they have heard about the place, and that is all (it will be up to the players to decide upon the value or veracity of such information).

To determine legends/rumors known, each player character will cast a 4-sided die in secret conference with the Dungeon Master (non-player characters or henchmen/hirelings will get no roll). The result of the roll will give the number of rumors/legends known by the individual rolling the die:

1 One legend known
2 Two legends known
3 Three legends known
4 No legends known

Rolls of 1, 2, or 3 will result in that many rolls on the Legend Table using d20. A roll of a 4 indicates that the adventurer has no knowledge of any rumors or legends pertaining to the stronghold; any information he desires he must attempt to obtain from the other players adventuring with him.

The legends/rumors known are determined by the player's roll of the 20-sided die, and the DM reads the appropriate information off the table to the player for each roll (this is done secretly where the other players cannot overhear). The DM then tells the player that this is the extent of background information known by his or her player character; whether or not the player chooses to share this information (all or only part of it) with the other players is a personal decision. In this manner each player is given a chance to see what bits of additional information their character knows before the adventure starts.

LEGEND TABLE (d20)

"F" denotes a false legend or rumor, but the player will not know it is false.

1) The name of the stronghold is Quasqueton.

2)F Zelligar had a wizard's workshop in the stronghold where he worked on magic stronger than any known to man.

3)F Rogahn owned a fantastic gem as big as a man's fist that was worth over 100,000 gold pieces; he kept it hidden in his personal quarters.

4) Zelligar and Rogahn had orc slaves to do the menial work, and some lived permanently at the stronghold.

5) The complex has two levels.

6) Part of the complex is unfinished.

7) The complex has a rear exit which is secret and well hidden.

8) No outsiders have ever entered the complex and returned to tell the tale.

9) Troglodytes have moved into the complex in the absence of its normal inhabitants.

10)F The place is protected by the gods themselves, and one member of any party of intruders is doomed to certain death.

11)F The treasures of Zelligar and Rogahn are safely hidden in a pool of water.

12)F The entire place is filled with guards left behind by Zelligar and Rogahn.

13) Rogahn's trophy room has battle relics and slain monster remains from his adventures.

14) There is a room with many pools of water within the complex.

15) The very walls speak to visitors.

16)F An enchanted stone within the stronghold will grant a wish to anyone who chips off a piece of it and places it within their mouth.

17)F All treasures of Zelligar and Rogahn are cursed to bring ill to any who possess them.

18)F Zelligar and Rogahn have actually returned to their stronghold, and woe be to any unwelcome visitors!

19) There are secret doors, rooms, and passageways in parts of the complex.

20) The complex has more than one level.

Note: when rolling on this table, roll again if any number duplicates one already rolled by the same player.

THE DUNGEON

This area for exploration is designed to challenge a party of 3-8 adventurers (player characters and henchmen or hirelings) of up to the third level of experience, and is specifically intended for use with Basic DUNGEONS & DRAGONS. Players will find it beneficial to have a mix of characters in their party who will complement each other and who will possess a variety of abilities due to their different classes (fighters, magic users, clerics, thieves, etc.). Additionally, the carrying of one or two useful magic items will likewise be of great help (although more numerous or more powerful such items will unbalance the situation).

If a Dungeon Master wishes to use the module with ADVANCED DUNGEONS & DRAGONS, a separate set of guidelines will be found at the end of the module to enable this conversion.

The Caverns of Quasqueton, as mentioned in the background description, are hewn from a great rock outcropping at the crest of a large wooded hill. Winds buffet the hill continuously, blowing and whistling through the trees, vines, and other vegetation which blanket the prominence on all sides. The rock itself is a heavy blackish slate, and is evident all throughout the caverns on both levels.

The air within the caverns is heavy, wet, and musty. In some portions of the complex, a layer of dust lies upon everything, undisturbed for years. Burning anything within is slow and difficult, for the entire atmosphere resists combustion. Torches and lanterns will burn smokily.

7

There are many doors within the dungeon (the term "dungeon" being used generically for the entire underground area, as it usually is in DUNGEONS & DRAGONS), and some of them are secret doors, discernible only by special examination or perhaps by an elf with his or her inborn ability to notice them. In all cases, unless otherwise noted, doors will be locked one-third of the time — and any roll of a 1 or 2 on a six-sided die (d6) will mean that they will bar entrance unless the lock is sprung or broken. Breaking the lock or breaking down the entire door will be a noisy undertaking, to be sure, and may serve to attract unwelcome monsters . . .

The two levels of the dungeon are approximately equal in size and are located one above the other. If the two maps could be placed over one another, the three access points between levels would directly correspond to their locations on the maps and lead directly to each other up and down.

THE CAVERNS OF QUASQUETON

KEY TO THE UPPER LEVEL

Within the complex, the upper level is a rather finished abode with generally good stonework and masonry overall. There are rough spots, or portions where workmanship is not as good as overall, but for the most part the construction and excavation are well done. The walls are relatively smoothly hewn and finished and in generally good repair. The floors, while uneven in places, are likewise in good condition. Corridors generally measure 10' in width, while ceilings for the most part are approximately 8' to 10' above the floor. The blackish stone from which the halls and caverns were hewn is evident overall. Doors are uniformly of heavy wooden construction, approximately five or six inches thick.

WANDERING MONSTERS

Check every third turn; 1 in 6 (roll a 6-sided die). If a monster is indicated, roll a six-sided die again and compare to the list below to determine what type of monster appears. Then check for surprise. The abbreviations which follow are the same as used and explained in the section entitled MONSTER LIST.

1. Orcs (1-4) — HP: 6, 4, 3, 1; #AT: 1; D: 1-6; AC 7/12; SA: None.

2. Giant Centipedes (1-2) — HP: 2 each; #AT: 1; D: Nil; AC 9/10; SA: Bite does no damage but save vs poison must be made (+4 on die).

3. Kobolds (1-6) — HP: 4, 3, 3, 2, 2, 1; #AT: 1; D: 1-4; AC 7/12; SA: None.

4. Troglodytes (1-2) — HP: 6, 5; #AT: 1; D: 1-6; AC 5/14; SA: Emit odor when enraged.

5. Giant Rats (2-5) — HP: 4, 3, 2, 1, 1; #AT: 1; D: 1-3; AC 7/12; SA: Bite has 5% chance of causing disease (save vs poison).

6. Berserkers (1-2) — HP: 5, 4; #AT: 1; D: 1-8; AC 7/12; SA: +2 on attacks vs normal men.

ENCOUNTER AREAS

ENTRANCE. A cave-like opening, somewhat obscured by vegetation, is noticeable at the end of a treacherous pathway which leads up to the craggy outcropping of black rock. By sweeping aside some of the vines and branches,

the opening becomes easily accessible to human-size explorers.

The opening leads straight into the rock formation, with a 10' wide corridor leading the way to a large wooden door. The door opens freely, and close examination will reveal that bits of wood have been chipped away from the edge, indicating that it has previously been forced (this fact will certainly be known if adventurers indicate they are examining the door; otherwise there will be a 10% chance per adventurer, cumulative, of this being noticed — 40% if four adventurers, etc.).

I. ALCOVES. There are three pairs of alcoves past the entrance, located as they are for purposes of defense against intruders or invaders. These guardpoints are all empty and barren of any markings.

The second pair of alcoves are actually secret one-way doors, but totally unnoticeable to anyone on the side of the entrance corridor (even if close examination is made). These one-way doors are also a defensive measure to allow guards to appear in the rear of any invading group which passes this point.

The third pair of alcoves contains a double **magic mouth** spell, and this magic omen will be triggered as soon as any adventurers reach the point in the corridor between the two alcoves. When this occurs, a **mouth** appears on the side wall of the east alcove, and another **mouth** appears on the side wall of the west alcove. The east **mouth** speaks first, in a booming voice: "WHO DARES ENTER THIS PLACE AND INTRUDE UPON THE SANCTUARY OF ITS INHABITANTS?" After but a moment, and drowning out any attempted reply by the party, comes the reply from the west **mouth**: "ONLY A GROUP OF FOOLHARDY EXPLORERS DOOMED TO CERTAIN DEATH!". Then both **mouths** will shout in unison, "WOE TO ANY WHO PASS THIS PLACE — THE WRATH OF ZELLIGAR AND ROGAHN WILL BE UPON THEM!" The **mouths** will then begin a loud and raucous laughter, which fades in intensity as the twin **mouths** disappear from view. They are a permanent feature of the stronghold, and will reappear on every visit.

Past the third pair of alcoves and at the end of the corridor from the entrance are two steps up. At the top of the steps, the corridor continues straight ahead, and corridors meet from east and west. At this intersection is a grisly sight — the remains of a hand-to-hand battle where no less than five combatants died.

Upon examination of the bodies (if the adventurers choose to do so), it will be seen that three of them were adventurers themselves, explorers from the outer world. This ill-fated trio obviously had their first and last battle at this spot. Their opponents, also slain here, are two guards. The bodies arrayed here, each in various states of decomposition, are as follows (the stench of decaying bodies is strong and repulsive, and the sight doubly so):

Body #1 — A human fighter, slumped against a wall. His broken sword, sheared off about eight inches above the pommel, tells the story of his demise. The body has been stripped of any armor, and there are no items of value on the remains, other than a belt pouch containing 5 gold pieces (g.p.).

Body #2 — A human magic-user, impaled against a wall. The killing sword, still thrust through the body, is lodged in the wall, which has a large section of wood at this point. If the sword is removed, the body will crumple to the floor, exposing a blood-stained carving. The carved letters

8

form the word "QUASQUETON" in the "common" language.

The sword, upon being removed, will prove worthless, since its handle is very loose and the overall quality of the weapon is poor.

The body is bereft of any items of great value. The magic-user's robe, now bloodstained and ruined, has a pocket and within it is a purse containing 2 g.p. and a pouch full of garlic buds.

Body #3 — A dwarf fighter, face down in the corridor just east of the intersection. In his right hand he still clutches his war hammer, and it appears that he crawled, wounded, to this point, since a trail of dried blood leads back to the battle location. A sack turned inside out lies alongside the body, now empty.

Armor has been stripped from the body, although the fighter's helm is still on his head. This headgear, however, has a noticeable dent in it which will make it unusable and thus worthless. There are no items of value on the remains.

Body #4 — A human berserker/fighter, obviously a guard who defended to the death. The body is sprawled on the floor, and a broken wooden shield lies nearby. The body has no armor on it. There is no weapon on the body or nearby, nor are there any other items of value on the remains.

Body #5 — A human berserker/fighter, another guard. This body, with a bashed head from the blow of a war hammer, lies on the floor face down. There is no armor or weapon on the body except for a small sheathed dagger on the belt. The belt is very ornately decorated leather, which would appear to be worth something, except for the bloodstains ruining its appearance.

Monster:

Treasure & Location:

II. KITCHEN. The food preparation area for the complex is a very long room with a variety of details. At the southwest corner of the room are two cooking pits, each large enough to cook an animal as large as a deer. One of the pits is slightly larger than the other, but both are about 3 feet in depth. The pits are full of ash and charred remains of cooking fuel. A chimney leads upward, but its small size prevents further investigation.

Long tables line each wall, and there are scattered containers on them, some upturned, with spilled contents moldering on the table top. There are spoiled pieces of food all around, and the smell in the room is very uninviting. One chunk of moldy cheese is particularly noxious, as a fuzzy green growth covers its entirety.

Hanging from above are a variety of utensils, and some other of these are scattered about on the floor of the room. These are nothing more than pots and pans of various sizes, although there is a large cast iron kettle suspended from the ceiling by a thick chain. The kettle is empty.

Monster:

Treasure & Location:

III. DINING ROOM. This room serves as the main dining hall for the complex, and it is here that guest banquets are held.

The room is moderately decorated, but frugally so, since there appear to be no items of great value which are part of the decor. A nicely carved wooden mantle surrounds the room at a height 7 feet off the floor, and the stone walls are also carved in simple yet pleasant designs.

There are a number of tables and chairs in the room, these being of wooden construction and quite utilitarian in nature. Only two chairs stand out from the rest, these being the personal seats of the stronghold's illustrious inhabitants, Zelligar and Rogahn. Both of these chairs are ornately carved walnut, formed from an enormous block of this wood which forms a portion of the wall in the northeast corner of the room. Upon closer examination, it will be seen that the chairs themselves are actually fixed seats connected to the wooden structure, thus being unremovable. Their great beauty is apparent, but is marred by a greenish fungus growing on portions of the walnut. It is obvious the seats have not been used for quite some length of time.

The lesser tables and chairs are scattered about, and several are overturned. All of these furnishings are of hard maple. They show wear, although they have obviously not been used recently.

The entire room has a musty, mildewy smell to it.

Monster:

Treasure & Location:

IV. LOUNGE. This anteroom is through a south door from the dining room, and apparently was designed for before-dinner and after-dinner activity. Drinking was apparently the most popular pastime here, for several earthenware tankard mugs hang from a row of hooks high on one wall (many more are missing, it appears). An ale keg, long since dry but still smelling slightly of the brew, stands in one corner.

The stone walls are strangely textured for an unusual effect, but are devoid of further markings or details. A long wooden bench seat, actually attached to the wall, is along each side of the room. Those seated on the bench all face toward the center of the room and the statue there.

At the center of the room is a carved statue, full-size, of a nude human female, beckoning with arms out front in a very alluring pose. This statue, apparently of white marble, is obviously of great value (over 5,000 g.p.). However, due to its tremendous weight and the fact that it seems anchored to the floor, it will be impossible to remove without a major engineering effort. Even characters with a strength of 18 will be unable to move it in any way.

Monster:

Treasure & Location:

V. WIZARD'S CHAMBER. Zelligar's personal chamber is actually a rather austere abode. The most noticeable feature seen upon entering is a very large and fairly detailed stone carving which runs most of the length of the north wall of the room. Some 70 feet in overall length, the wall carving depicts a mighty wizard (obviously Zelligar) on a hilltop casting a spell in the air over a valley below, with an entire army fleeing in confused panic.

The east and west walls are devoid of detail, although there are several wall pegs on each, apparently for hanging garments.

There is a minimum of furniture within the room. Zelligar's

9

bed, located in the southeast corner of the chamber, is a frame of ornately carved rosewood. The headboard, besides showing the carved designs to advantage, boldly features Zelligar's name highlighted in gold leaf. The bed, obviously of value, is of fine workmanship and construction. Because of its sturdiness, it cannot be removed from the room without dismantling, and doing so will be difficult and likely to cause damage to the various pieces. If this is done, the baseboard and sides would be worth 100 g.p. each, and the headboard up to 500 g.p. However, anyone trying to sell the headboard for its value will run an 80% risk that the purchaser will recognize the original owner's name (since the fame of Zelligar is widely known) — and if this word spreads at large, the seller may have attendant problems, since it will be obvious from where the headboard was obtained.

A rosewood nightstand/table is beside the bed, and it has one locked drawer. The brass handle to the drawer has a pin trap which will be tripped by anyone grasping it, inflicting 1 hit point of damage. An oily substance on the pins is not a poison, but it does inflict unusual pain which will make the grasping hand unusable by the victim for 2-5 (d4 + 1) turns. If a key is inserted into the lock before the handle is grasped, the trap will be negated. Any key of a size comparable to the actual key (which is nowhere to be found) will accomplish this function. The drawer itself is empty (unless treasure in this room is to be located within the drawer).

Elsewhere in the room is a table and three chairs, none of which is of any exceptional worth or value. Upon the table is a pewter pitcher and three pewter mugs. The pitcher has a value of 15 g.p., and the mugs are worth 5 g.p. each.

Monster:

Treasure & Location:

VI. CLOSET. Zelligar's closet lies through a door on the south wall of his chamber. The room is rather large for a closet, but is actually somewhat barren for its size.

In one corner of the room, several bolts of cloth are stacked, well covered with dust and partially moth-eaten and deteriorated. These are of no particular value.

On one wall, several garments are hung, mostly coats and cloaks. These are quite musty in smell, as well as being dusty and dingy in appearance. Of the five pieces of apparel there, only one is remarkable, being studded with circular bits of pewter for ornamentation. This bit of garb, however, also has suffered the ravages of age. While the first four garments are of no value, the last one could possibly bring up to 15 g.p. if sold.

A wooden stand in the corner of the room farthest from the door holds several books upon it. These large volumes are four in number, and apparently belong in the library (room XII.).

Book #1 — A historical work, this book, written in the common tongue, outlines the history of the civilized area within 100 miles of the stronghold location. It contains nothing remarkable.

Book #2 — This tome is apparently an encyclopedia of various types of plants. Although the various illustrations given within provide a clue to its topic, it is written in the language of elves, so it will not be understandable to a reader who does not know the elven tongue (unless a **read languages** spell is used).

Book #3 — This volume appears unremarkable at first glance, seeming to be a notebook with many hand-written entries of undecipherable runes and markings. It is actually a diary kept by Zelligar, and it details one of his adventures from the distant past, written in his own hand. The writing is not discernible unless a **read languages** spell is used. This book is really of no value to any finder, but a book dealer/scribe/librarian would pay up to 50 g.p. for it. Of course, if the book is sold in this manner, the seller risks a 40% chance of word of its sale getting out as a rumor, with attendant problems developing as those who hear of it seek out the finder for further details.

Book #4 — This work, written in the common language, discusses weather. Although well-illustrated with drawings of meteorological phenomena, descriptive text is sparse. Some cryptic notes written in the margins were apparently made by Zelligar, but these are undecipherable without a **read languages** spell and are actually nothing more than notes such as a student would make in studying the work to highlight important points.

Along one of the walls within the closet is an oil lantern which contains no fuel and which has obviously been unused for a great deal of time. If fuel is provided, the lantern will be perfectly usable.

In another corner is a small table with a stack of papers upon it. These are very dusty, and they are held in place by a stone slab paperweight which is monogrammed with a fancy letter Z. The papers are written in the common language and upon examination will be seen to deal with mundane matters: an inventory of foodstuffs, a financial accounting of expenses, notes on construction work for the complex, a couple of routine messages received by Zelligar, and other unremarkable writings. The most recent date on any of the papers is still more than three decades in the past.

Monster:

Treasure & Location:

VII. WIZARD'S ANNEX. Another room off of Zelligar's chamber is the unusually-shaped annex. This room apparently was for meditation and study, as well as the practice of magic spells. The triangular widening at the south end of this room was apparently for this purpose, and the stone wall (although not noticeable to adventurers) is actually thicker than elsewhere in the complex. The floor near the south wall is bumpy and darkly discolored, as if charred and partially melted by intense heat (this will not be noticeable until the **illusion** described below is dispelled).

At the south end of the room is a magnificent sight visible when explorers enter the door and cast light within. The spectacle is indeed impressive: two large wooden chests, each studded with jewels, overflowing with riches. A pile of gold pieces is arrayed around and within them, and scattered among this treasure trove is an assortment of glittering gems and jewels.

10

The massive treasure is in reality a permanent **illusion,** and it will be temporarily dispelled as soon as the first bit of ''treasure'' is touched by any creature. The **illusion,** once dispelled, reappears in the same place again within 24 hours.

In reality the room is empty (and it is recommended that no treasure be placed here).

Monster:

Treasure & Location:

VIII. WIZARD'S WORKROOM. Zelligar's workroom and laboratory (room IX.) are located adjacent to each other, with a limited access by secret doors.

The workroom is a facility designed for various purposes related to the study and practice of magic. There are several large wooden tables within the room, one of which is overturned on its side, as well as one central table made of stone. The top of this prominent table is a slab of smooth black slate, although its cold black beauty is hidden by a thick layer of dust. None of the tables have anything upon them. There are several chairs and stools scattered about the room.

Along the north wall to both sides of the door leading to the laboratory are wooden cabinets on the wall, approximately 4 feet off the floor. The cabinets are not locked, and contain various chemical compounds and supplies of no particular value in glass or earthen containers. There are forty such containers, as well as one larger jar (described below). If the adventurers choose to open and examine the contents of any particular container, roll a die (d20) to determine the contents:

	Contents	Possible Types
1	Sand	White, brown, black
2	Water	Pure, brackish, holy, urine
3	Salt	Common, mineral
4	Sulphur	-----
5	Wood chips	Hickory, pine, oak, ash, maple, walnut
6	Herbs	Dill, garlic, chives, basil, catnip, parsley
7	Vinegar	Red, white, yellow
8	Tree sap (hardened)	Pine, maple
9	Carbon	Coal, ash, graphite
10	Crushed stone	Quartz, granite, marble, shale, pumice, obsidian
11	Metal filings	Iron, tin, copper, brass
12	Blood	Human, orcish, dwarven, elven, dragon, halfling
13	Dung (hardened)	Human, canine, feline, dragon
14	Wine	White, red, alcohol (spoiled), fruit
15	Fungus powder	Mushroom, other
16	Oil	Vegetable, animal, petroleum, mineral
17	Insect bodies	Bees, flies, beetles, ants
18	Bone powder	Human, animal
19	Spice	Pepper, cinnamon, clove, paprika, oregano, nutmeg
20	Empty	-----

If a die roll gives a duplication, use the column at the right of each entry to determine differentiation between different substances of similar types. If adventurers try to ingest any substance, the Dungeon Master will handle the situation accordingly. In not all cases will the contents be immediately identifiable — in the case of uncertain substances not ob-

viously identifiable, multiply a character's wisdom times 5 to give the percentage chance of positive identification. Up to 2 characters may try to identify any given substance, but if both fail, the material will be a mystery to the entire party.

The larger jar is of clear glass and seemingly contains a black cat's body floating in a clear, colorless liquid. If the large cork lid is unstopped, the liquid will instantaneously evaporate, the cat will suddenly spring to life, jump out of the jar, meow loudly, and run for the door. If the door is open, the cat will dash through and disappear. If the door is not open, the cat will be seen to pass through the door and disappear. In neither case will the feline be seen again. (This occurrence has no special meaning other than to surprise and/or mystify the adventurers, as well as provide some fun for the Dungeon Master.)

Monster:

Treasure & Location:

IX. WIZARD'S LABORATORY. The wizard's lab is a strange but fascinating place. Zelligar's experimentation with many kinds of magic led to a collection of equipment and devices which was stored here, scattered about this 50' by 30' room.

Dominating the room is a large human skeleton suspended from the ceiling and hanging in the northeast corner of the laboratory. The skull is cracked. (Were there any way to know, it would be discovered to be a barbarian chieftain's remains . . .)

About the room are several large wooden tables, just as found in the workroom (room VIII.), and another heavy stone table which is likewise similar to the one appearing next door. The tables are bare, except for a single stoppered smoked glass bottle on one of them. If the cork is removed, the gas within will immediately issue forth with a whoosh. The vapors are pungent and fast-acting, and all characters within ten feet must make an immediate save vs poison or be affected by laughing gas. The gas itself is not poisonous, but will cause any characters failing their saving throw to immediately lapse into uncontrollable raucous laughter for 1-6 melee turns (check each individually). During this time, the characters will have a 50% chance of dropping anything they are holding or carrying and will rock with spasms of great laughter, staggering about the room, chuckling and bellowing with great glee. The noise will necessitate a special additional check for wandering monsters being attracted to the ruckus, and even if a monster appears, the affected characters will be unable to oppose it until the gas effects wear off (if a monster does come, roll a 4-sided die to see how many melee turns it appears after the laughing starts). Characters under the influence of the gas will not respond to any efforts by others to snap them out of its effects (even slapping the face will do no more than cause more laughing), although if a **dispel magic** spell is thrown, it will make them sober immediately. Otherwise, the only way to stop the laughter is to wait for the effects to wear off.

11

Several pine logs are piled underneath one of the tables, and if these are moved, a shiny "gold" ring will be found. Although it appears brilliant and seems to be worth up to 100 g.p., it is actually worthless. It has no special magical properties.

Along the west wall is a large wooden rack, apparently from some kind of torture chamber, since it is obviously sized for human bodies. A trickle of dried blood stains the oaken construction on the front.

On the south wall is a stretched leather skin with magical writings which will be undecipherable unless a **read magic** spell is cast. The legend, if interpreted, will read: "What mysterious happenings have their birth here? Only the greatest feats of wizardry, for which every element of earth, water and sky is but a tool!" The skin is old and extremely fragile, and any attempts to remove it will cause irreparable harm and render it useless because of the skin crumbling away.

A sunken fire pit, blackened and cold, is noticeable as the centerpiece of the room. The pit is only 2' deep, although it appears slightly less than that due to several inches of ashes resting within it. An iron bracing and bar across the 4' wide opening suspend a cast iron pot which is empty except for a harmless brown residue sticking to its interior sides and bottom. Another similar pot which is more shallow lies on the floor alongside the pit, and it is empty. Both pots are extremely heavy, and it takes great effort by two or more characters of 14 or greater strength to even move them.

Off in the southwest corner are two vats, each of approximately 100 gallon capacity. Both are made of wood and both are empty. A third vat nearby, only half the size of its neighbors, is half filled with murky, muddy water.

A stone block used as a table or stand is next to the vats, and along the west wall. It has six earthen containers just like those found in the workroom (room VIII.), and any contents within them should be determined in the same manner as described there. There are also pieces of glassware of various types on the top of the stand, as well as on the floor next to it. Some are clean, some show residues, but all are empty and dusty.

An empty wooden coffin, quite plain and utilitarian, rests upright in the northwest corner. It opens easily and is empty. The wood seems to be rotting in places.

Two kegs rest against the north wall, and examination will show them to be similar to those found in the storeroom (room X.). Each has a letter code to denote its contents, and a roll should be made in the same manner as described there to determine what is within if they are opened.

Wooden shelving on the north wall holds more glassware and three more containers (as those in room VIII. and likewise determined). Two small trays hold powdered incense of different colors, and the smell of their aroma will give away their identity.

Monster:

Treasure & Location:

X. STOREROOM. This irregularly shaped room, hidden by a secret door, contains quantities of supplies which are only a bare fraction of its capacity. Although the casks and barrels storing the commodities have prevented spoilage, the contents are by no means "fresh". Although usable or edible still, they nonetheless have an off-taste which suggests staleness.

Approximately 60 barrels and casks are within the room, in two stacks — one against the northwest wall and the other along the east wall in the southern portion of the room. These containers are each marked in some letter code to denote contents. If any individual barrel or cask is chosen for examination, a die (d20) is rolled on the following table to determine its code marking, and if it is broken open, the appropriate contents will be discovered:

	Code Letter(s)	Contents
1	TL	Whole barley
2	B	Wheat flour
3	FT	Rye flour
4	MK	Salt pork
5	GG	Dill pickles
6	HU	Raisins
7	EJ	Fish in brine
8	Y	Dried apples
9	PF	Whole peas
10	SD	Ale
11	Z	Honey
12	AW	Wine
13	OG	Water
14	XR	Soft soap
15	LC	Salt
16	VW	Lard
17	QS	Seasoning
18	RH	Sunflower seeds
19	UT	Hard candy
20	JS	Dried mushrooms

Note that any container opened and left unsealed, or containers whose contents have been spilled, will (over a period of time) attract vermin and/or monsters. Spilled or uncovered material will also be subject to spoilage and rot. This is important if more than one foray into the stronghold is made, and time elapses between such adventures.

Monster:

Treasure & Location:

XI. SUPPLY ROOM. The stronghold's supply room is also rather empty, containing mostly construction supplies.

Going through the room will reveal the following materials:

    A coil of very heavy rope, 200' in length
    A box of iron spikes (50)
    A box of metal nails
    A pile of wooden beams, each 10' in length and 6" by 6" in width (80)
    A sack of building mortar, almost empty
    A stack of stone blocks, each about 6" by 6" by 12" in size (400)
    Six wooden doors, leaning in a row against a wall
    A large box of assorted hardware (including several locks of various types, door hinges, clasps and hasps, door handles, assorted metal bolts, and similar items)
    A jug of dried glue

Monster:

Treasure & Location:

XII. LIBRARY. Quasqueton's library lies behind a pair of ornately carved oaken doors. The floor of the room is covered with dust, but beneath is a beautiful and shiny surface of polished red granite. The stone is inlaid in large blocks and extends uniformly to within a foot of each of the walls. In the very center of the room within the floor surface are blocks of white granite within the red stone, and these

12

form the letters R and Z with an ampersand between.

There are three large oaken tables within the room, one in each of the west, north, and east wings of the room. There are several wooden chairs scattered about. In two corners of the room are plush divans, each covered with a rich, fleecy upholstering that makes them very comfortable for reclining. These, however, are rather dusty and dingy due to their age and lack of use.

Wall sconces designed to hold torches for illumination are mounted on the walls all around the room. Small cages inset into the north wall contain numerous fire beetles, and these unusual insects give off an eerie, glowing light from their bodies — enough to illuminate this portion of the room. The reddish glow from this source will appear as forbidding and mysterious when viewed from the entrance to the library, seeming to be a luminosity of varying intensity totally alien to anything viewed before. The insects themselves seem to be thriving in their captive abode, but their food source and longevity are totally puzzling . . . There is no way to open or force the cages themselves, so releasing the insects or gaining access to them is impossible to any adventurers.

The library is rather modestly supplied with books, volumes, and tomes of various sizes. There are likewise only a few scrolls, these being stored in a rack along the east wall. None of the books or scrolls is of any particular use or special interest to the adventurers, despite how many they examine.

Monster:

Treasure & Location:

XIII. IMPLEMENT ROOM. This elongated room is used primarily for storage of tools, equipment, and implements of various types. In the room are the following items:

A box of wooden pegs
A coil of light rope, 50'
A coil of heavy chain, 70'
A coil of fine copper wire, 20'
Mining picks (32), all unusable and in poor repair
Chisels (15)
Shovels (13)
Empty barrels (11)
Mallets (8)
Iron bars (29, each measuring 1" in diameter, 8' in length)
An iron vise (12" jaws)
Mining jacks (2), broken
Crosscut saws (2, 2-man)
Hacksaws (4)
A mason's toolbox (containing trowel, stone chisel, plumb line, etc.)
A cobbler's toolbox (containing small hammer, knife, heavy needles, etc.)
A small barrel of unfletched arrows (60, all normal)
An empty wooden bench, 10' long

On the north wall, fairly well concealed considering its size, is a counterweight mechanism for the portcullis trap in the corridor just outside the room, as well as a lever to raise the barrier once it has been tripped. No more than two men/dwarves/elves, etc. at a time can attempt to use the lever to raise the portcullis, and their combined strength ratings must total at least 30. This gives them a 20% chance to raise the impediment, with an additional 5% chance for each point of the total beyond 30 (for example, two men with strengths of 15 and 18 trying together would have a 35% chance to raise the portcullis). Each combination of characters (including henchmen/hirelings) can attempt to raise the barrier but

once, although different attempts can be made with different combinations of two persons making the try.

The trap itself is in the corridor outside the door of the room and just beyond it to the east. The trap will be sprung when one or more adventurers reach a point 10' in front of the dead end wall, in which case the portcullis is noisily dropped 20' to the rear of that point. Thieves in the front of the party will have a chance for their percentage chance on the "remove trap" category, in which case they discover the trap and alert the party without triggering it — provided the thief is the first one to reach the trigger point, of course.

The bars of the portcullis are fairly strong and sturdy. There are twelve vertical bars and several crossmembers. Persons who are very strong may attempt to escape the trap by either **bending the bars** or **lifting the gate** itself. However, each person has but one attempt at each, and if the attempts fail, that person will never be able to do so with that barrier. Adventurers with a strength rating of 13, 14, or 15 have a 5% chance to bend bars or lift the gate, those with a strength of 16 have a 10% chance of doing so, and those with a 17 or 18 have a 15% chance at accomplishing each. Either method will negate the trap through success, thus allowing trapped persons to escape.

If some way can be employed to use the hacksaws to cut through the portcullis, there will be a time delay of 24 hours if one saw is used, 18 if two are used, 12 hours if three are employed, and 6 hours if all four are utilized (no more than one saw per person). The sawing will make noise of some sort, and this may attract wandering monsters at the Dungeon Master's discretion beyond normal chances. Additionally, each saw has a 20% chance of its blade breaking in any 6 hour period — and there are no extra blades.

If all attempts to escape fail, the persons trapped will be doomed to their fate.

Monster:

Treasure & Location:

XIV. AUXILIARY STOREROOM. This extra storeroom is empty of goods and supplies. In one corner is a pile of rock rubble.

Monster:

Treasure & Location:

13

XV. & XVI. TELEPORTATION ROOMS. A strong magic causing **teleportation** has been permanently placed upon these two rooms of equal size and shape. This is a trick to fool and confuse unwary adventurers and is designed to upset their directional sense.

Both rooms function in the same manner once their doors are opened. In each room, at the corner farthest from the door, is a shiny, sparkling outcropping of crystalline rock which will dazzle when light is reflected off of it; in both rooms the outcroppings are identical. Once adventurers enter the room to investigate this, the entire party is instantly **teleported** to identical locations at the other room — whether they be in the room itself or nearby in the hallway. This teleportation occurs without the adventurers noticing that it has occurred; that is, they have no way of "feeling" that anything unusual has happened. And of course, this means that, although they are in a different location facing in different directions, the adventurers will still have reason to believe that they entered the room through a door which is on the east wall (if they originally entered room XV.) or through a door which is on the south wall (if they originally entered room XVI.). To reflect this fact without tipping off the players, the Dungeon Master must turn his map on its side in order to be able to correspond to the directions the players **believe** they are facing. Of course, when the players emerge from the room and attempt to follow their maps, they will be confused by the fact that details outside the room are not as they expect. They may question the Dungeon Master and even suspect he has made a mistake (with such comments as "wait a minute, that **can't** be like that, we just **came** that way!"). When this occurs, the DM should avoid argument and simply state things as they are in the new location, letting players puzzle over the problem and arrive at their own conclusions and/or solutions.

Once the teleportation has been triggered in a room, it will not occur again until the room is empty and the door has been closed from the outside. It will thereafter be triggered when the door is opened and the room is entered. The door of the receiving room (the one to which the party is being teleported) will always appear exactly as the door of the first room entered. Doors to both rooms will automatically close themselves and the rooms will become "ready" to be triggered whenever all adventurers have passed to a point at least 120' from either door, as measured down any corridors. It is possible, however, that a party could trigger the trick, be teleported to the other room, then blunder back upon the original room, see that the two were identical but in different locations, and discover what had occurred. On the other hand, the adventurers could become totally confused, lose their way with an inaccurate map, and experience all kinds of difficulty — whatever does happen will depend upon players' actions and their ability to recognize and cope with the situation.

Note: it is recommended that no monsters or treasures be located in either of these rooms.

Monster:

Treasure & Location:

XVII. CHAR STORAGE CELLAR. This 20' by 20' room is used for storing fuel for the smithy across the hallway. The room is full of blackish soot and dust, but there is only a small pile of fuel against the north wall.

There is a false door on the west wall of the room. It cannot be opened, although it does seem to rest in a frame and even will rattle or move ever so slightly when great strength is applied.

Monster:

Treasure & Location:

XVIII. SMITHY. The smithy is an irregularly shaped room which actually seems to be almost two separate parts. An eerie wind whistles through the upper areas of the room near the ceiling, and this natural effect provided exhaust venting when the fires, long since silent, were stoked with fuel.

Three fire pits lie dormant in the northeast 20' by 20' portion of the room, and these are located on the north wall, in the northeast corner, and on the east wall. In the center of the room is a gigantic forging anvil. A hand bellows hangs on the wall to the west.

The larger southwest portion of the smithy is mostly barren, although an assortment of blacksmith's tools and irons hang on the walls.

Monster:

Treasure & Location:

XIX. ACCESS ROOM. This room adjoins the smithy, and also provides a vertical access to the lower level of the stronghold.

In the northeast corner of the room and along the north wall are log sections of various size (8"-24" in diameter, 1'-4' in length) stacked in a pile, apparently as additional fuel for the blacksmith's fires. The room is otherwise empty.

In the scutheast portion of the room there is a large hole in the floor about 3' across. If light is held from above and observation is attempted, it will be impossible to see how deep the hole is or to where it gives access. If a light source (such as a torch) is cast down the hole, it will come to rest on the floor of the lower level, and from above it will be seen that this is approximately 40' down.

There is a large iron ring anchored to the south wall near the hole, and if a rope is fastened to it, it can be used to assist in descending to the lower level. The fastening, however, is a bit loose, and each person using the rope will have a 1 in 6 chance (non-cumulative) of pulling the ring out of the wall, causing them and the rope to fall to the floor of the lower level. This chance is 2 in 6 for any persons with sizable encumbrance (the equivalent of 500 or more gold pieces in weight). If any person falls, they will do so near the bottom and will take 1-4 hit points of damage (determined by the roll of a four-sided die). Once the ring has been removed from the wall, it cannot be replaced to be usable again.

As an alternative to use of the ring, clever adventurers could use one of the logs in the room measuring 4' in length, tie the rope around it, place it across the 3' opening, and climb down the suspended cord.

For purposes of descent, any rope used must be at least 30' in length. In order to allow a return back up, the rope must be at least 35' in length so that it can be reached from below while suspended.

The final method for possible descent is to use a rope and grapple, either attaching the hook to the iron ring or anchoring it to one of the two doorways. If a grapple is used anchored at the south doorway, add 10' to required length, or 20' if the north doorway is used as the anchor point.

Monster:

Treasure & Location:

14

XX. DEAD END ROOM. A turning corridor winds inward until ending in a dead end room. The walls are unfinished, and apparently this area of the stronghold was reserved for future development — although no one can say for sure.

Monster:

Treasure & Location:

XXI. MEETING ROOM. This long and narrow room apparently served as some kind of auditorium or meeting room. There are ten wooden benches scattered about the room, each about 15' in length. A large stone slab at the north end of the room serves as a sort of stage, rising 10 inches off the floor to accommodate any speakers and place them in full view of any assemblage.

On the north wall are four decorative cloth banners of red, green, blue, and yellow. Although once attractive, they are now deteriorated and rotting, thus being of no particular value.

Monster:

Treasure & Location:

XXII. GARDEN ROOM. Once the showplace of the entire stronghold, the garden room has, over the passage of time, become a botanical nightmare. With no one to tend the gardens, the molds and fungi have grown out of control.

The room has two major portions, a north arm and a west arm. At the end of each of these extensions are large semi-circular stone formations overgrown with fungoid matter. In the southeast corner of the room is another similar outcropping likewise covered with the underground vegetation. In the center of the northern wing are two large sunken pits, each 10' x 20' in size.

Approaching the room from the corridor to the south reveals an eerie and forbidding sight, as unusual growths have extended themselves from within the room into the corridor, spreading inexorably onward and away from the garden room. Passing this feature and entering the room will reveal a sight totally unlike any ever seen in the outside world . . .

The floor is covered with a carpet of tufted molds that extends to all the walls and even onto parts of the ceiling, obscuring the rock surface. The molds appear in a rainbow assortment of colors, and they are mixed in their appearance, with splotches, clumps, swirls, and patches presenting a nightmarish combination of clashing colors. This is indeed a fuzzy fairyland of the most forbidding sort, although beautiful in its own mysterious way . . .

All around the room are fungi of a hundred different kinds. These are scattered in patches and clumps of growth. There are many different types of mushrooms (including an incredible "grove" of the giant variety, with stems looking like tree trunks and caps fully 8' in diameter), as well as such common fungi as shelf types, giant puffballs, coral fungi, and morels. The various growths all seem to be thriving, although any nutrient source is well covered by their proliferation. Perhaps some strange magic or extraordinary means keeps this incredible garden alive and growing . . .

Although passage through the room is possible, the various types of growth hinder movement. Furthermore, any kind of mass movement or commotion (such as a melee) will raise small clouds of spores which will obscure vision and be unpleasant to breathe.

If any adventurer attempts to ingest a certain type of fungus, there is a 30% chance of it being poisonous (a save vs poison is necessary).

Monster:

Treasure & Location:

XXIII. STORAGE ROOM. This room is used primarily for furniture storage, although it is mostly empty. There are three large oaken tables, a number of chairs, and fourteen wooden stools stacked against the walls. In the corner opposite the door is a woodworking table with a crude vise attached, and small saws and other carpenter's equipment are thereon. There are wood chips and some sawdust scattered about the floor.

Monster:

Treasure & Location:

XXIV. MISTRESS' CHAMBER. This room is more tastefully decorated than the rather spartan living quarters found elsewhere in the stronghold. It is the personal chamber of Rogahn's mistress and lover, who apparently lived at the stronghold for some time. But now it appears that she, along with so many others who lived here, has long since been gone.

There is a large walnut bed against the west wall, rather ornately carved (somewhat resembling the bed in room V. — see the description there — but with no name engraved on the headboard). The bed has a large canopy of embroidered green cloth with a striking reddish trim, but it is very dusty like everything else in the room.

Next to the bed is a small table/nightstand with a single drawer. Beside it against the wall is a chest of drawers made of red cedar, which, despite its age, still has the characteristic smell. In the drawers are an assortment of leather items, old clothing, and personal effects like combs, brushes, and hairpins. One comb is a silver plated item which is of moderate value, being worth 5 g.p. On top of the chest is a tortoiseshell dish which is empty except for a single gold piece coin lying in it, and this rests upon a frilly lace cloth along with two small capped bottles half full of perfume.

On the north wall just to the west of the secret door is a large full-length wall mirror in a wooden frame. The crown of the frame is carved into attractive curving designs, and there is an inscription hewn into the finished wood which says in the common language, "To the fairest of all in my eyes".

In the northwest corner of the room is an attractive water basin which is sculpted from the same rock which forms the wall of the room. Indeed, this protrusion is an integral part of the wall itself. A hole in the bottom of the basin is stopped with a rotting cork; this crude drain lets water drop to an inclined piece of rock which drains into a crack in the wall. There is no running water in the room, however.

A small tapestry measuring 3' x 4' hangs on the east wall. It depicts a handsome and robust warrior carrying off a beautiful maiden in a rescue scene set in a burning village, with a horde of ominous-looking enemies viewing from afar. Embroidered in gold cloth at the top of the scene are the words, "Melissa, the most dearly won and greatest of all my treasures". The tapestry is within a wooden frame, and is firmly anchored to the wall. It cannot be removed without damaging it, in which case it will only carry a value of 40 g.p.

15

Monster:

Treasure & Location:

XXV. ROGAHN'S CHAMBER. Rogahn's personal quarters are rather simple and spartan, showing his taste for the utilitarian rather than regal.

The curving walls of the room are immediately noticeable as different from all others in the stronghold, not only due to their layout, but also because of their covering. The walls are covered with vertical strips of rough-finished fir wood, and these narrow planks run in single pieces from floor to ceiling. The construction is not remarkable nor is it fancy in any respect, but the result is strikingly pleasing to the eye. If any of the wood is removed from the wall, nothing save back bracing and the rock surface wall will be discovered.

In each of the four curved corners of the room is a different wall hanging. These tapestries are each 6' wide and approximately 8' high. The four subjects depicted are: a dragon being slain by a group of warriors, with one standing prominently at the front of the group, thrusting the killing sword into the dragon's neck; a great battle in a mountain pass, with a small band of fighters led by a great wizard and a single hero putting an entire army to flight; a warrior and a maiden on horseback against a backdrop of mountains, holding hands with joyful expressions; and a depiction of a hero and a wizard joining in a firm handclasp on a deserted hilltop, with only a sunset in the background. The principals in all of these panoramas, of course, as well as the tapestry in room XXIV., are the same — the warrior/hero is Rogahn, the wizard is Zelligar, and the beautiful maiden is the fair Melissa, Rogahn's mistress. The tapestries, if removed, will be heavy (equal to 600 g.p. in weight each) and bulky; they are worth 100 g.p. each.

Opposite the secret door on the west wall is a bed which is made of maple, with a feather mattress. The baseboard has an engraved letter R on it, but the bed is otherwise devoid of particular detail.

A free-standing cabinet of wood matching the bed is alongside it. Inside are some garments of general use: cloaks, a leather vest, a buckskin shirt, a metal corselet, etc., as well as a pair of boots. None are of any exceptional value.

A wooden stool is near the cabinet, but there is no other furniture in the room.

Monster:

Treasure & Location:

XXVI. TROPHY ROOM. The stronghold's trophy room consists of an assortment of various curiosities accumulated over the years.

Covering most of the north wall is an immense dragon's skin, its brassy scales reflecting any illumination brightly. At the west end of the room is a basilisk frozen in stone, its menacing gaze forbidding but no longer a threat. On the east wall is a dwarven skeleton, suspended from a pair of irons near the ceiling, giving the entire chamber a macabre presence. Elsewhere on the walls are a variety of mementoes: two gigantic sets of moose antlers each on a large head, four dragon paws with claws extended, a stuffed cockatrice, a largish black shield which could only be used by a giant, a pair of ram's horns, a pair of crossed swords, a bearskin, an entire door bearing religious symbols, and a set of three colorful flags which will be immediately recognizable as belonging to prominent barbarian tribes.

Monster:

Treasure & Location:

XXVII. THRONE ROOM. The throne room, mostly for show, consists of two great chairs on a raised stone platform overlooking a rectangular court. The court is flanked on each side by a set of four large stone pillars.

The area is reminiscent of a ballroom of small size, although it is impossible to know the room's actual purpose. The floor is smooth slate, while the pillars and raised platform seem to be constructed of great blocks of red granite. The two chairs are sculpted from gigantic blocks of white marble, and due to their bulk and weight, are for all intents and purposes permanent fixtures.

Great draperies in alternating panels of yellow and purple hang on the wall behind the raised platform. These are of no unusual value, although they add considerably to the appearance of the room (despite their color clash with the various shades of stone).

Monster:

Treasure & Location:

XXVIII. WORSHIP AREA. The stronghold's worship area is no more than a token gesture to the gods, it would seem.

On the back wall of the room, opposite the door, is a rock carving of a great idol which is actually sculpted from the wall itself. The image (of a horned head with an evil visage) appears about 4' wide and 6' high, and is surrounded by religious symbols and runes.

The floor is smooth black slate. In the center of the room is a circular depression, or pit, which measures 5' across and slopes to a maximum depth of 3'. This sacrifice pit is open and mostly empty, except for a small quantity of residual ash covering the bottom.

Monster:

Treasure & Location:

XXIX. CAPTAIN'S CHAMBER. Home for Erig, Rogahn's friend and comrade in arms, is a rather simple room with few furnishings.

The door to the room is a large wooden construction just like the others in the stronghold, but its exterior surface is embellished with an irregular-shaped leather skin covering, which is studded with circular bits of brass which form the word "ERIG" prominently.

The door opens into a rather barren room. In the southeast corner is a crude bed, and alongside it is a table. On top of the table is a small stoneware crock with cover which contains 5 g.p., a large earthenware tankard mug, and a small hand mirror. On the south wall is a wooden chest which is locked. If opened, it will reveal its contents: several garments, including a pair of pants, several cloaks, a heavy cloth coat, and two pairs of boots. A broken dagger at the bottom of the chest underneath the clothing. A leather pouch also therein contains an unusual memento, a walnut plaque with an inlaid piece of silver engraved with the words, "To Erig, great and trusted fighter by my side, and captain of the guard at Quasqueton — against all foes we shall prevail!" It is signed with an embellished "R". This

16

plaque is of some value, and could bring up to 25 g.p. if sold.

In the northeast corner of the room is a wooden keg stand with a single barrel upon it. The barrel is marked with a letter code of "SD" and is full and untapped. If the keg is broken open, ale will issue forth.

On the wall at the western extremity of the room are numerous pegs and brackets, apparently for holding arms and armor. The wall is mostly empty, however, except for two shields and a heavy mace hanging thereon.

Monster:

Treasure & Location:

XXX. ACCESS ROOM. This room is devoid of detail or contents, giving access to the lower level of the stronghold by a descending stairway. This stairway leads down and directly into room XXXVIII on the lower level.

Monster:

Treasure & Location:

XXXI. ROOM OF POOLS. This room is the largest one on the upper level, and is quite different from all the others.

Although the walls are the same as elsewhere (rough blackish stone), the floor of this room is covered with ceramic tiles arranged in mosaic fashion. The majority of the thousands of tiles are golden brown in color, but patterns of white and black tiles appear in various places to enhance the effect of the very striking designs thus formed. The designs (various flowing lines, etc.) are purely decorative, and carry no mysterious message or meaning.

Arrayed throughout the room are fourteen different pools, each about ten feet in diameter, with sides sloping to a maximum depth of five feet in the center. This mystical arrangement is doubly amazing, since all the contents of the pools are different . . .

The individual pools are letter coded A to N, and examination of any particular pool will reveal the following:

a) Pool of healing — This pool contains a strange pinkish liquid that will cause instantaneous healing when ingested. It will also cure disease, but will not restore hit points in doing so. Whenever a drink is taken, 1-6 hit points of individual damage are restored immediately to the drinker, although this can only be done once per day per person (any further consumption will have no additional effect). Although the liquid can be placed into containers and removed from the pool, the healing properties will immediately disappear once it is taken from this room. Note: this pool disappears and reappears from time to time magically, so if adventurers make a return to this room, there is only a 30% chance that the liquid will be present again then (although it will always be there upon their first visit).

b) Acid pool — This pool is filled to the brim with a clear, fizzing liquid which gives off a strange and unpleasant aroma to those near it. It is full of acid, and most deadly. If any adventurer falls or leaps within it, certain and immediate death will result. Putting a hand or other body member within it will result in an immediate 2-5 hit points of damage (roll a 4-sided die and add 1 to the result) — more if a greater portion of the body is exposed to the liquid. Drinking any of the liquid (even but a sip) will cause immediate gagging and cause no less than 5 hit points of damage, plus a saving throw against poison to survive. Putting just a drop or two to the tongue will cause the loss of 1 hit point, plus induce gagging and choking for two melee rounds of time (twenty seconds), although no saving throw for poison will be necessary. Weapons or other objects dipped into the acid will deteriorate (swords will be marked and weakened, wooden items warped and cracked, etc.) and may even be ruined completely at the discretion of the Dungeon Master (who can roll a die for each item to determine how adversely it is affected). The strength of the acid is such that it will eat through any type of container within two melee rounds of time.

A single brass key of large size (about six inches long) is visible at the bottom of the pool, seemingly unaffected by the acid. This key, if somehow retrieved, will be worthless, and it does not correspond to any of the locks within the stronghold.

c) Pool of sickness — This pool is filled with a murky gray

17

syrup. If any of it is consumed (even but a sip), the victim will begin to suffer sickness, but not until six turns (one hour) afterwards. If this occurs, there is no loss of hit points, but the victim suffers from strong and recurring stomach pains for 1-4 hours (roll a four-sided die) which make fighting and even movement impossible for that period (although a victim could be carried by others), after which all symptoms pass and the character returns to normal. Placing a drop of liquid upon the tongue will give a sweet taste, but will cause no symptoms. Weapons or other items placed within the liquid will be totally unaffected. Any portion of the liquid removed from the pool will lose its special properties within three melee rounds (thirty seconds).

d) **Green slime pool** — The horrid contents of this pool are immediately obvious to any gazing into it. The slime (HP: 20) is covering the walls of the basin most of the way from the bottom to the edge.

e) **Drinking pool** — This pool is filled with ice cold spring water which will refresh anyone who takes a drink from it. The water is pure and good, but has no other special characteristics.

f) **Pool of wine** — This pool is filled with powerful wine of a deep red color. Not only is it excellent wine, it has a taste so inviting that anyone tasting it will be prone to drink more and more until intoxicated! If a sip is taken, the taster will have a 60% chance of drinking more (regardless of the player's wishes). If this is done, three 6-sided dice are thrown and compared to the character's constitution rating; if the number rolled is greater than the character's constitution score, then the difference is figured, and this is the number of **hours** the character will be intoxicated (if the roll is equal or less, the character "holds his liquor" and is unaffected). Any character so intoxicated will suffer the following penalties: -2 on all rolls "to hit" in combat, -3 to dexterity rating, and any other disadvantages to being drunk that the DM may deem in effect (prone to loud and boisterous speech, stumbling about, a greater chance to be surprised, etc.). After the allotted number of hours have passed, the character returns to normal. Any intoxicated character who returns to the pool of wine will have a 90% chance of drinking too much again, and the check against constitution will then be necessitated once more. If any of the wine is removed from the room, it will immediately lose its potency and be considered as normal wine, but actually rather weak in its effects.

g) **Dry pool** — This depression is completely dry, and there is no trace of any liquid within it, nor any clue as to whether any type of matter was ever within it. The basin itself seems to be of some kind of yellowish ceramic origin, but it will be impervious to striking or any similar attempt at cracking or fracturing.

h) **Hot pool** — This steaming and bubbling cauldron is filled with boiling water, which will be obvious to any observer. The water itself is completely normal in all other respects, although it has a relatively high mineral content, as evidenced by a whitish crust built up around the edge of the pool.

i) **Aura pool** — This pool of shimmering water (which otherwise appears normal in every respect) is less full than many of the others. The water itself seems to glisten and sparkle, and will be seen to radiate magic if an attempt to detect it is made. The water tastes normal in every respect, but those drinking as little as a single sip will experience a strange effect. Upon swallowing the liquid,

the drinker will feel his entire body tingle, and at the same time he and others around him will see a visual phenomenon: an aura of color will glow around his entire body for approximately a full minute. The color apparent will depend totally upon the character's alignment. It will glow blue for an alignment of lawful good, green for an alignment of chaotic good, yellow for chaotic evil, and red for lawful evil, while any neutral characters will exhibit a white aura. Of course, upon first consuming the liquid, players will have no idea what the strange appearing colors may mean, so they may be puzzled by the effects — and there are no clues around the pool to explain the colors. The water will retain its special magical characteristics even if it is removed from the pool, but there are only 10 suitable drinks possible due to the small amount of liquid present. This pool, just like the pool of healing previously described, disappears and reappears from time to time (see a. above for details and percentage chance of reappearance for future visits).

j) **Pool of sleep** — This pool is full of a greenish liquid of varying shades, with a swirling pattern evident on its stagnant surface. Putting a drop on the tongue reveals a sort of fruity taste, but no special effects will be noticeable. Taking a sip will be tasty refreshment, but within ten seconds a real drowsiness will set in which may even cause (50% chance) an immediate sleep to begin, which will last from 1-6 minutes. Drinking any greater volume of the liquid will certainly induce a comatose slumber of from 1-8 hours, with no saving throw possible. Any removal of the liquid from the room will totally negate its effectiveness, although removing anyone who has consumed the stuff will not awaken them.

k) **Fish pool** — This pool of normal lake water holds numerous small fish. It has no other special properties, nor are the fish unusual in any way.

l) **Ice pool** — This basin is filled with steaming dry ice, although for some unknown reason it never seems to dissipate. The ice is "hot" to the touch due to its extremely low temperature. Since it is highly doubtful any character has ever seen dry ice, the entire spectacle will be highly mysterious, appearing as some kind of whitish rock giving off eerie vapors and feeling hot to the touch. If any pieces are broken off and removed from the pool, they will dissipate into carbon dioxide gas as normal dry ice would do. Such pieces could be handled with a gloved hand, but the nature of the substance will still likely be unapparent.

m) **Treasure pool** — This basin, filled with normal water, seems to hold a great treasure underneath the water. A pile of gold pieces appears to lie on the bottom of the pool, and the golden image is sprinkled with an assortment of sparkling jewels. Alas, this treasure trove is nothing more than a magical **illusion**, which will be dispelled once the surface of the water is broken or disturbed. Once the waters are calm again, the image will reappear.

n) **Pool of muting** — This pool is almost empty, but a small amount of water remains. Although the liquid appears to be normal water (and has no unusual odor or taste to belie its actual nature), it is actually a magical substance. This liquid, when swallowed, causes a complete loss of voice and verbal capabilities for 1-6 hours. This muting will become apparent only when it has been swallowed; merely putting a drop to the tongue will give no clue as to its effect, and it will seem like normal water. Any character drinking the water will suffer the effects,

18

and that means that the players will be affected likewise. Thus, the referee informs the player or players of their limitation, and they are barred from any further communication by verbal means with the other players in the party for the duration of the muting effects (1-6 game hours, determined by rolling a six-sided die). In such cases, they must remain completely silent (no grunts or groans allowed) and can only communicate with other players via nods, head shaking, hand signals, etc. If any player who is caller for the group is so affected, another player must take his place. Written communication is possible only if the muted player has an intelligence of 14 or more, and any such message can only be read by another character with a similar intelligence rating.

Monster:

Treasure & Location:

XXXII. ADVISOR'S CHAMBER. Access to this room is only via a secret door on its west wall which gives access to the Room of Pools (XXXI.). The chamber is the dwelling area for Marevak, advisor to Zelligar and Rogahn.

The decor is rather pleasant, although uninspired. The floor is the most striking aspect of the room, for it is a continuation of the colored mosaic patterns of golden brown, white and black which are evidenced in the adjacent Room of Pools. There are some minimal furnishings in the room — a common bed, three chairs, a makeshift desk with a single drawer (locked), and a battered old table. The walls are barren rock, except for a framed picture hanging over the desk showing two figures standing side by side: a warrior of impressive proportions, and a wizened magic user in a purple robe. This is actually a full-color painting, beautifully rendered, and in one corner is written in the elvish language the words: "To wise Marevak, worthy advisor and counselor, from a grateful Zelligar and Rogahn". These words are readable only to those who know the elven language (or via a **read languages** spell), but the signed names of Zelligar and Rogahn will be apparent upon a close examination. In another corner of the painting is the signed name Tuflor — this being the artist who painted the picture, but this fact certainly not obvious to anyone finding the painting other than through deduction or by a character "asking around" once back in the civilized world.

The painting is quite large and bulky, as well as heavy, when removed from the wall. If carried undamaged out of the stronghold and back to civilization, it could bring up to 300 g.p. if sold. However, anyone trying to sell the painting for its value will run a 60% risk that the purchaser will recognize the origin of the painting — and if this word spreads at large, the seller may have attendant problems, since it will be obvious from where it was obtained.

The desk in the room is mostly empty, except for several attached sheets with various notes written in elvish. The first sheet is headed with the title, "Suggestions for the Further Development of Quasqueton", and the notes relate to certain details of construction for the stronghold (although there is no information of a sort to assist the adventurers, and no maps). The document (discernible only by those who know the elven language or by a **read languages** spell) is signed at the bottom of each page by Marevak.

The locked drawer of the desk is well-secured, and any tampering (with the exception of a successful "remove trap" by a thief) will cause the release of a terrible gaseous emission which will be so penetrating as to drive all characters from the room for 1-4 hours, with no saving throw (this happens only once). The lock can only be picked by a thief

character at his normal chances, but he can make only a single try — if he fails, the lock cannot be opened by him. However, access to the drawer can be gained by dismantling the desk, although this will require heavy blows from some kind of weapon (due to the noise, an extra check for wandering monsters must be made if this occurs). The contents of the drawer are determined by rolling a single twelve-sided die (only one roll is taken, for there is but a single item within): 1 Potion: **levitation**; 2 Elven boots; 3 10-100 g.p.; 4 A 50 g.p. gem (moonstone); 5 A golden medallion worth 20 g.p.; 6 **Read languages** scroll; 7 **Web** scroll; 8 **Cursed** scroll (permanently removes 1 point from charisma rating of first person to read it — **remove curse** will not counteract it); 9 **Ring of protection** + 1; 10 Potion of **healing** (two doses); 11 A +1 dagger with ornately carved handle; 12 Nothing.

Monster:

Treasure & Location:

XXXIII. BARRACKS. This large, open room is the dwelling place for the guards and men-at-arms of the stronghold (most of whom left on the last adventure with Rogahn and Zelligar). Scattered throughout the room are about 40 common beds, and about half that number of chairs and stools. There are several large wooden tables along various walls, and at the south wall is a large wooden chest of drawers which is empty except for a few old socks, some common footwear, a few cloth vestments, and other similar items of no special value.

In the southwest corner of the room the floor slants toward the wall steeply and an opening (too small to give any access) leads into the wall. From the faint smell, it is apparent that this is some kind of crude toilet area.

The walls of the room are rough stone, but there are wall sconces designed to hold torches, and various pegs upon the wall. There are some odds and ends hanging from several of the pegs: an old battered shield, an empty canteen, a 20' section of light chain, a sheathed sword (old and rusty), and a bearskin.

Monster:

Treasure & Location:

XXXIV. ARMORY. This irregularly-shaped room is designed to house the arms supply of the stronghold. It is mostly empty now, however, since many of the arms were taken along on the last foray by the inhabitants of the hideaway.

When the room is entered, a slight whistling sound can be heard if the adventurers stand quietly. If the door is closed (unless spiked open it will close automatically one round after everyone has entered, and even if so secured, there is a 50% chance that it will close anyway) and the second exit is likewise closed, a howling wind will immediately result, with an 80% chance of putting out any torch carried by the adventurers, or a 50% chance to extinguish each lantern carried. The wind will cease whenever either or both of the exits is opened. Upon examination of the ceiling of the room (which is a full 20' from the floor), two sizable vents will be noticeable (neither providing usable access) to show that this is a natural, rather than magical, phenomenon.

The rock walls of this room are mostly smooth, and there are carved ledges within several of them. Wooden pegs also abound, and there are some items still left in place on the wall: a number of battered shields (several broken and in otherwise poor repair), bits and pieces of body armor (in

19

uniformly poor condition), several crude bows (-2 "to hit" if used), a quiver of normal arrows, two swords (one in good condition), a dozen spears, two hand axes (one with a split handle), a flail, a two-handed sword with broken blade, and a dagger. None of the items appears remarkable, although the flail, the dagger, and one of the swords seem to be usable and of normal value for such an item.

In the extreme southwest corner of the room are two locked chests, but they are empty. Both are large and bulky, as well as heavy.

Monster:

Treasure & Location:

XXXV. GUEST CHAMBER. There are three identical guest chambers side by side, all opening into the same corridor. The rooms are all similarly furnished, with rough rock walls, and a minimum of furnishings: a wooden bed, a small table, and a single chair.

The middle chamber differs from the other two in one respect: there is a false door on its eastern wall. Although it seems to move just as a normal door would, it resists opening. If it is battered down, it will reveal only a stone wall behind it.

Monster:

Treasure & Location:

XXXVI. UTILITY ROOM. This extra room is empty and unused. Two special features of note near the room are described below:

FALSE STEPS. Although the steps here are very real, the entire area north of this room (the various winding corridors) is specially designed to confuse any explorers. The corridor leading past the guest chambers is on an upward slant which will be unnoticeable to casual adventurers (except dwarves, who will have a 2 in 6 chance to notice it). The stairs (8 of them) then lead downward, as if to another level — although this is only the impression created.

PIT TRAP. Just to the east of this room is a dead end to the corridor, with a false door on the north wall where the corridor stops. When any adventurer approaches the door (within 5'), his weight will trigger the trap, causing the entire 20' section of floor between the false door and the wall opposite it to open up. A giant crack opens in the center of the floor as the middle drops open and the sides slant inward, dropping all characters and their equipment through the 4' wide opening. The bottom of the trap, some 40' below, is a pool of cold spring water in room L. of the lower level. Those falling through the trap will sustain 1-4 hit points each when they hit the water below. In addition, since the pool is about 8' deep, characters heavily encumbered (more than 500 gold pieces of weight equivalent) will risk drowning unless they free themselves of the bulk and weight after landing in the water. If any character heavily encumbered does not, he or she will have a 90% chance of drowning, modified by a -5% per point of dexterity (for instance, a heavily encumbered character who elects not to unencumber himself and has a dexterity of 12 will have only a 30% chance of drowning — 90% -(12 x 5%) = 30%). Items dropped to the bottom of the pool will be retrievable, but due to the extremely cold temperature of the water, characters will depend upon their constitution rating to see if they can stand the water enough to dive for things on the bottom. One check can be made for each character, with a 5% chance per point of constitution that they will be able to

take the cold water (for example, a character with a constitution rating of 11 would have a 55% chance of being able to take the cold water and dive effectively). If characters dive for items at the bottom of the pool, only one item at a time is retrievable and each dive takes one round (ten seconds) with two rounds between each dive for air. In any event, no character can stand to stay in the water for more than ten rounds — and a full turn (one hour) is required for rest and recovery after each diving session to dry off, fully warm up again, etc.

The trap, after being triggered and dropping persons from above to the pool, will close again until triggered once more from above. Refer to the room description of room L. of the lower level for adventurers deposited here, and begin their progress from that location on the lower level map.

Monster:

Treasure & Location:

XXXVII. RECREATION ROOM. This room is designed for recreation and training, and was designed specially for Rogahn's use. The carved door, heavy and thick, bears a fancy "R" on its outer face.

The room is made for a variety of activities, as is apparent from its furnishings and contents. On the east and west walls, which are covered with pocked wood, are large archery targets, and six arrows are still stuck into the eastern target. Although there are several quivers of arrows around, there are no bows in the room.

There are several iron bars of varying length and weight in one corner of the room. These vary in circumference, and are apparently designed for weight lifting, although this fact is best discovered by the deduction of the players.

In another corner of the room, a metal bar is attached to the two walls and is about 7' off the floor. Nearby, a rope is suspended from the ceiling 20' above. Except for two heavy benches and a single stool, there are no furnishings in the room other than five heavy woven mats lying atop each other to form a sort of floor cushion measuring 20' by 20'. Hanging on the wall are several very heavy weapons which appear normal but which weigh almost double normal weight — a notched sword, a battle axe, a flail, and a mace. Leaning against the wall are two heavily battered shields.

Monster:

Treasure & Location:

20

KEY TO THE LOWER LEVEL

The lower level of the complex is rough and unfinished. The walls are irregular and coarse, not at all like the more finished walls of the level above (except for the two rooms on this level which are more like those in the upper portion and in a state of relative completion). The corridors are roughly 10' wide, and they are irregular and rough, making mapping difficult. The floors are uneven, and in some cases rock chips and debris cover the pathways between rooms and chambers. The doors are as in the upper level, but the secret doors are either rock or disguised by rock so as to appear unnoticeable.

WANDERING MONSTERS

Check every third turn; 1 in 6 (roll a 6-sided die). If a monster is indicated, roll a six-sided die again and compare to the list below to determine what type of monster appears. Then check for surprise. The abbreviations which follow are the same as used and explained in the section entitled MONSTER LIST.

1. Troglodytes (1-4) — HP: 9, 8, 5, 4; #AT: 1; D: 1-6; AC 5/14; SA: Emit odor when enraged.

2. Huge Spider (1) — HP: 12; #AT: 1; D: 1-6; AC 6/13; SA: Bite necessitates save vs poison (+1 on die).

3. Kobolds (2-7) — HP: 4, 4, 3, 3, 2, 2, 1; #AT: 1; D: 1-4; AC 7/12; SA: None.

4. Orcs (1-8) — HP: 6, 5, 5, 4, 4, 3, 3, 2; #AT: 1; D: 1-6; AC 7/12; SA: None.

5. Zombies (1-2) — HP: 8, 7; #AT: 1; D: 1-8; AC 8/11; SA: None.

6. Goblins (2-7) — HP: 5, 5, 4, 4, 3, 2, 1; #AT: 1; D: 1-6; AC 6/13; SA: None.

ENCOUNTER AREAS

XXXVIII. ACCESS ROOM. This room is filled with piles of rock and rubble as well as mining equipment: rock carts, mining jacks, timbers, pickaxes, etc. It is apparent that there has been no mining activity for quite some time.

Monster:

Treasure & Location:

XXXIX. MUSEUM. This room is an unfinished museum, a special monument to the achievements of the stronghold's most illustrious inhabitants.

The west wall is a sectioned fresco showing various events and deeds from the life of Rogahn, and the several views pictured are: a young boy raising a sword, a young man slaying a wild boar, a warrior carrying off a dead barbarian, and a hero in the midst of a large battle hacking barbarian foes to pieces.

The east wall is a similar sectioned fresco showing cameos from the life of Zelligar: a boy gazing upward at a starry night sky, a young man diligently studying a great tome, an earnest magician changing water to wine before a delighted audience, and a powerful wizard casting a type of death fog over an enemy army from a hilltop.

The north wall section is unfinished, but several sections of

frescoes show the two great men together: shaking hands for the first time in younger days, winning a great battle against barbarians in a hill pass, gazing upward together from the wilderness to a craggy rock outcropping (recognizable to the adventurers as the place where the stronghold was built), with a fourth space blank. Next to the frescoes are other mementoes from the past: a parchment letter of thanks for help in the war against the barbarians from a prominent landowner, a barbarian curved sword, and a skeleton of the barbarian chief (so identified by a wall plaque in the common language). There is more blank space on the wall, apparently for further additions to the room's collection of items.

The frescoes are painted and they cannot be removed. None of the mementoes are of any particular worth or value.

Monster:

Treasure & Location:

XL.-LVI. CAVERNS OF QUASQUETON. The bulk of the lower level of the complex is a series of unfinished caves and caverns, which are mostly devoid of special detail — all being characterized by irregular walls of rough rock, uneven floors strewn with bits of rock and rubble, and joined by winding corridors. The majority of the rooms are empty of furnishings.

XL. SECRET CAVERN.

Monster:

Treasure & Location:

XLI. CAVERN.

Monster:

Treasure & Location:

XLII. WEBBED CAVE. The entrance to this room is covered with silky but sticky webs, which must be cut or burned through to gain access to it. See **web** spell for details in Basic D & D booklet.

Monster:

Treasure & Location:

XLIII. CAVERN.

Monster:

Treasure & Location:

XLIV. CAVERN.

Monster:

Treasure & Location:

XLV. CAVERN OF THE MYSTICAL STONE. This ante-chamber is the resting place for a large, glowing chunk of rock which appears to be mica. The stone radiates magic strongly.

The stone rests permanently in its place and is not removable. Although chips can easily be broken off the rock by hand, only one chip at a time may be broken away; until anything is done with it, the rest of the rock will remain impervious to breaking.

Once a chip is removed, its glow will begin to fade, and after three rounds (thirty seconds) it will be a normal piece of mica with no magical properties (as will be the case if it is removed from this room). The chip's magical properties are manifested only if it is consumed (or placed in the mouth) by any character before three rounds have passed after breaking off from the chunk. The magical effects are highly variable, and each individual can only be once affected — even if a future return to the rock is made at a later time. If any character places a chip within his or her mouth, a 20-sided die is rolled to determine the effect according to the following table:

1 Immediately teleports the character and his gear to the webbed cave (room XLII.)

2 Immediately blinds the character for 1-6 hours of game time (no combat, must be led by other adventurers)

3 Raises strength rating permanently by 1 point

4 Raises charisma rating permanently by 1 point

5 Raises wisdom rating permanently by 1 point

6 Raises intelligence rating permanently by 1 point

7 Raises dexterity rating permanently by 1 point

8 Lowers strength rating permanently by 1 point

9 Lowers charisma rating permanently by 1 point

10 Lowers intelligence rating permanently by 1 point

11 Grants a **limited wish**

12 Causes **invisibility** for 1-6 hours of game time (subject to normal restrictions)

13 Poison (saving throw at + 1)

14 Makes a 500 g.p. gem (pearl) appear in character's hand

15 Gives a permanent + 1 to any single weapon carried by character (if more than one now carried, roll randomly to determine which)

16 Heals all lost hit points of character (if any)

17 Causes idiocy for 1-4 hours (unable to function intelligently or fight, must be led by other adventurers)

18 Gives a special one-time bonus of 1-6 hit points to the character (these are the first ones lost the next time damage or injury is taken)

19 Gives a **curse**: the character will sleep for 72 hours straight each month, beginning one day before and ending one day after each new moon (can only be removed by a **remove curse** spell)

20 Has no effect

Monster:

Treasure & Location:

XLVI. SUNKEN CAVERN. This small cavern lies at the bottom of a short, sloping corridor. The walls are wet with moisture, and glisten in any reflected light.

Monster:

Treasure & Location:

XLVII. CAVERN.

Monster:

Treasure & Location:

XLVIII. ARENA CAVERN. This cavern, designed as a small theatre or arena, is unfinished. The center portion of the room is sunken about 15' below the floor level, and the sides slope downward from the surrounding walls to form a small amphitheater.

Monster:

Treasure & Location:

XLIX. PHOSPHORESCENT CAVE. This medium-sized cavern and its irregularly-shaped eastern arm present an eerie sight to explorers. A soft phosphorescent glow bathes the entire area independent of any other illumination, and the strange light is caused by the widespread growth (on walls, ceiling, and even parts of the floor) of a light purplish mold. The mold itself is harmless.

Monster:

Treasure & Location:

L. WATER PIT. This room contains the 8' deep pool of water into which any unwary adventurers are precipitated from the trap on the upper level (see the special description of the trap under the description of room XXXVI.). As described there, the water is extremely cold. Anyone entering the water (whether voluntarily or not) must spend a full hour recovering from its chilly effects.

The pool is about 20' across and is filled by a cold spring.

Monster:

Treasure & Location:

LI. SIDE CAVERN. This cavern is unusual only in that its eastern rock wall is striated with irregular diagonal streaks of a bluish ore (of no unusual use or value to adventurers).

Monster:

Treasure & Location:

LII. RAISED CAVERN. This room, off the southeast corner of the grand cavern, is accessible by climbing four upward steps. Its eastern wall also shows diagonal streaks of the same bluish ore noticeable in room LI. The room has a low ceiling (only 5'), so some humans may find it difficult to stand fully erect.

Monster:

Treasure & Location:

LIII. GRAND CAVERN OF THE BATS. This majestic cave is the largest in the complex, and is impressive due to its size and volume, for the ceiling is almost 60' above. A corridor sloping downward into the cavern (noticeable even by non-dwarves) gives primary access to the room on its south wall. A secondary entrance/exit is via a secret door to the west, while steps to the southeast lead up to room LII.

A southwestern arm of the room leads to an alcove of rock pillars of unusual and irregular shape, and these run from floor to ceiling to form a very meager catacomb.

When it is daytime in the outer world, a small opening in the ceiling just off a midway point of the north wall will show daylight. (If the DM has not been meticulously charting time as night vs day, there will be a 60% chance of daylight being visible at the time the adventurers enter the room; if not, it will be very difficult to notice the opening — only a 10% chance per adventurer observing the ceiling). The opening in the ceiling (which will be totally inaccessible to any and all attempts by adventurers to reach it) is used by the many thousands of bats which live on the ceiling of the cavern by day and which venture out at sunset each day for feeding. (Again, if exact time is not being tracked, a die roll may be necessary to determine what time of day the adventurers reach the cavern and whether or not the bats are present or active.)

The bats are nocturnal animals, but the species living in this particular cavern is very easily agitated. Any party of adventurers entering the cavern with torches or other bright sources of light (including unshielded lanterns) will have a base 5% chance per light source per turn (10 minutes) of disturbing the bats and causing them to swarm. In addition, any noises above subdued conversation will add another 10% to the chance of disturbing the bats, assuming of course that they are present in the cave when the party enters. (For example, a party with 4 torches would have a 20% chance of disturbing the bats and causing them to swarm, or 30% if they are arguing in addition).

If the bats are disturbed, first a few begin squeaking and flying around (this will of course occur if any sleeping bats are physically prodded or awakened), then more and more until the mass becomes a giant churning swarm (this will take only two melee rounds, or twenty seconds). The swarming bats will squeak and squawk, flying madly about. They will fill the grand cavern and overflow into adjacent areas and corridors, but those flying out of the cavern will soon return. While swarming, the bats will buzz and harry any persons in the cavern or adjacent corridors, zooming past them at high speed while others hover about. Occasionally, one of the bats will try to land on a character (50% chance each round) to deliver a pinching bite which is unpleasant but harmless.

If adventurers leave the grand cavern and remove their light sources with them, the swarm of bats will slowly cease their activity and return to their inverted perches (this takes about 30 minutes). If the adventurers stay in the room, extinguish their lights, and lie silently on the floor for the same period of time, the bats will return to their dormant state.

Characters fighting swarming bats will find the task hopeless due to their sheer number, but attempts can be made using any hand held weapon larger than a dagger, with an 18, 19 or 20 needed to hit with a 20-sided die. Bats landing to bite can be hit on any roll of 7 or above. A single hit will kill any bat.

Characters fighting or otherwise enduring swarming bats will automatically be caught by surprise if any wandering monster comes upon them while they are doing so. Fighting the bats makes enough noise to necessitate an additional special roll for wandering monsters.

A sort of fluffy and dusty guano covers the floor of the grand cavern, quite different from the droppings of most other species of bats.

The bats will swarm and leave at sunset each day until returning as a swarm at the following dawn.

Monster:

Treasure & Location:

LIV. TREASURE CAVE. This secret room, itself opening to a corridor shielded by secret doors on either end, was designed as the hiding place for valuables in the stronghold. There is a scattering of gold pieces (11-30; roll a twenty-sided die and add 10) on the floor of the room, and three locked chests (which are empty unless noted below).

Two short human statues (appearing life-like, as if made from wax) are within the room. As soon as any item of value is touched or disturbed, both will immediately spring to life and draw their swords and attack the party. These are magical berserkers (4 Hit Points each, Armor Class 7) who will fight to the death. Neither has any treasure on his person.

Monster:

Treasure & Location:

LV. EXIT CAVE. This large cavern is otherwise unremarkable, except for the fact that a secret one-way passage out of the stronghold is hidden in the northeast corner of the cave. This secret exit is triggered by pushing on a loose rock within the wall, at which time the opening occurs in the wall, leading to the outside world. The opening allows access for only 10 seconds, at which time it closes once more, and will not be triggered for another 24 hours.

If characters take advantage of this exit, they will find themselves on a rock ledge about 3 feet wide and 20 feet long. If they use ropes to scale down, they can rappel without too much difficulty to a location some 40 feet below where the drop is less steep and a descent can be made through the trees and vegetation toward the valley below. If the characters stand on the ledge and observe the view, they will notice that they are on the north face of the massive outcropping which houses the stronghold, whereas the other entrance is on the south face. Because of the wilderness which surrounds the entire area, it may take some doing to return to civilization or home.

The secret exit is but a one-way access, and allows only egress from the stronghold, never entrance. There is no way to trigger the door from the outside, and even if this were possible, a permanent magic spell upon the exit totally prevents movement into the complex via the opening.

Monster:

Treasure & Location:

LVI. CAVERN OF THE STATUE. In the southern end of this cavern is a solitary stone figure, roughly sculpted from the same black stone of the cavern walls and firmly anchored to the floor. The figure, obviously a human male (although lacking any finished detail), stands some 5 feet high, with both arms slightly outstretched and pointing to the jagged rock outcropping which divides the two corridors to the north-northeast. The statue is too heavy to be moved, and will completely resist any attempts to budge or topple it.

PIT TRAP. Just outside this cavern, in the corridor which leads eastward, is a large covered pit at the intersection of three corridors. The pit is about 12' across and 10' deep. A

23

fall into this pit will inflict 1-4 hit points of damage, and any characters reaching the area will have a basic 70% chance of falling in, with a 30% chance of noticing the trap (the danger would be greater if, for instance, they were running rather than simply exploring). If characters in the first rank of a party fall in, there is only a 20% chance of the next row of characters falling, and each checks separately as before. The trap, once sprung, does not shield the pit any further, and the pit will be noticeable.

Monster:

Treasure & Location:

THIS ENDS THE MODULE "SEARCH FOR THE UNKNOWN"

KEYING THE DUNGEON

Once the Dungeon Master has read the entire module over one or more times and has gained a working familiarity with it, he is ready to key it. In doing so, he will take the basic descriptive framework and add his own ideas as to how and where the various monsters and treasures are located. The result will be a dungeon with his own indelible stamp, a bit different from all others — even those using the same descriptive outline.

With over sixty rooms and chambers noted on the two level maps by Roman numerals (and several other unmarked open areas), there is plenty of space to explore (though this dungeon is actually quite small compared to most). With 15 to 25 listed treasures (plus a few items of value that are part of the basic furnishings) and 16 to 20 monsters to place, the DM is offered a real choice in setting up the dungeon, for it is he who will decide on which areas are forbidding with danger or rich in reward.

The monsters (number keyed 1. to 25.) and the treasures (lettered A to HH) should be placed with care and consideration, and in many cases there should be a reason or rationale why something is located where it is. Just as there is a logical explanation behind the entire setting or scenario, so too should there be a similar thought behind what is to be found within the dungeon. Of course, in some cases, the unexpected or the inexplicable will be the exception — not everything should follow the normal order of things or be too predictable for the players.

As mentioned previously elsewhere, not every room or chamber will have a monster, a treasure, or both. As a matter of fact, quite a number of places will simply be empty, while others may hold a monster with no treasure, or, rarely, a treasure without a monster guarding it. In the latter instance, the unguarded treasure will likely be well-hidden (as indeed any treasure can be) or concealed to make the room *appear* empty. Finally, in some instances, a room may contain a monster (being in his lair) as well as a treasure he is guarding, either wittingly (if it is his trove) or unwittingly (if his appearance there was only coincidental). In such a case, it will be necessary to defeat (either by killing or driving away) the monster or monsters before any attempt to discover or garner the treasure is made . . .

Although monsters will inevitably make their presence known, treasures are usually not obvious. It is up to players to locate them by telling the DM how their characters will conduct any attempted search, and it is quite conceivable that they could totally miss seeing a treasure which is hidden or concealed. In fact, any good dungeon will have undiscovered treasures in areas that have been explored by the players, simply because it is impossible to expect that they will find every one of them.

Once the DM has decided on where to place the various monsters and treasures, he keys both the maps and the descriptive copy within this booklet by using the letter and number codes for treasures and monsters, respectively. On the two game maps, he marks (preferably using a colored pencil for readibility and possible erasure) the letter (for treasure) in each room containing a treasure from the master list. He then places a number (for monsters) in each room which will contain a monster, and may also make a note on the map what type of monster is there ("orcs" or "trogs", for instance). Each monster or treasure listing should appear but once on the game map when he is finished. He then refers to the descriptions of each room or chamber within the body copy of this booklet, and fills in the blanks following the proper sections corresponding to the marked map with the pertinent details and any side notes on: what monster is located there (if any), where it hides (if it does so — not all will hide), what treasure is located within the room (if any), where it is located, and how it is hidden or protected (if it is). Any remaining space should be reserved for further notes, especially listing of the effects caused by subsequent player adventuring — monsters scared away to new locations, creatures slain, treasures removed, equipment abandoned, etc. Of course, notes on the map can likewise be made as desired.

Once the dungeon has been keyed, it is ready for exploration by the players. Good luck, and have fun! Follow these guidelines when setting up your own dungeon from scratch, and you should be successful.

MONSTER LIST

The monsters occupying the area to be explored are an assortment of creatures, some of which are former inhabitants (orc and kobold slaves), and some of which have moved into the dungeon by unknown means.

The monsters (keeping in mind that the term refers to any encounter, no matter what the creature type) can be encountered in two ways: either in their "lair" (the particular room or chamber where they live, as keyed by the Dungeon Master), or as "wandering monsters". The latter encounters are more irregular, uncertain, and unpredictable as adventurers happen to meet the monsters on a random basis while exploring.

The monster list below is keyed by number for easy reference, and shows the monsters which will be shown on the game map as being in their "lair". The wandering monster lists appear within the descriptive copy of the module and are given prior to the information on each of the two levels of the dungeon — one being for the upper level, and the other for the lower level.

Monsters are shown on the list with pertinent details given (consult the descriptions within the D & D game booklet for further information on each type), thus allowing them to be employed by the DM when encountered without additional dice rolling (except for the initial roll to determine number appearing). **Important: although there are 25 listings, the Dungeon Master should use only 16 to 20 of them in the dungeon, placing some on each of the two levels in the rooms and chambers desired. The remainder are unused.**

The abbreviations below are used on the list which follows —

(1-4, etc.) =   possible number of the monster type appearing; roll appropriate die

HP	=	number of hit points each monster can take (if less than the maximum number are appearing, roll randomly to see which specific strengths are represented in the encounter)
#AT	=	number of attacks/melee round the monster is allowed
D	=	damage in hit points to victim if monster scores a hit
AC	=	armor class of the monster; this number is followed by the base number required by a 1st-3rd level fighter to score a hit, thus: AC 7/12
SA	=	any special attacks or abilities possessed by the monster

Note: All monster saving throws are taken at the same level as a 1st-3rd level fighter.

MONSTERS

1. Orcs (1-4) — HP: 5, 4, 3, 2; #AT: 1; D: 1-6; AC 7/12; SA: None.

2. Troglodytes (1-2) — HP: 7, 3; #AT: 1; D: 1-6; AC 5/14; SA: Emit odor when enraged.

3. Kobolds (2-9) — HP: 4, 4, 3, 3, 3, 3, 2, 2, 1; #AT: 1; D: 1-4; AC 7/12; SA: None.

4. Ghouls (1-2) — HP: 6, 4; #AT: 1; D: 1-3; AC 6/13; SA: Touch necessitates saving throw vs paralyzation.

5. Giant Centipedes (1-4) — HP: 2 each; #AT: 1; D: Nil; AC 9/10; SA: Bite does no damage but save vs poison must be made (+4 on die).

6. Carrion Crawler (1) — HP: 6; #AT: 8; D: Nil; AC 7/12; SA: Tentacles do no damage but necessitate save vs paralyzation.

7. Orcs (2-7) — HP: 5, 5, 4, 4, 3, 2, 1; #AT: 1; D: 1-6; AC 7/12; SA: None.

8. Large Spiders (1-3) — HP: 4, 3, 3; #AT: 1; D: 1; AC 8/11; SA: Bite necessitates save vs poison (+2 on die).

9. Troglodytes (1-2) — HP: 10, 4; #AT: 1; D: 1-6; AC 5/14; SA: Emit odor when enraged.

10. Giant Tick (1) — HP: 13; #AT: 1; D: 1-4; AC 4/15; SA: Bite drains 4 HP of blood per round after first and causes disease.

11. Stirges (2-5) — HP: 4, 4, 3, 2, 2; #AT: 1; D: 1-3; AC 7/12; SA: Bite drains 1-4 HP of blood per round after first. Attacks at +2 on all die rolls.

12. Gnolls (1-4) — HP: 13, 7, 6, 3; #AT: 1; D: 1-6; AC 5/14; SA: None.

13. Shriekers (1-4) — HP: 14, 10, 10, 8; #AT: 0; D: Nil; AC 7/12; SA: Light within 30' or movement within 10' will trigger shriek for 1-3 melee rounds, with 50% chance to attract a wandering monster.

14. Skeletons (1-6) — HP: 4, 4, 3, 3, 2, 1; #AT: 1; D: 1-6; AC 8/11; SA: None.

15. Hobgoblins (2-5) — HP: 9, 8, 6, 4, 3; #AT: 1; D: 1-8; AC 6/13; SA: None.

16. Goblins (1-8) — HP: 7, 5, 4, 3, 3, 3, 2, 1; #AT: 1; D: 1-6; AC 6/13; SA: None.

17. Giant Rats (2-7) — HP: 4, 3, 3, 2, 2, 1, 1; #AT: 1; D: 1-3; AC 7/12; SA: Bite has 5% chance of causing disease (save vs poison if disease occurs).

18. Zombies (1-2) — HP: 10, 7; #AT: 1; D: 1-8; AC 8/11; SA: None.

19. Kobolds (2-5) — HP: 4, 3, 3, 2, 1; #AT: 1; D: 1-4; AC 7/12; SA: None.

20. Bandits (1-4) — HP: 7, 5, 4, 2; #AT: 1; D: 1-6; AC 6/13; SA: None.

21. Ochre Jelly (1) — HP: 16; #AT: 1; D: 2-12; AC 8/11; SA: Will destroy wood, leather or cloth. Only affected by fire or cold.

22. Gnomes (2-5) — HP: 7, 5, 4, 2, 1; #AT: 1; D: 1-6; AC 5/14; SA: None (only 50% likely to fight unless provoked; otherwise will ignore adventurers and offer only minimal aid).

23. Orcs (2-7) — HP: 8, 6, 5, 4, 4, 2, 2; #AT: 1; D: 1-6; AC 7/12; SA: None.

24. Huge Spider (1) — HP: 7; #AT: 1; D: 1-6; AC 6/13; SA: May leap up to 30 feet to attack prey, bite necessitates save vs poison (+1 on die).

25. Goblins (1-6) — HP: 6, 5, 5, 4, 3, 2; #AT: 1; D: 1-6; AC 6/13; SA: None.

TREASURE LIST

Listed below are 34 different treasures, each letter-coded for easy reference.

Considering their very nature, treasures, in most instances, should be concealed or hidden cleverly. The Dungeon Master should use his imagination in devising ways to hide items from discovery. Some suggestions for treasure location might be: inside an ordinary item in plain view, within a secret compartment in a container, disguised to appear as something else, under or behind a loose stone in the floor or wall, under a heap of trash or dung, or similarly hidden. Occasionally a treasure may be easily noticed, but this should be the exception rather than the rule.

In some instances, valuable treasure will be protected by locks, traps, or protective magic. The more deadly protections are reserved for more experienced adventurers, so any such devices will be uncommon in dungeons designed for beginning players, such as this one. The DM should feel free to create an occasional protection which may confuse or delay characters attempting to find a particular treasure, however.

Remember that all coin values are based on a gold piece (g.p.) standard, with equivalent values being: 50 copper pieces (c.p.) = 10 silver pieces (s.p.) = 2 electrum pieces (e.p.) = 1 gold piece (g.p.) = 1/5 platinum piece (p.p.). All coin weights and sizes are approximately equal.

A) Leather pouch with 10 e.p.

B) 15 g.p.

25

C) 28 g.p.

D) Small wooden box with 35 g.p.

E) Dagger with jeweled handle (2 50 g.p. gems, onyx)

F) 200 s.p.

G) 8 10 g.p. gems (agate)

H) +1 mace

I) False map (shows room and adjacent corridor in detail; nothing else is accurate)

J) +2 spear

K) 120 g.p.

L) Silver medallion on chain worth 500 s.p.

M) 100 g.p. gem (pearl)

N) 2450 c.p.

O) Onyx statue worth 200 g.p.

P) 820 s.p.

Q) 4 100 g.p. gems (garnets)

R) 620 g.p. in locked chest

S) Scroll of 2 Spells (Cleric): 2 **cure light wounds** (or roll at random for determination)

T) False **magic wand** (finely detailed; radiates magic but has no other magical properties)

U) **bag of devouring**

V) 500 g.p. gem (peridot)

W) +1 shield

X) Bronze statuette, inlaid with silver and copper, worth 115 g.p.

Y) Silver mirror of exceptional quality, 90 g.p. value

Z) +1 chainmail

AA) Gold ring (non-magical) worth 10 g.p.

BB) Scroll of 1 Spell (Magic User): **sleep** (or roll at random for determination)

CC) Silver bracelet, worth 80 s.p.

DD) 840 c.p., 290 s.p., 120 e.p., 25 g.p. in locked chest

EE) **Ring of protection** +1

FF) 4 small gold rods, each worth 30 g.p.

GG) Crystal goblet, worth 15 g.p. (engraved with the word "Quasqueton")

HH) Potion: **invisibility** (2 doses, each with a duration of 2 hours)

Special note: Even though 34 treasures are listed here, only between 15 to 25 of them should actually be placed in the dungeon by the Dungeon Master. The remainder should go unused. When treasures are chosen and placed, a good assortment of items should be represented: some very valuable, some worthless, most in between. The letter type treasures listed under the monster specifications in the Basic D & D booklet are ignored in this module, as the above treasure list replaces them and monsters encountered will possess or guard the appropriate treasure assigned by the referee's listings.

THE CHARACTER LISTS

The character lists are designed for multi-purpose use. First of all, they can be used by players to select a player character if they choose to do so rather than roll up abilities of their own. And secondly, they can be used as non-player characters in the positions of henchmen or hirelings. In either case, certain dice rolls will be made to determine various particulars about each character. There are separate lists of 12 characters each for the four classes of fighting men, clerics, magic users, and thieves. The guidelines below explain how to use the lists depending upon desired applications.

Selecting A Player Character From The Character Lists

If a player prefers to choose a character from the lists rather than roll one up himself, he first determines the class of character he wishes to play. He then examines the list of character names and races which appears on the back side of the "Players' Background Sheet", and either chooses one he likes or rolls a 12-sided die to determine which one will be used. In any event, his choice is made without knowing further details about the character's exact ability ratings, which will be given to him by the Dungeon Master once his decision is made. The ability ratings are fixed, and may not be adjusted.

Once a player has gotten his character in this manner, he records the ability ratings and selects his character's alignment (lawful evil, chaotic evil, neutral, chaotic good, or lawful good — the latter three prevailing in this module setting). The player then determines wealth owned, purchases equipment, determines hit points, and chooses spells as normally. All characters will begin at first level of experience.

Using The Character Lists For Henchmen Or Hirelings

Players about to embark on an adventure may well wish to have additional assistance on the part of other fellow explorers, and these other adventurers are non-player characters who will serve either for pay (as hirelings) or out of respect and loyalty (as henchmen).

Hirelings, although not always plentiful, are nonetheless easier to find than henchmen. They will serve for a fee, as well as a cut of any treasure gained — their exact price to be determined by the DM, who then interacts with the players if any bargaining is necessary, taking the part of the non-player character.

Henchmen are usually characters who will be willing to serve a particular character out of admiration or respect without special regard for compensation, although the term could also denote a character who simply wishes to join an adventure without demanding payment other than a share of any treasure gained. The former type will be attracted depending upon the player character's charisma, while the latter's decision would be independent; in any case, with only 1st level characters, players cannot expect to attract henchmen until they have accomplished enough to gain a bit of a reputation and notice. Thus, any non-player character gained for an adventure will have only a 20% chance of being a henchman. (Of course, this fact is not crucial to the immediate adventure, but may bear upon future considerations . . .). Note that no henchman will serve a character of lower level.

The number of non-player characters available to a party of player characters is determined by consulting the table below, and by appropriate dice rolls as noted. The number of henchmen/hirelings available depends upon the number of player characters in the party — the more player characters participating, the fewer henchmen/hirelings available.

AVAILABILITY OF HENCHMEN/HIRELINGS

Player Characters	Chance for Henchmen/Hirelings & Number Available
2	100% chance of 1-4
3	75% chance of 1-3
4	50% chance of 1-2
5	25% chance of 1
6 or more	None

Once a party of players has determined that one or more non-player characters will be willing to join their adventuring group (dependent upon the financial arrangements being finalized), a 12-sided die is rolled for each such hireling or henchmen to determine their character class based on the following table:

CHARACTER CLASSES OF HENCHMEN/HIRELINGS

1	Fighting man	5	Cleric	9	Magic User
2	Fighting man	6	Thief	10	Any class desired
3	Fighting man	7	Thief	11	Any class desired
4	Cleric	8	Magic User	12	Any class desired

Example: Three player characters — a magic user, fighting man, and thief — wish to bolster the strength of their adventuring band by having others join the group. They have a 75% chance of locating 1-3 interested non-player characters who will listen to their offer and, if reasonable, likely be agreeable to joining the party for at least a single adventure. If they fail to locate any willing non-player characters, they will be forced to adventure without them, at least initially.

Once a class for each non-player character has been determined (this can be done prior to any terms being offered by the player characters), a 12-sided die should be rolled on the specific table corresponding to that type of character class to determine the individual character's name and race (although his ability ratings will not be known by the players until he actually joins their group). If the arrangement is finalized, the DM gives the players specifics on the non-player character's abilities, as well as other pertinent details (which are described following each character list depending upon the particular class). The alignment of any non-player character will generally be compatible with the rest of the group, although there is a slight (10%) chance that a non-player character will be chaotic evil while professing otherwise, thus seeking to hoodwink the party and perhaps take advantage of them when the opportunity arises.

Non-player characters will carry no wealth other than 1-6 gold pieces for incidental expenses. In most cases, they will carry their own weapon and/or armor. However, player characters may purchase additional equipment, arms, or armor for them to use while adventuring — either as a loan or an outright gift — or even give them their own. Attention must be paid to character class restrictions in this regard, however.

Important: non-player characters may vary widely in personality. The Dungeon Master plays their part to a great degree, although the players indicate what instructions or orders they are giving to the non-player characters during the course of the adventure. The DM can choose any personality he wants for a non-player character, or can determine the various aspects by rolling for the categories of attitude, disposition, courage, and loyalty on the following chart. Players are never informed of the exact personalities of non-player characters; they will discover them through interaction with the characters (as portrayed by the DM) and by observing them in the course of the adventure.

NON-PLAYER CHARACTER PERSONALITY

Attitude
1 Helpful/cooperative
2 Helpful/cooperative
3 Helpful/cooperative
4 Apathetic/lazy
5 Unreliable
6 Obstinate/argumentative/ domineering

Courage
1 Reckless/daring
2 Courageous
3 Normal
4 Normal
5 Hesitant
6 Cowardly

Disposition
1 Greedy/selfish
2 Normal
3 Normal
4 Normal
5 Normal
6 Unselfish

Loyalty
1 Loyal
2 Loyal
3 Normal
4 Normal
5 Fickle
6 Fickle

Any hireling surviving an adventure, if well treated and amply rewarded, may decide to become a follower (or loyal henchman) of one of the player characters. This will depend upon numerous factors: the non-player character's personality, the rewards or benefits obtained by the non-player character in previous adventuring, the treatment he received from the player characters, the competence of the player characters, and — of considerable importance — the charisma of a particular player character. All these factors must be weighed by the Dungeon Master, as well as consideration of the fact that the player characters may or may not have any accomplishments or reputation that would serve to attract others to their service. If he deems it appropriate, he assigns a reasonable chance for a character to gain a particular follower, and rolls the dice. *Keep in mind, however, that players may find it difficult to attract henchmen until they have increased their experience and fame.*

The loyalty of any follower will likewise be subject to continual checks depending upon similar considerations as above.

27

CLERICS

1. Farned of the Great Church (Human)
   Str 7, Int 10, Wis 14, Con 9, Dex 14, Cha 9

2. Dohram, Servant of Saint Carmichael (Human)
   Str 10, Int 12, Wis 14, Con 10, Dex 11, Cha 12

3. The Mystical One (Human)
   Str 12, Int 10, Wis 15, Con 15, Dex 8, Cha 14

4. Mulgar the Merciful (Human)
   Str 10, Int 10, Wis 18, Con 8, Dex 12, Cha 17

5. Seeful the Unforgiving (Human)
   Str 6, Int 8, Wis 12, Con 12, Dex 11, Cha 10

6. Philgo (Human)
   Str 9, Int 10, Wis 13, Con 9, Dex 7, Cha 12

7. Tassit, Servant of Saint Cuthbert (Human)
   Str 11, Int 9, Wis 12, Con 10, Dex 7, Cha 11

8. Wilberd the Silent (Human)
   Str 13, Int 8, Wis 17, Con 12, Dex 9, Cha 10

9. Kracky the Hooded One (Human)
   Str 8, Int 14, Wis 16, Con 8, Dex 8, Cha 12

10. Grampal of the Secret Church (Human)
    Str 12, Int 11, Wis 12, Con 10, Dex 9, Cha 10

11. Nupo, Servant of The Bringer (Human)
    Str 10, Int 7, Wis 15, Con 17, Dex 10, Cha 8

12. Eggo of the Holy Brotherhood (Human)
    Str 7, Int 10, Wis 13, Con 8, Dex 9, Cha 11

Non-player clerics will usually possess holy water as a matter of course, as well as a single non-edged weapon. A 6-sided die can be rolled once for each category shown below to determine the arms and armor of any non-player cleric:

Arms	Armor
1 Club	1 None
2 Club	2 Leather armor
3 Quarter staff	3 Leather armor
4 Hammer	4 Leather and shield
5 Flail	5 Chainmail
6 Mace	6 Chainmail and shield

All non-player clerics are of first level and use one 6-sided die to determine hit points, except for an independent henchman (one joining the adventure on his own rather than out of loyalty or for a fee other than a treasure share). An independent henchman cleric will be of either first, second, or third level depending upon a roll on the table which follows:

	Level	Hit Dice	Spells Known
1	First (Acolyte)	1d6	None
2	First (Acolyte)	1d6	None
3	Second (Adept)	2d6	Use table C, one roll
4	Second (Adept)	2d6	Use table C, one roll
5	Third (Priest)	3d6	Use table C, two rolls
6	Third (Priest)	3d6	Use table C, two rolls

Table C below is used to determine randomly which spell or spells any non-player cleric knows. First level clerics have no spell ability. Player character clerics do not utilize this table; they choose which spells they wish to use according to the guidelines in the Basic D & D booklet.

Table C

1 Cure Light Wounds
2 Cure Light Wounds
3 Cure Light Wounds
4 Detect Evil
5 Detect Magic
6 Detect Magic
7 Light
8 Light
9 Protection From Evil
10 Purify Food and Water
11 Remove Fear
12 Resist Cold

FIGHTING MEN

1. Brandon (Human)
   Str 14, Int 8, Wis 11, Con 13, Dex 9, Cha 12

2. Evro (Elf)
   Str 14, Int 13, Wis 7, Con 12, Dex 11, Cha 9

3. Glendor the Fourth (Human)
   Str 17, Int 10, Wis 9, Con 14, Dex 9, Cha 14

4. Zeffan (Dwarf)
   Str 14, Int 11, Wis 8, Con 8, Dex 14, Cha 7

5. Alho Rengate (Human)
   Str 12, Int 10, Wis 9, Con 11, Dex 12, Cha 12

6. Krago of the Mountains (Dwarf)
   Str 18/54, Int 9, Wis 15, Con 16, Dex 9, Cha 14

7. Pendor (Halfling)
   Str 12, Int 9, Wis 8, Con 10, Dex 11, Cha 9

8. Mohag the Wanderer (Human)
   Str 13, Int 12, Wis 9, Con 10, Dex 6, Cha 10

9. Norrin the Barbarian (Human)
   Str 15, Int 8, Wis 10, Con 14, Dex 9, Cha 9

10. Lefto (Halfling)
    Str 11, Int 10, Wis 11, Con 18, Dex 8, Cha 10

11. Webberan of the Great North (Human)
    Str 16, Int 10, Wis 13, Con 10, Dex 7, Cha 7

12. Sho-Rembo (Elf)
    Str 9, Int 11, Wis 9, Con 18, Dex 9, Cha 15

To determine arms and armor for non-player fighting men, roll once on each of the tables below with a 12-sided die:

Arms	Armor
1 Dagger and hand axe	1 Shield only
2 Dagger and sword	2 Leather armor
3 Hand axe	3 Leather and shield
4 Mace	4 Leather and shield
5 Sword	5 Leather and shield
6 Sword	6 Leather and shield +1
7 Sword +1	7 Chainmail
8 Pole arm	8 Chainmail
9 Pole arm	9 Chainmail and shield
10 Morning star	10 Chainmail and shield +1
11 Flail	11 Plate mail
12 Short bow and 12 arrows	12 Plate mail and shield

All non-player fighting men are of first level and use one 8-

28

sided die to determine hit points, except for an independent henchman (one joining the adventure on his own rather than out of loyalty or for a fee other than a treasure share). An independent henchman will be of either first, second, or third level depending upon a roll on the following table:

	Level	Hit Dice*
1	First (Veteran)	1d8
2	First (Veteran)	1d8
3	Second (Warrior)	2d8
4	Second (Warrior)	2d8
5	Third (Swordsman)	3d8
6	Third (Swordsman)	3d8

* Halfling and elven fighting men use 6-sided hit dice of the appropriate number.

MAGIC USERS

1. Presto (Elf)
   Str 9, Int 17, Wis 11, Con 14, Dex 11, Cha 14

2. Mezlo (Elf)
   Str 11, Int 14, Wis 8, Con 9, Dex 12, Cha 13

3. Nickar (Human)
   Str 11, Int 15, Wis 8, Con 12, Dex 5, Cha 13

4. Shobaffum (Human)
   Str 7, Int 13, Wis 9, Con 13, Dex 11, Cha 10

5. Yor (Human)
   Str 11, Int 14, Wis 8, Con 12, Dex 5, Cha 13

6. Ralt Gaither (Human)
   Str 11, Int 18, Wis 7, Con 9, Dex 14, Cha 10

7. Fencig (Elf)
   Str 8, Int 17, Wis 10, Con 5, Dex 11, Cha 9

8. Glom the Mighty (Human)
   Str 12, Int 15, Wis 15, Con 7, Dex 10, Cha 11

9. Trebbelos, Boy Magician (Human)
   Str 9, Int 16, Wis 9, Con 7, Dex 12, Cha 13

10. Beska Miltar (Human)
    Str 10, Int 13, Wis 12, Con 15, Dex 8, Cha 14

11. Lappoy the Unexpected (Elf)
    Str 11, Int 14, Wis 9, Con 10, Dex 7, Cha 9

12. Surfal (Human)
    Str 12, Int 14, Wis 11, Con 8, Dex 12, Cha 5

Non-player magic users will wear no armor and generally will be armed with nothing other than a dagger. All non-player magic users are of first level and use one 4-sided die to determine hit points, except for an independent henchman (one joining the adventure on his own rather than out of loyalty or for a fee other than a treasure share). An independent henchman magic user will be of either first, second, or third level depending upon a roll on the table which follows:

	Level	Hit Dice	Spells Known
1	First (Medium)	1d4	Use table A, one roll
2	First (Medium)	1d4	Use table A, one roll
3	Second (Seer)	2d4	Use table A, two rolls
4	Second (Seer)	2d4	Use table A, two rolls
5	Third (Conjurer)	3d4	Use table A, two rolls and table B, one roll
6	Third (Conjurer)	3d4	Use table A, two rolls and table B, one roll

Tables A and B below are used to determine randomly which spell or spells any non-player magic user knows. All first level magic users make but a single roll on table A. Player character magic users do not utilize this table; they check which spells they can know according to the guidelines in the Basic D & D booklet.

	Table A	Table B
1	Charm Person	Audible Glamer
2	Charm Person	Continual Light
3	Dancing Lights	Darkness
4	Detect Magic	Detect Evil
5	Detect Magic	Detect invisible
6	Enlargement	ESP
7	Hold Portal	Invisibility
8	Light	Invisibility
9	Light	Knock
10	Magic Missile	Levitate
11	Magic Missile	Locate Object
12	Protection From Evil	Magic Mouth
13	Read Languages	Mirror Image
14	Read Magic	Phantasmal Forces
15	Shield	Pyrotechnics
16	Sleep	Ray of Enfeeblement
17	Sleep	Ray of Enfeeblement
18	Sleep	Strength
19	Tenser's Floating Disc	Web
20	Ventriloquism	Wizard Lock

29

THIEVES

1. Luven Lightfinger (Halfling)
   Str 13, Int 14, Wis 9, Con 12, Dex 16, Cha 13

2. Treddo (Halfling)
   Str 10, Int 9, Wis 7, Con 11, Dex 17, Cha 14

3. Bozomus (Human)
   Str 5, Int 9, Wis 12, Con 6, Dex 13, Cha 12

4. Estra Zo (Elf)
   Str 12, Int 12, Wis 11, Con 7, Dex 16, Cha 12

5. Laggamundo (Human)
   Str 11, Int 10, Wis 9, Con 13, Dex 13, Cha 6

6. Feggener the Quick (Human)
   Str 10, Int 9, Wis 7, Con 11, Dex 17, Cha 14

7. Mezron (Dwarf)
   Str 5, Int 9, Wis 12, Con 6, Dex 13, Cha 12

8. Drebb (Human)
   Str 7, Int 12, Wis 10, Con 11, Dex 12, Cha 11

9. Postue (Elf)
   Str 10, Int 8, Wis 7, Con 10, Dex 18, Cha 12

10. Harg of the City Afar (Human)
    Str 9, Int 13, Wis 10, Con 6, Dex 15, Cha 8

11. Afton Borr (Human)
    Str 11, Int 11, Wis 8, Con 10, Dex 13, Cha 9

12. Sporragha (Dwarf)
    Str 10, Int 7, Wis 11, Con 14, Dex 12, Cha 18

To determine the arms and armor of any non-player thieves, roll a 6-sided die once on each of the following tables:

Arms		Armor	
1	None	1	None
2	None	2	None
3	Dagger	3	Leather armor
4	Dagger	4	Leather armor
5	Dagger	5	Leather armor
6	Dagger + 1	6	Leather armor + 1

All non-player thieves are of first level and use one 4-sided die to determine hit points, except for an independent henchman (one joining the adventure on his own rather than out of loyalty or for a fee other than a treasure share). An independent henchman will be of either first, second or third level depending upon a roll on the following table:

	Level	Hit Dice	Thief Ability Category
1	First (Apprentice)	1d4	A
2	First (Apprentice)	1d4	A
3	Second (Footpad)	2d4	B
4	Second (Footpad)	2d4	B
5	Third (Robber)	3d4	C
6	Third (Robber)	3d4	C

30

PLAYERS' BACKGROUND SHEET

Here is the standard background setting for all players to read prior to their first adventure:

Rogahn the Fearless and Zelligar the Unknown are legendary names. Even you, a young fledgling in a town far from the great cities of your world, know of their reputation — even though their tale begins long before you were born. The elders and the sages speak both names with respect, even awe, in a distant admiration for the memories of the two legendary figures . . .

You have heard parts of the story before, but never enough to know all of it, or even what is true and what is only legend or speculation. But it is a great and fascinating beginning in your own quest to learn more.

Rogahn the Fearless earned his name as a great warrior, and his reputation spread far and wide across the land. Zelligar the Unknown, equally renowned, earned his respected status and power as a foremost practitioner of the mystical arts of magic and sorcery.

hills, and decisively turned back the invasion. Rogahn slew a horde of barbarians single-handedly and Zelligar's powerful magic put their army to flight. It was a great victory, and a grateful populace rewarded the pair and their consorts with considerable treasure. After that, the two heroes returned to their mystical hideaway, and rumor has it that the spoils of victory were spent to further its construction, although some of it may yet be hidden somewhere.

The most exciting portions of the legend are the most recent. Some years ago, perhaps in the decade before you were born, Rogahn and Zelligar apparently decided upon a joint foray into the lands of the hated barbarians. Taking most of their henchmen and associates along with them in a great armed band, the two personages, it seems, disappeared into the forbidding alien lands to the north on a great adventure which some say may have been asked by the very gods themselves.

No one knows what occurrence or coincidence brought these two men together, but tales tell of their meeting and forming a strong bond of friendship, a union that would last for the ages. As this occurred, legend has it, the two men virtually disappeared from the view of civilization. Stories occasionally surfaced about a rumored hideaway being built deep in the wilderness, far from the nearest settlement, away from traveled routes, and high upon a craggy hill — but no one seemed to know any more than that, or where this supposed hideaway really was located, if indeed it was. No one knows for sure, but some say their motive was to pursue the common goals of personal greed and some kind of vague (or chaotic) evil. In any case, they jointly led a hermit life with but a few occasional forays into the outside world to add to their own reputations.

Many years passed, until one day a great barbarian invasion came from the lands to the north, threatening to engulf the entire land with the savage excesses of the unchecked alien horde. Just when things seemed the darkest, Rogahn the Fearless and Zelligar the Unknown made their unexpected yet most welcome reappearance. Joining their powerful forces, they and their band of loyal henchmen met the barbarian army in a great battle at a narrow pass in the

Word just reaching civilization tells of some great battle in the barbarian lands where the legendary Rogahn and Zelligar have met their demise. This rumored clash must have occurred some years ago, and there are few details — and no substantiation of the story. The only thing certain is that, if all this is true, Rogahn and Zelligar have been gone far too long . . . If only one had the knowledge and wherewithal to find their hideaway, he would have great things to explore!

Now, just recently, came the most promising bit of information — a crude map purporting to show the way to the hideaway of the two men, a place apparently called "Q". You or one of your acquaintances has this map, and if it is accurate, it could perhaps lead you to the mystical place that was their home and sanctuary. Who knows what riches of wealth and magic might be there for the taking??? Yes, the risk is great, but the challenge cannot be ignored. Gathering a few of your fellows, you share the secret and embark on an adventure in search of the unknown . . .

Note: Individual players may know of additional information in the form of rumors or legends as given to them by the Dungeon Master.

31

PLAYERS' LIST OF POTENTIAL CHARACTERS

Listed here are 12 characters of each of the four character classes, showing name and race. The Dungeon Master has a more complete listing of each character's ability scores and other information.

Clerics

1. Farned of the Great Church (Human)
2. Dohram, Servant of Saint Carmichael (Human)
3. The Mystical One (Human)
4. Mulgar the Merciful (Human)
5. Seeful the Unforgiving (Human)
6. Philgo (Human)
7. Tassit, Servant of Saint Cuthbert (Human)
8. Wilberd the Silent (Human)
9. Kracky the Hooded One (Human)
10. Grampal of the Secret Church (Human)
11. Nupo, Servant of The Bringer (Human)
12. Eggo of the Holy Brotherhood (Human)

Fighting Men

1. Brandon (Human)
2. Evro (Elf)
3. Glendor the Fourth (Human)
4. Zeffan (Dwarf)
5. Alho Rengate (Human)
6. Krago of the Mountains (Dwarf)
7. Pendor (Halfling)
8. Mohag the Wanderer (Human)
9. Norrin the Barbarian (Human)
10. Lefto (Halfling)
11. Webberan of the Great North (Human)
12. Sho-Rembo (Elf)

Magic Users

1. Presto (Elf)
2. Mezlo (Elf)
3. Nickar (Human)
4. Shobaffum (Human)
5. Yor (Human)
6. Ralt Gaither (Human)
7. Fencig (Elf)
8. Glom the Mighty (Human)
9. Trebbelos, Boy Magician (Human)
10. Beska Miltar (Human)
11. Lappoy the Unexpected (Elf)
12. Surfal (Human)

Thieves

1. Luven Lightfinger (Halfling)
2. Treddo (Halfling)
3. Bozomus (Human)
4. Estra Zo (Elf)
5. Laggamundo (Human)
6. Feggener the Quick (Human)
7. Mezron (Dwarf)
8. Drebb (Human)
9. Postue (Elf)
10. Harg of the City Afar (Human)
11. Afton Borr (Human)
12. Sporragha (Dwarf)

Your Dungeon Master has a complete list of guidelines for the use of these lists; they appear for your reference only.

TIPS FOR PLAYERS

Beginning players would do well to profit from some basic advice before beginning their D & D careers, and with that in mind, the following points are offered for consideration:

1) Be an organized player. Keep accurate records on your character (experience, abilities, items possessed, etc.) for your own purposes and to aid the Dungeon Master.

2) Always keep in mind that the Dungeon Master is the moderator of the game, and as such, deserves the continued cooperation, consideration and respect of all the players. If you disagree with him, present your viewpoint with deference to his position as game judge, but be prepared to accept his decision as final — after all, keep in mind that you may not know all aspects of the overall game situation, and that in any case, not everything will always go your way!

3) Cooperate with your fellow players and work together when adventuring. Remember that on any foray into the dungeon or wilderness, a mix of character classes will be beneficial, since the special abilities of the various characters will complement each other and add to the overall effectiveness of the party.

4) Be neither too hasty or too sluggish when adventuring. If you are too fast in your exploration, you may recklessly endanger yourself and your fellow adventurers and fall prone to every trick and trap you encounter. If you are too slow, you will waste valuable time and may be waylaid by more than your share of wandering monsters without accomplishing anything. As you gain playing experience you will learn the proper pace, but rely on your DM for guidance.

5) Avoid arguing. While disagreements about a course of action will certainly arise from time to time, players should quickly discuss their options and reach a concensus in order to proceed. Bickering in the dungeon will only create noise which may well attract wandering monsters. Above all, remember that D & D is just a game and a little consideration will go far toward avoiding any hard feelings . . .

6) Be on your guard. Don't be overly cautious, but be advised that some non-player characters may try to hoodwink you, players may doublecross you, and while adventuring, tricks and traps await the unwary. Of course, you won't avoid every such pitfall (dealing with the uncertainties is part of the fun and challenge of the game), but don't be surprised if everything is not always as it seems.

7) Treat any hirelings or henchmen fairly. If you reward them generously and do not expose them to great risks of life and limb that your own character would not face, then you can expect a continuing loyalty (although there may be exceptions, of course).

8) Know your limits. Your party may not be a match for every monster you encounter, and occasionally it pays to know when and how to run away from danger. Likewise, a dungeon adventure may have to be cut short if your party suffers great adversity and/or depleted strength. Many times it will take more than one adventure to accomplish certain goals, and it will thus be necessary to come back out of a dungeon to heal wounds, restore magical abilities and spells, and reinforce a party's strength.

9) Use your head. Many of the character's goals in the game can be accomplished through the strength of arms or magic. Others, however, demand common sense and shrewd judgment as well as logical deduction. The most successful players are those who can effectively use both aspects of the game to advantage.

10) D & D is a role playing game, and the fun of the game comes in playing your character's role. Take on your character's persona and immerse yourself in the game setting, enjoying the fantasy element and the interaction with your fellow players and the Dungeon Master.

Enjoy yourself, and good luck!

32

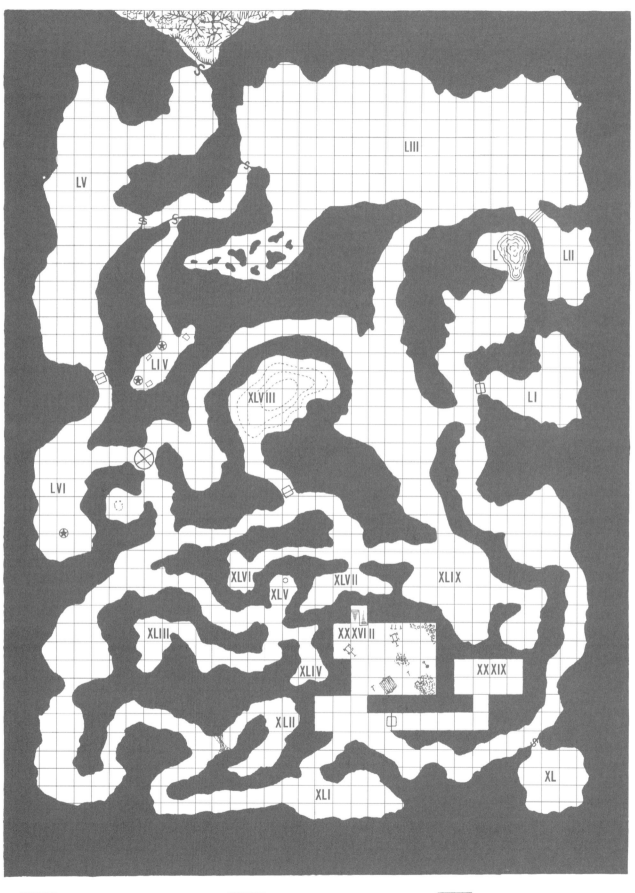

POOL   DEPRESSION   WEBS

This item is only one of the many popular aids for DUNGEONS & DRAGONS® produced by TSR Hobbies, Inc. Other D & D accessory items currently available include:

Dungeon Geomorphs, Set One (Basic Dungeon)
Dungeon Geomorphs, Set Two (Caves & Caverns)
Dungeon Geomorphs, Set Three (Lower Dungeon)

Outdoor Geomorphs, Set One (Walled City)

Monster & Treasure Assortment, Set One (Levels One to Three)
Monster & Treasure Assortment, Set Two (Levels Four to Six)
Monster & Treasure Assortment, Set Three (Levels Seven to Nine)

D & D Character Record Sheets Pad

Dungeon Module B1 (In Search of the Unknown)

The entire selection of this series of Dungeon Modules for ADVANCED DUNGEONS & DRAGONS® is comprised of the following items:

Dungeon Module G1 (Steading of the Hill Giant Chief)
Dungeon Module G2 (Glacial Rift of the Frost Giant Jarl)
Dungeon Module G3 (Hall of the Fire Giant King)
Dungeon Module D1 (Descent into the Depths of the Earth)
Dungeon Module D2 (Shrine of the Kuo-Toa)
Dungeon Module D3 (Vault of the Drow)
Dungeon Module S1 (Tomb of Horrors)

Other releases of additional items relating to D & D are planned for the future.

TSR Hobbies publishes a complete line of fantasy, science fiction, and historical games and rules. A complete catalog on the entire selection of TSR items is available for $2.00 from TSR Hobbies, POB 756, Lake Geneva, WI 53147.

Dungeon Module B1
In Search of the Unknown
by Mike Carr

INTRODUCTORY MODULE FOR CHARACTER LEVELS 1-3

This package (a cover folder with maps and descriptive booklet within) forms a complete module for use with DUNGEONS & DRAGONS Basic Set. It is especially designed as an instructional aid for beginning Dungeon Masters and players, especially created to enable new Dungeon Masters to initiate play with a minimum of preperation.

In addition to descriptive and situational material, this module also includes special informational sections giving: background history and legends, listings of possible monsters and treasures and how to place them, a list of adventuring characters, tips on various aspects of play for the Dungeon Master, and helpful advice for starting players.

If you enjoy this module, look for more releases in the D&D family from TSR, The Game Wizards.

DUNGEONS & DRAGONS and D&D are registered trademarks owned by TSR Hobbies Inc.

TM
TSR
The GameWizards
© 1980 TSR Hobbies, Inc. All Rights Reserved

PRINTED IN U.S.A.

Special
Instructional
Module

©1979, 1981 TSR Hobbies, Inc.
All Rights Reserved

TSR HOBBIES, INC.
POB 756
LAKE GENEVA, WI 53147

9023

UPPER LEVEL

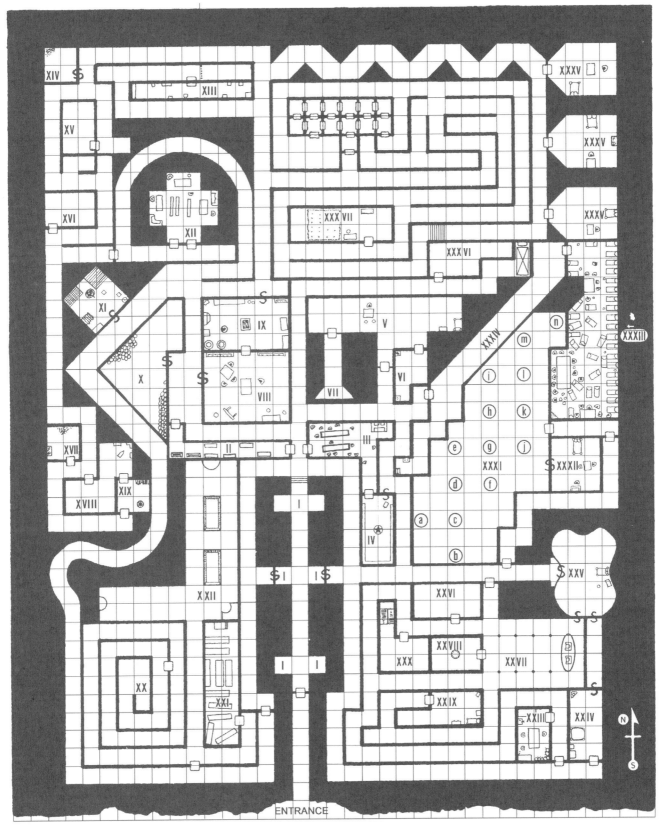

ENTRANCE

DOOR

S SECRET DOOR

FALSE DOOR

STAIRS, UP

STAIRS, DOWN

STATUE

PITS, COVERED

Dungeon Module B1
In Search of the Unknown

by Mike Carr

INTRODUCTORY MODULE FOR CHARACTER LEVELS 1-3

This package (a cover folder with maps and descriptive booklet within) forms a complete module for use with DUNGEONS & DRAGONS® BASIC SET. It is especially designed as an instructional aid for beginning Dungeon Masters and players, specifically created to enable new Dungeon Masters to initiate play with a minimum of preparation.

In addition to descriptive and situational material, this module also includes special informational sections giving: background history and legends, listings of possible monsters and treasures and how to place them, a list of adventuring characters, tips on various aspects of play for the Dungeon Master, and helpful advice for starting players.

If you enjoy this module, look for more releases in the D&D® family from TSR, The Game Wizards.

Distributed to the book trade in the United States by Random House, Inc. and in Canada by Random House of Canada, Ltd. Distributed to the toy and hobby trade by regional distributors.
©1979, 1981 TSR Hobbies, Inc. All Rights Reserved
DUNGEONS & DRAGONS® and D&D® are registered trademarks owned by TSR Hobbies, Inc.

©1980 TSR Hobbies, Inc. All Rights Reserved

TSR HOBBIES, INC.
POB 756
LAKE GENEVA, WI 53147

PRINTED IN U.S.A.
ISBN 0-935696-04-0

Special Instructional Module

DUNGEONS & DRAGONS® Basic Set
Special Instructional Dungeon Module #B1
IN SEARCH OF THE UNKNOWN
by Mike Carr

Introduction: This package forms a special instructional module for play of DUNGEONS & DRAGONS® Basic Set, and as such, is specifically designed for beginning players and Dungeon Masters. Due to its special design, it has numerous applications and services a multiplicity of purposes.

Most material within this module is that contained in the D&D® Basic Set game booklet. In some instances, new material (such as additional monsters, magic items, etc.) is included, and when this is so, every effort has been made to provide a pertinent explanation of important aspects and effects.

Those who would intend to be beginning players using this module would be well advised to stop reading this now and to avoid further examination of the module details or game map. The reason for this is that enjoyment of the module will be enhanced when the challenge of the unknown and unexpected confronts the participants, who will not be able to benefit from any familiarity with the game situation other than the background provided by the referee. This element of the unknown and the resultant exploration in search of unknown treasures (with hostile monsters and unexpected dangers to outwit and overcome) is precisely what a DUNGEONS & DRAGONS adventure is all about, and "knowing too much" can greatly spoil the fun of the experience that makes D&D gaming so special. So, if you're going to be a player in this module, stop reading here, resist the temptation (which will be considerable) to go further in examining the contents, put the module aside, and wait for your Dungeon Master to get ready to use this package for gaming. You won't be sorry!

NOTES FOR THE DUNGEON MASTER

As a beginning Dungeon Master, you will find this module helpful in many ways. First of all, it serves as a graphic example of a beginning dungeon. For this reason, it should prove illustrative to fledgling Dungeon Masters who will benefit from a look at what another dungeon design "looks like." Those designing their own dungeons will want to note various aspects of this dungeon which will give them valuable insights into the creative process which allows them to formulate their own unique dungeon and gaming setting. Those going on to design their own dungeons and campaigns should be advised of the various playing aids available from TSR as official DUNGEONS & DRAGONS accessories—most notably the various sets of geomorphs (see the products list on the D&D Basic Set booklet for details) which allow preparation of large map areas with a minimum of time and effort.

Second, this package provides an almost "ready-made" game situation which can be utilized for one or more playings. Some initial preparation is necessary in addition to reading the material through one or more times before using it in a game. The preparation, however, is interesting and fun as well as instructional, for it shows how a Dungeon Master (or DM) "stocks" the dungeon with assorted treasures and monsters before any adventuring begins. Separate lists of monsters and treasures to key with the various locations inside the dungeon insure that no two similar modules will be the same when set up by different DM's, and will also guarantee that players will not know what to expect in any given room or location. As for player characters, participants can use their own characters rolled up according to the guidelines within the DUNGEONS & DRAGONS Basic rulebook or choose from a list of pre-generated characters supplied here (including possible retainers to accompany the player characters in their adventuring).

Thirdly, there are several salient points of good dungeon design illustrated in this module which new DM's would be wise to note. Likewise, they should keep these factors in mind when they start to design their own game maps and situations:

1) Since it is important to offer a challenge commensurate to the players' level, this two-level dungeon design is made specifically for exploration by beginning players in a party of 3 to 6 adventurers (player and non-player characters combined). This is reflected in various ways:

    a) In general, this dungeon is less deadly and more forgiving than one designed to test experienced players. It is designed to be fairly challenging, however, and is by no means "easy." Careless adventurers will pay the penalty for a lack of caution—only one of the many lessons to be learned within the dungeon!

    b) The dungeon is designed to be instructive for new players. Most of it should be relatively easy to map, although there are difficult sections—especially on the lower level where irregular rock caverns and passageways will prove a real challenge.

    c) The monsters encountered will generally be commensurate with the adventurers' ability to defeat them. For the few that are too formidable, the adventurers will have to learn the necessary art of fleeing or else employ more powerful means against them.

    d) The treasures to be found will generally be small, although a couple of more lucrative finds are possible if the adventurers are clever or lucky.

2) The dungeon includes a good assortment of typical features which players can learn to expect, including some interesting tricks and traps:

    a) Several one-way secret doors

    b) Illusions and magic mouths

    c) A wind corridor which may extinguish torches and open flames

    d) A room of mysterious pools

    e) A room of doors

    f) A water pit trap which suddenly drops adventurers to the lower level

    g) A portcullis trap where vertical bars drop behind the party in a dead end corridor

    h) A pair of teleport rooms to confuse explorers

    i) Several magical treasures—most beneficial, some cursed

    j) Mysterious containers with a variety of contents for examination

3) There is a legend or story explaining some details of the setting and providing a background (i.e., why it exists, its background, how the characters became involved with it, etc.). Of course, players/adventurers will probably only know bits of this information—or perhaps only rumors of dubious reliability. Most good dungeons (and indeed, entire game campaigns) rest upon a firm basis of interesting background and "history" as set for the players by the game moderator, or Dungeon Master.

2

4) The setting is neither too simple nor too difficult. Adventurers can exit by either returning to the entrance or locating the other secret exit. Two ways down to the lower level are available for discovery, and a trap may also bring adventurers unexpectedly there.

PREPARATION FOR THE USE OF THE MODULE

The use of this module by the Dungeon Master first requires a working familiarity with its layout and various design features. Therefore, the first step is to completely read the module, doing so with care and with reference to the two maps provided to learn the basic layout and location of the various parts described in the written commentary. A second and third reading will also prove beneficial in preparing for a game employing the module.

Once the DM has obtained a background knowledge of the situation and the various features of the areas to be explored, he or she must **key** the two maps by placing various monsters and treasures within the dungeon complex. To do so, the DM utilizes the two lists provided which follow within this booklet, taking advantage of the special system to allow easy setup and reference.

Upon examination of the two game maps, it will be noticed that each prominent room or chamber has a number for designation purposes. Each number corresponds to a written description within the body commentary which accompanies the maps and which is contained in this booklet. Thus, a description of each such area of the dungeon is easily referenced by locating the written material within the booklet, and these are arranged in numerical order. The basic descriptions are standard, but in most cases there is no mention of either monsters inhabiting a particular area or specific treasures to be found within (except for occasional items which are part of the furnishings and which may have some unusual value). A space exists after each description with a brief area for listing either a monster or a treasure (or both) which may be within that room; exactly what will appear in each room, however, is up to the Dungeon Master, who will fill in some of the spaces to denote their presence. This is done easily through the use of the number and letter-coded lists provided for monsters and treasures, respectively. It is important to note, however, that not every room will contain a monster, a treasure, or both—in fact, a fair number of rooms will contain neither, and in some cases the treasure will be hidden or concealed in some manner. Further details on the use of the two lists is contained in the description which precedes them in the section entitled KEYING THE DUNGEON.

Once the dungeon has been keyed and the Dungeon Master's preparation is complete, he or she must assist the players in getting ready for the adventure. The first step is in providing them with the background outline which sets the stage for the game. This "Player's Background Sheet" (which differs in some ways from the more detailed description/background for the referee) is on a perforated sheet at the end of this booklet. It is designed to be removed and handed to the players prior to the adventure (or simply read aloud to them if you do not wish to remove it from the booklet).

Once the players know the background, they can prepare their characters for the adventure. If new characters are needed (as they will be if the players are just starting their first game), they can be rolled up by using the dice and following the prescribed procedure within the DUNGEONS & DRAGONS Basic rule booklet. Each player also determines his or her amount of starting money (the number of gold pieces he or she has to begin with), and this amount is available for the purchase of arms and equipment for adventur-

ing. Once the players have decided upon the equipment they will be carrying, as well as their own arms and armor, they are ready to start play. A written record of abilities, wealth, and equipment owned and carried is kept by each player.

As an alternative to spending time rolling the characters up, a list of assorted adventuring characters is included on the reverse side of the "Player's Background Sheet." If the Dungeon Master decides to do so, the players can choose one of the characters listed there as their player character. In such a case, the DM then provides the pertinent specifications and ability ratings of the character to the player, who makes a note of it on the side. The DM's master list of character abilities is within this booklet.

If there are only two or three players, or if a party wishes additional assistance, one or more retainers (non-player characters who will be a part of the party but who will not be under the total control of the players) can be added to the group of adventurers at the Dungeon Master's discretion. These characters can also be from the list, and their specifications and ability ratings are also on the master list for the Dungeon Master.

When players have retainers (characters who serve out of admiration or loyalty), the Dungeon Master must use common sense in their employment within the game. Obviously, allowing players to assemble large bands of armed assistants at this stage of the game would be unfair and unbalancing, so it will be unusual to see more than one or two non-player characters appearing in the first games. Only after players have survived to earn some repute and wealth to attract (and afford) them will they be able to locate additional adventurers to aid their exploration.

Seeking retainers is a matter to be handled by the Dungeon Master. A player's success in attracting retainers will depend upon the charisma of the seeker. Once a retainer has decided to join a group (this usually being determined by a secret dice roll by the Dungeon Master), the non-player character will generally function according to the directions of the player character being served. However, in some situations —most notably those involving great risk or danger—the Dungeon Master serves as the "conscience" of the retainer, and may cause him or her to balk at ordered action or perhaps even desert in the face of danger or as a result of unrewarded courage or accomplishment. For example, if a party is facing a hazardous situation and a player tells his or her retainer to do something which would seem more dangerous than the actions pursued by the other player adventurers, the retainer may hesitate to act upon the order—or in some cases might simply run away if the chance of death is great (this being determined by the DM's secret morale role plus modifiers of his or her choosing, depending upon the situation). Likewise, if a retainer successfully executes a hazardous action (slaying a dragon without much help, for instance) and does not get a proportional reward, he or she will understandably consider deserting the player character who illtreated him or her. In such cases, the DM will determine the outcome and, as always, the DM's decisions (often the result of die rolls at appropriate chances which he or she determines) are final.

An alternative to having retainers under player control is simply to have non-player adventurers available for singlegame participation. In this case, an additional character accompanies the group and participates, but is independent of player control other than to be helpful and generally cooperative. The Dungeon Master runs the character in essence,

3

although his or her actions will generally follow the desires and suggestions of the players (unless an unduly hazardous action is demanded). The independent character participates in return for a share of the treasure gained, and this share (which will at least be proportional if the character is better than the player characters) must be agreed upon before the adventure starts. If your players are trying to attract such help, roll a die to see how hard a bargain the extra character drives in order to be convinced that participating is worthwhile . . . After the adventure has been completed, the extra character might simply take his or her treasure share and disappear from further use, or if the DM desires, be available for similar service in future quests. The section entitled THE CHARACTER LISTS gives additional suggestions for the employment of non-player characters or retainers.

Once the players have completed their preparations for the game, the referee finishes "setting the stage" by bringing the player characters from the background story to the place where the game adventure will begin. This is usually simply a matter of providing a brief narrative (such as, "Your group, after purchasing supplies and getting organized, left their town and went cross country till a deserted pathway was found which led into the hills, and finally to a craggy outcropping of rock . . ."). Use of the LEGEND TABLE (described elsewhere in this booklet) is also made at this time.

To start the adventure, the players must decide on an order of march for all of the characters in their group—who will be in front, who in the middle, who at the rear, and so on. This should be diagrammed on a sheet of paper and given to the Dungeon Master for reference, and any change in the order of march during the adventure should be noted. In a standard 10' wide corridor, the most common arrangement is two adventurers side by side in each rank, although three characters could operate together in a single rank if all of their weapons were short and easily wielded (daggers or small axes, for instance).

One player in the group should be designated as the leader, or "caller" for the party, while another one or two players can be selected as mappers (at least one is a must!). Although individual players have the right to decide their own actions and relay them to the Dungeon Master as play progresses, the caller will be the one who gives the DM the details on the group's course of action as they move around and explore (such instructions as "We'll move slowly down this corridor to the east . . ." or "We'll break down this door while so-and-so covers our rear . . ." are typical directions given by a caller to the DM). In the course of the adventure, the caller will naturally discuss the options available to the party with the rest of the adventurers, but it is this person who the DM relies upon for the official instructions (although individual players can still pursue alternate courses of action at appropriate times, if they insist, by telling the Dungeon Master). Once a caller (or any player) speaks and indicates an action is being taken, it is begun—even if the player quickly changes his or her mind (especially if the player realizes he or she has made a mistake or error in judgment). Use your discretion in such cases.

The player or players mapping the explored area should use graph paper. Orient them according to the same directions on the referee's map (with the top being north in almost all cases). After that, allow them to draw their maps from your descriptions as they wish—but make certain that your verbal descriptions of the areas they explore are accurate (although you can say such things as "approximately sixty feet," especially in large or open areas or places where there are irregular rock surfaces). Above all, avoid the considerable temptation to correct their maps once they have drawn them. It will not be uncommon for players to show you their map (especially if they're confused) and ask you, "Is this right?" In most such instances, you should avoid correcting any mistakes there, unless it would be obvious through the eyes of the adventuring characters. Encourage good mapping skills and an attention to detail rather than falling into the rut of continual player map questions.

Exploration of the entire area comprising the module may well take more than one game session. It is also quite possible that adventurers (especially if wounded or reduced in number) may want to pull out of the stronghold and prepare for a return visit when refreshed or reinforced. If this is done, they must work their way to an exit and discuss with you the pertinent details and time passage until their return. In such cases, the exact status of areas already explored will depend upon your judgment—whether areas cleared of monsters might in some cases be reoccupied by new ones, doors left open closed again and locked, or whatever.

If the exploring adventurers wish to suspend the game temporarily during a rest period (when the adventuring characters stop to sleep, as they must do every 24 hours), appropriate notes should be made of each adventurer's status so that resumption of the game can begin at the same point on the next meeting of the players. Their choice of where to camp is a factor to consider, as well, since in this dungeon a check for wandering monsters must be made up to three times for any 8-hour period they remain there (these checks are made at a normal 1 in 6 chance). It is customary to have one or more adventurers in the party standing guard at any one time, as the party members sleep in shifts in order to always have continual protection (although the devious DM may give a slight chance of a guard being asleep if a monster comes . . .). Just as with march order, it is important that players provide the DM with the sleeping location of each member and the placement of the guard or guards, since this may be crucial if and when a monster approaches from a given direction.

Experience points earned and any benefits gained will only be applicable if and when the adventurers successfully exit the dungeon; experience gained in an adventure is only credited after the adventure is complete. However, successfully exiting the dungeon and then returning later would allow the characters to use experience gained on the previous foray, if applicable.

TIME

As adventures go on, the Dungeon Master is responsible for keeping track of time elapsed.

In normal movement and exploration, each turn is considered to be ten minutes. If an encounter or melee occurs, the Dungeon Master immediately (but temporarily, for the duration of the encounter) adjusts the time frame to melee rounds consisting of ten 10-second melee rounds.

Every third turn of adventuring, the DM should take a die roll for the possible appearance of wandering monsters at the indicated chances (which are normally 1 in 6, but which may vary depending upon location and dungeon level). Some occurrences (such as noise and commotion caused by adventurers) may necessitate additional checks.

Paper and pencil can be used to tally time, and the DM should monitor its passage as he or she sees fit, but keeping in mind that exploring, mapping and examining various features takes up considerable time—with the larger the area

4

and the greater the care taken in examining, the more time consumed. Wasted time is also a factor which should be noted, as players may waste time arguing or needlessly discussing unimportant matters or by simply blundering around aimlessly. On the other hand, time can pass quickly if adventurers move rapidly through the areas which have been previously explored and mapped. In all cases the DM should use good judgment and common sense.

Generally, eight hours of each twenty-four must be spent resting and sleeping, and prudent adventurers will sleep in shifts with a guard always awake. In this dungeon, three checks will be made each "night" for possible wandering monsters.

COMPUTING EXPERIENCE

At the conclusion of an adventure (the party's emergence from the dungeon), the surviving characters divide the treasure (with equal shares generally awarded to each and magical or special items diced for by eligible characters) and experience is computed. Retainers usually get an equal share of any treasure, although their experience point award may vary at the Dungeon Master's discretion from half to the full amount awarded to player characters, depending upon their accomplishments.

As an example, let us assume that the first level player characters (a magic-user and a fighter) and a first-level retainer (a fighter) survive an adventure and return to the outside world from a dungeon which has claimed several of their comrades. The treasure they carry out with them amounts to the following: 630 g.p., 9—50 g.p. gems, a scroll of 2 magic-user spells, a **sword +1** and a **ring of protection +1**. In the course of their adventure, their party slew the following monsters: 8 kobolds, 5 orcs, and a black widow spider.

In this instance, the treasure is rather easily divided: the gold pieces are split into 210 apiece, 3 gems are awarded to each character, the scroll goes to the magic-user (since he is the only one who can use it), and the two fighters roll dice for the sword and the ring, with one going to each (in some instances, a non-player character may end up with the best treasure this way, but such is the luck of the dice . . .). This gives each adventurer the equivalent of 210 g.p. cash, plus 150 g.p. in gems (if traded or sold for gold pieces), plus one other item which can be retained and used.

The monsters slain are considered for experience point values as follows (see page 12 of the D&D Basic Set booklet): the 8 kobolds are worth 5 points apiece as creatures under 1 hit die, the 5 orcs are worth 10 points each as 1 hit die monsters, and the spider is worth 50 points (35 points as a 3 hit die creature plus 15 points for its special ability of poison). The total value of all monsters killed is thus 140 experience points—40 for the kobolds, 50 for the orcs, and 50 for the spider. This divides to 46 experience points per surviving adventurer for monsters slain.

Total experience points for each adventurer would be 360 (the g.p. equivalent of coins and gems) plus 46 (for the monsters killed), or 406 points each. No additional points are awarded for the special or magical items.

Once enough points are accumulated, a character can rise to the next higher level of experience, and gain the benefits of the new level. Wealth obtained, besides counting initially for experience, can be used to purchase equipment or supplies, defray everyday expenses, attract retainers, sponsor various enterprises, or can be spent in any manner (including payments of tithes to the church, especially for clerics!).

HOW TO BE AN EFFECTIVE DUNGEON MASTER

The Dungeon Master, as referee, is the pivotal figure in any DUNGEONS & DRAGONS game. Accordingly, the DM's ability and expertise—as well as fairness—will be important factors in whether or not the game will be enjoyable for all of the participants.

The D&D game is a role-playing game, and is unlike traditional games which have a firm basis of regulated activity and repetitious action. A D&D adventure is free-flowing, and often goes in unknown and unpredictable directions—and that is precisely the reason it is so different and challenging. The Dungeon Master is best described as the moderator of the action, for the DM oversees the whole process, keeps the game moving, resolves the action based upon events occurring and player choices made, and monitors the actions and events outside the player group (i.e., handles monsters encountered, determines the actions of non-player characters encountered, etc.). The DM's responsibilities are considerable, but his or her foremost concern should be to provide an enjoyable game which is challenging to the players. This means that risk should be balanced with reward and that game situations are neither too "easy" nor too deadly. Above all, the DM must be fair, reasonable (without giving in to the unreasonable demands of the players), and worthy of the respect of all the participants.

Beginning Dungeon Masters who are not familiar with the game often ask the most common first question, "Exactly how do you referee the game?" The answer is that there is no single best way—different DM's have different styles, just as individual players do. However, there are certain guidelines which are important to follow . . .

First, it is crucial to keep in mind that this is a game based on player interaction and player choice. The game generally follows the course of the player's actions—if not always their plans! As moderator, you present an ever-changing situation as it occurs (sort of like an unfolding story, or even a movie, if you like to think in those terms), and the players respond pretty much as they desire. As the game goes on, you are presenting them with a hundred different opportunities and choices—exactly how the game goes will depend upon their response to those opportunities and choices. For instance, if players decide to walk down a corridor and find a dead end with three doors, they have a number of choices—simply turn around and ignore the doors, listen at one or more before proceeding elsewhere, try to open one or more (either normally, by forcing them, or even by simply bashing them in), or whatever. You describe the situation, then await their decision as to a course of action. Of course, some decisions will be more difficult, or quick, or crucial to survival—and as always, imagination and resourcefulness, as well as quick thinking, will usually be rewarded.

Second, a good DM remains "above the battle" and does not attempt to influence player actions or channel the activity in a particular direction. The Dungeon Master should do everything possible to assist players in their quest without actually providing important information unless the players themselves discover it or put the pieces of a puzzling problem together through deduction or questioning, or a combination of the two. A large part of the game consists of player questions, many of which are, "What do we see?" Your job as gamemaster is to answer those questions without giving too much away. You need not hint to players any information that they do not ask for on their own, except in unusual instances. Allow them to ask the questions, and allow them to make the choices.

In the same vein, as Dungeon Master you will enjoy watching players wrestle with the problems you present them with. Although you may set up situations to challenge them, you must understand that you are not their adversary, nor are you necessarily out to "defeat" them. You will enjoy moderating a well-played game where players respond to the challenges encountered much more than one where the adventurers foolishly meet their demise in quick time. However, if your players abandon caution or make stupid mistakes, let them pay the price—but be fair. In many cases, a danger due to lack of caution can be overcome, or a mistake in judgment countered by quick thinking and resourcefulness, *but let your players do the thinking and the doing.*

As Dungeon Master, you are the game moderator. This means you set the tempo of the game and are reponsible for keeping it moving. Above all, *you* remain in control of the situation, although with reasonable players your game should always be in control. If players are unusually slow or dilly-dally unnecessarily, remind them that time is wasting. If they persist, allow additional chances for wandering monsters to appear—or at least start rolling the dice to make the players think that you are doing so. If players are argumentative with each other, remind them their noise also serves to attract unwelcome monsters; if they persist, show them that this is true.

Lastly, it is important to remember that the Dungeon Master is the final arbiter in his or her game. If players disagree with you, hear them out and reasonably consider their complaint. However, **you** are the final judge—and they should understand that, as well as the fact that not everything will go their way, or as they expect. Be fair, but be firm. With human nature as it is, players will undoubtedly attempt to try to talk you into (or out of) all sorts of things; part of the fun of being a DM is this verbal interplay. But in the end, what you say is what goes.

BACKGROUND

Many years ago, rumor has it, two noted personages in the area, Rogahn the Fearless (a fighter of renown) and Zelligar the Unknown (a magic-user of mystery and power) pooled their resources and expertise to construct a home and stronghold for the two of them to use as a base of operations. The location of this hidden complex was chosen with care, since both men disliked visitors and intruders. Far from the nearest settlement, away from traveled routes, and high upon a craggy hill, the new construction took shape. Carved out of the rock protrusion which crested the heavily forested

hill, this mystical hideaway was well hidden, and its rumored existence was never common knowledge. Even less well known was its name, the Caverns of Quasqueton.

Construction of the new complex, it is said, took over a decade, even with the aid of magic and the work of hundreds of slaves and laborers. Vast amounts of rock were removed and tumbled off the rough cliffs into large piles now overgrown with vegetation. A single tower was constructed above ground for lookout purposes, even though there was little to see other than a hilly, forested wilderness for miles around.

Rogahn and Zelligar lived in their joint sanctuary for quite some time, conducting their affairs from within except for occasional adventures in the outside world where both men attempted to add to their reputations as foremost practitioners of their respective arts.

The deeds and adventures of these two characters were never well known, since they both kept their distance from civilization. Some say, and perhaps rightly so, that their motives were based on greed and some kind of vague (or chaotic) evil. No one knows for sure.

What is known more widely is the reputation of each. Despite their questionable alignment, both Rogahn and Zelligar capped their reputation of power when they joined forces to stop a barbarian invasion threatening the great valley below. In a crucial battle at a narrow pass in the hills, the two combined powerful forces and decisively turned back the invasion. Rogahn slew a horde of barbarians single-handedly and Zelligar's powerful magic put their army to flight. A grateful populace rewarded the pair and their henchmen with considerable treasure, after which the two retired to their hideaway. Most of the reward treasure was apparently used to finance the further construction of Quasqueton, although some of it may yet be hidden somewhere. In any case, the hill stronghold was not completed in its entirety when, years later, the intrepid pair apparently embarked on their last adventure.

Some years ago, Rogahn and Zelligar apparently decided upon a joint foray into the lands of the hated barbarians. Taking most of their henchmen and associates along in a great armed band, the two personages disappeared into the forbidding alien lands to the north, far from the hills and forests surrounding Quasqueton.

Word just reaching civilization tells of some great battle in the barbarian lands where Rogahn and Zelligar have met their demise. This rumored clash must have occurred some years ago, and there are few details—and no substantiation of the story. The only thing certain is the Rogahn and Zelligar have been gone far too long. If only one had the knowledge and wherewithal to find their hideaway, there would be great things to explore! And who knows what riches of wealth and magic might be there for the taking???

LEGEND TABLE

Prior to the first adventure into the stronghold, the Dungeon Master will utilize this table to impart "background knowledge" (from rumors or legends known) to the adventurers. The table itself includes bits and scraps of information regarding the place to be explored—most of it accurate; however, legends and rumors being what they are, some of the information is false and misleading. It will be up to the players to act upon the information they "know"; the Dungeon Master will tell them that these are legends or rumors they have heard about the place, and that is all (it will be up to the players to decide upon the value or veracity of such information).

To determine legends/rumors known, each player character will cast a 4-sided die in secret conference with the Dungeon Master (non-player characters or henchmen/hirelings will get no roll). The result of the roll will give the number of rumors/legends known by the individual rolling the die:

1 One legend known

2 Two legends known

3 Three legends known

4 No legends known

Rolls of 1, 2, or 3 will result in that many rolls on the Legend Table using d20. A roll of 4 indicates that the adventurer has no knowledge of any rumors or legends pertaining to the stronghold; any information the player desires he or she must attempt to obtain from the other players.

The legends/rumors known are determined by the player's roll of the 20-sided die, and the DM reads the appropriate information off the table to the player for each roll (this is done secretly where the other players cannot overhear). The DM then tells the player that this is the extent of background information known by his or her player character; whether or not the player chooses to share this information (all or only part of it) with the other players is a personal decision. In this manner each player is given a chance to see what bits of additional information their character knows before the adventure starts.

LEGEND TABLE (d20)

"F" denotes a false legend or rumor, but the player will not know it is false.

1)   The name of the stronghold is Quasqueton.

2) F Zelligar had a wizard's workshop in the stronghold where he worked on magic stronger than any known to man.

3) F Rogahn owned a fantastic gem as big as a man's fist that was worth over 100,000 gold pieces; he kept it hidden in his personal quarters.

4)   Zelligar and Rogahn had orc slaves to do the menial work, and some lived permanently at the stronghold.

5)   The complex has two levels.

6)   Part of the complex is unfinished.

7)   The complex has a rear exit which is secret and well hidden.

8)   No outsiders have ever entered the complex and returned to tell the tale.

9)   Troglodytes have moved into the complex in the absence of its normal inhabitants.

10) F The place is protected by the gods themselves, and one member of any party of intruders is doomed to certain death.

11) F The treasures of Zelligar and Rogahn are safely hidden in a pool of water.

12) F The entire place is filled with guards left behind by Zelligar and Rogahn.

13)   Rogahn's trophy room has battle relics and slain monster remains from his adventures.

14)   There is a room with many pools of water within the complex.

15)   The very walls speak to visitors.

16) F An enchanted stone within the stronghold will grant a wish to anyone who chips off a piece of it and places it within their mouth.

17) F All treasures of Zelligar and Rogahn are cursed to bring ill to any who possess them.

18) F Zelligar and Rogahn have actually returned to their stronghold, and woe be to any unwelcome visitors!

19)   There are secret doors, rooms, and passageways in parts of the complex.

20)   The complex has more than one level.

Note: When rolling on this table, roll again if any number duplicates one already rolled by the same player.

THE DUNGEON

This area for exploration is designed to challenge a party of 3-8 adventurers (player characters and henchmen or hirelings) of up to the third level of experience, and is specifically intended for use with DUNGEONS & DRAGONS Basic set. Players will find it beneficial to have a mix of characters in their party who complement each other and who will possess a variety of abilities due to their different classes (fighters, magic-users, clerics, thieves, etc.). Additionally, the carrying of one or two useful magic items will likewise be of great help (although more numerous or more powerful such items will unbalance the situation).

The Caverns of Quasqueton, as mentioned in the background description, are hewn from a great rock outcropping at the crest of a large wooded hill. Winds buffet the hill continuously, blowing and whistling through the trees, vines and other vegetation which blanket the prominence on all sides. The rock itself is a heavy blackish slate, and is evident all throughout the caverns on both levels.

The air within the caverns is heavy, wet, and musty. In some portions of the complex, a layer of dust lies upon everything, undisturbed for years. Burning anything within is slow and difficult, for the entire atmosphere resists combustion. Torches and lanterns will burn smokily.

There are many doors within the dungeon (the term "dungeon" being used generically for the entire underground area, as it usually is in DUNGEONS & DRAGONS games), and some of them are secret doors, discernible only by special examination or perhaps by an elf with his or her inborn ability

7

to notice them. In all cases, unless otherwise noted, doors will be locked one-third of the time—and any roll of a 1 or 2 on a six-sided die (d6) will mean that they will bar entrance unless the lock is sprung or broken. Breaking the lock or breaking down the entire door will be a noisy undertaking, to be sure, and may serve to attract unwelcome monsters . . .

The two levels of the dungeon are approximately equal in size and are located one above the other. If the two maps could be placed over one another, the three access points between levels would directly correspond to their locations on the maps and lead directly to each other up and down.

THE CAVERNS OF QUASQUETON

KEY TO THE UPPER LEVEL

Within the complex, the upper level is a rather finished abode with generally good stonework and masonry overall. There are rough spots, or portions where workmanship is not as good as overall, but for the most part the construction and excavation are well done. The walls are relatively smoothly hewn and finished and in generally good repair. The floors, while uneven in places, are likewise in good condition. Corridors generally measure 10' in width, while ceilings for the most part are approximately 8' to 10' above the floor. The blackish stone from which the halls and caverns were hewn is evident overall. Doors are uniformly of heavy wooden construction, approximately five or six inches thick.

WANDERING MONSTERS

Check every second turn; 1 in 6 (roll a 6-sided die). If a monster is indicated, roll a six-sided die again and compare to the list below to determine what type of monster appears. Then check for surprise. The abbreviations which follow are the same as used and explained in the section entitled MONSTER LIST.

1. Orcs (1-4)—AC 6, HD 1, hp 6,4,3,1, #AT 1, D 1-6 or by weapon, MV 90' (30'), Save F1, ML 8

2. Giant Centipedes (1-2)—AC 9, HD ½, hp 2,2, #AT 1, D poison, MV 60' (20'), Save NM, ML 7

3. Kobolds (1-6)—AC 7, HD ½, hp 4,3,3,2,2,1, #AT 1, D 1-4 or weapon -1, MV 90' (30'), Save NM, ML 6

4. Troglodytes (1-2)—AC 5, HD 2*, hp 6,5, #AT 3, D 1-4/1-4/1-4, MV 120' (40'), Save F2, ML 9

5. Giant Rats (2-5)—AC 7, HD ½, hp 4,3,2,1,1, #AT 1, D 1-3 + disease, MV 120' (40') swimming 60' (20'), Save NM, ML 8

6. Berserkers (1-2)—AC 7, HD 1+1*, hp 5,4, #AT 1, D 1-8 or by weapon, MV 90' (30'), Save F1, ML 12

ENCOUNTER AREAS

ENTRANCE. A cave-like opening, somewhat obscured by vegetation, is noticeable at the end of a treacherous pathway which leads up to the craggy outcropping of black rock. By sweeping aside some of the vines and branches, the opening becomes easily accessible to human-size explorers.

The opening leads straight into the rock formation, with a 10' wide corridor leading the way to a large wooden door. The door opens freely, and close examination will reveal that bits of wood have been chipped away from the edge, indicating that it has previously been forced (this fact will certainly be known if adventurers indicate they are examining the door; otherwise, there will be a 10% chance per adventurer, cumulative, of this being noticed—40% if four adventurers, etc.).

1. ALCOVES. There are three pairs of alcoves past the entrance, located as they are for purposes of defense against intruders or invaders. These guardpoints are all empty and barren of any markings.

The second pair of alcoves are actually secret one-way doors, but totally unnoticeable to anyone on the side of the entrance corridor (even if close examination is made). These one-way doors are also a defensive measure to allow guards to appear in the rear of any invading group which passes this point.

The third pair of alcoves contains a double **magic mouth** spell, and this magic omen will be triggered as soon as any adventurers reach the point in the corridor between the two alcoves. When this occurs, a **mouth** appears on the side wall of the east alcove, and another **mouth** appears on the side wall of the west alcove. The east **mouth** speaks first, in a booming voice: "WHO DARES ENTER THIS PLACE AND INTRUDE UPON THE SANCTUARY OF ITS INHABITANTS?" After but a moment, and drowning out any attempted reply by the party, comes the reply from the west **mouth**: "ONLY A GROUP OF FOOLHARDY EXPLORERS DOOMED TO CERTAIN DEATH!" Then both **mouths** will shout in unison, "WOE TO ANY WHO PASS THIS PLACE—THE WRATH OF ZELLIGAR AND ROGAHN WILL BE UPON THEM!" The **mouths** will then begin a loud and raucous laughter, which fades in intensity as the twin **mouths** disappear from view. They are a permanent feature of the stronghold, and will reappear on every visit.

Past the third pair of alcoves and at the end of the corridor from the entrance are two steps up. At the top of the steps, the corridor continues straight ahead, and corridors meet from east to west. At this intersection is a grisly sight—the remains of a hand-to-hand battle where no less than five combatants died.

Upon examination of the bodies (if the adventurers choose to do so), it will be seen that three of them were adventurers themselves, explorers from the outer world. This ill-fated trio obviously had their first and last battle at this spot. Their opponents, also slain here, are two guards. The bodies arrayed here, each in various states of decomposition, are as follows (the stench of decaying bodies is strong and repulsive, and the sight doubly so):

Body #1—A human fighter, slumped against a wall. His broken sword, sheared off about eight inches above the pommel, tells the story of his demise. The body has been stripped of any armor, and there are no items of value on the remains, other than a belt pouch containing 5 gold pieces (g.p.).

Body #2—A human magic-user, impaled against a wall. The killing sword, still thrust through the body, is lodged in the wall, which has a large section of wood at this point. If the sword is removed, the body will crumple to the floor, exposing a blood-stained carving. The carved letters form the word "QUASQUETON" in the "common" language.

8

The sword, upon being removed, will prove worthless, since its handle is very loose and the overall quality of the weapon is poor.

The body is bereft of any items of great value. The magic-user's robe, now bloodstained and ruined, has a pocket and within it is a purse containing 2 g.p. and a pouch full of garlic buds.

Body #3—A dwarf fighter, face down in the corridor just east of the intersection. In his right hand he still clutches his war hammer, and it appears that he crawled, wounded, to this point, since a trail of dried blood leads back to the battle location. A sack turned inside out lies alongside the body, now empty.

Armor has been stipped from the body, although the fighter's helm is still on his head. This headgear, however, has a noticeable dent in it which will make it unusable and thus worthless. There are no items of value on the remains.

Body #4—A human berserker/fighter, obviously a guard who defended to the death. The body is sprawled on the floor, and a broken wooden shield lies nearby. The body has no armor on it. There is no weapon on the body or nearby, nor are there any other items of value on the remains.

Body #5—A human berserker/fighter, another guard. This body, with a bashed head from the blow of a war hammer, lies on the floor face down. There is no armor or weapon on the body except for a small sheathed dagger on the belt. The belt is very ornately decorated leather, which would appear to be worth something, except for the bloodstains ruining its appearance.

Monster:

Treasure & Location:

2. KITCHEN. The food preparation area for the complex is a very long room with a variety of details. At the southwest corner of the room are two cooking pits, each large enough to cook an animal as large as a deer. One of the pits is slightly larger than the other, but both are about 3 feet in depth. The pits are full of ash and charred remains of cooking fuel. A chimney leads upward, but its small size prevents further investigation.

Long tables line each wall, and there are scattered containers on them, some upturned, with spilled contents moldering on the table top. There are spoiled pieces of food all around, and the smell in the room is very uninviting. One chunk of moldy cheese is particularly noxious, as a fuzzy green growth covers its entirety.

Hanging from above are a variety of utensils, and some other of these are scattered about on the floor of the room. These are nothing more than pots and pans of various sizes, although there is a large cast iron kettle suspended from the ceiling by a thick chain. The kettle is empty.

Monster:

Treasure & Location:

3. DINING ROOM. This room serves as the main dining hall for the complex, and it is here that guest banquets are held.

The room is moderately decorated, but frugally so, since there appear to be no items of great value which are part of the decor. A nicely carved wooden mantle surrounds the room at a height 7 feet off the floor, and the stone walls are also carved in simple yet pleasant designs.

There are a number of tables and chairs in the room, these being of wooden construction and quite utilitarian in nature. Only two chairs stand out from the rest, these being the personal seats of the stronghold's illustrious inhabitants, Zelligar and Rogahn. Both of these chairs are ornately carved walnut, formed from an enormous block of wood which forms a portion of the wall in the northeast corner of the room. Upon closer examination, it will be seen that the chairs themselves are actually fixed seats connected to the wooden structure, thus being unremovable. Their great beauty is apparent, but is marred by a greenish fungus growing on portions of the walnut. It is obvious the seats have not been used for quite some length of time.

The lesser tables and chairs are scattered about, and several are overturned. All of these furnishings are of hard maple. They show wear, although they have obviously not been used recently.

The entire room has a musty, mildewy smell to it.

Monster:

Treasure & Location:

4. LOUNGE. This anteroom is through a south door from the dining room, and apparently was designed for before-dinner and after-dinner activity. Drinking was apparently the most popular pastime here, for several earthenware tankard mugs hang from a row of hooks high on one all (many more are missing, it appears). An ale keg, long since dry but still smelling slightly of the brew, stands in one corner.

The stone walls are strangely textured for an unusual effect, but are devoid of further markings or details. A long wooden bench seat, actually attached to the wall, is along each side of the room. Those seated on the bench all face toward the center of the room and the statue there.

At the center of the room is a carved statue, full-size, of a nude human female, beckoning with arms out front in a very alluring pose. This statue, apparently of white marble, is obviously of great value (over 5,000 g.p.). However, due to its tremendous weight and the fact that it seems anchored to the floor, it will be impossible to remove without a major engineering effort. Even characters with a strength of 18 will be unable to move it in any way.

Monster:

Treasure & Location:

5. WIZARD'S CHAMBER. Zelligar's personal chamber is actually a rather austere abode. The most noticeable feature seen upon entering is a very large and fairly detailed stone carving which runs most of the length of the north wall of the room. Some 70 feet in overall length, the wall carving depicts a mighty wizard (obviously Zelligar) on a hilltop casting a spell in the air over a valley below, with an entire army fleeing in confused panic.

The east and west walls are devoid of detail, although there are several wall pegs on each, apparently for hanging garments.

9

There is a minimum of furniture within the room. Zelligar's bed, located in the southeast corner of the chamber, is a frame of ornately carved rosewood. The headboard, besides showing the carved designs to advantage, boldly features Zelligar's name highlighted in gold leaf. The bed, obviously of value, is of fine workmanship and construction. Because of its sturdiness, it cannot be removed from the room without dismantling, and doing so will be difficult and likely to cause damage to the various pieces. If this is done, the baseboard and sides would be worth 100 g.p. each, and the headboard up to 500 g.p. However, anyone trying to sell the headboard for its value will run an 80% risk that the purchaser will recognize the original owner's name (since the fame of Zelligar is widely known)—and if this word spreads at large, the seller may have attendant problems, since it will be obvious from where the headboard was obtained.

A rosewood nightstand/table is beside the bed, and it has one locked drawer. The brass handle to the drawer has a pin trap which will be tripped by anyone grasping it, inflicting 1 hit point of damage. An oily substance on the pins is not a poison, but it does inflict unusual pain which will make the grasping hand unusable by the victim for 2-5 (d4 + 1) turns. If a key is inserted into the lock before the handle is grasped, the trap will be negated. Any key of a size comparable to the actual key (which is nowhere to be found) will accomplish this function. The drawer itself is empty (unless treasure in this room is to be located within the drawer).

Elsewhere in the room is a table and three chairs, none of which is of any exceptional worth or value. Upon the table is a pewter pitcher and three pewter mugs. The pitcher has a value of 15 g.p., and the mugs are worth 5 g.p. each.

Monster:

Treasure & Location:

6. CLOSET. Zelligar's closet lies through a door on the south wall of his chamber. The room is rather large for a closet, but is actually somewhat barren for its size.

In one corner of the room, several bolts of cloth are stacked, well covered with dust and partially moth-eaten and deteriorated. These are of no particular value.

On one wall, several garments are hung, mostly coats and cloaks. These are quite musty in smell, as well as being dusty and dingy in appearance. Of the five pieces of apparel there, only one is remarkable, being studded with circular bits of pewter for ornamentation. This bit of garb, however, has also suffered the ravages of age. While the first four garments are of no value, the last one could possibly bring up to 15 g.p. if sold.

A wooden stand in the corner of the room farthest from the door holds several books upon it. These large volumes are four in number, and apparently belong in the library (room 12).

Book #1—A historical work, this book, written in the common tongue, outlines the history of the civilized area within 100 miles of the stronghold location. It contains nothing remarkable.

Book #2—This tome is apparently an encyclopedia of various types of plants. Although the various illustrations given within provide a clue to its topic, it is written in the language of elves, so it will not be understandable to a reader who does not know the elfin tongue (unless a **read languages** spell is used).

Book #3—This volume appears unremarkable at first glance, seeming to be a notebook with many handwritten entries of undecipherable runes and markings. It is actually a diary kept by Zelligar, and it details one of his adventures from the distant past, written in his own hand. The writing is not discernible unless a **read languages** spell is used. This book is really of no value to any finder, but a book dealer/scribe/librarian would pay up to 50 g.p. for it. Of course, if the book is sold in this manner, the seller risks a 40% chance of word of its sale getting out as a rumor, with attendant problems developing as those who hear of it seek out the finder for further details.

Book #4—This work, written in the common language, discusses weather. Although well-illustrated with drawings of meteorological phenomena, descriptive text is sparse. Some cryptic notes written in the margins were apparently made by Zelligar, but these are undecipherable without a **read languages** spell and are actually nothing more than notes such as a student would make in studying the work to highlight important points.

Along one of the walls within the closet is an oil lantern which contains no fuel and which has obviously been unused for a great deal of time. If fuel is provided, the lantern will be perfectly usable.

In another corner is a small table with a stack of papers upon it. These are very dusty, and they are held in place by a stone slab paperweight which is monogrammed with a fancy letter Z. The papers are written in the common language and upon examination will be seen to deal with mundane matters: an inventory of foodstuffs, a financial accounting of expenses, notes on construction work for the complex, a couple of routine messages received by Zelligar, and other unremarkable writings. The most recent date on any of the papers is still more than three decades in the past.

Monster:

Treasure & Location:

7. WIZARD'S ANNEX. Another room off of Zelligar's chamber is the unusually-shaped annex. This room apparently was for meditation and study, as well as the practice of magic spells. The triangular widening at the south end of this room was apparently for this purpose, and the stone wall (although not noticeable to adventurers) is actually thicker than elsewhere in the complex. the floor near the south wall is bumpy and darkly discolored, as if charred and partially melted by intense heat (this will not be noticeable until the **illusion** described below is dispelled).

At the south end of the room is a magnificent sight visible when explorers enter the door and cast light within. The spectacle is indeed impressive: two large wooden chests, each studded with jewels, overflowing with riches. A pile of gold pieces is arrayed around and within them, and scattered among this treasure trove is an assortment of glittering gems and jewels.

The massive treasure is in reality a permanent **illusion**, and it will be temporarily dispelled as soon as the first bit of "treasure" is touched by any creature. The **illusion**, once dispelled, reappears in the same place again within 24 hours.

In reality the room is empty (and it is recommended that no treasure be placed here).

Monster:

Treasure & Location:

8. WIZARD'S WORKROOM. Zelligar's workroom and laboratory (room 9) are located adjacent to each other, with a limited access by secret doors.

The workroom is a facility designed for various purposes related to the study and practice of magic. There are several large wooden tables within the room, one of which is overturned on its side, as well as one central table made of stone. The top of this prominent table is a slab of smooth black slate, although its cold black beauty is hidden by a thick layer of dust. None of the tables have anything upon them. There are several chairs and stools scattered about the room.

Along the north wall to both sides of the door leading to the laboratory are wooden cabinets on the wall, approximately 4 feet off the floor. The cabinets are not locked, and contain various chemical compounds and supplies of no particular value in glass or earthen containers. There are forty such containers, as well as one larger jar (described below). If the adventurers choose to open and examine the contents of any particular container, roll a die (d20) to determine the contents:

	Contents	Possible Types
1	Sand	White, brown, black
2	Water	Pure, brackish, holy, urine
3	Salt	Common, mineral
4	Sulphur	—
5	Wood chips	Hickory, pine, oak, ash, maple, walnut
6	Herbs	Dill, garlic, chives, basil, catnip, parsley
7	Vinegar	Red, white, yellow
8	Tree sap (hardened)	Pine, maple
9	Carbon	Coal, ash, graphite
10	Crushed stone	Quartz, granite, marble, shale, pumice, obsidian
11	Metal filings	Iron, tin, copper, brass
12	Blood	Human, orcish, dwarfin, elfin, dragon, halfling
13	Dung (hardened)	Human, canine, feline, dragon
14	Wine	White, red, alcohol (spoiled), fruit
15	Fungus powder	Mushroom, other
16	Oil	Vegetable, animal, petroleum, mineral
17	Insect bodies	Bees, flies, beetles, ants
18	Bone powder	Human, animal
19	Spice	Pepper, cinnamon, clove, paprika, oregano, nutmeg
20	Empty	—

If a die roll gives a duplication, use the column at the right of each entry to determine differentiation between different substances of similar types. If adventurers try to ingest any substance, the Dungeon Master will handle the situation accordingly. In not all cases will the contents be immediately identifiable—in the case of uncertain substance not obviously identifiable, multiply a character's wisdom times 5 to give the percentage chance of positive identification. Up to 2 characters may try to identify any given substance, but if both fail, the material will be a mystery to the entire party.

The larger jar is of clear glass and seemingly contains a black cat's body floating in a clear, colorless liquid. If the large cork lid is unstopped, the liquid will instantaneously evaporate, the cat will suddenly spring to life, jump out of the jar, meow loudly, and run for the door. If the door is open, the cat will dash through and disappear. If the door is not open, the cat will be seen to pass through the door and disappear. In neither case will the feline be seen again. (This occurrence has no special meaning other than to surprise and/or mystify the adventurers, as well as provide some fun for the Dungeon Master.)

Monster:

Treasure & Location:

9. WIZARD'S LABORATORY. The wizard's lab is a strange but fascinating place. Zelligar's experimentation with many kinds of magic led to a collection of equipment and devices which was stored here, scattered about this 50' by 30' room.

Dominating the room is a large human skeleton suspended from the ceiling and hanging in the northeast corner of the laboratory. The skull is cracked. (Were there anyway to know, it would be discovered to be a barbarian chieftain's remains . . .)

About the room are several large wooden tables, just as found in the workroom (room 8), and another heavy stone table which is likewise similar to the one appearing next door. The tables are bare, except for a single stoppered smoked glass bottle on one of them. If the cork is removed, the gas within will immediately issue forth with a whoosh. The vapors are pungent and fast-acting, and all characters within ten feet must make an immediate save vs. poison or be affected by laughing gas. The gas itself is not poisonous, but will cause any characters failing their saving throw to immediately lapse into uncontrollable raucous laughter for 1-6 melee rounds (check each indivirually). During this time, the characters will have a 50% chance of dropping anything they are holding or carrying and will rock with spasms of great laughter, staggering about the room, chuckling and bellowing with great glee. The noise will necessitate a special additional check for wandering monsters being attracted to the ruckus, and even if a monster appears, the affected characters will be unable to oppose it until the gas effects wear off (if a monster does come, roll a 4-sided die to see how many melee rounds it appears after the laughing starts). Characters under the influence of the gas will not respond to any efforts by others to snap them out of its effects (even slapping the face will do no more than cause more laughing), although if a **dispel magic** spell is thrown, it will make them sober immediately. Otherwise, the only way to stop the laughter is to wait for the effects to wear off.

11

Several pine logs are piled underneath one of the tables, and if these are moved, a shiny "gold" ring will be found. Although it appears brilliant and seems to be worth up to 100 g.p., it is actually worthless. It has no special magical properties.

Along the west wall is a large wooden rack, apparently from some kind of torture chamber, since it is obviously sized for human bodies. A trickle of dried blood stains the oaken construction on the front.

On the south wall is a stretched leather skin with magical writings which will be undecipherable unless a **read magic** spell is cast. The legend, if interpreted, will read: "What mysterious happenings have their birth here? Only the greatest feats of wizardry, for which every element of earth, water and sky is but a tool!" The skin is old and extremely fragile, and any attempts to remove it will cause irreparable harm and render it useless because of the skin crumbling away.

A sunken fire pit, blackened and cold, is noticeable as the centerpiece of the room. The pit is only 2' deep, although it appears slightly less than that due to several inches of ashes resting within it. An iron bracing and bar across the 4' wide opening suspend a cast iron pot which is empty except for a harmless brown residue sticking to its interior sides and bottom. Another similar pot which is more shallow lies on the floor alongside the pit, and it is empty. Both pots are extremely heavy, and it takes great effort by two or more characters of 14 or greater strength to even move them.

Off in the southwest corner are two vats, each of approximately 100 gallon capacity. Both are made of wood and both are empty. A third vat nearby, only half the size of its neighbors, is half filled with murky, muddy water.

A stone block used as a table or stand is next to the vats, and along the west wall. It has six earthen containers just like those found in the workroom (room 8), and any contents within them should be determined in the same manner as described there. There are also pieces of glassware of various types on the top of the stand, as well as on the floor next to it. Some are clean, some show residues, but all are empty and dusty.

An empty wooden coffin, quite plain and utilitarian, rests upright in the northwest corner. It opens easily and is empty. The wood seems to be rotting in places.

Two kegs rest against the north wall, and examination will show them to be similar to those found in the storeroom (room 6). Each has a letter code to denote its contents, and a roll should be made in the same manner as described there to determine what is within if they are opened.

Wooden shelving on the north wall holds more glassware and three more containers (as those in room 8 and likewise determined). Two small trays hold powdered incense of different colors, and the smell of their aroma will give away their identity.

Monster:

Treasure & Location:

10. STOREROOM. This irregularly shaped room, hidden by a secret door, contains quantities of supplies which are only a bare fraction of its capacity. Although the casks and barrels storing the commodities have prevented spoilage, the contents are by no means "fresh." Although usable or edible still, they nonetheless have an off-taste which suggests staleness.

Approximately 60 barrels and casks are within the room, in two stacks—one against the northwest wall and the other along the east wall in the southern portion of the room. These containers are each marked in some letter code to denote contents. If any individual barrel or cask is chosen for examination, a die (d20) is rolled on the following table to determine its code marking, and if it is broken open, the appropriate contents will be discovered:

	Code Letter(s)	Contents
1	TL	Whole barley
2	B	Wheat flour
3	FT	Rye flour
4	MK	Salt pork
5	GG	Dill pickles
6	HU	Raisins
7	EJ	Fish in brine
8	Y	Dried apples
9	PF	Whole peas
10	SD	Ale
11	Z	Honey
12	AW	Wine
13	OG	Water
14	XR	Soft Soap
15	LC	Salt
16	VW	Lard
17	QS	Seasoning
18	RH	Sunflower seeds
19	UT	Hard candy
20	JS	Dried mushrooms

Note that any container opened and left unsealed, or containers whose contents have spilled, will (over a period of time) attract vermin and/or monsters. Spilled or uncovered material will also be subject to spoilage and rot. This is important if more than one foray into the stronghold is made, and time elapses between such adventures.

Monster:

Treasure & Location:

11. SUPPLY ROOM. The stronghold's supply room is also rather empty, containing mostly construction supplies.

Going through the room will reveal the following materials:

    A coil of very heavy rope, 200' in length
    A box of iron spikes (50)
    A box of metal nails
    A pile of wooden beams, each 10' in length and 6" by 6" in width (80)
    A sack of building mortar, almost empty
    A stack of stone blocks, each about 6" by 6" by 12" in size (400)
    Six wooden doors, leaning in a row against a wall
    A large box of assorted hardware (including several locks of various types, door hinges, clasps and hasps, door handles, assorted metal bolts, and similar items)
    A jug of dried glue

Monster:

Treasure & Location:

12. LIBRARY. Quasqueton's library lies behind a pair of ornately carved oaken doors. The floor of the room is covered with dust, but beneath is a beautiful and shiny surface of polished red granite. The stone is inlaid in large blocks and extends uniformly to within a foot of each of the walls. In the very center of the room within the floor surface are blocks of white

granite within the red stone, and these form the letters R and Z with an ampersand between.

There are three large oaken tables within the room, one in each of the west, north, and east wings of the room. There are several wooden chairs scattered about. In two corners of the room are plush divans, each covered with a rich, fleecy upholstering that makes them very comfortable for reclining. These, however, are rather dusty and dingy due to their age and lack of use.

Wall sconces designed to hold torches for illumination are mounted on the walls all around the room. Small cages inset into the north wall contain numerous fire beetles, and these unusual insects give off an eerie, glowing light from their bodies—enough to illuminate this portion of the room. The reddish glow from this source will appear as forbidding and mysterious when viewed from the entrance to the library, seeming to be a luminosity of varying intensity totally alien to anything viewed before. The insects themelves seem to be thriving in their captive abode, but their food source and longevity are totally puzzling . . . There is no way to open or force the cages themselves, so releasing the insects or gaining access to them is impossible to any adventurers.

The library is rather modestly supplied with books, volumes, and tomes of various sizes. There are likewise only a few scrolls, these being stored in a rack along the east wall. None of the books or scrolls is of any particular use or special interest to the adventurers, despite how many they examine.

Monster:

Treasure & Location:

13. IMPLEMENT ROOM. This elongated room is used primarily for storage of tools, equipment, and implements of various types. In the room are the following items:

    A box of wooden pegs
    A coil of light rope, 50'
    A coil of heavy chain, 70'
    A coil of fine copper wire, 20'
    Mining picks (32), all unusable and in poor repair
    Chisels (15)
    Shovels (13)
    Empty barrels (11)
    Mallets (8)
    Iron bars (29, each measuring 1" in diameter, 8' in length)
    An iron vise (12" jaws)
    Mining jacks (2), broken
    Crosscut saws (2, 2-man)
    Hacksaw (4)
    A mason's toolbox (containing trowel, stone chisel, plumb line, etc.)
    A cobbler's toolbox (containing small hammer, knife, heavy needles, etc.)
    A small barrel of unfletched arrows (60, all normal)
    An empty wooden bench, 10' long

On the north wall, fairly well concealed considering its size, is a counterweight mechanism for the portcullis trap in the corridor just outside the room, as well as a lever to raise the barrier once it has been tripped. No more than two men/dwarves/elves, etc. at a time can attempt to use the lever to raise the portcullis, and their combined strength ratings must total at least 30. This gives them a 20% chance to raise the impediment, with an additional 5% chance for each point of the total beyond 30 (for example, two men with strengths of 15 and 18 trying together would have a 35% chance to raise the portcullis). Each combination of characters (including

henchmen/hirelings) can attempt to raise the barrier but once, although different attempts can be made with different combinations of two persons making the try.

The trap itself is in the corridor outside the door of the room and just beyond it to the east. The trap will be sprung when one or more adventurers reach a point 10' in front of the dead end wall, in which case the portcullis is noisily dropped 20' to the rear of that point. Thieves in the front of the party will have a chance for their percentage chance on the "remove trap" category, in which case they discover the trap and alert the party without triggering it—provided the thief is the first one to reach the trigger point, of course.

The bars of the portcullis are rusty and weak. There are twelve vertical bars and several crossmembers. Persons who are very strong may attempt to escape the trap; however, each person has but one attempt, and if the attempt fails, that person will never be able to do so with that barrier. Adventurers with a strength rating of 13, 14, or 15 have a 5% chance to bend bars or lift the gate, those with a strength of 16 have a 10% chance of doing so and those with a 17 or 18 have a 15% chance of success.

If some way can be employed to use the hacksaws to cut through the portcullis, there will be a time delay of 24 hours if one saw is used, 18 if two are used, 12 hours if three are employed, and 6 hours if all four are utilized (no more than one saw per person). The sawing will make noise of some sort, and this may attract wandering monsters at the Dungeon Master's discretion beyond normal chances. Additionally, each saw has 20% of its blade breaking in any 6 hour period —and there are no extra blades.

If all attempts to escape fail, the persons trapped will be doomed to their fate.

Monster:

Treasure & Location:

14. AUXILIARY STOREROOM. This extra storeroom is empty of goods and supplies. In one corner is a pile of rock rubble.

Monster:

Treasure & Location:

15. & 16. TELEPORTATION ROOMS. A strong magic causing **teleportation** has been permanently placed upon these two

13

rooms of equal size and shape. This is a trick to fool and confuse unwary adventurers and is designed to upset their directional sense.

Both rooms function in the same manner once their doors are opened. In each room, at the corner farthest from the door, is a shiny, sparkling outcropping of crystalline rock which will dazzle when light is reflected off of it; in both rooms the outcroppings are identical. Once adventurers enter the room to investigate this, the entire party is instantly **teleported** to identical locations at the other room—whether they be in the room itself or nearby in the hallway. This teleportation occurs without the adventurer noticing that it has occurred; that is, they have no way of "feeling" that anything unusual has happened. And of course, this means that, although they are in a different location facing in different directions, the adventurers will still have reason to believe that they entered the room through a door which is on the east wall (if they originally entered room 15), or through a door which is on the south wall (if they originally entered room 16). To reflect this fact without tipping off the players, the Dungeon Master must turn his or her map on its side in order to be able to correspond to the directions the players **believe** they are facing. Of course, when the players emerge from the room and attempt to follow their maps, they will be confused by the fact that the details outside the room are not as they expect. They may question the Dungeon Master and even suspect a mistake has been made (with such comments as, "Wait a minute, that **can't** be like that, we just **came** that way!") When this occurs, the DM should avoid argument and simply state things as they are in the new location, letting players puzzle over the problem and arrive at their own conclusions and/or solutions.

Once the teleportation has been triggered in a room, it will not occur again until the room is empty and the door has been closed from the outside. It will thereafter be triggered when the door is opened and the room is entered. The door of the receiving room (the one to which the party is being teleported) will always appear exactly as the door of the first room entered. Doors to both rooms will automatically close themselves and the rooms will become "ready" to be triggered whenever all adventurers have passed to a point at least 120' from either door, as measured down any corridors. It is possible, however, that a party could trigger the trick, be teleported to the other room, then blunder back upon the original room, see that the two were identical but in different locations, and discover what had occurred. On the other hand, the adventurers could become totally confused, lose their way with an inaccurate map, and experience all kinds of difficulty—whatever does happen will depend upon players' actions and their ability to recognize and cope with the situation.

Note: It is recommended that no monsters or treasures be located in either of these rooms.

Monster:

Treasure & Location:

17. CHAR STORAGE CELLAR. This 20' by 20' room is used for storing fuel for the smithy across the hallway. The room is full of blackish soot and dust, but there is only a small pile of fuel against the north wall.

There is a false door on the west wall of the room. It cannot be opened, although it does seem to rest in a frame and even will rattle or move ever so slightly when great strength is applied.

Monster:

Treasure & Location:

18. SMITHY. The smithy is an irregularly shaped room which actually seems to be almost two separate parts. An eerie wind whistles through the upper areas of the room near the ceiling, and this natural effect provided exhaust venting when the fires, long since silent, were stoked with fuel.

Three fire pits lie dormant in the northeast 20' by 20' portion of the room, and these are located on the north wall, in the northeast corner, and on the east wall. In the center of the room is a gigantic forging anvil. A hand bellows hangs on the wall to the west.

The larger southwest portion of the smithy is mostly barren, although an assortment of blacksmith's tools and irons hang on the walls.

Monster:

Treasure & Location:

19. ACCESS ROOM. This room adjoins the smithy, and also provides a vertical access to the lower level of the stronghold.

In the northeast corner of the room and along the north wall are log sections of various size (8"-24" in diameter, 1'-4' in length) stacked in a pile, apparently as additional fuel for the blacksmith's fires. The room is otherwise empty.

In the southeast portion of the room there is a large hole in the floor about 3' across. If light is held from above and observation is attempted, it will be impossible to see how deep the hole is or to where it gives access. If a light source (such as a torch) is cast down the hole, it will come to rest on the floor of the lower level, and from above it will be seen that this is approximately 40' down.

There is a large iron ring anchored to the south wall near the hole, and if a rope is fastened to it, it can be used to assist in descending to the lower level. The fastening, however, is a bit loose, and each person using the rope will have a 1 in 6 chance (non-cumulative) of pulling the ring out of the wall, causing them and the rope to fall to the floor of the lower level. This chance is 2 in 6 for any persons with sizable encumbrance (the equivalent of 500 or more coins in weight). If any person falls, they will do so near the bottom and will take 1-4 hit points of damage (determined by the roll of a four-sided die). Once the ring has been removed from the wall, it cannot be replaced to be usable again.

As an alternative to use of the ring, clever adventurers could use one of the logs in the room measuring 4' in length, tie the rope around it, place it across the 3' opening, and climb down the suspended cord.

For purposes of descent, any rope must be at least 30' in length. In order to allow a return back up, the rope must be at least 35' in length so that it can be reached from below while suspended.

The final method for possible descent is to use a rope and grapple, either attaching the hook to the iron ring or anchoring it to one of the two doorways. If a grapple is used anchored at the south doorway, add 10' to required length, or 20' if the north doorway is used as the anchor point.

Monster:

Treasure & Location:

14

20. DEAD END ROOM. A turning corridor winds inward until ending in a dead end room. The walls are unfinished, and apparently this area of the stronghold was reserved for future development—although no one can say for sure.

Monster:

Treasure & Location:

21. MEETING ROOM. This long and narrow room apparently served as some kind of auditorium or meeting room. There are ten wooden benches scattered about the room, each about 15' in length. A large stone slab at the north end of the room serves as a sort of stage, rising 10 inches off the floor to accommodate any speakers and place them in full view of any assemblage.

On the north wall are four decorative cloth banners of red, green, blue, and yellow. Although once attractive, they are now deteriorated and rotting, thus being of no particular value.

Monster:

Treasure & Location:

22. GARDEN ROOM. Once the showplace of the entire stronghold, the garden has, over the passage of time, become a botanical nightmare. With no one to tend the gardens, the molds and fungi have grown out of control.

The room has two major portions, a north arm and a west arm. At the end of each of these extensions are large semicircular stone formations overgrown with fungoid matter. In the southeast corner of the room is another similar outcropping likewise covered with the underground vegetation. In the center of the northern wing are two large sunken pits, each 10' x 20' in size.

Approaching the room from the corridor to the south reveals an eerie and forbidding sight, as unusual growths have extended themselves from within the room into the corridor, spreading inexorably onward and away from the garden room. Passing this feature and entering the room will reveal a sight totally unlike any ever seen in the outside world.

The floor is covered with a carpet of tufted molds that extends to all the walls and even onto parts of the ceiling, obscuring the rock surface. The molds appear in a rainbow assortment of colors, and they are mixed in their appearance, with splotches, clumps, swirls, and patches presenting a nightmarish combination of clashing colors. This is indeed a fuzzy fairyland of the most forbidding sort, although beautiful in its own mysterious way . . .

All around the room are fungi of a hundred different kinds. These are scattered in patches and clumps of growth. There are many different types of mushrooms (including an incredible "grove" of the giant variety, with stems looking like tree trunks and caps fully 8' in diameter), as well as such common fungi as shelf types, giant puffballs, coral fungi, and morels. The various growths all seem to be thriving, although any nutrient source is well covered by their proliferation. Perhaps some strange magic or extraordinary means keeps this incredible garden alive and growing . . .

Although passage through the room is possible, the various types of growth hinder movement. Furthermore, any kind of mass movement or commotion (such as a melee) will raise small clouds of spores which will obscure vision and be unpleasant to breathe.

If any adventurer attempts to ingest a certain type of fungus, there is a 30% chance of it being poisonous (a save vs. poison is necessary).

Monster:

Treasure & Location:

23. STORAGE ROOM. This room is used primarily for furniture storage, although it is mostly empty. There are three large oaken tables, a number of chairs, and fourteen wooden stools stacked against the walls. In the corner opposite the door is a woodworking table with a crude vise attached, and small saws and other carpenter's equipment are thereon. There are wood chips and some sawdust scattered about the floor.

Monster:

Treasure & Location:

24. MISTRESS' CHAMBER. This room is more tastefully decorated than the rather spartan living quarters found elsewhere in the stronghold. It is the personal chamber of Rogahn's mistress and lover, who apparently lived at the stronghold for some time. But now it appears that she, along with so many others who lived here, has long since been gone.

There is a large walnut bed against the west wall, rather ornately carved (somewhat resembling the bed in room 5—see the description there—but with no name engraved on the headboard). The bed has a large canopy of embroidered green cloth with a striking reddish trim, but it is very dusty like everything else in the room.

Next to the bed is a small table/nightstand with a single drawer. Beside it against the wall is a chest of drawers made of red cedar, which, despite its age, still has the characteristic smell. In the drawers are an assortment of leather items, old clothing, and personal effects like combs, brushes, and hairpins. One comb is a silver-plated item which is of moderate value, being worth 5 g.p. On top of the chest is a tortoiseshell dish which is empty except for a single gold piece coin lying in it, and this rests upon a frilly lace cloth along with two small capped bottles half full of perfume.

On the north wall just to the west of the secret door is a large full-length wall mirror in a wooden frame. The crown of the frame is carved into attractive curving designs, and there is an inscription hewn into the finished wood which says in the common language, "To the fairest of all in my eyes."

In the northwest corner of the room is an attractive water basin which is sculpted from the same rock which forms the wall of the room. Indeed, this protrusion is an integral part of the wall itself. A hole in the bottom of the basin is stopped with a rotting cork; this crude drain lets water drop to an inclined piece of rock which drains into a crack in the wall. There is no running water in the room, however.

A small tapestry measuring 3' x 4' hangs on the east wall. It depicts a handsome and robust warrior carrying off a beautiful maiden in a rescue scene set in a burning village, with a horde of ominous-looking enemies viewing from afar. Embroidered in gold cloth at the top of the scene are the words, "Melissa, the most dearly won and greatest of all my treasures." The tapestry is within a wooden frame, and is firmly anchored to the wall. It cannot be removed without damaging it, in which case it will only carry a value of 40 g.p.

15

Monster:

Treasure & Location:

25. ROGAHN'S CHAMBER. Rogahn's personal quarters are rather simple and spartan, showing his taste for the utilitarian rather than regal.

The curving walls of the room are immediately noticeable as different from all others in the stronghold, not only due to their layout, but also because of their covering. The walls are covered with vertical strips of rough-finished fir wood, and these narrow planks run in single pieces from floor to ceiling. The construction is not remarkable nor is it fancy in any respect, but the result is strikingly pleasing to the eye. If any of the wood is removed from the wall, nothing save back bracing and the rock surface wall will be discovered.

In each of the four curved corners of the room is a different wall hanging. These tapestries are each 6' wide and approximately 8' high. The four subjects depicted are: a dragon being slain by a group of warriors, with one standing prominently at the front of the group, thrusting the killing sword into the dragon's neck; a great battle in a mountain pass, with a small band of fighters led by a great wizard and a single hero putting an entire army to fight; a warrior and a maiden on horseback against a backdrop of mountains, holding hands with joyful expressions; and a depiction of a hero and a wizard joining in a firm handclasp on a deserted hilltop, with only a sunset in the background. The principals in all of these panoramas, of course, as well as the tapestry in room 26, are the same—the warrior/hero is Rogahn, the wizard is Zelligar, and the beautiful maiden is the Fair Melissa, Rogahn's mistress. The tapestries, if removed, will be heavy (equal to 600 g.p. in weight each) and bulky; they are worth 100 g.p. each.

Opposite the secret door on the west wall is a bed which is made of maple, with a feather mattress. The baseboard has an engraved letter R on it, but the bed is otherwise devoid of particular detail.

A free-standing cabinet of wood matching the bed is alongside it. Inside are some garments of general use: cloaks, a leather vest, a buckskin shirt, a metal corselet, etc., as well as a pair of boots. None is of any exceptional value.

A wooden stool is near the cabinet, but there is no other furniture in the room.

Monster:

Treasure & Location:

26. TROPHY ROOM. The stronghold's trophy room consists of an assortment of various curiosities accumulated over the years.

Covering most of the north wall is an immense dragon's skin, its brassy scales reflecting any illumination brightly. At the west end of the room is a basilisk frozen in stone, its menacing gaze forbidding but no longer a threat. On the east wall is a dwarfin skeleton, suspended from a pair of irons near the ceiling, giving the entire chamber a macabre presence. Elsewhere on the walls are a variety of mementoes: two gigantic sets of moose antlers each on a large head, four dragon paws with claws extended, a stuffed cockatrice, a largish black shield which could only be used by a giant, a pair of ram's horns, a pair of crossed swords, a bearskin, an entire door bearing religious symbols, and a set of three colorful flags which will be immediately recognizable as belonging to prominent barbarian tribes.

Monster:

Treasure & Location:

27. THRONE ROOM. The throne room, mostly for show, consists of two great chairs on a raised stone platform overlooking a rectangular court. The court is flanked on each side by a set of four large stone pillars.

The area is reminiscent of a ballroom of small size, although it is impossible to know the room's actual purpose. The floor is smooth slate, while the pillars and raised platform seem to be constructed of great blocks of red granite. The two chairs are sculpted from gigantic blocks of white marble and due to their bulk and weight, are for all intents and purposes permanent fixtures.

Great draperies in alternating panels of yellow and purple hang on the wall behind the raised platform. These are of no unusual value, although they add considerably to the appearance of the room (despite their color clash with the various shades of stone).

Monster:

Treasure & Location:

28. WORSHIP AREA. The stronghold's worship area is no more than a token gesture to the gods, it would seem.

On the back wall of the room, opposite the door, is a rock carving of a great idol which is actually sculpted from the wall itself. The image (of a horned head with an evil visage) appears about 4' wide and 6' high, and is surrounded by religious symbols and runes.

The floor is smooth black slate. In the center of the room is a circular depression, or pit, which measures 5' across and slopes to a maximum depth of 3'. This sacrifice pit is open and mostly empty, except for a small quantity of residual ash covering the bottom.

Monster:

Treasure & Location:

29. CAPTAIN'S CHAMBER. Home for Erig, Rogahn's friend and comrade in arms, is a rather simple room with few furnishings.

The door to the room is a large wooden construction just like the others in the stronghold, but its exterior surface is embellished with an irregular-shaped leather skin covering, which is studded with circular bits of brass which form the word "ERIG" prominently.

The door opens into a rather barren room. In the southeast corner is a crude bed, and alongside it is a table. On top of the table is a small stoneware crock with cover which contains 5 g.p., a large earthenware tankard mug, and a small hand mirror. On the south wall is a wooden chest which is locked. If opened, it will reveal its contents: several garments, including a pair of pants, several cloaks, a heavy cloth coat, and two pairs of boots. A broken dagger is at the bottom of the chest underneath the clothing. A leather pouch also therein contains an unusual memento, a walnut plaque with an inlaid piece of silver engraved with the words, "To Erig, great and trusted fighter by my side, and captain of the guard at Quasqueton—against all foes we shall prevail!" It is signed with an embellished "R." This plaque is of some value, and could bring up to 25 g.p. if sold.

16

In the northeast corner of the room is a wooden keg stand with a single barrel upon it. The barrel is marked with a letter code of "SD" and is full and untapped. If the keg is broken open, ale will issue forth.

On the wall at the western extremity of the room are numerous pegs and brackets, apparently for holding arms and armor. The wall is mostly empty, however, except for two shields and a heavy mace hanging thereon.

Monster:

Treasure & Location:

30. ACCESS ROOM. This room is devoid of detail or contents, giving access to the lower level of the stronghold by a descending stairway. This stairway leads down and directly into room 38 on the lower level.

Monster:

Treasure & Location:

31. ROOM OF POOLS. This room is the largest one on the upper level, and is quite different from all the others.

Although the walls are the same as elsewhere (rough blackish stone), the floor of this room is covered with ceramic tiles arranged in mosaic fashion. The majority of the thousands of tiles are golden brown in color, but patterns of white and black tiles appear in various places to enhance the effect of the very striking designs thus formed. The designs (various flowing lines, etc.) are purely decorative, and carry no mysterious message or meaning.

Arrayed throughout the room are fourteen different pools, each about ten feet in diameter, with sides sloping to a maximum depth of five feet in the center. This mystical arrangement is doubly amazing, since all the contents of the pools are different . . .

The individual pools are letter coded A to N, and examination of any particular pool will reveal the following:

a) Pool of healing—This pool contains a strange pinkish liquid that will cause instantaneous healing when ingested. It will also cure disease, but will not restore hit points in doing so. Whenever a drink is taken, 1-6 hit points of individual damage are restored immediately to the drinker, although this can only be done once per day per person (any further consumption will have no additional effect). Although the liquid can be placed into containers and removed from the pool, the healing properties will immediately disappear once it is taken from this room. Note: this pool disappears and reappears from time to time magically, so if adventurers make a return to this room, there is only a 30% chance that the liquid will be present again then (although it will always be there upon their first visit).

b) Acid pool—This pool is filled to the brim with a clear, fizzing liquid which gives off a strange and unpleasant aroma to those near it. It is full of acid, and most deadly. If any adventurer falls or leaps within it, certain and immediate death will result. Putting a hand or other body member within it will result in an immediate 2-5 hit points of damage (roll a 4-sided die and add 1 to the result)—more if a greater portion of the body is exposed to the liquid. Drinking any of the liquid (even but a sip) will cause immediate gagging and cause no less than 5 hit points of damage, plus a saving throw against poison to survive. Putting just a drop or two to the tongue will cause the loss of 1 hit point, plus induce gagging and choking for two melee rounds of time (twenty seconds), although no saving throw for poison will be necessary. Weapons or other objects dipped into the acid will deteriorate (swords will be marked and weakened, wooden items warped and cracked, etc.) and may even be ruined completely at the discretion of the Dungeon Master (who can roll a die for each item to determine how adversely it is affected). The strength of the acid is such that it will eat through any type of container within two melee rounds of time.

A single brass key of large size (about six inches long) is visible at the bottom of the pool, seemingly unaffected by the acid. This key, if somehow retrieved, will be worthless and it does not correspond to any of the locks within the stronghold.

c) Pool of sickness—This pool is filled with a murky gray syrup. If any of it is consumed (even but a sip), the victim will begin

to suffer sickness, but not until six turns (one hour) afterwards. If this occurs, there is no loss of hit points, but the victim suffers from strong and recurring stomach pains for 1-4 hours (roll a four-sided die) which make fighting and even movement impossible for that period (although a victim could be carried by others), after which all symptoms pass and the character returns to normal. Placing a drop of liquid upon the tongue will give a sweet taste, but will cause no symptoms. Weapons or other items placed within the liquid will be totally unaffected. Any portion of the liquid removed from the pool will lose its special properties within three melee rounds (thirty seconds).

d) Green slime pool—The horrid contents of this pool are immediately obvious to any gazing into it. The slime (HP: 20) is covering the walls of the basin most of the way from the bottom to the edge.

e) Drinking pool—This pool is filled with icy cold spring water which will refresh anyone who takes a drink from it. The water is pure and good, but has no other special characteristics.

f) Pool of wine—This pool is filled with powerful wine of a deep red color. Not only is it excellent wine, it has a taste so inviting that anyone tasting it will be prone to drink more and more until intoxicated! If a sip is taken, the taster will have a 60% chance of drinking more (regardless of the player's wishes). If this is done, three 6-sided dice are thrown and compared to the character's constitution rating; if the number rolled is greater than the character's constitution score, then the difference is figured, and this is the number of **hours** the character will be intoxicated (if the roll is equal or less, the character "holds his liquor" and is unaffected). Any character so intoxicated will suffer the following penalties: -2 on all rolls "to hit" in combat, -3 to dexterity rating, and any other disadvantages to being drunk that the DM may deem in effect (prone to loud and boisterous speech, stumbling about, a greater chance to be surprised, etc.). After the allotted number of hours have passed, the character returns to normal. Any intoxicated character who returns to the pool of wine will have a 90% chance of drinking too much again, and the check against constitution will then be necessitated once more. If any of the wine is removed from the room, it will immediately lose its potency and be considered as normal wine, but actually rather weak in its effects.

g) Dry pool—This depression is completely dry, and there is no trace of any liquid within it, nor any clue as to whether any type of matter was ever within it. The basin itself seems to be some kind of yellowish ceramic origin, but it will be impervious to striking or any similar attempt at cracking or fracturing.

h) Hot pool—This steaming and bubbling cauldron is filled with boiling water, which will be obvious to any observer. The water itself is completely normal in all other respects, although it has a relatively high mineral content, as evidenced by a whitish crust built up around the edge of the pool.

i) Aura pool—This pool of shimmering water (which otherwise appears normal in every respect) is less full than many of the others. The water itself seems to glisten and sparkle, and will be seen to radiate magic if an attempt to detect it is made. The water tastes normal in every respect, but those drinking as little as a single sip will experience a strange effect. Upon swallowing the liquid, the drinker will feel his or her entire body tingle, and at the same time the character and others in the area will see a visual phenomenon: an aura of color will glow around the character's entire body for approximately a full minute. The color apparent will depend totally upon the character's alignment. It will glow blue for an alignment of lawful, yellow for chaotic, while any neutral characters will exhibit a white aura. Of course, upon first consuming the liquid, the players will have no idea what the strange appearing colors may mean, so they may be puzzled by the effects—and there are no clues around the pool to explain the colors. The water will retain its special magical characteristics even if it is removed from the pool, but there are only 10 suitable drinks possible due to the small amount of liquid present. This pool, just like the pool of healing previously described, disappears and reappears from time to time (see "a" above for details and percentage chance of reappearance for future visits).

j) Pool of sleep—This pool is full of a greenish liquid of varying shades, with a swirling pattern evident on its stagnant surface. Putting a drop on the tongue reveals a sort of fruity taste, but no special effects will be noticeable. Taking a sip will be tasty refreshment, but within ten seconds a real drowsiness will set in which may even cause (50% chance) an immediate sleep to begin, which will last from 1-6 minutes. Drinking any greater volume of the liquid will certainly induce a comatose slumber of from 1-8 hours, with no saving throw possible. Any removal of the liquid from the room will totally negate its effectiveness, although removing anyone who has consumed the stuff will not awaken them.

k) Fish pool—This pool of normal lake water holds numerous small fish. It has no other special properties, nor are the fish unusual in any way.

l) Ice pool—This basin is filled with steaming dry ice, although for some unknown reason it never seems to dissipate. The ice is "hot" to the touch due to its extremely low temperature. Since it is highly doubtful any character has ever seen dry ice, the entire spectacle will be highly mysterious, appearing as some kind of whitish rock giving off eerie vapors and feeling hot to the touch. If any pieces are broken off and removed from the pool, they will dissipate into carbon dioxide gas as normal dry ice would do. Such pieces could be handled with a gloved hand, but the nature of the substance will still likely be unapparent.

m) Treasure pool—This basin, filled with normal water, seems to hold a great treasure underneath the water. A pile of gold pieces appears to lie on the bottom of the pool, and the golden image is sprinkled with an assortment of sparkling jewels. Alas, this treasure trove is nothing more than a magical **illusion**, which will be dispelled once the surface of the water is broken or disturbed. Once the waters are calm again, the image will reappear.

n) Pool of muting—This pool is almost empty, but a small amount of water remains. Although the liquid appears to be normal water (and has no unusual odor or taste to belie its actual nature), it is actually a magical substance. This liquid, when swallowed, causes a complete loss of voice and verbal capabilities for 1-6 hours. This muting will become apparent only when it has been swallowed; merely putting a drop on the tongue will give no clue as to its effect, and it will seem like normal water. Any character drinking the water will suffer the effects, and that means that the players will be affected likewise. Thus, the referee informs the player or players of their limitation, and they are barred from any further communication by verbal means with the other players in the party for the duration

18

of the muting effects (1-6 game hours, determined by rolling a six-sided die). In such cases, they must remain completely silent (no grunts or groans allowed), and can only communicate with other players via nods, head shaking, hand signals, etc. If any player who is caller for the group is so affected, another player must take his place. Written communication is possible only if the muted player has an intelligence of 14 or more, and any such message can only be read by another character with a similar intelligence rating.

Monster:

Treasure & Location:

32. ADVISOR'S CHAMBER. Access to this room is only via a secret door on its west wall which gives access to the Room of Pools (31). The chamber is the dwelling area for Marevak, advisor to Zelligar and Rogahn.

The decor is rather pleasant, although uninspired. The floor is the most striking aspect of the room, for it is a continuation of the colored mosaic patterns of golden brown, white and black which are evidenced in the adjacent Room of Pools. There are some minimal furnishings in the room—a common bed, three chairs, a makeshift desk with a single drawer (locked), and a battered old table. The walls are barren rock, except for a framed picture hanging over the desk showing two figures standing side by side: a warrior of impressive proportions, and a wizened magic-user in a purple robe. This is actually a full-color painting, beautifully rendered, and in one corner is written in the elfish language the words: "To wise Marevak, worthy advisor and counselor, from a grateful Zelligar and Rogahn." These words are readable only to those who know the elfin language (or via a **read languages** spell), but the signed names of Zelligar and Rogahn will be apparent upon a close examination. In another corner of the painting is the signed name Tuflor—this being the artist who painted the picture, but this fact certainly not obvious to anyone finding the painting other than through deduction or by a character "asking around" once back in the civilized world.

The painting is quite large and bulky, as well as heavy, when removed from the wall. If carried undamaged out of the stronghold and back to civilization, it could bring up to 300 g.p. if sold. However, anyone trying to sell the painting for its value will run a 60% risk that the purchaser will recognize the origin of the painting—and if this word spreads at large, the seller may have attendant problems, since it will be obvious from where it was obtained.

The desk in the room is mostly empty, except for several attached sheets with various notes written in elfin. The first sheet is headed with the title, "Suggestions for the Further Development of Quasqueton," and the notes relate to certain details of construction for the stronghold (although there is no information of a sort to assist the adventurers, and no maps). The document (discernible only by those who know the elfin language or by a **read languages** spell) is signed at the bottom of each page by Marevak.

▶ The locked drawer of the desk is well-secured, and any tampering (with the exception of a successful "remove trap" by a thief) will cause the release of a terrible gaseous emission which will be so penetrating as to drive all characters from the room for 1-4 hours, with no saving throw (this happens only once). The lock can only be picked by a thief character at his or her normal chances, but only a single try can be made —if he or she fails, the lock cannot be opened by that character. However, access to the drawer can be gained by dis-

mantling the desk, although this will require heavy blows from some kind of weapon (due to the noise, an extra check for wandering monsters must be made if this occurs). The contents of the drawer are determined by rolling a single twelve-sided die (only one roll is taken, for there is but a single item within): 1 Potion of **levitation**; 2 **Elven boots**; 3 10-100 g.p.; 4 A 50 g.p. gem (moonstone); 5 a golden medallion worth 20 g.p.; 6 **Read languages** scroll; 7 **Web** scroll; 8 **Cursed** scroll (permanently removes 1 point from charisma rating of first person to read it—**remove curse** (see D&D Expert rules) will not counteract it); 9 **Ring of protection +1**; 10 Potion of **healing** (two doses); 11 A **dagger +1** with ornately carved handle; 12 Nothing.

Monster:

Treasure & Location:

33. BARRACKS. This large, open room is the dwelling place for the guards and men-at-arms of the stronghold (most of whom left on the last adventure with Rogahn and Zelligar). Scattered throughout the room are about 40 common beds, and about half that numbr of chairs and stools. There are several large wooden tables along various walls, and at the south wall is a large wooden chest of drawers which is empty except for a few old socks, some common footwear, a few cloth vestments, and other similar items of no special value.

In the southwest corner of the room the floor slants toward the wall steeply and an opening (too small to give any access) leads into the wall. From the faint smell, it is apparent that this is some kind of crude toilet area.

The walls of the room are rough stone, but there are wall sconces designed to hold torches, and various pegs upon the wall. There are some odds and ends hanging from several of the pegs: an old battered shield, an empty canteen, a 20' section of light chain, a sheathed sword (old and rusty), and a bearskin.

Monster:

Treasure & Location:

34. ARMORY. This irregularly-shaped room is designed to house the arms supply of the stronghold. It is mostly empty now, however, since many of the arms were taken along on the last forway of the inhabitants of the hideaway.

When the room is entered, a slight whistling sound can be heard if the adventurers stand quietly. If the door is closed (unless spiked open it will close automatically one round after everyone has entered, and even if so secured, there is a 50% chance that it will close anyway) and the second exit is likewise closed, a howling wind will immediately result, with an 80% chance of putting out any torch carried by the adventurers, or a 50% chance to extinguish each lantern carried. The wind will cease whenever either or both of the exits is opened. Upon examination of the ceiling of the room (which is a full 20' from the floor), two sizable vents will be noticeable (neither providing usable access) to show that this is a natural, rather than magical, phenomenon.

The rock walls of this room are mostly smooth, and there are carved ledges within several of them. Wooden pegs also abound, and there are some items still left in place on the wall: a number of battered shields (several broken and in otherwise poor repair), bits and pieces of body armor (in uniformly poor condition), several crude bows (-2 "to hit" if used), a quiver of normal arrows, two swords (one in good condition), a dozen spears, two hand axes (one with a split

19

handle), a flail, a two-handed sword with broken blade, and a dagger. None of the items appears remarkable, although the flail, the dagger, and one of the swords seem to be usable and of normal value for such an item.

In the extreme southwest corner of the room are two locked chests, but they are empty. Both are large and bulky, as well as heavy.

Monster:

Treasure & Location:

35. GUEST CHAMBER. There are three identical guest chambers side by side, all opening into the same corridor. The rooms are all similarly furnished, with rough rock walls, and a minimum of furnishings: a wooden bed, a small table, and a single chair.

The middle chamber differs from the other two in one respect: there is a false door on its eastern wall. Although it seems to move just as a normal door would, it resists opening. If it is battered down, it will reveal only a stone wall behind it.

Monster:

Treasure & Location:

36. UTILITY ROOM. This extra room is empty and unused. Two special features of note near the room are described below:

FALSE STEPS. Although the steps here are very real, the entire area north of this room (the various winding corridors) is specially designed to confuse any explorers. The corridor leading past the guest chambers is on an upward slant which will be unnoticeable to casual adventurers (except dwarves, who will have a 2 in 6 chance to notice it). The stairs (8 of them) then lead downward, as if to another level—although this is only the impression created.

PIT TRAP. Just to the east of this room is a dead end to the corridor, with a false door on the north wall where the corridor stops. When any adventurer approaches the door (within 5'), the weight will trigger the trap, causing the entire 20' section of floor between the false door and the wall opposite it to open up. A giant crack opens in the center of the floor as the middle drops down and the sides slant inward, dropping all characters and their equipment through the 4' wide opening. The bottom of the trap, some 40' below, is a pool of cold spring water in room 50 of the lower level. Those falling through the trap will sustain 1-4 hit points each when they hit the water below. In addition, since the pool is about 8' deep, characters heavily encumbered (more than 50 coins of weight equivalent) will risk drowning unless they free themselves of the bulk and weight after landing in the water. If any character heavily encumbered does not, he or she will have a 90% chance of drowning, modified by a -5% per point of dexterity (for instance, a heavily encumbered character who elects not to unencumber and has a dexterity of 12 will only have a 30% chance of drowning—90% -[12 x 5%] = 30%). Items dropped to the bottom of the pool will be retrievable, but due to the extremely cold temperature of the water, characters will depend upon their constitution rating to see if they can stand the water enough to dive for things on the bottom. One check can be made for each character, with a 5% chance per point of constitution that they will be able to take the cold water (for example, a character with a constitution rating of 11 would have a 55% chance of being able

to take the cold water and dive effectively). If characters dive for items at the bottom of the pool, only one item at a time is retrievable and each dive takes one round (ten seconds) with two rounds between each dive for air. In any event, no character can stand to stay in the water for more than ten rounds—and one hour is required for rest and recovery after each diving session to dry off, fully warm up again, etc.

The trap, after being triggered and dropping persons from above to the pool, will close again until triggered once more from above. Refer to the room description of room 50 of the lower level for adventurers deposited here, and begin their progress from that location on the lower level map.

Monster:

Treasure & Location:

37. RECREATION ROOM. This room is designed for recreation and training, and was designed specially for Rogahn's use. The carved door, heavy and thick, bears a fancy "R" on its outer face.

The room is made for a variety of activities, as is apparent from its furnishings and contents. On the east and west walls, which are covered with pocked wood, are large archery targets, and six arrows are still stuck into the eastern target. Although there are several quivers of arrows around, there are no bows in the room.

There are several iron bars of varying length and weight in one corner of the room. These vary in circumference, and are apparently designed for weight lifting, although this fact is best discovered by the deduction of the players.

In another corner of the room, a metal bar is attached to the two walls and is about 7' off the floor. Nearby, a rope is suspended from the ceiling 20' above. Except for two heavy benches and a single stool, there are no furnishings in the room other than five heavy woven mats lying atop each other to form a sort of floor cushion measuring 20' by 20'. Hanging on the wall are several very heavy weapons which appear normal but which weigh almost double normal weight—a notched sword, a battle axe, a flail, and a mace. Leaning against the wall are two heavily battered shields.

Monster:

Treasure & Location:

KEY TO THE LOWER LEVEL

The lower level of the complex is rough and unfinished. The walls are irregular and coarse, not at all like the more finished walls of the level above (except for the two rooms on this level which are more like those in the upper portion and in a state of relative completion). The corridors are roughly 10' wide, and they are irregular and rough, making mapping difficult. The floors are uneven, and in some cases rock chips and debris cover the pathways between rooms and chambers. The doors are as in the upper level, but the secret doors are either rock or disguised by rock so as to appear unnoticeable.

WANDERING MONSTERS

Check every second turn; 1 in 6 (roll a 6-sided die). If a monster is indicated, roll a six-sided die again and compare to the list below to determine what type of monster appears. Then check for surprise. The abbreviations which follow are the same as used and explained in the section entitled MONSTER LIST.

1. Troglodytes (1-4)—AC 5, HD 2*, hp 9,8,5,4, #AT 3, D 1-4/1-4/1-4, MV 120' (40'), Save F2, ML 9

2. Crab Spider (1)—AC 7, HD 2*, hp 12, #AT 1, D 1-8 + poison, MV 120' (40'), Save F1, ML 7

3. Kobolds (2-7)—AC 7, HD ½, hp 4,4,3,3,2,2,1, #AT 1, D 1-4 or weapon -1, MV 90' (30'), Save NM, ML 6

4. Orcs (1-8)—AC 6, HD 1, hp 6,5,5,4,4,3,3,2, #AT 1, D 1-6 or by weapon, MV 90' (30'), Save F1, ML 8

5. Zombies (1-2)—AC 8, HD 2, hp 8,7, #AT 1, D 1-8 or by weapon, MV 90' (30'), Save F1, ML 12

6. Goblins (2-7)—AC 6, HD 1-1, hp 5,5,4,4,3,2,1, #AT 1, D 1-6 or by weapon, MV 90' (30'), Save NM, ML 7

ENCOUNTER AREAS

38. ACCESS ROOM. This room is filled with piles of rock and rubble, as well as mining equipment: rock carts, mining jacks, timbers, pickaxes, etc. It is apparent that there has been no mining activity for quite some time.

Monster:

Treasure & Location:

39. MUSEUM. This room is an unfinished museum, a special monument to the achievements of the stronghold's most illustrious inhabitants.

The west wall is a sectioned fresco showing various events and deeds from the life of Rogahn, and the several views pictured are: a young boy raising a sword, a young man slaying a wild boar, a warrior carrying off a dead barbarian, and a hero in the midst of a large battle hacking barbarian foes to pieces.

The east wall is a similar sectioned fresco showing cameos from the life of Zelligar: a boy gazing upward at a starry night sky, a young man diligently studying a great tome, an earnest magician changing water to wine before a delighted audience, and a powerful wizard casting a type of death fog over an enemy army from a hilltop.

The north wall section is unfinished, but several sections of frescoes show the two great men together: shaking hands for the first time in younger days, winning a great battle against barbarians in a hill pass, gazing upward together from the wilderness to a craggy rock outcropping (recognizable to the adventurers as the place where the stronghold was built), with a fourth space blank. Next to the frescoes are other mementoes from the past: a parchment letter of thanks for help in the war against the barbarians from a prominent landowner, a barbarian curved sword, and a skeleton of the barbarian chief (so identified by a wall plaque in the common language). There is more blank space on the wall, apparently for further additions to the room's collection of items.

The frescoes are painted and they cannot be removed. None of the mementoes is of any particular worth or value.

Monster:

Treasure & Location:

40.-56. CAVERNS OF QUASQUETON. The bulk of the lower level of the complex is a series of unfinished caves and caverns, which are mostly devoid of special detail—all being characterized by irregular walls of rough rock. Uneven floors strewn with bits of rock and rubble, and joined by winding corridors. The majority of the rooms are empty of furnishings.

40. SECRET CAVERN.

Monster:

Treasure & Location:

41. CAVERN.

Monster:

Treasure & Location:

42. WEBBED CAVE. The entrance to this room is covered with silky but sticky webs, which must be cut or burned through to gain access to it. See **web** spell for details in D&D Basic booklet.

Monster:

Treasure & Location:

43. CAVERN.

Monster:

Treasure & Location:

44. CAVERN.

Monster:

Treasure & Location:

45. CAVERN OF THE MYSTICAL STONE. This ante-chamber is the resting place for a large, glowing chunk of rock which appears to be mica. The stone radiates magic strongly.

The stone rests permanently in its place and is not removable. Although chips can easily be broken off the rock by hand, only one chip at a time may be broken away; until anything is done with it, the rest of the rock will remain impervious to breaking.

21

Once a chip is removed, its glow will begin to fade, and after three rounds (thirty seconds) it will be a normal piece of mica with no magical properties (as will be the case if it is removed from this room). The chip's magical properties are manifested only if it is consumed (or placed in the mouth) by any character before three rounds have passed after breaking off from the chunk. The magical effects are highly variable and each individual can only be once affected—even if a future return to the rock is made at a later time. If any character places a chip within his or her mouth, a 20-sided die is rolled to determine the effect according to the following table:

1 Immediately teleports the character and his gear to the webbed cave (room 42)

2 Immediately blinds the character for 1-6 hours of game time (no combat, must be led by other adventurers)

3 Raises strength rating permanently by 1 point

4 Raises charisma rating permanently by 1 point

5 Raises wisdom rating permanently by 1 point

6 Raises intelligence rating permanently by 1 point

7 Raises dexterity rating permanently by 1 point

8 Lowers strength rating permanently by 1 point

9 Lowers charisma rating permanently by 1 point

10 Lowers intelligence rating permanently by 1 point

11 Cures all damage on one character

12 Causes **invisibility** for 1-6 hours of game time (subject to normal restrictions)

13 Poison (saving throw at +1)

14 Makes a 500 g.p. gem (pearl) appear in character's hand

15 Gives a permanent +1 to any single weapon carried by character (if more than one now carried, roll randomly to determine which)

16 Heals all lost hit points of character (if any)

17 Causes idiocy for 1-4 hours (unable to function intelligently or fight, must be led by other adventurers)

18 Gives a special one-time bonus of 1-6 hit points to the character (these are the first ones lost the next time damage or injury is taken)

19 Gives a **curse**: the character will sleep for 72 hours straight each month, beginning one day before and ending one day after each new moon (can only be removed by a **remove curse** spell)

20 Has no effect

Monster:

Treasure & Location:

46. SUNKEN CAVERN. This small cavern lies at the bottom of a short, sloping corridor. The walls are wet with moisture, and glisten in any reflected light.

Monster:

Treasure & Location:

47. CAVERN.

Monster:

Treasure & Location:

48. ARENA CAVERN. This cavern, designed as a small theatre or arena, is unfinished. The center portion of the room is sunken about 15' below the floor level, and the sides slope downward from the surrounding walls to form a small amphitheatre.

Monster:

Treasure & Location:

49. PHOSPHORESCENT CAVE. This medium-sized cavern and its irregularly-shaped eastern arm present an eerie sight to explorers. A soft phosphorescent glow bathes the entire area independent of any other illumination, and the strange light is caused by the widespread growth (on walls, ceiling, and even parts of the floor) of a light purplish mold. The mold itself is harmless.

Monster:

Treasure & Location:

50. WATER PIT. This room contains the 8' deep pool of water into which any unwary adventurers are precipitated from the trap on the upper level (see the special description of the trap under the description of room 36). As described there, the water is extremely cold. Anyone entering the water (whether voluntarily or not) must spend a full hour recovering from its chilly effects.

The pool is about 20' across and is filled by a cold spring.

Monster:

Treasure & Location:

51. SIDE CAVERN. This cavern is unusual only in that its eastern rock wall is striated with irregular diagonal streaks of a bluish ore (of no unusual use or value to the adventurers).

Monster:

Treasure & Location:

52. RAISED CAVERN. This room, off the southeast corner of the grand cavern, is accessible by climbing four upward steps. Its eastern wall also shows diagonal streaks of the same bluish ore noticeable in room 51. The room has a low ceiling (only 5'), so some humans may find it difficult to stand fully erect.

Monster:

Treasure & Location:

53. GRAND CAVERN.OF THE BATS. This majestic cave is the largest in the complex, and is impressive due to its size and volume, for the ceiling is almost 60' above. A corridor sloping downward into the cavern (noticeable even by non-dwarves) gives primary access to the room on its south wall. A secondary entrance/exit is via a secret door to the west, while steps to the southeast lead up to room 52.

A southwestern arm of the room leads to an alcove of rock pillars of unusual and irregular shape, and these run from floor to ceiling to form a very meager catacomb.

When it is daytime in the outer world, a small opening in the ceiling just off a midway point of the north wall will show daylight. (If the DM has not been meticulously charting time as night vs. day, there will be a 60% chance of daylight being visible at the time the adventurers enter the room; if not, it will be very difficult to notice the opening—only a 10% chance per adventurer observing the ceiling.) The opening in the ceiling (which will be totally inaccessible to any and all attempts by adventurers to reach it) is used by the many thousands of bats which live on the ceiling of the cavern by day and which venture out at sunset each day for feeding. (Again, if exact time is not being tracked, a die roll may be necessary to determine what time of day the adventurers reach the cavern and whether or not the bats are present or active.)

The bats are nocturnal animals, but the species living in this particular cavern is very easily agitated. Any party of adventurers entering the cavern with torches or other bright sources of light (including unshielded lanterns) will have a base 5% chance per light source per turn (10 minutes) of disturbing the bats and causing them to swarm. In addition, any noises above subdued conversation will add another 10% to the chance of disturbing the bats, assuming of course that they are present in the cave when the party enters. (For example, a party with 4 torches would have a 20% chance of disturbing the bats and causing them to swarm, or 30% if they are arguing in addition.)

If the bats are disturbed, first a few begin squeaking and flying around (this will of course occur if any sleeping bats are physically prodded or awakened), then more and more until the mass becomes a giant churning swarm (this will take only two melee rounds, or twenty seconds). The swarming bats will squeak and squawk, flying madly about. They will fill the grand cavern and overflow into adjacent areas and corridors, but those flying out of the cavern will soon return. While swarming, the bats will buzz and harry any persons in the cavern or adjacent corridors, zooming past them at high speed while others hover about. Occasionally, one of the bats will try to land on a character (50% chance each round) to deliver a pinching bite which is unpleasant but harmless.

If adventurers leave the grand cavern and remove their light sources with them, the swarm of bats will slowly cease their activity and return to their inverted perches (this takes about 30 minutes). If the adventurers stay in the room, extinguish their lights, and lie silently on the floor for the same period of time, the bats will return to their dormant state.

Characters fighting swarming bats will find the task hopeless due to their sheer number, but attempts can be made using any hand held weapon larger than a dagger, with an 18, 19 or 20 needed to hit with a 20-sided die. Bats landing to bite can be hit on any roll of 7 or above. A single hit will kill any bat.

Characters fighting or otherwise enduring swarming bats will automatically be caught by surprise if any wandering monster comes upon them while they are doing so. Fighting the bats makes enough noise to necessitate an additional special roll for wandering monsters.

A sort of fluffy and dusty guano covers the floor of the grand cavern, quite different from the droppings of most other species of bats.

The bats will return and leave at sunset each day until returning as a swarm at the following dawn.

Monster:

Treasure & Location:

54. TREASURE CAVE. This secret room, itself opening to a corridor shielded by secret doors on either end, was designed as the hiding place for the valuables in the stronghold. There is a scattering of gold pieces (11-30; roll a twenty-sided die and add 10) on the floor of the room, and three locked chests (which are empty unless noted below).

Two short human statues (appearing lifelike, as if made from wax) are within the room. As soon as any item of value is touched or disturbed, both will immediately spring to life and draw their swords and attack the party. These are magical berserkers (4 Hit Points each, Armor Class 7) who will fight to the death. Neither has any treasure on his person.

Monster:

Treasure & Location:

35. EXIT CAVE. This large cavern is otherwise unremarkable, except for the fact that a secret one-way passage out of the stronghold is hidden in the northeast corner of the cave. This secret exit is triggered by pushing on a loose rock within the wall, at which time the opening occurs in the wall, leading to the outside world. The opening allows access for only 10 seconds, at which time it closes once more, and will not be triggered for another 24 hours.

If characters take advantage of this exit, they will find themselves on a rock ledge about 3 feet wide and 20 feet long. If they use ropes to scale down, they can rappel without too much difficulty to a location some 40 feet below where the drop is less steep and a descent can be made through the trees and vegetation toward the valley below. If the characters stand on the ledge and observe the view, they will notice that they are on the north face of the massive outcropping which houses the stronghold, whereas the other entrance is on the south face. Because of the wilderness which surrounds the entire area, it may take some doing to return to civilization or home.

The secret exit is but a one-way access, and allows only egress from the stronghold, never entrance. There is no way to trigger the door from the outside, and even if this were possible, a permanent magic spell upon the exit totally prevents movement into the complex via the opening.

Monster:

Treasure & Location:

56. CAVERN OF THE STATUE. In the southern end of this cavern is a solitary stone figure, roughly sculpted from the same black stone of the cavern walls and firmly anchored to the floor. The figure, obviously a human male (although lacking any finished detail), stands some 5 feet high, with both arms slightly outstretched and pointing to the jagged rock outcropping which divides the two corridors to the north-north-east. The statue is too heavy to be moved, and will completely resist any attempts to budge or topple it.

PIT TRAP. Just outside this cavern, in the corridor which leads eastward, is a large covered pit at the intersection of three corridors. The pit is about 12' across and 10' deep. A fall into this pit will inflict 1-4 hit points of damage, and any characters

23

reaching the area will have a basic 70% chance of falling in, with a 30% chance of noticing the trap (the danger would be greater if, for instance, they were running rather than simply exploring). If characters in the first rank of a party fall in, there is only a 20% chance of the next row of characters falling, and each checks separately as before. The trap, once sprung, does not shield the pit any further, and the pit will be noticeable.

Monster:

Treasure & Location:

THIS ENDS THE MODULE "SEARCH FOR THE UNKNOWN"

KEYING THE DUNGEON

Once the Dungeon Master has read the entire module over one or more times and has gained a working familiarity with it, he or she is ready to key it. In doing so, the DM will take the basic descriptive framework and add his or her own ideas as to how and where the various monsters and treasures are located. The result will be a dungeon with his or her own indelible stamp, a bit different from all others—even those using the same descriptive outline.

With over fifty rooms and chambers noted on the two level maps by numbers (and several other unmarked open areas), there is plenty of space to explore (though this dungeon is actually quite small compared to most). With 15 to 25 listed treasures (plus a few items of value that are part of the basic furnishings) and 16 to 20 monsters to place, the DM is offered a real choice in setting up the dungeon, for it is he or she who will decide on which areas are forbidding with danger or rich with reward.

The monsters (number keyed 1. to 25.) and the treasures (lettered A to HH) should be placed with care and consideration and in many cases there should be a reason or rationale *why* something is located where it is. Just as there is a logical explanation behind the entire setting or scenario, so too should there be a similar thought behind what is to be found within the dungeon. Of course, in some cases, the unexpected or the inexplicable will be the exception—not everything should follow the normal order of things or be too predictable for the players.

As mentioned previously elsewhere, not every room or chamber will have a monster, a treasure, or both. As a matter of fact, quite a number of places will simply be empty, while others may hold a monster with no treasure, or, rarely, a treasure without a monster guarding it. In the latter instance, the unguarded treasure will likely be well-hidden (as indeed any treasure can be) or concealed to make the room *appear* empty. Finally, in some instances, a room may contain a monster (being in its lair) as well as a treasure it is guarding, either wittingly (if it is its trove) or unwittingly (if its appearance there was only coincidental). In such a case, it will be necessary to defeat (either by killing or driving away) the monster or monsters before any attempt to discover or garner the treasure is made . . .

Although monsters will inevitably make their presence known, treasures are usually not obvious. It is up to players to locate them by telling the DM how their characters will conduct any attempted search, and it is quite conceivable that they could totally miss seeing a treasure which is hidden or concealed. In fact, any good dungeon will have undiscovered treasures in areas that have been explored by the players, simply because it is impossible to expect that they will find every one of them.

Once the DM has decided on where to place the various monsters and treasures, he or she keys both the maps and the descriptive copy within this booklet by using the letter and number codes for treasures and monsters, respectively. On the two game maps, he or she marks (preferably using a colored pencil for readability and possible erasure) the letter (for treasure) in each room containing a treasure from the master list. The DM then places a number (for monsters) in each room which will contain a monster, and may also make a note on the map what type of monster is there ("orcs" or "trogs," for instance). Each monster or treasure listing should appear but once on the game map when finished. The DM then refers to the descriptions of each room or chamber within the body copy of this booklet, and fills in the blanks following the proper sections corresponding to the marked map with the pertinent details and any side notes on: what monster is located there (if any), where it hides (if it does so—not all will hide), what treasure is located within the room (if any), where it is located, and how it is hidden or protected (if it is). Any remaining space should be reserved for further notes, especially listing of the effects caused by subsequent player adventuring—monsters scared away to new locations, creatures slain, treasures removed, equipment abandoned, etc. Of course, notes on the map can likewise be made as desired.

Once the dungeon has been keyed, it is ready for exploration by the players. Good luck, and have fun! Follow these guidelines when setting up your own dungeon from scratch, and you should be successful.

MONSTER LIST

The monsters occupying the area to be explored are an assortment of creatures, some of which are former inhabitants (orc and kobold slaves), and some of which have moved into the dungeon by unknown means.

The monsters (keeping in mind that the term refers to any encounter, no matter what the creature type) can be encountered in two ways: either in their "lair" (the particular room or chamber where they live, as keyed by the Dungeon Master), or as "wandering monsters." The latter encounters are more irregular, uncertain, and unpredictable as adventurers happen to meet the monsters on a random basis while exploring.

The monster list below is keyed by number for easy reference, and shows the monsters which will be shown on the game map as being in their "lair." The wandering monster lists appear within the descriptive copy of the module and are given prior to the information on each of the two levels of the dungeon—one being for the upper level, and the other for the lower level.

Monsters are shown on the list with pertinent details given (consult the descriptions within the D&D game booklet for further information on each type), thus allowing them to be employed by the DM when encountered without additional dice rolling (except for the initial roll to determine number appearing). **Important: although there are 25 listings, the Dungeon Master should use only 16 to 20 of them in the dungeon, placing some on each of the two levels in the rooms and chambers desired. The remainder are unused.**

The following are brief explanations of the abbreviations used in the monster lists. **Name**—an asterisk (*) after a name indicates that a special weapon or attack form is needed to hit this monster, **(#)**—number appearing, this type of die

24

should be rolled to determine the number of monsters, **AC**—armor class, **HD**—hit dice, an asterisk (*) after hit dice means that the special abilities bonus should be added when calculating experience, **hp**—hit points, the number of hit points that each monster has, **#AT**—number of attacks, **D**—damage done by each attack given in ranges of hit points, **MV**—move of the monster in feet per turn (and feet per round), **Save**—the class and level at which the monster makes it saving throws, D = dwarf, F = fighter, NM = normal man, T = thief, **ML**—morale (optional, see page B27 of the D&D Basic rulebook).

MONSTERS

1. Orcs (1-4)—AC 6, HD 1, hp 5,4,3,2, #AT 1, D 1-6 or by wea-pon, MV 90' (30'), Save F1, ML 8

2. Troglodytes (1-2)—AC 5, HD 2*, hp 7,3, #AT 3, D 1-4/1-4/1-4, MV 120' (40'), Save F2, ML 9

3. Kobolds (2-9)—AC 7, HD ½, hp 4,4,3,3,3,3,2,2,1 #AT 1, D 1-4 or weapon -1, MV 90' (30'), Save NM, ML 6

4. Ghouls (1-2)—AC 6, HD 2*, hp 6,4, #AT 3, D 1-3 each + special, MV 90' (30'), Save F2, ML 9

5. Giant Centipedes (1-4)—AC 9, HD ½, hp 2,2, #AT 1, D poison, MV 60' (20'), Save NM, ML 8

6. Carrion Crawler (1)—AC 7, HD 3+1*, hp 6, #AT 8, D paralysis, MV120' (40'), Save F2, ML 9

7. Orcs (2-7)—AC 6, HD 1, hp 5,5,4,4,3,2,1, #AT 1, D 1-6 or by weapon, MV 90' (30'), Save F1, ML 8

8. Crab Spiders (1-2)—AC 7, HD 2*, hp 6,5, #AT 1, D 1-8 + poison, MV 120' (40'), Save F1, ML 7

9. Troglodytes (1-2)—AC 5, HD 2*, hp 10,4, #AT 3, D 1-4/1-4/1-4, MV 120' (40'), Save F2, ML 9

10. Black Widow Spider (1)—AC 6, HD 3*, hp 13, #AT 1, D 2-12 + poison, MV 60' (20'), in web 120' (40'), Save F2, ML 8

11. Stirges (2-5)—AC 7, HD 1*, hp 4,4,3,2,2, #AT 1, D 1-3, MV 30' (10'), flying 180' (60'), Save F2, ML 9

12. Gnolls (1-4)—AC 5, HD 2, hp 13,7,6,3, #AT 1, D 2-8 or by weapon +1, MV 90' (30'), Save F2, ML 8

13. Shriekers (1-4)—AC 7, HD 3, hp 14,10,10,8 #AT special, D nil, MV 9' (3'), Save F1, ML 12

14. Skeletons (1-6)—AC 7, HD 1, hp 4,4,3,3,2,1, #AT 1, D 1-6 or weapon, MV 60' (20'), Save F1, ML 12

15. Hobgoblins (2-5)—C 6, HD 1+1, hp 9,8,6,4,3, #AT 1, D 1-8 or by weapon, MV 90' (30'), Save F1, ML 8

16. Goblins (1-8)—AC 6, HD 1-1, hp 7,5,4,3,3,3,2,1, #AT 1, D 1-6 or by weapon, MV 90' (30'), Save NM, ML 7

17. Giant Rats (2-7)—AC 7, HD ½, hp 4,3,3,2,2,1,1, #AT 1, D 1-3 + disease, MV 120' (40'), swimming 60' (20'), Save NM, ML 8

18. Zombies (1-2)—AC 8, HD 2, hp 10,7, #AT 1, D 1-8 or by weapon, MV 60' (20'), Save F1, ML 12

19. Kobolds (2-5)—AC 7, HD ½, hp 4,4,4,2,1, #AT 1, D 1-4 or weapon -1, MV 90' (30'), Save NM, ML 6

20. Bandits (1-4)—AC 6, HD 1, hp 7,5,4,2, #AT 1, D 1-6 or by weapon, MV 90' (30'), Save T1, ML 8

21. Ochre Jelly* (1)—AC 8, HD 5*, hp 16, #AT 1, D 2-12, MV 30' (10'), Save F3, ML 12

22. Gnomes (2-5)—AC 5, HD 1, hp 7,5,4,2,1, #AT 1, D 1-6 or by weapon, MV 60' (20'), Save D1, ML 8

23. Orcs (2-7)—AC 6, HD 1, hp 8,6,5,4,4,2,2, #AT 1, D 1-6 or by weapon, MV 90' (30'), Save F1, ML 8

24. Crab Spiders (1) AC 7, HD 2*, hp 7, #AT 1, D 1-8 + poison, MV 120' (40'), save F1, ML 7

25. Goblins (1-1)—AC 6, HD 1-1, hp 6,5,5,4,3,2, #AT 1, D 1-6 or by weapon, MV 90' (30'), Save NM, ML 7

TREASURE LIST

Listed below are 34 different treasures, each letter-coded for easy reference.

Considering their very nature, treasures, in most instances, should be concealed or hidden cleverly. The Dungeon Master should use his or her imagination in devising ways to hide items from discovery. Some suggestions for treasure location might be: Inside an ordinary item in plain view, within a secret compartment in a container, disguised to appear as something else, under or behind a loose stone in the floor or wall, under a heap of trash or dung, or similarly hidden. Occasionally a treasure may be easily noticed, but this should be the exception rather than the rule.

In some instances, valuable treasure will be protected by locks, traps, or protective magic. The more deadly protections are reserved for more experienced adventurers, so any such devices will be uncommon in dungeons designed for beginning players, such as this one. The DM should feel free to create an occasional protection which may confuse or delay characters attempting to find a particular treasure, however.

Remember that all coin values are based on a gold piece (g.p.) standard, with equivalent values being: 100 copper pieces (c.p.) = 10 silver pieces (s.p.) = 2 electrum pieces (e.p.) = 1 gold piece (g.p.) = 1/5 platinum piece (p.p.). All coin weights and sizes are approximately equal.

A) Leather pouch with 10 e.p.

B) 15 g.p.

C) 28 g.p.

D) Small wooden box with 35 g.p.

E) Dagger with jeweled handle (2—50 g.p. gems, onyx)

F) 20 s.p.

G) 8—10 g.p. gems (agate)

H) **Mace +1**

I) False map (shows room and adjacent corridor in detail; nothing else is accurate)

J) **Spear +2**

K) 120 g.p.

L) Silver medallion on chain worth 500 s.p.

M) 100 g.p. gem (pearl)

N) 2450 c.p.

O) Onyx statue worth 200 g.p.

P) 820 s.p.

Q) 4—100 g.p. gems (garnets)

R) 620 g.p. in locked chest

S) Scroll of 2 Spells (Cleric): 2 **cure light wounds** (or roll at random for determination)

T) False **magic wand** (finely detailed; radiates magic but has no other magical properties)

U) **Bag of devouring**

V) 500 g.p. gem (peridot)

W) **Shield +1**

X Bronze statuette, inlaid with silver and copper, worth 115 g.p.

Y) Silver mirror of exceptional quality, 90 g.p. value

Z) **Chainmail +1**

AA) Gold ring (non-magical) worth 10 g.p.

BB) Scroll of 1 Spell (Magic-User): **sleep** (or roll at random for determination)

CC) Silver bracelet worth 80 s.p.

DD) 840 c.p., 290 s.p., 120 e.p., 25 g.p. in locked chest

EE) **Ring of protection +1**

FF) 4 small gold rods, each worth 30 g.p.

GG) Crystal goblet worth 15 g.p. (engraved with the word "Quasqueton")

HH) Potion: **invisibility** (2 doses, each with a duration of 2 hours)

Special note: Even though 34 treasures are listed here, only between 15 to 25 of them should actually be placed in the dungeon by the Dungeon Master. The remainder should go unused. When treasures are chosen and placed, a good assortment of items should be represented: some very valuable, some worthless, most in between. The letter type treasures listed under the monster specifications in the D&D Basic booklet are ignored in this module, as the above treasure list replaces them and monsters encountered will possess or guard the appropriate treasure assigned by the referee's listings.

THE CHARACTER LISTS

The character lists are designed for multi-purpose use. First of all, they can be used by players to select a player character if they choose to do so rather than roll up abilities of their own. And secondly, they can be used as non-player charac-

ters in the position of retainers. In either case, certain dice rolls will be made to determine various particulars about each character. There are separate lists of 12 characters each. The guidelines below explain how to use the lists depending upon desired applications.

Selecting A Player Character From The Character Lists

If a player prefers to choose a character from the lists rather than roll one up, he or she first determines the class of character he or she wishes to play. The player then examines the list of character names and races which appears on the back side of the "Players' Background Sheet," and either chooses one or rolls a 12-sided die to determine which one will be used. In any event the choice is made without knowing further details about the character's exact ability ratings, which will be given to the player by the Dungeon Master once the decision is made. The ability ratings are fixed, and may not be adjusted.

Once a player has gotten a character in this manner, he or she records the ability ratings and selects the character's alignment (lawful, chaotic or neutral, with law or neutrality prevailing in this module setting). The player then determines wealth owned, purchases equipment, determines hit points, and chooses spells as normally. All characters will begin at first level of experience.

Using The Character Lists For Retainers or NPC's

Players about to embark on an adventure might well wish to have additional assistance on the part of other fellow explorers, and these other adventurers are non-player characters who will serve either for pay (as hirelings) or out of respect and loyalty (as henchmen).

Non-player characters, although not always plentiful, are nonetheless easier to find than retainers. They will serve for a fee, as well as a cut of any treasure gained—their exact price to be determined by the DM, who then interacts with the players if any bargaining is necessary, taking the part of the non-player character.

Retainers are usually characters who will be willing to serve a particular character out of admiration or respect without special regard for compensation. In any case, with only 1st level characters, players cannot expect to attract retainers until they have accomplished enough to gain a bit of reputation and notice. Thus, any non-player character gained for an adventure will have only a 20% chance of being a retainer. (Of course, this fact is not crucial to the immediate adventure, but may bear upon future considerations . . .) Note that no retainer will serve a character of lower level.

The number of non-player characters available to a party of player characters is determined by consulting the table below, and by appropriate dice rolls as noted. The number of NPC's available depends upon the number of player characters in the party—the more player characters participating, the fewer NPC's available.

AVAILABILITY OF NON-PLAYER CHARACTERS

Player Characters	Chance for Non-Player Characters & Number Available
2	100% chance of 1-4
3	75% chance of 1-3
4	50% chance of 1-2
5	25% chance of 1
6 or more	None

Once a party of players has determined that one or more non-player characters will be willing to join their adventuring group (dependent upon the financial arrangements being finalized), a 12-sided die is rolled for each NPC to determine their character class based on the following table:

CHARACTER CLASSES OF HENCHMEN/ HIRELINGS

1 Fighter*
2 Fighter*
3 Fighter*
4 Cleric
5 Cleric
6 Thief
7 Thief
8 Magic-user**
9 Magic-user**
10 Any class desired
11 Any class desired
12 Any class desired

*Also Dwarves and Halflings
**Also Elves

Example: Three player characters—a magic-user, fighting man, and thief—wish to bolster the strength of their adventuring band by having others join the group. They have a 75% chance of locating 1-3 intrested non-player characters who will listen to their offer and, if reasonable, likely be agreeable to joining the party for at least a single adventure. If they fail to locate any willing non-player characters, they will be forced to adventure without them, at least initially.

Once a class for each non-player character has been determined (this can be done prior to any terms being offered by the player characters), a 12-sided die should be rolled on the specific table corresponding to that type of character class to determine the individual character's name and race (although his or her other ability ratings will not be known by the players until he or she actually joins their group. If the arrangement is finalized, the DM gives the players specifics on the non-player character's abilities, as well as other pertinent details) which are described following each character list depending upon the particular class). The alignment of any non-player character will generally be compatible with the rest of the group, although there is a slight (10%) chance that a non-player character will be chaotic while professing otherwise, thus seeking to hoodwink the party and perhaps take advantage of them when the opportunity arises.

Non-player characters will carry no wealth other than 1-6 gold pieces for incidental expenses. In most cases, they will carry their own weapon and/or armor. However, player characters may purchase additional equipment, arms, or armor for them to use while adventuring—either as a loan or an outright gift—or even give them their own. Attention must be paid to character class restrictions in this regard, however.

Important: non-player characters may vary widely in personality. The Dungeon Master plays their part to a great degree, although the players indicate what instructions or orders they are giving to the non- player characters during the course of the adventure. The DM can choose any personality he wants for a non-player character, or can determine the various aspects by rolling for the categories of attitude, disposition, courage, and loyalty on the following chart. Players are never informed of the exact personalities of non-player characters: they will discover them through interaction with the characters (as portrayed by the DM) and by observing them in the course of the adventure.

NON-PLAYER CHARACTER PERSONALITY

Attitude		Courage	
1	Helpful/cooperative	1	Reckless/daring
2	Helpful/cooperative	2	Courageous
3	Helpful/cooprative	3	Normal
4	Apathetic/lazy	4	Normal
5	Unreliable	5	Hesitant
6	Obstinate/ argumentative/ domineering	6	Cowardly

Disposition		Loyalty	
1	Greedy/selfish	1	Loyal
2	Normal	2	Loyal
3	Normal	3	Normal
4	Normal	4	Normal
5	Normal	5	Fickle
6	Unselfish	6	Fickle

CREDITS

DESIGN . . . . Mike Carr

DEVELOPMENT . . . . Mike Carr

EDITING . . . . Allen Hammack
Timothy Jones

SECOND EDITION . . . . Patrick L. Price
Edward G. Sollers
Stephen D. Sullivan

LAYOUT . . . . Mike Carr
Stephen D. Sullivan

COVERS . . . . Darlene Pekul

ART . . . . David C. Sutherland III
David A. Trampier

27

CLERICS

1. Farned of the Great Church
   Str 7, Int 10, Wis 14, Con 9, Dex 14, Cha 9

2. Dohram, Servant of Saint Carmichael
   Str 10, Int 10, Wis 14, Con 10, Dex 11, Cha 12

3. The Mystical One
   Str 12, Int 10, Wis 15, Con 15, Dex 8, Cha 14

4. Mulgar the Merciful
   Str 10, Int 10, Wis 18, Con 8, Dex 12, Cha 17

5. Seeful the Unforgiving
   Str 6, Int 8, Wis 12, Con 12, Dex 11, Cha 10

6. Philgo
   Str 9, Int 10, Wis 13, Con 9, Dex 7, Cha 12

7. Tassit, Servant of Saint Cuthbert
   Str 11, Int 9, Wis 12, Con 10, Dex 7, Cha 11

8. Wilberd the Silent
   Str 13, Int 8, Wis 17, Con 12, Dex 9, Cha 10

9. Kracky the Hooded One
   Str 8, Int 14, Wis 16, Con 8, Dex 8, Cha 12

10. Grampal of the Secret Church
    Str 12, Int 11, Wis 12, Con 10, Dex 9, Cha 10

11. Nupo, Servant of The Bringer
    Str 10, Int 7, Wis 15, Con 17, Dex 10, Cha 8

12. Eggo of the Holy Brotherhood
    Str 7, Int 10, Wis 13, Con 8, Dex 9, Cha 11

Non-player clerics will usualy possess holy water as a matter of course, as well as a single non-edged weapon. A 6-sided die can be rolled once for each category shown below to determine the arms and armor of any non-player cleric:

Arms		Armor	
1	Club	1	None
2	Club	2	Leather armor
3	Hammer	3	Leather armor
4	Hammer	4	Leather and shield
5	Flail	5	Chainmail
6	Mace	6	Chainmail and shield

All non-player clerics are of first level and use one 6-sided die to determine hit points, except for an independent NPC (one joining the adventure on his or her own rather than out of loyalty or for a fee other than a treasure share). An independent NPC cleric will be of either first, second, or third level depending upon a roll on the table which follows:

	Level	Hit Dice	Spells Known
1	First	1d6	None
2	First	1d6	None
3	Second	2d6	Use table C, one roll
4	Second	2d6	Use table C, one roll
5	Third	3d6	Use table C, two rolls
6	Third	3d6	Use table C, two rolls

Table C below is used to determine randomly which spell or spells any non-player cleric knows. First level clerics have no spell ability. Player character clerics do not utilize this table; they choose which spells they wish to use according to the guidelines in the D&D Basic booklet.

Table C

1	Cure Light Wounds
2	Cure Light Wounds
3	Cure Light Wounds
4	Detect Evil
5	Detect Magic
6	Detect Magic
7	Light
8	Light
9	Protection from Evil
10	Purify Food and Water
11	Remove Fear
12	Resist Cold

FIGHTERS, DWARVES & HALFLINGS

1. Brandon (Human)
   Str 14, Int 8, Wis 11, Con 13, Dex 9, Cha 12

2. Evro (Human)
   Str 14, Int 13, Wis 7, Con 12, Dex 11, Cha 9

3. Glendor the Fourth (Human)
   Str 17, Int 10, Wis 9, Con 14, Dex 9, Cha 14

4. Zeffan (Dwarf)
   Str 14, Int 11, Wis 8, Con 8, Dex 14, Cha 7

5. Alho Rengate (Human)
   Str 12, Int 10, Wis 9, Con 11, Dex 12, Cha 12

6. Krago of the Mountains (Dwarf)
   Str 18/54, Int 9, Wis 15, Con 16, Dex 9, Cha 14

7. Pendor (Halfling)
   Str 12, Int 9, Wis 8, Con 10, Dex 6, Cha 10

8. Mohag the Wanderer (Human)
   Str 13, Int 12, Wis 9, Con 10, Dex 6, Cha 10

9. Norrin the Barbarian (Human)
   Str 15, Int 8, Wis 10, Con 14, Dex 9, Cha 9

10. Lefto (Halfling)
    Str 11, Int 10, Wis 11, Con 18, Dex 8, Cha 10

11. Webberan of the Great North (Human)
    Str 16, Int 10, Wis 13, Con 10, Dex 7, Cha 7

12. Sho-Rembo (Halfling)
    Str 9, Int 11, Wis 9, Con 18, Dex 9, Cha 15

To determine arms and armor for non-player fighters, halflings, dwarves or elves, roll once on each end of the tables below with a 12-sided die:

Arms		Armor	
1	Dagger and hand axe	1	Shield only
2	Dagger and sword	2	Leather armor
3	Hand axe	3	Leather and shield
4	Mace	4	Leather and shield
5	Sword	5	Leather and shield
6	Sword	6	Leather and shield +1
7	Sword +1	7	Chainmail
8	Pole arm	8	Chainmail
9	Pole arm	9	Chainmail and shield +1
10	Morning star	10	Chainmail and shield +1
11	Flail	11	Plate mail
12	Short bow and 12 arrows	12	Plate mail and shield

28

All non-player fighters, dwarves and halflings are of first level and use one 8-sided die (or d6 for halflings) to determine hit points, except for an independent NPC (one joining the adventure on his or her own rather than out of loyalty or for a fee other than a treasure share). An independent NPC will be of either first, second, or third level depending upon a roll on the following table:

	Level	Fighters' & Dwarves' Hit Dice	Halflings' Hit Dice
1	First	1d8	1d6
2	First	1d8	1d6
3	Second	2d8	2d6
4	Second	2d8	2d6
5	Third	3d8	3d6
6	Third	3d8	3d6

MAGIC USERS & ELVES

1. Presto (Elf)
   STR 9, Int 17, Wis 11, Con 14, Dex 11, Cha 14

2. Mezlo (Elf)
   Str 11, Int 14, Wis 8, Con 9, Dex 12, Cha 13

3. Nickar (Human)
   Str 11, Int 15, Wis 8, Con 12, Dex 5, Cha 13

4. Shobaffum (Human)
   Str 7, Int 13, Wis 9, Con 13, Dex 11, Cha 10

5. Yor (Human)
   Str 11, Int 14, Wis 8, Con 12, Dex 5, Cha 13

6. Ralt Gaither (Human)
   Str 11, Int 18, Wis 7, Con 9, Dex 14, Cha 10

7. Fencig (Elf)
   Str 8, Int 17, Wis 10, Con 5, Dex 11, Cha 9

8. Glom the Mighty (Human)
   Str 12, Int 15, Wis 15, Con 7, Dex 10, Cha 11

9. Trebbelos, Boy Magician (Human)
   Str 9, Int 16, Wis 9, Con 7, Dex 12, Cha 13

10. Beska Miltar (Human)
    Str 10, Int 13, Wis 12, Con 15, Dex 8, Cha 14

11. Lappoy the Unexpected (Elf)
    Str 11, Int 14, Wis 9, Con 10, Dex 7, Cha 9

12. Surfal (Human)
    Str 12, Int 14, Wis 11, Con 8, Dex 12, Cha 5

Non-player magic-users will wear no armor and generally will be armed with nothing other than a dagger. All non-player magic users are of first level and use one 4-sided die to determine hit points, except for an independent NPC (one joining the adventure on his or her own rather than out of loyalty or for a fee other than a treasure share). An independent NPC magic-user will be of either first, second, or third level depending upon a roll on the table which follows:

Level		Magic-Users' Hit Dice	Elves' Hit Dice	Spells Known
1	First	1d4	1d6	Use table A, one roll
2	First	1d4	1d6	Use table A, one roll
3	Second	2d4	2d6	Use table A, two rolls
4	Second	2d4	2d6	Use table A, two rolls
5	Third	3d4	3d6	Use table A, two rolls and Table B, one roll
6	Third	3d4	3d6	Use table A, two rolls and Table B, one roll

Non-player elves are determined as above but use the fighters' arms and armor tables to determine equipment.

Tables A and B below are used to determine randomly which spell or spells any non-player magic-user or elf knows. All first level magic-users and elves make but a single roll on Table A. Player character magic-users and elves do not utilize this table; they check which spells they can know according to the guidelines in the D&D Basic booklet.

	Table A	Table B
1	Charm Person	Continual Light
2	Charm Person	Continual Light
3	Charm Person	Detect Evil
4	Detect Magic	Detect Invisible
5	Detect Magic	ESP
6	Floating Disc	ESP
7	Hold Portal	Invisibility
8	Light	Invisibility
9	Light	Knock
10	Magic Missile	Knock
11	Magic Missile	Levitate
12	Protection from Evil	Levitate
13	Read Languages	Locate Object
14	Read Magic	Magic Mouth
15	Shield	Mirror Image
16	Shield	Mirror Image
17	Sleep	Phantasmal Forces
18	Sleep	Web
19	Sleep	Web
20	Ventriloquism	Wizard Lock

29

THIEVES

1. Luven Lightfinger
   Str 13, Int 14, Wis 9, Con 12, Dex 16, Cha 13

2. Treddo
   Str 10, Int 9, Wis 7, Con 11, Dex 17, Cha 14

3. Bozomus
   Str 5, Int 9, Wis 12, Cn 6, Dex 13, Cha 12

4. Estra Zo
   Str 12, Int 12, Wis 11, Con 7, Dex 16, Cha 12

5. Laggamundo
   Str 11, Int 10, Wis 9, Con 13, Dex 13, Cha 6

6. Feggener the Quick
   Str 10, Int 9, Wis 7, Con 11, Dex 17, Cha 14

7. Mezron
   Str 5, Int 9, Wis 12, Con 6, Dex 13, Cha 12

8. Drebb
   Str 7, Int 12, Wis 10, Con 11, Dex 12, Cha 11

9. Postue
   Str 10, Int 8, Wis 7, con 10, Dex 18, Cha 12

10. Harg of the City Afar
    Str 9, Int 13, Wis 10, Con 6, Dex 15, Cha 8

11. Afton Borr
    Str 11, Int 11, Wis 8, Con 10, Dex 13, Cha 9

12. Sporragha
    Str 10, Int 7, Wis 11, Con 14, Dex 12, Cha 18

To determine the arms and armor of any non-player thieves, roll a 6-sided die once on each of the following tables:

	Arms		Armor
1	None	1	None
2	None	2	None
3	Dagger	3	Leather armor
4	Dagger	4	Leather armor
5	Dagger	5	Leather armor
6	Dagger +1	6	Leather armor +1

All non-player thieves are of first level and use one 4-sided die to determine hit points, except for an independent NPC (one joining the adventure on his or her own rather than out of loyalty or for a fee other than a treasure share). An independent NPC will be of either first, second, or third level depending upon a roll on the following table:

	Level	Hit Dice	Thief Ability Category
1	First (Apprentice)	1d4	1
2	First (Apprentice)	1d4	1
3	Second (Footpad)	2d4	2
4	Second (Footpad)	2d4	2
5	Third (Robber)	3d4	3
6	Third (Robber)	3d4	3

30

PLAYERS' BACKGROUND SHEET

Here is the standard background setting for all players to read prior to their first adventure:

Rogahn the Fearless and Zelligar the Unknown are legendary names. Even you, a young fledgling in a town far from the great cities of your world, know of their reputation—even though their tale begins long before you were born. The elders and the sages speak both names with respect, even awe, in a distant admiration for the memories of the two legendary figures . . .

You have heard parts of the story before, but never enough to know all of it, or even what is true and what is only legend or speculation. But it is a great and fascinating beginning in your own quest to learn more.

Rogahn the Fearless earned his name as a great warrior, and his reputation spread far and wide across the land. Zelligar the Unknown, equally renowned, earned his respected status and power as a foremost practitioner of the mystical arts of magic and sorcery.

and decisively turned back the invasion. Rogahn slew a horde of barbarians single-handedly and Zelligar's powerful magic put their army to fight. It was a great victory, and a grateful populace rewarded the pair and their consorts with considerable treasure. After that, the two heroes returned to their mystical hideaway, and rumor has it that the spoils of victory were spent to further its construction, although some of it may yet be hidden somewhere.

The most exciting portions of the legend are the most recent. Some years ago, perhaps in the decade before you were born, Rogahn and Zelligar apparently decided upon a joint foray into the lands of the hated barbarians. Taking most of their henchmen and associates along with them in a great armed band, the two personages, it seems, disappeared into the forbidding alien lands to the north on a great adventure which some say may have been asked by the very gods themselves.

No one knows what occurrences or coincidence brought these two men together, but tales tell of their meeting and forming a strong bond of friendship, a union that would last for the ages. As this occurred, legend has it, the two men virtually disappeared from the view of civilization. Stories occasionally surfaced about a rumored hideaway being built deep in the wilderness, far from the nearest settlement, away from traveled routes, and high upon a craggy hill—but no one seemed to know any more than that, or where this supposed hideaway really was located, if indeed it was. No one knows for sure, but some say their motive was to pursue the common goals of personal greed and some kind of vague (or chaotic) evil. In any case, they jointly led a hermit life with but a few occasional forays into the outside world to add to their own reputations.

Many years passed, until one day a great barbarian invasion came from the lands to the north, threatening to engulf the entire land with the savage excesses of the unchecked alien horde. Just when things seemed the darkest, Rogahn the Fearless and Zelligar the Unknown made their unexpected yet most welcome reappearance. Joining their powerful forces, they and their band of loyal henchmen met the barbarian army in a great battle at a narrow pass in the hills,

Word just reaching civilization tells of some great battle in the barbarian lands where the legendary Rogahn and Zelligar have met their demise. This rumored clash must have occurred some years ago, and there are few details—and no substantiation of the story. The only thing certain is that, if all this is true, Rogahn and Zelligar have been gone far too long . . . if only one had the knowledge and wherewithal to find their hideaway, he or she would have great things to explore!

Now, just recently, came the most promising bit of information—a crude map purporting to show the way to the hideaway of the two men, a place apparently called "Q." You or one of your acquaintances has this map, and if it is accurate, it could perhaps lead you to the mystical place that was their home and sanctuary. Who knows what riches of wealth and magic might be there for the taking??? Yes, the risk is great, but the challenge cannot be ignored. Gathering a few of your fellows, you share the secret and embark on an adventure in search of the unknown . . .

Note: Individual players may know of additional information in the form of rumors or legends as given to them by the Dungeon Master.

31

PLAYERS' LIST OF POTENTIAL CHARACTERS

Listed here are 12 characters of each of the four character classes, showing name and race. The Dungeon Master has a more complete listing of each character's ability scores and other information.

Clerics

1. Farned of the Great Church
2. Dohram, Servant of Saint Carmichael
3. The Mystical One
4. Mulgar the Merciful
5. Seeful the Unforgiving
6. Philgo
7. Tassit, Servant of Saint Cuthbert
8. Wilberd the Silent
9. Kracky the Hooded One
10. Grampal of the Secret Church
11. Nupo, Servant of The Bringer
12. Eggo of the Holy Brotherhood

Fighters, Dwarves & Halflings

1. Brandon (Human)
2. Evro (Human)
3. Glendor the Fourth (Human)
4. Zeffan (Dwarf)
5. Alho Rengate (Human)
6. Krago of the Mountains (Dwarf)
7. Pendor (Halfling)
8. Mohag the Wanderer
9. Norrin the Barbarian
10. Lefto (Hafling)
11. Webberan of the Great North (Human)
12. Sho-Rembo (Halfling)

Magic-Users & Elves

1. Presto (Elf)
2. Mezlo (Elf)
3. Nickar (Human)
4. Shobaffum (Human)
5. Yor (Human)
6. Ralt Gaither (Human)
7. Fencig (Elf)
8. Glom the Mighty (Human)
9. Trebbelos, Boy Magician (Human)
10. Beska Miltar (Human)
11. Lappoy the Unexpected (Elf)
12. Surfal (Human)

Thieves

1. Luven Lightfinger
2. Treddo
3. Bozomus
4. Estra Zo
5. Laggamundo
6. Feggener the Quick
7. Mezron
8. Drebb
9. Postue
10. Harg of the City Afar
11. Afton Borr
12. Sporragha

Your Dungeon Master has a complete list of guidelines for the use of these lists; they appear for your reference only.

TIPS FOR PLAYERS

Beginning players would do well to profit from some basic advice before beginning their D&D careers, and with that in mind, the following points are offered for consideration:

1) Be an organized player. Keep accurate records on your character (experience, abilities, items possessed, etc.) for your own purposes and to aid the Dungeon Master.

2) Always keep in mind that the Dungeon Master is the moderator of the game, and as such, deserves the continued cooperation, consideration and respect of all the players. If you disagree with him or her, present your viewpoint with deference to the DM's position as game judge, but be prepared to accept his or her decision as final—after all, keep in mind that you may not know all aspects of the overall game situation, and in that case, not everything will always go your way!

3) Cooperate with your fellow players and work together when adventuring. Remember that on any foray into the dungeon or wilderness, a mix of character classes will be beneficial, since the special abilities of the various characters will complement each other and add to the overall effectiveness of the party.

4) Be neither too hasty nor too sluggish when adventuring. If you are too fast in your exploration, you may recklessly endanger yourself and your fellow adventurers and fall prone to every trick and trap you encounter. If you are too slow, you will waste valuable time and may be waylaid by more than your share of wandering monsters without accomplishing anything. As you gain playing experience you will learn the proper pace, but rely on your DM for guidance.

5) Avoid arguing. While disagreements about a course of action will certainly arise from time to time, players should quickly discuss their options and reach a consensus in order to proceed. Bickering in the dungeon will only create noise which may well attract wandering monsters. Above all, remember that this is just a game and a little consideration will go far toward avoiding any hard feelings . . .

6) Be on your guard. Don't be overly cautious, but be advised that some non-player characters may try to hoodwink you, players may doublecross you, and while adventuring, tricks and traps await the unwary. Of course, you won't avoid every such pitfall (dealing with the uncertainties is part of the fun and challenge of the game), but don't be surprised if everything is not always as it seems.

7) Treat any retainers or NPCs fairly. If you reward them generously and do not expose them to great risks of life and limb that your own character would not face, then you can expect a continuing loyalty (although there may be exceptions, of course).

8) Know your limits. Your party may not be a match for every monster you encounter, and occasionally it pays to know when and how to run away form danger. Likewise, a dungeon adventure may have to be cut short if your party suffers great adversity and/or depleted strength. Many times it will take more than one adventure to accomplish certain goals, and it will thus be necessary to come back out of a dungeon to heal wounds, restore magical abilities and spells, and reinforce a party's strength.

9) Use your head. Many of the characters' goals in the game can be accomplished through the strength of arms or magic. Others, however, demand common sense and shrewd judgment as well as logical deduction. The most successful players are those who can effectively use both aspects of the game to advantage.

10) The fun of a D&D game comes in playing your character's role. Take on your character's persona and immerse yourself in the game setting, enjoying the fantasy element and the interaction with your fellow players and the Dungeon Master.

Enjoy yourself, and good luck!

LOWER LEVEL

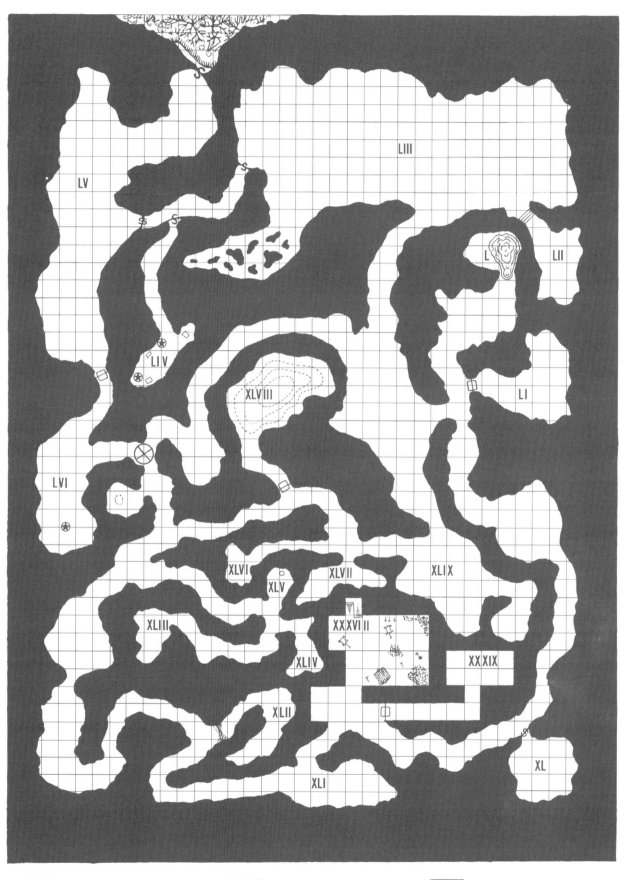

LIII

LV

L

LII

LIV

LI

XLVIII

LVI

XLVI

XLVII

XLIX

XLV

XXXVIII

XLIII

XXXIX

XLIV

XLII

XL

XLI

 POOL

 DEPRESSION

 WEBS

This item is only one of the many popular playing aids for DUNGEONS & DRAGONS Fantasy Adventure Game produced by TSR Hobbies, Inc. Other playing aids for the D&D game system currently include:

DUNGEONS & DRAGONS Basic Set (contains everything DMs and players need to get started, detailing character creation, spells, and dungeon levels 1-3)

DUNGEONS & DRAGONS Expert Set (designed to be used *with* the Basic Set, the Expert Set covers higher-level characters, deeper dungeon levels, and adventure in wilderness areas)

Dungeon Module B1 (In search of the Unknown)

Dungeon Module B2 (The Keep on the Boarderlands)

Dungeon Module X1 (the Isle of Dread)

Monster and Treasure Assortment, Sets One to Three: Levels One through Nine (makes the job of stocking dungeon levels easy)

Dungeon Geomorphs (allows the DM to create thousands of different dungeon levels by arranging the geomorphs in different combinations)

D&D Player Character Record Sheets (allows players to record all important information about their characters in an easy-to-use formet)

Other releases of additional items relating to the D&D game system are planned for the future. TSR Hobbies publishes a complete line of games, playing aids, and gaming accessories available from better hobby, game, and department stores nationwide. If you desire a complete catalog write to: TSR Hobbies, Inc., POB 756, Lake Geneva, WI 53147.

116-F-9023
ISBN 0-935696-04-0

394-51572-2TSR0550

CHAPTER THREE
Stocked Examples of B1 Dungeon

B1: In Search of the Unknown is unusual among early TSR adventures in that the rooms lack monsters and treasure. They are not yet "stocked," so to speak. This was an intentional design feature, which Mike Carr adopted to allow the neophyte Dungeon Master a "guided opportunity" to populate his first dungeon. For this reprint edition, we have asked Chris Doyle, Michael Curtis and Tim Wadzinski to provide their own "stocked" versions of B1. Every DM has their own approach to populating a dungeon, and you'll see those examples in the interpretations of B1 that follow!

Stocked Example of B1, Version A

by Chris Doyle

Author's Note: By modern standards, it might appear that the original *B1: In Search of the Unknown* was sparsely populated with monsters to battle. This was the intention, because back in the day, exploration was just as big a part of a D&D session as battling marauding humanoids, or twisted aberrations. Fifth edition brought this old-school mentality full circle with the concept of the *Three Pillars of Adventure*. The Pillars are defined as Exploration, Social Interaction, and (of course) Combat. So even this modern paradigm features about one third exploration and another one third combat. These two Pillars are often explicitly detailed in the key of the dungeon. Meanwhile, the Social Interaction Pillar is left to the players to provide, although its often cultivated by the Dungeon Master. Remember, it's not always about combat in the dungeon. There is always another locked door, concealed secret door, a false bottom in a chest, or a mysterious room of pools.

UPPER LEVEL

1.	Alcoves	Goblins (5)-AC 6, MV 6", HD 1-1, hp 7,6,5,5,3, #AT 1, D 1-6 or by weapon
The goblins are rifling through the belongings of the bodies at the end of the hall.		
Treasure: The goblins carry 15 gp among themselves.		

2.	Kitchen	Monster: None
Treasure: None		

3.	Dining Room	Giant Centipedes (4)-AC 9, MV 15", HD 1/4, hp 2,2,1,1, #AT 1, D poison
The centipedes have a nest in a pile of wood debris that was once several chairs.		
Treasure: None		

4.	Lounge	Monster: None
Treasure: None		

5.	Wizard's Chamber	Monster: None
Locked inside the nightstand drawer is a **false magic wand**. It radiates magic but has no other magical properties.		

6.	Closet	Monster: None
Treasure: None		

7.	**Wizard's Annex**	Monster: None

Treasure: None

8.	**Wizard's Workroom**	**Ghouls (2)**-AC 6, MV 9", HD 2, hp 10,8, #AT 3, D 1-3/1-3/1-6 + paralysis

The ghouls appear to be manacled to the tables, but this is but a ruse.

Treasure: Hidden in the jar of wood chips are 8 agates worth 10 gp each.

9.	**Wizard's Laboratory**	Monster: None

Treasure: None

10.	**Storeroom**	Monster: None

Treasure: None

11.	**Supply Room**	Monster: None

Treasure: None

12.	**Library**	**Goblins (4)**-AC 6, MV 6", HD 1-1, hp 6,6,5,2, #AT 1, D 1-6 or by weapon

These goblins can't read, but they can throw books at each other.

A false map is tucked into one of the books.

13.	**Implement Room**	**Goblins (6)**-AC 6, MV 6", HD 1-1, hp 6,5,5,4,4,2, #AT 1, D 1-6 or by weapon

These six goblins are sleeping on bedrolls.

The leader carries a pouch with 10 ep.

14.	**Auxiliary Room**	Monster: None

Treasure: None

15.	**Teleportation Room**	Monster: None

Treasure: None

16.	Teleportation Room	Monster: None

Treasure: None

17.	**Char Storage Cellar**	Monster: None

Treasure: None

| **18.** | **Smithy** | **Skeletons (5)**-AC 5, MV 12", HD 1, hp 4,4,3,3,3, #AT 1 D 1-8 |

These undead were smith assistants, but now have donned chain mail and armed themselves with longswords to defend the smithy.

One of the longswords wielded by a skeleton has a 500 gp peridot mounted in the pommel.

| **19.** | **Access Room** | **Crab Spiders (2)**-AC 7, MV 12", HD 2, hp 10,6, #AT 1, D 1-8 + poison |

One of the crab spiders hides in the pile of lumber, while the second hides down the access shaft to the lower level.

Treasure: None

| **20.** | **Dead End Room** | Monster: None |

Treasure: None

| **21.** | **Meeting Room** | **Goblins (8)**-AC 6, MV 6", HD 1-1, hp 6,6,5,4,3,2,2,1 #AT 1, D 1-6 or by weapon |

One goblin (1 hp) is on the stage wearing a scholarly cloak addressing his fellow goblins, while they pelt him with rotten fruit and vegetables.

The largest goblin carries a sack with worthless junk and 28 gp.

| **22.** | **Garden Room** | **Carrion Crawler (1)**-AC 3/7, MV 12", HD 3+1, hp 16, #AT 8, D paralysis |

A carrion crawler, itself covered with fungal growth, hides on the ceiling to attack via dangling.

A sack containing 820 sp is buried under the fungal growth in the northern pit.

| **23.** | **Storage Room** | Monster: None |

Treasure: None

| **24.** | **Mistress' Chamber** | Monster: None |

A gold ring (non-magical) worth 50 gp lies discarded under the bed.

| **25.** | **Rogahn's Chamber** | Monster: None |

Treasure: None

| **26.** | **Trophy Room** | **Goblins (2)**-AC 6, MV 6", HD 1-1, hp 7,5, #AT 1, D 1-6 or by weapon |

These goblins are ransacking the trophy room.

A suit of **chain mail +1** hangs on a rack.

| **27.** | **Throne Room** | **Goblins (8)**-AC 6, MV 6", HD 1-1, hp 7,6,5,4,4,4,4,2, #AT 1, D 1-6 or by weapon |

The band of goblins exploring the ruins are based in this chamber.

Under a few tapestries is a locked chest with 840 cp, 290 sp, 120 ep, and 25 gp.

| **28.** | **Worship Area** | **Zombies (2)**-AC 8, MV 6", HD 2, hp 10,7, #AT 1, D 1-8 or by weapon |

The zombies wear black clerical vestments and perpetually worship the idol.

Treasure: One of the zombies wields a **mace +1**.

29.	Captain's Chamber	Monster: None
Treasure: None		

30.	Access Room	Monster: None
Treasure: None		

31.	Room of Pools	Monster: None
Treasure: None		

32.	Advisor's Chamber	Monster: None
Treasure: None		

33.	Barracks	Orcs (6)-AC 6, MV 9", HD 1, hp 6,6,5,5,4,3, #AT 1, D 1-8 or by weapon
This orc pack is exploring this level from the lower level.		
Treasure: None		

34.	Armory	Monster: None
Treasure: None		

35.	Guest Chamber	Monster: None
Treasure: None		

36.	Utility Room	Monster: None
Treasure: None		

37.	Recreation Room	Giant Centipedes (3)-AC 9, MV 16", HD 1/4, hp 2,2,1, #AT 1, D poison
The giant centipedes infest the pile of woven mats.		
Treasure: None		

38.	Access Room	Monster: None

Treasure: None

39.	Museum	Monster: None

Treasure: None

40.	Secret Cavern	Skeletons (6)-AC 7, MV 12", HD 1, hp 6,4,4,3,3,3, #AT 1 D 1-6

These skeletal guards stand at attention awaiting orders that never came.

Treasure: None

41.	Cavern	Monster: None

Treasure: None

42.	Webbed Cavern	Black Widow Spider (1)-AC 6, MV 6"*12", HD 3, hp 13, #AT 1, D 2-12 + poison

A giant black widow spider hides in this web-filled cave.

The husk of an orc with 20 sp in his pouch dangles from the ceiling.

43.	Cavern	Crab Spider (1)-AC 7, MV 12", HD 2, hp 11, #AT 1, D 1-8 + poison

A crab spider lurks on the ceiling just above the entrance to this chamber.

Treasure: None

44.	Cavern	Monster: None

Treasure: None

45.	Cavern of the Mystical Stone	Monster: None

Treasure: None

46.	Sunken Cavern	Orcs (3)-AC 6, MV 9", HD 1, hp 4,4,3, #AT 1, D 1-8 or by weapon

These three orc slackers have split off of the main group and are fast asleep in this chamber.

Treasure: None

47.	Cavern	Orcs (4)-AC 6, MV 9", HD 1, hp 4,4,4,3, #AT 1, D 1-8 or by weapon

A detachment of four orcs are posted as guards here, sparring with longswords to pass the time.

One of the orcs has a silver bracelet (worth 80 gp) as a nose ring.

48.	Arena Cavern	Kobolds (4)-AC 7, MV 6", HD 1/2, hp 3,3,2,1, #AT1, D 1-4 or by weapon
These four unfortunate humanoids are prisoners of the orcs, forced to fight in this arena for their enjoyment.		
Treasure: None		

49.	Phosphorescent Cave	Orcs (7)-AC 6, MV 9", HD 1, hp 8,6,6,5,4,4,3, #AT 1, D 1-8 or by weapon
This is the main encampment of the orcs exploring the ruins.		
Treasure: The leader (8 hp) carries a **spear +2.**		

50.	Water Pit	Ochre Jelly (1)-AC 8, MV 3", HD 6, hp 22, #AT 1, D 3-12
An ochre jelly lives in the pool.		
At the bottom of the pool, under a thin layer of mud, is a crystal goblet engraved with "Quasqueton" (15 gp value).		

51.	Side Cavern	Monster: None
Treasure: None		

52.	Raised Cavern	Stirges (5)-AC 8, MV 3"/18", HD 1+1, hp 4,3,3,3,2, #AT 1, D 1-3 + blood drain
The stirges cling to the ceiling.		
Treasure: None		

53.	Grand Cavern of the Bats	Stirges (5)-AC 8, MV 3"/18", HD 1+1, hp 4,3,3,3,2, #AT 1, D 1-3 + blood drain
Among the bats, five stirges hang on the ceiling of this grand chamber.		
Treasure: None		

54.	Treasure Cave	Animated Statues (2)-AC 7, MV 12", HD 1, hp 4,4, #AT 1, D 1-6
Two animated statues guard the chest as indicated in the room description.		
In a locked chest there are 2,450 cp, 120 gp, and four garnets worth 100 gp each.		

55.	Exit Cave	Monster: None
Treasure: None		

56	Cavern of the Statue	Monster: None
Hidden in one hand of the statue is a pearl (100 gp value).		

Stocked Example of B1, Version B
by Michael Curtis

Author's Note: Compared to the school of modern adventure design, the following list of encounters may seem slight. This is intentional. Given the heritage of *In Search of the Unknown*, the author intentionally embraced the principles of old school adventure creation. In the words of Gary Gygax, "Roughly one-third of the rooms should remain empty. One-third should contain monsters with or without treasure, one-sixth traps and/or tricks, and the remaining one-sixth should be specially designed areas with monsters and treasures selected by the DM (rather than randomly determined). Slides, teleport areas, and sloping passages should be added sparingly." Although the percentage of monsters on the list below may be low, parties exploring Quasqueton shall quickly discover there are a lot of interesting features (magic pools, teleportation pads, cats in jars, etc.) present to challenge their wits and baffle their senses. And don't forget the regular chance of encountering those pesky, no-treasure-carrying, wandering monsters! Between those dangers and the monsters presented, there's more than enough going on in Quasqueton to keep the party (and players) occupied.

UPPER LEVEL

1.	Alcoves	Monster: None
Treasure: None		

2.	Kitchen	Zombies (2)-AC 8, MV 6", HD 2, hp 10,9, #AT 1, D 1-8 or 1-6 (kitchen knives)
Two zombies, former cooks of Quasqueton still carrying their kitchen cutlery, try to prepare intruders for an evening meal.		
Treasure: None		

3.	Dining Room	Monster: None
Treasure: None		

4.	Lounge	Goblins (6)-AC 6, MV 6", HD 1-1, hp 7,6,5,5,3,2, #AT 1, D 1-6 or by weapon
Two goblins are inside the ale cask, licking the interior, while the remaining four gaze lasciviously at the statue.		
The goblins carry a total of 20 sp among them.		

5.	Wizard's Chamber	Monster: None
A dozen plain brass rings and one **ring of protection +1** are strung together on a leather thong and locked inside the nightstand drawer.		

6.	Closet	Monster: None
Treasure: None		

7.	**Wizard's Annex**	Monster: None

Treasure: None

8.	Wizard's Workroom	Monster: None

A **bag of devouring** sits atop one of the cabinets and a **potion of invisibility** (two doses, each with a duration of 3-6 turns) is inside the left-hand cabinet.

9.	**Wizard's Laboratory**	Monster: None

Four small gold rods (30 gp value each) are in a tin on the north shelves.

10.	**Storeroom**	**Giant Rats (2)**-AC 7, MV 12"//6", HD 1/2, hp 3,3, #AT 1, D 1-3 + disease

Two giant rats have chewed a hole in the back of the apple barrel and feast among the delicacies inside.

Treasure: None

11.	**Supply Room**	Monster: None

Treasure: None

12.	**Library**	**Kobolds (5)**-AC 7, MV 6", HD 1/2, hp 4,4,3,2,2, #AT 1, D 1-4 or by weapon

Five kobolds are gathering flammable materials to bring back to their brethren at the Smithy (#18).

A scroll containing two **cure light wounds** spells, with an annotation of "Useless!" on it, is mixed in among the material gathered by the kobolds.

13.	**Implement Room**	Monster: None

Treasure: None

14.	**Auxiliary Storeroom**	Monster: None

Treasure: None

15.	**Teleportation Room**	Monster: None

Treasure: None

16.	Teleportation Room	Monster: None

Treasure: None

17.	**Char Storage Cellar**	Monster: None	
Four large leather sacks containing a total of 2,450 sp are buried beneath the charcoal by the north wall.			

18.	**Smithy**	**Kobolds (8)**-AC 7, MV 6", HD 1/2, hp 4,4,3,3,3,3,2,2, #AT 1, D 1-4 or by weapon	
A band of kobolds, believing themselves to be better smiths than dwarves, are trying to get this smithy operational and are waiting on fuel for the fire pits from their colleagues in the Library (#12).			
The two largest kobolds (4 hp) each wear a necklace strung with unworked agates (40 gp value per necklace).			

19.	**Access Room**	Monster: None	
Treasure: None			

20.	Dead End Room	Monster: None	
Treasure: None			

21.	**Meeting Room**	Monster: None	
A crystal goblet, its base engraved with the word "Quasqueton," (15 gp value) lies forgotten beneath one of the benches.			

22.	**Garden Room**	**Crab Spider (1)**-AC 7, MV 12", HD 2, hp 8, #AT 1, D 1-8 + poison	
A crab spider dwells among the fungi, ambushing those who enter its territory.			
An onyx statue depicting a cavorting faun (200 gp value) stands on the southeast outcropping, covered by fungi growth.			

23.	**Storage Room**	Monster: None	
Treasure: None			

24.	Mistress' Chamber	Monster: None	
An exceptionally made silver mirror (90 gp value) is in the nightstand's single drawer.			

25.	**Rogahn's Chamber**	Monster: None	
In the pocket of one vest is a gold ring (non-magical) worth 50 gp.			

26.	**Trophy Room**	**Goblins (6)**-AC 6, MV 6", HD 1-1, hp 7,5,5,4,4,3, #AT 1, D 1-6 or by weapon	
A band of goblins is attempting to pry the trophies from the walls when the party enters.			
A bronze spear hanging on the wall is a **spear +2** and the dragon skin is worth 5,000 gp to certain buyers, but weighs 250 lbs.			

27.	Throne Room	Gnolls (4)-AC 5, MV 9", HD 2, hp 12,10,10,5, #AT 1, D 2-8 or by weapon
A small party of gnolls occupy this room, convinced that by doing so they are the rightful rulers of Quasqueton.		
The gnoll keep 637 gp and a large ruby (500 gp value) in a small keg stashed under one of the thrones.		

28.	Worship Area	Skeletons (5)-AC 7, MV 12", HD 1, hp 8,8,5,2,1, #AT 1, D 1-6
Bones beneath the ashes in the sacrificial pit are actually five skeletons that animate 1-4 rounds after the room is entered.		
Treasure: None		

29.	Captain's Chamber	Monster: None
The mace hanging on the wall is actually a **mace +1**.		

30.	Access Room	Monster: None
Treasure: None		

31.	Room of Pools	Monster: None
Treasure: None		

32.	Advisor's Chamber	Monster: None
Treasure: None		

33.	Barracks	Orcs (7)-AC 6, MV 9", HD 1, hp 8,6,5,4,3,2,2, #AT 1, D 1-8 or by weapon
A squad of orcs playing mumblety peg and throwing dice occupy this chamber.		
The dice game has a pot of 28 gp piled on the center of one of the tables.		

34.	Armory	Monster: None
Treasure: None		

35.	Guest Chamber	Monster: None
Treasure: None		

36.	Utility Room	Monster: None
Treasure: None		

37.	Recreation Room	Orcs (2)-AC 6, MV 9", HD 1, hp 6,5, #AT 1, D 2-9 or by weapon +1
Two muscular (+1 to damage rolls) orcs are lifting weights in this chamber.		
The orcs carry 15 gp and a single pearl (100 gp value) between them.		

LOWER LEVEL

38.	**Access Room**	Monster: None

Treasure: None

39.	**Museum**	Monster: None

Treasure: None

40.	**Secret Cavern**	**Ghouls (2)**-AC 6, MV 9", HD 2, hp 10,8, #AT 3, D 1-3/1-3/1-6 + paralysis

A pair of ghouls dwell here among grim bones, rotted meat, and a gore-streaked chest.

The chest is unlocked and contains 840 cp, 410 sp, 150 ep, and 100 gp.

41.	**Cavern**	**Stirges (4)**-AC 8, MV 3"/18", HD 1+1, hp 8,8,2,2, #AT 1, D 1-3

Four stirges cling to the roof of this cavern, lurking above the bone- and dirt-covered floor.

Treasure: None

42.	**Webbed Cave**	**Black Widow Spider (1)**-AC 6, MV 6"*12", HD 3, hp 13, #AT 1, D 2-12 + poison

A giant black widow spider lurks at the heart of this web-filled cave.

A silver medallion on chain (50 gp value) hangs around the neck of a desiccated previous meal.

43.	**Cavern**	**Carrion Crawler (1)**-AC 3/7, MV 12", HD 3+1, hp 18, #AT 8, D paralysis

A carrion crawler makes its home here and is often found dangling from the ceiling above a pile of bones and debris.

A bronze statuette, inlaid with silver and copper and depicting a howling wolf (115 gp value) is buried in the bone and debris pile.

44.	Cavern	Monster: None

Treasure: None

45.	**Cavern of the Mystical Stone**	Monster: None

Treasure: None

46.	**Sunken Cavern**	**Ochre Jelly (1)**-AC 8, MV 3", HD 6, hp 31, #AT 1, D 3-12

An ochre jelly lurks in a small crevice directly over the entrance to this cave, attacking those who enter with a pseudopod.

Treasure: None

47.	**Cavern**	Monster: None

Treasure: None

48.	Arena Cavern	Monster: None
Treasure: None		

49.	Phosphorescent Cave	Troglodytes (4)-AC 5, MV 12", HD 2, hp 10,9,6,4, #AT 3 or 1, D 1-3/1-3/2-5 or by weapon
Four phosphorescent mold-covered troglodytes are camouflaged against the walls, waiting to attack with surprise.		
Treasure: None		

50.	Water Pit	Monster: None
Treasure: None		

51.	Side Cavern	Monster: None
Treasure: None		

52.	Raised Cavern	Hobgoblins (4)-AC 5, MV 9", HD 1+1, hp 8,7,6,4, #AT 1, D 1-8 or by weapon
A group of hobgoblins are inspecting the curious blue veins in this chamber, convinced it is a sign of magical ore.		
The largest hobgoblin (8 hp) carries a leather pouch containing 10 ep and a piece of amber (25 gp value).		

53.	Grand Cavern of the Bats	Monster: None
Treasure: None		

54.	Treasure Cave	Animated Statues (2)-AC 7, MV 12", HD 1, hp 4,4, #AT 1, D 1-6
Two animated statues guard the chests as indicated in the room description.		
The three locked chests in the area contain 1,000 gp (chest #1), 2,467 sp and four emeralds worth 100 gp each (chest #2), and a suit of human-sized **chainmail +1** (chest #3).		

55.	Exit Cave	Monster: None
Treasure: None		

56.	Cavern of the Statue	Troglodytes (2)-AC 5, MV 12", HD 2, hp 7,3, #AT 3 or 1, D 1-3/1-3/2-5 or by weapon
A pair of troglodytes lurk here, waiting for unwary adventurers to fall into the nearby pit trap and then attack them with surprise.		
One of the troglodytes has a silver armband worth 80 gp.		

Stocked Example of B1, Version C

by Tim Wadzinski

Author's Note: I still have my original copy of *In Search of the Unknown*—probably the second module I owned—and this encounter list is taken directly from its ragged pages. There is very little rhyme or reason to the way these monsters and treasures were placed back in 1983, as my 12-year-old Monty Haul DM self (clearly) wasn't yet very adept at "making sense" with dungeon layout.

(Logic? Bah! Let's just do cool stuff!) Still, it was lots of fun to go back through my pencil-scrawled notes and reproduce them here, updated to Advanced Dungeons & Dragons specifications. I hope you get a kick out of this chaotically messy version of Quasqueton—and that you appreciate how most of the treasure comes in multiples of 10 coins, to make calculating encumbrance that much easier!

UPPER LEVEL

1.	Alcoves	Large Spiders (5)-AC 8, MV 6"*15", HD 1+1, hp 9,7,5,3,2, #AT 1, D 1 + poison

Five large spiders are on the ceiling above the bodies. Two dead spiders are (freshly) squashed on one of the walls.

There is a pile of coins—totaling 55 cp, 40 sp, 30 ep, 10 gp, and 20 pp—lying in the hall up around the corner from the bodies.

2.	Kitchen	Adepts (4)-AC 5, MV 9", HD 2, hp 9,8,5,4, #AT 1, D 1-6

Four adepts (2nd-level clerics) are here, exploring Quasqueton in search of treasures they can bring back to fund their chapel. Each is equipped with chain mail, a club, and a holy symbol. One also wields a **rod of cancellation**. They have the following spells prepared: **detect evil**, **light** (#1); **cure light wounds**, **remove fear** (#2); **cure light wounds**, **resist cold** (#3); **bless**, **command** (#4). Their leader is in the Dining Room (#3) across the hall.

The adepts carry bags filled with a total of 700 sp and 300 ep.

3.	Dining Room	Priest (1)-AC 4, MV 9", HD 3, hp 14, #AT 1, D 2-7

A priest (3rd-level cleric) sits in Zelligar's seat, cleaning spider guts off of his mace. His acolytes will run to assist if he calls out. He has chain mail, a shield, and a holy symbol, and he has the following spells prepared: **detect magic**, **sanctuary**, **find traps**.

A locked iron trunk behind the "thrones" contains 1,050 ep and nine violet garnets worth 500 gp each.

4.	Lounge	Huge Spider (1)-AC 6, MV 18", HD 2+2, hp 16, #AT 1, D 1-6 + poison

A huge spider is curled up beneath the eastern section of the bench seat.

A secret compartment in the base of the statue holds 900 gp and 350 pp.

5.	Wizard's Chamber	Giant Fire Beetles (6)-AC 4, MV 12", HD 1+2, hp 9,8,7,7,6,5, #AT 1, D 2-8

A small swarm of giant fire beetles has tunneled up from below and makes its nest beneath Zelligar's bed. The light from their glands causes an eerie glow to emanate from beneath the bed.

A **potion of levitation** and 450 gp are tucked away in a bag inside the nightstand.

6.	Closet	Giant Rats (6)-AC 7, MV 12"//6", HD 1/2, hp 4,4,4,3,3,2 #AT 1, D 1-3 + disease

The stacks of cloth are home to a nest of giant rats, who will rush forth and attack if disturbed.

Behind the wooden stand is a small unlocked chest containing 200 cp.

7.	Wizard's Annex	Monster: None

Treasure: None

8.	Wizard's Workroom	Giant Spider (1)-AC 4, MV 3"*12", HD 4+4, hp 24, #AT 1, D 2-8 + poison

A **dagger +1**, 1,300 cp, and an amethyst (100 gp value) are jammed into a false timber in the upright wooden table.

9.	Wizard's Laboratory	Skeletons (3)-AC 7, MV 12", HD 1, hp 8,6,4, #AT 1, D 1-6 or 2-7

Skeletons—the large obvious one, wielding a **spear +1**, and two more hidden in the empty vats—will animate and attack if anything in the room is disturbed.

A small purple bag with a golden drawstring sits near the trays of incense; it contains 20 sp.

10.	Storeroom	Footpads (2)-AC 7, MV 12", HD 2, hp 9,8, #AT 1, D 1-8

Two footpads (2nd-level thieves) will either be standing in the middle of the room (if surprised) or hiding around the corner just north of the secret door (if the party is surprised). They wear leather armor and wield long swords.

The footpads carry 70 pp between them, squirreled away in various pouches and hidden pockets.

11.	Supply Room	Skeletons (4)-AC 7, MV 12", HD 1, hp 7,6,6,2, #AT 1, D 1-6

Skeletons were led here by some forgotten evil NPC cleric, and forgotten.

A stash of 600 sp is hidden beneath a false bottom in the large box.

12.	Library	Giant Centipedes (4)-AC 9, MV 15", HD 1/4, hp 2,2,1,1, #AT 1, D poison

Giant centipedes live in the divans.

A large bag containing 600 sp lies beneath the scroll rack.

13.	Implement Room	Giant Rats (5)-AC 7, MV 12"//6", HD 1/2, hp 4,3,2,2,1 #AT 1, D 1-3 + disease

Five hungry giant rats live inside two of the empty barrels.

Another of the empty barrels holds a small sack containing 100 sp.

14.	Auxiliary Storeroom	Giant Toads (2)-AC 6, MV 6" + 6" hop, HD 2+4, hp 10,9 #AT 1, D 2-8

Two emaciated giant toads are poking through the rubble, hunting for food.

Hidden in the rubble is an unlocked wooden box containing 100 cp.

15.	Teleportation Room	Monster: None

Treasure: None

16.	Teleportation Room	Monster: None

Treasure: None

---

17. Char Storage Cellar Black Widow Spider (1)-AC 6, MV 6"*12", HD 3, hp 15, #AT 1, D 2-12 + poison

Jostling the false door will cause the black widow spider living inside it to emerge and bite.

A small leather pouch containing 10 ep sits on the floor near the false door.

---

18. Smithy Skeletons (6)-AC 7, MV 12", HD 1, hp 4,4,3,3,2,1, #AT 1, D 1-6

Another group of skeletons from the same band as those in the Supply Room (#11) rushes to the attack.

One of the skeletons wears a belt with a pouch that contains a single bloodstone (50 gp value).

---

19. Access Room Giant Centipedes (2)-AC 9, MV 15", HD 1/4, hp 2,2, #AT 1, D poison

Hidden amidst the logs is a small nest of giant centipedes.

A crumpled **bag of devouring** lies in a heap next to the hole in the floor.

---

20. Dead End Room Gnomes (4)-AC 5, MV 6", HD 1, hp 7,6,5,5, #AT 1, D 1-6 or by weapon

A party of four kobold-hunting gnomes is arguing about where to search the maze for a trap door in the floor. The PCs gain automatic surprise due to the noise. The gnomes are armed with clubs and spears.

The gnomes carry 60 gp between them.

---

21. Meeting Room Kobolds (8)-AC 7, MV 6", HD 1/2, hp 4,4,4,3,3,3,3,2, #AT 1, D 1-4 or by weapon

A pack of kobolds is attempting to organize itself here, before battling the gnomes they've spotted prowling around the Dead End Room (#20).

The kobolds' amassed treasure of 1,100 cp is stored in sacks scattered about the room.

---

22. Garden Room Yellow Mold (5 patches)-AC 9, MV 0", HD -, hp -, #AT 1, D 1-8 + poison

Five patches of yellow mold are scattered throughout the room; two are near the sunken pits and three are in the room's west arm.

A small pile of 20 sp lies beneath one of the yellow mold patches.

---

23. Storage Room Kobolds (4)-AC 7, MV 6", HD 1/2, hp 4,3,2,2, #AT 1, D 1-4 or by weapon

A scout party of kobolds is looking for equipment to bring back to the Meeting Room (#21).

Concealed by the stacked wooden stools are a **spear +1** and a sack containing 820 sp.

---

24. Mistress' Chamber Goblins (4)-AC 6, MV 6", HD 1-1, hp 7,7,5,2, #AT 1, D 1-6 or by weapon

These goblins are aware of the kobolds on this level, and are contemplating the best way to dominate and rule them. They are armed with spears.

Behind and beneath the chest of drawers is a sack containing 800 ep.

25.	Rogahn's Chamber	Footpads (2)-AC 7, MV 12", HD 2, hp 6,5, #AT 1, D 1-8

Two footpads clad in leather armor and armed with long swords are searching the room for loot.

The thieves are carrying loot bags holding 300 gp.

26.	Trophy Room	Giant Rats (9)-AC 7, MV 12"//6", HD 1/2, hp 4,4,4,3,3,3,2,2,2 #AT 1, D 1-3 + disease

The dragon paws are partially hollowed out and now home to a nest of giant rats.

Treasure: None

27.	Throne Room	Crab Spider (1)-AC 7, MV 12", HD 2, hp 8, #AT 1, D 1-8 + poison

Clinging to a pillar is a crab spider. It will leap to attack anyone approaching the thrones.

Scattered behind the thrones are 100 cp.

28.	Worship Area	Giant Poisonous Snake (1)-AC 5, MV 15", HD 4+2, hp 17, #AT 1, D 1-3 + poison

The mouth of the idol leads to a narrow tunnel system, wherein lurks a giant albino rattlesnake.

Each of the idol's eyes is a piece of white jade (100 gp value).

29.	Captain's Chamber	Skeletons (4)-AC 7, MV 12", HD 1, hp 4,3,2,1, #AT 1, D 1-6

Anyone entering the room will be attacked by skeletons.

Inside the locked wooden chest is a sack containing 200 sp.

30.	Access Room	Monster: None

Treasure: None

31.	Room of Pools	Black Widow Spider (1)-AC 6, MV 6"*12", HD 3, hp 18, #AT 1, D 2-12 + poison

Webs hang from the ceiling in several places. A black widow spider lurks in them, near the secret door.

A sack on the floor near the secret door holds 500 ep and 100 gp.

32.	Advisor's Chamber	Monster: None

Treasure: None

33.	Barracks	Zombies (2)-AC 8, MV 6", HD 2, hp 16,13, #AT 1, D 1-8

Two zombies lie in beds near the toilet area, appearing to be dead bodies.

A small belt pouch filled with 30 gp sits next to the toilet hole.

34.	Armory	Berserkers (6)-AC 7, MV 12", HD 2-7 hp, hp 7,7,7,6,6,6, #AT 1 (or 2), D by weapon

A roving band of berserkers is rummaging through the equipment. They are armed with battle axes, long swords, and scimitars.

The berserkers carry a total of 107 ep.

35.	Guest Chamber	Bugbears (5)-AC 5, MV 9", HD 3+1, hp 21,20,20,18,16, #AT 1, D 2-8 or by weapon

Five bugbears are inspecting the middle chamber and have just begun scrutinizing the false door.

Between them the bugbears are carrying 833 gp, a pearl (100 gp value), and a red garnet (100 gp value).

36.	Utility Room	Orcs (8)-AC 6, MV 9", HD 1, hp 8,7,6,6,6,5,5,5, #AT 1, D 1-8 or by weapon

Several dim-witted orcs are carefully inspecting the empty room for secret things. The leader (8 hp) is overseeing the futile search. They are all armed with long swords.

The orcs have 30 gp in a large bag.

37.	Recreation Room	Giant Centipedes (2)-AC 9, MV 15", HD 1/4, hp 2,2, #AT 1, D poison

There is a giant centipede on the rope, and another behind the battered shields.

Treasure: None

LOWER LEVEL

38.	Access Room	Troglodytes (2)-AC 5, MV 12", HD 2, hp 8,8, #AT 3 or 1, D 1-3/1-3/2-5 or by weapon

Two troglodytes are digging through the mining equipment, looking for anything useful.

Unbeknownst to the troglodytes, one of the overturned rock carts covers a pile of 200 cp, 100 sp, and 18 rock crystals worth 50 gp each.

39.	Museum	Giant Rats (5)-AC 7, MV 12"//6", HD 1/2, hp 4,4,3,3,3 #AT 1, D 1-3 + disease

Scratching noises can be heard behind the east wall; if a PC investigates giant rats burst forth into the room.

Treasure: None

40.	Secret Cavern	Shadows (3)-AC 7, MV 12", HD 3+3, hp 17,15,12, #AT 1, D 2-5 + strength drain

A trio of halfling-sized shadows wait patiently for victims.

Treasure: None

41.	Cavern	Cave Bears (2)-AC 6, MV 12", HD 6+6, hp 31,28, #AT 3, D 1-8/1-8/1-12 + hug

A mated pair of cave bears lair here. Their sleeping area is in the far east end of the cavern.

Buried near an obvious marker stone is an unlocked wooden box containing 182 ep.

42.	Webbed Cave	Crab Spiders (4)-AC 7, MV 12", HD 2, hp 9,7,7,5, #AT 1, D 1-8 + poison

Crab spiders hide around the bend and will leap to attack the first creature they see.

Lying on the floor near the webs are 82 gp.

43.	Cavern	Orcs (6)-AC 6, MV 9", HD 1, hp 6,6,6,5,5,4, #AT 1, D 1-8 or by weapon

Three orcs bearing torches are watching their comrades use rocks to scrape crude artwork onto the cavern walls. Once they become aware of the party they will snuff the torches and rely on infravision.

Treasure: None

44.	Cavern	Merchants (3)-AC 10, MV 12", HD 1-6 hp, hp 6,4,2, #AT 1, D by weapon

A group of three frightened merchants is camping here. Their guards have all been killed. If pressed into combat the merchants will fight with clubs and thrown rocks.

The merchants have a total of 82 cp and 65 pp in various small bags and sacks.

45.	Cavern of the Mystical Stone	Rock Baboons (6)-AC 6, MV 18", HD 2, hp 12,10,9,9,7,7, #AT 2, D 1-6/1-3

A family of demented rock baboons lives here, worshiping the stone as a god.

The dominant male (12 hp) wears a crude necklace with two chunks of turquoise worth 10 gp each.

46.	Sunken Cavern	Monster: None

Treasure: None

47.	Cavern	Robber Flies (6)-AC 6, MV 12"/24", HD 2, hp 10,9,8,8,6,6, #AT 1, D 1-8

There is a hole in the western wall, 10' off the ground, that serves as an entrance to a nest of robber flies.

Treasure: None

48.	Arena Cavern	Prestidigitators (4)-AC 12, MV 12", HD 1, hp 4,3,2,2, #AT 1, D 1-4

Four wandering prestidigitators (1st-level magic-users) occupy this room, plotting and scheming. Each is equipped with robes, a dagger, torches, and a spell book. They have the following spells prepared: **charm person** (#1); **spider climb** (#2); **magic missile** (#3); **dancing lights** (#4).

Besides their spell books (which can be detailed at the DM's discretion) the prestidigitators carry 98 sp between them.

49.	Phosphorescent Cave	Monster: None

Treasure: None

50.	Water Pit	Lizard Men (5)-AC 5, MV 6"//12", HD 2+1, hp 12,11,9,9,7, #AT 3, D 1-2/1-2/1-8

Five feral lizard men have adapted to the pool's cold water, and attack anything that enters the room.

Scattered about the bottom of the pool are 5,000 cp, 1,000 gp, a large pink crystal (worthless), and a waterproof lockbox containing a **potion of polymorph**, a **potion of levitation**, and a **wand of fear** (5 charges).

51.	Side Cavern	Monster: None

Treasure: None

52.	Raised Cavern	Blink Dogs (2)-AC 5, MV 12", HD 4, hp 26,19, #AT 1, D 1-6

A pair of scruffy blink dogs are nosing around in the rubble.

A severed hand wearing three jewel-encrusted rings is partially buried in the debris on the floor. The jewels are a pink pearl (100 gp value), a yellow topaz (500 gp value), and a black pearl (500 gp value).

53.	Grand Cavern of the Bats	Monster: None

Treasure: None

54.	Treasure Cave	Berserker Statues (2)-AC 7, MV 12", HD 1, hp 4,4, #AT 1, D 1-6

Two berserker statues guard the chests as indicated in the room description.

There are 21 gp scattered on the floor. The first two locked chests contain 2,000 sp and a **potion of undead control (skeletons)**, respectively.

55.	Exit Cave	Wood Golem (1)-AC 7, MV 12", HD 2, hp 9, #AT 1, D 1-8

Zelligar's old wood golem is trapped inside this cave, and wanders around aimlessly.

A sack containing 550 gp lies near the magical secret exit.

56	Cavern of the Statue	Living Statue (1)-AC 4, MV 6", HD 5, hp 28, #AT 2, D 2-12/2-12

If anyone approaches within 10' of the rock statue without first saying "Rogahn" or "Zelligar" it will animate and attack.

There is a **shield +1** and a **potion of invisibility** at the bottom of the pit trap.

CHAPTER FOUR
B2: The Keep on the Borderlands
Original Publication

B2: *The Keep on the Borderlands* went through a total of eight printings and was included in the D&D Basic Set for a period of time (specifically the sixth through eleventh printings of that set).

B2 was published in two very different formats. The interior art changed considerably in the first three printings. The second printing added two illustrations that weren't present in the first printing, then the third and subsequent printings changed six illustrations. You can see the differences in art on these pages: 5, 6, 7, 9, 20, and 23.

The minotaur image on page 20 is for many gamers one of the most iconic illustrations of their early D&D experience. How interesting to see that there were *two, different* minotaur illustrations! Which one do you remember?

(Astute readers may also recognize the illustration on page 6 as also appearing in the subsequent printings of B1.)

Additionally, Dexterity scores were included in monster stats on the earlier printings. You can see their removal in the later printing shown here.

In this volume we present complete scans of the second and fourth printings.

B2

Dungeon Module B2
The Keep on the Borderlands

by Gary Gygax

INTRODUCTORY MODULE FOR CHARACTER LEVELS 1-3

This module includes a cover folder with maps and a complete description booklet to form a ready-made scenario for BASIC DUNGEON & DRAGONS®. It has been specially designed for use by beginning Dungeon Masters so that they may begin play with a minimum of preparations.

Within are many features to aid novice players and Dungeon Masters: legends, history and background information, a list of adventuring characters, tips on how to be an effective Dungeon Master, plus an interesting area for characters to base themselves in (the Keep) before setting out to explore the Caves of Chaos!

If you enjoy this module, look for more releases in the D&D® family from TSR, The Game Wizards.

© 1980 by TSR Hobbies, Inc.

TSR Hobbies, Inc.
POB 756
LAKE GENEVA, WI 53147

PRINTED IN U.S.A.

Special Instructional Module

9034

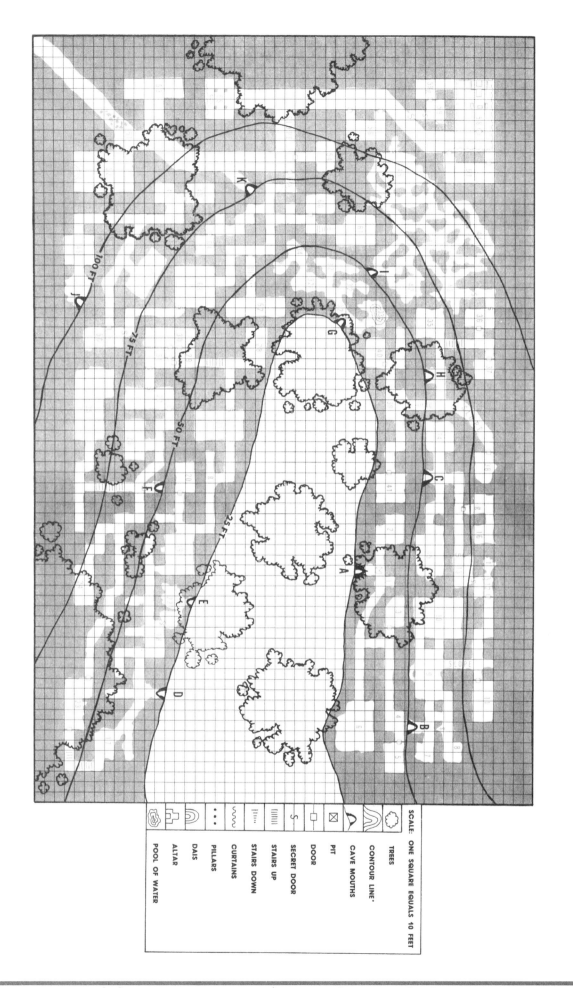

SCALE: ONE SQUARE EQUALS 10 FEET

	TREES
	CONTOUR LINE
	CAVE MOUTHS
⊠	PIT
▭	DOOR
S	SECRET DOOR
‖‖‖	STAIRS UP
‖····	STAIRS DOWN
～～	CURTAINS
• • •	PILLARS
	DAIS
	ALTAR
	POOL OF WATER

Dungeon Module B2
The Keep on the Borderlands

by Gary Gygax

INTRODUCTORY MODULE FOR CHARACTER LEVELS 1-3

This module includes a cover folder with maps and a complete description booklet to form a ready-made scenario for BASIC DUNGEONS & DRAGONS®. It has been specially designed for use by beginning Dungeon Masters so that they may begin play with a minimum of preparations.

Within are many features to aid novice players and Dungeon Masters: legends, history and background information, a list of adventuring characters, tips on how to be an effective Dungeon Master, plus an interesting area for characters to base themselves in (the Keep) before setting out to explore the Caves of Chaos!

If you enjoy this module, look for more releases in the D&D® family from TSR, The Game Wizards.

Distributed to the book trade in the United States by Random House, Inc. and in Canada by Random House of Canada, Ltd. Distributed to the toy and hobby trade by regional distributors.
© 1980 by TSR Hobbies, Inc., All Rights Reserved

TSR Games
POB 756
LAKE GENEVA, WI 53147

PRINTED IN U.S.A.
ISBN 0-935696-19-9

Special Instructional Module

9034

Basic Dungeons & Dragons

Dungeon Module #B2

The Keep on the Borderlands

Introduction: Welcome to the land of imagination. You are about to begin a journey into worlds where magic and monsters are the order of the day, where good and evil, law and chaos are forever at odds, where adventure and heroism are the meat and drink of all who would seek their fortunes in uncommon pursuits. This is the realm of DUNGEONS & DRAGONS®.

If you plan to play in this module and participate in the fun of adventuring, **stop** reading now. The information in the rest of the module is for your Dungeon Master or DM, so that he or she may guide you and other players through a thrilling adventure. Knowing too much about the contents of this module will spoil the surprises and excitement of the game.

Dungeon Masters, if many copies of this module are available to the players, you may wish to alter sections of the Keep and the Caves of Chaos. If you do this, you will be sure to have new surprises for players who might be familiar with some of the contents of the module. You are not entering this world in the usual manner, for you are setting forth to be a **Dungeon Master.** Certainly there are stout fighters, mighty magic-users, wily thieves, and courageous clerics who will make their mark in the magical lands of D&D. You, however, are above even the greatest of these, for as DM you are to become the Shaper of the Cosmos. It is you who will give form and content to all the universe. You will breathe life into the stillness, giving meaning and purpose to all the actions which are to follow. The others in your group will assume the roles of individuals and play their parts, but each can only perform within the bounds you will set. It is now up to you to create a magical realm filled with danger, mystery, and excitement, complete with countless challenges. Though your role is the greatest, it is also the most difficult. You must now prepare to become all things to all people.

NOTES FOR THE DUNGEON MASTER

The basic instruction book for DUNGEONS & DRAGONS® has given you the information necessary to understand D&D and start play. This module is another tool. It is a scenario which will help you to understand the fine art of being a Dungeon Master as you introduce your group of players to your own fantasy world, **your** interpretation of the many worlds of DUNGEONS & DRAGONS®. **THE KEEP ON THE BORDERLANDS** is simply offered as a vehicle for your use, a way to move smoothly and rapidly into your own special D&D campaign. Read the module thoroughly; you will notice that the details are left in your hands. This allows you to personalize the scenario, and suit it to what you and your players will find most enjoyable.

This module has been designed to allow **six to nine player characters of first level** to play out many adventures, gradually working up to second or third level of experience in the process. **The group is assumed to have at least one magic-user and one cleric in it.** If you have fewer than six players, be sure to arrange for them to get both advice and help in the KEEP. For example, they should have advice from a friendly individual to "stay near the beginning of the ravine area, and enter the lower caves first", to avoid their getting into immediate trouble with higher level monsters. Likewise, the services of several men-at-arms **must** be available to smaller parties. If only two or three player characters are to adventure, be sure to have a non-player charac-

ter or two go along, as well as a few men-at-arms. In addition, give the player characters a magic dagger or some magic arrows and at least one **potion of healing** — family bequests to aid them in finding their fame and fortune when they go against Chaos.

The DM should be careful to give the player characters a reasonable chance for survival. If your players tend to be a bit rash and unthinking, it might be better to allow them to have a few men-at-arms along even if the party is large, and they actually don't attempt to hire such mercenaries. Hopefully, they will quickly learn that the monsters here will act together and attack with reasonable intelligence, if applicable. If this lesson is not learned, all that can be done is to allow the chips to fall where they may. Dead characters cannot be brought back to life here!

Using the KEEP as "home base", your players should be able to have quite a number of adventures (playing sessions) before they have exhausted all the possibilities of the **Caves of Chaos** map. Assuming that they have played well, their player characters will certainly have advanced a level or two in experience when the last minion of darkness falls before their onslaught. While your players will have advanced in their understanding and ability, you will likewise have taken great strides in your skill as DM. In fact, before they have finished all the adventure areas of this module, it is likely that you will have begun to add your own separate maps to the setting. The KEEP is only a small section of the world. You must build the terrain and towns which surround it. You must shape the societies, create the kingdoms, and populate the countryside with men and monsters.

The KEEP is a microcosm, a world in miniature. Within its walls your players will find what is basically a small village with a social order, and will meet antagonists of a sort. Outside lies the way to the **Caves of Chaos** where monsters abound. As you build the campaign setting, you can use this module as a guide. Humankind and its allies have established strongholds — whether fortresses or organized states — where the players' characters will base themselves, interact with the society, and occasionally encounter foes of one sort or another. Surrounding these strongholds are lands which are hostile to the bold adventurers. Perhaps there are areas of wilderness thick with dangerous creatures, or maybe the neighboring area is a land where chaos and evil rule. There are natural obstacles to consider, such as mountains, marshes, deserts, and seas. There can also be magical barriers, protections, and portals. Anything you can imagine could be part of your world if you so desire. The challenge to your creativity is to make a world which will bring the ultimate in fabulous and fantastic adventure to your players. A world which they may believe in.

NOTE: For your convenience, whenever a monster or NPC* is described in the text, the details will be listed in the following order:

Name (Dexterity, Armor Class, Level **or** Hit Dice, hit points, Number of Attacks per round, Damage per attack)

Dexterity = **DX**, Armor Class = **AC**, Level = **LVL**, Hit Dice = **HD**, hit points = **hp**, Number of Attacks = **#AT**, Damage = **D**. Note that the term **Hit Dice** applies only to monsters, while the term **Level** is used to refer to Level of Experience.

Examples: Taverner (DX 13, AC 9, LVL 0, hp 6)
　　　　　Guard (DX 14, AC 4, LVL 1, hp 7, #AT ½, D 1-6)
　　　　　Kobold (DX 13, AC 5, HD ½, hp 3, #AT 1, D 1-4)

LVL 0 indicates that the person is a normal man.
#AT ½ indicates that the weapon may only be used once every 2 rounds.
#AT ¼ this weapon may only be used once every 4 rounds.

2

Determining Armor Class:

Armor Class	Type of Armor
9	None
8	Shield only
7	Leather
6	Leather & Shield
5	Chainmail
4	Chainmail & Shield
3	Plate Mail
2	Plate Mail & Shield
1	Plate Mail & magic + 1 Shield (or other combinations)

Note that an Armor Class (AC) of less than 2 is possible for characters wearing magic armor, carrying a magic shield, and/or wearing a **ring of protection**. Players using these items will **subtract** bonuses from their AC — for example, a fighter using both + 1 Plate Mail and + 1 Shield would have AC 0.

Using the Combat Tables:

To find the die roll needed to hit any Armor Class, look at the charts on pages 18-19 of the **BASIC D&D** rulebook. Compare the Level (if a character) or Hit Dice (if a monster) with the AC of the target to find the number needed 'to hit'. For Armor Classes lower than 2, adjust the number upwards; a character needing a roll of 17 to hit AC 2 would need an 18 to hit AC 1, 19 to hit AC 0, and so forth. Unless magic or silver weapons are needed to cause damage (and not available), a roll of **20** will **always** hit, and a roll of **1** will always **miss**!

A bonus of + 1 should be added to the "to hit" die roll of high level characters, for they have more training and experience in fighting. This bonus will apply to Fighters of 4th level or above, to Clerics and Thieves of 5th level or above, and to Magic-Users of 6th level or above.

Movement in Combat:

Combat movement is short and swift, and usually done by sprinting. In a combat situation, only short charges or retreats are allowed. After combat is resolved, movement rates return to normal. The movement speed for characters is:

Unarmored, unencumbered man:	**20** feet per melee round	
Armored **or** encumbered man	: **10** feet per melee round	
Armored, encumbered man	: **5** feet per melee round	

To determine a monster's movement speed in combat, divide its base movement speed by **12**.

When dice are used to randomly determine a number, the type of dice used are abbreviated 'd#' ('d4' means a four-sided die, 'd6' a six-sided, and so forth). If more than one is rolled, the number required is placed before the 'd' ('2d6' means two six-sided dice). If any number is to be added to the total of the dice, it is indicated afterward ('d4 + 2' means to roll a four-sided die and add 2 to the total; '2d8 + 1' will thus give a number from 3 to 17). You will quickly get to know all of these abbreviations, and may use them when you design your **own** dungeon.

Become familiar with this module, then make whatever additions, changes, or amendments you feel are appropriate for **your** campaign. Once you are satisfied, gather the players together and have them create their characters. This will take some time, so at first, don't plan on getting much actual adventuring done unless there is a lot of time available. After each person has rolled the numbers for his

or her characteristics (strength, intelligence, etc.), selected a race, chosen a profession, and found how much money he or she has to begin, you should introduce them to the setting by reading the **Background** section to them. As an aside, feel free to limit race or profession as suits your conception of the setting. You might wish to disallow the presence of elves or halflings in the KEEP, or you might not want any thieves as beginning characters. It is all up to you as DM to decide the shape of the campaign. Likewise, you can opt to give the player characters a special item of equipment to begin with — possibly mounts, a weapon, some trade goods, or virtually anything of small value (within reason).

After you have outlined the circumstances, allow your players to begin interacting with their characters. Give them time to wander around the KEEP, learning what is there, finding the limits of their freedom, and meeting the other "inhabitants" of the place. They may quickly establish their base in the **Traveler's Inn**, purchase their equipment, and then visit the tavern — where they may gather bits of information about their coming adventures. All of this preliminary play, just as what will come afterwards, demands that the players assume the personae (personalities) that they will have throughout the length of the campaign, barring the unforeseen. You, however, have a far greater challenge and obligation! You not only must order and create the cosmos, you must also play the part of each and every creature that the player characters encounter. You must be gate guard and merchant, innkeeper and orc, oracle and madman as the situation dictates. The role of DM is all-powerful, but it also makes many demands. It is difficult to properly play the village idiot at one moment and the sage the next, the noble clergyman on one hand and the vile monster on the other. In one role you must be cooperative, in the next uncaring and non-commital, then foolish, then clever, and so on. Be prepared!

Whether in the first session of play or in the next, the participants will set forth to find and explore the many **Caves of Chaos**. You must describe the journey to the place and what the characters see, and allow them to choose how they will go about their adventuring. In such situations, the DM must be a true disinterested party, giving information as required by questioning and proper action, but neither helping nor hindering otherwise. When the players experience their first encounter with a monster, you must be ready to play the part fully. If the monster is basically unintelligent, you must have it act accordingly, enlivening the meeting with the proper dramatics of the animal sort — including noises! If the encounter is with a monster of the more intelligent sort, it is up to the DM to not only provide an exciting description but also to correctly act the part of the monster. Rats, for instance, will swarm chitteringly from their burrows — a wave of lice-ridden hunger seeking to consume the adventurers with sheer numbers, but easily driven off squealing with blows and fire. Goblins, on the other hand, will skulk and hide in order to ambush and trap the party — fleeing if overmatched, but always ready to set a new snare for the unwary character.

If all of this seems too much to handle, never fear! Just as your players are learning and gaining real experience at D&D, so too will you be improving your ability as a DM. The work necessary to become a master at the art is great, far greater than that necessary to be a top player, but the rewards are proportionate. You will bring untold enjoyment to many players in your role as DM, and all the while you will have the opportunity to exercise your imagination and creative ability to the fullest. May each of your adventure episodes always be a wondrous experience!

NOTE: Several words in the following text will be followed by an asterisk (*). This means that the word will be explained in the **Glossary** at the end of this module.

3

HOW TO BE AN EFFECTIVE DUNGEON MASTER

As Dungeon Master, the beginner is faced with a difficult problem. The DM is the most important person in the D&D game. He or she sets up and controls all situations, makes decisions, and acts as the link between the players and the world he or she has created. Perhaps the most common question faced by a beginning Dungeon Master is, "What do I do to run a game?" It is possible to read through the rules and become slightly lost by all the things that must be prepared or known before DMing a game.

Unlike most boardgames, D&D relies on information, both from the players and the DM. In boardgames, the way the game is played is obvious. First one person moves, and then another. Actions and choices are few. In D&D, the action is only limited by the abilities of the character, the imagination of the player, and the decisions of the DM. The play will often go in unexpected directions and the DM will sometimes be required to decide on situations not covered in the rules. The DM is the judge.

As a judge, moderator, or referee, the DM must constantly deal with the players. Just as the referee of a sporting event, the DM must be fair. He or she cannot be "out to get the players", nor should he or she be on their side all the time. The DM must be **neutral**. If a party has played well and succeeded, the DM should not punish them by sending more and more monsters at them or thwart their plans; on the other hand, if the players have acted foolishly, they should get their "just rewards". In combat, the DM should play the monsters to the best of the monster's ability. If the creature is stupid, it may be easily tricked or may not always do the smartest thing. If the monster is clever or intelligent, it will fight to its best advantage. The DM must be fair, but the players must play wisely.

The DM is also the designer of the situations and must bear in mind the abilities of his or her players. It is the job of the DM to see that the situations and characters balance. If things are too difficult, the players will become discouraged; too easy and they will become bored. Is it possible for a good player to win, yet still a challenge and a risk in doing so? Is the amount of treasure gained appropriate for the danger of trying to get it? As DM, much satisfaction comes from watching players overcome a difficult situation. But they should do it on their own!

To defeat monsters and overcome problems, the DM must be a dispenser of information. Again, he or she must be fair — telling the party what it can see, but not what it cannot. Questions will be asked by players, either of the DM or of some character the party has encountered, and the DM must decide what to say. Information should never be given away that the characters have not found out — secret doors may be missed, treasure or magic items overlooked, or the wrong question asked of a townsperson. The players must be allowed to make their own choices. Therefore, it is important that the DM give accurate information, but **the choice of action is the players' decision.**

Throughout all this — making decisions, playing roles, handling monsters — the DM must remember that he or she is in control. The DM is the judge, and it is his or her game. The DM should listen to the players and weigh their cases fairly when disagreements arise, but the final decision belongs to the DM. The Dungeon Master's word is law!

TIME

The Dungeon Master is responsible for keeping track of elapsed time. Inside the dungeon, a normal turn is ten minutes (adventure time). A normal turn is determined by the distance the party can travel, using the **MOVEMENT TABLE** on page 9 of the **BASIC D&D** rule book. For example, a party whose slowest member moves at 120 feet per turn, would travel 120 feet in a turn. When the party has mapped 120 feet of dungeon, one turn has elapsed.

If fighting should occur, the time reference shifts to a **melee turn** which is subdivided into ten, 10 second melee **rounds**. The concept of a melee turn is designed to simulate the quick exchange of blows in combat. For the sake of convenience, a DM can consider one entire melee turn to equal one normal turn (that is, 10 minutes), no matter how many melee rounds the combat took. The extra time is spent recovering one's breath, checking for wounds, resharpening blunted weapons, etc.

The **actual** (clock-time) length of a turn varies. A turn might take longer than ten actual minutes, particularly if extensive combat has taken place. On the other hand, a turn may be quite short in actual time, if the party is heading back through a previously mapped area.

In general, a party should rest and sleep eight hours in every 24. Prudent player characters will sleep in shifts, with a guard always awake.

Remember that player characters heal 1-3 points naturally every 24 hours of full rest.

DIVIDING TREASURE AND COMPUTING EXPERIENCE

After the party exits the dungeon safely, all surviving player characters should divide up treasure and be awarded their experience points. Division of treasure is the players' responsibility. Awarding experience points is the Dungeon Master's responsibility.

Ideally, treasure should be divided equally among surviving player characters, with henchmen and hirelings usually receiving an equal share (minus any advance payment already given them). Magical items are generally given only to character classes that could use them. For example, a fighter should take a magical sword as part of his or her share in preference to a scroll.

Non-magical treasure is usually divided first, since it is easier to divide equally. It is seldom possible to divide magic items equally. A suggested solution to division of magic items is to have each character roll percentile dice and let the highest score have first pick, second highest score second pick, and so on until there are no more magical items. Henchmen and hirelings may, or may not, be excluded from an equal chance for a magic item. If they are excluded, a DM should note the fact and take it into account when it next comes time to test the henchman's or hireling's loyalty.

For example, a party consisting of a fighter, a magic-user, and a hireling (all first level) arrives safely back at the Keep. Their recovered treasure equals 520 gold pieces, 1000 silver pieces, a necklace worth 400 gold pieces, a **+ 1 sword**, and a **ring of water walking**. The total value of all non-magical treasure is 1020 gold pieces. Without selling the necklace, it would be impossible for the party to split the treasure equally. The two player characters compromise by giving the necklace to the hireling, to insure his loyalty with a greater share of treasure. They each take only 310 gold pieces, but the magic-user keeps the ring and the fighter keeps the sword.

Experience points are awarded by the DM to player characters on the basis of non-magical treasure recovered and monsters killed or overcome. Experience points for recovered treasure are calculated at one experience point for every gold piece worth of non-magical treasure. Experience points for monsters overcome or killed is calculated by using the **Experience Points for Monsters Overcome** chart on page 11 of the **Basic DUNGEONS & DRAGONS** rule book.

Unless a player character has earned extra treasure through the use of his or her class abilities (for example, a thief who steals treasure which he did not report to the party), the DM should **divide the experience points**

4

earned through treasure recovery equally among all surviving party members. Since, in the above example, the entire party recovered 1020 gold pieces worth of non-magical treasure, the fighter and the magic-user each receive 340 experience points for the treasure recovered. The hireling receives ½ normal experience, since presumably he was only following orders, and not doing his own thinking. The hireling thus receives only 170 experience points for recovered treasure.

To recover the treasure, it was necessary for the party members to kill 19 orcs, 7 skeletons, and an ogre. The party should receive 10 points of experience for each orc killed, as orcs have 1 hit die. The party should receive 5 experience points for each skeleton. For killing the ogre, they should receive 125 experience points, since it has 4 + 1 hit dice, plus 75 further experience points since it does more than normal damage due to its large size and great strength. The total experience points for overcoming monsters would be 425. When this is divided, the magic-user and fighter each receive 142 additional experience points. The hireling receives only one-half, 71 additional experience points. The total experience for each player character is 482 (340 + 142) experience points apiece. The hireling receives 241 experience points.

When enough experience points are accumulated, a player character rises to the next higher level, and gains the benefits of that level (an additional hit die, a new spell, etc.). Earned wealth can be used to purchase new equipment, to pay for everyday expenses, and to attract hirelings.

PREPARATION FOR THE USE OF THE MODULE

The use of this module first requires a working familiarity with its layout and design. Therefore, the first step is to completely read through the module, referring to the maps provided to learn the locations of the various features. A second (and third!) reading will be helpful in learning the nature of the monsters, their methods of attack and defense, and the treasures provided.

Certain buildings of the KEEP will frequently be visited by the adventurers (such as the Travelers Inn, Taverner, and Provisioner). Floor plans are very useful in visualizing these areas. For information on their preparation, refer to the section entitled "Designing Floor Plans" near the end of the module.

Once you are familiar with the areas described in the module and have drawn whatever additional plans you wish, assist the players in preparing their characters by reading them the section entitled **Background**. This will set the stage for the game.

After the background is given, the players may prepare their characters. Full details are given in the **BASIC D&D** book. A written record of each character should be kept by the players.

As an alternative to rolling up new characters, the players may (at the DM's option) select characters from the NPC• list in this module. Note that the personalities given are for the DM's use with NPC's **only**, and are **not** to be used by the players.

Before the players enter the KEEP, the DM may privately give each player one rumor about the CAVES OF CHAOS. This information may be shared or kept secret, as the **players** wish. The DM should avoid interfering with their choices whatever the result. Additional information may be gathered in the KEEP itself; use the **Rumors Table** in the "DM Notes About the Keep" for this purpose, or create your own based on the CAVES.

To start an adventure outside the KEEP, the players must decide on an order of march — who will be in the first rank, middle, and at the rear of the party. This should be drawn on a sheet of paper and given to the DM for his or her reference. Any changes in the order (due to injuries, special procedures, etc.) should be noted on the sheet as they occur. In a standard 10' wide corridor, the most common arrangement is two adventurers, side by side, in each rank; however, three characters could occupy a single rank if all of their weapons were small (such as daggers and hand axes).

One player in the group should be selected as leader and 'caller' for the party; another one or two should take care of necessary mapping. INDIVIDUAL PLAYERS MAY DECIDE ON THEIR ACTIONS, but it is the 'caller' who gives the DM the details on the party's course of action (such as "We'll head down the eastern corridor."). The caller should discuss the party's actions with the players, and inform the DM of the decisions of the group. When a player speaks and indicates that an action is being taken, **it has begun** — even if the player changes his mind. Use your discretion in these cases, and remember that the DM has the final say in all matters.

The players should use graph paper to map the areas being explored. Have them indicate which direction is north, and use compass directions to describe details and direction of travel ("We'll go west and turn north at the next intersection"). Use the same method to describe areas to them ("You see a corridor which goes about 30' south and then turns west"). Be sure to keep your descriptions accurate, though you may say such things as 'about forty feet', especially in open areas or when describing irregular surfaces. Players will often show you their map and ask "Is this right?" Do not correct their mistakes unless the error would be obvious in the eyes of the adventurers, and remember that, in most cases, maps do not have to be exact. Encourage good mapping skills and an attention to detail, and avoid falling into a rut of continually answering map questions.

Exploration of the CAVES OF CHAOS will take more than one game session. When the players want to stop play, they must find an exit and (preferably) return to the KEEP. You may divide treasure and award experience when this occurs. Remember to make adjustments to the areas they visited — the monsters may build new defenses, reoccupy areas that were cleaned out, and so forth.

If the adventurers wish to stop exploring temporarily for a rest period (for example, the customary 8 hours rest each night), they should tell the DM exactly where they plan to stay and who is standing guard. Just as with marching order, it is important that the guard and sleeping positions be noted on paper, since this may be crucial if and when a monster approaches.

During play, make careful notes on the monsters killed, the amount of treasure taken, experience gained, and any other details of interest. It is then a simple matter to compute the totals at the end of a play session. See the section of this module entitled "DIVIDING TREASURE AND COMPUTING EXPERIENCE" for more information.

5

BACKGROUND

The Realm of mankind is narrow and constricted. Always the forces of Chaos press upon its borders, seeking to enslave its populace, rape its riches, and steal its treasures. If it were not for a stout few, many in the Realm would indeed fall prey to the evil which surrounds them. Yet, there are always certain exceptional and brave members of humanity, as well as similar individuals among its allies — dwarves, elves, and halflings — who rise above the common level and join battle to stave off the darkness which would otherwise overwhelm the land. Bold adventurers from the Realm set off for the Borderlands to seek their fortune. It is these exceptional individuals who, provided they survive the challenge, carry the battle to the enemy. Such adventurers meet the forces of Chaos in a testing ground where only the fittest will return to relate the tale. Here, these exceptional individuals will become skilled in their calling, be it fighter or magic-user, cleric or thief. They will be tried in the fire of combat, those who return, hardened and more fit. True, some few who do survive the process will turn from law and good and serve the masters of Chaos, but most will remain faithful and ready to fight evil wherever it threatens to infect the Realm.

You are indeed members of that exceptional class, adventurers who have journeyed to the **KEEP ON THE BORDERLANDS** in search of fame and fortune. Of course you are inexperienced, but you have your skills and a heart that cries out for adventure. You have it in you to become great, but you must gain experience and knowledge and greater skill. There is much to learn, and you are willing and eager to be about it! Each of you has come with everything which could possibly be given you to help. Now you must fend for yourselves; your fate is in your hands, for better or worse.

Ahead, up the winding road, atop a sheer-walled mount of stone, looms the great KEEP. Here, at one of civilization's bulwarks* between good lands and bad, you will base yourselves and equip for forays against the wicked monsters who lurk beyond. Somewhere nearby, amidst the dark forests and tangled fens, are the **Caves of Chaos** where fell creatures lie in wait. All this you know, but before you dare adventure into such regions you must become acquainted with the other members of your group, for each life will depend upon the ability of the others to cooperate against the common foe. Now, before you enter the grim fortress, is the time for introductions and an exchange of information, for fate seems to have decreed that you are to become an adventurous band who must pass through many harrowing experiences together on the path which leads towards greatness.

START:

You have travelled for many days, leaving the Realm and entering into the wilder area of the Borderlands. Farms and towns have become less frequent and travellers few. The road has climbed higher as you enter the forested and mountainous country.

You now move up a narrow, rocky track. A buttress*-like wall of natural stone is on your left, the land falling away to a sheer cliff on the right. There is a small widening ahead, where the main gate to the KEEP is. The blue-clad men-at-arms* who guard the entrance shout at you to give your names and state your business. All along the wall you see curious faces peering down at you — eager to welcome new champions of Law, but ready with crossbow and pole arm* to give another sort of welcome to enemies.

(**DM Note:** Have each player identify his or her character's name and profession. Have them answer in their own words why they seek entrance to the place. If the answer sounds unnatural, assume the role of the corporal of the watch, and begin to cross-examine the speaker. Now is the time to make the players realize that whatever they say — as speech or relating their actions — will be noted by you, as Dungeon Master, and acted upon accordingly in whatever role is appropriate to the situation. A courteous and full reply might well win a friend amongst the soldiers who might be of aid sometime. Rudeness and discourtesy may bring suspicion and enemies to trouble the course of things within the otherwise safe base area. When you are satisfied that the scene is played out, have the group enter.)

DM Notes About The Keep:

I. This whole place is well-organized for security and for defense. In time of need, many civilians will arm and help man the walls, while non-combatants bring ammunition, food, and water to the walls and help the wounded. Sentries are alert. A patrol of guards makes a round of the walls, but irregularly, and a command-type checks every half hour to hour. It is very unlikely that persons can enter or leave without being seen, unless magic is used. (You can have **magic mouth** spells placed in key areas to shout "ALARM" whenever an invisible creature passes within 10' or so!)

Within the Keep itself, the townspeople are generally law-abiding and honest. Boorishness and ill manners will be frowned upon. If any member of a party should be caught in a criminal act, the alarm will be sounded instantly. Citizens will try to prevent the escape of any lawbreakers (without sacrificing their lives) until the guard arrives in 1-2 turns. If met with resistance, the guard will not hesitate to use force, even killing if they must. Those offenders taken prisoner will be locked in the dungeons under the Keep and punished for their crimes.

— indicates a ballista, a huge heavy crossbow manned by two men. It fires like a heavy crossbow, but has a range of 480 feet, hits as if it were fired by a fighter of 1st-3rd level, and does 2 six-sided dice of damage plus two points (4-14 points of damage per hit). Each ballista has 12 missiles. They may only be fired once every four rounds (requiring 3 rounds to prepare and 1 to fire).

— indicates a light catapult with a range of 241 to 480 feet which fires half as often as a ballista (once per 8 rounds). Each requires two crewmen to operate, hits as if fired by a normal man, but can hit 1-6 targets in any close group (or one large target) for 1 six-sided die of damage each (6 dice if one large target). There is ammunition for six catapult shots per machine.

II. Floor plans might be useful. Note that most areas have two or more stories, and there is furniture in the rooms not shown. Also left out are details of heating, light, and descriptive touches such as color, rafters, decoration, etc. If you have time, floor plans and detailing of each area might be very helpful, exceptionally so in places frequented by the adventurers. See the appendix covering this near the end of the module.

III. Information from inhabitants of the KEEP might be gained by player characters. You may give one rumor (at random, using d20) to each player as starting information. Other rumors may be keyed to other persons in the KEEP. For example: "Talking with the Taverner (**#15**) might reveal either rumor #18 or #19; he will give the **true** rumor if his reaction is good."

Do not give out **all** the rumors. You may add whatever false rumors you wish, but adding to the amount of true information is not recommended.

The false rumors are noted by an 'F' after the number.

1. A merchant, imprisoned in the caves, will reward his rescuers.
2.F A powerful magic-user will rain spells on cave invaders.
3. Tribes of different creatures live in different caves.
4. An ogre sometimes helps the cave dwellers.
5. A magic wand was lost in the caves' area.
6.F All of the cave entrances are trapped.
7. If you get lost, beware the eater of men!
8. Altars are very dangerous.
9.F A fair maiden is imprisoned within the caves.
10.F "Bree-yark" is goblin-language for "we surrender"!
11. Beware of treachery from within the party.
12. The big dog-men live very high in the caves.
13. There are hordes of tiny dog-men in the lower caves.
14.F Piles of magic armor are hoarded in the southern caves.
15.F The bugbears in the caves are afraid of dwarves!
16. Lizard-men live in the marshes.
17. An elf once disappeared across the marshes.
18. Beware the mad hermit of the north lands.
19.F Nobody has ever returned from an expedition to the caves.
20. There is more than one tribe of orcs within the caves.

IV. Entrance to the Inner Bailey* can be gained if the adventurers perform a heroic act in behalf of the KEEP, if they bring back an exceptional trophy or valuable prisoners, or if they contribute a valuable magic item or 1,000 or more gold pieces to the place. They will be invited to a feast and revel, and then closely watched and carefully questioned. If the Castellan* likes the looks of the group, and his assistants agree, he will ask them to perform a special mission (suitable to their ability, but difficult — use the area map or the **Caves of Chaos** to find a suitable goal. On the other hand, if they are rude or behave badly, he will simply retire early, ending the revel, and they will never be aided or invited back. If they try to steal or are threatening, the group will be attacked and killed immediately (if this can be managed, of course).

Groups sent on a mission will be **blessed** and given up to 100 g.p. each for any needed supplies. If they succeed, they will be given passes to the Inner Bailey and can ask the Castellan for aid if there is a major foe to overcome (in the **Caves'** area). He will send a minimum of one corporal and 3 archers in plate, or at maximum the sergeant, a corporal, and a dozen men-at-arms.

V. After the normal possibilities of this module are exhausted, you might wish to continue to center the action of your campaign around the KEEP by making it the base for further adventures which you may devise. For example (assuming that the group has done good service for the Castellan), have a large force of bandits move into the area, and then appoint the group to command an expedition of KEEP troops, mercenaries, and so on to wipe them out. Or the party might become "traders" operating out of the place, hoping to find adventures as they travel in the surrounding area.

AREAS OF THE KEEP

1. **MAIN GATE:** Two towers 30' high with battlements*, flank a gatehouse 20' high. All have holes for bow and crossbow fire. A deep crevice in front of the place is spanned by a drawbridge (usually up). There is a portcullis* at the entry and large gates at the far end of the passage. The passage is about 10' wide and high, the ceiling above pierced with murder holes*, the walls to either side slitted for archery. It is obvious that this construction is of great blocks of the hardest granite, undoubtedly common throughout the whole fortress. Two men-at-arms will appear when the drawbridge is lowered and the portcullis raised. Each is clad in platemail and carries a pole arm* which will strike the first blow when used against a charging foe. (DX 18, AC 3, LVL 0, hp 5 each, #AT ½, D 1-6.) They require that persons entering the KEEP put their weapons away, and then will escort them through the short tunnel into area **3.**.

2. **FLANKING TOWERS:** Atop each tower are four crossbowmen with heavy crossbows cocked and ready to fire. Each is clad in chain (AC 5), wearing a sword and dagger, and has a shield (AC 4 when picked up) nearby. (DX 12, LVL 0, hp 4 each, #AT ¼ with heavy crossbow, D 1-6.) Inside each tower are 12 other men-at-arms, four being "on-duty" and armored and armed as the men-at-arms on the tower tops. The other eight in the tower are resting, and it will take one full turn for these men to ready themselves for battle. They are exactly like the others, except instead of heavy crossbows, they carry regular bows. (DX 14, AC 4, LVL 0, hp 4, #AT 1, D 1-6.) The three floors of these towers will contain supplies of bolts and arrows, spears, rocks, and several barrels of oil (all for hurling down on attackers). There will also be pallets* for sleeping, pegs with clothing belonging to the soldiers, and some small tables, stools, and benches. Each man-at-arms will have (d6) copper pieces and (d4) silver pieces on his person.

3. **ENTRY YARD:** This narrow place is paved. All entrants, save those of the garrison, will be required to dismount and stable their animals (area **4.**, below). The **corporal of the watch** is here. He is dressed in plate mail and carries a shield (AC 2), with sword and dagger at his waist. (DX 16, AC 2, LVL 2 fighter, hp 15, and his sword is a + 1 magic weapon. The corporal is rather grouchy and abrasive, with a low charisma, but he admires outspoken, brave fighters and is easily taken in by a pretty girl.) Beside him is a man in robes (a scribe) who records the name of each person who enters or leaves, and flanking each man is another man-at-arms in plate with pole arms as noted in **1.**, above. (DX 18, AC 3, LVL 0, hp 5 each, #AT ½, D 1-6.) When dismounted, lackeys* will come from area **4.** (the stable) to take the mounts. Any goods which are not carried by entrants will be stored in area **5.** (the warehouse). Another lackey will then show entrants to the Traveler's Inn.

4. **COMMON STABLE:** This long building is about 15' high, with a 3' parapet* atop its flat roof, so that it can be used in defense of the gate. The gateside wall is pierced for archery. There are always 5-8 (d4 + 4) lackeys inside tending to horses and gear. Each is unarmored (AC 9) but can fight with various available weapons (pitch forks and the like — treat as pole arms) and each has 1-4 hit points, dexterity rolled at random. There will be various light and draft horses here (2-8 of each) and mules as well (1-6).

5. **COMMON WAREHOUSE:** Visiting merchants and other travelers who have quantities of goods are required to keep their materials here until they are either sold to the persons at the KEEP or taken elsewhere. The building is the same as the stable (**4.**, above) with respect to height, parapet, etc. Its double doors are chained and padlocked, and the **corporal of the watch** must be called to gain entry, as he has the keys. Inside are two wagons, a cart, many boxes, barrels, and bales — various food items, cloth, arrows, bolts, salt, and two tuns* of wine. (Average value is 100 gold pieces per wagon-load.)

6. **BAILIFF'S TOWER:** The superintendent (or bailiff) of the outer bailey of the fortress is quartered here. (DX 14, AC 2, LVL 3 fighter, hp 22. He is wearing + 1 plate mail, wields a + 1 magic sword, and is also able to use a longbow which is hanging on the wall.) He and the scribe share offices on the lower floor. Their quarters are on the second story. (Usual furnishings of bed, chest, armoire*, table, chairs, rug, etc.) (The bailiff has (3d6) gold pieces with him always, the scribe has (2d6) silver pieces and (d4) gold pieces in his purse. There are 50 gold pieces hidden in the bailiff's old boots in the armoire*, and hanging on his wall is a quiver with 20 arrows, 3 of which are + 1 magic shafts. The scribe has a jewelled ink pot worth 100 gold pieces, but it is dirty and ink covered, looks worthless, and is on his table in plain sight.) The third floor is a storage area, and the fourth story quarters 12 men-at-arms. Six are armored in leather and shield (AC 6) with pole arm and axe, the other six have chainmail (AC 5), light crossbow, and sword and serve as the escort of the bailiff from time to time. (DX 10, LVL 0, hp 4 each, and each carries 2d6 copper pieces and 1d6 silver pieces.) Their room contains pallets, pegs with cloaks and other clothing, two long tables with benches, a supply of 180 bolts, and several dozen large rocks. The whole tower is 40' high, with a 5' crenellated* battlement atop it. All walls are pierced for archery.

7. **PRIVATE APARTMENTS:** Special quarters are available for well-to-do families, rich merchants, guildmasters, and the like. The five small apartments along the south wall are occupied by families of persons dwelling within the Outer Bailey of the KEEP. The two large ones (indicated by **7a.** and **7b.**) currently house a jewel merchant and a priest:

a. **Jewel Merchant:** This normal man and his wife are guarded by a pair of 2nd level fighters in chainmail and shield with sword and dagger. (DX 13, AC 4, LVL 2, hp 17 and 12.) The four are lodged in the eastern portion of the building, the merchant and his wife being in the upper floor most of the time. Each guard commands a huge dog trained to kill. (DX 9, AC 6, HD 3, hp 12 and 11, #AT 1, D 1-6.) The merchant has a locked iron box with 200 platinum pieces and 100 gold pieces inside. Secreted in his belt are 10 gems of 100 gold piece value each. He will buy gems at 60% to 90% (d4 × 10 + 50%) of value. He sells at 110% to 140% (d4 × 10 + 100%) of value. His wife wears a jeweled bracelet, necklace, and earrings (600, 1,200, and 300 gold piece value respectively), also available for sale as per gems. They are awaiting a caravan back to the Realm. All persons here have 3d6 silver pieces each upon their person. The apartment is well-furnished, but there is nothing of particular interest or value, except for the coins, gems, and jewelry noted.

b. Priest: The western portion houses the jovial **priest** who is taking advantage of his stopover at the KEEP to discuss theology with learned folk and to convert others. Everyone speaks well of him, although the two **acolytes** with him are avoided, as they never speak — the priest says they must follow vows of silence until they attain priestly standing. His well-appointed chambers are comfortably furnished, and guests are always welcomed with a cozy fire and plenty of ale or wine. The priest is a very fine companion and an excellent listener. He does not press his religious beliefs upon any unwilling person. He is outspoken in his hatred of evil, and if approached by a party of adventurers seeking the **Caves of Chaos,** he will certainly accompany them. He has + 1 magic plate armor and a + 1 shield (AC 0) and a + 1 war hammer, and has a dexterity of 15. (He also has a magic cleric scroll with a **hold person** and a **silence, 15' radius** spell on it.) He appears very robust (18 **hit points**), as do his assistants. The latter wear chain, carry shields and have maces. (DX 12, AC 4, LVL 1 clerics, hp 7 each.) **(Note:** All are chaotic and evil, being in the KEEP to spy and defeat those seeking to gain experience by challenging the monsters in the **Caves of Chaos.** Once in the caves the **priest** will use a **cause light wounds** or a **darkness** spell as needed to hinder and harm adventurers. Betrayal will always occur during a crucial encounter with monsters.) Each cleric carries (4d6) silver pieces, and each wears a gold chain worth 100 gold pieces (the **priest's** has a bloodstone gem worth 500 gold pieces in addition). (A small sack hidden in the **priest's** chair contains 30 each of platinum, gold, electrum, silver, and copper pieces, plus one jeweled clasp worth 300 gold pieces. These are for bribes for subversion or to use to gain freedom if necessary.)

8. SMITHY AND ARMORER: This building is about 20' high, with the usual 5' parapet above and walls pierced for defense. The lower floor is occupied by a forge, bellows, and other items. Here horses and mules are shod, weapons made, armor repaired and similar work done. The smith is also an armorer, and has two assistants. (Smith: DX 14, AC 7 from leather armor, LVL 1 fighter, hp 11; he uses his hammer as a weapon. Assistants: DX 13, AC 9, LVL 0, hp 5 each; they will pick up any weapons handy if need be.) There are 2 swords, 1 mace, a suit of man-sized chainmail, and 11 finished spears in the shop. In the second story are rooms where the smith, his family, and his assistants live. (Normal furnishings, but a jar in the smith's bed chamber holds 27 electrum pieces.) The smith carries (d4) gold pieces, and each assistant has (2d6) silver pieces.

9. PROVISIONER: This low building houses a shop where all of the equipment needed for dungeon adventures (as listed in the rulebook) are sold. (Obvious exceptions are wagons, boats, and large or unusual items for such a place as an outpost.) He does not sell weapons other than spears, daggers, arrows and bolts. He has a few (7) shields, but does not sell armor or mounts. He will direct any persons interested in such items to the trader next door. Prices are as shown in the rules. He will buy like equipment from adventurers at 50% of listed price. The provisioner is a normal man; in time of need he has leather armor and shield (AC 6) and will man the walls or otherwise fight with a spear. (DX 8, AC 9, LVL 0, hp 3.) His wife and two children live in a small apartment in the place. He carries d6 gold pieces. He has a strong box with 100 gold pieces, 16 electrum pieces, and 30 copper pieces.

10. TRADER: This place deals in all armor, weapons, mounts (kept at the stable **4.**, above) and large quantities of goods such as salt, spices, cloth, rare woods, etc. The trader is very interested in obtaining furs. (Prices are as per the rule book, purchases **from** adventurers are at 50% of listed cost, except for furs which will be bought by him at whatever their stated value is **if the seller demands.**) He is a normal man (DX 9, AC 9, LVL 0, hp 2); his two sons are likewise (DX 10, AC 9, LVL 0, hp 3 each). All have leather armor and shields (AC 6) and pole arms and swords for use when necessary. (Hidden under the floorboards of their small apartment are 500 gold pieces and 1,110 silver pieces. Each carries 2d6 gold pieces in his purse.)

11. LOAN BANK: Here anyone can change money or gems for a 10% fee. The banker will also keep a person's wealth stored somewhat safely at no charge if it is left for at least one month, otherwise there is a 10% fee. Loans at an interest rate of 10% per month can be obtained for up to 5 gold pieces with no security deposit; over 5 gold pieces requires some item of at least twice the value of the loan. A sign on the shop states clearly that this place is under direct protection of the KEEP, and there is always a man-at-arms in chainmail with bow and sword watching the place from tower 12. (DX 10, AC 5, LVL 0, hp 4.) (The banker is a retired 3rd level fighter, DX 14, hp 12, with a sword handy, and plate and shield stored in his apartment above. He carries 6 platinum pieces and 12 gold pieces with him.) There is a scrawny old clerk in the place as well (2nd level magic-user, 5 **hit points**, with **sleep** and **ventriloquism** spells ready) who typically handles transactions. A hired mercenary fighter (DX 9, AC 3, LVL 0, hp 7) in plate mail and armed with axe and light crossbow is on guard inside the door. Displayed for sale are the following items:

1 carved ivory tusk — price 50 g.p.

1 silver cup — 20 g.p.

1 crystal decanter* — price 45 g.p. (actual worth 10 g.p.)

1 jade ring — price 250 g.p. (actual worth 400 g.p.)

1 dagger with jeweled scabbard — price 600 g.p.

1 fur-trimmed cape — price 75 g.p.

3 blank vellum* books — price 20 g.p. each

1 gold & silver belt — price 90 g.p.

1 set of thief's tools — price 100 g.p. (actual worth 35 g.p.)

1 iron box with secret lock — price 50 g.p.

9

The strong room of the place is in the cellar. It is protected by a locked iron door which leads to a small vault with 12 compartments each protected by locks with hidden poison needles (save versus poison at + 1 or die). These compartments hold the following items:

#1, #4, #11 empty.

#2 has 277 g.p. and 1 gem worth 500 g.p.

#3 has a gold altar service set worth 6,000 g.p.

#5 is **trapped** with a sleeping gas — no save, sleep for 3 turns; characters above 4th level save vs. poison to avoid effect.

#6 has 1,000 each platinum, gold, electrum, silver and copper pieces.

#7 has four poisonous adders (DX 15, AC 5 due to small size and great speed, HD 1 + 1, hp 5, #AT 1, each can bite for 1 hit point of damage and save versus poison at + 2 or die).

#8 has 3 gems of 1,000 g.p. value, 4 of 500 g.p., 11 of 100 g.p., 25 of 50 g.p., and 18 of 10 g.p. value.

#9 has an arrow trap which will always hit anyone in front of its door — 4 arrows each doing 1-6 points of damage (Divide arrows amongst persons in front).

#10 has an alabaster and gold statue worth 3,000 g.p. in a rare wood and silk case worth 600 g.p.

#12 has a sack with 58 platinum pieces and 91 electrum pieces in it.

(Empty compartments indicate funds out on loan. **Bold-faced** numbers are those belonging to the banker.)

12. WATCH TOWER: This 45' tall tower has all of the usual defensive devices. It houses six men-at-arms in chain (AC 5) with bows and swords, 6 others in leather and carrying shields (AC 6) and pole arms (DX 10, LVL 0, hp 4 each), and the **captain of the watch** (DX 15, AC 2, LVL 3 fighter, hp 20, + 1 **flaming sword** and + 1 dagger). The captain dwells on the first floor (with the usual furnishings, but he has a silver flagon and tankard worth 750 g.p.). He is known to carry quite a bit of money with him (20 platinum pieces, 11 gold pieces, 8 silver pieces), although the soldiers have only small coins (2d6 silver pieces each). The second and third floors are barracks for the men-at-arms. The upper story holds a supply of 200 arrows, many rocks, 2 barrels of oil, and 24 spears.

13. FOUNTAIN SQUARE: There is a large, gushing fountain in the center of the square. On holidays, local farmers and tradesmen set up small booths to sell their goods in this place.

14. TRAVELERS INN: This long, low structure has five small private rooms and a large common sleeping room for a full dozen. (Servants and the like always sleep in the stables, **4.**, of course.) Private rooms cost 1 g.p. per night, but sleeping in the common room is only 1 silver piece per night. The innkeeper and his family live in a small loft above the inn. They are obviously normal persons of no fighting ability. This building is some 18' high.

15. TAVERN: This place is the favorite of visitors and regulars alike. The food is excellent, the drinks generous and good. The place is always active, with 4-16 (4d4) patrons at any time of day or night. The bill of fare reads:

ALE	1 e.p.	SOUP	1 s.p.
SMALL BEER	1 s.p.	STEW	1 e.p.
WINE	1 e.p.	ROAST FOWL	1 g.p.
HONEY MEAD	1 g.p.	ROAST JOINT	2 g.p.
BARK TEA	1 s.p.	HOT PIE	1 e.p.
BREAD	1 c.p./slice	CHEESE	1 s.p./wedge
PUDDING	1 s.p./bowl	FRUIT	1 s.p.

The barkeep, if talking with a good customer and drinking to his health, will sometimes talk about the lands around the keep (1 drink per story, half of which may be true). He is known to hate small beer and love honey mead. There is a 50% chance that 2-5 (d4 + 1) of the patrons will be mercenary men-at-arms looking for work. (DX 11, AC 6, LVL 0, hp 5 each.) Each will have leather armor & shield, and sword and dagger; all other desired equipment must be purchased by the employer, including missile weapons, mounts, and dungeon gear. Wages for dangerous duty include all gear purchased, room and board, and 1 s.p. per day of service. If no gear is purchased, the cost rises to 1 g.p. per day. (Note that a mere spear or minor equipment is considered as **no gear**.) It is always necessary to buy mercenaries a drink before discussing terms of employment. There is a 10% chance that each of the following persons will be in the tavern at any given time:

CORPORAL OF THE WATCH
CAPTAIN OF THE WATCH
BAILIFF (see **6.**, above)
PRIEST (see **7b.**, above)
2-4 WATCHMEN (see **12.**, above)
SERGEANT OF THE GUARD (see **18.**, below)
 WANDERER (a 2nd or 3rd level fighter; human, dwarf, elf, or halfling as the DM decides, with complete equipment for adventuring; such a wanderer is 75% likely to join an expedition if offered 25% of the treasure gained, but 1 in 6 will be of evil intent and alignment.)

The taverner is a normal man (DX 13, AC 9, LVL 0, hp 6), as are his son and the pot boy* (DX 10, AC 9, LVL 0, hp 5 and 2), but in time of need they will don leather armor, carry shields (AC 6), and bear arms against attackers. The place is also served by his wife, daughter, a serving wench, and a scullion*. (The owner and his son each have 2d6 gold pieces in their purses, the wife d6, all others 2d6 coppers.) The cellar is where drink and food are stored and prepared, and where the servants sleep. The family sleeps in the small loft. (Hidden in an old crock under empty flour bags in the back room are 82 copper pieces, 29 silver pieces, 40 electrum pieces, and 17 gold pieces.)

16. GUILD HOUSE: When members of any guild (merchants, craft, artisans, etc.) travel to this area, they are offered the hospitality of this two-story building. This is a fee collection and administrative post, and the staff is careful to observe what traffic passes through the KEEP. Any trader who passes through must pay guild dues of 5% of the value of his merchandise, but he then gains the protection of the Guild House, assuming he is not a regular member. Craftsmen and artisans must gain Guild permission to enter or leave the land, paying a fee of 2d6 gold pieces either way (depending on the value of their trade). The lower floor contains the Guild Master's and his two clerks' quarters and an office (all sparsely furnished, but the Master has a gold ring worth 50 g.p., and 2d6 g.p. in his purse; each clerk has d4 each of gold, silver, and copper pieces. A strongbox under the Master's bed holds 712 gold pieces.) They are normal men (DX 12, AC 9, LVL 0, hp 4 each), with chainmail (AC 5), crossbows, and swords kept in a closet for quick use. There are two non-combatant servants who have quarters in the cellar. The upper floor is divided into two private rooms and a dormitory for guests. The Master is very influential, and his favor or dislike will be reflected in the treatment of persons by fortress personnel. Four men-at-arms with leather armor and shields and armed with spear and sword are on duty at all times, two on the first floor, two above (DX 14, AC 6, LVL 0, hp 6 each). They are fanatical Guildsmen who will obey any order from the Master. Guests of the Guild eat here. Drinking is frowned upon.

17. CHAPEL: The spiritual center of the Keep is opposite the Guild House. This building has a peaked roof two stories tall; the interior is one large room. The altar is located at the eastern end, with a colored glass window (worth 350 g.p. intact) above it; the window is 20' tall and 8' wide. An offering box is fastened securely atop a heavy pedestal in the southeast corner; it contains 1-100 c.p. and 1-100 s.p. at any time of the day. It is emptied each evening by the **Curate**, who deposits the coins with the Banker (**11.**, above). A small stairway in the northwest corner, behind the bare wooden pews, leads to the cellar, where the Curate and his three assistants have their quarters.

The **Curate** (5th level cleric) is the most influential person in the Keep except for the **Castellan** (**26.**, below). He has a +1 'to hit', due to his high level; Dexterity 13, 24 h.p., +1 magic Plate armor, normal shield, and a +1 **ring of protection** (AC 0). He wields a +1 magic mace or a **snake staff** (+1 to hit, 1 d6 +1 point of damage per hit; on command it will coil around the person hit, rendering him helpless until the Curate releases him or for 1-4 (d4) turns; it will crawl back to the Curate on command). He rarely wears his armor (unless the Keep is threatened), but is never without his ring and Staff. His three **Acolytes** (1st level clerics, hp 6, 5, 5, dexterity 15, 13, and 12 respectively) have plate and shield (AC 2) and mace. They are normally clothed in robes (AC 9) but will arm for battle on command of the Curate.

The Curate normally carries the following spells: **cure light wounds, detect magic, bless, hold person**. He will only use the **cure** on a member of his church, such as an officer of the Guard or a shopkeeper.

All of the clerics' armor and weapons are stored in the Curate's locked room in the Chapel cellar, which has normal but sparse furnishings. The Chapel also owns many magic potions (3 of **healing**, 1 of **haste**, 1 of **flying**) and a magic scroll with one **cure disease**, one **hold person**, and three **cure light wounds** spells on it. All of these magic items are hidden in a secret compartment underneath the offering box pedestal. The door of the compartment cannot be found unless the pedestal is moved. The door has two locks in it; the Curate and the Castellan have the only sets of keys.

If questioned closely by a friend, the Curate might (50% of the time) reveal his distrust of the Priest (**7b.**, above) who visits the Keep regularly. The Acolytes, however, think very highly of the Priest, and will say so to any who ask about him.

18. INNER GATEHOUSE: This stone structure is itself like a small fort. The southern portion is only about 15' high, plus battlement; the rear part is some 30' tall, plus battlement. There are arrow slits in the southern section of course, and along the walls of the 20' wide, 10' high passage through to the north. This passage slopes upwards towards the inner courtyard. The heavy gates are doublebound with iron and spiked. There are six guards on duty at all times (two inside the gateway, two on the lower battlement, two on the upper), plus one officer on call (see below). No visitor is allowed beyond this point except by invitation or unless he or she has special permits.

The first floor of the place is the main armory. There are dozens of shields and of each sort of weapon. Two small rooms are quarters for the **Sergeant** and **Captain of the Guard** (furnishings are sparse). The second story on the north houses the Guardsmen stationed here.

Captain of the Guard: (DX 16, AC 0 from +1 plate armor and +1 shield, LVL 3 fighter, hp 24, +1 spear and +2 sword.) This man is very personable and an excellent leader and tactician. (He will sometimes move about in the Outer Bailey disguised as a mercenary.) He has 15 gold pieces and a 100 g.p. gem in the pommel* of his dagger.

Sergeant of the Guard: (DX 14, AC 2 from chainmail with magic shield +1 and **ring of protection** +1, LVL 2 fighter, hp 18, +1 sword, +2 dagger.) This very strong fellow (strength 17) is a hard fighter and loves to drink and brawl. He carries d6 each of gold, electrum, and silver pieces. (There is a potion of **healing** in a chest in his room under a spare cape.)

Guardsmen: There are 24 quartered here. Each has chainmail and shield, sword, dagger, and throwing axe. Eight are crossbowmen, eight are bowmen, and eight have pole arms. (DX usually 10, AC 4, LVL 0, hp 5 each.) Two from each group are on duty at any given time; the rest take a full turn to armor and arm and turn out. (Each has 2d6 silver pieces.)

19. SMALL TOWER: This typical tower houses eight guardsmen who are all armored in chainmail (AC 5) and carry crossbows and swords. Shields are stored below, so in hand-to-hand combat they are AC 4. (DX usually 10, LVL 0, hp 5 each, 2d6 s.p. each.) Two are on duty atop the tower at all times. The other six are in the chamber below. The base is solid except for the small stair up.

20. GUARD TOWER: This 50' high structure houses 24 guardsmen (as in **18.**, above). Their commander is the **corporal of the guard**. (DX 15, AC 2 from plate & shield, LVL 1, hp 9, sword and +1 dagger.) There are supplies of food, weapons, and oil on the upper floor. The rest of the building is taken up with barracks and a room for the leader.

21. INNER BAILEY: This entire area is grass-covered. The troops drill here, and there are practice and jousting areas. During the daylight hours there will always be a dozen or more soldiers engaged in weapons practice.

22. CAVALRY STABLES: There are 12 heavy warhorses and 18 medium warhorses kept within. They are tended by 2 lackeys (DX 9, AC 9, LVL 0, hp 2) and guarded by two men-at-arms with chainmail & shield, sword and dagger. (DX 11, AC 4, LVL 0, hp 4 each.) In addition, there are always from 1-4 light horses kept here for use by couriers or messengers.

23. GREAT TOWER: This 60' high structure houses 24 guardsmen, one-third with crossbows, one-third with bows, one-third with pole arms (DX usually 10, AC 4, LVL 0, hp 5 each), and another **corporal** as per **20.**, above. (See **20.** for tower details and so on.)

24. THE KEEP FORTRESS: This place has many tiers and is solidly built to withstand a siege. The lowest level consists of a 15' high front section. The round flanking towers are 60' high, while the main building is 30' high. All sections have battlements. The door is solid iron. Inside are a great hall, an armory for the cavalry, and several side chambers for small dinners or meetings. The cellars below have vast stores of provisions, quarters for a score of servants, a cistern*, and a dungeon area with four stout cells.

The **Castellan*** resides in area **27.** (see below), but he and his assistants will be in the lower part of the place during the day, tending to business and holding audience. There will always be eight guardsmen in plate (AC 3) with crossbows and swords on duty on the walls, and a like number with plate & shield (AC 2) and swords stationed inside. (DX 12, LVL 0, hp 5 each.) The whole place is well-appointed, and the furniture is heavy and upholstered.

11

Second Floor: There are rooms here for up to 36 cavalrymen, plus two chambers for special guests. There are 12 heavy cavalrymen with plate & shield and sword and dagger (DX 12, AC 2, LVL 1, hp 8 each; lances are stored below). There are also 18 medium cavalrymen in chainmail, each with light crossbow and axe, quartered here. (DX 11, AC 5, LVL 0, hp 6 each; each has 2d6 gold pieces.) Their rooms are spartan, with cot, chair, and armoire* for each. Two couriers, men-at-arms with leather armor and swords, are currently quartered in one side chamber. (DX 16, AC 7, LVL 0, hp 3 each.)

25. TOWER: Each is 40' high, with battlements, and pierced with arrow slits to cover the east and west corner areas. The fortress men-at-arms are housed in these structures and in the towers indicated by **26**.

26. CENTRAL TOWERS: These structures rise 20' above the roof of the fortress, with a 5' battlement above their roof. Their two upper stories house 12 men-at-arms each; 6 in plate (AC 3) with crossbow and sword, 6 in plate and shield (AC 2) with sword (DX 12, LVL 0, hp 5 each) who are off-duty. It will take one turn for them to be ready for battle. In the two lower floors are the **Castellan's** assistants.

> **Scribe:** This individual is a 2nd level cleric, armored in plate & shield, with a mace. (DX 9, AC 2, LVL 2, hp 11.) He has a **hold person** spell on a scroll he carries; his own spell is **light** which he may cast on an opponent's eyes to blind him. His chamber is austere, and there is nothing of value within except a gold holy symbol worth 150 gold pieces. He has 48 gold pieces in his purse.

> **Advisor:** This individual is an elf who speaks eight languages. He is a fighter/magic-user of 3rd level, DX 16, AC 2 from +1 plate mail, hp 18, sword, +1 magic bow, and a **ring of fire resistance**. His spells are **charm person, read magic,** and **web**. Tapestries and carpets are all about the room (one tapestry is worth 500 g.p.); he has very comfortable furniture. He wears a jeweled pendant worth 1,000 g.p. and carries 6 platinum and 10 gold pieces in purse.

27. CASTELLAN'S CHAMBER: This portion of the fortress is 10' above the main roof and has battlements. Inside is the private room of the commander of the whole Keep. It is lavishly furnished, with a silver mirror (worth 300 g.p.) on the wall, a malachite bowl (worth 750 g.p.) on a table, and a fox robe (worth 1,200 g.p.) in his armoire*. He has a small silver case (worth 450 g.p.) which contains 40 platinum pieces and 12 gems worth 100 g.p. each. There is a +1 spear on the wall by the door.

> **Castellan:** 6th level fighter (+2 to hit due to his high level), DX 16, AC -1 from +1 magic plate, +1 shield, and **ring of protection**, hp 48, +3 sword, +2 dagger, **elven cloak and boots**. (He also carries a potion of **flying** and a potion of **haste** with him at all times.) His chain of office is silver with gems (worth 1,800 g.p.), and he carries 10 each of platinum, gold, and electrum pieces, plus a gem worth 500 g.p. He is a very clever fellow, but at times he can be too hasty in his decisions. His bravery and honesty are absolute. If a guest asks him any question, he will do his best to answer, providing that it does not compromise the security of the KEEP.

ADVENTURES OUTSIDE THE KEEP

After the group establishes itself and obtains equipment, they will either follow clues gained in conversation with residents of the KEEP or set out exploring on their own (or both). Naturally, they will be trying to find the **Caves of Chaos**, but this will take a bit of trekking, and in the meantime they might well run into more than they can handle. Thus there are two maps — an AREA MAP for use while they search for their prime objective, and the CAVES OF CHAOS MAP which is essentially a dungeon level map. Leaving the latter for later, take a look at the AREA MAP.

The "Realm" is to the west, off the map. The road branches, one path to the KEEP ON THE BORDERLANDS, the other leading off into the forsaken wilderness beyond the ken of Law. Note that most features are unnamed, so you can name them as suits your campaign. Inspection of the map will also show that there are five special areas. Numbers 1-4 indicate outside encounters and are detailed below. The **Cave of the Unknown** area is left for you to use as a place to devise your own cavern complex or dungeon maze. You may also wish to expand on the other encounter areas, designing camps, lairs or lost ruins to permit more adventuring. If you do not wish to undertake this at first, simply DO NOT ALLOW YOUR PLAYERS TO LOCATE IT EVEN IF THEY THOROUGHLY SEARCH THE VERY SPACE IT IS IN. (It was hidden by a magical illusion so as to be undetectable . . .)

The normal movement rate is 1 square per hour searching, 3 walking, 6 riding. Walking in the fens is at the rate of 1 square per hour; no riding is possible. Both walking and riding in the forest are at the same speed, 2 squares per hour. Mounted movement along the road can be increased to 12 squares for one hour, but then the horse must rest for an hour within the next six turns, or it can be held at 8 squares per hour for 6 hours with a 2 hour rest thereafter.

Camping Outdoors Overnight: Nothing will molest the party when so camped, unless they are within six squares of a numbered encounter area. For each square they are within the six square range there is a 1 in 6 chance that the monsters there will seek them out; so at 6 squares there is a 1 in 6 chance, at 5 there is a 2 in 6, at 4 there is a 3 in 6, at 3 there is a 4 in 6, at 2 there is a 5 in 6 and at 1 square a 6 in 6 — automatic encounter. Treat otherwise as a normal encounter.

Organized parties should post at least one guard in shifts throughout the night. However, if the party posts no guards, surprise will be automatic as they are sleeping and unaware. If the party has a fire going, the monsters will never be surprised, even though the party may be.

Also take note of what provisions are brought with the party. They are adventuring, not hunting, and so they should not expect to find food. They should bring ample food and water with them. If not, when the party runs out, they will either have to try their luck at hunting (1 chance in 6 to catch food for **one** day for d6 men), or return to the Keep to restock their supplies. Stress to them in some manner that they will probably prefer to return to the Keep, knowing that they will fare better there, and not risk encountering monsters while hunting.

If the party attempts to move off the map, have a sign, a wandering stranger, a friendly talking magpie, or some other "helper" tell them that they are moving in the wrong direction.

Area Map Encounter Areas:

1. MOUND OF THE LIZARD MEN: The streams and pools of the fens* are the home of a tribe of exceptionally evil lizard men. Being nocturnal, this group is unknown to the residents of the KEEP, and they will not bother

individuals moving about in daylight unless they set foot on the mound, under which the muddy burrows and dens of the tribe are found. One by one, males will come out of the marked opening and begin attacking the party. There are 6 males total (DX 10, AC 5, HD 2 + 1, hp 12, 10, 9, 8, 7, and 5, #AT 1, D 1-8) who will attack, and if all are killed, the remainder of the tribe will hide in the lair. Each has only crude weapons; the largest has a necklace worth 1,100 gold pieces.

In the lair is another male (DX 9, AC 5, HD 2 + 1, hp 11), 3 females (who are equal to males, but attack as 1 + 1 hit dice monsters, DX 9, and have 8, 6, and 6 hit points respectively), 8 young (with 1 hit point each and do not effectively attack), and 6 eggs. Hidden under the nest with the eggs are 112 copper pieces, 186 silver pieces, a gold ingot worth 90 gold pieces, a **healing** potion and a **poison** potion. The first person crawling into the lair will always lose the initiative to the remaining lizard man and the largest female, unless the person thrusts a torch well ahead of his or her body.

2. **SPIDERS' LAIR:** 3 large spiders (DX 12, AC 8, HD 1 + 1, hp 7, 6, and 5, #AT 1, D 1 point, plus save vs. poison at + 2 on the roll) have spun their webs amongst the trees here. Under a pile of leaves nearby is the skeleton of a victim, a hapless elf. Everything he bore has turned to rot and ruin, save a filthy shield which appears quite worthless (but cleaning and oiling will return it to + 1 magic status).

3. **BANDIT CAMP:** A party of a dozen bandits has camped here — close enough to be able to spy on the KEEP, far enough away so as to be unlikely to be discovered by patrols. The members of this group are:

Leader:	DX 14, AC 5 (chainmail), LVL 2 fighter, hp 12, bow and spear
Lieutenant:	DX 12, AC 6 (leather & shield), LVL 1 fighter, hp 7, spear and sword
2 Bowmen:	DX 13, AC 7 (leather), LVL 0, hp 4 each, daggers, bows
8 Spearmen:	DX 10, AC 6 (leather & shield), LVL 0, hp 5 each, daggers, spears

Each has 3d6 silver pieces, the lieutenant having an additional d6 gold pieces, and the leader having an additional 2d6 gold pieces. They each have a light

horse, saddle, saddle bags, and bed roll. Bowmen have an extra quiver of 20 arrows near their horses, and there is a cask of good wine on a tree stump in the camp. Several game animals are hung from branches and can be eaten or carried along as they are cleaned.

4. **THE MAD HERMIT:** For many years a solitary hermit has haunted this area of the forest, becoming progressively wilder and crazier and more dangerous. His dwelling is in a huge hollow oak, the entrance to the trunk cavity concealed by a thick bush. Inside is a mound of leaves and a couple of pieces of crude furniture. Even his cup and plate are handmade of wood and are of no value. (There is a small chest buried under a few inches of dirt under the leaves of the Mad Hermit's "bed". In this container are 31 gold pieces, 164 silver pieces, a potion of **invisibility**, and a + 1 **dagger**.) The hermit also has a "pet", a puma, which lurks in hiding on a limb of the oak, ready to spring upon any unwary intruder. (This creature will always get first attack.)

Mad Hermit: 3rd level thief, DX 17, AC 6, (wears a + 1 **ring of protection** and leather armor), hp 15, 30% chance to **move silently**, 20% chance to **hide in shadows**, + 2 bonus to hit when attacking (due to his madness), and + 2 on damage when a hit is scored, due to his madman's strength (bonus for striking from behind is + 6 to hit and double normal damage + 2 points). He carries no treasure (other than the ring he wears!).

Puma: DX 18, AC 6, HD 3 + 3, hp 15, #AT 3, D 1-6 each. (This creature will always attack first in each round. If it leaps down upon an opponent, it gains + 2 to hit on each of its attacks that combat round. Usually it will attack by jump, and thereafter it will stay on the ground and fight normally. If it is not engaged in combat during any round, however, it will take the opportunity to leap into a tree and then spring down on the next round.)

(You may opt to have the Mad Hermit approach the group on friendly terms, claiming to be a holy man seeking goodness in nature — perhaps he actually believes that at times. He will suddenly turn on the group when the opportunity presents itself, striking from behind, and calling his ferocious "pet" to his aid.)

13

THE CAVES OF CHAOS

(DM Note: When the players discover the ravine area, read the following paragraph to them. Add whatever you feel is appropriate to the description of what they see, but be careful not to give anything away or mislead them. Information on how you should handle the whole area is given before the encounter area descriptions.)

START: The forest you have been passing through has been getting more dense, tangled, and gloomier than before. The thick, twisted tree trunks, unnaturally misshapen limbs, writhing roots, clutching and grasping thorns and briars all seem to warn and ward you off, but you have forced and hacked your way through regardless. Now the strange growth has suddenly ended — you have stepped out of the thicket into a ravine-like area. The walls rise rather steeply to either side to a height of about 100' or so — dark, streaked rock mingled with earth. Clumps of trees grow here and there, both on the floor of the ravine and up the sloping walls of the canyon. The opening you stand in is about 200' wide. The ravine runs at least 400' west (actually 440') to where the western end rises in a steep slope. Here and there, at varying heights on all sides of the ravine, you can see the black mouths of cave-like openings in the rock walls. The sunlight is dim, the air dank, there is an oppressive feeling here — as if something evil is watching and waiting to pounce upon you. There are bare, dead trees here and there, and upon one a vulture perches and gazes hungrily at you. A flock of ravens rise croaking from the ground, the beat of their wings and their cries magnified by the terrain to sound loud and horrible. Amongst the litter of rubble, boulders, and dead wood scattered about on the ravine floor, you can see bits of gleaming ivory and white — closer inspection reveals that these are bones and skulls of men, animals, and other things . . . .

You know that you have certainly discovered the **Caves of Chaos.**

NOTES FOR THE DM ON THE CAVES OF CHAOS

CAVE AREA MAP: There are woods overlays and rough contour lines* shown on the map. These are only for surface movement references, and once your players are underground you should ignore these markings.

WOODS: The small groves and copses are thick growths, tangled and forbidding. You may, at your option, have characters encounter occasional monsters herein — stirges, humanoids (kobolds, orcs, etc.) from the caves nearby, or the like. Movement through these wooded areas is slow and difficult. Characters must move in single file. Even though not shown, there are single trees, shrubs, and bushes elsewhere.

UNDERGROUND: The caves, passages, and rooms of the complex are on different levels. Passages slope upwards and downwards between the contours, even where stairways are not shown. Areas are roofed by at least 5' of solid rock.

INTERIORS: Except where noted otherwise, all underground areas are natural or hewn from living rock. All surfaces are rough (and easy to climb for a thief) with small ledges, minor cracks, small openings, etc.

RANSOMING PRISONERS: Organized tribes can optionally be allowed to take player characters prisoner, freeing one to return to the KEEP in order to bring a ransom back to free the captives. Set the sums low — 10 to 100 gold pieces (or a magic item which the ransoming monsters would find useful) per prisoner. If the ransom is paid, allow the characters to go free. Then, without telling the players, assume that this success brought fame to the capturing monsters, so their numbers will be increased by 2-12 additional members, and the tribe will also be very careful to watch for a return of the adventurers seeking revenge for their humiliating captivity. The period of extra alertness will last for 1-4 weeks; the increase in numbers is permanent.

TRIBAL ALLIANCES AND WARFARE: You might allow player characters to somehow become aware that there is a constant skirmishing going on between the goblins and hobgoblins on one side and the orcs, sometimes with gnoll allies, on the other — with the kobolds hoping to be forgotten by all, and the bugbears picking off any stragglers who happen by. With this knowledge, they might be able to set tribes to fighting one another, and then the adventurers can take advantage of the weakened state of the feuding humanoids. Be careful to handle this whole thing properly; it is a device you may use to aid players who are few in number but with a high level of playing skill. It will make it too easy if there are many players, or if players do not actually use wits instead of force when the opportunity presents itself.

MONSTERS LEARNING FROM EXPERIENCE: Allow intelligent monsters (even those with only low intelligence) to learn from experience. If player characters use flaming oil against them, allow the monsters to use oil as soon as they can find some. If adventurers are always sneaking up on them, have the monsters set warning devices to alert them of intruders. If characters run from overwhelming numbers, have the monsters set up a ruse by causing a few to shout and make noise as if there were many coming, thus hopefully frightening off the intruders. This method of handling monsters is basic to becoming a good DM. Apply the principle wherever and whenever you have reason.

EMPTIED AREAS: When monsters are cleared out of an area, the place will be deserted for 1-4 weeks. If no further intrusion is made into the area, however, the surviving former inhabitants will return or else some other monster will move in. For instance, a troll might move into the minotaur's cave complex (I.), bringing with him whatever treasure he has.

Encounter Areas:

A. **KOBOLD LAIR:** There is a 2 in 6 chance that as the group enters the cave-like tunnel, 8 kobolds will come out from hiding in the trees above and attack first. Kobolds: DX 13, AC 7, HD ½, hp 3 each, #AT 1, D 1-4, + 3 on all saving throws except dragon breath. Each carries d8 silver pieces.

   Note: 30' inside the entrance is a **pit** (⊠). There is a 3 in 6 chance that each person in the front rank will fall in unless they are probing ahead. There is a 1 in 6 chance that individuals in the second rank will also fall in, but only if they are close to the first rank and the character ahead has fallen in. The pit is 10' deep, and those falling in will take 1-6 points of damage. The pit lid will close, and persons within cannot escape without aid from the outside. The noise will attract creatures from areas **1.** and **2.** Planks for crossing the pit are stored at #**1.**, beyond.

1. **GUARD ROOM:** 6 kobold guards, DX 13, AC 7, HD ½, hp 3 each, D 1-4, 2 attacks on first round as they have javelins to hurl. Each carries d6 silver pieces. One will run to alert areas **4.** and **6.** The guards will be alerted by loud noises or lights.

2. **GIANT RATS** (amidst garbage and waste): There are 18 giant rats, DX 8, AC 7, HD ½, hp 2 each, #AT 1, D 1-3, and 1 in 20 chance per wound caused that disease will result. (Starting 48 hours after infection, the disease will cause weakness for 1 week and end in death, unless cured.) These monsters are the pets of the kobolds, living off the garbage and waste of their hosts. They will

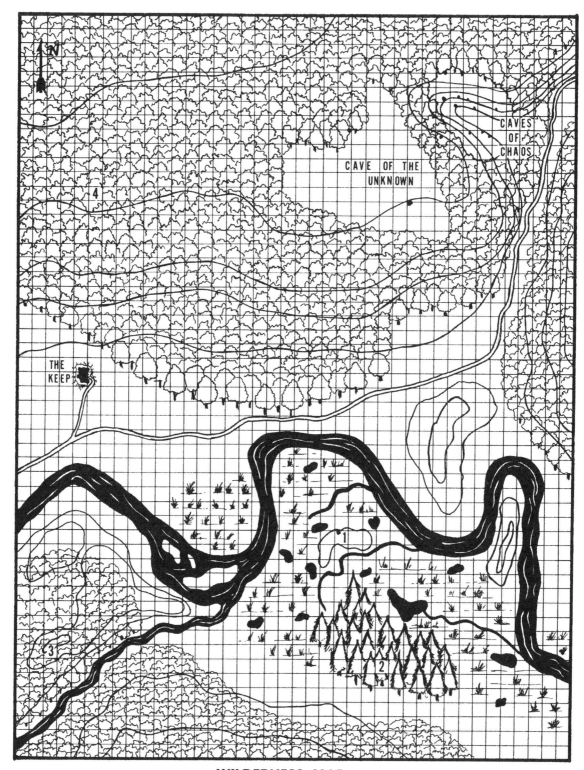

WILDERNESS MAP

SCALE: ONE SQUARE EQUALS 100 YARDS

FOREST

RIVER

CONTOUR LINE

FENS

ROAD

TAMARACK STAND

WATER

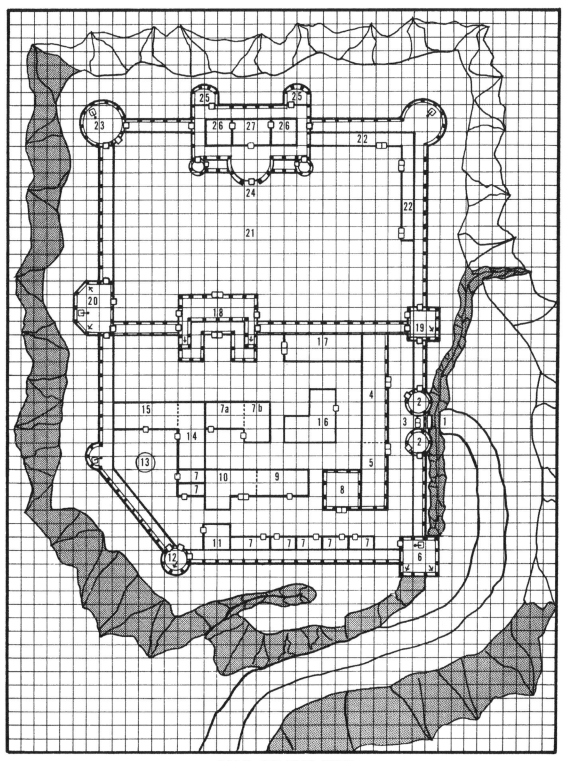

MAP OF THE KEEP

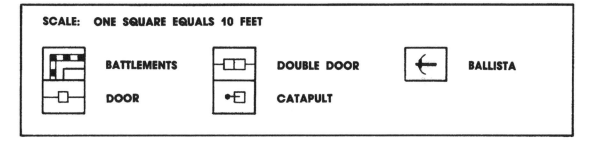

SCALE: ONE SQUARE EQUALS 10 FEET

BATTLEMENTS

DOOR

DOUBLE DOOR

CATAPULT

← BALLISTA

MAGIC-USER SPELLS

Book of First Level Spells:

Charm Person	Protection from Evil
Dancing Lights	Read Languages
Detect Magic	Read Magic
Enlargements	Shield
Hold Portal	Sleep
Light	Tenser's Floating Disc
Magic Missile	Ventriloquism

Book of Second Level Spells:

Audible Glamer	Locate Object
Continual Light	Magic Mouth
Darkness	Mirror Image
Detect Evil	Phantasmal Forces
Detect Invisible	Pyrotechnics
ESP	Ray of Enfeeblement
Invisibility	Strength
Knock	Web
Levitate	Wizard Lock

Book of Third Level Spells:

Clairaudience	Invisibility 10'
Clairvoyance	Lightning Bolt
Dispel Magic	Monster Summoning I
Explosive Runes	Protection/Evil 10'
Fire Ball	Protection/Normal Missiles
Fly	Rope Trick
Haste Spell	Slow Spell
Hold Person	Suggestion
Infravision	Water Breathing

CLERICAL SPELLS

Clerics of the first level can not cast any spells. When they reach the second level, however, they are capable of one spell per game/day. Since clerical spells are divinely given, they do not have to be studied to master them. A second level cleric can call on any first level spell he wants to use, thus the entire gamut of spells is available to him for selection **prior** to the adventure. However, only that spell or spells selected can be used during the course of the adventure.

Book of First Level Spells:

Cure Light Wounds	Protection from Evil
Detect Evil	Purify Food and Water
Detect Magic	Remove Fear
Light	Resist Cold

Book of Second Level Spells:

Bless	Resist Fire
Find Traps	Silence: 15' Radius
Know Alignment	Snake Charm
Hold Person	Speak with Animals

DUNGEONS & DRAGONS®

REFERENCE TABLES

(This page is perforated for easy removal)

Saving Throw Table — Levels 1 to 3
(Use a 20-sided die)

Class	Spell or Magic Staff	Magic Wand	Death Ray or Poison	Turned to Stone	Dragon Breath
Normal man, Kobold, Goblin, etc.	17	14	13	15	16
Fighting Man, Thief, Hobgoblin, etc.	16	13	12	14	15
Magic-user	15	14	13	13	16
Cleric	15	12	11	14	16
Dwarves & Halflings	14	11	10	12	14

COST OF EQUIPMENT AND WEAPONS

Item	Cost	Item	Cost
Barding (Horse Armor)	150	Silver Mirror, small	15
50' of Rope	1	Wooden Cross	2
10' Pole	1	Silver Cross	25
12 Iron Spikes	1	Holy Water/Vial	25
Small Sack	1	Wolvesbane, bunch	10
Large Sack	2	Garlic, bud	5
Leather Back Pack	5	Wine, quart	1
Water/Wine Skin	1	Iron rations (for dungeon	
6 Torches	1	expeditions) 1 person/	
Lantern	10	1 week	15
Flask of Oil	2	Standard rations for 1	
		person/1 week	5
Tinder Box	3		
		Other items cost may be	
3 Stakes & Mallet	3	calculated by comparing	
		to similar items listed	
Steel Mirror	5	above.	

Item	Cost	Item	Cost
Dagger	3	Case with 30 Quarrels	10
Hand Axe	3	20 Arrows/30 Quarrels	5
Mace	5	Silver Tipped Arrow	5
Sword	10	Mule	20
Battle Axe	7	Draft Horse	30
Morning Star	6	Light Horse	40
Flail	8	Warhorse, Medium	100
Spear	2	Warhorse, Heavy	200
Pole Arm	7	Saddle	25
Halberd	7	Saddle Bags	10
Two-Handed Sword	15	Cart	100
Lance	4	Wagon	200
Pike	5	Raft	40
Short Bow	25	Small Boat	100
Long Bow	40	Leather Armor	15
Composite Bow	50	Chain-type Mail	30
Light Crossbow	15	Plate Mail	50
Heavy Crossbow	25	Helmet	10
Quiver of 20 Arrows	10	Shield	10

WANDERING MONSTER TABLE

One Level Below Ground	Die	Two Levels Below Ground	Die	Three Levels Below Ground	Die
Kobolds (3-12)	1	Orcs (5-20)	1	Hobgoblins (5-20)	1
Goblins (2-8)	2	Hobgoblins (2-8)	2	Zombies (2-5)	2
Bandits (1-4)	3	Gnomes (2-5)	3	Bugbears (2-8)	3
Orcs (2-5)	4	Ghouls (1-4)	4	Ogres (1-4)	4
Skeletons/Zombies (1-6/1-4)	5	Bandits (2-5)	5	Wights (1-3)	5
Bandits (2-5)	6	Skeletons (1-4)	6	Displacer Beasts (1-2)	6
Berserkers (1-4)	7	Bandits (2-5)	7	Dopplegangers (1-4)	7
Stirges (2-5)	8	Orcs (2-8)	8	Grey Ooze (1)	8
Orcs (1-4)	9	Dwarves (4-16)	9	Blink Dogs (2-5)	9
Dwarves (2-5)	10	Elves (3-12)	10	Harpies (1-3)	10
Elves (1-6)	11	Giant Ticks (1-3)	11	Wererats (1-4)	11
Gelatinous Cube (1)	12	Carrion Crawler (1)	12	Ochre Jelly (1)	12

CLERICS VS. UNDEAD TABLE
(use 2d6)

Undead Type

Cleric Level	Skeleton	Zombie	Ghoul	Wight	Wraith	Mummy	Spectre	Vampire
1	7	9	11	no effect.				
2	T	7	9	11	no effect.			
3	T	T	7	9	11	no effect . .		

Number = score this number or greater to turn away
T = automatically turned away, up to 2 dice in number

DIE ROLL FOR CHARACTER TO SCORE A HIT,
BY OPPONENT'S ARMOR CLASS
(use 1d20)

Armor Class	9 No Armor	8 Shield	7 Leather Armor	6 Leather & Shield	5 Chain Mail	4 Chain Mail & Shield	3 Plate Mail	2 Plate & Shield
Normal Man	11	12	13	14	15	16	17	18
1st-3rd Level Character	10	11	12	13	14	15	16	17

Score of number shown or higher is a hit.

DIE ROLL FOR MONSTER TO SCORE A HIT, BY DEFENDER'S ARMOR CLASS
(use 1d20)

Armor Class	9	8	7	6	5	4 Chain Mail & Shield	3	2
Monster's Hit Dice	No Armor	Shield	Leather	Leather & Shield	Chain Mail		Plate Mail	Plate & Shield
up to 1	10	11	12	13	14	15	16	17
1 + 1 to 2	9	10	11	12	13	14	15	16
2+ to 3	8	9	10	11	12	13	14	15
3+ to 4	6	7	8	9	10	11	12	13
4+ to 6+	5	6	7	8	9	10	11	12
7 to 8+	4	5	6	7	8	9	10	11
9 to 10+	2	3	4	5	6	7	8	9
11 up	0	1	2	3	4	5	6	7

rush to the sound of the trap door closing or battle. They have nothing of value in their lair or on their bodies, but their leader (rat #18) who will be at the back of the pack, a huge fellow (DX 12, AC 5 due to speed and cunning, HD 1-1, hp 4, #AT 2, D 2-4, i.e. 1-3 + 1) wears a thin silver chain set with 5 small gems (jewelry value 400 gold pieces, chain value 50 gold pieces, each gem worth 50 gold pieces). The weight of a few rats will not trigger the pit trap.

3. FOOD STORAGE ROOM: The door is locked. This place contains various sorts of dried and salted meat, grain, and vegetables in sacks, boxes, barrels, and piles. There are also bits and pieces of past human victims. There is nothing of value here; even the wine in a large cask is thin and vinegary.

4. GUARD ROOM: Here are 3 very large kobold guards with chainmail and bows to fire down the passage at attackers (DX 13, AC 5, HD 1 + 1, hp 5 each, #AT 1, D 1-6). The guards will hide behind the corner for cover, so all missiles fired at them will be at -2 "to hit". Each carries an axe in his belt and a purse with 2d6 gold pieces.

5. KOBOLD CHIEFTAIN'S ROOM: This huge kobold is equal to a 2 hit dice monster, has 8 hit points, chainmail & shield (AC 4), with a large gem on a great golden chain about his neck (value 1,200 gold pieces). He has the key to the storage room (#3.). He hits for 2-8 (2d4) points of damage with a large battle axe. (DX 12, AC 4, HD 2, hp 8, #AT ½, D 2-8.) There are 5 female kobolds in the room also. (DX 10, AC 7, HD ½, hp 2 each, #AT 1, D 1-3.) There are heaps of cloth and bits of battered furniture in the place. Hidden in an old blanket hanging on the wall are 50 gold pieces (sewn into the hem). Each female has d6 gold pieces. A locked chest holds 203 copper, 61 silver, and 22 electrum pieces.

6. COMMON CHAMBER: The bulk of the kobold tribe dwells here. There are 17 males (DX 13, AC 7, HD ½, hp 3 each, #AT 1, D 1-4), 23 females (DX 10, AC 7, HD ½, hp 2 each, #AT 1, D 1-3), and 8 young (which do not attack). If their caves are invaded, those able will help in its defense. Males have d6 silver pieces each, females d4 silver pieces each; the young have nothing. Amidst the litter of cloth and bits and scraps of odds-and-ends there is a piece of silk worth 15 gold pieces. (If the party does not search it will not be located.)

(DM Note: Kobold losses will not be replaced, though injured kobolds will heal. If the attackers hurl oil at the kobolds, they will retreat if possible, rather than suffer damage. Should they have the opportunity to find any flasks of oil, the kobolds will use them against attacking characters!)

B. ORC LAIR: Upon entering, the party will see that the wall 30' to the north is decorated with heads and skulls (human, elven, dwarven) in various stages of decay. These cheerful greetings are placed in niches which checker about 100 square feet of the surface of the wall. Close inspection will show that one is orcish (see **g.** below). Sounds of activity can be heard from the west, but all is quiet to the east.

> **Area g:** This narrowing area is a guard post, the watcher (Orc: DX 10, AC 7, HD 1, hp 5, #AT 1, D 1-6 sword) having a small, window-like opening from which he can observe the entrance to the lair. A piece of gray canvas behind gives the impression that the guard's head is another of the ghastly trophies which decorate the wall. If adventurers enter, he will quickly duck down, slipping a goblin head into the place his own was, and alert the orcs at **7.**

7. GUARD ROOM: 4 orcs: DX 10, AC 7, HD 1, hp 5 each. These guards are armed with spears. Each carries one for hurling and one to melee with. They have d8 electrum pieces each. When alerted, they will rush to engage intruders, raising a hue and cry when they see them. There is nothing of value in their chamber, there being only pallets and shabby clothing hanging on pegs.

8. The watcher (**g.**) will alert the 4 guards here (exactly as in **7.**, above) who will rush west and then south to flank or surround intruders threatening area **7.** or **9.** or approaching their own quarters.

9. BANQUET AREA: There is a great fireplace on the south wall and many tables and benches in this 30' x 50' chamber — the table at the north end having a large chair at its head where the orc leader usually holds court. The place is empty of orcs although there is a small fire of charcoal burning in the fireplace.

10. COMMON ROOM: Here are quartered 12 male orcs (DX 10, AC 7, HD 1, hp 4 each) and 18 females and 9 young (who do not fight). The males have 2d6 silver pieces each, the others have nothing of worth. The few furnishings in the room are likewise of no value.

11. STORAGE CHAMBER: The door is locked. Amidst the stacks and heaps of supplies are goods here (see **3.**, above), there are 3 shields, 17 spears, and 2 axes in excellent condition (by some quirk of fate). A small crate in the far northeast corner contains a long-forgotten light crossbow and 60 bolts. There is nothing else of value in the place.

12. ORC LEADER'S ROOM: This large creature is clad in chainmail, has a +1 magic shield, and carries a mace. He fights as a 3 hit dice monster, has 12 hit points, and adds +2 to damage he causes when successfully striking an opponent (thus, 3-8 points of damage). This is due to his strength and skill. He carries 31 gold pieces, and wears a ring set with a gem (total value 700 g.p.).

The room is carpeted, has tapestries upon the walls (note one of these covers the entrance to the small cave to the west), and battered but still serviceable furniture and a cot. His two mates sleep on cushions at the foot of his resting place. The two females in the place fight as males (DX 12, AC 7, HD 1, hp 3 each), and each has 2d6 gold pieces on her person. The chests and other furniture have nothing of value.

If hard pressed, the leader will wiggle behind the tapestries on the south wall and attempt to work the catch on the secret door to the south and go to the rival tribe for help, but his very life must be in great peril before he will do so. (Adventurers can only spring this catch by rolling a 1 (on a d6) twice in a row, or having two characters do so simultaneously.)

> **Area t:** This alcove is used by the orc leader to store arms and treasure. There are two complete suits of chainmail here (man-sized and dwarf-sized), 4 swords, and a locked iron chest which holds 205 copper, 386 silver, 81 gold, and 13 platinum pieces. A small niche in the back wall, with a boulder in front covering it, hides a **potion of healing** and a scroll with a 6-die **fire ball** spell on it.

(DM Note: Orc losses cannot be replaced, but after an initial attack by adventurers, the males at location **10.** will move four of their number into area **9.**, arm these orcs with light crossbows, and lay an ambush for intruders. If the leader is slain, all surviving orcs from this locale will seek refuge under the tribe at **C.** (see below), taking everything of value (and even of no value) with them, and **B.** will thereafter be deserted.)

C. ORC LAIR: Similar to the orcs at area **B.**, these monsters inhabit cave areas **14.-16.** These orcs, however, do not rely upon a continual watch being kept; instead, they have a series of nearly invisible strings running across the entry passage, about 11' from the entrance. When any of these strings is tripped, a heavy, weighted net suspended from the ceiling will drop upon intruders, and metal pieces tied to it will create an alarm sound. (The trip strings will be spotted only if careful observation is asked for, each observer having a 1 in 6 chance of seeing the devices. The camouflaged net is 10' wide and 18' long, made of thick, tarred ropes, and will entrap the victim for 1-4 rounds. Meanwhile, orcs from area **14.** will be there in 1 round . . . .)

13. FORGOTTEN ROOM: Only the two orc leaders (from this area and from **B.**) know of this place. They secretly meet here on occasion to plan co-operative ventures or discuss tribal problems, for although separate tribes are not exactly friendly, both leaders are aware of the fact that there is strength in numbers. A small table and two chairs are in the middle of the room. There is a wooden chest to one side which holds a bow, a quiver of 20 arrows, 2 swords, and 2 daggers. Two shields are hung on the south wall. There are only odds and ends otherwise, except that in the southeast corner, hidden beneath an old bucket (which is filled with black, stagnant water) are two small pouches, each holding 1 gem of 50 gold piece value, 10 gold pieces, and 20 silver pieces. Nesting under these small pouches are 2 **giant centipedes**: DX 13, AC 9, HD ¼, hp 2 each, #AT 1, bite causes no damage, but the victim must save versus poison at + 4 or victim will die.

14. COMMON CHAMBER: Here there are quartered 9 male orcs with shields and swords (DX 10, AC 6, HD 1, hp 3 each, #AT 1, D 1-6) and 8 females and 3 young who do not fight. The males have d20 silver pieces each, the females d4 copper pieces, the young have nothing. The place is a mess, and there is nothing of value in it. The males will go to the entrance if they hear the net falling, arriving in 1 round.

15. COMMON HALL: General meetings are held here, and food is likewise cooked and eaten here. There are 6 males here, 2 with light crossbows (DX 10, AC 6, HD 1, hp 3 each) and 4 females (non-combatant), dwelling in the western forepart. Each has treasure on their person equal to **14.**, above. The males here will also go to the entrance if they hear the noise of the net falling, arriving in 3 rounds.

16. LEADER'S ROOM: A guard (**g.**) is always posted just inside the door, and he cannot be surprised. (Orc: DX 10, AC 5, HD 1 + 1, hp 6, carries 2d6 silver and d4 gold pieces.) He immediately shouts an alarm if any intruders attempt to enter. Behind him are stacks of barrels and boxes and sacks — extra supplies for the tribe. (One small wine barrel, 400 gold pieces in weight, contains a good quality wine worth 55 gold pieces.) None of the other items here have value, and the foodstuffs is not up to human standards.

The area to the east houses the leader, a very large orc who wears plate and carries a shield, uses a sword, and attacks as a 3 hit dice monster. (DX 12, AC ½, HD 3, hp 16.) At his belt is a magic + 1 axe which he will hurl at an opponent, and he can do so and still attack normally in the same round of combat. His belt is of silver, with a gold buckle (total value 160 gold pieces), and his sword has a 100 gold piece gem set in its pommel*. In his purse are 8 gold pieces, 17 electrum pieces, and 5 silver pieces. His mate is equal to a male orc in combat (DX 10, AC 6, HD 1, hp 5), and she has a bracelet of ivory which is worth 100 gold pieces. The area is well furnished, and a small chest of drawers

contains a sack with 50 platinum pieces tied shut with a **rope of climbing**. There is also a copper bowl, finely wrought and chased with silver, on a small table near the bed. However, it is filled with garbage and very tarnished, so it looks only as if it were worth 10 silver pieces, rather than the actual 50 gold pieces, unless it is closely inspected.

(DM Note: Orc losses cannot be replaced. If this tribe is attacked, they will have the males at area **15.** watching the entrance, ready for a second try by the adventurers. If the leader is slain, the survivors will seek safety in area **B.**, if possible; otherwise, they will flee the place entirely, carrying their goods away.)

D. GOBLIN LAIR: The natural cave quickly turns into the worked stone tunnels typical of this whole complex. The passageways here are very busy, and for every 10' distance covered by the party there is a 1 in 6 chance that they will encounter a group of goblins (see below). Check each time the party travels 30' (a 3 in 6 chance) until wandering goblins are encountered, then check no further. When an encounter occurs, the entire bunch of goblins will attack and cry out an alarm (Bree-Yark!) at the same time. Wandering goblins are in addition to those found in numbered areas.

Wandering Goblins: 6 males, DX 11, AC 6, HD 1-1, hp 3 each. Each will have d6 silver pieces. (They are patrolling and carrying messages back and forth. The group will also be carrying several bags (d6) of fairly good foodstuffs — not worth much, but quite suitable for human fare.)

17. GUARD CHAMBER: 6 goblin guards with javelins and clubs (DX 11, AC 6, HD 1-1, hp 3 each) are alertly watching both passages here for intruders of any sort, including hobgoblins from the south. They each have d4 × 10 copper and d4 silver pieces. The chamber has a barrel with 72 small javelins, a small table, 2 benches and a keg of water.

18. GUARD CHAMBER: This is the same as **17.**, above, except the goblins watch mainly to the east. If there is a cry of "BREE-YARK" (similar to "Hey Rube!"), 2 of these guards will rush to the secret door, toss a sack with 250 gold pieces in it to the ogre (**E., 22.**, below) and ask him to help them. The ogre will accept the payment and will enter the goblins' lair and move to attack intruders immediately, if possible. The sack of gold coins is hidden in a water barrel in the corner by the secret door.

19. COMMON ROOM: There are 10 males (DX 11, AC 6, HD 1-1, hp 3 each) and 14 females and 6 young (who do not fight) dwelling here. Food is prepared and eaten here, and general meetings are likewise held here. There are heaps of bedding, tables, stools, benches, etc. all around the whole place, making it very cluttered. Each male has d6 silver pieces, each female has 2d6 copper pieces. If the wandering group of goblins has not been encountered when the adventurers enter this area, be certain to have those 6 additional males in this chamber.

20. CHIEFTAIN'S ROOM: The goblin leader (DX 13, AC 4, HD 2 + 1, hp 11, + 1 on damage due to strength and skill, so 2-7 points per hit), 3 guards (DX 12, AC 5, HD 1 + 1, hp 7 each), and several females are quartered here. The chief has a purse with 18 gold and 2 platinum pieces in it; each of his guards has 8 electrum pieces and d6 silver pieces. There is a silver cup (value 90 gold pieces) under his bed. He and the guards have bows hung on the wall, and if there is time they will take them down and use them. If hard-pressed, 2 of the female goblins can fight as well as males, and will do so (2 female goblins, DX 10, AC 7, HD 1-1, hp 2 each); the other females do not fight.

This place has quite a bit of good furniture in it — all scaled to goblin-size, of course. A low bench near the bed has a secret drawer under the seat, and inside is stored the treasure of the goblins: a tapestry with silver and gold threads which is worth 900 gold pieces. Nearby is a stand with a pewter bowl which holds 273 silver and 321 copper pieces.

21. STORAGE CHAMBER: Note that at position **g** there are 4 goblin guards on duty (DX 11, AC 6, HD 1-1, hp 4 each), armed with ready light crossbows and swords. Many bales, boxes, crates, barrels, and sacks are stacked and heaped in the large chamber. They contain cloth, food, beer, and wine — all of no special worth. The hard-working but not-too-bright goblins continually bring supplies of stolen and looted goods to this place. They do not realize that their large cousins, the hobgoblins at area **F.**, below, use a secret door known only to them to steal the best of the foodstuffs and drink. If the adventurers stay in this chamber for more than 1 turn, a party of 4 hobgoblins will come through the secret door:

4 Hobgoblins: DX 10, AC 6, HD 1 + 1, hp 6 each, #AT 1, D 1-8, + 1 on morale, saves versus fear. Each carries d4 gold pieces.

(DM Note: Goblin losses cannot be replaced. If they are being soundly defeated by intruders, the goblins will attempt to hide or flee east. Those who do so will go from area **17.** to area **23.**, inform the hobgoblins, and join forces with them, so adjust encounters appropriately.)

E. OGRE CAVE: Persons entering this place will notice a strong, sour odor and then notice what appears to be a huge bear sprawled asleep in the southwestern part of the cave. This is nothing more than the skin of a huge bear which the ogre killed and uses as a bed, making it more comfortable by heaping leaves underneath. The ogre sits in the eastern portion of his lair, and noise will certainly bring him ready to do battle. This huge ogre has AC 4, due to another thick bearskin he wears for protection. He strikes opponents for 3-12 (d10 + 2) points of damage, the extra 2 points of damage caused by his strength. (DX 8, AC 4, HD 4 + 1, hp 25, #AT 1, D 3-12.) The ogre has grown wealthy by serving as a mercenary — generally on the side of the goblins (and their occasional allies, the hobgoblins), although he has been bought off by the orcs and gnolls from time to time. He will rush to aid the goblins when they toss him the sack of coins (see **18.**, above). If anyone offers him a greater fee — one which he can actually see and feel — it is 90% likely that he will simply take it (and the goblins' money too!), and return to his lair.

22. The ogre sits here on top of a great leather bag. In this bag are seven large sacks which contain:

#1: 287 silver pieces; #2: a hard cheese; #3: 182 copper pieces and 91 electrum pieces; #4: 289 gold pieces; #5: a keg of brandy (value 80 gold pieces); #6: 303 copper pieces; #7: 241 gold pieces (actually lead coins with a wash of gold, so value of each is only 1 copper!).

If intruders offer him a bribe of 20 or more gold piece value, the ogre will be 90% likely to allow them to leave unmolested, but if he catches them again, he will attempt to kill them, whatever the offers. Hidden under a heap of old bones in the southern portion of his cave are 6 + 1 magic arrows, a **potion of invisibility**, and a magic scroll with 2 cleric spells — **cure light wounds, find traps.**

F. HOBGOBLIN LAIR: Seldom are these fierce creatures troubled by marauders, for the entrance to their lair is guarded by a stout, barred door at the back of the entry cave. Skulls are lined along the walls, and several are affixed to the oaken door to highlight a warning written in common runes: "Come in — we'd like to have you for dinner!" (Which **could** be misinterpreted as a cordial invitation to dine . . . .) Careful inspection of the barred door has a 1 in 6 chance per person examining it of detecting a secret mechanism which allows a person outside to slide the bar back so the portal can be entered. If it is forced open, it will require three 1s (on a d6) to indicate the bar has been broken, and the noise will alert area **26.** If a **knock** spell is used to open the door, the noise of the falling bar will be heard, but guards will not have time to react, so the intruders will have two rounds of time before the guards will come.

23. COMMON ROOM: This place quarters 5 males (DX 10, AC 6, HD 1 + 1, hp 5 each, #AT 1, D 1-8) with d4 × 10 silver pieces each; 8 females (DX 12, AC 7, HD 1, hp 4 each, #AT 1, D 1-6) with 2d6 silver pieces each, and 3 young which do not fight and have no treasure. There are heaps of cloth and skins for beds, some odds and ends of furniture, a small barrel of beer, buckets, etc. in the place, all worthless. The males are watching the east door which communicates with the goblin lair (**D.**, above) and are battle-ready.

24. TORTURE CHAMBER/PLAYROOM/FOOD STORAGE: There are 2 very large, ugly hobgoblins here. Each is equal to a 2 + 1 hit dice monster, one having 10 hit points, the other 8 hit points, and both wear chainmail (AC 5). One also has a whip, as well as a sword, so that he can strike at opponents up to 15' distant, and if a hit is scored, the whip will jerk the victim off his or her feet and stun him or her for 1-2 melee rounds. However, once closely engaged, the hobgoblin cannot make use of his whip, so he will cast it aside. Each of these monsters has a purse with d6 each copper, silver, and electrum pieces. The larger also has a silver armlet worth 135 gold pieces. They guard 6 prisoners who are chained to the walls. There are two chairs, a small table, a central fire pit, and various implements of torture in the chamber. The keys to the prisoners' chains are hanging on the wall in the southwest corner. The prisoners are:

#1: A plump, half-dead merchant, scheduled to be eaten tonight in a special banquet. If he is rescued and returned to the KEEP, the Guild will pay a 100 gold piece reward, grant the rescuers honorary Guild status, and exempt them for one year from any fees, dues, taxes, and the like which the Guild would normally collect.

#2: An orc (DX 10, AC 7, HD 1, hp 4) who will fight goblins and hobgoblins gladly, if handed a weapon (of course he will seek to escape from the adventurers at first chance, taking whatever he can with him, and informing his fellows at **B.** (above), of what happened).

#3: A man-at-arms (DX 12, AC 9, LVL 0, hp 5) who formerly served as a guard for the merchant. He will take service with rescuers for 1 year if an offer is made, for room and board only, if given armor and weapons.

#4: A normal female, the merchant's wife, in fact, who is also slated for the big feast. She will personally reward her rescuers by giving them a + 1 magic dagger she has in her room back at the KEEP.

#5: A crazy gnoll (DX 9, AC 9 due to no armor, HD 2, hp 9) who will snatch up a weapon and attack his rescuers if he is freed. (He will cause only 1-6 points of damage due to his weakened condition.)

#6: Another man-at-arms as #3, above, who will behave the same way his companion will.

25. **COMMON CHAMBER:** This large place is used for meals, meetings, and general revels of the hobgoblin tribe. There are many tables and benches set out now, as the place is being readied for the coming feast. 4 males (DX 10, AC 6, HD 1 + 1, hp 5 each, #AT 1, D 1-8), 5 females (DX 12, AC 7, HD 1, hp 4 each, #AT 1, D 1-6), and 9 young (who will not fight) are working here. Males have d4 gold pieces each, females 2d6 silver pieces. The head table has a set of pewter dishes on it, and their value is 25 g.p. for the set.

26. **GUARD ROOM:** 6 hobgoblins (DX 10, AC 6, HD 1 + 1, hp 6 each), 3 with heavy crossbows which they'll fire once before dropping and taking their maces for close combat. Each carries d4 each gold, silver, and copper pieces. If they hear the door being battered, or the bar falling, all but one will immediately rush to the entry, while the other will alert area **27.**, and then join his fellows. It takes two rounds for them to reach the entry, and the sixth will join the other guards on round four.

27. **ARMORY:** 3 hobgoblin guards (DX 10, AC 5 due to large shields, HD 1 + 1, hp 6 each, #AT 1, D 1-8) are on duty here at all times. If warning comes, two will move to the door to wait in ambush, and the other will pass through the secret entrance (to area **31.**) to alert the chief. Each guard has 2d4 each of silver and electrum pieces. In the chamber are the following:

    1 suit of man-sized plate mail
    1 suit of dwarf-sized plate mail
    3 suits of man-sized chainmail
    2 suits of elf-sized chainmail
    7 suits of man-sized leather armor
    11 shields
    6 daggers
    1 axe
    4 maces
    3 swords
    2 bows (short)
    1 longbow
    11 light crossbows
    2 heavy crossbows
    11 score* arrows (14 arrows have silver heads)
    9 score* bolts
    51 spears
    19 pole arms
    42 helmets of various sizes

Armor-type items are standing or hung from racks. Weapons are in chests or on pegs or in racks.

28. **STOREROOM:** Goods stolen from the stupid goblins are kept here until needed above. There will be a single guard (DX 15, AC 6, HD 1 + 1, hp 5, #AT 1, D 1-8) on duty here at all times. He has 2d8 electrum pieces. (If the looting party does not encounter adventurers in area **21.**, they will also be here: 4 hobgoblins (DX 10, AC 6, HD 1 + 1, hp 6 each, #AT 1, D 1-8). Each of the four carries d4 gold pieces.

29. **GUARD ROOM:** 2 hobgoblin guards with light crossbows and swords stand here. (DX 12, AC 6, HD 1 + 1, hp 5 each, #AT 1, D 1-8.) With them are 2 females who will fight (DX 12, AC 7, HD 1, hp 4 each, #AT 1, D 1-6). Males have 2d6 each silver and copper pieces, females have no treasure. There are two cots, a bench, a stool, and a large box (filled with soiled clothing) in the room. If attackers are seen, one female will alert area **30.**, the other area **31.**; then both will fight.

30. **HOBGOBLIN CHIEF'S QUARTERS:** This great, ugly creature is particularly tough, fighting as a 3 + 1 hit dice monster, AC 2 due to his plate armor and shield, and adding + 1 to damage from his hits. (DX 15, AC 2, HD 3 + 1, hp 17, #AT 1, D 2-9). He has 5 platinum and 31 gold pieces in his purse. He wears a silver and gem studded belt (value 600 gold pieces). With him are 4 large female hobgoblins, each equal to a male (DX 12, AC 6, HD 1 + 1, hp 6 each, #AT 1, D 1-8), and each has 2d6 gold pieces. The room is crowded with furniture and junk — all of no real worth, except that there is a false bottom in a huge iron box filled with mangy animal skins. The secret portion of the iron box holds 25 platinum, 200 gold, 115 electrum, and 400 silver pieces plus a 100 gold piece gem and a potion of **poison**. Amidst a heap of kindling wood near the fireplace (southeast corner) there is concealed a **wand of paralyzation**, but it has only 17 charges left in it.

31. **GUARD ROOM:** 4 hobgoblins (DX 10, AC 5 due to large shields, HD 1 + 1, hp 5 each, #AT 1, D 1-8), each with 2d6 electrum, silver, and copper pieces. They are alert for danger, and when notified, they will pass the word to areas **29.**, **30.**, and/or **27.**, as required. The room is rather bare, having only 2 pallets, a stool, and a large water barrel.

(**DM Note:** As usual, hobgoblin losses cannot be replaced during the course of normal play, which is a period of only several days or weeks of action. The hobgoblins are fairly smart, well-organized, and alert. If their chief is killed, they will typically seek to escape alive, unless their opponents are obviously weak and inferior. Survivors will reinforce the goblins at **D.**, above, unless their attackers are very dangerous and the hobgoblins can see that the whole **Caves'** area is in trouble . . . .)

G. **SHUNNED CAVERN:** Even the normal inhabitants of this area, including the ogre, stay away from here, for the creatures who dwell herein are exceptionally dangerous. Any creature foolish enough to venture out at night becomes fair game. A horrible stench is noticed as soon as creatures enter the cavern area.

32. **EMPTY GALLERY:** The odor of these places is awful. Bones and rotting corpses are spread here and there amidst a litter of dead leaves and old branches. If a careful search is made, adventurers will find a coin every round: 1-2 = 1 copper piece, 3-4 = 1 silver piece, 5-6 = 1 electrum piece. The sound of such searching might bring visitors! Roll on the table below for an encounter:

    1 = Owl bear from **34.**, below

    2 = 2-12 giant rats (DX 8, AC 7, HD ½, hp 2 each, #AT 1, D 1-3)

    3 = Gray ooze from **33.**, below

    4-6 = Nothing is attracted to the noise

33. **SHALLOW POOL:** This portion of the cavern is very wet, and all of the walls and the floor have a sheen from the dampness. There is a large pool of shallow water (as shown), and a few white, blind fish are swimming therein. There is a jewel-encrusted goblet worth 1,300 gold pieces in the water. There are 3 gray ooze monsters in this place (only 2 if 1 has already been encountered in a **32.** area). Each causes 1-8 hit points of damage on the first round, unless attacking from above, because half of their damage will be taken up in destroying the foot and leg protection of the victim. Thereafter, attacks cause 2-16 points damage, as do attacks from above. (DX 11, AC 8, HD 3, hp 15 each, #AT 1, D 1-8 1st round, then 2-16.) The pair always in the place are the one at the south edge of the pool and the one on the ceiling in

the southwestern portion of the area. There is only a 1 in 20 chance of noticing either unless a pole device is used to prod the area before the pool or unless two or more torches are held aloft so as to fully light the ceiling area. The third gray ooze will be on the ceiling to the left of the entrance, if present.

34. OWL BEAR'S DEN: Owl bear: DX 10, AC 5, HD 5, hp 30, #AT 3, D 1-8 each. It sleeps in the most southerly part of its den, digesting a meal of gnoll it just caught at dawn. If aroused, the beast will roar and rush out, striking with its two great paws and toothy beak for 1-8 points of damage per hit, with three such attacks per round, i.e. a claw, another clawing attack, and then a snap of its beak. It has no treasure, but amidst the many sticks and bones it sleeps on is a bone tube (1 in 6 chance of noticing it for each person searching the heap, with a check for each once per round) with a **protection from undead** scroll within it.

H. BUGBEAR LAIR: The group of bugbears is not numerous, but what it lacks in numbers, it makes up for in strength and cunning. There are signs beside the entrance cave in kobold, orcish, goblin, etc. Each says: "Safety, security and repose for all humanoids who enter — WELCOME! (Come in and report to the first guard on the left for a hot meal and bed assignment.)"

35. GUARD ROOM: 3 bugbears (DX 10, AC 5, HD 3 + 1, hp 11 each, #AT 1, D 2-8) with 2d10 gold pieces each. These creatures lounge on stools near a smoking brazier which has skewers of meat toasting over the coals. Each will ignore his great flail when intruders enter, reaching instead for the food. Though they do not speak common, they will grab and eat a chunk, then offer the skewers to the adventurers — and suddenly use them as swords to strike first blow (at + 2 bonus to hit due to surprise!) unless the victims are very alert. There are two cots in the place and a large gong. If the battle goes badly, one will smite the gong to warn the others in the complex.

36. CHIEFTAIN'S ROOM: This tough old bugbear is equal to an ogre (DX 8, AC 4, HD 4 + 1, hp 18, #AT 1, D 3-12, i.e. d10 + 2). He has a pouch with a key, 29 platinum pieces, and 3 50 g.p. gems in it. With him is a female bugbear equal to a male (DX 9, AC 5, HD 3 + 1, hp 12, #AT 1, D 2-8). She has gold earrings worth 100 g.p. The furnishings of the room are battered and crude, but several pieces of silk are mixed up with the bedding, in all 6 may be found; the party will be able to sell them for 20 g.p. each. There is a gray chest stuck up on a ledge near the ceiling which will only be spotted if the room is carefully searched. It contains 1,462 silver pieces, a 30 pound statue of alabaster and ivory (worth 200 gold pieces), and 2 potions of **healing** (which will break if the chest is roughly handled). It will take three or four strong characters to bring this down safely. There is a + 1 battle axe on the wall, and if the chieftain has the chance, he will take it down and hurl it first, then close for full melee. He knows of the secret door — it is his escape route in desperate situations.

37. SPOILS ROOM: The heavy door is locked, and the key is in the pouch of the chieftain (**36.**, above). Inside are a + 1 magic shield, being used as a tray to hold a heap of dried herbs (catnip, something these particular bugbears relish), various boxes and crates of high quality dried or salted foodstuffs, leather hides in a stack, 3 barrels of ale, a tun of wine, and a small keg of oil (20 flask capacity). (If all but the shield and oil are sold at the KEEP, the value will be 400 gold pieces.) Breaking the lock of smashing the door will bring the guards from **35.** and the chieftain and his mate from **36.**

38. COMMON ROOM: 3 males (DX 8, AC 5, HD 3 + 1, hp 12 each, #AT 1, D 2-8) with 2d6 each of gold and silver pieces, 7 females (DX 8, AC 6, HD 2, hp 8 each, #AT 1, D 1-8), and 3 young bugbears (DX 8, AC 7, HD 1, hp 3 each, #AT 1, D 1-4) dwell here. There are piles of bedding and old garments here and there. Blackened by soot, there is a silver urn worth 175 g.p. near the fireplace, but only close examination will reveal its true value.

39. GUARD ROOM: Watching here are 2 males (DX 8, AC 5, HD 3 + 1, hp 10 each, #AT 1, D 2-8) with 2d8 gold pieces each, and 3 females (DX 8, AC 6, HD 2, hp 7 each, #AT 1, D 1-8), each with d10 gold pieces. Each has a spear in addition to normal weapons, so that they can hurl this missile and then close to fight hand-to-hand. These bugbears tend to the slaves as well as help to guard the entrance to their lair. There are bedrolls, a bench, a long table, a water pail, and sacks of meal scattered here and there in the chamber. Keys to the doors to **40.** and **41.** are on the wall opposite the stairs. Both corridors to the slave pens have meal sacks and small boxes and barrels of provisions and watered wine along their length.

40. SLAVE PEN: The iron door is secured by a bar, chain, and heavy padlock. Inside is a litter of straw, a bucket, and the following slaves: 3 kobolds (DX 13, AC 9, HD ½, hp 2 each), 1 goblin (DX 11, AC 9, HD 1-1, hp 3 each), 4 orcs (DX 10, AC 9, HD 1, hp 5 each), and 2 humans (DX 11, AC 9, LVL 0 men-at-arms, hp 4 each) — optionally add 1 dwarf (DX 13, AC 9, LVL 2 fighter, hp 12) and 2 elves (DX 14, AC 9, HD 1 + 1, hp 7 each) in place of 2 of the kobolds and 1 of the orcs. They are chained to the wall with a common chain and a heavy padlock. All will fight against the bugbears if given weapons. (Treat as AC 9 unless protection is provided.) The humans will serve as those noted in **F., 24.**, above. The dwarf and elves, if used by the DM, may agree to help the adventurers as long as they stay in the **Caves'** area continuously and fight. The other creatures will desert at first opportunity.

41. SLAVE PEN: Another barred, chained, and padlocked iron door keeps safe the following slaves: 3 hobgoblins (DX 10, AC 8, HD 1 + 1, hp 6 each), 2 gnolls (DX 9, AC 8, HD 2 + 1, hp 9 each), 1 (rebel) bugbear (DX 8, AC 7, HD 3 + 1, hp 14) and 1 huge human — a seeming wildman, with mighty muscles, shaggy hair and beard, and staring eyes (a hero, or 4th level fighter, with 18 strength, DX 15, AC 9, hp 24, + 2 on hit probability and damage due to his great strength and level). (He is prone to fits of berserk fury due to his enslavement, and if armed and in combat it is 50% likely per round that he will strike a friend instead of a foe in his lust to slay!) If freed, these slaves will attempt to flee, although they will attack bugbears who are in the way of their escape. There are two exceptions: the big bugbear hates his fellows, and will take arms and fight against them or any of the other inhabitants of the whole area; he will continue to do so for as long as the party stays there. The hero is a chaotic evil person; once he is armed, and after battle madness leaves him, he will either kill the adventurers who freed him, so as to have all their treasure for himself, or else he will steal whatever is most valuable and then sneak off — but only if he knows the party is too strong for him.

(DM Note: There are 2 bugbears out hunting, and they will return with a human corpse and 83 gold pieces the day after adventurers first enter the bugbear lair. They will be placed on guard duty at **35.**, if appropriate, and their statistics are the same as the guards there. Bugbears will stay in the place until all are dead, save the chieftain, who will seek help from the minotaur at **I., 45.)**

19

I. CAVES OF THE MINOTAUR: This labyrinth* houses a number of nasty things, but the worst is a fiendishly clever minotaur who abides herein. Immediately upon entering the place, adventurers will feel slightly dizzy — the effects of a powerful spell which will cause them to lose all sense of direction.

The minotaur will agree to help the bugbears against invaders at the cost of one human slave every three days of service — of course, the slave is eaten in that period. The minotaur keeps only the choicest of treasures, tossing unwanted loot to whomever happens to find it at the mouth of the labyrinth.

(DM Notes: You may allow players to find a few low-value coins, normal equipment, weapons, or armor at the entrance. After 30' past the cave mouth, the spell of **direction confusion** will begin to function, so start to misdirect them by naming incorrect directions, i.e. **south**east instead of **north**east, east instead of west, etc. Don't worry about calling the same passage as a different direction should they travel over the same route twice — that's the effect of the magic on **them**. You may wish to allow the mapping character a secret saving throw every couple of turns, a 19 or 20 indicating that the effect has been thrown off.)

42. STIRGE CAVE: There are 13 of these flying monsters here: DX 10, AC 7, HD 1, hp 3 each, #AT 1, D 1-3 points; the creature strikes at + 2 on attacks; if opponent is hit, stirge will automatically suck blood each round thereafter, doing 1-4 hit points of damage due to blood drain until victim is dead or stirge is killed. The minotaur loves to catch and eat these creatures, so they avoid him, and they are quite hungry. In fact, this hunger makes it 90% likely that they will be squeaking and hooting to one another, so the party won't be surprised. They have no treasure.

43. FIRE BEETLES: Three dwell in this area: DX 9, AC 4, HD 1 + 2, hp 7 each, #AT 1, D 2-8. They too are hungry and will hasten to attack any persons entering their area. They have no treasure, but 2 glands above their eyes and one in their abdomen will glow with a red light, 10' radius, for 1-6 days after the beetle is killed.

44. FIRE BEETLES: There are 2 of these creatures here, in all respects like those in **43.**, above.

45. THE MINOTAUR: This huge monster has AC 4 due to a great chainmail coat he wears, and carries a + 1 magic spear. When he attacks he rushes and stabs with it for 2-7 points of damage, followed by a butt at the same opponent (1-6 points of damage for each horn that hits), and then a fierce bite for 1-6 hit points at the same person, or another within 5' of him. (DX 12, AC 6, HD 6, hp 35, #AT 4, D 2-7/1-6/1-6.) When not charging the minotaur may only use his spear and bite **or** horns and bite.

When intruders enter the area, the minotaur immediately moves to attack. He knows this area so well that the only way for victims to escape is to go through the secret door into area **36.**, or else to run out of the place and climb a large tree.

The cave the minotaur dwells in has skulls and bones arrayed in decorative patterns. The secret door is actually a slab of stone which takes not less than 3 humans to move. (It will be noticed by careful checking of the walls, but how it is moved requires a roll of a 1 on a six-sided die to indicate the searcher has found where it can be grasped. All of the minotaur's treasure is behind this slab of rock. It hides:

1 locked chest (with poison needle in lock) — contents 930 gold and 310 electrum pieces

1 **staff of healing**

1 suit of man-sized (optionally elf-sized) + 1 magic plate armor

1 locked coffer — contents 3 potion bottles (**gaseous form, delusionary healing, giant strength**)

1 locked chest — contents 3 pieces of jewelry worth 1,600, 900, and 600 g.p. respectively

J. GNOLL LAIR: The entry into this place is a small cave, and only at the end will worked stone be visible. If the adventurers have a light or make much noise, the guards (**46.**) will certainly be alerted and ready.

46. GUARD ROOM: There are always 4 gnolls (DX 9, AC 5, HD 2, hp 9 each, #AT 1, D 2-8) on duty here. Two have bows, and will shoot at intruders until melee takes place; they will then run for help while the other two fight. Each gnoll has d8 each of electrum, silver, and copper pieces.

47. GUARD ROOM: 3 males (DX 9, AC 5, HD 2, hp 8 each, #AT 1, D 2-8) and 5 females (DX 8, AC 6, HD 1 + 1, hp 5 each, #AT 1, D 1-8) are quartered here. They will be ready to fight immediately. The males have d6 gold pieces each, the females have d4. There is a scattering of rude furniture in the place, heaps of bedding on the floor, several hides and pelts on the walls (one is a valuable sable cloak worth 450 g.p.), and a barrel of water in the southwest corner of the room.

48. LOCKED ROOM: This chamber is a store room and armory. Besides the usual provisions, there are 7 shields, a suit of dwarf-sized chainmail, 12 battle axes, 3 longbows, 5 quivers of arrows (20 in each), and a magic sword (-2, **cursed**). One barrel of exceptionally fine ale is leaking, and the odor will tempt adventurers to taste it. It is so good, in fact, that there is a 5 in 6 chance per taste that he or she will draw a healthy draught and then spend the next 1-4 turns drinking. (If this occurs, be sure that you have the appropriate characters sing, make noise, and act foolishly. Any of their attacks will be at -2 to hit; this will continue for as many turns as they spent drinking, i.e. 1-4).

49. COMMON ROOM: This place quarters the gnoll tribe — 6 males (DX 9, AC 5, HD 2, hp 8 each, #AT 1, D 2-8), 11 females (DX 8, AC 6, HD 1 + 1, hp 5 each, #AT 1, D 1-8), and 18 young who do not fight. Males have d6 each of electrum and silver pieces, females d10 silver pieces each. There is the usual clutter of worthless furniture in the room.

50. GNOLL CHIEFTAIN'S QUARTERS: The gnoll leader is DX 12, AC 3 due to pieces of plate mail he wears, HD 3, hp 17, #AT 1, and 4-10 (2d4 +2) points of damage per attack due to his ability and strength. With him are his two sons (DX 11, AC 4 due to chainmail and shield, HD 2 + 1, hp 10 each, #AT 1, D 3-9), and 4 females (DX 8, AC 6, HD 1 + 1, hp 5 each, #AT 1, D 1-8). The chieftain has a pair of silver armbands worth 50 gold pieces each, and there are 39 gold pieces in his belt pouch. His sons have d10 each of gold, electrum, and silver pieces. Each female wears a silver neck chain worth 30 gold pieces and has 2d6 electrum pieces in addition. The furnishings of the place are crude and battered. A large metal pot beneath a flagstone in the fireplace alcove hides 200 copper, 157 silver, 76 electrum, and 139 gold pieces.

The secret door and passage to area **K., 63.**, is unknown to all parties. Just inside the entrance is the skeleton of a human thief, his leg is broken and he must have died here trying to escape through the secret door. The rotten leather armor and corroded weapons are valueless, but the purse at his belt holds 12 gems of 50 g.p. base value each, and the **elven boots** upon his bony feet are still in usable shape.

(DM Note: Losses by the gnolls cannot be replaced. They are in a loose alliance with the orcs, so if there are surviving gnolls, they will move to the orc areas and vice versa. If you wish, allow the chieftain to be able to escape enemies by climbing up the chimney of the fireplace in his area.)

K. SHRINE OF EVIL CHAOS: A faint, foul draft issues from the 20' wide cave mouth which is the entrance to this place. The worn path through the copse of obscenely twisted and oddly bloated trees gives those approaching along its length an eerie sense of unease, and as soon as they enter the cave mouth a dim awareness of lurking evil will pervade their senses. Red strata intertwines with bulging black veins running through the hewn rock walls beyond the entrance. The wide corridors and chambers are deathly still. A faint groaning sound, and a shrill piping may be occasionally heard, barely perceptible even if the party is absolutely silent and listening.

The floors are smooth and worn by the tread of countless feet of the worshipers at this grim place. The footsteps of intruders will echo alarmingly in these vaulted halls (+2 chance of being surprised), and extreme care must be taken to muffle such sounds if the party has any hopes of remaining undetected until the moment of their choosing. Continual noise will bring a group of zombie guards to investigate:

> 8 zombies: DX 6, AC 8, HD 2, hp 8 each, #AT ½, D 1-8. These ghastly monsters are clad in filthy red and black striped uniforms. Each carries a cleaver-like battle axe. (One wears an amulet* with a **protection from good** spell cast upon it, so attempts by a cleric to turn them are made as if they were **ghouls** rather than zombies.)

51. BOULDER FILLED PASSAGE: Large rocks and boulders have been placed here in order to seal off this tunnel. It will take 100 man-turns to open a way large enough for a human to pass through into the area beyond. (You have the option of allowing this passage to lead to the outside somewhere to the southwest of the **Caves of Chaos**, or you may choose to have it go all the way to the **Cave of the Unknown**. If you opt for the latter case, you must, of course, prepare an appropriate underground area map and stock it with monsters and treasures.)

52. HALL OF SKELETONS: This unusual audience chamber has a dais and throne-like chair set with 4 large red gems (500 g.p. each) at the south end. It is otherwise empty except for a dozen skeletons, clad in rags of chainmail and bearing battered shields and rusty scimitars, propped against the walls. These bony guards do not move, and any attempt to turn them immediately upon entering the chamber will have no effect, as they are obviously not animated. However, as soon as intruders touch the dais or throne chair, these monsters will spring to action from their positions on either wall of the chamber. Each has a **protection from good** and **haste** spell upon it, so they are turned by a cleric as if they were **zombies**, and each attacks twice per round of combat, once at the beginning and once at the end. (AC 6, HD ½, hp 3 each, #AT 2, D 1-6.) They have no treasure.

Once the skeletons are disposed of, it is an easy matter to pry the 4 garnets (gems) from the back of the chair.

53. GUARD ROOM: There will always be 8 zombies (DX 8, AC 8, HD 2, hp 8 each, #AT ½, D 1-8, turned as if they were ghouls due to a **protection from good** amulet) hulking silently here, 4 at either end of the hall. Anyone entering will be attacked unless they are robed (see area **54.**, below) and have an amulet identical to the ones which the zombie guard groups have. There is no treasure here.

54. ACOLYTES' CHAMBER: There are 4 acolytes (1st level clerics) here, DX 11, AC 5, hp 4 each, all dressed in rusty-red robes, with black cowls*. Under these robes each wears chainmail and a mace at his belt. Each carries 10 gold pieces in his purse, and the leader wears an amulet of **protection from good**. (The effect of this amulet on living **evil** creatures is to increase their armor class by +1, thus effectively making all 4 evil clerics AC 4 as long as they are within a 10' radius of the amulet and being attacked by opponents who are on the side of **good**.) Their room contains four hard pallets*, a brazier*, a table, four stools, a cabinet for clothing, a water pail, a waste bucket, and a flagon* of wine and four cups. There is nothing of value amongst these items.

55. EVIL CHAPEL: This place is of red stone, the floor being a mosaic checkerboard of black and red. The south wall is covered by a huge tapestry which depicts a black landscape, barren trees, and unidentifiable but horrible black shapes in silhouette — possibly demons of some sort — holding aloft a struggling human. A gray sky is torn by wisps of purple clouds, and a bloody moon with a skull-like face on it leers down upon the scene. Four black pillars support the domed ceiling some 25' overhead. Between these columns, just in front of the tapestry, is a stone altar of red veined black rock, rough-hewn and stained brown with dried blood. Upon it are 4 ancient bronze vessels — a shallow bowl, a pair of goblets, and a ewer, a vase-shaped pitcher. They are also bloodstained but obviously worth a great deal of money. (The value is 1,000 g.p. for each cup, and 2,000 g.p. for each of the other items, but these are relics of chaos, and any character possessing them will **not** part with them or sell them nor allow others to handle them. For each character who picks up one of these objects, the DM should roll a secret saving throw vs. magic at -2. Any who save successfully will get a "feeling of great evil" about the object, and he or she may voluntarily put it down. If the save fails, the character will rapidly fall under the influence of a demonic spell and within 6 days become a servant of chaos and evil, returning to this chapel to replace the relics, and then staying as a guard forever after. If someone attempts to destroy these relics the great bell (see **58.**, below) will sound and the Shrine's residents will come running in 3 rounds. If a **detect evil** spell is cast upon these items, they will glow an ugly purple, and all good characters will feel instant loathing for them. If the character who has taken them has a **dispel magic** and then a **bless** spell cast upon him or her, there is a 60% chance of removing the evil on the first day, 50% on the 2nd, 40% on the 3rd, 30% on the 4th, 20% on the 5th, and 10% on the 6th. Otherwise, not even a **wish** will be able to save the character!)

56. ADEPTS' CHAMBER: There are 4 adepts (2nd level clerics) here, each clad in a black robe with a maroon colored cowl*. (DX 12, AC 3 or 2, hp 8 each.) They have plate mail beneath their garments, and each bears a mace. Their waists are circled with copper chains (worth 40 g.p. each) with skull-shaped clasps fashioned of bone. Each carries a purse with 20 gold and 5 platinum pieces, and each wears an amulet of **protection from good**, which makes their effective armor class 2 vs. good creatures. The first and second have **cause light wounds** spells, the third a **darkness** spell, the fourth a **cause fear** spell. They will use their spells first, if possible, before engaging in combat with weapons. In the room are four beds, four small stands, a table, four chairs, four chests for clothing, and various books and scrolls of evil nature — nothing of value. However, on the table are copper dishes and vessels (total weight 300 g.p.) of exceptional craftsmanship which are worth 175 gold pieces. (If the party opts to destroy the evil writings, they should receive an additional 600 experience points for the act, unless they are themselves evil, in which case they should receive points for keeping and

reading these works.) If hard pressed, these evil clerics will attempt to flee and warn their master by striking the great bell (**58.**).

57. HALL OF UNDEAD WARRIORS: There are four files of the undead here, two of 10 skeletons each, two of 10 zombies each. The former face south, the latter north.

20 skeletons: DX 11, AC 6 (chainmail rags & shields), HD ½, hp 3 each, #AT 1, D 1-6, turned as zombies.

20 zombies: DX 6, AC 5 (chainmail shirts), HD 2, hp 8 each, #AT 1, D 1-8, turned as if they were ghouls.

Upon striking of the great iron bell at **58.**, below, the skeletons will issue forth from the south door of the place and march into the temple (**58.**) to line the south wall, while the zombies plod out the north exit to line the north wall of the temple. If intruders enter room **57.**, are in the passage to the temple, or are within the temple itself, these undead warriors will attack. Proper garments and amulets will prevent attack unless the head cleric commands the undead to do so. They have no treasure.

58. TEMPLE OF EVIL CHAOS: This huge area has an arched ceiling some 30' or more in height. The floor is of polished black stone which has swirling patterns of red veins through it. The walls behind the draperies, and the ceiling as well, are of dull black rock, while the west wall is of translucent red stone which is seemingly one piece, polished to mirror-like smoothness. A great bell of black iron stands near the entrance point, with a pair of mallets beside its supports. To the south are several long benches or pews. There are three stone altars to the west, the northernmost of pure black, the middle one of streaked red and black, the last of red with black flecks. At the western end of the temple area is a dais of black stone, with four lesser chairs on its lower tier and a great throne above. The chairs are of bone; the ivory throne is set with gold and adorned with gems of red and black (10 black stones each worth 100 gold pieces, 10 red stones each worth 500 gold pieces, and one large red stone worth 1,000 g.p.). The signs and sigils upon these seats are of pure chaos and evil. The other walls are covered by draperies of deep purple with embroidered symbols and evil sayings, done in scarlet and gold and black thread. As soon as the party enters the place, black candles in eight great candelabras on either side of the place will come alight magically, shooting forth a disgusting red radiance. Shapeless forms of purple, yellow and green will dance and sway on the western wall, and if anyone looks at them for more than a moment, they must save versus magic or be mesmerized into chanting a hymn to chaotic evil. Should three or more voices be so raised, the iron bell will sound automatically by magic, but even one such chant will alert the guards of the head cleric (see below). Zombie guards will enter here in 3 rounds after entry, even if the party is quiet.

59. THE CHAMBERS OF THE EVIL PRIEST: Location 59.g is the anteroom where special visitors are entertained by the chief cleric. There are lavish furnishings here, although none are of particular value except for a golden flagon and cups (flagon worth 500 g.p., each of the nine cups has 100 g.p. value). Two zombies are on guard here. They once were 3rd level fighters so treat as 3 + 1 hit dice monsters (DX 8, AC 2 from plate mail and shield, HD 3 + 1, hp 17 each, #AT 1, D 1-8). They stand unmoving unless they are summoned by a chant from the temple area, someone enters their area, or they are commanded by the evil priest.

Location **59.** is the private chamber of the evil priest. He is 3rd level, wears magic +1 armor, has a +1 shield, and wears an **amulet of protection from good**, which adds a further + 1 to his armor class when attacked by good creatures. (DX 16, AC 0 or –1, LVL 3, hp 14.) He attacks with a **snake staff** (+ 1 chance to hit, 2-7 (d6 + 1) points of damage per hit, and will coil around opponents upon command). He also has a normal mace hanging from his belt. He has a gold ring with a black gem (value 1,400 gold pieces) and a purse with 51 platinum pieces in it. He wears a black cape and cowl, with red robes beneath. His spells are: **cause light wounds** and **cause fear**. He also has a scroll with three cleric spells on it: **detect magic, hold person, silence, 15' radius**. He has a **potion of gaseous form** which he will use to escape through the boulder-filled corridor, **51.**, when all else fails.

His room is furnished lavishly, with a red carpet, furniture of black wood with velvet upholstery of scarlet, and a large bed covered with silken covers of black and red cushions and pillows. A demon idol leers from the wall to the north, directly over the bed. If anyone other than the priest touches it it will topple over upon the person, causing 2-12 points of damage. It has two gem eyes (100 g.p. value each). The evil priest will dart behind a screen in the southeast corner, enter a wardrobe there, slip through a secret door in its back, and then down a short passage and out into the corridor through another secret door, should his life be in danger. When the secret door in the back of the wardrobe is opened by the party, 500 gold pieces and 50 gems of 10 gold piece value each will spill from the wardrobe into the room to hopefully cause pursuers to stop for the loot. The priest will meanwhile either try to rally his forces, or else escape (assuming that most of his fellows have been eliminated already).

60. GUEST CHAMBER: This lower room is for important guests of the place. It contains a large bed, table, chairs, etc. There is nothing of value within, although the tapestries adorning the walls (things picturing evil cruelties and obscene rites) appear expensive. Beneath a velvet cloth on the table is a polished mirror.

61. TORTURE CHAMBER: There are various implements of torture here, both large and small — a rack, iron maiden, tongs, pincers, whips, etc. Comfortable chairs are scattered along the walls, evidently so placed to allow visitors an enjoyable view of the proceedings. The **torturer** lives in the forepart of the place, and he will attack unauthorized persons who enter. He is a 3rd level fighter, DX 17, hp 19, with chainmail under his black leather garments (AC 4). His weapon is a huge axe which inflicts 3-9 hit points of damage per blow (due to his strength). Hidden in his mattress are 135 gold pieces and a bracelet worth 700 gold pieces.

62. THE CRYPT: The door to this room is bolted shut. This long hall is of roughly hewn stone, with a low ceiling. In it are many coffins and large sarcophagi with the remains of servants of the Temple of Chaos. The sixth tomb opened will contain a **wight**: DX 7, AC 5, HD 3, hp 13, #AT 1, D 1-6 **plus** drains one energy (experience) level. There is no treasure buried with any of the remains, but there is a secret compartment in the wight's tomb; this contains a + 1 **flaming sword**, a scroll of **protection from undead**, a **helm of evil**, and a silver dagger worth 800 gold pieces because of the gems set into its pommel*.

63. STORAGE CHAMBER: There are many piles of boxes, crates, barrels, sacks, and so forth here — the supplies of the temple are kept here. There is nothing of value, and if the party stays within the place for longer than 3 rounds, a **gelatinous cube** will move down the corridor into the place and block it: DX 5, AC 8, HD 4, hp 22, #AT

1, D 2-8, plus deadens touched flesh so as to make it unresponsive for 2-12 rounds (thus an arm will hang useless for that time if the monster touches it!). Inside the creature are d12 each of copper, silver, electrum, gold, and platinum pieces, as well as several bones — evidently parts of a victim not yet wholly digested. (One of the "bones" is actually a **wand of fire balls** with 9 charges left. If it is not gotten out of the monster within 1 turn, it will be ruined by digestive juices.) The secret door in the room leads to the gnoll chieftain's cave (**50.**, above).

64. CELL: The door is of iron, locked and barred, but a window is set in the door. This is the place where prisoners are kept until tortured to death or sacrificed in the area above. There are several skeletons still chained to the wall, and one scantily clad female — a fair maiden obviously in need of rescuing! As she is partly around a corner, at first only her shapely legs and body up to the shoulders can be seen. Those who enter and approach closer are in for a rude shock! This is actually a **medusa** recently taken by the evil priest's zombie guards. (DX 14, AC 8, HD 4, hp 20, #AT 1, D 1-6 from asp-hair biting, plus opponent so hit must save versus poison or be slain.) Persons looking at the creature — including those fighting her from the front — must save versus being turned to stone by the medusa.

Not being above such things, the cleric had plans for removing its snakes, blinding it, and then eventually sacrificing it at a special rite to a demon. The medusa will spare one or two of the adventurers from her gaze, promising them she has magic which will turn their companions back to flesh again, if they will free her from her chains. She does, in fact, have a special elixir*, a potion of **stone to flesh** in a small vial, enough liquid to turn six persons back to normal, but she does not intend to give it away. If freed she will attempt to "stone" her rescuers.

CREDITS:

Designed and written by: Gary Gygax

Layout: Harold Johnson

Editing: David Cook, Harold Johnson, Jeff R. Leason, Frank Mentzer, Tom Moldvay, Lawrence Shick, Jean Wells

Art: David S. LaForce, Erol Otus, Jim Roslof

23

NON-PLAYER CHARACTERS (NPCs)

Whenever the players encounter a person, it is helpful to have the characteristics of that person at ready. Before play, roll the strength, intelligence, etc. for each NPC. Make the adjustments as permitted in the BASIC book, select a personality, and equip the character (if details are not already given).

The tables below will help get you started. You may select from the list of personalities or roll (d20) at random, giving one or two types to each NPC. Use common sense — a character can't be rude and courteous, for example. Feel free to add to this list; it gives just a few examples for you to begin with.

PERSONALITIES

1. Brave	11. Kind
2. Careless	12. Lazy
3. Cautious	13. Modest
4. Cheerful	14. Nosy
5. Courteous	15. Prankish
6. Dishonest	16. Rude
7. Forgiving	17. Suspicious
8. Friendly	18. Talkative
9. Helpful	19. Trusting
10. Honest	20. Wasteful

For your convenience, you may key the characteristics listed below to the persons mentioned in the module. For instance, a note after the Taverner 'c#4'' would indicate that when the players meet him, the DM is to use the characteristics of #4 (below) to represent him. Remember to make as many listings as you need! The class designations (Ftr, etc.) do not apply to normal men, of course, and may be ignored when used to represent normal men.

HUMANS

Race/Class	Str	Int	Wis	Dex	Con	Cha	Personality
1. Ftr	14	13	7	11	12	14	Cheerful, honest
2. Ftr	16	10	9	9	11	15	Talkative, careless
3. Ftr	17	8	13	10	15	12	Brave, forgiving
4. Ftr	15	8	11	14	16	6	Honest, wasteful
5. Ftr	18	10	7	11	13	9	Kind, trusting
6. Ftr	14	8	10	13	17	11	Helpful, forgiving
7. Ftr	13	10	6	10	14	17	Kind, dishonest
8. Thf	11	12	8	14	11	7	Prankish, rude
9. Thf	14	6	11	16	12	10	Nosy, suspicious
10. Thf	8	9	11	17	8	16	Modest, careless
11. Cl	11	10	14	8	13	9	Lazy, trusting
12. Cl	13	7	15	11	10	10	Friendly, wasteful
13. Cl	7	11	17	9	16	8	Courteous, helpful
14. M-U	10	17	12	6	9	11	Cautious, modest

DEMI-HUMANS

Race	Str	Int	Wis	Dex	Con	Cha	Personality
15. Elf	16	14	7	9	13	10	Suspicious, dishonest
16. Elf	14	15	10	17	14	5	Cautious, rude
17. Hflg	17	12	8	14	10	9	Courteous, nosy
18. Hflg	15	10	11	11	11	7	Prankish, friendly
19. Dwarf	18	8	9	12	9	13	Brave, talkative
20. Dwarf	16	9	15	8	17	11	Cheerful, lazy

DESIGNING FLOOR PLANS

Once you have become familiar with the KEEP — who its residents are, where the main buildings are located, and so forth — it will be helpful to have details about the layout and contents of certain places. Players can easily 'see' an area they are visiting if you have prepared a floor plan. The Guild House (#16) will be used as an example of this procedure.

On the map of the KEEP, the Guild House is shown to be an 'L' shape about 40' long. Draw a large version of it on a piece of graph paper (the kind with ¼'' squares usually works best). Leave room for a **key** (noting what symbols are being used) and index the sheet for easy reference.

The outer walls should have the same dimensions as the building's outline. Note the **scale** (what map length represents what real length) at the bottom of the key. In the example given, ¼'' equals two feet of 'real' length. Since the walls in a normal building are from six inches to one foot thick, they may be represented by single lines; an outer wall should be indicated by double lines.

Now look closely at the description of the building in the text. The lower floor contains the Guild Master's quarters, two clerks' quarters, and an office. Give equal spaces to the clerks, more to the Guild Master, and the most to the office (as it represents the main purpose of the building). The rooms may be in whatever order you like; just remember that the outer door shown on the map probably opens into the office, not into a private bedroom. Most doors are 3 to 5 feet wide. Be sure to include steps down to the cellar and up to the rooms on the second floor. Add some windows and a back door.

Try and think of what items would be in a sparsely furnished office in the KEEP (probably chairs, tables, desks, a lockbox or chest, and a cabinet or two). Consider how necessities would be provided: heat (fireplaces), water (barrels), and food (a kitchen in the cellar). The fireplaces should be located first — chimneys go straight up, and must be placed in the same area on each floor. Most buildings have one or two chimneys. Remember to heat each room, if possible! Add other furnishings wherever you wish, including any information provided in the text.

The completed office in this example has the Master's desk along the west wall under a window, flanked by records cabinets. The clerks' desk (they share one) and collection table are just inside a railing, which keeps visitors from wandering into the work area. A coat rack and waiting chairs are placed for the Guild members' convenience. A secret door in the fireplace leads to the Master's bedroom — a quick escape route in case of trouble. The locked chest is for money received in Guild dues, but is usually empty due to a clever 'drop' system. It is triggered by a lever under the Master's desk, which dumps the chest's contents down a short chute into a cellar storage room! (You may add whatever tricks and traps you wish.)

24

Arrange the bedroom furnishings (table, chairs, bed, armoire, etc.) in a similar manner. On the second floor (divided into private bedrooms and dormitory, according to the text) build the rooms off of the stairs, hallways, and fireplaces. It's easy!

Now **you** design the cellar, remembering a few key facts:

1. The stairs and chimneys **must** connect properly to the first floor.
2. Two servants live in the cellar, but not as richly as the clerks or the Guild Master.
3. A heavily barred, locked room must be under the office to receive the Guild fees from the chute.
4. A kitchen must be located by one of the fireplaces.

You won't have to worry about windows or outside doors — but you might wish to include a secret entrance to a long-forgotten dungeon (which, of course, you must design and stock with monsters and treasure)!

Adding the details to a house, church, or other structure can take a lot of time, but it's **not** as hard as you might think. Before playing the module, lay out as many buildings of the KEEP as you can. The most commonly used buildings will be the TRAVELERS' INN (**14.**), the TAVERN (**15.**), the GUILD HOUSE (**16.**), and the CHAPEL (**17.**). You may add just a few·simple furnishings to each if you wish, leaving the many smaller details for later. By designing floor plans, you can experiment with many of your own ideas before starting a major project — like the CAVES OF THE UNKNOWN.

TIPS TO THE PLAYERS

It often helps for beginning players to have advice on how to play **D&D**. Many points are overlooked by novices in their eagerness to get on with the adventure. The following points are given to help these players.

Most importantly, players should be organized and cooperative. Each player should have complete information on his or her character easily on hand and should supply the DM with this information quickly and accurately if asked. As parties will usually involve a variety of races, alignments, and classes, players should work together to use their abilities effectively. Arguing among players will cause delays, attract monsters, and often result in the deaths of some or all of the members.

Cooperation should also be given to the DM. He or she is the judge of the game and his or her decisions are final. If a player disagrees, he or she should calmly state why, and accept whatever the DM decides. Shouting, crying, pouting, or refusing to accept decisions only angers the other players. The game should be fun for all involved. Not everything will go the way players want it.

Planning is another important part of play. Players should be well equipped, comparing each member's list and balancing the items on each. No character should be overburdened nor under-equipped. This may mean sharing the costs of extra items. Rope, oil, torches, spikes, and other useful items should always be carried. Plans should be considered for encountering monsters and casting spells.

Caution is also necessary and is a part of planning. A party that charges forward without preparation is almost certainly doomed. Danger should be expected at any moment and from any direction, possibly even from one's own party. Lying and trickery are not unknown. Cautious play will help avoid many (but not all) tricks and traps and may save a life. However, too much caution is as dangerous as too little. Many instances will require bold and quick actions on the part of the players, before all is lost.

Above all a player must think. The game is designed to challenge the minds and imaginations of the players. Those who tackle problems and use their abilities, wits, and new ideas will succeed more often than fail. The challenge of thinking is a great deal of the fun of the game.

GLOSSARY

amulet — A charm inscribed with a magic symbol.

armoire — A large trunk or closet where clothes are kept.

bailey — The outer wall of a castle, or an area within such a wall.

battlement — A parapet with open spaces atop a wall, used for defense or decoration.

brazier — A pan for holding hot coals, usually on a tripod.

bulwark — A solid wall for defense, or any strong projection or support.

buttress — A projecting structure for supporting a wall or building.

Castellan — A governor or warden of a castle or fort.

cistern — A reservoir for storing liquids, especially water.

contour line — A line connecting points having the same elevation on a map.

cowl — The hood on a cloak.

crenellate — To furnish with battlements.

decanter — A vessel used to pour or store liquids; usually used for wines and other liquids containing sediment.

elixir — A sweet liquid, or a cure-all.

fen — Low land which is covered, wholly or partially, by water; a swamp.

flagon — A large vessel or bottle of metal or porcelain, usually with a lid.

hilt — The handle of a sword or dagger.

labyrinth — A confusing maze, usually of tunnels underground.

lackey — A servant, usually very low in class.

Man-at-Arms — A soldier of the most common type.

mercenary — A soldier who fights for wages rather than allegiance.

murder holes — Slits cut into a ceiling so that victims passing below may be attacked from above.

NPC — A non-playing character, controlled by the Dungeon Master rather than one of the players.

pallet — A straw-filled mattress or small, hard bed.

parapet — A wall or elevation of earth or stone to protect soldiers.

pole arm — A large, heavy weapon on a long pole. There are many types, all of which are considered equal for BASIC D&D combat.

pommel — The knob on the hilt of a sword or dagger.

portcullis — An iron grate hung over a gateway and lowered between grooves to prevent passage.

pot boy — A young servant or slave who works in a tavern or inn.

sarcophagus — A stone coffin (Plural — sarcophagi.)

scenario — An outline of a possible course of events.

score — 20 items.

scullion — A kitchen helper, usually very low in class.

tun — A measure of wine: 252 gallons, or 8 barrels.

vellum — A very strong cream-colored paper.

25

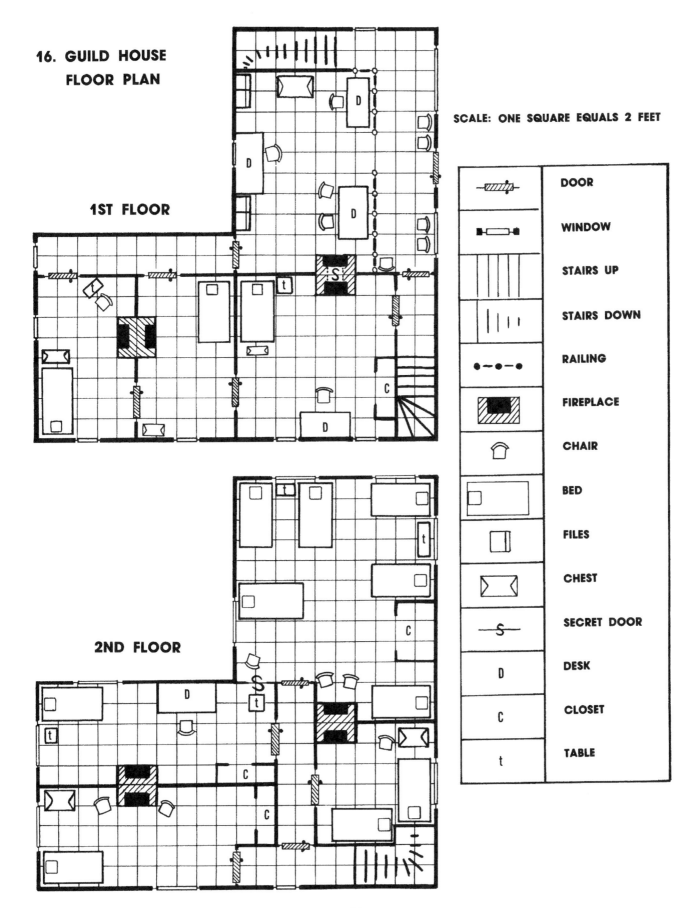

16. GUILD HOUSE FLOOR PLAN

1ST FLOOR

2ND FLOOR

SCALE: ONE SQUARE EQUALS 2 FEET

	DOOR
	WINDOW
	STAIRS UP
	STAIRS DOWN
	RAILING
	FIREPLACE
	CHAIR
	BED
	FILES
	CHEST
S	SECRET DOOR
D	DESK
C	CLOSET
t	TABLE

26

DRAW YOUR OWN FLOOR PLAN

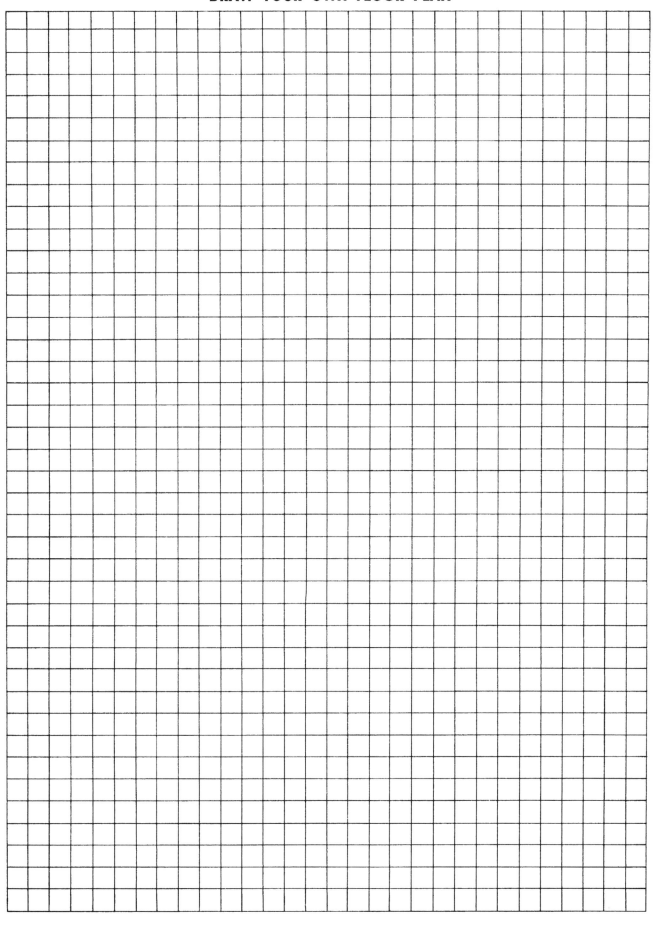

ADDITIONAL NON-PLAYER CHARACTERS

Use this sheet to list persons in the KEEP or in the CAVES OF CHAOS. Profession could be Fighter, Innkeeper, and so forth. Special refers to spells, valuables, and other details you may wish to include. Place should be noted by building or cave number.

	Name	Class/ Profession	Level	AC	hp	Str	Int	Wis	Dex	Con	Cha	Personality	Special	Place
1.														
2.														
3.														
4.														
5.														
6.														
7.														
8.														
9.														
10.														
11.														
12.														
13.														
14.														
15.														
16.														
17.														
18.														
19.														
20.														
21.														
22.														
23.														
24.														
25.														
26.														
27.														
28.														
29.														
30.														
31.														
32.														

28

This item is only one of the many popular playing aids for DUNGEONS & DRAGONS produced by TSR Hobbies, Inc. Other playing aids for D&D currently available include:

Dungeon Module B1 (In Search of the Unknown), another beginning instructional module

Dungeon Geomorphs , Set One (Basic Dungeon)
Dungeon Geomorphs , Set Two (Caves & Caverns)
Dungeon Geomorphs , Set One (Lower Dungeon)

Outdoor Geomorphs, Set One (Walled City)

Monster & Treasure Assortment, Set One (Levels One to Three)
Monster & Treasure Assortment, Set Two (Levels Four to Six)
Monster & Treasure Assortment, Set Three (Levels Seven to Nine)

TSR also publishes the ADVANCED DUNGEONS & DRAGONS family of games and playing aids:

Players Handbook (everything the AD&D player needs to know)
Dungeon Masters Guide (essential reference work for DMs)
Monster Manual (over 350 monsters, profusely illustrated)

The World of Greyhawk (fantasy world setting approved for use with AD&D)

AD&D Dungeon Masters Screen (combat and saving throws reference)
Rogues Gallery (100's of pre-rolled chracters for AD&D)

AD&D Player Character Sheets
AD&D Permanent Character Folder and Adventure Record Sheets
AD&D Non-Player Character Sheets

Dungeon Module G1 (Steading of the Hill Giant Chief)
Dungeon Module G2 (Glacial Rift of the Frost Giant Jarl)
Dungeon Module G3 (Hall of the Fire Giant King)
Dungeon Module D1 (Descent into the Depths of the Earth)
Dungeon Module D2 (Shrine of the Kuo-Toa)
Dungeon Module D3 (Vault of the Drow)

Dungeon Module S1 (Tomb of Horrors)
Dungeon Module S2 (White Plume Mountain)
Dungeon Module S3 (Expedition to the Barrier Peaks)

Dungeon Module T1 (Village of Hommlet)
Dungeon Module C1 (Hidden Shrine of Tamoachan)

Other releases of additional items relating to D&D are planned for the future. TSR Hobbies pub-lishes a complete line of fantasy, science fiction and historical games and rules which are available from better hobby, game, and department stores nationwide. If you desire a complete catalog,write to: TSR Hobbies, POB 756 Lake Geneva, WI 53147.

ISBN 0-935696-47-4

Dungeon Module B2
The Keep on the Borderlands

by Gary Gygax

INTRODUCTORY MODULE FOR CHARACTER LEVELS 1-3

This module includes a cover folder with maps and a complete description booklet to form a ready-made scenario for DUNGEONS & DRAGONS®Basic Set. It has been specially designed for use by beginning Dungeon Masters so that they may begin play with a minimum of preperations.

Within are many features to aid novice players and Dungeon Masters: legends, history and background information, a list of adventuring characters, tips on how to be an effective Dungeon Master, plus and interesting area for characters to base themselves in (the Keep) before setting out to explore the Caves of Chaos!

If you enjoy this module, look for more releases in the D&D®family from TSR, the Game Wizards.

TSR Hobbies, Inc.
POB 756
LAKE GENEVA, WI 53147

PRINTED IN U.S.A.

Special Instructional Module

9034

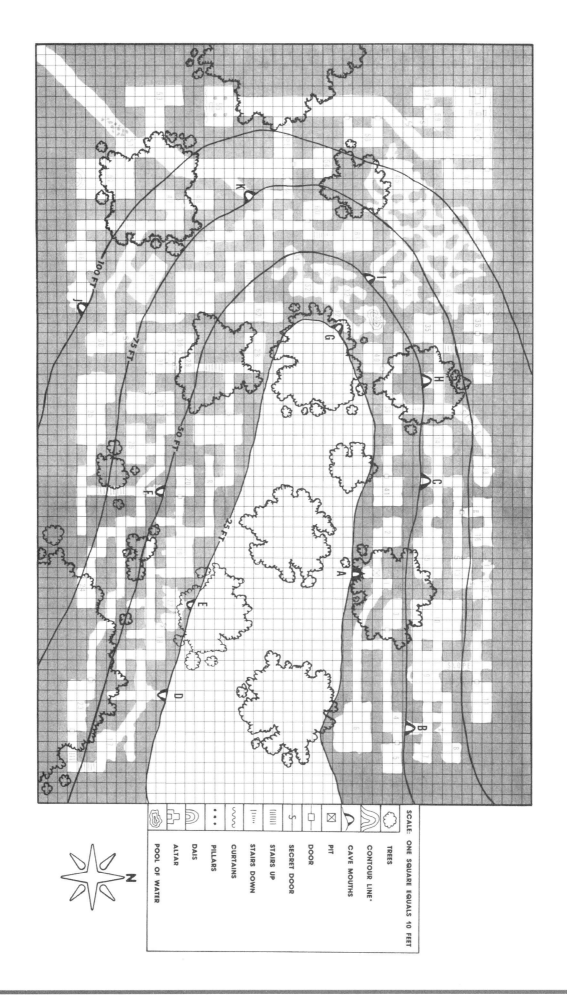

SCALE: ONE SQUARE EQUALS 10 FEET

Symbol	Meaning
	TREES
	CONTOUR LINE
	CAVE MOUTHS
	PIT
	DOOR
S	SECRET DOOR
	STAIRS UP
	STAIRS DOWN
	CURTAINS
	PILLARS
	DAIS
	ALTAR
	POOL OF WATER

N

Dungeon Module B2
The Keep on the Borderlands

by Gary Gygax

INTRODUCTORY MODULE FOR CHARACTER LEVELS 1-3

This module includes a cover folder with maps and a complete description booklet to form a ready-made scenario for DUNGEONS & DRAGONS® Basic Set. It has been specially designed for use by beginning Dungeon Masters so that they may begin play with a minimum of preparations.

Within are many features to aid novice players and Dungeon Masters: legends, history and background information, a list of adventuring characters, tips on how to be an effective Dungeon Master, plus an interesting area for characters to base themselves in (the Keep) before setting out to explore the Caves of Chaos!

If you enjoy this module, look for more releases in the D&D® family from TSR, The Game Wizards.

Distributed to the book trade in the United States by Random House, Inc. and in Canada by Random House of Canada, Ltd. Distributed to the toy and hobby trade by regional distributors.
© 1981 by TSR Hobbies, Inc., All Rights Reserved.
DUNGEONS & DRAGONS® and D&D® are registered trademarks owned by TSR Hobbies, Inc.

© 1980 TSR Hobbies, Inc. All Rights Reserved

TSR Hobbies, Inc.
POB 756
LAKE GENEVA, WI 53147

PRINTED IN U.S.A.
ISBN 0-935696-47-4

Special Instructional Module

Dungeons & Dragons®

Dungeon Module #B2

The Keep on the Borderlands

Introduction: Welcome to the land of imagination. You are about to begin a journey into worlds where magic and monsters are the order of the day, where law and chaos are forever at odds, where adventure and heroism are the meat and drink of all who would seek their fortunes in uncommon pursuits. This is the realm of DUNGEONS & DRAGONS® Adventure Game.

If you plan to play in this module and participate in the fun of adventuring, **stop** reading now. The information in the rest of the module is for your Dungeon Master or DM, so that he or she may guide you and other players through a thrilling adventure. Knowing too much about the contents of this module will spoil the surprises and excitement of the game.

Dungeon Masters, if many copies of this module are available to the players, you may wish to alter sections of the Keep and the Caves of Chaos. If you do this, you will be sure to have new surprises for players who might be familiar with some of the contents of the module. You are not entering this world in the usual manner, for you are setting forth to be a **Dungeon Master**. Certainly there are stout fighters, mighty magic-users, wily thieves, and courageous clerics who will make their mark in the magical lands of D&D® adventure. You, however, are above even the greatest of these, for as DM you are to become the Shaper of the Cosmos. It is you who will give form and content to all the universe. You will breathe life into the stillness, giving meaning and purpose to all the actions which are to follow. The others in your group will assume the roles of individuals and play their parts, but each can only perform within the bounds you will set. It is now up to you to create a magical realm filled with danger, mystery, and excitement, complete with countless challenges. Though your role is the greatest, it is also the most difficult. You must now prepare to become all things to all people.

NOTES FOR THE DUNGEON MASTER

The basic instruction book for DUNGEONS & DRAGONS® Game has given you the information necessary to understand this game and start play. This module is another tool. It is a scenario or setting which will help you to understand the fine art of being a Dungeon Master as you introduce your group of players to your own fantasy world, **your** interpretation of the many worlds of DUNGEONS & DRAGONS® Adventure. **THE KEEP ON THE BORDERLANDS** is simply offered for your use as a way to move smoothly and rapidly into your own special continuing adventures or campaigns. Read the module thoroughly; you will notice that the details are left in your hands. This allows you to personalize the scenario, and suit it to what you and your players will find most enjoyable.

NOTE: Several words in the following text will be followed by an asterisk (*). This means that the word will be explained in the **Glossary** at the end of this module.

This module has been designed to allow **six to nine player characters of first level** to play out many adventures, gradually working up to second or third level of experience in the process. **The group is assumed to have at least one magic-user and one cleric in it.** If you have fewer than six players, be sure to arrange for them to get both advice and help in the KEEP. For example, they should have advice from a friendly individual to "stay near the beginning of the ravine area, and enter the lower caves first", to avoid their getting into immediate trouble with higher level monsters. Likewise, the services of several men-at-arms* **must** be available to smaller parties. If only two or three player char-

acters are to adventure, be sure to have a non-player character or two go along, as well as a few men-at-arms. In addition, give the player characters a magic dagger or some magic arrows and at least one **potion of healing** — family bequests to aid them in finding their fame and fortune when they go against Chaos.

The DM should be careful to give the player characters a reasonable chance to survive. If your players tend to be rash and unthinking, it might be better to allow them to have a few men-at-arms accompany them even if the party is large, and they don't attempt to hire such mercenaries*. Hopefully, they will quickly learn that the monsters here will work together and attack intelligently, if able. If this lesson is not learned, all that can be done is to allow the chips to fall where they may. Dead characters cannot be brought back to life here!

Using the KEEP as "home base", your players should be able to have quite a number of adventures (playing sessions) before they have exhausted all the possibilities of the **Caves of Chaos** map. Assuming that they have played well, their player characters will certainly have advanced a level or two in experience when the last minion of darkness falls before their might. While your players will have advanced in their understanding and ability, you will likewise have increased your skills as DM. In fact, before they have finished all the adventure areas of this module, it is likely that you will have begun to add your own separate maps to the setting. The KEEP is only a small section of the world. You must build the towns and terrain which surround it. You must shape the societies, create the kingdoms, and populate the countryside with men and monsters.

The KEEP is a microcosm, a world in miniature. Within its walls your players will find what is basically a small village with a social order, and will meet opponents of a sort. Outside lies the way to the **Caves of Chaos** where monsters abound. As you build the campaign setting, you can use this module as a guide. Humankind and its allies have established strongholds — whether fortresses or organized countries — where the players' characters will base themselves, interact with the society, and occasionally encounter foes of one sort or another. Surrounding these strongholds are lands which may be hostile to the bold adventurers. Perhaps there are areas of wilderness filled with dangerous creatures, or maybe the neighboring area is a land where chaos and evil rule (for wilderness adventures, see DUNGEONS & DRAGONS® EXPERT SET). There are natural obstacles to consider, such as mountains, marshes, deserts, and seas. There can also be magical barriers, protections, and portals. Anything you can imagine could be part of your world if you so desire. The challenge to your imagination is to make a world which will bring the ultimate in fabulous and fantastic adventure to your players. A world which they may believe in.

NOTE: For your convenience, whenever a monster or non-player character (NPC*) is described in the text, the details will be listed in the following order:

Name (Armor Class, Class/Level **or** Hit Dice, hit points, Number of Attacks per round, Damage per attack, Movement (per round), Save as class and level, Morale)

Armor Class = **AC**; Class: Cleric = **C**, Fighter = **F**, Magic-user = **M**, Thief = **T**, Dwarf = **D**, Elf = **E**, Halfling = **H**, Normal Man = **LVL 0** or **NM**; Level = **#**, Hit Dice = **HD**, hit points = **hp**, Number of Attacks = **#AT**, Damage = **D**, Movement = **MV**, Save = **Save**, Morale = **ML**.

Class/Level is only used for non-player characters (NPCs), while **Hit Dice** is used for all other monsters. Movement in a game turn is three times the movement given for one combat round. NPCs **save** at the same level as their class level of experience.

2

Examples: Taverner (AC 9, LVL 0, hp 6, #AT 1, D 1-6, ML 8)
Guard (AC 4, F 1, hp 7, #AT 1, D 1-6, ML 10)
Kobold (AC 7, HD ½, hp 3, #AT 1, D 1-4, MV (40'),
Save NM, ML 6)

#AT ½ indicates that the player may only attack once every 2 rounds.

* An asterisk after Hit Dice indicates an experience point bonus.
** Two asterisks after Hit Dice indicates double the normal experience point bonus.

Determining Armor Class:

Armor Class	Type of Armor
9	None
8	Shield only
7	Leather
6	Leather & Shield
5	Chainmail
4	Chainmail & Shield
3	Plate Mail
2	Plate Mail & Shield
1	Plate Mail & magic **Shield +1** (or other combinations)

Note that an Armor Class (AC) of less than 2 is possible for characters wearing magic armor, carrying a magic shield, having a higher than normal Dexterity score, and/or wearing a **ring of protection**. Players using these items will **subtract** bonuses from their AC — for example, a fighter using both **Plate Mail +1** and **Shield +1** would have AC 0.

Using the Combat Tables:

To find the die roll needed to hit any Armor Class, look at the **HOW TO ATTACK** section in the **D&D® Basic Set** rulebook. Compare the Level (if a character) or Hit Dice (if a monster) with the AC of the target to find the number needed 'to hit'. For Armor Classes lower than 2, adjust the number upwards; a character needing a roll of 17 to hit AC 2 would need an 18 to hit AC 1, 19 to hit AC 0, and so forth. Unless magic or silver weapons are needed to cause damage (and not available), a roll of **20** will **always** hit, and a roll of **1** will always **miss**!

A bonus of +1 should be added to the "to hit" die roll of high level characters, for they have more training and experience in fighting. This bonus will apply to Fighters of 4th level or above, to Clerics and Thieves of 5th level or above, and to Magic-Users of 6th level or above.

Movement in Combat:

Combat movement is usually very short and quick. In a combat situation, only short charges or retreats are allowed. After combat is resolved, movement rates return to normal. The movement speed for characters is:

Unarmored, unencumbered man:	**40** feet per melee round
Metal armored **or** encumbered man:	**20** feet per melee round
Metal armored, encumbered man:	**10** feet per melee round

To determine a monster's movement speed in combat, divide its base movement speed by **3**.

Note: Movement speed may be different if the optional encumbrance rule is used.

When dice are used to randomly determine a number, the type of dice used are abbreviated 'd#' ('d4' means a four-sided die, 'd6' a six-sided, and so forth). If more than one is rolled, the number required is placed before the 'd' ('2d6' means two six-sided dice). If any number is to be added to the total of the dice, it is indicated afterward ('d4 + 2' means to roll a four-sided die and add 2 to the total; '2d8 + 1' will thus give a number from 3 to 17). You will quickly get to know all of these abbreviations, and may use them when you design your **own** dungeon.

Become familiar with this module, then make whatever additions or changes you feel are necessary for **your** campaign. Once you are satisfied, gather the players together and have them create their characters. This will take some time, so at first, don't plan on getting much playing done unless there is a lot of time available. After each person has rolled the numbers for his or her characteristics (Strength, Intelligence, etc.), selected a class, and found how much money he or she has to begin, you should introduce them to the setting by reading the **Background** section to them. If you wish, feel free to limit the classes your players may choose as suits your setting. You might wish to not have elves or halflings in the KEEP, or you might not want any thieves as beginning characters. It is all up to you as DM to decide the shape of the campaign. Likewise, you can opt to give the player characters a special item of equipment to begin with — possibly mules, a weapon, some trade goods, or virtually anything of small value (within reason).

After you have explained the background, allow your players to begin interacting with their characters. Give them time to wander around the KEEP, learning what is there, finding the limits of their freedom, and meeting the other "inhabitants" of the place. They may quickly establish their base in the **Traveler's Inn**, purchase their equipment, and then visit the tavern — where they may gather bits of information for their coming adventures. All of this play, as well as what will come afterwards, requires that the players play the personae (personalities) of the characters that they will have throughout the length of the campaign, much like an actor plays a role in a play. You, however, have a far greater challenge and obligation! You not only must order and create the world, you must also play the part of each and every creature that the player characters encounter. You must be gate guard and merchant, innkeeper and orc, oracle and madman as the situation dictates. The role of DM is all-powerful, but it also makes many demands. It is difficult to properly play the village idiot at one moment and the wise man the next, the noble clergyman on one hand and the vile monster on the other. In one role you must be cooperative, in the next uncaring and non-commital, then foolish, then clever, and so on. Be prepared!

Whether the first time you play or the next, the players will set forth to find and explore the many **Caves of Chaos.** You must describe the journey to the place and what the characters see, and allow them to choose how they will go about their adventuring. In such situations, the DM must be a truly disinterested party, giving information as required by questioning and proper action, but neither helping nor hindering otherwise. When the players experience their first encounter with a monster, you must be ready to play the part fully. If the monster is basically unintelligent, you must have it act accordingly. Make the encounter exciting with the proper dramatics of the animal sort — including noises! If the encounter is with an intelligent monster, it is up to the DM to not only provide an exciting description but also to correctly act the part of the monster. Rats, for instance, will swarm chitteringly from their burrows — a wave of lice-ridden hunger seeking to overrun the adventurers with sheer numbers, but easily driven off squealing with blows and fire. Goblins, on the other hand, will skulk and hide in

3

order to ambush and trap the party — fleeing from more powerful foes, but always ready to set a new snare for the unwary character.

If all of this seems too difficult, never fear! Just as your players are learning and gaining experience at D&D® play, so too will you be improving your ability as a DM. The work necessary to become a master at the art is great, far greater than that necessary to be a top player, but the rewards are even greater. You will bring untold enjoyment to many players in your role as DM, and all the while you will have the opportunity to exercise your imagination and creative ability to the fullest. May each of your dungeon adventure episodes always be a wondrous experience!

HOW TO BE AN EFFECTIVE DUNGEON MASTER

As Dungeon Master, the beginner is faced with a difficult problem. The DM is the most important person in the D&D® game. He or she sets up and controls all situations, makes decisions, and acts as the link between the players and the world he or she has created. Perhaps the most common question asked by a beginning Dungeon Master is, "What do I do to run a game?" It is possible to read through the rules and become slightly lost by all the things that must be prepared or known before DMing a game.

Unlike most boardgames, D&D play relies on information, both from the players and the DM. In boardgames, the way the game is played is obvious. First one person moves, and then another. Actions are limited and choices are few. In this game, the action is only limited by the abilities of the character, the imagination of the player, and the decisions of the DM. The play will often go in unexpected directions and the DM will sometimes be required to decide on situations not covered in the rules. The DM is the judge.

As a judge, moderator, or referee, the DM must constantly deal with the players. Just as the referee of a sporting event, the DM must be fair. He or she cannot be "out to get the players", nor should he or she be on their side all the time. The DM must be **neutral**. If a party has played well and succeeded, the DM should not punish them by sending more and more monsters at them or thwart their plans; on the other hand, if the players have acted foolishly, they should get their "just rewards". In combat, the DM should play the monsters to the best of the monster's ability. If the creature is stupid, it may be easily tricked or may not always do the smartest thing. If the monster is clever or intelligent, it will fight to its best advantage. The DM must be fair, but the players must play wisely.

The DM is also the designer of the situations and must bear in mind the abilities of his or her players. It is the job of the DM to see that the situations and characters balance. If things are too difficult, the players will become discouraged; too easy and they will become bored. Is it possible for a good player to win, yet still be a challenge and a risk in doing so? Is the amount of treasure gained equal to the danger of trying to get it? As DM, much satisfaction comes from watching players overcome a difficult situation. But they should do it on their own!

To defeat monsters and overcome problems, the DM must be a dispenser of information. Again, he or she must be fair — telling the party what it can see, but not what it cannot. Questions will be asked by players, either of the DM or of some character the party has encountered, and the DM must decide what to say. Information should never be given away that the characters have not found out — secret doors may be missed, treasure or magic items overlooked, or the wrong question asked of a townsperson. The players must be allowed to make their own choices. There-

fore, it is important that the DM give accurate information, but **the choice of action is the players' decision.**

Throughout all this — making decisions, playing roles, handling monsters — the DM must remember that he or she is in control. The DM is the judge, and it is his or her game. The DM should listen to the players and weigh their arguments fairly when disagreements arise, but the final decision belongs to the DM. The Dungeon Master's word is law!

TIME

The Dungeon Master is responsible for keeping a track of game time. Inside the dungeon, a normal turn is ten minutes long (adventure time). A normal turn is determined by the distance the slowest party member can travel, using the **CHARACTER MOVEMENT TABLE** in the **Dungeons & Dragons® Basic Set** rulebook. For example, a party whose slowest member moves at 120 feet per turn, would travel 120 feet in a turn. When the party has mapped 120 feet of dungeon, one turn has passed.

If fighting should occur, the time reference shifts to melee **rounds** of 10 seconds each. Melee rounds are used to simulate the quick exchange of blows in combat. For convenience, a DM should consider one entire melee* to last as long as one normal turn (that is, 10 minutes), no matter how many melee rounds the combat actually took. The extra time is spent recovering one's breath, bandaging wounds, resharpening blunted weapons, etc.

The **actual** (clock-time) length of a turn varies. A turn might take longer than ten actual minutes, especially if a long combat has taken place. On the other hand, a turn may be quite short in actual time, if the party is heading back through a familiar area.

In general, a party should rest and sleep eight hours every 24. Cautious player characters will sleep in shifts, with a guard always awake.

Remember that player characters heal 1-3 points naturally every 24 hours of **full** rest.

DIVIDING TREASURE AND COMPUTING EXPERIENCE

After the party leaves the dungeon safely, all surviving player characters should divide the treasure and be awarded their experience points. Division of treasure is the players' responsibility. Awarding experience points is the Dungeon Master's responsibility.

Ideally, treasure should be divided equally among surviving player characters, with retainers* usually receiving a share (minus any advance payment already given them). Players may decide to only give magical items to character classes that could use them. For example, a fighter should take a magical sword as part of his or her share in preference to a scroll.

Non-magical treasure is usually divided first, since it is easier to divide equally. It is seldom possible to divide magic items equally. A suggested solution to division of magic items is to have each character roll percentile dice and let the highest score have first pick, second highest score second pick, and so on until there are no more magical items. Retainers may, or may not, be given an equal chance for a magic item. If they are excluded, a DM should note the fact and take it into account when it next comes time to test the retainers' loyalty.

For example, a party consisting of a fighter, a magic-user, and a retainer (all first level) returns safely to the Keep. Their recovered treasure equals 520 gold pieces, 1000 silver pieces, a necklace worth 400 gold pieces, a **sword +1** and a **ring of water walking**. The total value of all non-magical treasure is 1020 gold pieces. Without selling the necklace, it would be impossible for the party to split the treasure

4

equally. The two player characters compromise by giving the necklace to their retainer, to insure his loyalty with a greater share of treasure. They each take only 310 gold pieces, but the magic-user keeps the ring and the fighter keeps the sword.

Experience points are awarded by the DM to player characters on the basis of non-magical treasure recovered and monsters killed or overcome. Experience points for recovered treasure are calculated at one experience point for every gold piece worth of non-magical treasure. Experience points for monsters overcome or killed is calculated by using the **Experience Points for Monsters** chart in the **DUNGEONS & DRAGONS® Basic Set** rulebook.

Unless a player character has earned extra treasure through the use of his or her class abilities (for example, a thief who steals treasure which he did not report to the party), the DM should **divide the experience points earned through treasure recovery equally among all surviving party members**. Since, in the above example, the entire party recovered 1020 gold pieces worth of non-magical treasure, the fighter and the magic-user each receive 340 experience points for the treasure recovered. The retainer receives ½ normal experience, since he was only following orders, and not doing his own thinking. The retainer thus receives only 170 experience points for recovered treasure.

To recover the treasure, it was necessary for the party members to kill 19 orcs, 7 skeletons, and an ogre. The party should receive 10 points of experience for each orc killed, as orcs have 1 hit die. The party should receive 5 experience points for each skeleton. For killing the ogre, they should receive 125 experience points, since it has 4 + 1 hit dice. The total experience points for defeating monsters would be 350. When this is divided, the magic-user and fighter each receive 117 additional experience points. The retainer receives only one-half, 59 additional experience points. The total experience for each player character is 457 (340 + 117) experience points apiece. The retainer receives 229 experience points.

When enough experience points are accumulated, a player character rises to the next higher level, and gains the benefits of that level (an additional hit die, a new spell, etc.). Wealth can be used to buy new equipment, to pay for everyday expenses, and to hire retainers.

PREPARATION FOR THE USE OF THE MODULE

The use of this module first requires that the DM be familiar with its contents. Therefore, the first step is to completely read through the module, referring to the maps provided to learn the locations of the various features. A second (and third!) reading will be helpful in learning the nature of the monsters, their methods of attack and defense, and the treasures guarded.

Certain buildings of the KEEP will frequently be visited by the adventurers (such as the Travelers Inn, Tavern, and Provisioner). Floor plans are very useful in visualizing these areas. For information on their preparation, refer to the section entitled "Designing Floor Plans" near the end of the module.

Once you are familiar with the areas described in the module and have drawn whatever additional plans you wish, assist the players in preparing their characters by reading them the section entitled **Background**. This will set the stage for the game.

After the background is given, the players may prepare their characters. Full details are given in the **D&D® BASIC SET** rulebook. A written record of each character should be kept by the players.

As an alternative to rolling up new characters, the players may (at the DM's option) select characters from the NPC* list in this module. Note that the personalities given are for the DM's use with NPC's **only**, and are **not** to be used by the players.

Before the players enter the KEEP, the DM may privately give each player one rumor about the CAVES OF CHAOS. This information may be shared or kept secret, as the **players** wish. The DM should avoid interfering with their choices whatever the result. Additional information may be gathered in the KEEP itself; use the **Rumors Table** in the "DM Notes About the Keep" for this purpose, or create your own based on the CAVES.

To start an adventure outside the KEEP, the players must decide on an order of march — who will be in the first rank, middle, and at the rear of the party. This should be drawn on a sheet of paper and given to the DM for his or her reference. Any changes in the order (due to injuries, special procedures, etc.) should be noted on the sheet as they occur. In a standard 10' wide corridor, the most common arrangement is two adventurers, side by side, in each rank; however, three characters could occupy a single rank if all of their weapons were small (such as daggers and hand axes).

One player in the group should be selected as leader and 'caller' for the party; another one or two should take care of necessary mapping. INDIVIDUAL PLAYERS MAY DECIDE ON THEIR ACTIONS, but it is the 'caller' who gives the DM the details on the party's course of action (such as "We'll head down the eastern corridor."). The caller should discuss the party's actions with the players, and inform the DM of the decisions of the group. When a player speaks and indicates that an action is being taken, **it has begun** — even if the player changes his mind. Use your discretion in these cases, and remember that the DM has the final say in all matters.

The players should use graph paper to map the areas being explored. Have them indicate which direction is north, and use compass directions to describe details and direction of travel ("We'll go west and turn north at the next intersection"). Use the same method to describe areas to them ("You see a corridor which goes about 30' south and then turns west"). Be sure to keep your descriptions accurate, though you may say such things as 'about forty feet', especially in open areas or when describing irregular

5

surfaces. Players will often show you their map and ask "Is this right?" Do not correct their mistakes unless the error would be obvious in the eyes of the adventurers, and remember that, in most cases, maps do not have to be exact. Encourage good mapping skills and an attention to detail, and avoid falling into a rut of continually answering map questions.

Exploration of the CAVES OF CHAOS will take more than one game session. When the players want to stop play, they must find an exit and (preferably) return to the KEEP. You may divide treasure and award experience when this occurs. Remember to make adjustments to the areas they visited — the monsters may build new defenses, reoccupy areas that were cleaned out, and so forth.

If the adventurers wish to stop exploring for a while and take a rest period (for example, the customary 8 hours rest each night), they should tell the DM exactly where they plan to stay and who is standing guard. Just as with marching order, it is important that the guard and sleeping positions be noted on paper, since this may be crucial if and when a monster approaches.

During play, make careful notes on the monsters killed, the amount of treasure taken, experience gained, and any other details of interest. It is then a simple matter to compute the totals at the end of a play session. See the section of this module entitled "DIVIDING TREASURE AND COMPUTING EXPERIENCE" for more information.

BACKGROUND

The Realm of mankind is narrow and constricted. Always the forces of Chaos press upon its borders, seeking to enslave its populace, rape its riches, and steal its treasures. If it were not for a stout few, many in the Realm would indeed fall prey to the evil which surrounds them. Yet, there are always certain exceptional and brave members of humanity, as well as similar individuals among its allies — dwarves, elves, and halflings — who rise above the common level and join battle to stave off the darkness which would otherwise overwhelm the land. Bold adventurers from the Realm set off for the Borderlands to seek their fortune. It is these adventurers who, provided they survive the challenge, carry the battle to the enemy. Such adventurers meet the forces of Chaos in a testing ground where only the fittest will return to relate the tale. Here, these individuals will become skilled in their profession, be it fighter or magic-user, cleric or thief. They will be tried in the fire of combat, those who return, hardened and more fit. True, some few who do survive the process will turn from Law and good and serve the masters of Chaos, but most will remain faithful and ready to fight chaos wherever it threatens to infect the Realm.

You are indeed members of that exceptional class, adventurers who have journeyed to the **KEEP ON THE BORDERLANDS** in search of fame and fortune. Of course you are inexperienced, but you have your skills and a heart that cries out for adventure. You have it in you to become great, but you must gain experience and knowledge and greater skill. There is much to learn, and you are willing and eager to be about it! Each of you has come with everything which could possibly be given you to help. Now you must fend for yourselves; your fate is in your hands, for better or worse.

Ahead, up the winding road, atop a sheer-walled mount of stone, looms the great KEEP. Here, at one of civilization's strongholds between good lands and bad, you will base yourselves and equip for forays against the wicked monsters who lurk in the wilds. Somewhere nearby, amidst the dark forests and tangled fens, are the **Caves of Chaos** where fell creatures lie in wait. All this you know, but before you dare adventure into such regions you must become acquainted with the other members of your group, for each life will depend upon the ability of the others to cooperate against the common foe. Now, before you enter the grim fortress, is the time for introductions and an exchange of information, for fate seems to have decreed that you are to become an adventurous band who must pass through many harrowing experiences together on the path which leads towards greatness.

START:

You have travelled for many days, leaving the Realm and entering into the wilder area of the Borderlands. Farms and towns have become less frequent and travellers few. The road has climbed higher as you enter the forested and mountainous country.

You now move up a narrow, rocky track. A sheer wall of natural stone is on your left, the path falling away to a steep cliff on the right. There is a small widening ahead, where the main gate to the KEEP is. The blue-clad men-at-arms* who guard the entrance shout at you to give your names and state your business. All along the wall you see curious faces peering down at you — eager to welcome new champions of Law, but ready with crossbow and pole arm* to give another sort of welcome to enemies.

(**DM Note:** Have each player identify his or her character's name and profession. Have them answer in their own words why they seek entrance to the place. If the answer sounds unnatural, assume the role of the corporal of the watch, and begin to cross-examine the speaker. Now is the time to make the players realize that whatever they say — as speech or relating their actions — will be noted by you, as Dungeon Master, and acted upon accordingly in whatever role is appropriate to the situation. A courteous and full reply might well win a friend amongst the soldiers who might be of aid sometime. Rudeness and discourtesy may bring suspicion and enemies to trouble the course of things within the otherwise safe base area. When you are satisfied that the scene is played out, have the group enter.)

DM Notes About The Keep:

I.   This whole place is well-organized for security and for defense. In time of need, many civilians will arm and help man the walls, while non-combatants bring ammunition, food, and water to the walls and help the wounded. Sentries are alert. A party of guards patrols the walls irregularly, and a commander checks every half hour to hour. It is very unlikely that persons can enter or leave without being seen, unless magic is used. (You can have magical traps placed in key areas to shout "ALARM" whenever an invisible creature passes within 10' or so!)

Within the Keep itself, the townspeople are generally law-abiding and honest. Boorishness and ill manners will be frowned upon. If any member of a party should be caught in a criminal act, the alarm will be sounded instantly. Citizens will try to prevent the escape of any lawbreakers (without sacrificing their lives) until the guard arrives in 1-2 turns. If met with resistance, the guard will not hesitate to use force, even killing if they must. Those offenders taken prisoner will be locked in the dungeons under the Keep and punished for their crimes.

┼   indicates a ballista, a huge, heavy crossbow manned by two men. It fires like a crossbow, but has a range of 480 feet, hits as if it were fired by a fighter of 1st-3rd level, and does 2 six-sided dice of damage plus two points (4-14 points of damage per hit).

6

Each ballista has 12 missiles. They may only be fired once every four rounds (requiring 3 rounds to load and 1 to fire).

indicates a light catapult with a range of 241 to 480 feet which fires half as often as a ballista (once per 8 rounds). Each requires two crewmen to operate, hits as if fired by a normal man, but can hit 1-6 targets in any close group (or one large target) for 1 six-sided die of damage each (6 dice if one large target). There is ammunition for six catapult shots per machine.

II. Floor plans might be useful. Note that most areas have two or more stories, and there is furniture in the rooms not shown. Also left out are details of heating, light, and descriptive touches such as color, rafters, decoration, etc. If you have time, floor plans and detailing of each area might be very helpful, exceptionally so in places frequented by the adventurers. See the appendix covering this near the end of the module.

III. Information from inhabitants of the KEEP might be gained by player characters. You may give one rumor (at random, using d20) to each player as starting information. Other rumors may be keyed to other persons in the KEEP. For example: "Talking with the Taverner (**#15**) might reveal either rumor #18 or #19; he will give the **true** rumor if his reaction is good."

Do not give out **all** the rumors. You may add whatever false rumors you wish, but adding to the amount of true information is not recommended.

The false rumors are noted by an 'F' after the number.

RUMOR TABLE

1. A merchant, imprisoned in the caves, will reward his rescuers.
2.F A powerful magic-user will destroy all cave invaders.
3. Tribes of different creatures live in different caves.
4. An ogre sometimes helps the cave dwellers.
5. A magic wand was lost in the caves' area.
6.F All of the cave entrances are trapped.
7. If you get lost, beware the eater of men!
8. Altars are very dangerous.
9.F A fair maiden is imprisoned within the caves.
10.F "Bree-yark" is goblin-language for "we surrender"!
11. Beware of treachery from within the party.
12. The big dog-men live very high in the caves.
13. There are hordes of tiny dog-men in the lower caves.
14.F Piles of magic armor are hoarded in the southern caves.
15.F The bugbears in the caves are afraid of dwarves!
16. Lizard-men live in the marshes.
17. An elf once disappeared across the marshes.
18. Beware the mad hermit of the north lands.
19.F Nobody has ever returned from an expedition to the caves.
20. There is more than one tribe of orcs within the caves.

IV. Entrance to the **Inner Bailey*** can be gained if the adventurers perform a heroic act in behalf of the KEEP, if they bring back an exceptional trophy or valuable prisoners, or if they contribute a valuable magic item or 1,000 or more gold pieces to the place. They will be invited to a feast and revel, and then closely watched and carefully questioned. If the Castellan* likes the looks of the group, and his assistants agree, he will ask them to perform a special mission (suitable to their ability, but difficult — use the area map or the **Caves of Chaos** to find a suitable goal). On the other hand, if they are rude or behave badly, he will simply retire early, ending the revel, and they will never be aided or invited back. If they try to steal or are threatening, the group will be attacked and killed immediately (if this can be managed, of course).

Groups sent on a mission will be **blessed** and given up to 100 g.p. each for any needed supplies. If they succeed, they will be given passes to the Inner Bailey and can ask the Castellan for aid if there is a major foe to overcome (in the **Caves'** area). He will send a minimum of one corporal and 3 archers in plate, or at maximum the sergeant, a corporal, and a dozen men-at-arms.

V. After the normal possibilities of this module are exhausted, you might wish to continue to center the action of your campaign around the KEEP by making it the base for further adventures which you may devise. For example (assuming that the group has done good service for the Castellan), have a large force of bandits move into the area, and then appoint the group to command an expedition of KEEP troops, mercenaries, and so on to drive them away. Or the party might become "traders" operating out of the KEEP, hoping to find adventures as they travel in the surrounding area (for wilderness adventures see the **D&D® EXPERT SET**).

7

AREAS OF THE KEEP

1. **MAIN GATE:** Two towers 30' high with battlements*, flank a gatehouse 20' high. All have holes for bow and crossbow fire. A deep crevice in front of the place is spanned by a drawbridge (usually up). There is a portcullis* at the entry and large gates at the far end of the passage. The passage is about 10' wide and high, the ceiling above pierced with murder holes*, and walls to either side slitted for archery. It is obvious that the building is constructed of great blocks of the hardest granite, undoubtedly common throughout the entire fortress. Two men-at-arms (AC 3, F 1, hp 5, #AT 1, D 1-6, ML 10) will approach when the drawbridge is lowered and the portcullis raised. Each is clad in plate mail and carries a pole arm*. They require that persons entering the KEEP put their weapons away, and then will escort them through the short tunnel into area **3.**.

2. **FLANKING TOWERS:** Atop each tower are four crossbowmen with crossbows cocked and ready to fire. Each is clad in chain mail (AC 5), wearing a sword and dagger, and has a shield (AC 4 when picked up) nearby. (AC 5 or 4, F 1, hp 4, #AT 1 or ½ with crossbow, D 1-6, ML 10.) Inside each tower are 12 other men-at-arms, four being "on-duty" and armored and armed as the men-at-arms on the tower tops. The other eight in the tower are resting, and it will take one full turn for these men to ready themselves for battle. They are exactly like the others, except instead of crossbows, they carry long bows. (AC 5 or 4, F 1, hp 4, #AT 1, D 1-6, ML 10.) The three floors of these towers will contain supplies of bolts and arrows, spears, rocks, and several barrels of oil (all for hurling down on attackers). There will also be pallets* for sleeping, pegs with clothing belonging to the soldiers, and some small tables, stools, and benches. Each man-at-arms will have (d6) copper pieces and (d4) silver pieces on his person.

3. **ENTRY YARD:** This narrow place is paved. All entrants, save those of the garrison, will be required to dismount and stable their animals (area **4.**, below). The **corporal of the watch** is here. He is dressed in plate mail and carries a shield, with sword and dagger at his waist. (AC 2, F 2, hp 15, #AT 1, D 2-7; his sword is a +1 magic weapon, ML 11.) The corporal is rather grouchy, with a low charisma, but he admires outspoken, brave fighters and is easily taken in by a pretty girl. Beside him is a man in robes (a scribe) who records the name of each person who enters or leaves, and flanking each man is another man-at-arms in plate with pole arms as noted in **1.**, above. (AC 3, F 1, hp 5, #AT 1, D 1-6, ML 10.) When dismounted, lackeys* will come from area **4.** (the stable) to take the mounts or mules. Any goods which are not carried by the adventurers will be stored in area **5.** (the warehouse). Another lackey will then show travelers to the Traveler's Inn.

4. **COMMON STABLE:** This long building is about 15' high, with a 3' parapet* atop its flat roof, so that it can be used in defense of the gate. The gateside wall is pierced for archery. There are always 5-8 (d4 + 4) lackeys inside tending to horses and gear. Each is unarmored (AC 9) but can fight with various available weapons (pitch forks and the like — treat as pole arms) and each has 1-4 hit points. There will be various light horses (AC 7, HD 2, hp 8 each, #AT 2, D 1-4/1-4, ML 7) and draft horses (AC 7, HD 2 + 1, hp 9 each, #AT 0) here, 2-8 of each, as well as 1-4 mules.

5. **COMMON WAREHOUSE:** Visiting merchants and other travelers who have quantities of goods are required to keep their materials here until they are either sold to the persons at the KEEP or taken elsewhere. The building is the same as the stable (**4.**, above) with respect to height, parapet, etc. Its double doors are chained and padlocked, and the **corporal of the watch** must be called to gain entry, as he has the keys. Inside are two wagons, a cart, many boxes, barrels, and bales — various food items, cloth, arrows, bolts, salt, and two tuns* of wine. (Average value is 100 gold pieces per wagon-load).

6. **BAILIFF'S TOWER:** The superintendent (or bailiff) of the outer bailey* of the fortress lives here. (AC 1, F 3, hp 22, #AT 1, D 2-7 due to **sword +1**, ML 12.) He is wearing magic **plate mail +1** or wields a **sword +1**, and is also able to use a longbow which is hanging on the wall. He and the scribe share offices on the lower floor. Their quarters are on the second story. (Usual furnishings of bed, chest, armoire*, table, chairs, rug, etc.) (The bailiff has 3d6 gold pieces with him always, the scribe has 2d6 silver pieces and d4 gold pieces in his purse. There are 50 gold pieces hidden in the bailiff's old boots in the armoire*, and hanging on his wall is a quiver with 20 arrows, 3 of which are magic **arrows +1**. The scribe has a jewelled ink pot worth 100 gold pieces, but it is dirty and ink covered, looks worthless, and is on his table in plain sight.) The third floor is a storage area, and the fourth story quarters twelve men-at-arms. Six are armored in leather and shield (AC 6) with pole arm and hand axe, the other six have chain mail (AC 5), crossbow, and sword and serve as the escort of the bailiff from time to time. (F 1, hp 4, #AT 1, D 1-6, ML 10.) Each carries 2d6 copper pieces and 1d6 silver pieces. Their room contains pallets, pegs with cloaks and other clothing, two long tables with benches, a supply of 180 bolts, and several dozen large rocks. The whole tower is 40' high, with a 5' tall battlement atop it. All walls are pierced for archery.

7. **PRIVATE APARTMENTS:** Special quarters are available for well-to-do families, rich merchants, guildmasters, and the like. The five small apartments along the south wall are occupied by families of persons dwelling within the Outer Bailey of the KEEP. The two large ones (indicated by **7a.** and **7b.**) currently house a jewel merchant and a priest:

a. **Jewel Merchant:** This normal man and his wife are guarded by a pair of 2nd level fighters in chainmail and shield with sword and dagger. (AC 4, F 2, hp 17, 12, #AT 1, D 1-6, ML 8.) The four are lodged in the eastern portion of the building, the merchant and his wife being on the upper floor most of the time. Each guard commands a huge dog trained to kill. (AC 6, HD 3, hp 12, 11, #AT 1, D 1-6, MV (60'), Save F 2, ML 9.) The merchant has a locked iron box with 200 platinum pieces and 100 gold pieces inside. Secreted in his belt are 10 gems of 100 gold piece value each. He will buy gems at 60% to 90% (d4 × 10 + 50%) of value. He sells at 110% to 140% (d4 × 10 + 100%) of value. His wife wears a jeweled bracelet, necklace, and earrings (600, 1,200, and 300 gold piece value respectively), also available for sale as per gems. They are awaiting a caravan back to more civilized lands. All persons here have 3d6 silver pieces each upon their person. The apart-

8

ment is well-furnished, but there is nothing of particular interest or value, except for the coins, gems, and jewelry noted.

b. Priest: The western portion houses the jovial **priest** who is taking advantage of his stopover at the KEEP to discuss theology with learned folk and to convert others. Everyone speaks well of him, although the two **acolytes** with him are avoided, as they never speak — the priest says they must follow vows of silence until they attain priestly standing. His well-appointed chambers are comfortably furnished and guests are always welcomed with a cozy fire and plenty of ale or wine. The priest is a very fine companion and an excellent listener. He does not press his religious beliefs upon any unwilling person. He is outspoken in his hatred of evil, and if approached by a party of adventurers seeking the **Caves of Chaos**, he will certainly accompany them. He has **plate mail +1** and a **shield +1** (AC -1) and a **mace +1**, and has a Dexterity of 15 (thus the low AC). He also has a magic cleric scroll with a **hold person** and a **silence, 15' radius** spell on it. He appears very robust (18 **hit points**), as do his assistants. The latter wear chain mail, carry shields and have maces. (AC 4, C 1, hp 7 each, #AT 1, D 1-6, ML 7.) **(Note:** All are chaotic and evil, being in the KEEP to spy and defeat those seeking to gain experience by challenging the monsters in the **Caves of Chaos**. Once in the caves the **priest** will use a **cause light wounds** (does 2-7 points of damage to the creature touched, a normal ''to hit'' roll must be made to touch the victim) or a **light** spell as needed to hinder and harm adventurers. Betrayal will always occur during a crucial encounter with monsters.) Each cleric carries 4d6 silver pieces, and each wears a gold chain worth 100 gold pieces (the **priest's** has a bloodstone gem worth 500 gold pieces in addition). (A small sack hidden in the **priest's** chair contains 30 each of platinum, gold, electrum, silver, and copper pieces, plus one jeweled clasp worth 300 gold pieces. These are for bribes for subversion or to use to gain freedom if necessary.)

8. SMITHY AND ARMORER: This building is about 20' high, with the usual 5' parapet above and walls pierced for defense. The lower floor is occupied by a forge, bellows, and other items. Here horses and mules are shod, weapons made, armor repaired and similar work done. The smith is also an armorer, and has two assistants. (Smith: AC 7 from leather armor, F 1, hp 11, #AT 1, D 1-6; he uses his hammer as a weapon, ML 8. His two assistants: AC 8, LVL 0, hp 5 each, #AT 1, D 1-6; they will pick up any weapons handy if need be, ML 8.) There are 2 swords, 1 mace, a suit of man-sized chain mail, and 11 finished spears in the shop. In the second story are rooms where the smith, his family, and his assistants live. (The rooms have normal furnishings, but a jar hidden in the smith's bedroom holds 27 electrum pieces.) The smith carries d4 gold pieces, and each assistant has 2d6 silver pieces.

9. PROVISIONER: This low building houses a shop where all of the equipment needed for dungeon adventurers (as listed in the rulebook) are sold. He does not sell weapons other than spears, daggers, arrows and bolts. He has a few (7) shields, but does not sell armor or mounts. He will direct any persons interested in such items to the trader next door. Prices are as shown in the

rules. He will buy equipment from adventurers at 50% of listed price. The provisioner is a normal man; in time of need he has leather armor and shield (AC 6) and will man the walls or otherwise fight with a spear. (In the shop he is AC 9, LVL 0, hp 3, #AT 1, D 1-6, ML 7.) His wife and two children live in a small apartment in the place. He carries d6 gold pieces. He has a strong box with 100 gold pieces, 16 electrum pieces, and 30 copper pieces.

10. TRADER: This place deals in all armor, weapons, and large quantities of goods such as salt, spices, cloth, rare woods, etc. The trader is very interested in obtaining furs. (Prices are as per the rulebook, purchases **from** adventurers are at 50% of listed cost, except for furs which will be bought by him at whatever their stated value is **if the seller demands**.) He is a normal man (AC 9, LVL 0, hp 2, #AT 1, D 1-6, ML 7); his two sons are likewise (AC 9, LVL 0, hp 3 each, #AT 1, D 1-6, ML 7). All have leather armor and shields (AC 6) and pole arms and swords for use when necessary. (Hidden under the floorboards of their small apartment are 500 gold pieces and 1,110 silver pieces. Each carries 2d6 gold pieces in his purse.)

11. LOAN BANK: Here anyone can change money or gems for a 10% fee. The banker will also keep a person's wealth stored safely at no charge if it is left for at least one month, otherwise there is a 10% fee. Loans at an interest rate of 10% per month can be obtained for up to 5 gold pieces with no security deposit; over 5 gold pieces requires some item of at least twice the value of the loan. A sign on the shop states clearly that this place is under direct protection of the KEEP, and there is always a man-at-arms in chain mail with long bow and sword watching the place from tower **12.**. (AC 5, F 1, hp 4, #AT 1, D 1-6, ML 10.) (The banker is a retired 3rd level fighter (AC 9, F 3, hp 12, #AT 1, D 1-6, ML 9) with a sword handy, and plate and shield (AC 2) stored in his apartment above. He carries 6 platinum pieces and 12 gold pieces with him.) There is a scrawny old clerk in the place as well (2nd level magic-user, 5 **hit points**, with **sleep** and **ventriloquism** spells ready) who typically handles transactions. A hired mercenary fighter (AC 3, F 1, hp 7, #AT 1 or ½ with crossbow, D 1-6, ML 8) in plate mail and armed with battle axe and crossbow is on guard inside the door. Displayed for sale are the following items:

1 carved ivory tusk — price 50 g.p.

1 silver cup — 20 g.p.

1 crystal decanter* — price 45 g.p. (actual worth 10 g.p.)

1 jade ring — price 250 g.p. (actual worth 400 g.p.)

1 dagger with jeweled scabbard — price 600 g.p.

1 fur-trimmed cape — price 75 g.p.

3 blank vellum* books — price 20 g.p. each

1 gold & silver belt — price 90 g.p.

1 set of thief's tools — price 100 g.p. (actual worth 35 g.p.)

1 iron box with secret lock — price 50 g.p.

The strong room of the place is in the cellar. It is protected by a locked iron door which leads to a small vault with 12 compartments each protected by locks with hidden poison needles (save versus Poison at +1 or die). These compartments hold the following items:

#1, #4, #11 empty.

#2 has 277 g.p. and 1 gem worth 500 g.p.

#3 has a gold altar service set forth 6,000 g.p.

#5 is **trapped** with a sleeping gas — no save, sleep for 3 turns; characters above 4th level save vs. Poison to avoid effect.

#6 has 1,000 each platinum, gold, electrum, silver and copper pieces.

#7 has four pit vipers (AC 6, HD 1*, hp 5 each, #AT 1, D 1-4 plus poison, MV (30'), Save F 1, ML 7).

#8 has 3 gems of 1,000 g.p. value, 4 of 500 g.p., 11 of 100 g.p., 25 of 50 g.p., and 18 of 10 g.p. value.

#9 has an arrow trap which will always hit anyone in front if its door — 4 arrows each doing 1-6 points of damage (Divide arrows amongst persons in front).

#10 has an alabaster and gold statue worth 3,000 g.p. in a rare wood and silk case worth 600 g.p.

#12 has a sack with 58 platinum pieces and 91 electrum pieces in it.

(Empty compartments indicate funds out on loan. **Bold-faced** numbers are those belonging to the banker.)

12. WATCH TOWER: This 45' tall tower has all of the usual defensive devices. It houses six men-at-arms in chain mail (AC 5) with bows and swords, 6 others in leather and carrying shields (AC 6) and pole arms (F 1, hp 4 each, #AT 1, D 1-6, ML 10), and the **captain of the watch** (AC 2, F 3, hp 20, #AT 1, D 2-7 with **dagger +1**, or 3-8 with **sword +2**, ML 11). The captain lives on the first floor (with the usual furnishings, but he has a silver flagon and tankard worth 750 g.p.). He is known to carry quite a bit of money with him (20 platinum pieces, 11 gold pieces, 8 silver pieces), although the soldiers have only small coins (2d6 silver pieces each). The second and third floors are barracks for the men-at-arms. The upper story holds a supply of 200 arrows, many rocks, 2 barrels of oil, and 24 spears.

13. FOUNTAIN SQUARE: There is a large, gushing fountain in the center of the square. On holidays, local farmers and tradesmen set up small booths to sell their goods in this place.

14. TRAVELERS INN: This long, low structure has five small private rooms and a large common sleeping room for a full dozen. (Servants and the like always sleep in the stables, **4.**, of course.) Private rooms cost 1 g.p. per night, but sleeping in the common room is only 1 silver piece per night. The innkeeper and his family live in a small loft above the inn. They are obviously normal persons of no fighting ability. This building is some 18' high.

15. TAVERN: This place is the favorite of visitors and inhabitants of the KEEP alike. The food is excellent, the drinks generous and good. The place is always active, with 4-16 (4d4) patrons at any time of day or night. The bill of fare reads:

ALE	1 e.p.	SOUP	1 s.p.
SMALL BEER	1 s.p.	STEW	1 e.p.
WINE	1 e.p.	ROAST FOWL	1 g.p.
HONEY MEAD	1 g.p.	ROAST JOINT	2 g.p.
BARK TEA	1 s.p.	HOT PIE	1 e.p.
BREAD	1 c.p./slice	CHEESE	1 s.p./wedge
PUDDING	1 s.p./bowl	FRUIT	1 s.p.

The barkeep, if talking with a good customer and drinking to his health, will sometimes talk about the lands around the keep (1 drink per story, half of which may be true). He is known to hate small beer and love honey mead. There is a 50% chance that 2-5 (d4 + 1) of the patrons will be mercenary men-at-arms looking for work. (AC 6, F 1, hp 5 each, #AT 1, D 1-6, ML 7.) Each will have leather armor & shield, and sword and dagger;

all other desired equipment must be purchased by the employer, including missile weapons, and dungeon gear. Wages for duty include all gear purchased, room and board, and 1 s.p. per day of service. If no gear is purchased, the cost rises to 1 g.p. per day. (Note that a mere spear or minor equipment is considered as **no gear**.) It is always necessary to buy mercenaries a drink before discussing terms of employment. There is a 10% chance that each of the following persons will be in the tavern at any given time:

    CORPORAL OF THE WATCH
    CAPTAIN OF THE WATCH
    BAILIFF (see **6.**, above)
    PRIEST (see **7b.**, above)
    2-4 WATCHMEN (see **12.**, above)
    SERGEANT OF THE GUARD (see **18.**, below)
    WANDERER (a 2nd or 3rd level fighter, dwarf, elf, or halfling as the DM decides, with complete equipment for adventuring; such a wanderer is 75% likely to join an expedition if offered 25% of the treasure gained, but 1 in 6 will be of chaotic alignment).

The taverner is a normal man (AC 9, LVL 0, hp 6, #AT 1, D 1-6, ML 7), as are his son and the pot boy* (AC 9, LVL 0, hp 5, 2, #AT 1, D 1-6, ML 7), but in time of need they will don leather armor, carry shields (AC 6), and bear arms against attackers. The place is also served by his wife, daughter, a serving wench, and a scullion*. (The owner and his son each have 2d6 gold pieces in their purses, the wife d6, all others have 2d6 coppers.) The cellar is where drink and food are stored and prepared, and where the servants sleep. The family sleeps in the small loft. (Hidden in an old crock under empty flour bags in the back room are 82 copper pieces, 29 silver pieces, 40 electrum pieces, and 17 gold pieces.)

16. GUILD HOUSE: When members of any guild (merchants, craft, artisans, etc.) travel to this area, they are offered the hospitality of this two-story building. This is a fee collection and administragive post, and the staff is careful to observe what traffic passes through the KEEP. Any trader who passes through must pay guild dues of 5% of the value of his merchandise, but he then gains the protection of the Guild House, assuming he is not a regular member. Craftsmen and artisans must gain Guild permission to enter or leave the land, paying a fee of 2d6 gold pieces either way (depending on the value of their trade). The lower floor contains the Guild Master's and his two clerks' quarters and an office (all sparsely furnished, but the Master has a gold ring worth 50 g.p., and 2d6 g.p. in his purse; each clerk has d4 each of gold, silver, and copper pieces. A strongbox under the Master's bed holds 712 gold pieces.) They are normal men (AC 9, LVL 0, hp 4 each, #AT 1, D 1-6, ML 7), with chain mail (AC 5), crossbows, and swords kept in a closet for quick use. There are two servants who will not fight and who have quarters in the cellar. The upper floor is divided into two private rooms and a dormitory for guests. The Master is very influential, and his favor or dislike will be reflected in the treatment of persons by fortress personnel. Four men-at-arms with leather armor and shields and armed with spear and sword are on duty at all times, two on the first floor, two above (AC 6, F 1, hp 6 each, #AT 1, D 1-6, ML 8). They are fanatical Guildsmen who will obey any order from the Master. Guests of the Guild eat here. Drinking is frowned upon.

17. CHAPEL: The spiritual center of the Keep is opposite the Guild House. This building has a peaked roof two stories tall; the interior is one large room. The altar is located at the eastern end, with a colored glass window (worth 350 g.p. intact) above it; the window is 20' tall and 8' wide. An offering box is fastened securely atop a heavy pedestal in the southeast corner; it contains 1-100 c.p.

10

and 1-100 s.p. at any time of the day. It is emptied each evening by the **Curate** (5th level cleric), who deposits the coins with the Banker (**11.**, above). A small stairway in the northwest corner, behind the bare wooden pews, leads to the cellar, where the Curate and his three assistants have their quarters.

The **Curate** is the most influential person in the Keep except for the **Castellan** (**26.**, below). He has a +1 'to hit', due to his high level; (AC 0 due to **plate mail +1**, normal shield, and a **ring of protection +1**, C 5, hp 24, #AT 1, D see below, ML 10). He will wield either a **mace +1** (D2-7) or a **snake staff**. The **snake staff** adds +1 to "to hit" rolls and does 2-7 (1d6+1) points of damage. On command the staff turns into a snake and coils around the person hit. The victim is held helpless until The Curate recalls the staff (or for 1d4 turns maximum). The snake staff crawls back to the cleric on command. He rarely wears his armor (unless the Keep is threatened), but is never without his ring and Staff. His three **Acolytes** (AC 9 or 2, C 1, hp 6, 5, 5, #AT 1, D 1-6, ML 7) have plate mail and shield (AC 2) and mace. They are normally clothed in robes (AC 9) but will arm for battle on command of the Curate.

The Curate normally carries the following spells: **cure light wounds, detect magic, bless, hold person**. He will only use the **cure** on a member of his congregation, such as an officer of the Guard or a shopkeeper.

All of the clerics' armor and weapons are stored in the Curate's locked room in the Chapel cellar, which has normal but sparse furnishings. The Chapel also owns many magic potions (3 of **healing**, 1 or **ESP**, 1 of **gaseous form**) and a magic scroll with one **cure disease** (a higher level spell which will cure any one normal disease), one **hold person**, and three **cure light wounds** spells on it. All of these magic items are hidden in a secret compartment underneath the offering box pedestal. The door of the compartment cannot be found unless the pedestal is moved. The door has two locks in it; the Curate and the Castellan have the only sets of keys.

If questioned closely by a friend, the Curate might (50% of the time) reveal his distrust of the Priest (**7b.**, above) who visits the Keep regularly. The Acolytes, however, think very highly of the Priest, and will say so to any who ask about him.

18. **INNER GATEHOUSE:** This stone structure is itself like a small fort. The southern portion is only about 15' high, plus battlement; the rear part is some 30' tall, plus battlement. There are arrow slits in the southern section of course, and along the walls of the 20' wide, 10' high passage through to the north. This passage slopes upwards towards the inner courtyard. The heavy gates are doublebound with iron and spiked. There are six guards on duty at all times (two inside the gateway, two on the lower battlement, two on the upper), plus one officer on call (see below). No visitor is allowed beyond this point except by invitation or unless he or she has special permits.

The first floor of the place is the main armory. There are dozens of shields and of each sort of weapon. Two small rooms are quarters for the **Sergeant** and **Captain of the Guard** (furnishings are sparse). The second story on the north houses the Guardsmen stationed here.

Captain of the Guard: (AC 0, due to **plate mail +1** and **shield +1**, F 3, hp 24, #AT 1, D 1-6 plus magical bonus, ML 11). He has a **sword +2** and a **spear +1**. This man is very kind, friendly and an excellent leader. (He will sometimes move about in the Outer Bailey disguised as a mercenary.) He has 15 gold pieces and a 150 g.p.

gem in the pommel* of his dagger.

Sergeant of the Guard: (AC 2, due to chain mail with a **shield +1**, and a **ring of protection +1**, F 2, hp 16, #AT 1, D 3-8 due to Strength plus magic weapon bonus, ML 11.) This very strong fellow (strength 17) is a hard fighter and loves to drink and brawl He wields a **sword +1** and a **dagger +1**. He carries d6 each of gold, electrum, and silver pieces. (There is a potion of **healing** in a chest in his room under a spare cape.)

Guardsmen: There are 24 quartered here. Each has chain mail and shield, sword, dagger, and hand axe. Eight are crossbowmen, eight are long bowmen, and eight have pole arms. (AC 4 or 5 when not using shield, F 1, hp 5 each, #AT 1 or ½ for crossbows, D 1-6, ML 10.) Two from each group are on duty at any given time; the rest take a full turn to armor and arm and turn out. (Each has 2d6 silver pieces.)

19. **SMALL TOWER:** This typical tower houses eight guardsmen who are all armored in chain mail (AC 5) and carry crossbows and swords. Shields are stored below, so in hand-to-hand combat they are AC 4. (AC 5 or 4, F 1, hp 5 each, #AT 1 or ½ for crossbows, D 1-6, ML 10.) Two are on duty atop the tower at all times. The other six are in the chamber below. The base of the tower is solid except for the small stair up.

20. **GUARD TOWER:** This 50' high structure houses 24 guardsmen (as in **18.**, above). Their commander is the **corporal of the guard** (AC 0, F 1, hp 9, #AT 1, D 1-6 plus magic bonus, ML 11.) He is armed with a sword and a **dagger +1**. There are supplies of food, weapons, and oil on the upper floor. The rest of the building is barracks and a room for the leader.

21. **INNER BAILEY:** This entire area is grass-covered. The troops drill here, and there are practice and jousting areas. During the daylight hours they will always be a dozen or more soldiers engaged in weapons practice.

22. **CAVALRY STABLES:** There are 30 war horses (AC 7, HD 3, hp 11 each, #AT 2, D 1-6/1-6, ML 8) and 1-4 riding horses (AC 7, HD 2, hp 8 each, #AT 2, D 1-4/1-4, ML 7) kept within. They are tended by two lackeys* (AC 9, LVL 0, hp 2 each, #AT 1, D 1-6, ML 7) and guarded by two men-at-arms (AC 4, F 1, hp 4, #AT 1, D 1-6, ML 8).

23. **GREAT TOWER:** This 60' high structure houses 24 guardsmen, one-third with crossbows, one-third with bows, one-third with pole arms, and another **corporal** as per **20.**, above. (See **18.** for tower details and so on.)

24. **THE KEEP FORTRESS:** This place has many tiers and is solidly built to withstand attack. The lowest level consists of a 15' high front section. The round flanking towers are 60' high, while the main building is 30' high. All sections have battlements. The door is solid iron. Inside are a great hall, an armory for the cavalry, and several side chambers for small dinners or meetings. The cellars below have vast stores of provisions, quarters for a score of servants, a cistern*, and a dungeon area with four stout cells.

The **Castellan*** lives in area **27.** (see below), but he and his assistants will be in the lower part of the building during the day, tending to business and holding audience. There will always be eight guardsmen in plate (AC 3) with crossbows and swords on duty on the wall, and the same number with plate & shield (AC 2) and swords stationed inside. (AC 2, F 1, hp 5 each, #AT 1 or ½ with crossbows, D 1-6, ML 8.) The whole place is well decorated, and the furniture is heavy and upholstered.

Second Floor: There are rooms here for up to 36 cavalrymen, plus two chambers for special guests. There are 12 heavy cavalrymen with plate & shield and

11

sword and dagger (AC 2, F 1, hp 8 each, #AT 1, D 1-6, ML 10). There are also 18 medium cavalrymen in chain, each with crossbow and axe, quartered here. (AC 5, F 1, hp 6 each, #AT 1 or ½ for crossbows, D 1-6, ML 10.) Their rooms are sparsely furnished with only a cot, chair, and armoire* for each. Two couriers, men-at-arms with leather armor and swords, are currently quartered in one side chamber. (AC 7, F 1, hp 3, #AT 1, D 1-6, ML 8.)

25. TOWER: Each is 40' high, with battlements, and pierced with arrow slits to protect the east and west corners of the building. The fortress men-at-arms are housed in these structures and in the towers indicated by **26**.

26. CENTRAL TOWERS: These structures rise 20' above the roof of the fortress, with a 5' battlement on their roof. Their two upper stories house 12 men-at-arms each; 6 in plate (AC 3) with crossbow and sword, 6 in plate and shield (AC 2) with sword (AC 3 or 2, F 1, hp 5, #AT 1 or ½ for crossbows, D 1-6, ML 10) who are off-duty. It will take one turn for them to get ready for battle. In the two lower floors are the **Castellan's** assistants.

Scribe: This individual is a 2nd level cleric, armored in plate & shield, with a mace. (AC 2, C 2, hp 11, #AT 1, D 1-6, ML 8.) He has a **hold person** spell on a scroll he carries; his own spell is **light** which he may cast on an opponent's eyes to blind him. The scribe's chamber is austere, and there is nothing of value within except a gold holy symbol worth 150 gold pieces. He has 48 gold pieces in his purse.

Advisor: This individual is a third level elf (AC 0 due to Dexterity 16 and **plate mail +1**, E 3, hp 18, #AT 1, D 1-6, ML 12). He wears a **ring of fire resistance** and carries a short bow (which he uses at +2 "to hit" due to high Dexterity) and 10 **arrows +1**. His spells are **charm person, read magic,** and **web.** Tapestries and carpets are all about the room (one tapestry is worth 500 g.p.); he has very nice furniture. He wears a jeweled pendant worth 1,000 g.p. and carries 6 platinum and 10 gold pieces in his purse.

27. CASTELLAN'S CHAMBER: This portion of the fortress is 10' above the main roof and has battlements. Inside is the private room of the commander of the whole Keep. It is lavishly furnished, with a silver mirror (worth 300 g.p.) on the wall, a malachite bowl (worth 750 g.p.) on a table, and a fox robe (worth 1,200 g.p.) in his armoire*. He has a small silver case (worth 450 g.p.) which contains 40 platinum pieces and 12 gems worth 100 g.p. each. There is a **spear +1** on the wall by the door.

Castellan: 6th level fighter (+1 to hit due to his high level), (AC -3 due to Dexterity 16, **plate mail +1, shield +1,** and **ring of protection +1,** hp 48, #AT 1, D 1-6 plus magical bonus, ML 12) with **sword +2, dagger +1,** and an **elven cloak and boots.** (He also carries a potion of **levitation** and a potion of **healing** with him at all times.) His chain of office is silver with gems (worth 1,800 g.p.), and he carries 10 each of platinum, gold, and electrum pieces, plus a gem worth 500 g.p. He is a very clever fellow, but at times he can be too hasty in his decisions. His bravery and honesty are absolute. If a guest asks him any question, he will do his best to answer, providing that it does not compromise the security of the KEEP.

ADVENTURES OUTSIDE THE KEEP

After the group establishes itself and obtains equipment, they will either follow clues gained in conversation with residents of the KEEP or set out exploring on their own (or both). Naturally, they will be trying to find the **Caves of Chaos,** but this will take some travelling, and in the meantime they might well run into more than they can handle. Thus there are two maps — an AREA MAP for use when the party searches for the caves, and the CAVES OF CHAOS MAP which is a dungeon level map. First, take a look at the AREA MAP.

The "Realm" is to the west, off the map. The road branches, one path to the KEEP ON THE BORDERLANDS, the other leading off into the forsaken wilderness beyond the ken of Law. Note that most features are unnamed, so you can name them as suits your campaign. Inspection of the map will also show that there are five special areas. Numbers 1-4 indicate outside encounters and are detailed below. The **Caves of the Unknown** area is left for you to use as a place to devise your own cavern complex or dungeon maze. You may also wish to expand on the other encounter areas, designing camps, lairs or lost ruins to permit more adventuring. If you do not wish to undertake this at first, simply DO NOT ALLOW YOUR PLAYERS TO LOCATE IT EVEN IF THEY THOROUGHLY SEARCH THE VERY SPACE IT IS IN. (It was hidden by a magical illusion so as to be undetectable . . .)

The normal movement rate is 1 square per hour searching, 3 walking. Walking in the fens is at the rate of 1 square per hour. Walking is done in the forest at 2 squares per hour.

(Wilderness adventures are more completely explained in the **D&D EXPERT SET** rulebook.)

Camping Outdoors Overnight: Nothing will bother the party when camped outdoors, unless they are within six squares of a numbered encounter area. For each square they are within the six square range there is a 1 in 6 chance that the monsters there will seek them; so at 6 squares there is a 1 in 6 chance, at 5 there is a 2 in 6, at 4 there is a 3 in 6, at 3 there is a 4 in 6, at 2 there is a 5 in 6 and at 1 square a 6 in 6 — automatic encounter. Treat otherwise as a normal encounter.

Organized parties should post at least one guard in shifts throughout the night. However, if the party posts no guards, the monsters will surprise automatically as the party was sleeping and unaware. If the party has a fire lit, the monsters will never be surprised, even though the party may be.

Also take note of what provisions are brought with the party. They are adventuring, not hunting, and so they should not expect to find food. They should bring enough food and water with them. If not, when the party eats all the food, they will either have to try their luck at hunting (1 chance in 6 to catch food for **one** day for d6 men), or return to the Keep to restock their supplies. Stress to them in some manner that they will probably prefer to return to the Keep, knowing that they will fare better there, and not risk encountering monsters while hunting.

If the party attempts to move off the map, have a sign, a wandering stranger, a friendly talking magpie, or some other "helper" tell them that they are moving in the wrong direction.

Area Map Encounter Areas:

1. MOUND OF THE LIZARD MEN: The streams and pools of the fens* are the home of a tribe of exceptionally evil lizard men. Being nocturnal, this group is unknown to the residents of the KEEP, and they will not bother individuals moving about in daylight unless they set foot on the mound, under which the muddy burrows and dens of the tribe are found. One by one, males will

come out of the marked opening and attack the party. There are 6 males total (AC 5, HD 2 + 1, hp 12, 10, 9, 8, 7, 5, #AT 1, D 2-7, MV (20'), Save F 2, ML 12) who will attack. If all these males are killed, the remainder of the tribe will hide in the lair. Each has only crude weapons; the largest has a necklace worth 1,100 gold pieces.

In the lair is another male (AC 5, HD 2 + 1, hp 11, #AT 1, D 2-7, Save F 2, ML 12), 3 females (who are equal to males, but attack as 1 + 1 hit dice monsters, and have 8, 6 and 6 hit points respectively), 8 young (with 1 hit point each and do not attack), and 6 eggs. Hidden under the nest with the eggs are 112 copper pieces, 186 silver pieces, a gold ingot worth 90 gold pieces, a **healing** potion and a **poison** potion. The first person crawling into the lair will always lose the initiative to the remaining lizard man and the largest female, unless the person thrusts a torch well ahead of his or her body.

2. **SPIDERS' LAIR:** Two black widow spiders (AC 6, HD 3*, hp 11, 10, #AT 1, D 2-12 plus poison, MV (20'), (40') in web, Save F 2, ML 8) have spun their webs amongst the trees here. Under a pile of leaves nearby is the skeleton of a victim, a hapless elf. Everything he bore has turned to rot and ruin, save a filthy shield which appears quite worthless (but cleaning and oiling will return it to **+1** magic status).

3. **RAIDER CAMP:** A party of a dozen chaotic fighters has camped here — close enough to be able to spy on the KEEP, far enough away so as to be unlikely to be discovered by patrols. The members of this group are:

Leader:	AC 5 (chain mail), F 2, hp 12, #AT 1, D 1-6, ML 10, bow and spear
Lieutenant:	AC 6 (leather and shield), F 1, hp 7, #AT 1, D 1-6, ML 9, spear and sword
2 Bowmen:	AC 7 (leather armor), F 1, hp 4 each, #AT 1, D 1-6, ML 8, bows and daggers
8 Spearmen:	AC 6 (leather and shield), F 1, hp 5 each, #AT 1, D 1-6, ML 8, spears and daggers

Each has 3d6 silver pieces, the lieutenant has an additional d6 gold pieces, and the leader has an additional 2d6 gold pieces. They each have a bed roll and the

bowmen have an extra quiver of 20 arrows. There is a cask of good wine on a tree stump in the camp. Several game animals are hung from branches and can be eaten or taken along as they are cleaned.

4. **THE MAD HERMIT:** For many years a solitary hermit has haunted this area of the forest, becoming progressively wilder and crazier and more dangerous. His home is in a huge hollow oak, the entrance to the hollow concealed by a thick bush. Inside is a mound of leaves and a couple of pieces of crude furniture. Even his cup and plate are handmade of wood and are of no value. (There is a small chest buried under a few inches of dirt under the leaves of the Mad Hermit's "bed". In this container are 31 gold pieces, 164 silver pieces, a potion of **Invisibility**, and a **dagger +1**.) The hermit also has a "pet", a mountain lion, which lurks on a limb of the oak, ready to spring upon any unwary intruder. (This creature will always get first attack.)

Mad Hermit: (3rd level thief, AC 4 due to leather armor, **ring of protection +1** and Dexterity 17, hp 15, #AT 1 at +2, D 3-8, ML 10.) The hermit has a 30% chance to **move silently** and a 20% chance to **hide in shadows**. His madness gives him a +2 bonus to hit and a +2 bonus on damage (thus the bonus for striking from behind is +6 to hit, and double normal damage +2 points). He carries no treasure (other than the ring he wears!).

Mountain Lion: AC 6, HD 3 + 2, hp 15, #AT 3, D 1-3/1-3/1-6, MV (50'), Save F 2, ML 8. (This creature will always attack first in each round. If it leaps down upon an opponent, it gains +2 to hit on each of its attacks that combat round. Usually it will first attack by jumping, and then it will stay on the ground and fight normally. If it is not engaged in combat during any round, however, it will take the opportunity to leap into a tree and then spring down on the next round.)

(The DM may choose to have the Mad Hermit approach the group on friendly terms, claiming to be a holy man seeking goodness in nature — perhaps he actually believes that at times. He will suddenly turn on the group when the opportunity presents itself, striking from behind, and calling his ferocious "pet" to his aid.)

13

THE CAVES OF CHAOS

(DM Note: When the players discover the ravine area, read the following paragraph to them. Add whatever you feel is appropriate to the description of what they see, but be careful not to give anything away or mislead them. Information on how you should handle the whole area is given before the encounter area descriptions.)

START: The forest you have been passing through has been getting more dense, tangled, and gloomier than before. The thick, twisted tree trunks, unnaturally misshapen limbs, writhing roots, clutching and grasping thorns and briars all seem to warn and ward you off, but you have forced and hacked your way through regardless. Now the strange growth has suddenly ended — you have stepped out of the thicket into a ravine-like area. The walls rise rather steeply to either side to a height of about 100' or so — dark, streaked rock mingled with earth. Clumps of trees grow here and there, both on the floor of the ravine and up the sloping walls of the canyon. The opening you stand in is about 200' wide. The ravine runs at least 400' west (actually 440') to where the western end rises in a steep slope. Here and there, at varying heights on all sides of the ravine, you can see the black mouths of cave-like openings in the rock walls. The sunlight is dim, the air dank, there is an oppressive feeling here — as if something evil is watching and waiting to pounce upon you. There are bare, dead trees here and there, and upon one a vulture perches and gazes hungrily at you. A flock of ravens rise croaking from the ground, the beat of their wings and their cries magnified by the terrain to sound loud and horrible. Amongst the litter of rubble, boulders, and dead wood scattered about on the ravine floor, you can see bits of gleaming ivory and white — closer inspection reveals that these are bones and skulls of men, animals, and other things . . . .

You know that you have certainly discovered the **Caves of Chaos.**

NOTES FOR THE DM ON THE CAVES OF CHAOS

CAVE AREA MAP: There are woods overlays and rough contour lines* shown on the map. These are only for surface movement references, and once your players are underground you should ignore these markings.

WOODS: The small groves and copses are thick growths, tangled and forbidding. You may, at your option, have characters encounter occasional monsters herein — stirges, humanoids (kobolds, orcs, etc.) from the caves nearby, or the like. Movement through these wooded areas is slow and difficult. Characters must move in single file. Even though not shown, there are single trees, shrubs, and bushes elsewhere.

UNDERGROUND: The caves, passages, and rooms of the complex are on different levels. Passages slope upwards and downwards between the contours, even where stairways are not shown. Areas are roofed by at least 5' of solid rock.

INTERIORS: Except where noted otherwise, all underground areas are natural or cut from living rock. All surfaces are rough (and easy for a thief to climb) with small ledges, minor cracks, small holes, etc.

RANSOMING PRISONERS: Organized tribes can optionally be allowed to take player characters prisoner, freeing one to return to the KEEP in order to bring a ransom back to free the captives. Set the sums low — 10 to 100 gold pieces (or a magic item which the ransoming monsters would find use-

ful) per prisoner. If the ransom is paid, allow the characters to go free. Then, without telling the players, assume that this success brought fame to the capturing monsters, so their numbers will be increased by 2-12 additional members, and the tribe will also be very careful to watch for a return of the adventurers seeking revenge for their humiliating captivity. The period of extra alertness will last for 1-4 weeks; the increase in numbers is permanent.

TRIBAL ALLIANCES AND WARFARE: You might allow player characters to somehow become aware that there is a constant fighting going on between the goblins and hobgoblins on one side and the orcs, sometimes with gnoll allies, on the other — with the kobolds hoping to be forgotten by all, and the bugbears picking off any stragglers who happen by. With this knowledge, they might be able to set tribes to fighting one another, and then the adventurers can take advantage of the weakened state of the feuding humanoids. Be careful to handle this whole thing properly; it is a device you may use to aid players who are few in number but with a high level of playing skill. It will make it too easy if there are many players, or if players do not actually use wits instead of force when the opportunity presents itself.

MONSTERS LEARNING FROM EXPERIENCE: Allow intelligent monsters (even those with only low intelligence) to learn from experience. If player characters use flaming oil against them, allow the monsters to use oil as soon as they can find some. If adventurers are always sneaking up on them, have the monsters set warning devices to alert them of intruders. If characters run from overwhelming numbers, have the monsters set up a ruse by causing a few to shout and make noise as if there were many coming, thus hopefully frightening off the intruders. This method of handling monsters is basic to becoming a good DM. Apply the principle wherever and whenever you have reason.

EMPTIED AREAS: When monsters are cleared out of an area, the place will be deserted for 1-4 weeks. If no further intrusion is made into the area, however, the surviving former inhabitants will return or else some other monster will move in. For instance, a thoul might move into the minotaur's cave complex (I.), bringing with him whatever treasure he has.

Encounter Areas:

A. KOBOLD LAIR: There is a 2 in 6 chance that as the group enters the cave-like tunnel, 8 kobolds will come out from hiding in the trees above and attack. Kobolds: AC 7, HD ½, hp 3 each, #AT 1, D 1-4, MV (40'), Save NM, ML 6). Each carries d8 silver pieces.

   Note: 30' inside the entrance is a **pit** (⊠). There is a 3 in 6 chance that each person in the front rank will fall in unless they are probing ahead. There is a 1 in 6 chance that individuals in the second rank will also fall in, but only if they are close to the first rank and the character ahead has fallen in. The pit is 10' deep, and those falling in will take 1-6 points of damage. The pit lid will close, and persons within cannot escape without aid from the outside. The noise will attract creatures from areas **1.** and **2.** Planks for crossing the pit are stored at **#1.**, beyond.

1. GUARD ROOM: 6 kobold guards (AC 7, HD ½, hp 3 each, #AT 1, D 1-4, Save NM, ML 6). They will throw their spears the first round if they have initiative. Each carries d6 silver pieces. One will run to warn areas **4.** and **6.**. The guards will be alerted by loud noises or lights.

2. GIANT RATS (amidst garbage and waste): There are 18 giant rats (AC 7, HD ½, hp 2 each, #AT 1, D 1-3 plus disease, MV (40'), Save F 1, ML 8). Each time a character

14

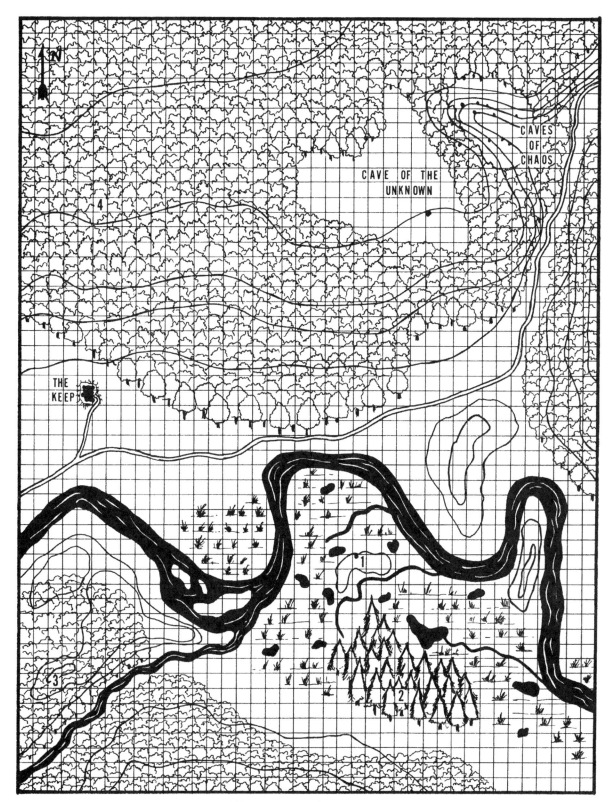

WILDERNESS MAP

SCALE: ONE SQUARE EQUALS 100 YARDS

 FOREST

 RIVER

CONTOUR LINE

FENS

ROAD

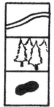 TAMARACK STAND

WATER

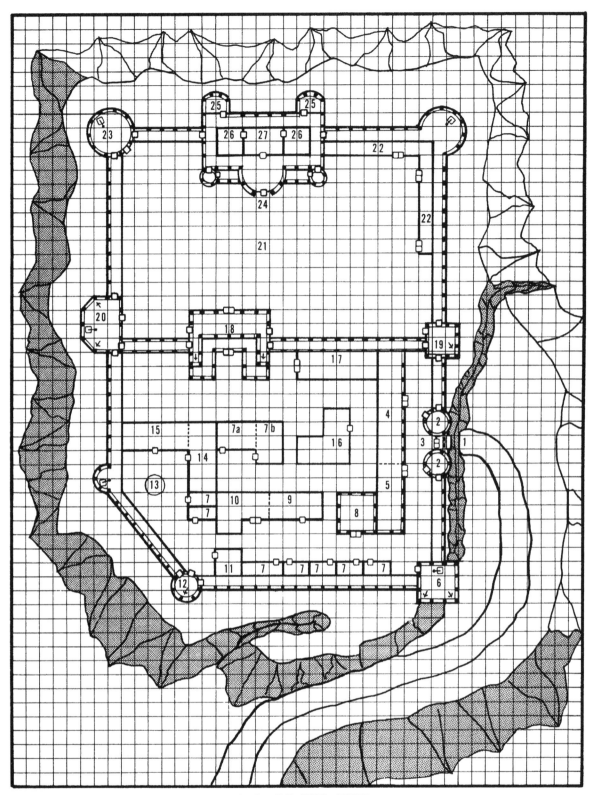

MAP OF THE KEEP

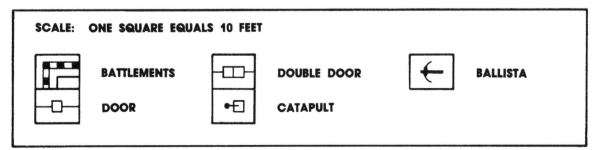

SCALE: ONE SQUARE EQUALS 10 FEET

BATTLEMENTS

DOOR

DOUBLE DOOR

CATAPULT

BALLISTA

CHARACTER ATTACKS

Attacker's Level	Defender's Armor Class												
	9	8	7	6	5	4	3	2	1	0	-1	-2	-3
(Normal man)	11	12	13	14	15	16	17	18	19	20	20	20	20
1st to 3rd	10	11	12	13	14	15	16	17	18	19	20	20	20
4th + higher*	9	10	11	12	13	14	15	16	17	18	19	20	20

* for NPCs or higher level characters

MONSTER ATTACKS

Monster's Hit Dice	Defender's Armor Class												
	9	8	7	6	5	4	3	2	1	0	-1	-2	-3
up to 1	10	11	12	13	14	15	16	17	18	19	20	20	20
1+ to 2	9	10	11	12	13	14	15	16	17	18	19	20	20
2+ to 3	8	9	10	11	12	13	14	15	16	17	18	19	20
3+ to 4	7	8	9	10	11	12	13	14	15	16	17	18	19
4+ to 5	6	7	8	9	10	11	12	13	14	15	16	17	18
5+ to 6	5	6	7	8	9	10	11	12	13	14	15	16	17
6+ to 7	4	5	6	7	8	9	10	11	12	13	14	15	16
7+ to 9	3	4	5	6	7	8	9	10	11	12	13	14	15
9+ to 11	2	3	4	5	6	7	8	9	10	11	12	13	14
11+ to 13	2	2	3	4	5	6	7	8	9	10	11	12	13
13+ to 15	2	2	2	3	4	5	6	7	8	9	10	11	12
15+ to 17	2	2	2	2	3	4	5	6	7	8	9	10	11
17+ or more	2	2	2	2	2	3	4	5	6	7	8	9	10

SAVING THROWS

Type of Attack

Character Class	Death Ray or Poison	Magic Wands	Paralysis or Turn To Stone	Dragon Breath	Rods, Stave, or Spells
Clerics	11	12	14	16	15
Dwarves and Halflings	10	11	12	13	14
Elves	12	13	13	15	15
Fighters	12	13	14	15	16
Magic-users	13	14	13	16	15
Thieves	13	14	13	16	15

Saving Throws for Higher Level Characters

In the D&D BASIC rules, NPCs higher than 3rd level should use the saving throws given above. In the D&D EXPERT SET, saving throws are given for higher level characters. In the more advanced game, a character's saving throws get easier to make as the character advances in experience level.

The DM may want to give higher level NPCs a bonus of +2 on all saving throw rolls to imitate their improved ability to save vs. special attacks. This should *not* be done, however, if the D&D EXPERT rules are used.

DUNGEONS & DRAGONS®

FANTASY ADVENTURE GAME
REFERENCE TABLES

(This page is perforated for easy removal.)

COST OF EQUIPMENT AND WEAPONS

Weapons

Item	Cost in gp
Axes:	
Battle Axe (two-handed)	7
Hand Axe	4
Bows:	
Crossbow (fires quarrels)	30
Case with 30 quarrels	10
Long Bow	40
Short Bow	25
Quiver with 20 arrows	5
1 silver-tipped arrow	5
Daggers:	
Normal dagger	3
Silver dagger	30
Swords:	
Short Sword	7
Sword (normal)	10
Two-handed Sword	15
Other weapons:	
Mace*	5
Club*	3
Pole Arm (two-handed)	7
Sling with 30 Sling Stones*	2
Spear	3
War Hammer*	5

* these weapons may be used by a cleric.

Armor

Item	AC	Cost in gp
Chain Mail Armor	5	40
Leather Armor	7	20
Plate Mail Armor	3	60
Shield	(-1)*	10

* deduct 1 from Armor Class number if shield is used.

Miscellaneous

Item	Cost in gp
Backpack	5
Flask of Oil	2
Hammer (small)	2
Holy Symbol	25
Holy Water (1 vial)	25
Iron Spikes (12)	1
Lantern	10
Mirror (hand-sized, steel)	5
Rations:	
Iron Rations (preserved food for 1 person/1 week)	15
Standard Rations (unpreserved food for 1 person/1 week)	5
Rope (50' length)	1
Sacks:	
Small	1
Large	2
Thieves' Tools	25
Tinder Box (flint & steel)	3
Torches (6)	1
Water/Wine Skin	1
Wolfsbane (1 bunch)	10
Wooden Pole (10' long)	1

Sometimes the characters may wish to buy an item not on this list. In this case, the DM must carefully consider whether such an item could be found for sale and, if so, how much it would cost. The item should then be added to this list.

CLERICAL ABILITIES

First Level Clerical Spells

1. Cure Light Wounds
2. Detect Evil
3. Detect Magic
4. Light
5. Protection from Evil
6. Purify Food and Water
7. Remove Fear
8. Resist Cold

Second Level Cleric Spells

1. Bless
2. Hold Person
3. Silence 15' radius

Clerics vs. Undead

Cleric's Level	Skeletons	Zombies	Ghouls	Wights	Wraiths
1	7	9	11	No effect	No effect
2	T	7	9	11	No effect
3	T	T	7	9	11

T means that the cleric automatically Turns the undead; a **number** is the roll needed (on 2d6) to Turn. A complete explanation of Turning **undead** is given in the class description of clerics.

VARIABLE WEAPON DAMAGE

Damage	Weapon Type
1-4 (1d4)	Torch
1-4 (1d4)	Dagger
1-4 (1d4)	Sling stone
1-4 (1d4)	Club
1-6 (1d6)	Arrow
1-6 (1d6)	Hand Axe
1-6 (1d6)	Mace
1-6 (1d6)	Quarrel* (Crossbow Bolt)
1-6 (1d6)	Short Sword
1-6 (1d6)	Spear
1-6 (1d6)	War Hammer
1-8 (1d8)	Battle Axe*
1-8 (1d8)	Sword
1-10 (1d10)	Pole Arm*
1-10 (1d10)	Two-handed Sword*

* Two-handed weapon

MAGIC-USER AND ELF SPELLS

First Level Spells

1. Charm Person
2. Detect Magic
3. Floating Disc
4. Hold Portal
5. Light
6. Magic Missile
7. Protection from Evil
8. Read Languages
9. Read Magic
10. Shield
11. Sleep
12. Ventriloquism

Second Level Spells

1. Continual Light
2. Detect Evil
3. Detect Invisible
4. ESP
5. Invisibility
6. Knock
7. Levitate
8. Locate Object
9. Mirror Image
10. Phantasmal Force
11. Web
12. Wizard Lock

Third Level Spells

1. Dispel Magic
2. Fire Ball
3. Fly

ARMOR CLASSES

Type of Armor	Armor Class
Clothing only	9
Shield only	8
Leather Armor	7
Leather Armor & Shield	6
Chain Mail Armor	5
Chain Mail Armor & Shield	4
Plate Mail Armor	3
Plate Mail Armor & Shield	2

Armor Class is a measure of how well a character is protected from physical attacks. As the Armor Class number gets lower, the character becomes harder to hit. Armor Class is affected by such things as magic, magic items, and Dexterity, as well as by the type of armor worn.

Armor Class may be lowered (improved) by Dexterity and magical bonuses. A fighter with a Dexterity score of 16, **plate mail +1**, and a **shield +1** would have a total Armor Class of -2. Magical protection pluses are *always* subtracted from the number of the Armor Class.

WANDERING MONSTERS: LEVEL 1

Die Roll	Wandering Monster	No.
1	Acolyte (A)	1-8
2	Bandit (N-C)	1-8
3	Beetle, Fire (N)	1-8
4	Dwarf (L)	1-6
5	Gnome (L)	1-8
6	Goblin (C)	2-8
7	*Green Slime (N)	1
8	Halfling (L)	3-18
9	Killer Bee (N)	1-10
10	Kobold (C)	4-16
11	Lizard, Gecko (N)	1-3
12	Orc (C)	2-8
13	Shrew, Giant (N)	1-10
14	Skeleton (C)	3-12
15	Snake, Cobra (N)	1-6
16	Spider, Crab (N)	1-4
17	Sprite (N)	3-18
18	Stirge (N)	1-10
19	Trader (A)	1-8
20	Wolf (N)	2-12

WANDERING MONSTERS: LEVEL 2

Die Roll	Wandering Monster	No.
1	Beetle, Oil (N)	1-8
2	Berserker (N)	1-6
3	Cat, Mt. Lion (N)	1-4
4	Elf (L/N)	1-4
5	Ghoul (C)	1-6
6	Gnoll (C)	1-6
7	*Gray Ooze (N)	1
8	Hobgoblin (C)	1-6
9	Lizard, Draco (N)	1-4
10	Lizard Man (N)	1-3
11	Neanderthal (N)	1-10
12	Noble (A)	2-12
13	Pixie (N)	2-8
14	Robber Fly (N)	1-6
15	Rock Baboon (N)	2-12
16	Snake, Pit Viper (N)	1-8
17	Spider, Black Widow (N)	1-3
18	Troglodyte (C)	1-8
19	Veteran (A)	2-8
20	Zombie (C)	2-8

WANDERING MONSTERS: LEVEL 3

Die Roll	Wandering Monster	No.
1	Beetle, Tiger (N)	1-6
2	Bugbear (C)	2-8
3	Carrion Crawler (N)	1-3
4	Doppleganger (C)	1-6
5	Driver Ant (N)	2-8
6	*Gargoyle (C)	1-6
7	Gelatinous Cube (N)	1
8	Harpy (C)	1-6
9	Living Statue, Crystal (N)	1-6
10	*Lycanthrope, Wererat (C)	1-8
11	Medium (A)	1-4
12	Medusa (C)	1-3
13	NPC Party (A)	5-8
14	*Ochre Jelly (N)	1
15	Ogre (C)	1-6
16	Shadow (C)	1-8
17	Spider, Tarantella (N)	1-3
18	Thoul (C)	1-6
19	White Ape (N)	1-6
20	*Wight (C)	1-6

is bitten there is a 1-in-20 chance of getting a disease, unless a save vs. Poison is made. If the saving throw failed, there is a 25% chance the character will die in 1-6 (1d6) days. Otherwise the character will be too sick to adventure for one game month. These monsters are the pets of the kobolds, living off the garbage and waste of their hosts. They will rush to the sound of the trap door closing or of battle. They have nothing of value in their lair or on their bodies, but their leader (rat #18) who will be at the back of the pack, a huge fellow (AC 5 due to speed and cunning, HD 1-1, hp 4, #AT 2, D 2-4/2-4, MV (40'), Save F 1, ML 8) wears a thin silver chain set with 5 small gems (jewelry value 400 gold pieces, chain value 50 gold pieces, each gem worth 50 gold pieces). The weight of a few rats will not trigger the pit trap.

3. **FOOD STORAGE ROOM:** The door is locked. This place contains various sorts of dried and salted meat, grain, and vegetables in sacks, boxes, barrels, and piles. There are also bits and pieces of past human victims. There is nothing of value here; even the wine in a large cask is thin and vinegary.

4. **GUARD ROOM:** Here are 3 very large kobold guards with chain mail and bows to fire down the passage at attackers (AC 5, HD 1+1, hp 5 each, #AT 1, D 1-6, MV (40'), Save NM, ML 6). The guards will hide behind the corner for cover, so all missiles fired at them will be at -2 "to hit". Each carries a hand axe in his belt and a purse with 2d6 gold pieces.

5. **KOBOLD CHIEFTAIN'S ROOM:** This huge kobold (AC 5, HD 2, hp 8, #AT 1, D 2-8 (2d4), MV (40'), Save F 1, ML 8) is so powerful that he fights with a battle axe. He has the key to the storage room (**#3.**) and a large gem on a great golden chain about his neck (value 1,200 gold pieces). Five female kobolds (AC 7, HD ½, hp 2 each, #AT 1, D 1-3, Save NM, ML 8 due to the chief) are also in the room. There are heaps of cloth and bits of battered furniture in the place. Hidden in an old blanket hanging on the wall are 50 gold pieces (sewn into the hem). Each female has d6 gold pieces. A locked chest holds 203 copper, 61 silver, and 22 electrum pieces.

6. **COMMON CHAMBER:** The rest of the kobold tribe lives here. There are 17 males (AC 7, HD ½, hp 3 each, #AT 1, D 1-4, MV (40'), Save NM, ML 6), 23 females (AC 7, HD ½, hp 2 each, #AT 1, D 1-3, Save NM, ML 6), and 8 young (which do not attack). If their caves are invaded, those able will help in its defense. Males have d6 silver pieces each, females d4 silver pieces each; the young have nothing. Amidst the litter of cloth and bits and scraps of odds-and-ends there is a piece of silk worth 150 gold pieces. (If the party does not search it will not be located.)

(DM Note: Kobold losses will not be replaced, though injured kobolds will heal. If the attackers hurl oil at the kobolds, they will retreat if possible, rather than suffer damage. Should they have the opportunity to find any flasks of oil, the kobolds will use them against attacking characters!)

B. ORC LAIR: Upon entering, the party will see that the wall 30' to the north is decorated with heads and skulls (human, elven, dwarven) in various stages of decay. These cheerful greetings are placed in niches which checker about 100 square feet of the surface of the wall. Close inspection will show that one is orcish (see **g.** below). Sounds of activity can be heard from the west, but all is quiet to the east.

Area g: This narrowing area is a guard post, the watcher (Orc: AC 7, HD 1, hp 5, #AT 1, D 1-6, MV (40'), Save F 1, ML 8) having a small, window-like opening from which he can observe the entrance to the lair. A piece of gray canvas behind gives the impression that the guard's head is another of the ghastly trophies which decorate the wall. If adventurers enter, he will quickly duck down, slipping a goblin head into the place his own was, and alert the orcs at **7.**

7. **GUARD ROOM:** 4 orcs: (AC 7, HD 1, hp 5 each, #AT 1, D 1-6, MV (40'), Save F 1, ML 8). These guards are armed with spears. Each carries one for hurling and one to melee with. They have d8 electrum pieces each. When alerted, they will rush to engage intruders, raising the alarm when they see them. There is nothing of value in their chamber, there being only pallets and shabby clothing hanging on pegs.

8. The watcher (**g.**) will alert the 4 guards here (exactly as in **7.**, above) who will rush west and then south to flank or surround intruders threatening area **7.** or **9.** or approaching their own quarters.

9. **BANQUET AREA:** There is a great fireplace on the south wall and many tables and benches in this 30' x 50' chamber — the table at the north end having a large chair at its head where the orc leader usually holds court. The place is empty of orcs although there is a small fire of charcoal burning in the fireplace.

10. **COMMON ROOM:** Here are quartered 12 male orcs (AC 7, HD 1, hp 4 each, #AT 1, D 1-6, Save F 1, ML 8) and 18 females and 9 young (who do not fight). The males have 2d6 silver pieces each, the others have nothing of worth. The few furnishings in the room are likewise of no value.

11. **STORAGE CHAMBER:** The door is locked. Amidst the stacks and heaps of supplies here (see **3.**, above), there are 3 shields, 17 spears, and 2 battle axes in excellent condition. A small crate in the far northeast corner contains a long-forgotten crossbow and 60 bolts. There is nothing else of value in the place.

12. **ORC LEADER'S ROOM:** This large creature is clad in chain mail, has a **shield +1**, and carries a mace. He fights as a 4 hit dice monster, has 15 hit points, and adds +2 to damage he causes when successfully striking an opponent (thus, 3-8 points of damage). This is due to his strength and skill. He carries 31 gold pieces, and wears a ring set with a gem (total value 700 g.p.).

The room is carpeted, has tapestries upon the walls (note one of these covers the entrance to the small cave to the west), and battered but still serviceable furniture and a cot. His two mates sleep on cushions at the foot of his resting place. The two females in the place fight as males (AC 7, HD 1, hp 3 each, #AT 1, D 1-6, Save F 1, ML 8), and each has 2d6 gold pieces on her person. The chests and other furniture have nothing of value.

If hard pressed, the leader will wiggle behind the tapestries on the south wall and attempt to work the catch on the secret door to the south and go to the rival tribe for help, but his very life must be in great peril before he will do so. (Adventurers can only spring this catch by rolling a 1 (on a d6) twice in a row, or having two characters do so simultaneously.)

Area t: This alcove is used by the orc leader to store arms and treasure. There are two complete suits of chain mail here (man-sized and dwarf-sized), 4 swords, and a locked iron chest which holds 205 copper, 286 silver, 81 gold, and 13 platinum pieces. A small niche in the back wall, with a boulder in front covering it, hides a **potion of healing** and a scroll with a 6-die **fire ball** spell on it.

(DM Note: Orc losses cannot be replaced, but after an initial attack by adventurers, the males at location **10.** will move four of their number into area **9.**, arm these orcs with crossbows, and lay an ambush for intruders. If the leader is slain, all surviving orcs from this locale will seek refuge with the tribe at **C.** (see below), taking everything of value (and even of no value) with them, and **B.** will thereafter be deserted.)

C. ORC LAIR: Similar to the orcs at area **B.**, these monsters inhabit cave areas **14.-16.** These orcs, however, do not rely upon a continual watch being kept; instead, they have a series of nearly invisible strings running across the entry passage, about 11' from the entrance. When any of these strings is tripped, a heavy, weighted net suspended from the ceiling will drop upon intruders, and metal pieces tied to it will create an alarm sound. (The trip strings will be spotted only if careful observation is asked for, each observer having a 1 in 6 chance of seeing the devices. The camouflaged net is 10' wide and 18' long, made of thick, tarred ropes, and will entrap the victim for 1-4 rounds. Meanwhile, orcs from area **14.** will be there in 1 round . . . .)

13. FORGOTTEN ROOM: Only the two orc leaders (from this area and from **B.**) know of this place. They secretly meet here on occasion to plan co-operative ventures or discuss tribal problems, for although separate tribes are not exactly friendly, both leaders are aware of the fact that there is strength in numbers. A small table and two chairs are in the middle of the room. There is a wooden chest to one side which holds a bow, a quiver of 20 arrows, 2 swords, and 2 daggers. Two shields are hung on the south wall. There are only odds and ends otherwise, except that in the southeast corner, hidden beneath an old bucket (which is filled with black, stagnant water) are two small pouches, each holding 1 gem of 50 gold piece value, 10 gold pieces, and 20 silver pieces. Nesting under these small pouches are 2 **giant centipedes**: (AC 9, HD ½, hp 2 each, #AT 1, D illness, MV (20'), Save NM, ML 7).

14. COMMON CHAMBER: Here there are quartered 9 male orcs with shields and swords (AC 6, HD 1, hp 3 each, #AT 1, D 1-6, MV (40'), Save F 1, ML 8) and 8 females and 3 young who do not fight. The males have d20 silver pieces each, the females d4 copper pieces, the young have nothing. The place is a mess, and there is nothing of value in it. The males will go the entrance if they hear the net falling, arriving in 1 round.

15. COMMON HALL: General meetings are held here, and food is likewise cooked and eaten here. There are 6 males here, 2 with crossbows, (AC 7, HD 1, hp 3 each, #AT 1 or ½ for crossbows, Save F 1, ML 8) and 4 females (non-combatant), dwelling in the western forepart. Each has treasure on their person equal to **14.**, above. The males here will also go to the entrance if they hear the noise of the net falling, arriving in 3 rounds.

16. LEADER'S ROOM: A guard (**g.**) is always posted just inside the door, and he cannot be surprised. (Orc: AC 5 for chain mail, HD 1 + 1, hp 6, #AT 1, D 1-6. Save F 1, ML 8, carries 2d6 silver and d4 gold pieces.) He immediately shouts an alarm if any intruders attempt to enter. Behind him are stacks of barrels and boxes and sacks — extra supplies for the tribe. (One small wine barrel, 400 coins in weight, contains a good quality wine worth 55 gold pieces.) None of the other items here have value, and the foodstuffs is not up to human standards.

The area to the east houses the leader (AC 2, HD 3, hp 16, #AT 1, D 1-6, Save F 3, ML 10). He is a very large orc who wears plate mail and carries a shield. He uses a sword and attacks as a 3 hit die monster. At his belt is a magic **hand axe +1** which he will hurl at an opponent, and he can do so and still attack normally in the same round of combat. His belt is made of silver, with a gold buckle (total value 160 gold pieces), and his sword has a 100 gold piece gem set in its pommel*. In his purse are 8 gold pieces, 17 electrum pieces, and 5 silver pieces. His mate is equal to a male orc in combat (AC 7, HD 1, hp 5, #AT 1, D 1-6, Save F 1, ML 10), and she has a bracelet of ivory which is worth 100 gold pieces. The area is well furnished, and a small chest of drawers contains a sack with 50 platinum pieces tied shut with a **rope of climbing**. There is also a copper bowl, finely wrought and chased with silver, on a small table near the bed. However, it is filled with garbage and very tarnished, so it looks as if it were worth 10 silver pieces, rather than the actual 50 gold pieces, unless it is closely inspected.

(DM Note: Orc losses cannot be replaced. If this tribe is attacked, they will have the males at area **15.** watching the entrance, ready for a second try by the adventurers. If the leader is slain, the survivors will seek safety in area **B.**, if possible; otherwise, they will flee the place entirely, carrying their goods away.)

D. GOBLIN LAIR: The natural cave quickly turns into the worked stone tunnels typical of this whole complex. The passageways here are very busy, and for every 10' distance covered by the party there is a 1 in 6 chance that they will encounter a group of goblins (see below). Check each time the party travels 30' (a 3 in 6 chance) until wandering goblins are encountered, then check no further. When an encounter occurs, the entire bunch of goblins will attack and cry out an alarm (Bree-Yark!) at the same time. Wandering goblins are in addition to those found in numbered areas.

Wandering Goblins: 6 males (AC 6, HD 1-1, hp 3 each, #AT 1, D 1-6, MV (20'), Save NM, ML 7). Each will have d6 silver pieces. (They are patrolling and carrying messages back and forth. The group will also be carrying several bags (d6) of fairly good foodstuffs — not worth much, but quite suitable for human fare.)

17. GUARD CHAMBER: 6 goblin guards with several spears each (AC 6, HD 1-1, hp 3 each, #AT 1, D 1-6, Save NM, ML 7) are alertly watching both passages here for intruders of any sort, including hobgoblins from the south. They each have d4 × 10 copper and d4 silver pieces. The chamber has a barrel with 60 spears, a small table, 2 benches and a keg of water.

18. GUARD CHAMBER: This is the same as **17.**, above, except the goblins watch mainly to the east. If there is a cry of "BREE-YARK" (similar to "Hey Rube!"), 2 of these guards will rush to the secret door, toss a sack with 250 gold pieces in it to the ogre (**E., 22.**, below) and ask him to help them. The ogre will accept the payment and will enter the goblins' lair and move to attack intruders immediately, if possible. The sack of gold coins is hidden in a water barrel in the corner by the secret door.

19. COMMON ROOM: There are 10 males (AC 6, HD 1-1, hp 3 each, #AT 1, D 1-6, Save NM, ML 7) and 14 females and 6 young (who do not fight) dwelling here. Food is prepared and eaten here, and general meetings are likewise held here. There are heaps of bedding, tables, stools, benches, etc. all around the whole place, making it very cluttered. Each male has d6 silver pieces,

16

each female has 2d6 copper pieces. If the wandering group of goblins has not been encountered when the adventures enter this area, be certain to have those 6 additional males in this chamber.

20. **CHIEFTAIN'S ROOM:** The goblin leader (AC 4 due to chain mail and shield, HD 3, hp 11, #AT 1, D 2-7 due to Strength and skill, Save F 2, ML 9), 3 guards (AC 6, HD 1+1, hp 7, #AT 1, D 1-6, Save NM, ML 9 due to presence of chief), and several females are quartered here. The chief has a purse with 18 gold and 2 platinum pieces in it; each of his guards has 8 electrum pieces and d6 silver pieces. There is a silver cup (value 90 gold pieces) under his bed. He and the guards have bows hung on the wall, and if there is time they will take them down and use them. If hard-pressed, 2 of the female goblins can fight as well as males, and will do so (2 female goblins (AC 7, HD 1-1, hp 2 each, #AT 1, D 1-6, MV (20'), Save NM, ML 9 due to the presence of the chief); the other females do not fight.

This place has quite a bit of good furniture in it — all scaled to goblin-size, of course. A low bench near the bed has a secret drawer under the seat, and inside is stored the treasure of the goblins: a tapestry with silver and gold threads which is worth 900 gold pieces. Nearby is a stand with a pewter bowl which holds 273 silver and 321 copper pieces.

21. **STORAGE CHAMBER:** Note that at position **g.** there are 4 goblin guards on duty (AC 7, HD 1-1, hp 4 each, #AT 1, D 1-6, Save NM, ML 7), armed with ready crossbows and swords. Many bales, boxes, crates, barrels, and sacks are stacked and heaped in the large chamber. They contain cloth, food, beer, and wine — all of no special worth. The hard-working but not-too-bright goblins continually bring supplies of stolen and looted goods to this place. They do not realize that their large cousins, the hobgoblins at area **F.**, below, use a secret door known only to them to steal the best of the foodstuffs and drink. If the adventurers stay in this chamber for more than 1 turn, a party of 4 hobgoblins will come through the secret door:

4 Hobgoblins: (AC 6, HD 1+1, hp 6 each, #AT 1, D 1-8, MV (30').) Each carries d4 gold pieces.

(**DM Note:** Goblin losses cannot be replaced. If they are being soundly defeated by intruders, the goblins will attempt to hide or flee east. Those who do so will go from area **17.** to area **23.**, inform the hobgoblins, and join forces with them, so adjust encounters appropriately.)

E. **OGRE CAVE:** Persons entering this place will notice a strong, sour odor and then notice what appears to be a huge bear sprawled asleep in the southwestern part of the cave. This is nothing more than the skin of a huge bear which the ogre killed and uses as a bed, making it more comfortable by heaping leaves underneath. The ogre sits in the eastern portion of his lair, and noise will certainly bring him ready to do battle. This huge Ogre has AC 4 due to his thick hide and another thick bearskin he wears for protection. Because of his high strength, he hits opponents for 3-12 (1d10+2) points of damage (AC 4, HD 4+1, hp 25, D 3-12, MV (30'), Save F 4, ML 10). The ogre has grown wealthy by serving as a mercenary — generally on the side of the goblins (and their occasional allies, the hobgoblins), although he has been bought off by the orcs and gnolls from time to time. He will rush to aid the goblins when they toss him the sack of coins (see **18.**, above). If anyone offers him a greater fee — one which he can actually see and feel — it is 90% likely that he will simply take it (and the goblins' money too!), and return to his lair.

22. The ogre sits here on top of a great leather bag. In this bag are seven large sacks which contain:

#1: 287 silver pieces; #2: a hard cheese; #3: 182 copper pieces and 91 electrum pieces; #4: 289 gold pieces; #5: a keg of brandy (value 80 gold pieces); #6: 303 copper pieces; #7: 241 gold pieces (actually lead coins with a wash of gold, so value of each is only 1 copper!).

If intruders offer him a bribe of 20 or more gold piece value, the ogre will be 90% likely to allow them to leave unmolested, but if he catches them again, he will attempt to kill them, whatever the offers. Hidden under a heap of old bones in the southern portion of his cave are 6 magic **arrows +1**, a **potion of invisibility**, and a magic scroll with 2 cleric spells — **cure light wounds, hold person**.

F. **HOBGOBLIN LAIR:** Seldom are these fierce creatures troubled by marauders, for the entrance to their lair is guarded by a stout, barred door at the back of the entry cave. Skulls are lined along the walls, and several are affixed to the oaken door to highlight a warning written in common runes: "Come in — we'd like to have you for dinner!" (Which **could** be misinterpreted as a cordial invitation to dine . . . .) Careful inspection of the barred door has a 1 in 6 chance per person examining it of detecting a secret mechanism which allows a person outside to slide the bar back so the portal can be entered. If it is forced open, it will require three 1s (on a d6) to indicate the bar has been broken, and the noise will alert area **26.** If a **knock** spell is used to open the door, the noise of the falling bar will be heard, but guards will not have time to react, so the intruders will have two rounds of time before the guards will come.

23. **COMMON ROOM:** This place quarters 5 males (AC 6, HD 1+1, hp 5 each, #AT 1, D 1-8, MV (30'), Save F 1, ML 8) with d4 × 10 silver pieces each; 8 females (AC 7, HD 1, hp 4 each, #AT 1, D 1-6, MV (30'), Save F 1, ML 7) with 2d6 silver pieces each, and 3 young which do not fight and have no treasure. There are heaps of cloth and skins for beds, some odds and ends of furniture, and a small barrel of beer, buckets, etc. in the place, all worthless. The males are watching the east door which communicates with the goblin lair (**D.**, above) and are battle-ready.

24. **TORTURE CHAMBER/PLAYROOM/FOOD STORAGE:** There are 2 very large, ugly hobgoblins here. Each is equal to a 2+1 hit dice monster, one having 10 hit points, the other 8 hit points, and both wear chain mail (AC 5). One also has a whip, as well as a sword, so that he can strike at opponents up to 15' distant, and if a hit is scored, the whip will jerk the victim off his or her feet and stun (paralyze) him or her for 1-2 melee rounds. However, once closely engaged, the hobgoblin cannot make use of his whip, so he will cast it aside. Each of these monsters has a purse with d6 each copper, silver, and electrum pieces. The larger also has a silver armlet worth 135 gold pieces. They guard 6 prisoners who are chained to the walls. There are two chairs, a small table, a central fire pit, and various implements of torture in the chamber. The keys to the prisoners' chains are hanging on the wall in the southwest corner. The prisoners are:

#1: A plump, half-dead merchant, scheduled to be eaten tonight in a special banquet. If he is rescued and returned to the KEEP, the Guild will pay a 100 gold piece reward, grant the rescuers honorary Guild status, and exempt them for one year from any fees, dues, taxes, and the like which the Guild would normally collect.

17

#2: An orc (AC 7, HD 1. hp 4, ML 8) who will fight goblins and hobgoblins gladly, if handed a weapon (of course, he will seek to escape from the adventurers at first chance, taking whatever he can with him, and informing his fellows at **B.** (above), of what happened).

#3: A man-at-arms (AC 9 due to no armor, F 1, hp 5, ML 7) who formerly served as a guard for the merchant. He will take service with rescuers for 1 year if an offer is made, for room and board only, if given armor and weapons.

#4: A normal female, the merchant's wife, in fact, who is also slated for the big feast. She will personally reward her rescuers by giving them a **dagger +1** she has in her room back at the KEEP.

#5: A crazy gnoll (AC 9 due to no armor, HD 2, hp 9, #AT 1, D 1-6, Save F 2, ML 8) who will snatch up a weapon and attack his rescuers if he is freed. (He will cause only 1-6 points of damage due to his weakened condition.)

#6: Another man-at-arms as #3, above, who will behave the same way his companion will.

25. COMMON CHAMBER: This large place is used for meals, meetings, and general revels of the hobgoblin tribe. There are many tables and benches set out now, as the place is being readied for the coming feast. 4 males (AC 6, HD 1 + 1, hp 5 each, #AT 1, D 1-8, MV (30'), Save F 1, ML 8), 5 females (AC 7, HD 1, hp 4 each, #AT 1, D 1-6, Save F 1, ML 7), and 9 young (who will not fight) are working here. Males have d4 gold pieces each, females 2d6 silver pieces. The head table has a set of pewter dishes on it, and their value is 25 g.p. for the set.

26. GUARD ROOM: 6 hobgoblins (AC 7 when using crossbows or 6, HD 1 + 1, hp 6 each, #AT 1 or ½ for crossbows, D 1-6, Save F 1, ML 8), 3 with crossbows which they'll fire once before dropping and taking their maces for close combat. Each carries d4 each gold, silver, and copper pieces. If they hear the door being battered, or the bar falling, all but one will immediately rush to the entry, while the other will alert area **27.**, and then join his fellows. It takes two rounds for them to reach the entry, and the sixth will join the other guards on round four.

27. ARMORY: 3 hobgoblin guards (AC 5 due to chain mail, HD 1 + 1, hp 6 each, #AT 1, D 1-8, Save F 1, ML 8) are on duty here at all times. If warning comes, two will move to the door to wait in ambush, and the other will pass through the secret entrance (to area **31.**) to alert the chief. Each guard has 2d4 each of silver and electrum pieces. In the chamber are the following:

1 suit of man-sized plate mail
1 suit of dwarf-sized plate mail
3 suits of man-sized chain mail
2 suits of elf-sized chain mail
7 suits of man-sized leather armor
11 shields
6 daggers
1 battle axe
4 maces
3 swords
2 bows (short)
1 longbow
13 crossbows
11 score* arrows (14 arrows have silver heads)
9 score* bolts
51 spears
19 pole arms
42 helmets of various sizes

Armor-type items are standing or hung from racks. Weapons are in chests or on pegs or in racks.

28. STOREROOM: Goods stolen from the stupid goblins are kept here until needed above. There will be a single guard (AC 6, HD 1 + 1, hp 5, #AT 1, D 1-8, Save F 1, ML 8) on duty here at all times. He has 2d8 electrum pieces. (If the looting party does not encounter adventurers in area **21.**, they will also be here: 4 hobgoblins (AC 6, HD 1 + 1, hp 6 each, #AT 1, D 1-8, Save F 1, ML 8). Each of the four carries d4 gold pieces.

29. GUARD ROOM: 2 hobgoblin guards with crossbows and swords stand here. (AC 7, HD 1 + 1, hp 5 each, #AT 1 or ½ for crossbows, D 1-6, Save F 1, ML 8.) With them are 2 females who will fight (AC 7, HD 1, hp 4 each, #AT 1, D 1-6, Save F 1, ML 7). Males have 2d6 each silver and copper pieces, females have no treasure. There are two cots, a bench, a stool, and a large box (filled with soiled clothing) in the room. If attackers are seen, one female will alert area **30.**, the other area **31.**; then both will fight.

30. HOBGOBLIN CHIEF'S QUARTERS: This great, ugly creature (AC 2 due to his plate mail and shield, HD 5, hp 22, #AT 1, D 3-10 due to Strength and skill, MV (30'), Save F 5, ML 10) has 5 platinum and 31 gold pieces in his purse. He wears a silver and gem studded belt (value 600 gold pieces). With him are 4 large female hobgoblins, each equal to a male (AC 6, HD 1 + 1, hp 6 each, #AT 1, D 1-8, Save F 1, ML 10 due to the chief), and each has 2d6 gold pieces. The room is crowded with furniture and junk — all of no real worth, except that there is a false bottom in a huge iron box filled with mangy animal skins. The secret portion of the iron box holds 25 platinum, 200 gold, 115 electrum, and 400 silver pieces plus a 100 gold piece gem and a potion of **poison**. Amidst a heap of kindling wood near the fireplace (southeast corner) there is concealed a **wand of paralyzation**, but it has only 7 charges left in it.

31. GUARD ROOM: 4 hobgoblins (AC 5 due to chain mail, HD 1 + 1, hp 5 each, #AT 1, D 1-8, Save F 1, ML 8), each with 2d6 electrum, silver, and copper pieces. They are alert for danger, and when notified, they will pass the word to areas **29.**, **30.**, and/or **27.**, as required. The room is rather bare, having only 2 pallets, a stool, and a large water barrel.

(DM Note: As usual, hobgoblin losses cannot be replaced during the course of normal play, which is a period of only several days or weeks of action. The hobgoblins are fairly smart, well-organized, and alert. If their chief is killed, they will typically seek to escape alive, unless their opponents are obviously weak and inferior. Survivors will reinforce the goblins at **D.**, above, unless their attackers are very dangerous and the hobgoblins can see that the whole **Caves'** area is in trouble . . . .)

G. SHUNNED CAVERN: Even the normal inhabitants of this area, including the ogre, stay away from here, for the creatures who dwell herein are exceptionally dangerous. Any creature foolish enough to venture out at night becomes fair game. A horrible stench is noticed as soon as creatures enter the cavern area.

32. EMPTY GALLERY: The odor of these places is awful. Bones and rotting corpses are spread here and there amidst a litter of dead leaves and old branches. If a careful search is made, adventurers will find a coin every round: 1-2 = 1 copper piece, 3-4 = 1 silver piece, 5-6 = 1 electrum piece. The sound of such searching might bring visitors! Roll on the table below for an encounter:

18

1 — Owl bear from **34.**, below

2 — 2-12 giant rats (AC 7, HD ½, hp 2 each, #AT 1, D 1-3 plus disease, MV (40'), Save F 1, ML 8)

3 — Gray ooze from **33.**, below

4-6 — Nothing is attracted to the noise

33. **SHALLOW POOL:** This portion of the cavern is very wet, and all of the walls and the floor have a sheen from the dampness. There is a large pool of shallow water (as shown), and a few white, blind fish are swimming therein. There is a jewel-encrusted goblet worth 1,300 gold pieces in the water. There are 3 gray ooze monsters in this place (only 2 if 1 has already been encountered in a **32.** area). Each causes 1-8 hit points of damage on the first round, unless attacking from above, because half of their damage will be taken up in destroying the foot and leg protection of the victim. Thereafter, attacks cause 2-16 points of damage, as do attacks from above. (AC 8, HD 3*, hp 15 each, #AT 1, D 1-8 first round, then 2-16 destroys armor, MV (3'), Save F 2, ML 12.) The pair always in the place are the one at the south edge of the pool and the one on the ceiling in the southwestern portion of the area. There is only a 1 in 20 chance of noticing either unless a pole device is used to prod the area before the pool or unless two or more torches are held aloft so as to fully light the ceiling area. The third gray ooze will be on the ceiling to the left of the entrance, if present.

34. **OWL BEAR'S DEN:** The owl bear (AC 5, HD 5, hp 30, #AT 3, D 1-8/1-8/1-8, MV (40'), Save F 3, ML 9) sleeps in the most southerly part of its den, digesting a meal of gnoll it just caught at dawn. If aroused, the beast will roar and rush out, striking with its two great paws and toothy beak for 1-8 points of damage per hit, with three such attacks per round, i.e. a claw, another clawing attack, and then a snap of its beak. It has no treasure, but amidst the many sticks and bones it sleeps on is a bone tube (1 in 6 chance of noticing it for each person searching the heap, with a check for each once per round) with a **protection from undead** scroll within it.

H. **BUGBEAR LAIR:** The group of bugbears is not numerous, but what it lacks in numbers, it makes up for in strength and cunning. There are signs beside the entrance cave in kobold, orcish, goblin, etc. Each says: "Safety, security and repose for all humanoids who enter — WELCOME! (Come in and report to the first guard on the left for a hot meal and bed assignment.)"

35. **GUARD ROOM:** 3 bugbears (AC 5, HD 3+1, hp 11 each, #AT 1, D 2-8, MV (30'), Save F 3, ML 9) with 2d10 gold pieces each. These creatures lounge on stools near a smoking brazier which has skewers of meat toasting over the coals. Each will ignore his great mace when intruders enter, reaching instead for the food. Though they do not speak common, they will grab and eat a chunk, then offer the skewers to the adventurers — and suddenly use them as swords to strike first blow (at +2 bonus to hit due to surprise!) unless the victims are very alert. There are two cots in the place and a large gong. If the battle goes badly, one will smite the gong to warn the others in the complex.

36. **CHIEFTAIN'S ROOM:** This tough old bugbear is equal to an ogre (AC 5, HD 4+1, hp 18, #AT 1, D 3-12 (d10+2), Save F 4, ML 9). He has a pouch with a key, 29 platinum pieces, and 3 50 g.p. gems in it. With him is a female bugbear equal to the male (AC 5, HD 3+1, hp 12, #AT 1, D 2-8, Save F 3, ML 9). She has gold earrings worth 100 g.p. The furnishings of the room are battered and crude, but several pieces of silk are mixed up with the bedding, in all 6 may be found; the party will be able to

sell them for 20 g.p. each. There is a gray chest stuck up on a ledge near the ceiling which will only be spotted if the room is carefully searched. It contains 1,462 silver pieces, a 30 pound statue of alabaster and ivory (worth 200 gold pieces), and 2 potions of **healing** (which will break if the chest is roughly handled). It will take three or four strong characters to bring this down safely. There is a **hand axe +1** on the wall, and if the chieftain has the chance, he will take it down and hurl it first, then close for full melee. He knows of the secret door — it is his escape route in desperate situations.

37. **SPOILS ROOM:** The heavy door is locked, and the key is in the pouch of the chieftain (**36.**, above). Inside are a **shield +1**, being used as a tray to hold a heap of dried herbs (catnip, something these particular bugbears relish), various boxes and crates of high quality dried or salted foodstuffs, leather hides in a stack, 3 barrels of ale, a tun of wine, and a small keg of oil (20 flask capacity). (If all but the shield and oil are sold at the KEEP, the value will be 400 gold pieces.) Breaking the lock or smashing the door will bring the guards from **35.** and the chieftain and his mate from **36.**.

38. **COMMON ROOM:** 3 males (AC 5, HD 3+1, hp 12 each, #AT 1, D 2-8, MV (30'), Save F 3, ML 9) with 2d6 each of gold and silver pieces, 7 females (AC 6, HD 2, hp 8 each, #AT 1, D 1-8, Save F 2, ML 8), and 3 young bugbears (AC 7, HD 1, hp 3 each, #AT 1, D 1-4, Save F 1, ML 7) live here. There are piles of bedding and old garments here and there. Blackened by soot, there is a silver urn worth 175 g.p. near the fireplace, but only close examination will reveal its true value.

39. **GUARD ROOM:** Watching here are 2 males (AC 5, HD 3+1, hp 10 each, #AT 1, D 2-8, Save F 3, ML 9) with 2d8 gold pieces each, and 3 females (AC 6, HD 2, hp 7 each, #AT 1, D 1-8, Save F 2, ML 8), each with d10 gold pieces. Each has a spear in addition to normal weapons, so that they can hurl this missile and then close to fight hand-to-hand. These bugbears tend to the slaves as well as help to guard the entrance to their lair. There are bedrolls, a bench, a long table, a water pail, and sacks of meal scattered here and there in the chamber. Keys to the doors to **40.** and **41.** are on the wall opposite the stairs. Both corridors to the slave pens have meal sacks and small boxes and barrels of provisions and watered wine along their length.

40. **SLAVE PEN:** The iron door is secured by a bar, chain, and heavy padlock. Inside is a litter of straw, a bucket, and the following slaves: 3 kobolds (AC 9, HD ½, hp 2 each, MV (40'), Save NM, ML 6), 1 goblin (AC 9, HD 1-1, hp 3 each, MV (20'), Save NM, ML 7), 4 orcs (AC 9, HD 1, hp 5 each, MV (40'), Save F 1, ML 8), and 2 humans (AC 9, F 1, hp 4 each, MV (40'), ML 7) — optionally add 1 dwarf (AC 9, D 2, hp 12, MV (40'), ML 8) and 2 elves (AC 9, E 1, hp 7 each, MV (40'), ML 8) in place of 2 of the kobolds and 1 of the orcs. They are chained to the wall with a common chain and a heavy padlock. All will fight against the bugbears if given weapons. (Treat as AC 9 unless protection is provided.) The humans will serve as those noted in **F., 24.**, above. The dwarf and elves, if used by the DM, may agree to help the adventurers as long as they stay in the **Caves'** area continuously and fight. The other creatures will desert at first opportunity.

41. **SLAVE PEN:** Another barred, chained, and padlocked iron door keeps safe the following slaves: 3 hobgoblins (AC 8, HD 1+1, hp 6 each, MV (30'), Save F 1, ML 8), 2 gnolls (AC 8, HD 2+1, hp 9 each, MV (30'), Save F 2, ML 8), 1 (rebel) bugbear (AC 7, HD 3+1, hp 14, MV (30'), Save F 3, ML 9) and 1 huge human — a seeming wildman, with mighty muscles, shaggy hair and beard, and staring eyes. He is a **Hero** (a 4th level fighter). His 18

19

Strength and +1 for his level give him a total of +4 "to hit" bonus and +3 to damage (AC 9 due to no armor, F 4, hp 24, #AT 1, D 4-9, ML 10). (He is prone to fits of berserk fury due to his enslavement, and if armed and in combat it is 50% likely per round that he will strike a friend instead of a foe in his lust to slay!) If freed, these slaves will attempt to flee, although they will attack bugbears who are in the way of their escape. There are two exceptions: the big bugbear hates his fellows, and will take arms and fight against them or any of the other inhabitants of the whole area; he will continue to do so for as long as the party stays there. The hero is an evil person; once he is armed, and after battle madness leaves him, he will either kill the adventurers who freed him, so as to have all their treasure for himself, or else he will steal whatever is most valuable and then sneak off — but only if he knows the party is too strong for him.

(DM Note: There are 2 bugbears out hunting, and they will return with a human corpse and 83 gold pieces the day after adventurers first enter the bugbear lair. They will be placed on guard duty at **35.**, if appropriate, and their statistics are the same as the guards there. Bugbears will stay in the place until all are dead, save the chieftain, who will seek help from the minotaur at **I., 45.**)

I. **CAVES OF THE MINOTAUR:** This labyrinth* houses a number of nasty things, but the worst is a fiendishly clever minotaur who abides herein. Immediately upon entering the place, adventurers will feel slightly dizzy — the effects of a powerful spell which will cause them to lose all sense of direction.

The minotaur will agree to help the bugbears against invaders at the cost of one human slave every three days of service — of course, the slave is eaten in that period. The minotaur keeps only the choicest of treasures, tossing unwanted loot to whomever happens to find it at the mouth of the labyrinth.

(DM Notes: You may allow players to find a few low-value coins, normal equipment, weapons, or armor at the entrance. After 30' past the cave mouth, a spell of **direction confusion** (a special spell) will begin to function, so start to misdirect them by naming incorrect directions, i.e. **south**east instead of **north**east, east instead of west, etc. Don't worry about calling the same passage as a different direction should they travel over the same route twice — that's the effect of the magic on **them**. You may wish to allow the mapping character a secret saving throw every couple of turns, a 19 or 20 indicating that the effect has been thrown off.)

42. **STIRGE CAVE:** There are 13 of these flying monsters here: (AC 7, HD 1, hp 3 each, #AT 1 at +2 to hit, D 1-3 first round plus 1-4 per additional round, MV (60'), Save F 1, ML 9). If opponent is hit, stirge will automatically suck blood each round thereafter, doing 1-4 hit points of damage due to blood drain until victim is dead or stirge is killed. The minotaur loves to catch and eat these creatures, so they avoid him, and they are quite hungry. In fact, this hunger makes it 90% likely that they will be squeaking and hooting to one another, so the party won't be surprised. They have no treasure.

43. **FIRE BEETLES:** Three dwell in this area: (AC 4, HD 1 + 2, hp 7 each, #AT 1, D 2-8 (2d4), MV (40'), Save F 1, ML 7). They too are hungry and will hasten to attack any persons entering their area. They have no treasure, but 2 glands above their eyes and one in their abdomen will glow with a red light, 10' radius, for 1-6 days after the beetle is killed.

44. **FIRE BEETLES:** There are 2 of these creatures here, in all respects like those in **43.**, above.

45. **THE MINOTAUR:** This huge monster has AC 4 due to a great chain mail coat he wears, and carries a **spear +1**. When he first attacks, the minotaur (AC 4, HD 6, hp 35, #AT 1 or 2, D 4-9 or 1-6/1-6, MV (40'), Save F 6, ML 12) will rush forward and stab with his spear for 4-9 (d6 + 3) points of damage, due to his strength. The next round he will gore and bite doing 1-6 points of damage with each successful attack. The minotaur may only use his spear **or** his horns and bite.

When intruders enter the area, the minotaur immediately moves to attack. He knows this area so well that the only way for victims to escape is to go through the secret door into area **36.**, or else to run out of the place and climb a large tree.

The cave the minotaur dwells in has skulls and bones arrayed in decorative patterns. The secret door is actually a slab of stone which takes not less than 3 humans to move. (It will be noticed by careful checking of the walls, but how it is moved requires a roll of a 1 on a six-sided die to indicate the searcher has found where it can be grasped. All of the minotaur's treasure is behind this slab of rock. It hides:

1 locked chest (with poison needle in lock) — contents 930 gold and 310 electrum pieces

1 **staff of healing**

1 suit of man-sized (optionally elf-sized) **plate mail +1**

1 locked coffer — contents 3 potion bottles (**gaseous form, healing, growth**)

1 locked chest — contents 3 pieces of jewelry worth 1,600, 900, and 600 g.p. respectively

J. GNOLL LAIR: The entry into this place is a small cave, and only at the end will worked stone be visible. If the adventurers have a light or make much noise, the guards (**46.**) will certainly be alerted and ready.

46. GUARD ROOM: There are always 4 gnolls (AC 5, HD 2, hp 9 each, #AT 1, D 2-8, MV (30'), Save F 2, ML 8) on duty here. Two have bows, and will shoot at intruders until melee takes place; they will then run for help while the other two fight. Each gnoll has d8 each of electrum, silver, and copper pieces.

47. GUARD ROOM: 3 males (AC 5, HD 2, hp 8 each, #AT 1, D 2-8, Save F 2, ML 8) and 5 females (AC 6, HD 1 + 1, hp 5 each, #AT 1, D 1-8, Save F 1, ML 8) are quartered here. They will be ready to fight immediately. The males have d6 gold pieces each, the females have d4. There is a scattering of rude furniture in the place, heaps of bedding on the floor, several hides and pelts on the walls (one is a valuable sable cloak worth 450 g.p.), and a barrel of water in the southwest corner of the room.

48. LOCKED ROOM: This chamber is a store room and armory. Besides the usual provisions, there are 7 shields, a suit of dwarf-sized chain mail, 12 hand axes, 3 longbows, 5 quivers of arrows (20 in each), and a **sword -1, cursed.** One barrel of exceptionally fine ale is leaking, and the odor will tempt adventurers to taste it. It is so good, in fact, that there is a 5 in 6 chance per taste that he or she will draw a healthy draught and then spend the next 1-4 turns drinking. (If this occurs, be sure that you have the appropriate characters sing, make noise, and act foolishly. Any of their attacks will be at -2 to hit; this will continue for as many turns as they spent drinking, i.e. 1-4).

49. COMMON ROOM: This place quarters the gnoll tribe — 6 males (AC 5, HD 2, hp 8 each, #AT 1, D 2-8, Save F 2, ML 8), 11 females (AC 6, HD 1 + 1, hp 5 each, #AT 1, D 1-8, Save F 1, ML 8), and 18 young who do not fight. Males have d6 each of electrum and silver pieces, females d10 silver pieces each. There is the usual clutter of worthless furniture in the room.

50. GNOLL CHIEFTAIN'S QUARTERS: The gnoll leader (AC 3 due to pieces of plate mail worn, HD 3, hp 17, #AT 1, D 4-10 (2d4 + 2) due to his strength, Save F 3, ML 10), his two sons (AC 4, HD 2 + 1, hp 10 each, #AT 1, D 3-9 (2d4 + 1), Save F 2, ML 10) and four female gnolls (AC 6, HD 1 + 1, hp 5 each, #AT 1, D 1-8, Save F 1, ML 9) are waiting in this room. The chieftain has a pair of silver armbands worth 50 gold pieces each, and there are 39 gold pieces in his belt pouch. His sons have d10 each of gold, electrum and silver pieces. Each female wears a silver neck chain worth 30 gold pieces and has 2d6 electrum pieces in addition. The furnishings of the place are crude and battered. A large metal pot beneath a flagstone in the fireplace alcove hides 200 copper, 157 silver, 76 electrum, and 139 gold pieces.

The secret door and passage to area **K., 63.,** is unknown to all. Just inside the entrance is the skeleton of a human thief, his leg is broken and he must have died here trying to escape through the secret door. The rotten leather armor and corroded weapons are valueless, but the purse at his belt holds 12 gems of 50 g.p. base value each, and the **elven boots** upon his bony feet are still in usable shape.

(DM Note: Losses by the gnolls cannot be replaced. They are in a loose alliance with the orcs, so if there are surviving gnolls, they will move to the orc areas and vice versa. If you wish, allow the chieftain to be able to escape enemies by climbing up the chimney of the fireplace in his area.)

K. SHRINE OF EVIL CHAOS: A faint, foul draft issues from the 20' wide cave mouth which is the entrance to this place. The worn path through the copse of obscenely twisted and oddly bloated trees gives those approaching along its length an eerie sense of unease, and as soon as they enter the cave mouth a dim awareness of lurking evil will pervade their senses. Red strata intertwines with bulging black veins running through the hewn rock walls beyond the entrance. The wide corridors and chambers are deathly still. A faint groaning sound, and a shrill piping may be occasionally heard, barely perceptible even if the party is absolutely silent and listening.

The floors are smooth and worn by the tread of countless feet of the worshipers at this grim place. The footsteps of intruders will echo alarmingly in these vaulted halls (+2 chance of being surprised), and extreme care must be taken to muffle such sounds if the party has any hopes of remaining undetected until the moment of their choosing. Continual noise will bring a group of zombie guards to investigate:

> 8 zombies: (AC 8, HD 2, hp 8 each, #AT 1, D 1-8, MV (40'), Save F 1, ML 12). These ghastly monsters are clad in filthy red and black striped uniforms. Each carries a cleaver-like battle axe. (Each wears an **amulet** of protection from turning, so attempts by a cleric to turn them are made as if they were **ghouls** rather than zombies.)

51. BOULDER FILLED PASSAGE: Large rocks and boulders have been placed here in order to seal off this tunnel. It will take 100 man-turns to open a way large enough for a human to pass through into the area beyond. (You have the option of allowing this passage to lead to the outside somewhere to the southwest of the **Caves of Chaos,** or you may choose to have it go all the way to the **Cave of the Unknown.** If you opt for the latter case, you must, of course, prepare an appropriate underground area map and stock it with monsters and treasures.)

52. HALL OF SKELETONS: This unusual audience chamber has a dais and throne-like chair set with 4 large red gems (500 g.p. each) at the south end. It is otherwise empty except for a dozen skeletons, clad in rags of chain mail and bearing battered shields and rusty scimitars (swords), propped against the walls. These bony guards do not move, and any attempt to turn them immediately upon entering the chamber will have no effect, as they are obviously not animated. However, as soon as intruders touch the dais or throne chair, these monsters will spring to life from their positions on either wall of the chamber. Each has an **amulet of protection from turning** upon it, so they are turned by a cleric as if they were **zombies** (AC 7, HD 1, hp 3 each, #AT 1, D 1-6, Save F 1, ML 12). They have no treasure.

Once the skeletons are disposed of, it is an easy matter to pry the 4 garnets (gems) from the back of the chair.

53. GUARD ROOM: There will always be 8 zombies (AC 8, HD 2, hp 8 each, #AT 1, D 1-8, Save F 1, ML 12), turned as if they were ghouls due to a **amulet of protection from turning** hulking silently here, 4 at either end of the hall. Anyone entering will be attacked unless they are robed in temple garb (see area **54.,** below) and have an amulet identical to the ones which the undead guard groups or priests wear. There is no treasure here.

54. ACOLYTES' CHAMBER: There are 4 acolytes (1st level clerics) here (AC 5, C 1, hp 4 each, #AT 1, D 1-6, ML 8), all dressed in rusty-red robes, with black cowls*. Under these robes each wears chain mail and a mace at his belt. Each carries 10 gold pieces in his purse, and the leader wears an amulet of **protection from good**. This amulet circles the wearer with a magic barrier. The amulet serves as some protection from good attacks (attacks by monsters of some alignment other than the wearer's alignment) by adding 1 to the wearer's saving throws, and subtracting 1 from the "to hit" die roll of these opponents. The spell will also keep out attacks from enchanted (magical) monsters (such as gargoyles), but not missile fire attacks from these creatures. Their room contains four hard pallets*, a brazier*, a table, four stools, a cabinet for clothing, a water pail, a waste bucket, and a flagon* of wine and four cups. There is nothing of value amongst these items.

55. CHAPEL OF EVIL CHAOS: This place is of red stone, the floor being a mosaic checkerboard of black and red. The south wall is covered by a huge tapestry which depicts a black landscape, barren trees, and unidentifiable but horrible black shapes in silhouette — possibly demons of some sort — holding aloft a struggling human. A gray sky is torn by wisps of purple clouds, and a bloody moon with a skull-like face on it leers down upon the scene. Four black pillars support the domed ceiling some 25' overhead. Between these columns, just in front of the tapestry, is a stone altar of red veined black rock, rough-hewn and stained brown with dried blood. Upon it are 4 ancient bronze vessels — a shallow bowl, a pair of goblets, and a ewer, a vase-shaped pitcher. They are also bloodstained but obviously worth a great deal of money. (The value is 1,000 g.p. for each cup, and 2,000 g.p. for each of the other items, but these are relics of evil, and any character possessing them will **not** part with them or sell them nor allow others to handle them.) For each character who picks up one of these objects, the DM should have the character roll a saving throw vs. Magic at -2. Any who save successfully will get a "feeling of great evil" about the object, and he or she may voluntarily put it down. If the save fails, the character will rapidly fall under the influence of a demonic spell and within 6 days become a servant of chaos and evil, returning to this chapel to replace the relics, and then staying as a guard forever after. If someone attempts to destroy these relics the great bell (see **58.**, below) will sound and the Shrine's residents will come running in 3 rounds. If a **detect evil** spell is cast upon these items, they will glow an ugly purple, and all good characters will feel instant loathing for them. If the character who has taken them has a **dispel magic** and then a **bless** spell cast upon him or her, there is a 60% chance of removing the evil on the first day, 50% on the 2nd, 40% on the 3rd, 30% on the 4th, 20% on the 5th, and 10% on the 6th. Otherwise, **nothing** will be able to save the character!)

56. ADEPTS' CHAMBER: There are 4 adepts (2nd level clerics) here, each clad in a black robe with a maroon colored cowl* (AC 3, C 2, hp 8 each, #AT 1, D 1-6, ML 8). They have plate mail beneath their garments, and each bears a mace. Their waists are circled with copper chains (worth 40 g.p. each) with skull-shaped clasps fashioned of bone. Each carries a purse with 20 gold and 5 platinum pieces, and each wears an amulet of **protection from good (#54.)**, which makes their effective armor class 2 vs. good creatures. The first and second have **cause light wounds** (does 2-7 points of damage to creature touched; normal "to hit" roll must be made to touch victim) spells, the third a **light** spell, the fourth a **cause fear** (those who fail to save vs. Spells must flee in terror for 1 turn. A normal "to hit" roll must be made to affect creature) spell. They will use their

spells first, if possible, before engaging in combat with weapons. In the room are four beds, four small stands, a table, four chairs, four chests for clothing, and various books and scrolls of evil nature — nothing of value. However, on the table are copper dishes and vessels (total weight 300 coins) of exceptional craftsmanship which are worth 175 gold pieces. (If the party opts to destroy the evil writings, they should receive an additional 600 experience points for the act, unless they are themselves evil, in which case they should receive points for keeping and reading these works.) If hard pressed, these evil clerics will attempt to flee and warn their master by striking the great bell (**58.**).

57. HALL OF UNDEAD WARRIORS: There are four files of the undead here, two of 10 skeletons each, two of 10 zombies each. The former face south, the latter north.

20 skeletons: AC 6 (due to chain mail rags and shields), HD 1, hp 3 each, #AT 1, D 1-6, Save F 1, ML 12, turned as if they were zombies.

20 zombies: AC 5 (due to chain mail), HD 2, hp 8 each, #AT 1, D 1-8, Save F 1, ML 12, turned as ghouls.

Upon striking of the great iron bell at **58.**, below, the skeletons will issue forth from the south door of the place and march into the temple (**58.**) to line the south wall, while the zombies plod out the north exit to line the north wall of the temple. If intruders enter room **57.**, are in the passage to the temple, or are within the temple itself, these undead warriors will attack. Proper garments and amulets will prevent attack unless the head cleric commands the undead to do so. They have no treasure.

58. TEMPLE OF EVIL CHAOS: This huge area has an arched ceiling some 30' or more in height. The floor is of polished black stone which has swirling patterns of red veins through it. The walls behind the draperies, and the ceiling as well, are of dull black rock, while the west wall is of translucent red stone which is seemingly one piece, polished to mirror-like smoothness. A great bell of black iron stands near the entrance point, with a pair of mallets beside its supports. To the south are several long benches or pews. There are three stone altars to the west, the northernmost of pure black, the middle one of streaked red and black, the last of red with black flecks. At the western end of the temple area is a dais of black stone, with four lesser chairs on its lower tier and a great throne above. The chairs are of bone; the ivory throne is set with gold and adorned with gems of red and black (10 black stones each worth 100 gold pieces, 10 red stones each worth 500 gold pieces, and one large red stone worth 1,000 g.p.). The signs and sigils* upon these seats are of pure chaos and evil. The other walls are covered by draperies of deep purple with embroidered symbols and evil sayings, done in scarlet and gold and black thread. As soon as the party enters the place, black candles in eight great candelabras on either side of the place will come alight magically, shooting forth a disgusting red radiance. Shapeless forms of purple, yellow and green will dance and sway on the western wall, and if anyone looks at them for more than a moment, they must save versus Spells or be mesmerized into chanting a hymn to chaotic evil. Should three or more voices be so raised, the iron bell will sound automatically by magic, but even one such chant will alert the guards of the head cleric (see below). Zombie guards will enter here in 3 rounds after entry, even if the party is quiet.

59. THE CHAMBERS OF THE EVIL PRIEST: Location **59.g** is the anteroom where special visitors are entertained by the chief cleric. There are lavish furnishings here, although none are of particular value except for a golden flagon and cups (flagon worth 500 g.p., each of the nine cups has 100 g.p. value). Three zombies are on guard here. (AC 2 due to plate mail and shield, HD 2, hp 13 each, #AT 1, D 1-8, Save F 1, ML 12.) They stand unmoving unless they are summoned by a chant from the temple area, someone enters their area, or they are commanded by the evil priest.

Location **59.** is the private chamber of the evil priest. He is 3rd level, wears **plate mail +1**, has a **shield +1**, and wears an **amulet of protection from good**, which adds a further +1 to his armor class when attacked by "good" creatures. (AC 0 or -1 due to magic armor and amulet, C 3, hp 14, #AT 1, D 2-7 (staff) or 1-6 (mace), ML 10). He attacks with a **snake staff**, which is +1 to hit. On command the staff will turn into a snake and coil around the person hit. The person is held helpless for 1d4 turns, or until the cleric recalls the staff. The staff then crawls back to the cleric on command. He also has a normal mace hanging from his belt. He has a gold ring with a black gem (value 1,400 gold pieces) and a purse with 51 platinum pieces in it. He wears a black cape and cowl, with red robes beneath. His spells are: **cause light wounds** (inflicts 2-7 points of damage) and **cause fear**. The priest must touch someone, strike to hit, for the spells to take affect. He also has a scroll with three cleric spells on it: **detect magic, hold person, silence, 15' radius**. He has a **potion of gaseous form** which he will use to escape through the boulder-filled corridor, **51.**, when all else fails.

His room is furnished lavishly, with a red carpet, furniture of black wood with velvet upholstery of scarlet, and a large bed covered with silken covers of black and red cushions and pillows. A demon idol leers from the wall to the north, directly over the bed. If anyone other than the priest touches it it will topple over upon the person, causing 2-12 points of damage. It has two gem eyes (100 g.p. value each). The evil priest will dart behind a screen in the southeast corner, enter a wardrobe there, slip through a secret door in its back, and then down a short passage and out into the corridor through another secret door, should his life be in danger. When the secret door in the back of the wardrobe is opened by the party, 500 gold pieces and 50 gems of 10 gold piece value each will spill from the wardrobe into the room to hopefully cause pursuers to stop for the loot. The priest will meanwhile either try to rally his forces, or else escape (assuming that most of his fellows have been eliminated already).

60. GUEST CHAMBER: This lower room is for important guests of the place. It contains a large bed, table, chairs, etc. There is nothing of value within, although the tapestries adorning the walls (things picturing evil cruelties and obscene rites) appear expensive. Beneath a velvet cloth on the table is a polished mirror.

61. TORTURE CHAMBER: There are various implements of torture here, both large and small — a rack, iron maiden, tongs, pincers, whips, etc. Comfortable chairs are scattered along the walls, evidently so placed to allow visitors an enjoyable view of the proceedings. The **torturer** lives in the forepart of the place, and he will attack unauthorized persons who enter. He is a third level fighter with chain mail under his black leather garments. His weapon is a huge battle axe. Torturer: AC 5, F 3, hp 19, #AT 1, D 3-8 (1d6 + 2 due to Strength), ML 8. Hidden in his mattress are 135 gold pieces and a bracelet worth 700 gold pieces.

62. THE CRYPT: The door to this room is bolted shut. This long hall is of roughly hewn stone, with a low ceiling. In it are many coffins and large sarcophagi with the remains of servants of the Temple of Chaos. The sixth tomb opened will contain a **wight**: (AC 5, HD 3*, hp 13, #AT 1, D drain one level, MV (30'), Save F 2, ML 12.) There is no treasure buried with any of the remains, but there is a secret compartment in the wight's tomb; this contains a **sword +2**, a scroll of **protection from undead**, a **helm of alignment change**, and a silver dagger worth 800 gold pieces because of the gems set into its pommel*.

63. STORAGE CHAMBER: There are many piles of boxes, crates, barrels, sacks, and so forth here — the supplies of the temple are kept here. There is nothing of value, and if the party stays within the place for longer than 3 rounds, a **gelatinous cube** will move down the corridor into the place and block it. (AC 8, HD 4*, hp 22, #AT 1, D 2-8 plus paralyzation, MV (20'), Save F 2, ML 12.) Inside the creature are d12 each of copper, silver, electrum, gold, and platinum pieces, as well as several bones — evidently parts of a victim not yet wholly digested. (One of the "bones" is actually a **wand of enemy detection** with 9 charges left. If it is not gotten out of the monster within 1 turn, it will be ruined by digestive juices.) The secret door in the room leads to the gnoll chieftain's cave (**50.**, above).

64. CELL: The door is of iron, locked and barred, but a window is set in the door. This is the place where prisoners are kept until tortured to death or sacrificed in the area above. There are several skeletons still chained to the wall, and one scantily clad female — a fair maiden obviously in need of rescuing! As she is partly around a corner, at first only her shapely legs and body up to the shoulders can be seen. Those who enter and approach closer are in for a rude shock! This is actually a **medusa** recently taken by the evil priest's zombie guards. (AC 8, HD 4**, hp 20, #AT 1, D 1-6 plus poison, MV (30'), Save F 4, ML 8.) An opponent hit by the medusa's attack has been bitten by the asp-hair and must save vs. Poison or die. Persons looking at the creature — including those fighting her from the front — must save versus being Turned to Stone by the medusa.

Not being above such things, the cleric had plans for removing its snakes, blinding it, and then eventually sacrificing it at a special rite to a demon. The medusa will spare one or two of the adventurers from her gaze, promising them she has magic which will turn their companions back to flesh again, if they will free her from her chains. She does, in fact, have a special elixir*, a potion of **stone to flesh** in a small vial, enough liquid to turn six persons, who have been turned to stone, back to normal, but she does not intend to give it away. If freed she will attempt to "stone" her rescuers.

CREDITS:

Designed and written by: Gary Gygax

Revised by: Dave Cook, Harold Johnson, Jon Pickens, Michael Price, Evan Robinson, Lawrence Schick, Stephen D. Sullivan

Editing: Mike Carr, David Cook, Harold Johnson, Jeff R. Leason, Frank Mentzer, Tom Moldvay, Lawrence Schick, Edward G. Sollers, Stephen D. Sullivan, Jean Wells

Art: David S. LaForce, Erol Otus, Jim Roslof

23

NON-PLAYER CHARACTERS (NPCs)

Whenever the players encounter a person, it is helpful to have the characteristics of that person at ready. Before play, roll the Strength, Intelligence, etc. for each NPC. Make the adjustments as permitted in the **D&D BASIC SET**, select a personality, and equip the character (if details are not already given).

The tables below will help get you started. You may select from the list of personalities or roll (d20) at random, giving one or two types to each NPC. Use common sense — a character can't be rude and courteous, for example. Feel free to add to this list; it gives just a few examples for you to begin with.

PERSONALITIES

1. Brave	11. Kind
2. Careless	12. Lazy
3. Cautious	13. Modest
4. Cheerful	14. Nosy
5. Courteous	15. Prankish
6. Dishonest	16. Rude
7. Forgiving	17. Suspicious
8. Friendly	18. Talkative
9. Helpful	19. Trusting
10. Honest	20. Wasteful

For your convenience, you may key the characteristics listed below to the persons mentioned in the module. For instance, a note after the Taverner 'c#4' would indicate that when the players meet him, the DM is to use the characteristics of #4 (below) to represent him. Remember to make as many listings as you need! The class designations (Ftr, etc.) do not apply to normal men, of course, and may be ignored when used to represent normal men.

HUMANS

Class	Str	Int	Wis	Dex	Con	Cha	Personality
1. Ftr	14	13	7	11	12	14	Cheerful, honest
2. Ftr	16	10	9	9	11	15	Talkative, careless
3. Ftr	17	8	13	10	15	12	Brave, forgiving
4. Ftr	15	8	11	14	16	6	Honest, wasteful
5. Ftr	18	10	7	11	13	9	Kind, trusting
6. Ftr	14	8	10	13	17	11	Helpful, forgiving
7. Ftr	13	10	6	10	14	17	Kind, dishonest
8. Thf	11	12	8	14	11	7	Prankish, rude
9. Thf	14	6	11	16	12	10	Nosy, suspicious
10. Thf	8	9	11	17	8	16	Modest, careless
11. Cl	11	10	14	8	13	9	Lazy, trusting
12. Cl	13	7	15	11	10	10	Friendly, wasteful
13. Cl	7	11	17	9	16	8	Courteous, helpful
14. M-U	10	17	12	6	9	11	Cautious, modest

DEMI-HUMANS

Class	Str	Int	Wis	Dex	Con	Cha	Personality
15. Elf	16	14	7	9	13	10	Suspicious, dishonest
16. Elf	14	15	10	17	14	5	Cautious, rude
17. Hflg	17	12	8	14	10	9	Courteous, nosy
18. Hflg	15	10	11	11	11	7	Prankish, friendly
19. Dwarf	18	8	9	12	9	13	Brave, talkative
20. Dwarf	16	9	15	8	17	11	Cheerful, lazy

DESIGNING FLOOR PLANS

Once you have become familiar with the KEEP — who its residents are, where the main buildings are located, and so forth — it will be helpful to have details about the layout and contents of certain places. Players can easily 'see' an area they are visiting if you have prepared a floor plan. The Guild House (**#16**) will be used as an example of this procedure.

On the map of the KEEP, the Guild House is shown to be an 'L' shape about 40' long. Draw a large version of it on a piece of graph paper (the kind with ¼" squares usually works best). Leave room for a **key** (noting what symbols are being used) and index the sheet for easy reference.

The outer walls should have the same dimensions as the building's outline. Note the **scale** (what map length represents what real length) at the bottom of the key. In the example given, ¼" equals two feet of 'real' length. Since the walls in a normal building are from six inches to one foot thick, they may be represented by single lines; an outer wall should be indicated by thicker lines.

Now look closely at the description of the building in the text. The lower floor contains the Guild Master's quarters, two clerks' quarters, and an office. Give equal spaces to the clerks, more to the Guild Master, and the most to the office (as it represents the main purpose of the building). The rooms may be in whatever order you like; just remember that the outer door shown on the map probably opens into the office, not into a private bedroom. Most doors are 3 to 5 feet wide. Be sure to include steps down to the cellar and up to the rooms on the second floor. Add some windows to help provide light.

Try and think of what items would be in a sparsely furnished office in the KEEP (probably chairs, tables, desks, a lockbox or chest, and a cabinet or two). Consider how necessities would be provided: heat (fireplaces), water (barrels), and food (a kitchen in the cellar). The fireplaces should be located first — chimneys go straight up, and must be placed in the same area on each floor. Most buildings have one or two chimneys. Remember to heat each room, if possible! Add other furnishings wherever you wish, including any information provided in the text.

The completed office in this example has the Master's desk along the west wall under a window, flanked by records cabinets. The clerks' desks and collection table are just inside a railing, which keep visitors from wandering into the work area. Waiting chairs are placed for the Guild members' convenience. A secret door in the fireplace leads to the Master's bedroom — a quick escape route in case of trouble. The locked chest is for money received in Guild dues, but is usually empty due to a clever 'drop' system. It is triggered by a lever under the Master's desk, which dumps the chest's contents down a short chute into a cellar storage room! (You may add whatever tricks and traps you wish.)

Arrange the bedroom furnishings (table, chairs, bed, armoire, etc.) in a similar manner. On the second floor (divided into private bedrooms and dormitory, according

24

to the text) build the rooms off of the stairs, hallways, and fireplaces. It's easy!

Now **you** design the cellar, remembering a few key facts:

1. The stairs and chimneys **must** connect properly to the first floor.
2. Two servants live in the cellar, but not as richly as the clerks or the Guild Master.
3. A heavily barred, locked room must be under the office to receive the Guild fees from the chute.
4. A kitchen must be located by one of the fireplaces.

You won't have to worry about windows or outside doors — but you might wish to include a secret entrance to a long-forgotten dungeon (which, of course, you must design and stock with monsters and treasure)!

Adding the details to a house, church, or other structure can take a lot of time, but it's **not** as hard as you might think. Before playing the module, lay out as many buildings of the KEEP as you can. The most commonly used buildings will be the TRAVELERS' INN (**14.**), the TAVERN (**15.**), the GUILD HOUSE (**16.**), and the CHAPEL (**17.**). You may add just a few simple furnishings to each if you wish, leaving the many smaller details for later. By designing floor plans, you can experiment with many of your own ideas before starting a major project — like the CAVES OF THE UNKNOWN.

TIPS TO THE PLAYERS

It often helps for beginning players to have advice on how to play **D&D**. Many points are overlooked by novices in their eagerness to get on with the adventure. The following points are given to help these players.

Most importantly, players should be organized and co-operative. Each player should have complete information on his or her character easily on hand and should supply the DM with this information quickly and accurately if asked. As parties will usually involve a variety of alignments and classes, players should work together to use their abilities effectively. Arguing among players will cause delays, attract monsters, and often result in the deaths of some or all of the members.

Cooperation should also be given to the DM. He or she is the judge of the game and his or her decisions are final. If a player disagrees, he or she should calmly state why, and accept whatever the DM decides. Shouting, crying, pouting, or refusing to accept decisions only angers the other players. The game should be fun for all involved. Not everything will go the way players want it.

Planning is another important part of play. Players should be well equipped, comparing each member's list and balancing the items on each. No character should be over-burdened nor under-equipped. This may mean sharing the costs of extra items. Rope, oil, torches, spikes, and other useful items should always be carried. Plans should be considered for encountering monsters and casting spells.

Caution is also necessary and is a part of planning. A party that charges forward without preparation is almost certainly doomed. Danger should be expected at any moment and from any direction, possibly even from one's own party. Lying and trickery are not unknown. Cautious play will help avoid many (but not all) tricks and traps and may save a life. However, too much caution is as dangerous as too little. Many instances will require bold and quick actions on the part of the players, before all is lost.

Above all a player must think. The game is designed to challenge the minds and imaginations of the players.

Those who tackle problems and use their abilities, wits, and new ideas will succeed more often than fail. The challenge of thinking is a great deal of the fun of the game.

GLOSSARY

amulet — A charm inscribed with a magic symbol.

armoire — A large trunk or closet where clothes are kept.

bailey — The outer wall of a castle, or an area within such a wall.

battlement — A parapet with open spaces atop a wall, used for defense or decoration.

brazier — A pan for holding hot coals, usually on a tripod.

Castellan — A governor or warden of a castle or fort.

cistern — A reservoir for storing liquids, especially water.

contour line — A line connecting points having the same elevation on a map.

cowl — The hood on a cloak.

decanter — A vessel used to pour or store liquids; usually used for wines and other liquids containing sediment.

elixir — A sweet liquid, or a cure-all.

fen — Low land which is covered, wholly or partially, by water; a swamp.

flagon — A large vessel or bottle of metal or porcelain, usually with a lid.

hilt — The handle of a sword or dagger.

labyrinth — A confusing maze, usually of tunnels underground.

lackey — A servant, usually very low in class.

man-at-arms — A soldier of the most common type.

melee — Hand-to-hand combat between groups of characters and monsters.

mercenary — A soldier who fights for wages rather than sworn loyalty.

murder holes — Slits cut into a ceiling so that victims passing below may be attacked from above.

NPC — A non-playing character, controlled by the Dungeon Master rather than one of the players.

pallet — A straw-filled mattress or small, hard bed.

parapet — A wall or elevation of earth or stone to protect soldiers.

pole arm — A large, heavy weapon on a long pole. There are many types, all of which are considered equal for D&D BASIC SET combat.

pommel — The knob on the hilt of a sword or dagger.

portcullis — An iron grate hung over a gateway and lowered between grooves to prevent passage.

pot boy — A young servant or slave who works in a tavern or inn.

retainer — Special NPC followers of player characters, who travel on adventures for a share of any treasure found.

sarcophagus — A stone coffin (Plural — sarcophagi.)

scenario — An outline of a possible course of events.

score — 20 items.

scullion — A kitchen helper, usually very low in class.

tun — A measure of wine: 252 gallons, or 8 barrels.

vellum — A very strong cream-colored paper.

25

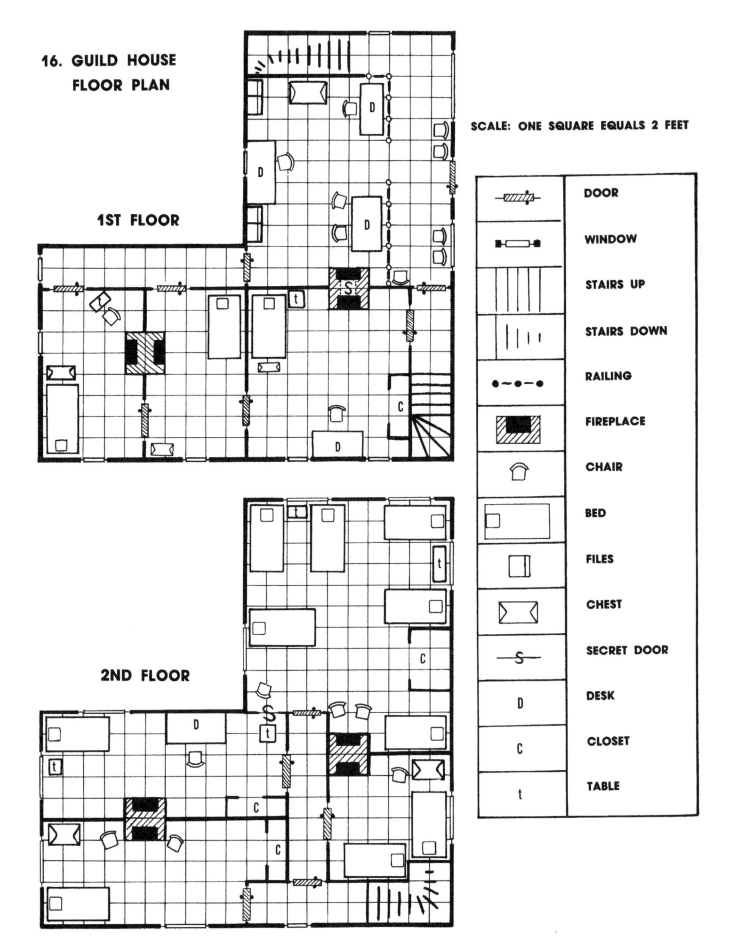

16. GUILD HOUSE FLOOR PLAN

1ST FLOOR

2ND FLOOR

SCALE: ONE SQUARE EQUALS 2 FEET

	DOOR
	WINDOW
	STAIRS UP
	STAIRS DOWN
	RAILING
	FIREPLACE
	CHAIR
	BED
	FILES
	CHEST
S	SECRET DOOR
D	DESK
C	CLOSET
t	TABLE

26

DRAW YOUR OWN FLOOR PLAN

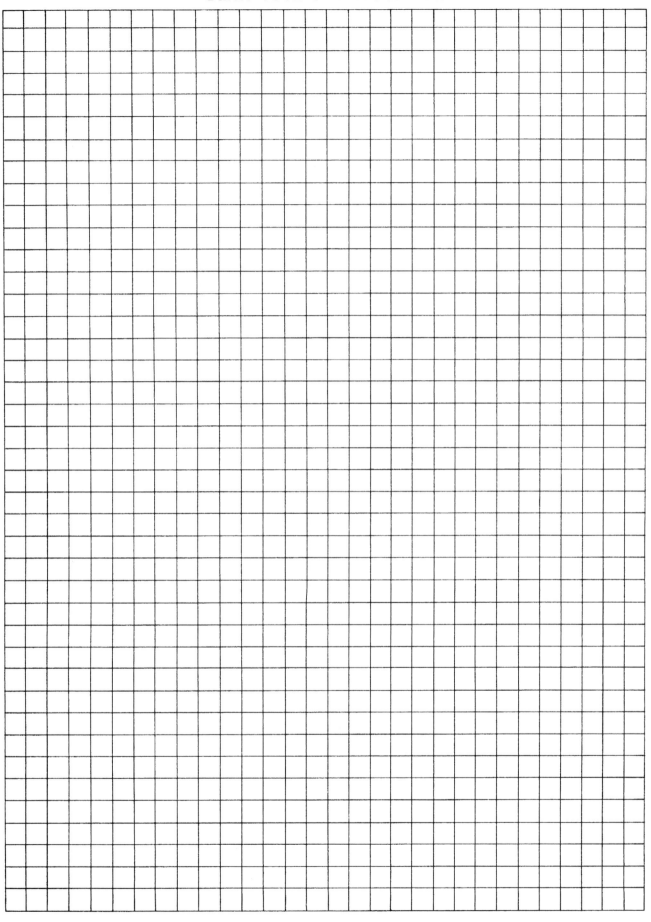

ADDITIONAL NON-PLAYER CHARACTERS

Use this sheet to list persons in the KEEP or in the CAVES OF CHAOS. Profession could be Fighter, Innkeeper, and so forth. Special refers to spells, valuables, and other details you may wish to include. Place should be noted by building or cave number.

	Name	Class/Profession	Level	AC	hp	Str	Int	Wis	Dex	Con	Cha	Personality	Special	Place
1.														
2.														
3.														
4.														
5.														
6.														
7.														
8.														
9.														
10.														
11.														
12.														
13.														
14.														
15.														
16.														
17.														
18.														
19.														
20.														
21.														
22.														
23.														
24.														
25.														
26.														
27.														
28.														
29.														
30.														
31.														
32.														

28

This item is only one of the many popular playing aids for DUNGEONS & DRAGONS Fantasy Adventure Game produced by TSR Hobbies, Inc. Other playing aids currently available for use with the D&D games system include:

Dungeon Module B1 (In Search of the Unknown)
Dungeon Module B2 (The Keep on the Borderlands)

Dungeon Module X1 (The Isle of Dread)
Monster and Treasure Assortment, Set One to Three: Levels One through Nine (makes the job of stocking dungeon
   levels easy)

Dungeon Geomorphs (allows the DM to create thousands of different dungeon levels by arranging them in different
   combinations)

D&D Player Character Record Sheets (allows players to record all important information about their characters in
   an easy-to-use format)

Other releases of additional items relateing to D&D Adventure Games are planned for the future. TSR Hobbies publishes a complete line of fantasy and science fiction games and rules which are available from better hobby, game, and department stores nationwide. If you desire a complete catalog, write to: TSR Hobbies, Inc., POB 756 Lake Geneva, WI 53147.

ISBN 0-935696-47-4

CHAPTER FIVE
Advice for Dungeon Masters

This package forms special instructional modules for play of the fifth edition of Dungeons & Dragons, and as such, is specifically designed for beginning players and Dungeon Masters. Due to its special design, it has numerous applications and services a multiplicity of purposes. Most material within these modules references that contained in the three fifth edition core rulebooks. In some instances, new material (such as new monsters, magic items, etc.) is included in the appendices.

Those who would intend to be beginning players using these modules would be well advised to stop reading this now and to avoid further examination of the modules' details or game maps. The reason for this is that enjoyment of the modules will be enhanced when the challenge of the unknown and unexpected confronts the participants, who will not be able to benefit from any familiarity with the game situation other than the background provided by the referee. This element of the unknown and the resultant exploration in search of unknown treasures (with hostile monsters and unexpected dangers to outwit and overcome) is precisely what a Dungeons & Dragons adventure is all about, and "knowing too much" can greatly spoil the fun of the experience that makes D&D gaming so special. So, if you're going to be a player in these modules, stop reading here, resist the temptation (which will be considerable) to go further in examining the contents, put the modules aside, and wait for your Dungeon Master to get ready to use this package for gaming. You won't be sorry!

THE BASICS OF ADVENTURING IN THE BORDERLANDS

Whether traveling the Borderlands, delving into the halls of Quasqueton, or exploring the Caves of Chaos, to start the adventure, the players must decide on a marching order for all of the characters in their group. The marching order determines who will be in front, who's in the middle, who's at the rear, and so on. This should be diagrammed on a sheet of paper and given to the Dungeon Master for reference, and any change in the order

of march during the adventure should be noted. Alternatively, miniatures can be utilized to depict the marching order. In a standard 10-foot-wide corridor, the most common arrangement is two adventurers side by side in each rank, although three characters could operate together in a single rank if all of their weapons were short and easily wielded (daggers or small axes, for instance). In the wilderness, the marching order could vary considerably based on the terrain.

One player in the group should be designated as the leader, or "Caller," for the party. Although individual players have the right to decide their own actions and relay them to the Dungeon Master as play progresses, the Caller is the one who gives the DM the details on the group's course of action as they move around and explore. For example, instructions as "We'll move slowly down this corridor to the east. . ." or "We'll break down this door while so-and-so covers the rear. . ." are typical directions given by a Caller to the DM. In the course of the adventure, the Caller will naturally discuss the options available to the party with the rest of the players, but it is this person whom the DM relies upon for the official instructions (although individual players can still pursue alternate courses of action at appropriate times, if they insist, by telling the Dungeon Master). Once a Caller (or any player) speaks and indicates an action is being taken, it is begun—even if the player quickly changes his or her mind (especially if the player realizes he or she has made a mistake or error in judgment). The DM must use discretion in such cases.

One player (or perhaps two players) should be encouraged to map the explored areas using graph paper. Orient them according to the same directions on the DM's map (with the top being north in almost all cases). After that, allow them to draw their maps from your descriptions as they wish—but make certain that your verbal descriptions of the areas they explore are accurate (although you can say such things as "approximately 60 feet," especially in large or open areas or places where there are irregular rock surfaces). Above all, avoid the considerable temptation to correct their maps once they have drawn them.

It will not be uncommon for players to show you their map (especially if they're confused) and ask you, "Is this right?" In most such instances, you should avoid correcting any mistakes there, unless it would be obvious through the eyes of the adventuring characters. Encourage good mapping skills and an attention to detail rather than falling into the rut of answering continual player map questions.

Exploration of Quasqueton or the Caves of Chaos will take more than one game session. It is also quite possible that adventurers (especially if wounded or reduced in number) may want to pull out of the adventuring site and prepare for a return visit when refreshed or reinforced. If this is done, they must work their way to an exit and discuss with you the pertinent details and time passage until their return. In such cases, the exact status of ar-

eas already explored will depend upon your judgment—whether areas cleared of monsters might in some cases be re-occupied by new ones, doors left open closed again and locked, or whatever. Some of the more intelligent monsters can even plan defenses and construct traps or obstacles the characters need to overcome when they resume their delve.

If the exploring adventurers wish to suspend the game temporarily during a long rest (when the adventuring characters stop to sleep, as they must do every 24 hours), appropriate notes should be made of each character's status so that resumption of the game can begin at the same point on the next meeting of the players. Their choice of where to camp is a factor to consider, as well, since in these dungeons a check for wandering monsters may be required according to the adventure text. It is customary to have one or more adventurers in the party standing guard at any one time, as the party members sleep in shifts in order to always have continual protection (although the devious DM may give a slight chance of a guard being asleep if a monster comes. . .). Just as with marching order, it is important that players provide the DM with the sleeping location of each member and the placement of the guard or guards, since this may be crucial if and when foes approach from a given direction.

During play, one player should record careful notes on the monsters defeated, the amount of treasure gathered, experience gained, and any other details of interest. These details could include a journal summary of the characters' exploits, locations of traps and secret doors, or clues and history regarding the adventuring site. It is then a simple matter to compute the experience and treasure totals at the end of a play session. Experience points (or XPs) earned and any benefits gained by additional levels are only applicable if and when the characters successfully exit an adventuring site.

B1 Notes for the Dungeon Master

As a beginning Dungeon Master, you will find this module helpful in many ways. First of all, it serves as a graphic example of a beginning dungeon. For this reason, it should prove illustrative to fledgling Dungeon Masters who will benefit from a look at what another dungeon design "looks like." Those designing their own dungeons will want to note various aspects of this dungeon, which will give them valuable insights into the creative process and allow them to formulate their own unique dungeon and gaming setting.

Second, this package provides an almost "ready-made" game situation which can be utilized for one or more sessions of play. Some initial preparation is necessary in addition to reading the material (chapters 6 and 7) through one or more times before using it in a game. The preparation, however, is interesting and fun as well as instructional, for it shows how a Dungeon Master (or DM) "stocks" the dungeon with assorted treasures and monsters before any adventuring begins. Separate lists of monsters and treasures to key with the various locations inside the dungeon (chapter 8) ensure that no two similar modules will be the same when set up by different DMs, and will also guarantee that players will not know what to expect in any given room or location. As for player characters (or PCs), participants can use their own characters rolled up according to the guidelines within the fifth edition Player's Handbook, or choose from a list of pre-generated characters available for download at www.goodman-games.com. This includes possible followers to accompany the player characters in their adventuring.

Thirdly, there are several salient points of good dungeon design illustrated in this module which new DMs would be wise to note. Likewise, they should keep these factors in mind when they start to design their own game maps and adventuring locales:

1. Since it is important to offer a challenge commensurate to the players' level, this two-level dungeon is designed specifically for exploration by beginning players in a party of three to six adventurers (player and nonplayer characters combined). This is reflected in various ways:

   a) In general, this dungeon is less deadly and more forgiving than one designed to test experienced players. It is designed to be fairly challenging, however, and is by no means "easy." Careless adventurers will pay the penalty for a lack of caution—only one of the many lessons to be learned within the dungeon.

   b) The dungeon is designed to be instructive for new players. Most of it should be relatively easy to map, although there are difficult sections—especially on the lower level where irregular rock caverns and passageways will prove a real challenge.

   c) The monsters encountered will generally be commensurate with the adventurers' ability to defeat them. For the few that are too formidable, the adventurers will have to learn the necessary art of fleeing or else employ more powerful means against them.

   d) The treasures to be found will generally be small, although a couple of more lucrative finds are possible if the adventurers are clever or lucky.

2. The dungeon includes a good assortment of typical features which players can learn to expect, including some interesting tricks and traps:

   a) Several one-way secret doors

   b) Illusions and *magic mouth* spells

   c) A wind corridor which may extinguish torches and open flames

   d) A room of mysterious pools

   e) A room of doors

   f) A water pit trap which suddenly drops adventurers to the lower level

   g) A portcullis trap where vertical bars drop behind the party in a dead-end corridor

   h) A pair of *teleport* rooms to confuse explorers

   i) Several magical treasures—most beneficial, some cursed

   j) Mysterious containers with a variety of contents for examination

3. There is a legend or story explaining some details of the setting and providing its lore (i.e., why it exists, its background, how the characters became involved with it, etc.). Of course, players/adventurers will probably

only know bits of this information—or perhaps only rumors of dubious reliability. Most good dungeons (and indeed entire game campaigns) rest upon a firm basis of interesting background and "history" as set for the players by the game moderator, or Dungeon Master.

4. The setting is neither too simple nor too difficult. Adventurers can leave by either returning to the entrance or locating the other secret exit. Two ways down to the lower level are available for discovery, and a trap may also bring adventurers there unexpectedly.

PREPARATION FOR THE USE OF THE MODULE B1

The use of this module by the Dungeon Master first requires a working familiarity with its layout and various design features. Therefore, the first step is to completely read the module, doing so with care and with reference to the maps provided to learn the basic layout and location of the various parts described in the written commentary. A second and third reading will also prove beneficial in preparing for a game employing the module. During these additional reviews, the DM should jot down notes in the margins, highlight relevant sections, and record notes on the maps proper to facilitate play at the game table.

This is a good time to mention Dungeon Dressing. It is the responsibility of the Dungeon Master to fully describe the environment beyond what is written in the individual encounter locations. These dungeon dressings can include noises, odors, air quality, general features, furnishings, and personal effects. The Dungeon Master's Guide (pp. 298-301) includes tables to randomly determine the various dressings to make the setting come alive. The DM can roll randomly on these tables, or simply select any entries that are appropriate. These should be noted in the individual encounter descriptions or directly on the maps.

The fifth edition conversion of this module comes fully prepared and stocked with monsters and treasures. Optionally, the DM may wish to stock the dungeon with his own monsters and treasures as per the original design. To do so, the DM utilizes the lists and tables provided in chapter 8, taking advantage of the special system to allow easy setup and reference. Refer also to the section Designing Challenging Encounters below.

Upon examination of the game maps, it will be noticed that each prominent room or chamber has a number for designation purposes. Each number corresponds to a written description within the body commentary which accompanies the maps, and which is contained in this book. Thus, a description of each such area of the dungeon is easily referenced by locating the written material within the book, and these are arranged in numerical order.

Once the Dungeon Master's preparation is complete, he or she must assist the players in getting ready for the adventure. The first step is in providing them with the background outline which sets the stage for the game. This Players' Background Sheet, which differs in some ways from the more detailed description/background for the DM, should be photocopied and distributed to the player for review and study. The DM may simply read it aloud to them if you wish.

Once the players know the background, they can prepare their characters for the adventure. If new characters are needed (as they will be if the players are just starting their first game), they can be rolled up by using dice and following the prescribed procedure within the Player's Handbook. Each player also determines his or her amount of starting money (the number of gold pieces he or she has at the beginning of play), and this amount is available for the purchase of arms and equipment for adventuring. Once the players have decided upon the equipment they will be carrying, as well as their own arms and armor, they are ready to start play. A written record of attributes, traits, and wealth, plus equipment owned and carried, is kept by each player.

As an alternative to spending time rolling the characters up, a list of assorted adventuring characters is available for download at www.goodman-games.com. If the Dungeon Master decides to do so, the players can choose one of the characters listed there as their player character. In such a case, the DM then provides the pertinent specifications and attributes of the character to the player, who makes a note of such statistics on a piece of paper. Alternatively, photocopies of the pre-generated characters can be provided.

If there are only two or three players, or if a party wishes additional assistance, one or more followers (nonplayer characters who will be a part of the party but who will not be under the total control of the players) can be added to the group of adventurers at the Dungeon Master's discretion. These characters can also be from the pre-generated list, or from the nonplayer character section of appendix C. These lists can also be used for nonplayer characters (or NPCs) encountered during the course of adventuring, or to replace player characters that fall in the line of adventuring.

When players have followers (characters who serve out of admiration or loyalty), the Dungeon Master must use common sense with their employment within the game. Obviously, allowing players to assemble large bands of armed assistants at this stage of the game would be unfair and unbalancing, so it will be unusual to have more than one or two NPCs appearing in the first games. Only after players have survived to earn some repute and wealth to attract (and afford) them will they be able to locate additional adventurers to aid their exploration.

Seeking followers is a matter to be handled by the Dungeon Master. A player's success in attracting followers will depend upon the Charisma of the seeker. Once a follower has decided to join a group (this usually being determined by a secret Charisma (Persuasion) check by the Dungeon Master), the nonplayer character will generally function according to the directions of the player character being served. However, in some situations—most notably those involving great risk or danger—the Dungeon Master serves as the "conscience" of the follower, and may cause him or her to balk at an ordered action, or perhaps even desert in the face of danger or as a result of unrewarded courage or accomplishment. For example, if a party is facing a hazardous situation and a player tells his or her follower to do something which would seem more dangerous than the actions pursued by the other PCs, the follower may hesitate to act upon the order—or in some cases might simply run away if the chance of death is great (this being determined by the DM's discretion, but is highly dependent upon the situation). Likewise, if a follower successfully executes a hazardous action (slaying a dragon without much help, for instance) and does not get a proportional reward, he or she will understandably consider deserting the player character that treated him or her unjustly. In such cases, the DM will determine the outcome and, as always, the DM's decisions (possibly the result of die rolls at appropriate chances which he or she determines) are final.

An alternative to having followers under player control is simply to have nonplayer characters available for single-game participation. In this case, an additional character accompanies the group and participates, but is independent of player control other than to be helpful and generally cooperative. The Dungeon Master runs the character in essence, although his or her actions will generally follow the desires and suggestions of the players (unless an unduly hazardous action is demanded). The independent character participates in return for a share of the treasure gained, and this share (which will be at least be proportional if the character is better than the player characters) must be agreed upon before the adventure starts. In general, if treated with respect and rewarded sufficiently, an NPC will remain in the employ of the characters.

Once the players have completed their preparations for the game, the referee finishes "setting the stage" by bringing the player characters from the background story to the place where the game adventure will begin. This is usually simply a matter of providing a brief narrative (such as, "Your group, after purchasing supplies and getting organized, left their town and went cross country till a deserted pathway was found which led into the hills, and finally to a craggy outcropping of rock. . ."). Use of the Legend Table (in chapter 6) is also made at this time.

B2 NOTES FOR THE DUNGEON MASTER

The three core rulebooks of the Dungeons & Dragons game have given you the information necessary to understand this game and start play. This module is another tool. It is a scenario or setting which will help you to understand the fine art of being a Dungeon Master as you introduce your group of players to your own fantasy world, your interpretation of the many worlds of Dungeons & Dragons adventure. *The Keep on the Borderlands* is simply offered for your use as a way to move smoothly and rapidly into your own special continuing adventures or campaigns. Read the module thoroughly; you will notice that many details are left in your hands. This allows you to personalize the scenario, and suit it to what you and your players will find most enjoyable.

This module has been designed to allow six to nine player characters of first level to play out many adventures, gradually working up to the second or third level of experience in the process. The group is assumed to have at least one wizard and one cleric in it. If you have fewer than six players, be sure to arrange for them to get both advice and help in the Keep. For example, they should have advice from a friendly individual to "stay near the beginning of the ravine area, and enter the lower caves first," to avoid their getting into immediate trouble with higher-level monsters. Likewise, the services of several hirelings must be available to smaller parties. If only two or three player characters are to adventure, be sure to have a nonplayer character or two go along, as well as a few men-at-arms. See appendix C for a list of suitable hirelings and nonplayer characters. In addition, give the player characters a magic dagger or some magic arrows and at least one *potion of healing*. These represent family bequests to aid them in finding their fame and fortune when they go against Chaos.

The DM should be careful to give the player characters a reasonable chance to survive. If your players tend to be rash and unthinking, it might be better to allow them to have a few men-at-arms accompany them even if the party is large, and they don't attempt to hire such mercenaries. Hopefully, they will quickly learn that the monsters here will work together and attack intelligently, if able. If this lesson is not learned, all that can be done is to allow the chips to fall where they may. Dead characters cannot be brought back to life here!

Using the Keep as "home base," your players should be able to have quite a number of adventures (playing sessions) before they have exhausted all the possibilities of the Caves of Chaos map. Assuming that they have played well, their player characters will certainly have advanced a level or two in experience when the last minion of darkness falls before their might. While your players will have advanced in their understanding and ability, you will likewise have increased your skills as DM. In fact, before they have finished all the adventure areas of this module, it is likely that you will have begun to add your own separate maps to the setting. The Keep is only a small section of the world. You must build the towns and terrain which surround it. You must shape the societies, create the kingdoms, and populate the countryside with men and monsters.

The Keep is a microcosm, a world in miniature. Within its walls your players will find basically a small village with a social order, and will meet opponents of a sort. Outside the safety of the Keep are dangerous wild lands and the way to the Caves of Chaos where monsters abound. As you build the campaign setting, you can use this module as a guide. Humankind and its allies have established strongholds—whether fortresses or organized countries—where the PCs can base themselves, interact with the society, and occasionally encounter foes of one sort or another. Surrounding these strongholds are lands which may be hostile to the bold adventurers. Perhaps there are areas of wilderness filled with dangerous creatures, or maybe the neighboring area is a land where chaos and evil rule. For wilderness adventures in the lands surrounding the Keep, refer to chapter 10. There are natural obstacles to consider, such as mountains, marshes, deserts, and seas. There can also be magical barriers, protections, and portals. Anything you can imagine could be part of your world if you so desire. The challenge to your imagination is to make a world which will bring the ultimate in fabulous and fantastic adventure to your players. A world which they may believe in.

Become familiar with this module, then make whatever additions or changes you feel are necessary for your campaign. Once you are satisfied, gather the players together and have them create their characters. This will take some time, so at first, don't plan on getting much playing done unless there is a lot of time available. After each person randomly determines his or her character's attributes (Strength, Intelligence, etc.), selects a class, and finds how much money he or she has to begin, you should introduce them to the setting by reading the Background section to them. If you wish, feel free to limit the classes and/or races your players may choose as suits your setting. You might wish not to have elves or halflings in the Keep, or you might not want any rogues as beginning characters. It is all up to you as DM to decide the shape of the campaign. Likewise, you can opt to give each PC a trinket (Player's Handbook pp. 159-161) to begin the game. Don't feel limited by the table, as virtually anything of small value (within reason) is appropriate.

After you have explained the background, allow your players to begin interacting with their characters. Give them time to wander around the Keep, learning what is there, finding the limits of their freedom, and meeting the other "inhabitants" of the place. They may quickly establish their base in the Traveler's Inn, purchase their equipment, and then visit the Tavern—where they may gather bits of information for their coming adventures. All of this play, as well as what will come afterwards, requires that the players play the personae (personalities) of the characters that they will have throughout the length of the campaign, much like an actor plays a role in a play. You, however, have a far greater challenge and obligation! You not only must order and create the world, you must also play the part of each and every creature that the player characters encounter. You must be the gate guard and the merchant, innkeeper and orc, oracle and madman as the situation dictates. The role of DM is all-powerful, but it also makes many demands. It is difficult to properly play the village idiot at one moment and the wise man the next, the noble clergyman on one hand and the vile monster on the other. In one role you must be cooperative, in the next uncaring and non-committal, then foolish, then clever, and so on. Be prepared!

Whether the first time you play or the next, the players will set forth to find and explore the many Caves of Chaos. You must describe the journey to the place and what the characters see, and allow them to choose how they will go about their adventuring. In such situations, the DM must be a truly disinterested party, giving information as required by questioning and proper action, but neither helping nor hindering otherwise. When the players experience their first encounter with a monster, you must be ready to play the part fully. If the monster is basically unintelligent, you must have it act accordingly. Make the encounter exciting with the proper dramatics of the animal sort—including noises! If the encounter is with an intelligent monster, it is up to the DM to not only provide an exciting description but also to correctly act the part of the monster. Rats, for instance, will swarm from their burrows—a wave of lice-ridden hunger seeking to overrun the adventurers with sheer numbers, but are easily driven off squealing with blows and fire. Goblins, on the other hand, will skulk and hide in order to ambush and trap the party—fleeing from more powerful foes, but always ready to set a new snare for the unwary character.

If all of this seems too difficult, never fear! Just as your players are learning and gaining experience at D&D play, so too will you be improving your ability as a DM. The work necessary to become a master at the art is great, far greater than that necessary to be a top player, but the rewards are even greater. You will bring untold enjoyment to many players in your role as DM, and all the while you will have the opportunity to exercise your imagination and creative ability to the fullest. May each of your dungeon adventure episodes always be a wondrous experience!

PREPARATION FOR THE USE OF THE MODULE B2

The use of this module first requires that the DM be familiar with its contents. Therefore, the first step is to completely read through the module (chapters 9 through 12), referring to the maps provided to learn the locations of the various features. A second (and third!) reading will be helpful in learning the nature of the monsters, their methods of attack and defense, and the treasures guarded.

Certain buildings of the Keep will frequently be visited by the adventurers (such as the Traveler's Inn, Tavern, and Provisioner). Floor plans are very useful in visualizing these areas. For information on their preparation, refer to the section below entitled Designing Floor Plans.

Once you are familiar with the areas described in the module and have drawn whatever additional maps you wish, assist the players in preparing their characters by reading them the section entitled Background. This will set the stage for the game.

After the background is given, the players may prepare their characters. A written record of each character should be kept by the players.

As an alternative to rolling up new characters, the players may (at the DM's option) select from a list of pre-generated characters available for download at www.goodman-games.com.

Before the players enter the Keep, the DM may privately give each player one rumor about the Caves of Chaos. This information may be shared or kept secret, as the players wish. The DM should avoid interfering with their choices whatever the result. Additional information may be gathered in the Keep itself; use the Rumor Table in the DM Notes About the Keep section for this purpose, or create your own based on the Caves and the surrounding wilderness. Please note that the characters can receive the same rumor more than once (perhaps slightly reworded).

DESIGNING FLOOR PLANS IN B2

Once you have become familiar with the Keep, who its residents are, where the main buildings are located, and so forth, it will be helpful to have details about the layout and contents of certain places. Players can easily "see" an area they are visiting if you have prepared a floor plan. The Guild House (area 16) will be used as an example of this procedure.

On the map of the Keep, the Guild House is shown to be an "L" shape about 40 feet long. Draw a large version of it on a piece of graph paper (the kind with 1/4-inch squares usually works best). Leave room for a key (noting what symbols are being used) and index the sheet for easy reference.

The outer walls should have the same dimensions as the building's outline. Note the scale (what map length represents what real length) at the bottom of the key. In the example given, 1/4 inch equals 2 feet of "real" length. Since the walls in a normal building are from 6 inches to 1 foot thick, they may be represented by single lines; an outer wall should be indicated by thicker lines.

Now look closely at the description of the building in the text. The lower floor contains the Guild Master's quarters, two clerks' quarters, and an office. Give equal spaces to the clerks, more to the Guild Master, and the most to the office (as it represents the main purpose of the building). The rooms may be in whatever order you like; just remember that the outer door shown on the map probably opens into the office, not into a private bedroom. Most doors are 3 to 5 feet wide. Be sure to include steps down to the cellar and up to the rooms on the second floor. Add some windows to help provide light.

Try to think of what items would be in a sparsely furnished office in the Keep (probably chairs, tables, desks, a lockbox or chest, and a cabinet or two). Consider how necessities would be provided: heat (fireplaces), water (barrels), and food (a kitchen in the cellar). The fireplaces should be located first—chimneys go straight up, and must be placed in the same area on each floor. Most buildings have one or two chimneys. Remember to heat each room, if possible! Add other furnishings wherever you wish, including any information provided in the text.

The completed office in this example has the Master's desk along the west wall under a window, flanked by records cabinets. The clerks' desks and collection table are just inside a railing, which keep visitors from wandering into the work area. Waiting chairs are placed for the Guild members' convenience. A secret door in the fireplace leads to the Master's bedroom—a quick escape route in case of trouble. The locked chest is for money received in Guild dues, but is usually empty due to a clever "drop" system. It is triggered by a lever under the Master's desk, which dumps the chest's contents down a short chute into a cellar storage room! You may add whatever tricks and traps you wish.

Arrange the bedroom furnishings (table, chairs, bed, armoire, etc.) in a similar manner. On the second floor (divided into private bedrooms and dormitory, according to the text) build the rooms off of the stairs, hallways, and fireplaces. It's easy!

Now you design the cellar, remembering a few key facts:

1. The stairs and chimneys must connect properly to the first floor.

2. Two servants live in the cellar, but not as richly as the clerks or the Guild Master.

3. A heavily barred, locked room must be under the office to receive the Guild fees from the chute.

4. A kitchen must be located by one of the fireplaces.

You won't have to worry about windows or outside doors, but you might wish to include a secret entrance to a long forgotten dungeon. Of course, you must design and stock with monsters and treasure, if you plan to have the characters explore this dungeon!

Adding the details to a house, church, or other structure can take a lot of time, but it's not as hard as you might think. Before playing the module, lay out as many buildings of the Keep as you can. The most commonly used buildings will be the Traveler's Inn (area 14), the Tavern (area 15), the Guild House (area 16), and the Chapel (area 17). You may add just a few simple furnishings to each if you wish, leaving the many smaller details for later. By designing floor plans, you can experiment with many of your own ideas before starting a major project—like the Caves of the Unknown.

HOW TO BE AN EFFECTIVE DUNGEON MASTER

The Dungeon Master, as referee, is the pivotal figure in any Dungeons & Dragons game. Accordingly, the DM's ability and expertise—as well as fairness—will be important factors in whether or not the game will be enjoyable for all of the participants. The DM is the most important person in the D&D game. He or she sets up and controls all situations, makes decisions, and acts as the link between the players and the world he or she has created.

The D&D game is a roleplaying game, and is unlike traditional tabletop board games which have a firm basis of regulated activity and repetitious action. A D&D adventure is free-flowing, and often goes in unknown and un-

be fair, reasonable (without giving in to the unreasonable demands of the players), and worthy of the respect of all the participants.

Beginning Dungeon Masters who are not familiar with the game often ask the most common first question, "Exactly how do you referee the game?" It is possible to read through the rules and become slightly lost by all the things that must be prepared or known before running a game as a DM. The answer is that there is no single best way—different DMs have different styles just as individual players do. However, there are certain guidelines which are important to follow.

First, it is crucial to keep in mind that this is a game based on player interaction and player choice. The game generally follows the course of the player's actions—if not always their plans! As moderator, you present an ever-changing situation as it occurs (sort of like an unfolding story, or even a movie, if you like to think in those terms), and the players respond pretty much as they desire. As the game goes on, you are presenting them with numerous different opportunities and choices—exactly how the game goes will depend upon their response to those opportunities and choices. For instance, if players decide to walk down a corridor and find a dead end with three doors, they have a number of choices: simply turn around and ignore the doors, listen at one or more before proceeding elsewhere, try to open one or more (either normally, by forcing them, or even by simply bashing them in), or whatever. You describe the situation, and then await their decision as to a course of action. Of course, some decisions will be more difficult, or quick, or crucial to survival—and as always, imagination and resourcefulness, as well as quick thinking, will usually be rewarded.

predictable directions—and that is precisely the reason it is so different and challenging. In a roleplaying game, the action is only limited by the abilities of the character, the imagination of the player, and the decisions of the DM. The Dungeon Master is best described as the moderator of the action, for the DM oversees the whole process, keeps the game moving, resolves the action based upon events occurring and player choices made, and monitors the actions and events outside the player group (i.e., handles monsters encountered, determines the actions of nonplayer characters encountered, etc.). The DM's responsibilities are considerable, but his or her foremost concern should be to provide an enjoyable game which is challenging to the players. This means that risk should be balanced with reward and that game situations are neither too "easy" nor too deadly. Above all, the DM must

Second, a good DM remains "above the battle" and does not attempt to influence player actions or channel the activity in a particular direction. The Dungeon Master should do everything possible to assist players in their quest without actually providing important information, unless the players themselves discover it or put the pieces of a puzzling problem together through deduction or questioning, or a combination of the two. A large part of the game consists of player questions, many of which are, "What do we see?" Your job as Dungeon Master is to answer those questions without giving too much away. You need not hint to players any information that they do not ask for on their own, except in unusual instances. Allow them to ask the questions, and allow them to make the choices.

In the same vein, as Dungeon Master you will enjoy watching players wrestle with the challenges you present to them. Although you may set up situations to challenge them, you must understand that you are not their adversary, nor are you necessarily out to "defeat" them. You will enjoy moderating a well-played game where players respond to the challenges encountered much more than one where the adventurers foolishly meet their demise in quick time. However, if your players abandon caution or make stupid mistakes, let them pay the price—but be fair. In many cases, a danger due to lack of caution can be overcome, or a mistake in judgment countered by quick thinking and resourcefulness, but let your players do the thinking and the doing.

As Dungeon Master, you are the game moderator. Just as the referee of a sporting event, the DM must be fair. He or she cannot be "out to get the players," nor should he or she be on their side all the time. The DM must be neutral. This also means you set the tempo of the game and are responsible for keeping it moving. Above all, you must remain in control of the situation, although with reasonable players your game should always be in control. If players are unusually slow or dilly-dally unnecessarily, remind them that time is wasting. If they persist, allow additional chances for wandering monsters to appear—or at least start rolling the dice to make the players think that you are doing so. If players are argumentative with each other, remind them their noise also serves to attract unwelcome monsters; if they persist, show them that this is true.

It is the job of the DM to see that the situations and characters balance. If things are too difficult, the players will become discouraged; too easy and they will become bored. Is it possible for a good player to win, yet still be a challenge and a risk in doing so? Is the amount of treasure gained equal to the danger of trying to get it? As DM, much satisfaction comes from watching players overcome a difficult situation. But they should do it on their own!

Lastly, it is important to remember that the Dungeon Master is the final arbiter in his or her game. If players disagree with you, hear them out and reasonably consider their complaint. However, you are the final judge, and they should understand that, as well as the fact that not everything will go their way, or as they expect. Be fair, but be firm. With human nature as it is, players will undoubtedly attempt to try to talk you into (or out of) all sorts of things; part of the fun of being a DM is this verbal interplay. But in the end, what you say is what goes.

TIME

The Dungeon Master is responsible for keeping a track of game time. Record time elapsed on a piece of scrap paper or use some other tracking method. Inside the dungeon, time is normally measured in **minutes**. Moving cautiously, in 1 minute a character can travel down a hallway, or search an object (such as a door or a chest) for traps. Searching a medium-sized chamber takes at least 10 minutes.

In combat, the time reference shifts to the **round**, a 6-second span of time. Melee rounds are used to simulate the quick exchange of blows in combat. For convenience, a DM should consider one entire melee to last as long as 10 minutes, no matter how many rounds the combat actually took. The extra time is spent recovering one's breath, bandaging wounds, sharpening blunted weapons, checking equipment, etc.

While moving through a city or the wilderness, a scale of **hours** is usually used to track the passage of time. Depending on the rate of pace (slow, normal, fast) characters can cover 2 to 4 miles per day in the wilderness. For longer overland journeys, the time scale can even be shifted to **days**.

Unless specified in the text of the module, every 30 minutes of adventuring, the DM should roll a die for the possible appearance of wandering monsters at the indicated chances (which are normally 1 in 6, but which may vary depending upon location and dungeon level). Some occurrences (such as noise and commotion caused by adventurers as detailed in the text of an encounter location) may necessitate additional checks.

A **short rest** is at least 1 hour long and consists of non-strenuous activity such as eating, reading, or tending minor wounds. At the end of a short rest, a character can regain hit points by spending up to his maximum number of Hit Dice (which is equal to his level). For each Hit Die spent, the player rolls the appropriate die and adds his Constitution modifier. For example, if a rogue with a 14 Constitution (+2) chooses to regain two Hit Dice following a short rest, he would roll 2d8 and add 4 to get the total hit points recovered. Spent Hit Dice are regained following a long rest.

A **long rest** is a period of extended downtime at least 8 hours long. During this time, light activity, standing guard, reading, or eating for no more than 2 hours is acceptable. Strenuous activity exceeding an hour in length negates the benefits of a long rest. At the end of long rest, some character class traits previously used become available, a character regains all lost hit points, and a character regains spent Hit Dice (up to half of his maximum number). A character can't benefit from more than one long rest in a 24-hour period.

DESIGNING CHALLENGING ENCOUNTERS

The DM must exercise caution when designing encounters for the party based on their number and level of experience. There are four categories of encounter difficulty: Easy, Medium, Hard, and Deadly. The XP value of all the monsters or NPCs is used to calculate the difficulty of the encounter. Most encounters should be Easy or Medium, with Hard and Deadly encounters reserved for boss battles. A typical, balanced party of adventurers with average luck and suitable equipment can handle six to eight Medium or Hard encounters before requiring a long rest. Use the tables below to design appropriate encounters when stocking a dungeon.

	Character Level	Easy	Medium	Hard	Deadly
	1st	100	200	300	400
	2nd	200	400	600	800
4 Characters	3rd	300	600	900	1,600
	4th	500	1,000	1,700	2,000
	5th	1,000	2,000	3,000	4,400
	1st	125	250	375	500
	2nd	250	500	750	1,000
5 Characters	3rd	375	750	1,125	2,000
	4th	625	1,250	1,875	2,500
	5th	1,250	2,500	3,750	5,500
	1st	150	300	450	600
	2nd	300	600	900	1,200
6 Characters	3rd	450	900	1,350	2,400
	4th	750	1,500	2,250	3,000
	5th	1,500	3,000	4,500	6,600

First, determine the number of characters in the party, including NPCs (on the left-hand side of the table). Next determine their average level; the table has XP budgets for levels 1 through 5, although the DM can expand the table to include higher levels (or more players). Then cross reference the XP budgets for the different encounter difficulties.

For example, if the party includes a 3rd-level wizard, a 4th-level rogue, a 2nd-level fighter, a 3rd-level cleric, and a 3rd-level ranger, we would have an average of five characters of 3rd level. An Easy encounter for this group would be 375 equivalent XP, while a Deadly encounter would be 2,000 equivalent XP.

To determine how difficult an encounter is, add up all the XP of all the monsters and then adjust the amount by using the multiplier in the table below based on the total number of monsters. Monster XP are based on Challenge Rating (CR) values and are included in the Monster Manual or statistics capsules provided. For example, a water weird (CR 3, 700 XP) would be a Medium encounter for our described party. But five orcs (CR 1/2, 100 XP each) plus an Ogre (CR 2, 450 XP) would be a Deadly encounter for our five 3rd-level characters (5 x 100 = 500 + 450 = 950 XP x 2 = 1,900 equivalent XP). Note that this calculation is the equivalent XP for the encounter. The characters are only awarded the actual experience points (in this case, 950 XP) for defeating this group of monsters.

# of Monsters Encountered	XP Multiplier
1	x 1
2	x 1.5
3-6	x 2
7-10	x 2.5
11-14	x 3
15+	x 4

DIVIDING TREASURE AND COMPUTING EXPERIENCE

After the party leaves the dungeon safely, all surviving player characters should divide the recovered treasure and be awarded their experience points. Division of treasure is the players' responsibility, while awarding experience points is the Dungeon Master's responsibility.

Ideally, treasure should be divided equally among surviving player characters, with followers and hirelings usually receiving a share (minus any advance payment already given them). Players should decide to only give magical items to character classes that could use them most effectively. For example, a fighter should take a magical sword as part of his or her share in preference to a *spell scroll*.

Nonmagical treasure is usually divided first, since it is easier to divide equally. It is seldom possible to divide magic items equally. A suggested solution to division of magic items is to have each character roll percentile dice and let the highest score have first pick, second highest score second pick, and so on until there are no more magical items. Nonplayer characters may, or may not, be given an equal chance for a magic item. If they are excluded, a DM should note the fact and take it into account in regards to the followers' or hirelings' loyalty.

For example, a party consisting of a fighter, a wizard, and an NPC (all first level) returns safely to the Keep. Their recovered treasure equals 520 gp, 1,000 sp, a necklace worth 400 gp, a *+1 longsword,* and a *ring of water walking.* The total value of all nonmagical treasure is 1,020 gold pieces. Without selling the necklace, it would be impossible for the party to split the treasure equally. The two player characters compromise by giving the necklace to the NPC, to ensure his loyalty with a greater share of treasure. They each take only 310 gold pieces, but the wizard keeps the ring and the fighter keeps the longsword.

Experience points are awarded by the DM to player characters on the basis of monsters defeated or overcome. Experience point values are based on challenge rating and are listed in the monster statistics, either in appendix B or in the Monster Manual.

Following a foray into the Caves of Chaos, the party defeated 19 orcs, 7 skeletons, and an ogre. The party should receive 100 points of experience for each orc defeated, as orcs are CR 1/2. The party should receive 50 experience points for each skeleton (CR 1/4). For killing the ogre,

they should receive 450 experience points, since it is CR 2. The total experience points for defeating monsters would be 2,700. When this is divided, the wizard, fighter, and NPC each receive 900 experience points.

At the DM's discretion, additional experience points can be awarded to reward fine roleplaying, superior tactics, or achieving goals. For example, if the party's rogue swipes a 500 gp gem from an NPC, the DM might decide to award the rogue character 25 experience points. Likewise, if the party rescues prisoners scheduled to be eaten at a feast later that night, the DM might decide to reward each character 50 experience points for the deed.

When enough experience points are accumulated, a player character rises to the next higher level, and gains the benefits of that level (an additional Hit Die, additional traits or spell slots, etc.). Wealth can be used to buy new equipment, to pay for everyday expenses, and to hire additional retainers or hirelings.

ADVICE: TIPS TO THE PLAYERS

It often helps for beginning players to have advice on how to play Dungeons & Dragons. Many points are overlooked by novices in their eagerness to get on with the adventure. The following points are given to help these neophyte players.

Most importantly, players should be organized and cooperative. Each player should have complete information on his or her character easily on hand and should supply the Dungeon Master with this information quickly and accurately if asked. An adventuring party will usually involve a variety of alignments and classes, so players should work together to use their abilities effectively. Arguing among players can cause delays, attract monsters, and often result in the wasting of precious resources or even the deaths of some or all of the members. While disagreements about a course of action certainly arise from time to time, players should quickly discuss their options and reach a consensus in order to proceed.

Cooperation should also be given to the DM. He or she is the judge of the game and his or her decisions are final. If a player disagrees, he or she should calmly state why, but accept whatever the DM decides. If necessary, the topic can be discussed outside of the game, but for the sake of all players, avoid prolonged disruptions of play. Shouting, crying, pouting, or refusing to accept decisions only angers the other players. The game should be fun for all involved. Not everything will go the way players want it. As such, the DM deserves the continued cooperation, consideration, and respect of all the players. Above all, remember that this is just a game and a little consideration can go far toward avoiding any hard feelings.

Planning is another important part of play. Players should be well equipped, comparing each member's list and balancing the items on each. No character should be overburdened nor under-equipped. This may mean sharing the costs of extra items. Rope, oil, torches, spikes, and other useful items should always be carried. Plans should be considered for encountering monsters and casting spells.

Caution is also necessary and is a part of planning. A party that charges forward without preparation is almost certainly doomed. Danger should be expected at any moment and from any direction, possibly even from one's own party. Lying and trickery are not unknown. Cautious play will help avoid many (but not all) tricks and traps and may save a character's life. However, too much caution is as dangerous as too little. Many instances will require bold and quick actions on the part of the players, before all is lost. As you gain playing experience you will learn the proper pace, but often it is wise to rely on your DM for guidance.

Treat any nonplayer characters, hirelings, or followers fairly. If you reward them generously and do not expose them to great risks of life and limb that your own character would not face, then you can expect a continuing loyalty. Although there may be exceptions, of course.

Know your character's limits. Your party may not be a match for every monster you encounter, and occasionally it pays to know when and how to run away from danger. Likewise, a dungeon adventure may have to be cut short if your party suffers great adversity and/or depleted resources. Often it takes more than one foray to accomplish certain goals, and it becomes necessary to come back out of a dungeon to heal wounds, restore magical abilities and spells, re-supply with equipment, and reinforce a party's strength. Plan accordingly for such retreats.

Above all, a player must think. The game is designed to challenge the minds and imaginations of the players. Those who tackle problems and use their abilities, wits, and new ideas will succeed more often than fail. Many of the characters' goals in the game can be accomplished through the strength of arms or magic. Others, however, demand common sense and shrewd judgment as well as logical deduction. The most successful players are those who can effectively use both aspects of the game to their advantage. The challenge of thinking is a great deal of the fun of the game. Be on your guard. Don't be overly cautious, but be advised that some enemies may try to hoodwink you, NPCs may double cross you, and while adventuring, tricks and traps await the unwary. Of course, you won't avoid every such pitfall (dealing with the uncertainties is part of the fun and challenge of the game), but don't be surprised if everything is not always as it seems.

The fun of a D&D game comes in playing your character's role. Take on your character's persona and immerse yourself in the game setting, enjoying the fantasy element and the interaction with your fellow players and the Dungeon Master. Remember, this is a game, and the object is for all to have fun.

CHAPTER SIX
In Search of the Unknown

Many years ago, rumor has it, two noted personages in the area, Rogahn the Fearless (a fighter of renown) and Zelligar the Unknown (a wizard of mystery and power), pooled their resources and expertise to construct a home and stronghold for the two of them to use as a base of operations. The location of this hidden complex was chosen with care, since both men disliked visitors and intruders. Far from the nearest settlement, away from traveled routes, and high upon a craggy hill, the new construction took shape. Carved out of the rock protrusion which crested the heavily forested hill, this mystical hideaway was well hidden, and its rumored existence was never common knowledge. Even less well known was its name, the Caverns of Quasqueton.

Construction of the new complex, it is said, took over a decade, even with the aid of magic and the work of hundreds of slaves and laborers. Vast amounts of rock were removed and tumbled off the rough cliffs into large piles now overgrown with vegetation. A single tower was constructed above ground for lookout purposes, even though there was little to see other than a hilly, forested wilderness for miles around.

Rogahn and Zelligar lived in their joint sanctuary for quite some time, conducting their affairs from within except for occasional adventures in the outside world where both men attempted to add to their reputations as foremost practitioners of their respective arts.

The deeds and adventures of these two characters were never well known, since they both kept their distance from civilization. Some say, and perhaps rightly so, that their motives were based on greed and some kind of vague (or chaotic) evil. No one knows for sure.

What is known more widely is the reputation of each. Despite their questionable alignment, both Rogahn and Zelligar capped their reputation of power when they joined forces to stop a barbarian invasion threatening the great valley below. In a crucial battle at a narrow pass in the hills, the two combined powerful forces and decisively turned back the invasion. Rogahn slew a horde of barbarians single-handedly and Zelligar's powerful magic put their army to flight. A grateful populace rewarded the pair and their henchmen with considerable treasure, after which the two retired to their hideaway. Most of the reward treasure was apparently used to finance the further construction of Quasqueton, although some of it may yet be hidden somewhere. In any case, the hill stronghold was not completed in its entirety when, years later, the intrepid pair apparently embarked on their last adventure.

Some years ago, Rogahn and Zelligar apparently decided upon a joint foray into the lands of the hated barbarians. Taking most of their henchmen and associates along in a great armed band, the two personages disappeared into the forbidding alien lands to the north, far from the hills and forests surrounding Quasqueton.

Word just reaching civilization tells of some great battle in the barbarian lands where Rogahn and Zelligar have met their demise. This rumored clash must have occurred some years ago, and there are few details—and no substantiation of the story. The only thing certain is the Rogahn and Zelligar have been gone far too long. If only one had the knowledge and wherewithal to find their hideaway, there would be great things to explore! And who knows what riches of wealth and magic might be there for the taking???

PLAYERS' BACKGROUND SHEET

Here is the standard background setting for all players to read prior to their first adventure. Either read this aloud before the adventure begins, or print out a copy for the players to read and refer to during their quest.

Rogahn the Fearless and Zelligar the Unknown are legendary names. Even you, a young fledgling in a town far from the great cities of your world, know of their reputation—even though their tale begins long before you were born. The elders and the sages speak both names with respect, even awe, in a distant admiration for the memories of the two legendary figures. . .

You have heard parts of the story before, but never enough to know all of it, or even what is true and what is only legend or speculation. But it is a great and fascinating beginning in your own quest to learn more. Rogahn the Fearless earned his name as a great warrior, and his reputation spread far and wide across the land. Zelligar the Unknown, equally renowned, earned his respected status and power as a foremost practitioner of the mystical arts of magic and sorcery.

No one knows what occurrences or coincidence brought these two men together, but tales tell of their meeting and forming a strong bond of friendship, a union that would last for the ages. As this occurred, legend has it, the two men virtually disappeared from the view of civilization. Stories occasionally surfaced about a rumored hideaway being built deep in the wilderness, far from the nearest settlement, away from traveled routes, and high upon a craggy hill—but no one seemed to know any more than that, or where this supposed hideaway really was located, if indeed it was. No one knows for sure, but some say their motive was to pursue the common goals of personal greed and some kind of vague (or chaotic) evil. In any case, they jointly led a hermit life with but a few occasional forays into the outside world to add to their own reputations.

Many years passed, until one day a great barbarian invasion came from the lands to the north, threatening to engulf the entire land with the savage excesses of the unchecked alien horde. Just when things seemed the darkest, Rogahn the Fearless and Zelligar the Unknown made their unexpected yet most welcome reappearance. Joining their powerful forces, they and their band of loyal henchmen met the barbarian army in a great battle at a narrow pass in the hills, and decisively turned back the invasion. Rogahn slew a horde of barbarians single-handedly and Zelligar's powerful magic put their army to flight. It was a great victory, and a grateful populace rewarded the pair and their consorts with considerable treasure. After that, the two heroes returned to their mystical hideaway, and rumor has it that the spoils of victory were spent to further its construction, although some of it may yet be hidden somewhere.

The most exciting portions of the legend are the most recent. Some years ago, perhaps in the decade before you were born, Rogahn and Zelligar apparently decided upon a joint foray into the lands of the hated barbarians. Taking most of their henchmen and associates along with them in a great armed band, the two personages, it seems, disappeared into the forbidding alien lands to the north on a great adventure which some say may have been asked by the very gods themselves.

Word just reaching civilization tells of some great battle in the barbarian lands where the legendary Rogahn and Zelligar have met their demise. This rumored clash must have occurred some years ago as there are few details, and no substantiation of the story. The only thing certain is that, if all this is true, Rogahn and Zelligar have been gone far too long. If only one had the knowledge and wherewithal to find their hideaway, he or she would have great things to explore!

Now, just recently, came the most promising bit of information—a crude map purporting to show the way to the hideaway of the two men, a place apparently called "Q." You or one of your acquaintances has this map, and if it is accurate, it could perhaps lead you to the mystical place that was their home and sanctuary. Who knows what riches of wealth and magic might be there for the taking? Yes, the risk is great, but the challenge cannot be ignored. Gathering a few of your fellows, you share the secret and embark on an adventure in search of the unknown.

DM Note: Individual players may know of additional information in the form of rumors or legends as given to them by the Dungeon Master.

LEGEND TABLE

Prior to the first adventure into the stronghold, the Dungeon Master (or DM) can utilize this table to impart "background knowledge" (from rumors or legends known) to the adventurers. The table itself includes bits and scraps of information regarding the place to be explored—most of it accurate; however, legends and rumors being what they are, some of the information is false and misleading.

To determine legends/rumors known, each player should roll a d4 in secret conference with the Dungeon Master. Nonplayer characters (NPCs), hirelings, and followers do not get a roll. The result of the roll determines the number of rumors/legends known by the individual rolling the die:

D4	Legends/Rumors
1	One legend known
2	Two legends known
3	Three legends known
4	No legends known

Rolls of 1, 2, or 3 will result in that many rolls on the Legend Table using 1d20. A roll of 4 indicates that the adventurer has no knowledge of any rumors or legends pertaining to the stronghold; any information the player desires he or she must attempt to obtain from the other players.

The legends/rumors known are determined by the player's roll of the 20-sided die, and the DM reads the appropriate information off the table to the player for each roll (this is done secretly where the other players cannot overhear). The DM then tells the player that this is the extent of background information known by his or her player character; whether or not the player chooses to share this information (all or only part of it) with the other players is a personal decision. In this manner each player is given a chance to see what bits of additional information their character knows before the adventure starts.

LEGEND TABLE

"F" denotes a false legend or rumor

D20	Legend/Rumor
1	The name of the stronghold is Quasqueton.
2	(F) Zelligar had a wizard's workshop in the stronghold where he worked on magic stronger than any known to man.
3	(F) Rogahn owned a fantastic gem as big as a man's fist that was worth over 100,000 gold pieces; he kept it hidden in his personal quarters.
4	Zelligar and Rogahn had orc slaves to do the menial work, and some lived permanently at the stronghold.
5	The complex has two levels.
6	Part of the complex is unfinished.
7	The complex has a rear exit which is secret and well-hidden.
8	No outsiders have ever entered the complex and returned to tell the tale.
9	Troglodytes have moved into the complex in the absence of its normal inhabitants.
10	(F) The place is protected by the gods themselves, and one member of any party of intruders is doomed to certain death.
11	(F) The treasures of Zelligar and Rogahn are safely hidden in a pool of water.
12	(F) The entire place is filled with guards left behind by Zelligar and Rogahn.
13	Rogahn's trophy room has battle relics and slain monster remains from his adventures.
14	There is a room with many pools of water within the complex.
15	The very walls speak to visitors.
16	(F) An enchanted stone within the stronghold will grant a wish to anyone who chips off a piece of it and places it within their mouth.
17	(F) All treasures of Zelligar and Rogahn are cursed to bring ill to any who possess them.
18	(F) Zelligar and Rogahn have actually returned to their stronghold, and woe be to any unwelcome visitors!
19	There are secret doors, rooms, and passageways in parts of the complex.
20	The complex has more than one level.

DM Note: When rolling on this table, reroll any duplicates rolled by the same player.

QUASQUETON: UPPER LEVEL

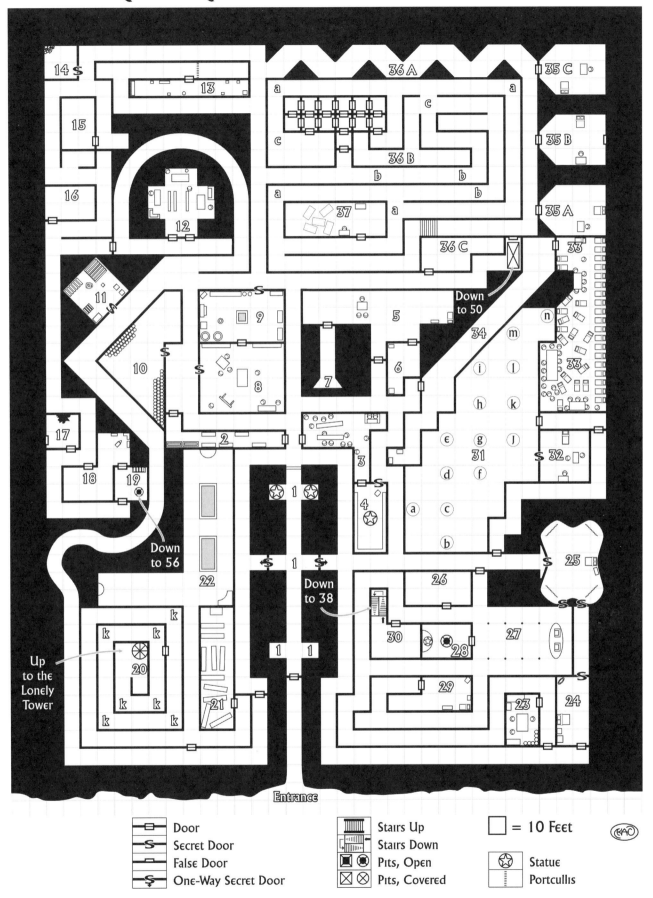

14 S
13
15
16
12
11
36 A
a
c
c
36 B
a
37
a
b
b
b
35 C
35 B
35 A
33
36 C
Down to 50
34
n
m
l
i
h
k
e
g
j
d
f
31
32 S
a
c
b
10
9
S
8
S
2
5
6
7
3
S
4
1
17
18
19
Down to 56
22
Down to 38
1
S
1
S
1
1
25
26
27
28
30
29
23
24
20
Up to the Lonely Tower
21
k
k
k
k
k
k

Entrance

	Door		Stairs Up		= 10 Feet
S	Secret Door		Stairs Down		Statue
	False Door		Pits, Open		Portcullis
S	One-Way Secret Door		Pits, Covered		

THE CAVERNS OF QUASQUETON

This area for exploration is designed to challenge a party of three to eight adventurers (player characters plus NPCs) of up to the third level of experience, and is specifically intended for use with the fifth edition of Dungeons & Dragons. Players will find it beneficial to have a mix of characters in their party who complement each other and who possess a variety of abilities due to their different classes (fighters, wizards, clerics, rogues, etc.). Additionally, characters with one or two useful magic items are likewise to be of great help, although more numerous or more powerful such items can unbalance the challenges herein.

UPPER LEVEL

GENERAL FEATURES

The Caverns of Quasqueton, as mentioned in the background description, are hewn from a great rock outcropping at the crest of a large wooded hill. Winds buffet the hill continuously, blowing and whistling through the trees, vines, and other vegetation which blanket the prominence on all sides. The rock itself is a heavy blackish slate, and is evident all throughout the caverns on both levels.

Environment. The air within the caverns is heavy, wet, and musty. In some portions of the complex, a layer of dust lies upon everything, undisturbed for years. Burning anything within is slow and difficult, for the entire atmosphere resists combustion. Torches and lanterns burn but emit smoke.

Light. The corridors and chambers of Quasqueton are generally unlit, unless the room description details otherwise.

Walls/Floors. The walls are relatively smoothly hewn and finished, typically in good repair. The floors, while uneven in places, are likewise in good condition. Climbing a standard wall requires a successful DC 15 Strength (Athletics) check.

Doors. Normal doors are uniformly of heavy wooden construction, approximately 5 or 6 inches thick (AC 15, 22 hit points). There are many doors within the dungeon (the term "dungeon" being used generically for the entire underground area), and some of them are secret doors. Secret doors are discernible only by special examination, requiring a successful Wisdom (Perception) check (with the DC being stated in the room description). In all cases, unless otherwise noted, doors are locked one-third of the time—and any roll of a 1 or 2 on a six-sided die (d6) indicates that they are barred unless the lock is sprung or broken. Picking a lock requires a successful Dexterity check with a set of thieves' tools (with the DC stated in the room text). Breaking the lock or breaking down the entire door requires a successful DC 15 Strength check, but this noisy process calls for an immediate wandering monster check.

Upper/Lower Levels. The two levels of the dungeon are approximately equal in size and are located one above the other. If the two maps could be placed over one another, the three access points between levels would directly correspond to their locations on the maps and lead directly to each other up and down. These include the opening from area 19 (to an unnumbered location east of area 56), the stairs from area 30 to area 38, and the trap in area 36 (to area 50).

Ceilings/Corridors. Within the complex, the upper level is a rather finished abode with generally good stonework and masonry overall. There are rough spots, or portions where workmanship is not as good as overall, but for the most part the construction and excavation are well done. Corridors generally measure 10 feet in width, while ceilings for the most part are approximately 8 to 10 feet above the floor. The blackish stone from which the halls and caverns were hewn is evident overall.

WANDERING MONSTERS

For every 30 minutes the characters explore the dungeon, make a wandering monster check. Roll 1d6, with a 1 in 6 chance of an encounter. If an encounter is indicated, roll 1d6 again to determine what type of monster that appears. Determine surprise as normal.

D6	Monster
1	Gnomes (see appendix B) (1-4)
2	Giant Centipedes (1-2)
3	Kobolds (1-6)
4	Troglodytes (1-2)
5	Giant Rats (2-5)
6	Barbarian Warriors (see appendix B) (1-2)

ENCOUNTER AREAS

ENTRANCE

When the characters approach the entrance to Quasqueton, read or paraphrase the following:

A cave-like opening, somewhat obscured by vegetation, is noticeable at the end of a treacherous pathway which leads up to the craggy outcropping of black rock. By sweeping aside some of the vines and branches, the opening becomes easily accessible.

The opening leads straight into the rock formation, with a 10-foot-wide corridor leading 60 feet to a large wooden door. The door opens freely, and close examination with a successful DC 10 Wisdom (Perception) check reveals that bits of wood have been chipped away from the edge, indicating that it has previously been forced. Nearby lies a concealed trail leading to the Lonely Tower (see chapter 7).

AREA 1 – ALCOVES

There are three pairs of alcoves past the entrance, located as they are for purposes of defense against intruders or invaders. The first pair is empty. The second pair of alcoves is also empty, but actually contains secret one-way doors, totally unnoticeable to anyone on the side of the entrance corridor (even if close examination is made). These one-way doors are also a defensive measure to allow guards to appear in the rear of any invading group which passes this point.

The third pair of alcoves each contains a stone statue, depicting a 6-foot-tall human adorned in chain mail and wielding a longsword. Two *magic mouth* spells are triggered as soon as any adventurers reach the point in the corridor between these two alcoves. When this occurs, a *mouth* appears on the statue's mouth in the east alcove, and another *mouth* appears on the statue in the west alcove.

The eastern one speaks first, in a booming voice: "WHO DARES ENTER THIS PLACE AND INTRUDE UPON THE SANCTUARY OF ITS INHABITANTS?" After but a moment, and drowning out any attempted reply by the party, comes the reply from the western one: "ONLY A GROUP OF FOOLHARDY EXPLORERS DOOMED TO CERTAIN DEATH!" Then both shout in unison, "WOE TO ANY WHO PASS THIS PLACE—THE WRATH OF ZELLIGAR AND ROGAHN WILL BE UPON THEM!" They then begin a loud and raucous laughter, which fades in intensity as the twin *mouths* disappear from view. They are a permanent feature of the stronghold, and repeat their message after 10 minutes the next time a living creature enters the area between these alcoves.

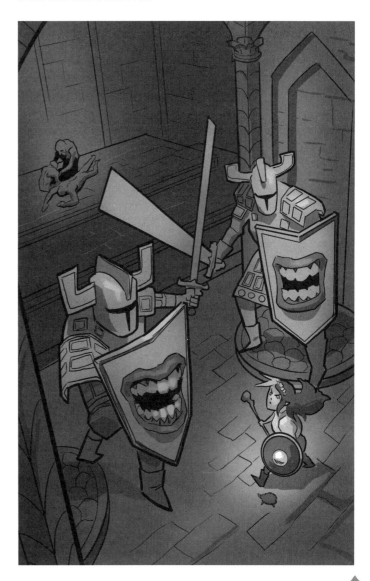

The statues are actually **living stone statues** (see appendix B), animated by Zelligar to guard the entrance to Quasqueton. Due to their False Appearance trait, they are indistinguishable from normal stone statues. Following the menacing speech delivered via *magic mouth*, both statues move to prevent characters from entering the complex, by blocking the way to the north. The statues attack, stalling and preventing combatants from pressing further into the complex. A successful DC 15 Dexterity (Acrobatics) check is required to dodge past the statues. Failure results in the character ending his movement and receiving an opportunity attack from one statue. Back in the day, this tactic allowed other guards to utilize the secret doors in the second alcove to attack from the rear; no such reinforcements arrive these days. The living stone statues only pursue targets 60 feet from this entrance hall. If targets move beyond that distance, the statues return to the alcoves. There once was a passphrase that could be delivered to the statues to allow safe passage but it has long been forgotten.

When the characters delve deeper into the complex, read the following:

Past the third pair of alcoves, at the end of the corridor from the entrance are two steps up. At the top of the steps, the corridor continues straight ahead, and corridors meet from east and west. At this intersection is a grisly sight—the remains of a hand-to-hand battle where no less than five combatants died.

Upon examination of the bodies (if the characters choose to do so), it is obvious that three of them were adventurers themselves, explorers from the outer world. This ill-fated trio obviously had their first and last battle at this spot. Their opponents, also slain here, were two barbarian warriors. The bodies arrayed here, each in various states of decomposition, are as follows (the stench of decaying bodies is strong and repulsive, and the sight doubly so):

Body #1. A human fighter, slumped against a wall. His broken sword, sheared off about 8 inches above the pommel, tells the story of his demise. The body has been stripped of any armor, and there are no items of value on the remains, other than a belt pouch containing 5 gp.

Body #2. A human wizard, impaled against a wall. The killing sword, still thrust through the body, is lodged in the wall, which has a large section of wood at this point. If the sword is removed, the body crumples to the floor,

exposing a bloodstained carving. The carved letters read "QUASQUETON" in Common. The sword, upon being removed, proves to be worthless, since its handle is very loose and the overall quality of the weapon is poor. The body is bereft of any items of great value. The wizard's robe, now bloodstained and ruined, has a pocket and within it is a purse containing 2 gp and a pouch full of moldy garlic buds.

Body #3. A dwarf fighter, lying facedown in the corridor just east of the intersection. In his right hand he still clutches his warhammer, and it appears that he crawled, wounded, to this point, since a trail of dried blood leads back to the battle location. A sack turned inside-out lies alongside the body, now empty. Armor has been stripped from the body, although the fighter's helm is still on his head. This headgear, however, has a noticeable dent and thus is worthless. There are no items of value on the remains.

Body #4. A human barbarian is sprawled on the floor, with a broken wooden shield nearby. The body has no armor on it. There is no weapon on the body or nearby, nor are there any other items of value on the remains.

Body #5. A human barbarian with a bashed head from the blow of a warhammer, lies on the floor facedown. There is no armor or weapon on the body except for a small sheathed dagger on the belt. The belt is very ornately decorated leather, which would appear to be valuable, except for the bloodstains ruining its appearance.

AREA 2 – KITCHEN

Although but 10 feet wide, this chamber stretches for 70 feet. Long tables line each wall, and there are scattered containers on them, some upturned with spilled contents moldering on the tabletop. At the southwest corner of the room are two cooking pits, each large enough to cook an animal as large as a deer. Hanging from above are a variety of utensils and cooking implements, and some other of these are scattered about on the floor of the room.

The food preparation area for the complex is a very long room with a variety of details. One of the cooking pits is slightly larger than the other, but both are about 3 feet in depth. The pits are full of ash and charred remains of cooking fuel. A chimney leads upward, but its small size prevents further investigation by creatures sized larger than Tiny.

There are spoiled pieces of food all around the room, and the smell in the room is very uninviting. One chunk of moldy cheese on a table is particularly noxious, as a fuzzy green growth covers its entirety. The hanging implements are nothing more than pots and pans of various sizes, although there is a large cast-iron kettle suspended from the ceiling by a thick chain. The kettle is empty.

AREA 3 – DINING ROOM

This room was the main dining hall for the complex, and it is here that guest banquets were once held.

This stately room is 20 feet wide and 40 feet long, appearing to once have served as a dining hall of sorts. A nicely carved wooden mantle surrounds the room at a height 7 feet off the floor, and the stone walls are carved in simple yet pleasant designs. There are a number of tables and chairs in the room, these being of wooden construction and quite utilitarian in nature. A pale green mold lightly covers many of the wooden surfaces. The entire room has a musty, mildew scent to it.

The room is moderately decorated, but frugally so, since there appear to be no items of great value which are part of the decor. Only two chairs stand out from the rest, these being the personal seats of the stronghold's illustrious inhabitants, Zelligar and Rogahn. Both of these chairs are ornately carved walnut, formed from an enormous block of wood which is joined into a portion of the wall in the northeast corner of the room. Upon closer examination, it can be discerned that the chairs themselves are actually fixed seats connected to the wooden structure. Their great beauty is apparent, but is marred by the harmless greenish fungus growing on portions of the wood. It is obvious the seats have not been used for quite some length of time.

Lesser tables and chairs are scattered about, and several are overturned. All of these furnishings are of hard maple. They show wear, although they have obviously not been used recently.

AREA 4 – LOUNGE

Off the dining room, this 20-foot-by-40-foot hall was perhaps a sitting room or lounge. Several earthenware tankard mugs hang from a row of hooks high on one wall. Numerous unadorned pegs are also present. A long wooden bench seat, actually attached to the wall, is along each side of the room, facing the center of the room. The centerpiece of the room is a full-sized carved statue of a nude human female, beckoning with arms out front in a very alluring pose. An ale keg, long since dry but still smelling slightly of the brew, is at rest in one corner.

This anteroom is through a south door from the dining room, and apparently was designed for before-dinner and after-dinner activity. Drinking was apparently the most popular pastime here, based on the presence of the numerous tankards and pegs for many more.

The stone walls are strangely textured for an unusual effect, but are devoid of further markings or details.

Those seated on the bench all face toward the center of the room and the statue there. This statue, apparently of white marble, is obviously of great value (worth at least 5,000 gp). However, due to its tremendous weight (approximately 1,200 pounds with the base) and the fact that it seems to be anchored to the floor, it is impossible to remove without a major engineering effort or the use of magic.

AREA 5 – WIZARD'S CHAMBER

Positioned in the center of this long hall is a rather plain table and three chairs. A detailed stone carving adorns most of the length of the north wall of the room. Some 90 feet in overall length, the wall carving depicts a mighty wizard on a hilltop casting a spell in the air over a valley below, with an entire army fleeing in confused panic. The east and west walls are devoid of detail, although there are several wall pegs on each, apparently for hanging garments. In the southeast corner of the room is an ornate wooden bed.

A diminutive humanoid wearing green robes is busy attempting to pry open a drawer in a nightstand near the bed.

The diminutive humanoid is a **gnome trickster** (see appendix B), Moth-gar, one of three triplets that have recently arrived at the dungeon searching for lost magic and wealth. See the sidebar for more information on these NPCs. Moth-gar assumes the characters are enemies and jumps behind the bed, gaining half cover. He casts a few offensive spells such as *chromatic orb* or *Tasha's hideous laughter*. Then he shouts an alarm, and casts *minor illusion* to simulate the sound of many guards approaching from area 7. He reserves *misty step* to escape out the door if reduced to 5 hit points or less.

This rather austere abode was Zelligar's personal chamber. The table and three chairs are typical wooden construction, if a bit dusty. Upon the table is a pewter pitcher (worth 15 gp) and three pewter mugs (each worth 5 gp).

Zelligar's bed, located in the southeast corner of the chamber, has a frame of ornately carved rosewood. The headboard, besides showing the carved designs to advantage, boldly features Zelligar's name highlighted in gold leaf. The bed, obviously of value, is of fine workmanship and construction. However, due to its sturdiness, it cannot be removed from the room without dismantling, and doing so is a difficult task likely to cause damage to the various pieces. If this is done, the baseboard and sides would be worth 100 gp each, and the headboard up to 500 gp. However, anyone trying to sell the headboard for its value runs an 80% risk that the purchaser recognizes the original owner's name (since the fame of Zelligar is widely known). If this word spreads at large, the seller may have attendant problems, since it will be obvious from where the headboard was obtained.

A rosewood nightstand/table is beside the bed, and it has one locked drawer. The brass handle to the drawer has a pin trap which is tripped by anyone grasping it, inflicting 1 piercing damage. An oily substance on the pin is not a poison, but it does inflict unusual pain which makes the grasping hand unusable by the victim for 20-50 ([1d4 + 1] x 10) minutes. If a key is inserted into the lock before the handle is grasped, the trap is disarmed. Any key of a size comparable to the actual key (which is nowhere to be found) can accomplish this function, or a successful DC 11 Dexterity check with another pointy object (a dagger tip, for example) also completes the task. The drawer itself contains a pouch of 17 ep, a large iron key (to the door in area 51), and two unlabeled potions. These are a *potion of healing* and a *potion of climbing*.

THE GNOME TRIPLETS

Three gnomish triplets (Moth-gar, Hoth-gar, and Roth-gar) have recently arrived at the complex with a band of gnomes (see areas 26 and 27). They are seeking long-lost lore and magic regarding Zelligar, and their leader (Roth-gar) thinks he can even locate the famous wizard's final resting place. The gnomes have all split up, each hoping to beat its other brothers to the ultimate prize. Assuming the characters encounter one of the tricksters and defeats him, subsequent encounters with the others should be confusing as they all dress the same. Each has barely discernible differing facial features, but it requires a successful DC 15 Intelligence (Investigation) check to determine they are different individuals.

AREA 6 – CLOSET

Zelligar's closet lies through a door on the south wall of his chamber.

The door opens to reveal a somewhat large closet, 20 feet by 20 feet, with an alcove situated in the opposite corner of the room. In one corner of the room, several bolts of cloth are stacked, and on one wall, several garments are hung, mostly coats and cloaks.

The room is rather large for a closet, but is actually somewhat barren for its size. The bolts of cloth are covered with dust, partially moth-eaten, and deteriorated. These are of no particular value. The cloaks and garments (five total) are quite musty in smell, as well as being dusty and dingy in appearance. Only one is remarkable, being studded with circular bits of pewter ornamentation. This bit of garb, however, has also suffered the ravages of age. While the first four garments are of no value, the last one could possibly bring up to 15 gp if sold.

A wooden stand in the corner of the room farthest from the door holds several books upon it. These large volumes are five in number, and apparently belong in the library (area 12).

Book #1. A historical work written in the Common tongue, this book outlines the history of the civilized area within 100 miles of the stronghold location. It contains nothing remarkable.

Book #2. This tome is apparently an encyclopedia of various types of plants. Although the various illustrations within provide a clue to its topic, it is written in Elvish, so it will not be understandable to a reader who does not know that tongue (unless a *comprehend languages* spell is used).

Book #3. This volume appears unremarkable at first glance, seeming to be a notebook with many handwritten entries of undecipherable runes and markings. It is actually a diary kept by Zelligar, and it details one of his adventures from the distant past, written in his own hand. The writing is not discernible unless a *comprehend languages* spell is used. This book is really of no value to any finder, but a book dealer/scribe/librarian would pay up to 50 gp for it. Of course, if the book is sold in this manner, the seller risks a 40% chance of word of its sale getting out as a rumor, with attendant problems developing as those who hear of it seek out the finder for further details.

Book #4. This work, written in Common, discusses weather. Although well-illustrated with drawings of meteorological phenomena, descriptive text is sparse. Some cryptic notes written in the margins were apparently made by Zelligar, but these are undecipherable without a *comprehend languages* spell and are actually nothing more than notes such as a student would make in studying the work to highlight important points.

Book #5. This book is titled "Outdoor Survival," penned by naturalist Sel Dourts in gnomish. It is a collection of short stories featuring a fictional (?) ranger named Aulfors and his trials of survival in the wilderness alone. This book would be very useful to the characters should they discover the teleportation portal in area 51 on the lower level.

Along one of the walls within the closet is an oil lantern which contains no fuel and which has obviously been unused for a great deal of time. If fuel is provided, the lantern is perfectly usable.

In the northwest corner of the closet is a small table with a stack of papers upon it. These are very dusty, and they are held in place by a stone slab paperweight which is monogrammed with a fancy letter "Z." The papers are written in Common and upon examination reveal notes on mundane matters: an inventory of foodstuffs, a financial accounting of expenses, notes on construction work for the complex, a couple of routine messages received by Zelligar, and other unremarkable writings. The most recent date on any of the papers is still more than three decades in the past.

AREA 7 – WIZARD'S ANNEX

The door reveals a 10-foot-wide passage that extends for 30 feet before widening. As your light source pierces the darkness, you are greeted by a magnificent sight. The spectacle is indeed impressive: two large wooden chests, each studded with jewels, overflowing with riches. A pile of gold pieces is arrayed around and within them, and scattered among this treasure trove is an assortment of glittering gems and jewels.

Another room off of Zelligar's chamber is this unusually-shaped annex. This room apparently was for meditation and study, as well as the practice of magic spells. The triangular widening at the south end of this room was apparently for this purpose, and the stone wall (although not noticeable to adventurers) is actually thicker than elsewhere in the complex. The floor near the south wall is bumpy and darkly discolored, as if charred and partially melted by intense heat. However, this fact is not discernible until the *programmed illusion* described below is dispelled.

In reality, the room is empty. The massive treasure is a *programmed illusion*, triggered by opening the door. The image lasts for 5 minutes, but it is temporarily dispelled as soon as the first bit of "treasure" is touched by any creature. Any character can spend an action to disbelieve the *programmed illusion* with a successful DC 17 Intelligence (Investigation) check. The illusion, once dispelled, reappears in the same place again within 10 minutes.

AREA 8 – WIZARD'S WORKROOM

Zelligar's workroom and laboratory (area 9) are located adjacent to each other, with limited access by secret doors. It has been recently discovered by one of the gnome trickster triplets, Hoth-gar. This chamber is hidden behind a secret door that can be found with a successful DC 15 Wisdom (Perception) check. Hoth-gar has left the secret door slightly ajar, so this check is made with advantage.

This chamber appears to be designed for various purposes related to the study and practice of magic. There are several large wooden tables within the room, one of which is overturned on its side, as well as one central table made of stone. The top of this prominent table is a slab of smooth black slate, although its cold black beauty is hidden by a thick layer of dust. None of the tables have anything upon them. There are several chairs and stools scattered about the room. Centered on the north wall is a door, flanked by numerous cabinets mounted on the wall about 4 feet high.

A short, somewhat portly figure in green robes balances on a wooden chair while rummaging through several opened cabinets along the north wall.

The portly figure is Hoth-gar, one of the **gnome trickster** (see appendix B) triplets, and he has just found a large jar of white powder. He carefully steps down off his perch and interacts with the characters while cradling the jar and edging his way to the stone table. After he determines the characters' intentions, he tosses the contents of the jar at a random target. The target needs to make a successful DC 11 Dexterity saving throw or become blinded by the powder. Next he tries to get under the stone table, gaining three-quarters cover, and casting *blur*. He follows this up with *ray of sickness* and *Melf's acid arrow*. Caught up in the thrill of battle, Hoth-gar fights to the death, and has a final trick up his sleeve.

He has recently found a *wand of wonder* but has no idea what it does. In desperation, he uses it with reckless abandon. The command word ("satunainen") for the wand is inscribed on the side, but in Draconic. The wand is fully charged, but has a thin crack. Each use carries a cumulative 10% chance of the wand breaking, releasing a burst of magical energy that causes 10 (3d6) force damage in a 10-foot burst. If this occurs the wand is rendered useless.

The cabinets are not locked, and contain various chemical compounds and supplies of no appreciable value in glass or earthen containers. There are 40 such containers, as well as one larger jar (described below). If the adventurers choose to open and examine the contents of any particular container, roll a die to determine the contents:

D20	Contents	Possible Types
1	Sand	White, brown, black
2	Water	Pure, brackish, holy, urine
3	Salt	Common, mineral
4	Sulfur	—
5	Wood chips	Hickory, pine, oak, ash, maple, walnut
6	Herbs	Dill, garlic, chives, basil, catnip, parsley
7	Vinegar	Red, white, yellow
8	Tree sap (hardened)	Pine, maple
9	Carbon	Coal, ash, graphite
10	Crushed stone	Quartz, granite, marble, shale, pumice, obsidian
11	Metal filings	Iron, tin, copper, brass
12	Blood	Human, orcish, dwarven, elven, dragon, halfling
13	Dung (hardened)	Human, canine, feline, dragon
14	Wine	White, red, alcohol (spoiled), fruit
15	Fungus powder	Mushroom, other
16	Oil	Vegetable, animal, petroleum, mineral
17	Insect bodies	Bees, flies, beetles, ants
18	Bone powder	Human, animal
19	Spice	Pepper, cinnamon, clove, paprika, oregano, nutmeg
20	Empty	—

If a die roll indicates duplication, use the column at the right of each entry to differentiate between substances of similar types. If adventurers try to ingest any substance, the Dungeon Master should handle the situation with reason accordingly. In not all cases will the contents be immediately identifiable. In the case of an uncertain substance not obviously identifiable, a successful DC 13 Intelligence check is needed to discern the contents. Up to two characters can attempt this skill check. If both fail, the contents remain a mystery.

The larger jar is of clear glass and seemingly contains a black cat's body floating in a clear, colorless liquid. If the large cork lid is unstopped, the liquid instantaneously evaporates, the cat suddenly springs to life, jumps out of the jar, meows loudly, and runs for the door. If the door is open, the cat dashes through and disappears. If the door is not open, the cat appears to pass through the door and disappears. The feline is not to be seen again. This occurrence has no special meaning other than to surprise and/or mystify the adventurers, as well as provide some fun for the Dungeon Master.

AREA 9 – WIZARD'S LABORATORY

The wizard's lab is a strange but fascinating place. Zelligar's experimentation with many kinds of magic led to a collection of equipment and devices which were stored here. This chamber is hidden behind a secret door that can be found with a successful DC 15 Wisdom (Perception) check.

Scattered about this 50-foot-by-30-foot chamber are several large wooden tables and a single heavy stone table. Dominating the room is a large human skeleton suspended from the ceiling in the northeast corner of the laboratory. A sunken fire pit, blackened and cold, is noticeable as the centerpiece of the room.

The tables, which are similar to those in area 8, are bare, except for a single stopped smoked glass bottle on one of them. If the cork is removed, the gas within immediately issues forth with a loud whoosh. The vapors are pungent and fast-acting, and all characters within 10 feet must make a successful DC 12 Wisdom saving throw. The gas itself is not poisonous, but magical in nature. A failed saving throw results in the target being affected by a *Tasha's hideous laughter* spell that lasts for 1 minute. Assuming one or more characters fail their save, the ensuing ruckus requires an immediate wandering monster check. If an encounter is indicated the monster(s) arrive in 1d4 rounds.

Although there is no way to determine this, the skeleton is the remains of a barbarian chieftain. The skull is cracked, but otherwise the skeleton is normal.

Several pine logs are piled underneath one of the tables, and if these are moved, a shiny gold ring can be found with a successful DC 10 Wisdom (Perception) check. Although it appears brilliant and seems to be worth up to 100 gp, a successful DC 13 Intelligence check reveals it is worthless and it has no special magical properties.

Along the west wall is a large wooden rack, apparently from some kind of torture chamber, since it is obviously sized for human bodies. A trickle of dried blood stains the oaken construction on the front.

On the south wall is a stretched leather skin with magical writings which are undecipherable without a successful DC 15 Intelligence (Arcana) check or a *comprehend languages* spell. The legend, if interpreted, reads: "What mysterious happenings have their birth here? Only the greatest feats of wizardry, for which every element of earth, water, and sky is but a tool!" The skin is old and extremely fragile, and any attempt to remove it causes irreparable harm and renders it useless because of the skin crumbling away.

The fire pit is only 2 feet deep, although it appears slightly less than that due to several inches of ashes resting within it. An iron bracing and bar across the 4-foot-wide opening suspends a cast-iron pot which is empty except for a harmless brown residue sticking to its interior sides and bottom. Another similar shallow pot, also empty, lies on the floor alongside the pit. Both pots are extremely heavy, weighing just over 75 pounds.

Off in the southwest corner are two vats, each of approximately 100-gallon capacity. Both are made of wood and both are empty. A third vat nearby, only half the size of its neighbors, is half-filled with murky, muddy water.

A stone block used as a table or stand is next to the vats situated along the west wall. It has six earthen containers just like those found in the workroom (area 8), and any contents within them should be determined in the same manner as described there. There are also pieces of glassware of various types on the top of the stand, as well as on the floor next to it. Some are clean and some show residues, but all are empty and dusty.

A wooden coffin rests upright in the northwest corner. Although the wood is rotting in places, it is quite plain and utilitarian and it opens easily. Inside is a nest of four **giant centipedes**, which burst forth to attack when the coffin is opened. Determine surprise as normal. The giant centipedes fight to the death, although if a character uses an action to slam the casket door shut, the giant centipedes eventually settle down back into their nest.

Two kegs rest against the north wall, and examination reveals them to be similar to those found in the storeroom (area 10). Each has a letter code to denote its contents, and a roll should be made in the same manner as described there to determine the contents if they are opened.

Wooden shelving on the north wall holds more glassware and three more containers (as those in area 8, with contents determined randomly). Two small trays hold powdered incense of different colors, and the smell of their aroma gives away their identity.

AREA 10 – STOREROOM

This chamber is hidden behind a secret door that can be found with a successful DC 15 Wisdom (Perception) check.

Beyond a secret door, this irregularly shaped room is somewhat triangular. It stretches for about 70 feet north to south, and nearly 40 feet east to west. Numerous casks and barrels are stacked along the walls, but there is plenty of room for additional supplies.

Approximately 60 barrels and casks are within the room, in two stacks. One stack is against the northwest wall and the other is along the east wall in the southern portion of the room. Although the casks and barrels storing the commodities have prevented spoilage, the contents are by no means "fresh." Although usable or edible still, they nonetheless have an off-taste which suggests staleness. These containers are each marked in some letter code to denote contents. If any individual barrel or cask is chosen for examination, a d20 is rolled on the following table to determine its code marking, and if it is broken open, the appropriate contents will be discovered:

D20	Code Letter(s)	Contents
1	TL	Whole barley
2	B	Wheat flour
3	FT	Rye flour
4	MK	Salt pork
5	GG	Dill pickles
6	HU	Raisins
7	EJ	Fish in brine
8	Y	Dried apples
9	PF	Whole peas
10	SD	Ale
11	Z	Honey
12	AW	Wine
13	OG	Water
14	XR	Soft soap
15	LC	Salt
16	VW	Lard
17	QS	Seasoning
18	RH	Sunflower seeds
19	UT	Hard candy
20	JS	Dried mushrooms

Note that any container opened and left unsealed, or containers whose contents have spilled, will attract vermin and/or monsters over a period of time. Spilled or uncovered material will also be subject to spoilage and rot. This is important if more than one foray into the stronghold is made, and time elapses between such adventures.

AREA 11 – SUPPLY ROOM

The stronghold's supply room is also rather empty, containing mostly construction supplies.

Going through the room reveals the following materials:

* A coil of very heavy rope, 200 feet in length
* A box of iron spikes (50)
* A box of metal nails (100)
* A pile of wooden beams, each 10 feet in length and 6 inches by 6 inches in width (80)
* A sack of building mortar, almost empty
* A stack of stone blocks, each about 6 inches by 6 inches by 12 inches in size (400)
* Six wooden doors, leaning in a row against a wall
* A large box of assorted hardware (including several locks of various types, door hinges, clasps and hasps, door handles, assorted metal bolts, and similar items)
* A jug of dried glue

AREA 12 – LIBRARY

Quasqueton's library lies behind a pair of ornately carved oaken doors.

The floor of the room is covered with dust, but beneath is a beautiful and shiny surface of polished red granite. The stone is inlaid in large blocks and extends uniformly to within a foot of each of the walls. In the very center of the room within the floor surface are blocks of white granite within the red stone, and these form the letters "R" and "Z" with an ampersand between. Wall sconces designed to hold torches for illumination are mounted on the walls all around the room.

There are three large oaken tables within the room, one in each of the west, north, and east wings of the room. There are several wooden chairs scattered about. In two corners of the room are plush divans, each covered with a rich, fleecy upholstering that makes them very comfortable for reclining. These, however, are rather dusty and dingy due to their age and lack of use.

Hanging from the sconces inset into the north wall are small metal cages, each containing a large beetle. These unusual insects give off an eerie, glowing light from their bodies, enough to illuminate this portion of the room with a forbidding reddish glow. Comfortably seated at a table in the northern alcove, engrossed in a voluminous tome, is short humanoid clad in thick green robes.

The short humanoid is one of the **gnome trickster** (see appendix B) triplets, Roth-gar. He is shocked by the characters' arrival, granting them surprise. Once he regains his composure he interacts, attempting to cast *charm person* on one or more of the characters. Should that fail, he tries to cast *sleep*, using a 2nd-level slot to affect more targets. He doesn't hesitate to pull an animal from his *brown bag of tricks* (see appendix A) to cover his escape.

Roth-gar carries a leather-bound diary full of notes on Zelligar. One page is earmarked pertaining to rumors regarding Zelligar's final resting place. It contains the phrase "Sel Dourts will show the way to Zelligar." Roth-gar knows Sel Dourts to be a famous author, and is searching for any books penned by him. There is one, but it is currently in area 6. A successful DC 15 Intelligence (History) check reveals who Sel Dourts was. But only another successful DC 24 Intelligence (History) check reveals that his most famous character created was Aulfors, a ranger survivalist, whose name is the password to activate the portal in area 51. Consulting a sage (at a cost of 25 gp and a few days' research) can reveal the name Aulfors as well.

The glowing beetles seem to be thriving in their captive abode, but their food source and longevity are totally puzzling. The cages lack any doors. Each of these insects is actually a variant *continual flame* spell.

The library is rather modestly supplied with books, volumes, and tomes of various sizes. There are likewise only a few nonmagical scrolls, these being stored in a rack along the east wall. None of the books or scrolls is of any particular use or special interest to the adventurers, despite how many they examine. Unless the DM has other designs…

AREA 13 – IMPLEMENT ROOM

DM Note: There is a trap in the corridor outside the door to this storeroom, just beyond it to the east. The trap is sprung when one or more adventurers reach a point 10 feet in front of the dead-end wall, in which case the portcullis is noisily dropped 20 feet to the rear of that point. The trap trigger can be discovered with a successful DC 15 Wisdom (Perception) check.

The bars of the portcullis are rusty and weak. There are 12 vertical bars and several cross members. The bars can be lifted or bent with a successful DC 22 Strength check.

This elongated room is used primarily for storage of tools, equipment, and implements of various types.

In the room are the following items:

- A box of wooden pegs
- A coil of light rope, 50 feet long
- A coil of heavy chain, 70 feet long
- A coil of fine copper wire, 20 feet long
- Mining picks (32), all unusable and in poor repair
- Chisels (15)
- Shovels (13)
- Empty barrels (11)
- Mallets (8)
- Iron bars (29), each measuring 1 inch in diameter by 8 feet long
- An iron vise (12-inch jaws)
- Mining jacks (2), broken
- Crosscut saws (2), two-man
- Hacksaws (4)
- A mason's toolbox (containing trowel, stone chisel, plumb line, etc.)
- A cobbler's toolbox (containing small hammer, knife, heavy needles, etc.)
- A small barrel of non-fletched arrows (60), all normal
- An empty wooden bench, 10 feet long

On the north wall, fairly well concealed considering its size, is a counterweight mechanism for the portcullis trap in the corridor just outside the room. It can be located with a successful DC 12 Wisdom (Perception) check. This lever can be used to raise the barrier once it has been tripped. No more than two characters at a time can attempt to use the lever to raise the portcullis, and it requires a successful DC 18 Strength check to activate.

The hacksaws can be used to cut through the portcullis, but this is a long and arduous process. If one saw is employed, it requires 24 hours of use to cut through the bars. Each additional hacksaw reduces the time by 6 hours, although a character can only employ one hacksaw. The sawing generates significant noise and at the Dungeon Master's discretion, this may attract wandering monsters beyond the normal chances. Additionally, each saw has a 20% chance of its blade breaking in any 6-hour period, and there are no extra blades. If all attempts to escape fail, the persons trapped are doomed to their fate.

AREA 14 – AUXILIARY STOREROOM

This chamber is hidden behind a secret door that can be found with a successful DC 15 Wisdom (Perception) check.

This 20-foot-by-20-foot chamber appears to be a storeroom. In the northwest corner of the room is a pile of rubble.

This extra storeroom is empty of goods and supplies. There is nothing unusual in the rubble.

AREAS 15 & 16 – TELEPORTATION ROOMS

A strong magic *teleport* effect has been permanently placed upon these two rooms of equal size and shape. Zelligar was fascinated with teleportation and magic portals, and these rooms were his first attempt to create permanent, linked teleport gates. The result is likely to confuse unwary adventurers and upset their directional sense.

The door opens to reveal a plain room 30 feet wide and 20 feet deep. In the corner of the room opposite the door is a sparkling outcropping of crystalline rock which shimmers with vibrant purple once reflected off your light source.

Both rooms appear identical and function in the same manner once their doors are opened. Once adventurers enter the room to investigate this, the entire party is instantly *teleported* to identical locations at the other room, whether the characters are in the room itself or nearby in the hallway. This *teleportation* occurs without the characters noticing that it has occurred; that is, they have no way of "feeling" that anything unusual has happened. And of course, this means that, although they are in a different location facing in different directions, the adventurers still have reason to believe that they entered the room through a door which is on the east wall (if they originally entered room 15), or through a door which is on the south wall (if they originally entered room 16). To reflect this fact without tipping off the players, the Dungeon Master must turn his or her map on its side in order to be able to correspond to the directions the players believe they are facing. Of course, when the players emerge from one of the rooms and attempt to follow their maps, they will be confused by the fact that the details outside the room are not as they expect. They may question the Dungeon Master and even suspect a mistake has been made (with such comments as, "Wait a minute, that can't be like that, we just came that way!"). When this occurs, the Dungeon Master should avoid argument and simply state things as they are in the new location, letting players puzzle over the problem and arrive at their own conclusions and/or solutions.

Once the *teleportation* has been triggered in a room, it will not occur again until the room is empty and the door has been closed from the outside. It will thereafter be triggered when the door is opened and the room is entered. The door of the receiving room (the one to which the party is being *teleported*) always appears exactly as the door of the first room entered. Doors to both rooms automatically close themselves and the rooms become "ready" to be triggered whenever all adventurers have passed to a point at least 120 feet from either door, as measured down any corridors. It is possible, however, that a party could trigger the trick, be *teleported* to the other room, then blunder back upon the original room, see that the two were identical but in different locations, and discover what had occurred. On the other hand, the characters could become totally confused, lose their way with an inaccurate map, and experience all kinds of difficulty.

AREA 17 – CHAR STORAGE CELLAR

This 20-foot-by-20-foot room is covered with blackish soot and dust. There is a small pile of coal against the north wall.

This room is used for storing fuel for the smithy across the hallway. There is a false door on the west wall of the room. It cannot be opened, although it does seem to rest in a frame and even rattles or moves ever so slightly when character tries to open it.

AREA 18 – SMITHY

This chamber is slightly cooler, with air not as stale as the previous chamber. A faint, almost haunting whistling can be heard. The door opens to a 30-foot-by-20-foot room that is mostly barren save for an assortment of tools and irons hanging on the walls, and a thick coat of dust. Off this main room, to the northeast, is another 20-foot-by-20-foot area, complete with three fire pits and a massive anvil.

The smithy is an irregularly shaped room, actually two separate areas. The larger, southwest portion of the smithy is mostly barren, with the blacksmith's tools and irons all being mundane and of typical use. Pokers, tongs, and hammers are all represented. Three fire pits lie dormant in the smaller, northeast section of the room. One is located along the north wall, one is in the northeast corner, and the last is on the east wall. In the center of the room is a gigantic forging anvil. A hand bellows hangs on the wall to the west.

The eerie wind (and pleasant, cooler, fresher air) that whistles through the room near the ceiling is a natural effect providing exhaust venting when the fires were stoked with fuel—but this smithy has not seen active use in decades.

AREA 19 – ACCESS ROOM

This room adjoins the smithy and provides a vertical access to the lower level of the stronghold.

In the northeast corner of this 20-foot-square room and along the north wall are log sections of various sizes stacked in a pile. A similar door is opposite the one just opened. In the southeast portion of the room there is a large hole in the floor about 3 feet across. The room is otherwise empty.

The wood sections range from 8 to 24 inches in diameter and 1 to 4 feet in length. They were apparently used as additional fuel for the blacksmith's fires.

If light is held from above and observation is attempted, it is impossible to see how deep the hole is or to where it gives access. If a light source (such as a torch) is cast down the hole, it comes to rest on the floor of the lower level, approximately 40 feet below. The floor below is a small cave just east of area 56 on the lower level.

There is a large iron ring anchored to the south wall near the hole, and if a rope is fastened to it, it can be used to assist in descending to the lower level. The fastening, however, is a bit loose, and each person using the rope has a 1 in 6 chance (non-cumulative) of pulling the ring out of the wall, causing them and the rope to fall to the floor of the lower level. This chance is 2 in 6 for any persons with sizable encumbrance (weighing in excess of 250 pounds). If any person falls, they do so near the end of the descent and thus only suffer 2 (1d4) bludgeoning damage. Once the ring has been removed from the wall, it cannot be replaced to be usable again.

As an alternative to using the ring, clever characters could use one of the logs in the room measuring 4 feet in length, tie the rope around it, place it across the 3-foot opening, and climb down the suspended cord. For purposes of descent, any rope must be at least 30 feet in length. In order to allow a return back up, the rope must be at least 35 feet in length so that it can be reached from below while suspended. Climbing down (or up) the rope requires a successful DC 10 Strength (Athletics) check.

The final method for possible descent is to use a rope and grapple, either attaching the hook or tying the rope to the iron ring, or anchoring it to one of the two doorways. If a rope is attached at the south doorway, add 10 feet to the required length. Add 20 feet if the north doorway is used as the anchor point.

AREA 20 – DEAD END ROOM

The room at the end of this corridor has been converted to a guard chamber by the band of kobolds that lair in the Lonely Tower, above. Seven **kobolds** are stationed here, each one located at one of the corners of the corridor. As soon as intruders approach, the kobolds alert the others via hand signals and then charge, leading with spears (+0 to hit, 1d8 - 2 piercing damage).

The turning corridor winds inward until ending in a dead-end room measuring 20 feet by 30 feet. The walls of this room are unfinished. The stuffy room smells faintly of animal, and seven straw pallets are strewn about the floor. A rickety metal spiral staircase disappears up a shaft into the ceiling.

The kobolds here have converted this room into a guard room, protecting the way above.

The staircase leads to the Lonely Tower, 30 feet above (see chapter 7). If more than 150 pounds of weight are placed on the staircase, there is a 35% chance per round that the staircase collapses. It takes 2 rounds to climb the staircase. The kobolds weight about 75 pounds each, so they only risk collapse if three of more use the stairs at a time. If the staircase does collapse, any creatures on it must make a DC 15 Dexterity saving throw, or suffer 10 (3d6) bludgeoning damage and gain the stunned condition for 1 minute. Success indicates only 3 (1d6) bludgeoning damage and no stunning effect. The access passage now requires a successful DC 10 Strength (Athletics) check to scale.

In one of the straw pallets is a hidden pouch that holds three jade playing pieces (each worth 15 gp). The pouch can be located with a successful DC 15 Wisdom (Perception) check.

Development. The kobolds fight to the death, although if four are defeated, one flees up the spiral staircase to alert the inhabitants of the Lonely Tower. If the staircase collapses, the occupants of the Lonely Tower are on alert.

AREA 21 – MEETING ROOM

The wooden door concealing this chamber is falling apart. On close examination it appears to have been chewed in locations, a hint regarding the current occupants of the room beyond.

This long and narrow room apparently served as some kind of auditorium or meeting area. There are 10 overturned wooden benches scattered about the room, each approximately 15 feet in length. A large stone slab at the north end of the room serves as a sort of stage, rising 10 inches off the floor to accommodate any speakers and place them in full view of any assemblage. On the north wall are four decorative cloth banners of red, green, blue, and yellow. Although once attractive, they are now deteriorated and rotting.

The wooden benches are normal, and the decorative banners were once valuable, but in their current condition are now worthless.

The jumble of benches and other debris serves as the nest for a pack of nine **giant rats**. Any character entering more than 10 feet into the chamber disturbs these rodents of unusual size, precipitating their attack. The debris and clutter of the benches is equivalent to difficult terrain to the characters, but not the giant rats. The agile rodents are adept at clambering over and under the morass of items strewn about, attacking with ease. The giant rats fight to the death.

A successful DC 13 Wisdom (Perception) check reveals a collection of shiny baubles underneath a pile of cloth, burlap, and deteriorated tapestries. Valuables include 11 sp, 5 gp, three small pieces of purple quartz (each worth 25 gp), and a silver pin set with three diminutive emeralds (worth 115 gp).

AREA 22 – GARDEN ROOM

Once the showplace of the entire stronghold, the garden has, over the passage of time, become a botanical nightmare. With no one to tend the gardens, the molds and fungi have grown out of control.

Approaching the room from the corridor to the south reveals an eerie and forbidding sight, as unusual growths have extended themselves from within the room into the corridor, spreading inexorably onward and away from the garden room. Passing this feature and entering the room reveals a sight totally unlike any ever seen in the outside world. Continue with the following:

The floor is covered with a carpet of tufted molds that extends to all the walls and even onto parts of the ceiling, obscuring the rock surface. The molds appear in a rainbow assortment of colors, and they are mixed in their appearance, with splotches, clumps, swirls, and patches presenting a nightmarish combination of clashing colors. This is indeed a fuzzy fairyland of the most forbidding sort, although beautiful in its own mysterious way . . .

The room has two major portions, a north arm and a west arm. At the end of each of these extensions are large semicircular stone formations overgrown with fungoid matter. In the southeast corner of the room is another similar outcropping likewise covered with the underground vegetation. In the center of the northern wing are two large sunken pits, each 10 feet by 20 feet in size.

All around the room are fungi of a hundred different kinds. These are scattered in patches and clumps of growth. There are many different types of mushrooms such as common toadstools, fungi as shelf types, giant puffballs, coral fungi, and morels. There is even a grove of giant fungi with tree-like stems and 8-foot-diameter caps. The various growths all seem to be thriving, although any nutrient source is well covered by their proliferation. Perhaps some strange magic or extraordinary means keeps this incredible garden alive and growing . . .

Although passage through the room is possible, the various types of growth are treated as difficult terrain. Furthermore, any kind of mass movement or commotion (such as a melee) releases small clouds of spores which obscure vision and are unpleasant to breathe. Targets are required to make a successful DC 10 Constitution saving throw, or gain the poisoned condition for 1 hour.

If any character attempts to ingest a certain type of fungus, roll 1d6 and consult the table below to determine the effects. The Dungeon Master is encouraged to create more effects as appropriate.

D6	Description	Effect
1	Purple toadstool	Poisonous (DC 12 Constitution saving throw or suffer 10 (3d6) poison damage and gain the poisoned condition for 1 hour)
2	Pink puffball	Tasty; provides nourishment for 1 day
3	Brown shelf fungus	Poisonous (DC 10 Constitution save or suffer 13 (3d8) poison damage and fall unconscious for 30 minutes)
4	Pasty white puffball	Poisonous (DC 10 Constitution saving throw or fall asleep for 4d6 minutes)
5	Red toadstool with white spots	Heals 1d3 hit points (1/day)
6	Blue-gray morel	Vile; turns tongue blue and induces nausea for 1d8 minutes

Near the sunken pits, scattered among the normal fungus is a trio of **shriekers**, indistinguishable from the other fungi due to their False Appearance trait. These man-sized toadstools come in a variety of colors and textures. If a character or light source approaches within 30 feet, they emit a piercing shriek until the source moves away. Even so, the sound continues for 1d4 more rounds. Although harmless, the shrieking does gain the attention of the kobolds in area 20, and 1d3 of the humanoids come to investigate in 1d4 rounds, approaching from the south, ready for a fight.

At the far north end of the garden are the remains of an adventurer that met its demise years ago. Its skeleton is covered with tiny spores and fungi, requiring a successful DC 17 Wisdom (Perception) check to discover. Its leather armor is ruined, as are the rotting remnants of clothes, belt, and boots. A normal shortsword lies nearby, and under the body (if moved, triggering a cloud of spores as described above) is a silver dagger with a black dragonskin-wrapped handle (worth 75 gp). Near the skeleton is a **violet fungus** which attacks with its rotting touch anyone examining the skeletal remains.

AREA 23 – STORAGE ROOM

This 20-foot-by-30-foot room is cluttered with three large oaken tables, a number of chairs, and numerous wooden stools stacked against the walls. In the corner opposite the door is a woodworking table with a crude vise attached, and small saws and other carpenter's equipment are thereon. Wood chips and sawdust are scattered about the stone floor.

This room is used primarily for furniture storage, although it is mostly empty now. There is a total of 14 stools, and all the furniture is sturdy, normal construction.

AREA 24 – MISTRESS' CHAMBER

This room is more tastefully decorated than the rather spartan living quarters found elsewhere in the stronghold. It was the personal chamber of Rogahn's mistress and lover, who apparently lived at the stronghold for some time. But now it appears that she, along with so many others who lived here, has long since been gone.

This room is 40 feet long and 20 feet wide. There is a large walnut bed against the west wall, rather ornately carved. The bed has a large canopy of embroidered green cloth with a striking reddish trim, but it is very dusty like everything else in the room. Next to the bed is a small table/nightstand with a single drawer. Beside it against the wall is a chest of drawers composed of reddish wood. A full-length mirror with a wooden frame rests centered on the north wall. On the east wall is a small tapestry.

The bed somewhat resembles a similar piece of furniture in area 5, but it lacks a name engraved on the headboard.

The chest of drawers is made from red cedar, which despite its age, still has the characteristic smell. In the drawers are an assortment of leather items, old clothing, and personal effects like combs, brushes, and hairpins. One comb is a silver-plated item which is of moderate value, being worth 5 gp. On top of the chest is a tortoiseshell dish which is empty except for a single gold coin lying in it, and this rests upon a frilly lace cloth along with two small capped bottles half full of perfume.

On the north wall is a secret door that can be discovered with a successful DC 20 Wisdom (Perception) check. Beyond is a 40-foot-long corridor that ends in a blank wall. Concealed on this wall is another secret door, but this one is relatively easy to find and trigger, requiring but a successful DC 12 Wisdom (Perception) check. This door opens to area 25.

To the left of the secret door in this room is a large full-length wall mirror in a wooden frame. The crown of the frame is carved into attractive curving designs, and there is an inscription hewn into the finished wood which says in Common, "To the fairest of all in my eyes."

In the northwest corner of the room is an attractive water basin which is sculpted from the same rock which forms the wall of the room. Indeed, this protrusion is an integral part of the wall itself. A hole in the bottom of the basin is stopped with a rotting cork. This crude drain lets water drop onto an inclined piece of rock which drains into a crack in the wall. There is no running water in the room, however.

A small tapestry measuring 3 feet by 4 feet hangs on the east wall. It depicts a handsome and robust warrior carrying off a beautiful maiden in a rescue scene set in a burning village, with a horde of ominous-looking enemies viewing from afar. Embroidered in gold cloth at the top of the scene are the words, "Melissa, the most dearly won and greatest of all my treasures." The tapestry is within a wooden frame, and is firmly anchored to the wall. It can only be removed without damaging it with a successful DC 17 Dexterity check. If damaged, the tapestry only fetches 40 gp, but if removed without damage, it is worth 160 gp.

AREA 25 – ROGAHN'S CHAMBER

This chamber is at the end of a hall, concealed behind a secret door that requires a successful DC 20 Wisdom (Perception) check to discover. Beyond, Rogahn's personal quarters are rather simple and spartan, showing his taste for the utilitarian rather than regal.

The curving walls of the room are immediately noticeable as different from all others in the stronghold, not only due to their layout, but also because of their covering. The walls are covered with vertical strips of rough-finished fir wood, and these narrow planks run in single pieces from floor to ceiling. The construction is not remarkable nor is it fancy in any respect, but the result is strikingly pleasing to the eye. Each corner of the room displays an ornate tapestry. Along the east wall is a bed of maple wood, with a feather mattress. The baseboard has an engraved letter "R" on it, but the bed is otherwise devoid of detail. A free-standing cabinet of wood matching the bed is alongside it.

Although unique, the bed is of no exceptional value. Discarded under the bed is a normal longsword with a fancy basket guard shaped like four claws extended toward the blade. This was Rogahn's first blade, but more importantly is needed to unlock the door in area 40 on the lower level.

Inside the cabinet are some garments of general use: cloaks, a leather vest, a buckskin shirt, a metal corselet, etc., as well as a pair of boots. None is of any exceptional value. A wooden stool is near the cabinet, but there is no other furniture in the room.

In addition to the secret door on the west wall, there are two additional secret doors on the south wall. One leads to area 24, while the other leads to area 27. The former served as access to Rogahn's mistress' chamber, while the latter served as an escape route. All three doors are triggered by depressing one of the wooden wall boards in just the right location. Each door can be located with a successful DC 20 Wisdom (Perception) check.

In each of the four curved corners of the room is a different wall hanging. These tapestries are each 6 feet wide and approximately 8 feet high. The four subjects depicted are:

- A dragon being slain by a group of warriors, with one standing prominently at the front of the group, thrusting the killing sword into the dragon's neck.

- A great battle in a mountain pass, with a small band of fighters led by a great wizard and a single hero putting an entire army to flight.

- A warrior and a maiden on horseback against a backdrop of mountains, holding hands with joyful expressions.

- A depiction of a hero and a wizard joining in a firm handclasp on a deserted hilltop, with only a sunset in the background.

The principals in all these panoramas—as well as the tapestry in room 24—are, of course, the same. The warrior/hero is Rogahn, the wizard is Zelligar, and the beautiful maiden is the Fair Melissa, Rogahn's mistress. The tapestries are bulky (each weighs 25 pounds), but they are worth 100 gp each.

AREA 26 – TROPHY ROOM

The stronghold's trophy room consists of an assortment of various curiosities accumulated over the years. A group of gnomes loyal to the gnome trickster triplets are initially here searching the room, but unless the characters dispatch their fellows in area 27 quietly, they respond to the battle in that location. If the gnomes are encountered here, be sure to modify the following read-aloud text:

This 40-foot-by-20-foot hall appears to be a museum or trophy room of sorts. Numerous odds and ends are displayed, including a reptilian hide on the north wall, a statue of a many-legged reptile in a menacing pose, and a diminutive yet stocky skeleton suspended in irons on the west wall. Displayed on the east wall is an entire wooden door, bound with black iron and bearing strange runes.

A variety of interesting mementos from Zelligar and Rogahn's exploits are displayed in this chamber. Most can be identified with a successful DC 15 Intelligence check. These include:

- Covering most of the north wall is an immense dragon's skin, its brassy scales revealing its type. The scales are polished to reflect any illumination brightly.

- The stone statue at the west end of the room is an actual basilisk frozen in stone, victim of its own gaze. Although menacing, its gaze is no longer a threat.

- On the east wall is a dwarf skeleton, suspended from a pair of irons near the ceiling, giving the entire chamber a macabre presence.

- Two gigantic sets of moose antlers each on a large moose skull.

- Four dragon paws with claws extended (brass).

- A stuffed cockatrice (worth 75 gp, as a curiosity).

- A massive black shield, usable only by a Huge creature.

- A pair of ram's horns.

- A pair of crossed greatswords. Although they appear normal, one is a *+1 greatsword*.

- A bearskin (worth 125 gp).

- An entire door bearing religious symbols. A successful DC 13 Intelligence (Religion) check reveals the deity and meaning of these runes (as determined by the Dungeon Master).

- A set of three colorful flags depicting a wolf, a toothed whale, and an ice bear. A successful DC 12 Intelligence (History) check reveals these to be the standards for several prominent barbarian tribes to the north.

Development. If encountered here, five **gnomes** (see appendix B) are searching the room for anything that might be valuable. When the characters open the door, they stop and draw weapons, ready for a fight. They are resistant to using their alchemist's fire in this room for fear of ruining any potential treasures, so instead they employ shortswords or light crossbows as appropriate. If three are defeated, the remaining two flee or surrender.

AREA 27 – THRONE ROOM

The throne room, mostly for show, is reminiscent of a ballroom of small size, although it is impossible to know the room's actual purpose. The bulk of gnomes loyal to the trickster triplets have set up camp here while their leaders explore the complex.

This great hall is 60 feet long and 40 feet wide, with an expanded ceiling reaching 20 feet above. The floor is smooth black slate. Four sets of two pillars lead to an elevated platform at the opposite end of the chamber, all constructed of great blocks of red granite. Two throne-like chairs are sculpted from gigantic blocks of white marble. Great draperies in alternating panels of yellow and purple hang on the wall behind the raised platform. Strewn about the hall are numerous bedrolls, and blankets tended by numerous small humanoids.

There is bedding for 12 **gnomes** (see appendix B), although only seven are present at the current time. These humanoids are evil to the core and seek to plunder the riches from this complex, and consider all others fierce competitors. They have already clashed with the kobolds and the barbarians elsewhere, and are ready for a fight. They use the pillars and thrones as cover and are fond of tossing vials of alchemist's fire. A few might flee down the southern west passage to loop around to attack the characters from the rear. This trek takes about 3 rounds. In general, they fight to the death although one or two might flee to alert one of the triplets.

The thrones, due to their bulk and weight, are for all intents and purposes permanent fixtures. The tapestries are of no unusual value, although they add considerably to the appearance of the room, despite their color clash with the various shades of stone. A small wooden box is hidden behind one of the thrones under a pile of burlap. The unlocked box contains 187 sp, 41 gp, and a small red garnet (worth 75 gp).

The secret door in the northeast corner of the room is concealed behind one of the great tapestries. The door is triggered by pulling down on a nearby empty torch sconce. Strangely, this is the only sconce in the entire hall, calling attention to the presence of the hidden door. Otherwise, a successful DC 15 Wisdom (Perception) check reveals the secret door.

Development. If a battle breaks out in this chamber, and the gnomes in area 26 have not been encountered yet, they burst out of the chamber with loaded crossbows and join the fray after 2 rounds.

AREA 28 – WORSHIP AREA

The stronghold's worship area is no more than a token gesture to the gods, it would seem.

On the back wall of the room, opposite the door, is a rock carving of a great idol which is actually sculpted from the wall itself. The idol depicts a humanoid with a horned head sporting an evil visage and appears to be about 4 feet wide and 6 feet high. The walls nearby are surrounded by religious symbols and runes. The floor is smooth black slate. In the center of the room is a circular pit, which measures 5 feet across.

The idol depicts a demonic figure. If closely examined, it becomes obvious that the eye sockets are empty. They once held precious gemstones, long since removed. If the dust is disturbed in the front of the idol, blackened char marks are discovered, evidence that a magical fire trap was triggered, likely during the removal of the gems.

The pit is open and slopes to a maximum depth of 3 feet. It is empty save for a few inches of residual ash at the bottom.

AREA 29 – CAPTAIN'S CHAMBER

This room was the living quarters for Erig, Rogahn's friend and comrade in arms. It is a rather simple room with few furnishings.

When the characters approach the exterior door to this chamber, continue below:

The door to the room is a large wooden construction just like the others in the stronghold, but its exterior surface is embellished with an irregularly-shaped leather skin covering, which is studded with circular bits of brass which form the word "ERIG" prominently.

When the characters open the door, continue below:

The door opens into a rather barren room. In the southeast corner is a crude bed, and alongside it is a table. On the south wall is a wooden chest with metal bands. In the northeast corner of the room is a wooden keg stand with a single barrel upon it. On the wall at the western extremity of the room are numerous pegs and brackets, apparently for holding arms and armor.

On top of the table is a small, covered stoneware crock which contains 5 gp, a large earthenware tankard mug, and a small hand mirror.

The wooden chest is locked and requires thieves' tools and a successful DC 18 Dexterity check to pick the lock. If opened, its contents are revealed: several garments including a pair of pants, several cloaks, a heavy cloth coat, and two pairs of boots. A broken dagger is at the bottom of the chest underneath the clothing. A leather pouch also therein contains an unusual memento, a walnut plaque with an inlaid piece of silver engraved with the words, "To Erig, great and trusted fighter by my side, and captain of the guard at Quasqueton—against all foes we shall prevail!" It is signed with an embellished "R." This plaque is of some value, and could bring up to 25 gp if sold.

The barrel is marked with a letter code of "SD" and is full and untapped. If the keg is broken open, ale will issue forth.

The wall pegs are mostly empty, except for two shields and a heavy mace hanging thereon.

AREA 30 – ACCESS ROOM

This room provides access to the lower level of the stronghold by a descending stairway.

This 30-foot-by-20-foot chamber is devoid of contents. The floor is smooth flagstone, and the stone walls are plain. An alcove in the northwest corner of the room leads to a stairway descending to a lower level.

This stairway leads directly down into area 38 on the lower level.

AREA 31 – ROOM OF POOLS

This is largest room on the upper level, and is quite different from all the others.

Although the walls are the typical rough blackish stone as the rest of the complex, the floor of this room is covered with ceramic tiles arranged in mosaic fashion. The majority of the thousands of tiles are golden brown in color, but patterns of white and black tiles appear in various places to enhance the effect of the very striking designs formed. Arrayed throughout the room are 14 different pools, each about 10 feet in diameter, with sides sloping down to the center. This mystical arrangement is doubly amazing, since all the contents of the pools appear to be different.

The designs (various flowing lines, etc.) are purely decorative, and carry no mysterious message or meaning. The secret door on the east wall can be found with a successful DC 20 Wisdom (Perception) check. The trigger is a concealed knob on the rough-hewn wall that needs to be depressed to open the door. The door hides passage to area 32.

The individual pools are each 5 feet deep. They are letter coded "a" to "n," corresponding to the map, and require close examination to reveal the details of each's contents:

a) Pool of Healing. This pool radiates evocation magic, and a clue to its function can be discerned with a successful DC 22 Intelligence (Arcana) check. It contains a strange pinkish liquid that causes instantaneous healing when ingested. It can also cure diseases as a *lesser restoration* spell, but does not restore hit points in doing so. Whenever a drink is taken, 1d6 hit points of individual damage are restored immediately to the drinker, although this can only be done once per day per person. Additional consumption by the same creature has no additional effect. Although the liquid can be placed into containers and removed from the pool, the healing properties immediately disappear once it is removed from this basin.

DM Note: Although this magical pool is always present on the characters' first visit to this room, this pool disappears and reappears from time to time magically. If characters return to this room, there is only a 30% chance that the liquid is present again.

b) Pool of Acid. This pool is filled to the brim with a clear, fizzing liquid which gives off a strange and unpleasant aroma to those near it. It is full of deadly acid. If any creature falls or leaps within it, certain and immediate death is the result. Putting a hand or other body member within it results in an immediate 3 (1d4 + 1) acid damage. At the Dungeon Master's discretion, increase the acid damage if a greater portion of the body is exposed to the liquid. Drinking any of the liquid (even but a sip) causes immediate gagging and 20 (5d6 + 3) acid damage, although a successful DC 15 Constitution saving throw reduces the damage by half. Putting just a drop or two to the tongue will cause the loss of 1 hit point, plus induce gagging and choking for 2 rounds. Weapons or other objects dipped into the acid are subject to acid damage as well and may even be ruined completely; consult pp. 246-247 of the Dungeon Master's Guide for information on damaging objects. The strength of the acid is such that it eats through any type of container within 1 minute. A single brass key, about 6 inches long, is visible at the bottom of the pool, seemingly unaffected by the acid. This key, if somehow retrieved, is worthless and it does not correspond to any of the locks within the stronghold. (At the DM's discretion, this key may unlock the door to Zelligar's Secret Laboratory—see chapter 7.)

c) Pool of Sickness. This pool is filled with a murky gray syrup. If any of it is consumed (even but a sip), the victim begins to suffer sickness, but not until 1 hour afterwards. If this occurs, there is no loss of hit points, but the victim suffers from strong and recurring stomach pains for 1d4 hours, after which all symptoms pass and the character returns to normal. Combat, skill checks, and all saving throws are at disadvantage and the character's movement is reduced to 0 feet for that period, although a victim could be carried by others. Placing a drop of liquid upon the tongue reveals a sweet taste, but incurs no symptoms. Weapons or other items placed within the liquid are totally unaffected. Any portion of the liquid removed from the pool will lose its special properties within 1 minute.

d) Green Slime Pool. The horrid contents of this pool are immediately obvious to any gazing into it with a successful DC 15 Intelligence (Nature) check. The **green slime** (see Dungeon Master's Guide p. 105) is covering the walls of the basin most of the way from the bottom to the edge. Its pseudopods can extend 5 feet to a target, although an aware target can make a DC 10 Dexterity saving throw to avoid it. If unaware, the target's saving throw is at disadvantage.

e) Drinking Pool. This pool is filled with icy cold spring water which refreshes anyone who takes a drink from it. The water is pure and quenching, but has no other special characteristics.

f) Pool of Wine. This pool is filled with powerful wine of a deep red color. Not only is it excellent wine, it has a taste so inviting that anyone tasting it is be prone to drink more and more until intoxicated! If a sip is taken, the taster needs to succeed at a DC 15 Wisdom saving throw or drink more. If the wine is consumed a second time, the target needs to succeed at a DC 15 Constitution saving throw, or become intoxicated for 6 hours. Each hour, another Constitution saving throw can be attempted to shake off the effects of drunkenness. Any character so intoxicated makes all attacks and skill checks at disadvantage, plus any other results of being drunk that the DM may deem

appropriate. This could include being prone to loud and boisterous speech, stumbling about, a greater chance to be surprised, etc. Any intoxicated character who returns to the pool of wine is required to make the Wisdom saving throw at disadvantage with failure requiring another Constitution saving throw. If any of the wine is removed from the room, it immediately loses its potency and is considered as normal wine.

g) Dry Pool. This depression is completely dry, and there is no trace of any liquid within it, or any clue as to whether any type of fluid was ever within it. The basin itself seems to be some kind of yellowish ceramic material, but it is impervious to striking or any similar attempt at cracking or fracturing.

h) Hot Pool. This steaming and bubbling cauldron is filled with boiling water, which will be obvious to any observer. The water itself is completely normal in all other respects, although it has a relatively high mineral content, as evidenced by a whitish crust built up around the edge of the pool.

i) Aura Pool. This pool of shimmering water (which otherwise appears normal in every respect) is less full than many of the others. The water itself seems to glisten and sparkle, and radiates divination magic if an attempt to *detect magic* is made. The water tastes normal in every respect, but those drinking as little as a single sip experience a strange effect. Upon swallowing the liquid, the drinker feels his or her entire body tingle, and at the same time the character and others in the area observe a visual phenomenon: an aura of color glows around the character's entire body for approximately a full minute. The color depends totally upon the character's alignment. The imbiber glows blue for an alignment of lawful, yellow for chaotic, while any neutral characters exhibit a white aura. Of course, upon first consuming the liquid, the characters have no idea what the strange appearing colors may mean, so they may be puzzled by the effects. There are no clues around the pool to explain the colors. The water retains its special magical characteristics even if it is removed from the pool, but there are only 10 suitable drinks possible due to the small amount of liquid present.

DM Note: This pool, just like the pool of healing previously described, disappears and reappears from time to time. There is a 30% chance this pool is not present on subsequent visits to the room, but it is always present on the initial visit.

j) Pool of Sleep. This pool is full of a greenish liquid of varying shades, with a swirling pattern evident on its stagnant surface. Putting a drop on the tongue reveals a sort of fruity taste, but no special effects are noticeable. Taking a sip is tasty refreshment, but within 1 minute a real drowsiness sets in, which requires a successful DC 13 Constitution saving throw or of the target falls asleep, as per a *sleep* spell. Drinking any greater volume of the liquid requires this saving throw to be attempted at disadvantage, and the effects last 1d8 hours. Any removal of the liquid from the room totally negates its effectiveness, although removing anyone who has consumed the stuff does not awaken them.

k) Fish Pool. This pool of normal lake water holds numerous small colorful fish. Reds, yellows, oranges, and even steel blues are all represented. The water radiates conjuration magic, but the water has no other special properties, nor are the fish unusual in any way.

l) Ice Pool. This basin is filled with steaming dry ice, although for some unknown reason it never seems to dissipate. The ice is "hot" to the touch due to its extremely low temperature. Touching the dry ice with unprotected flesh causes 2 (1d4) cold damage, although it should be described as a burning effect. Since it is highly doubtful any character has ever seen dry ice, the entire spectacle is highly mysterious, appearing as some kind of whitish rock giving off eerie vapors and feeling hot to the touch. If any pieces are broken off and removed from the pool, they dissipate into carbon dioxide gas as normal dry ice would do. Such pieces could be handled with a gloved hand, but the nature of the substance is still likely unapparent.

m) Treasure Pool. This basin, filled with normal water, seems to hold a great treasure underneath the water. A pile of gold pieces appears to lie on the bottom of the pool, and the golden image is sprinkled with an assortment of sparkling jewels. Alas, this treasure trove is nothing more than a magical illusion that is temporarily dispelled once the surface of the water is broken or disturbed. Once the waters are calm again, the illusionary image reappears. The **water weird** that inhabits the pool is real, and is undetectable while fully immersed. The water weird attempts to establish a grapple on a target to drown it. Once a target ceases to struggle it releases it and attacks another target, if within reach (10 feet).

n) Pool of Muting. This pool is almost empty, but a small amount of water remains. Although the liquid appears to be normal water and has no unusual odor or taste, it is actually a magical substance that radiates necromancy. This liquid, when swallowed, causes a complete loss of voice and verbal capabilities for 1d6 hours. This muting becomes apparent only when it has been swallowed; merely putting a drop on the tongue gives no clue as to its effect, and it seems in all respects like normal water. Any character drinking the water suffers the muting effect on a failed DC 12 Constitution saving throw. Thus, the Dungeon Master should inform the player or players of their limitation, and they are barred from any further communication by verbal means with the other players in the party for the duration of the muting effects. In such cases, they must remain completely silent (no grunts or groans allowed), and can only communicate with other players via nods, head shaking, hand signals, etc. Written communication is of course possible assuming the PCs understand the written language being used. The Dungeon Master may allow a DC 10 Intelligence check to decipher what a muted character is trying communicate.

AREA 32 – ADVISOR'S CHAMBER

Access to this room is only via a secret door on its west wall which connects to the Room of Pools (area 31). The chamber was the dwelling for Marevak, an elven advisor to Zelligar and Rogahn.

The decor of this 30-foot-square chamber is rather pleasant, although uninspired. The floor is the most striking aspect of the room, for it is a continuation of the colored mosaic patterns of golden brown, white, and black, similar to the adjacent room of pools. There are some minimal furnishings in the room, including a common bed, three chairs, a makeshift desk with a single drawer, and a battered old table. The walls are barren rock, except for a framed picture hanging over the desk showing two figures standing side by side: a warrior of impressive proportions, and an aging wizard in a purple robe.

The full-color painting is beautifully rendered. In one corner, written in Elvish, are the words: "To wise Marevak, worthy advisor and counselor, from a grateful Zelligar and Rogahn." These words are understandable only to those who know Elvish (or via a *comprehend languages* spell), but the signed names of Zelligar and Rogahn can be discerned upon a close examination, or with a DC 12 passive Perception check. In another corner of the painting is the signed name Tuflor—the artist who painted the picture. Tuflor has quite a bit of renown in the region, and this fact can be discovered by a character "asking around" once back in the civilized world, or by making a successful DC 15 Intelligence check. The painting is quite large and bulky, weighing the equivalent of 40 pounds. If carried undamaged out of the stronghold and back to civilization, it could bring up to 300 gp if a buyer of fine art can be located. However, anyone trying to sell the painting for its value runs a 60% chance that the purchaser recognizes the origin of the painting. If this word spreads at large, the seller may have attendant problems, since it is obvious from where the painting was likely obtained.

The desk in the room is mostly empty, except for several attached sheets with various notes written in Elvish. The first sheet is headed with the title, "Suggestions for the Further Development of Quasqueton," and the notes relate to certain details of construction for the stronghold, mostly regarding the lower level. Although there is no information of a sort to assist the characters, and no maps, the Dungeon Master is encouraged to give astute characters a few pieces of information about the lower level. The document, penned in Elvish, is signed at the bottom of each page by Marevak. There is also a crude map leading to wilderness area 11 (see chapter 10), the ancient portal Zelligar discovered that inspired his study of *teleportation*.

The locked drawer of the desk is well-secured, and requires thieves' tools and a successful DC 20 Dexterity check to open. However, access to the drawer can also be gained by dismantling the desk, although this requires heavy blows from some kind of weapon. Treat the desk as AC 15 and having 15 hit points. Due to the noise required to destroy the desk, an extra check for wandering monsters is required if this task is performed. The desk drawer is trapped, which can be found by a character searching for traps and a successful DC 20 Wisdom (Perception) check. The trap is triggered if this check is failed, or the desk is smashed open. The trap releases poison gas which fills the entire room in 3 rounds. Exposure to the gas requires a DC 15 Constitution check, or the target takes 7 (2d6) poison damage each round and gains the poisoned condition. A successful saving throw or exposure to fresh air ends the damage, but it takes an hour for the poisoned condition to wear off. The gas remains potent in this chamber for 1d4 hours before dissipating.

The contents of the drawer are determined by rolling a d12 and consulting the table below. Only one roll is made, for there is but a single item within the drawer.

D12	Item
1	*Potion of levitation* (see appendix A) (destroyed if the desk is smashed)
2	*Boots of elvenkind*
3	Pile of 10-100 gp (roll 10d10)
4	50 gp gem (moonstone)
5	Golden medallion worth 20 gp
6	*Spell scroll* of *comprehend languages*
7	*Spell scroll* of *web*
8	*Cursed scroll* (character loses 1 point from Charisma permanently)
9	*Ring of protection*
10	Two *potions of healing* (destroyed if the desk is smashed)
11	*+1 dagger* with ornately carved handle
12	Nothing

AREA 33 – BARRACKS

This large, open room was the dwelling for the guards and men-at-arms of the stronghold, most of whom left on the ill-fated last adventure with Rogahn and Zelligar. Recently a small band of barbarians, descendants of old enemies of Rogahn and Zelligar, have arrived at the complex seeking revenge. After several clashes with kobolds and gnomes, they are holed up in this chamber and area 34.

This room is huge, at least 100 feet long and 30 feet wide, although in places even wider. Scattered throughout the room are about 40 common beds, and about half that number of chairs and stools. There are several large wooden tables along various walls, and at the south wall is a large wooden chest of drawers. The walls of the room are rough stone, but there are sconces designed to hold torches, and various pegs upon the walls. Your presence disturbs several bulky humans adorned with animal pelts and armed with spears.

Three **barbarian warriors** (see appendix B), led by a **berserker**, have set up camp in this room. If they didn't respond to intruders in area 34, they are here resting. The berserker needs to retrieve his nearby greataxe, which takes his entire first turn. Meanwhile, the barbarian warriors assume the characters are aggressive, and attack. They begin the encounter about 60 feet from the door. Each has two spears, one to hurl and one for melee. They close with the characters throwing a spear, while attempting to block passage to their leader until he picks up his weapon. Then, they rage with bloodcurdling screams and fight to the death.

The large wooden chest of drawers is empty except for a few old socks, some common footwear, a few cloth vestments, and other similar items of no special value.

In the southwest corner of the room the floor slants toward the wall steeply and an opening (too small to give any access) leads into the wall. From the faint smell, it is apparent that this is some kind of crude toilet area.

Some odds and ends are hanging from several of the pegs: an old battered shield, an empty canteen, a 20-foot piece of light chain, a sheathed longsword (old and rusty), and a damaged bearskin (worthless).

AREA 34 – ARMORY

This irregularly-shaped room is designed to house the arms supply of the stronghold. It is mostly empty now, however, since many of the arms were taken along on the last foray of the inhabitants of the hideaway.

On opening the door to this room, a faint whistling can be heard. The rock walls of this room are mostly smooth, and there are carved ledges within several of them. Wooden pegs also abound, and there are some items still left in place on the wall. To the north, several human figures sit cross-legged in a rough circle in the middle of casual conversation. Each has tanned, weathered skin, and wears leather armor amid animal pelts and furs. Nearby, several spears lean against the wall, and a wooden cart bristling with numerous spears rests nearby.

The tribal warriors holed up in area 33 left three **barbarian warrior** guards (see appendix B) in this chamber with access to the barracks. The characters likely surprise these brutes, but unless they are neutralized quickly and quietly, the rest of the band in area 33 responds to the sounds of battle, and join the fray in 1d4 rounds. With their first actions, one barbarian warrior bangs on the door and shouts an alarm in a strange dialect of Common. He then grabs a spear and prepares to hurl it at a target that approaches. Meanwhile, the other two spring into action by pushing the wagon adorned with spears down the hallway toward the characters. During the next round, the cart makes a melee attack with a +6 bonus against all targets in a 10-foot-wide path. On a hit a target suffers 7 (1d8 + 3) piercing and 7 (2d6) bludgeoning damage, although a successful DC 13 Dexterity saving throw reduces the bludgeoning damage by half. The cart is destroyed by the single attack, so the following round the barbarian warriors attack with spears and begin to rage. They fight to the death.

Even if spiked open, there is a 50% chance the door slams behind the characters after they pass through. If the door is closed and the second exit is likewise closed, a howling wind immediately results, with an 80% chance of putting out any torch carried by the characters, or a 50% chance to extinguish each lantern carried. The wind ceases whenever either or both of the exits is opened. Upon examination of the ceiling of the room (which is a full 20 feet from the floor), two sizable vents can be located (neither providing usable access) which demonstrates that this is a natural, rather than magical, phenomenon.

The following items are still hanging on the wall pegs: a number of battered shields (several broken and in otherwise poor repair), bits and pieces of body armor (in uniformly poor condition), several crude bows (if used, all attack rolls are at disadvantage), a quiver of normal arrows, two longswords (one in good condition), a few spears, two handaxes (one with a split handle), a flail, a greatsword with a broken blade, and a dagger. None of the items appears remarkable, although the flail, the dagger, and one of the longswords seem to be usable and of normal value for such an item.

In the extreme southwest corner of the room are two locked chests, requiring thieves' tools and a successful DC 15 Dexterity check to open. Both are large and bulky, measuring 2 feet wide by 4 feet long by 3 feet high. However, both chests are empty.

AREA 35 – GUEST CHAMBER

There are three identical guest chambers side by side, all opening into the same corridor. Use the same description for each chamber, but each is slightly different as described below.

This 30-foot-by-30-foot room with rough rock walls is furnished with a wooden bed, a small table, and a single chair.

A. This room has a pungent smell as it has become the living quarters for the kobold leader of the tribe that inhabits area 37. A **kobold chieftain** (see appendix B) and three **elite kobolds** (see appendix B) lazily lounge about the chamber. The chieftain's pet **giant weasel** skulks nearby. The chieftain sits in a large wooden chair (his throne) covered with smelly furs and animal pelts (all worthless). The elite kobolds rest on grimy pillows, drinking watery mead and consuming meat of unknown origin. The elite kobolds rush the characters to protect the chieftain. These kobolds understand they are cut off from their tribe, so they fight to the death. The kobold chieftain has a *+1 shield* (AC 17).

A keg of watery mead is in the corner of the room. Six battered pewter flagons (although still worth 5 gp each) are scattered about the room. Under the chieftain's throne is an unlocked wooden box that contains a mess of coins: 265 sp, 31 ep, 87 gp, and 4 pp.

B. The middle chamber has a false door on its eastern wall. Although it seems to move just as a normal door would, it resists opening. If it is battered down, a stone wall is revealed behind it.

C. Zelligar reserved this room for practical jokes and the occasional enemy. In addition to the normal furniture, this room contains a plush red carpet 12 feet long by 8 feet wide, positioned in the center of the room. A DC 10 passive Perception check reveals one corner slightly turned up, exposing a wooden trapdoor in the floor. The trapdoor is false, but the carpet is actually a **rug of smothering** that attacks if disturbed (such as examining the trapdoor) or walked on.

AREA 36 – UTILITY ROOM

This extra room is empty and unused.

The door opens to reveal an unadorned 30-foot-by-20-foot chamber with smooth walls. To the northeast is a 10-foot-wide alcove that extends to 20 feet deep.

Three special features of note near the room are described below:

A. False Steps. Although the steps here are very real, the entire area north of this room (the various winding corridors) is specially designed to confuse any explorers. The twisting corridor west of the guest chambers is on an upward grade which is unnoticeable to most, except characters with Stonecunning. A character with Stonecunning can attempt a DC 15 Intelligence (History) check to discern this sloping effect. The stairs (eight of them) then lead downward, as if to another level—although this is only the impression created.

B. Winding Corridors and Cells. These twisting corridors and passages are patrolled by six **kobolds**. They have set up numerous crude traps in the corridors (as indicated on the map in letters and described below) to discourage investigation, and engage in hit-and-run tactics for further discouragement. This entails shouting obscene phrases and a few sling stone volleys before fleeing toward the cells, and luring characters away from area 37 (where the females of the tribe reside). Six more **kobolds** reside in cells at the center of the maze. Any surviving kobolds from the corridor retreat here to assist with an ambush in the second cell. This cell has doors on all four walls. Each door has a peephole about 3 feet high, used by the kobolds to spring an attack on all four sides! The kobolds fight to the death here.

a) Crossbow Trap. At the end of this corridor is a heavy crossbow mounted on a crude tripod. About 60 feet away is a tripwire that triggers the crossbow. The tripwire can be detected with a successful DC 15 Wisdom (Perception) check. The tripwire can be disabled with thieves' tools with a successful DC 14 Dexterity check. If triggered, the crossbow makes a ranged attack with a +4 bonus. On a hit a target takes 6 (1d10 + 1) piercing damage.

b) Caltrops. The kobolds have spread caltrops in this 10-foot section of the corridor. The kobolds arranged the caltrops with safe spots so they can cross without reducing their speed. A creature that enters the area at full speed must succeed on a DC 15 Dexterity saving throw. Failure indicates the creature must stop moving and take 1 piercing damage, and until healed at least 1 hit point, the creature's walking speed is reduced to 10 feet. Moving at half speed through the caltrops doesn't require the saving throw.

c) Net Trap. A net is concealed at the ceiling, triggered by a tripwire. Spotting the net or tripwire requires a successful DC 13 Wisdom (Perception) check. The mechanical trap can be disarmed with thieves' tools and a successful DC 15 Dexterity check. If triggered the net falls in a 10-foot-by-10-foot section of the corridor; trapped creatures in the area are restrained, and knocked prone if they fail a DC 10 Strength saving throw. A creature can use its action to attempt a DC 10 Strength check, to free itself or another target. The net has AC 10 and 20 hit points, although dealing 5 points of slashing damage is suitable to free one creature and destroy that 5-foot section of net.

C. Pit Trap. Just to the east of this room is a dead end to the corridor, with a false door on the north wall where the corridor terminates. When any character approaches within 5 feet of the door, the weight triggers the trap, causing the entire 20-foot section of floor between the false door and the wall opposite it to open. A giant crack opens in the center of the floor as the middle drops down and the sides slant inward, dropping all characters and their equipment through the 4-foot-wide opening. The bottom of the trap, some 40 feet below, is a pool of cold spring water in area 50 of the lower level. Those falling through the trap sustain 2 (1d4) bludgeoning damage when they hit the water below. In addition, since the pool is about 8 feet deep, encumbered characters (those carrying equipment weighing more than 5 times their Strength) risk drowning unless they free themselves of the bulk after landing in the water. Each round, an encumbered character needs to make a successful DC 15 Strength (Athletics) check to stay afloat. Heavily encumbered characters (those carrying more than 10 times their Strength in equipment), make this check is at disadvantage. Failure indicates the creature begins to drown. (See Encumbrance on p. 176 and Suffocating on p. 183 of the Player's Handbook.) Items dropped to the bottom of the pool can be retrieved, but the extremely cold temperature of the water is dangerous. For every round beyond the first spent in the water, a character must make a successful DC 13 Constitution saving throw; failure results in suffering 2 (1d4) cold damage. A character that takes cold damage this way must spend 1 hour recovering. During this time all the character's attack rolls are at disadvantage. The trap, after being sprung, closes again until triggered once more from above.

AREA 37 – RECREATION ROOM

This room was designed for recreation and training, specifically for Rogahn's use. The carved wooden door is heavy, thick, and bears a fancy "R" on its outer face.

This room is 60 feet long but only 20 feet wide. On the east and west walls, which are covered with pocked wood, are large archery targets, and several arrows are still stuck into the eastern target. There are several iron bars of varying length and weights in one corner of the room. In another corner of the room, a metal bar is attached to the two walls and is about 7 feet off the floor. Nearby, a rope is suspended from the ceiling 20 feet above. Hanging on the wall are several weapons, including a notched sword, a battleaxe, a flail, and a mace. Leaning against one wall are two heavily battered shields.

Numerous reptilian humanoids, about 3 feet tall with reddish-black hides, appear to inhabit the chamber, and clamber to alertness as you peer about.

This is the remainder of the kobold tribe that resides on the upper level of the complex, descendants of the servants that reported to Zelligar and Rogahn. Thirteen female **kobolds** (see appendix B) guard clutches of eggs deposited in the woven sleeping mats. Although ineffective combatants, they fight nevertheless to defend their lair.

There are five such mats that could be used to cover a 20-foot-by-20-foot section of the floor.

The weapons are worn, but functional. Each weighs double that of a typical weapon, and if wielded attack rolls are at disadvantage. They were used for training only. The shields are normal, but also double the weight. If used for defense, they only provide a +1 bonus to Armor Class.

The iron bars vary in circumference, and are apparently designed for weightlifting, although this fact is best discovered by the deduction of the characters. Wooden scraps from two heavy benches and a single stool round out the furnishings in the room.

LOWER LEVEL

GENERAL FEATURES

The lower level of the complex is rough and unfinished. The walls are irregular and coarse, not at all like the more finished walls of the level above (except for the areas 38 and 39 which are more like those in the upper portion and in a state of relative completion). The corridors are roughly 10 feet wide, and they are irregular and rough, making mapping difficult. The floors are uneven, and in some cases rock debris covers the pathways between rooms and chambers. The doors are as in the upper level, but the secret doors are either rock or disguised by rock so as to appear unnoticeable.

WANDERING MONSTERS

Check every 30 minutes with a 1 in 6 chance of an encounter. In addition, many of the caverns of Quasqueton are empty and devoid of any furnishings. Each time the characters enter one of these chambers, the DM should make another wandering monster check. If a monster is indicated, roll 1d6 again and compare to the list below to determine what type of monster appears.

D6	Monster
1	Troglodytes (1-4)
2	Giant Wolf Spider (1)
3	Kobolds (2-7)
4	Giant Rats (2-9)
5	Giant Fire Beetles (2-4)
6	Piercers (2-5)

ENCOUNTER AREAS

AREA 38 – ACCESS ROOM

Stairs from the upper level (area 30) lead to this chamber. Adjust the read-aloud text if the characters approach from the corridor to the south.

This 60-foot-by-40-foot room is filled with rock piles and rubble, as well as mining equipment. Everything is covered with a thick layer of dust as it is apparent that there has been no mining activity for quite some time.

This chamber was a staging area for the expansion of the lower level. Slaves and servants alike toiled to carve and improve many of the existing passages.

A pair of rock carts, still partially filled with rubble, are present. Several mining jacks and three piles of rotting timbers are scattered about. Four pickaxes lean against wall, although two have broken handles. They can be used in combat in a pinch (1d6 piercing damage), but due to their unwieldiness, all attack rolls are made at disadvantage.

QUASQUETON: LOWER LEVEL

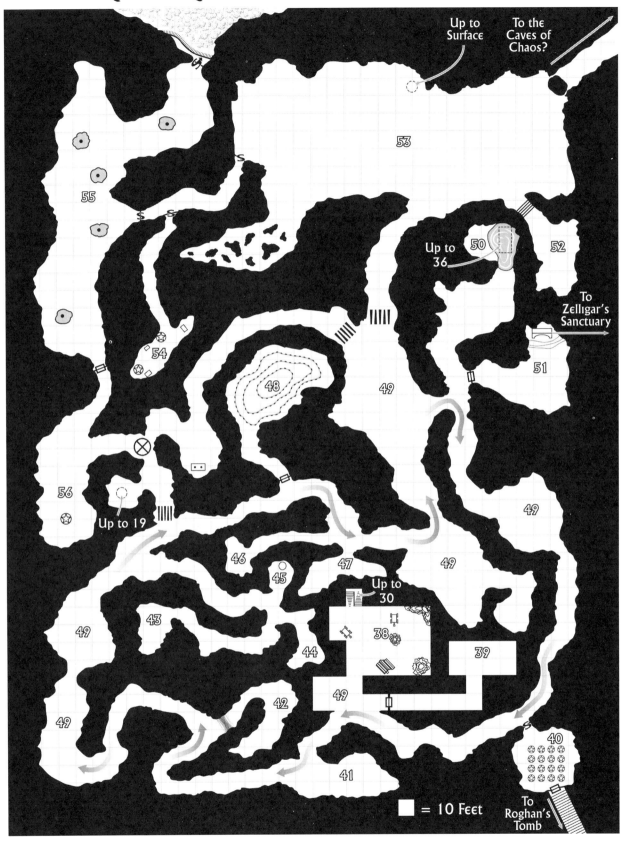

Up to Surface

To the Caves of Chaos?

53

55

Up to 36

50

52

54

To Zelligar's Sanctuary

51

48

49

56

Up to 19

49

49

46

45

47

Up to 30

49

43

49

38

44

39

49

49

42

41

40

To Roghan's Tomb

■ = 10 Feet

Door
Secret Door
One-Way Secret Door

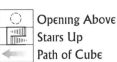
Opening Above
Stairs Up
Path of Cube

Altar
Depression
Pool

Statue
Pits, Covered
Pile of Rocks

Stalagmite
Webs

AREA 39 – MUSEUM

The actual door to this chamber rotted away years ago. The current door is a hungry **mimic** that is indistinguishable from a real door due to its False Appearance trait. This predator arrived at the complex years ago, and moves around seeking prey to satiate its hunger. When a character attempts to open the door (or search it for traps), they are subject to its Adhesive trait. On its next turn, the mimic attacks with its bite or pseudopod as appropriate. However, if outnumbered, the mimic does not seek to kill, but instead strike a bargain. This mimic is cunning and unusually intelligent (Intelligence 11), and can speak broken phrases of Common, although it often confuses the meaning of words and phrases. In return for some food (enough for one Medium humanoid for 1 day), it allows the characters to enter the room beyond. Of course, they need to pay to exit as well! And the fee might increase to "per character" at a whim. If the characters continue to interact with this strange monstrosity, additional bribes of food could glean tidbits about the lower level, at the DM's discretion. Such information could include:

"Bad tasting reptile men lair nearby."

"Beware the shambling ooze."

"Small but tasty dragon-like humanoids occasional explore this level."

"Nearby the rock wall hides a door."

The room beyond is an unfinished museum, a special monument to the achievements of the stronghold's most illustrious inhabitants. Continue with the read-aloud below:

The corridor turns to the north before opening into a smooth finished chamber, some 40 feet wide and 20 feet deep. Several of the walls are decorated with elaborate, painted frescoes. Near the frescos other mementos are displayed, similar to a museum. These include a framed parchment letter hanging on the wall, a curved sword mounted on a wooden plaque, and the skeletal remains of a large humanoid.

The frescoes are painted and they cannot be removed. The west wall is a sectioned fresco showing various events and deeds from the life of a great warrior (Rogahn). The several views pictured are: a young boy raising a sword, a young man slaying a wild boar with a spear in a forest, a warrior carrying off a dead barbarian, and a hero in the midst of a large battle, hacking barbarian foes to pieces.

The east wall is a similarly sectioned fresco showing cameos from the life of wizard (Zelligar). These scenes include a boy gazing upward at a starry night sky, a young man diligently studying a great tome, an earnest magician changing water to wine before a delighted audience, and a powerful wizard casting a type of death fog over a barbarian army from a hilltop.

The north wall's fresco is unfinished, but several sections show the two great men together. These scenes include shaking hands for the first time in younger days, winning a great battle against barbarians in a hill pass, and gazing upward together from the wilderness to a craggy rock outcropping (recognizable to the characters as the place where this very stronghold was constructed), with a fourth space blank.

The framed parchment is a letter of gratitude for help in the war against the barbarians, from the castellan of a keep. The curved sword belonged to a barbarian chief, and is still functional; treat this weapon as a greatscimitar (1d10 slashing damage, Heavy, Two-Handed). The skeleton, of the barbarian chief, is identified by a wall plaque in Common: "Itchor, Chief of the Ice Bear Clan." There is more blank space on the wall, apparently for further additions to the room's collection of items.

AREA 40 – SECRET CAVERN

A secret door conceals this chamber to the casual explorer. The door is constructed of rock and pivots on a central metal pin, which needs to be unlocked by pressing an unassuming stony protrusion. This requires a successful DC 22 Wisdom (Perception) check. Knowledge of this door's presence (from the mimic in area 39) grants advantage on this check. If discovered and opened, continue with the read-aloud:

As you push the rocky door open you are greeted by a blast of stale air. Beyond is a rough-hewn cavern, perhaps 30 feet in diameter. The floor is occupied by rank upon rank of reddish clay warriors depicted in wicker armor and helms. Each of the unmoving guards sports a human visage, and holds a shield and mace at its side. Along the opposite wall is a sealed iron door.

This secret cavern hides the entrance to Rogahn's tomb. The statues are terra cotta shells, each covering a human skeleton armed with a mace and shield. There are four ranks of four warriors. The terra cotta shells can be easily smashed (AC 13, 6 hit points, vulnerable to bludgeoning damage). Eight of the **skeletons** are animated, but they are under instructions to attack only if disturbed or if the iron door is touched. Skeletons still encased in terra cotta must use an action to free themselves, before they can attack. These skeletons have shields (AC 14) and wield maces (1d6 bludgeoning damage). They fight until destroyed.

The iron door does not have a handle or an obvious lock. Instead of a knob, there is a 3-inch horizontal slot surrounded by four round holes, each about a half inch in diameter. Touching the door triggers a *magic mouth* spell that gives a clue how to open the door. In a booming voice it states, "FOOLISH MORTALS! ONLY THE GUARD CAN OPEN THIS PORTAL!"

The characters likely mistake the skeletal guards (or the terra cotta shells) as the key to opening the door, but this is purposely misleading. The "guard" refers to the guard on a sword handle. If the blade of the longsword found in area 25 is slid into the horizontal slit with the four claw quillons lined up into the holes, the door unlocks. The door can be unlocked with thieves' tools but this is very difficult and requires a successful DC 22 Dexterity check. If a regular blade is inserted in the slot, pressure still needs to be applied in the four holes, but this is easier to accomplish, so grant advantage to the Dexterity check. The door reveals a steep flight of stone steps that leads to Rogahn's Tomb (see chapter 7).

AREA 41 – CAVERN

This rough-hewn cavern is about 60 feet long and 25 feet wide. Aside from a few scattered piles of rubble, the chamber appears empty.

Unless a wandering monster is indicated here, this cavern is empty.

AREA 42 – WEBBED CAVE

The entrance to this room is covered with silky—but sticky—webs, which must be cut or burned to access the area beyond. The webbed area is considered difficult terrain. A creature entering the webs must make a DC 12 Dexterity saving throw to avoid becoming restrained. A restrained creature needs to make a successful DC 12 Strength check to break free. A 5-foot cube of webs can be burned in 1 round, although anyone restrained by the webs suffer 5 (2d4) fire damage.

This chamber is perhaps 20 feet in diameter but it's difficult to ascertain due to the numerous webs stretched from wall to wall and ceiling to floor. Scattered about the webs are 1-foot-diameter cocoons, and one large humanoid-sized cocoon is suspended about 6 feet off the floor.

The ceiling here is about 25 feet high. Past the entrance, the webs are less obtrusive and don't hamper movement. However, combat in this chamber requires a successful DC 10 Dexterity check each round, to avoid becoming entangled in the webs.

The cavern extends about 30 feet to the south, the lair of a **giant spider**. The giant spider hangs back in the southern portion of the cavern, using its web action to hinder characters. If a character becomes ensnared, the giant spider moves in to deliver a quick bite before retreating out of reach near the ceiling, waiting for its web action to recharge. If reduced to less than 7 hit points, it either attempts to flee or cowers in a corner niche at the ceiling.

The humanoid husk is the remains of a troglodyte drained of blood. Its crude club is wrapped into the cocoon as well. Around its neck, it wears a leather throng of animal teeth (worthless). In a cloth pouch on its harness are several dried algae wafers and a rough piece of pink amethyst (worth 100 gp).

AREA 43 – CAVERN

This unadorned rough-hewn cavern is about 25 feet in diameter. The ceiling is about 15 feet high with a few scattered stalactites. The floor slopes to the south, and is clean of any debris.

This cavern is empty.

AREA 44 – CAVERN

This cavern is damp, with a vaulted ceiling about 25 feet overhead. The ceiling is covered with stalactites, slick with moisture. The floor is covered with rocky debris and other refuse, including the glint of metal from your light source.

Examination of the refuse reveals red stains on it and the floor itself. These are bloodstains, left by the creatures that lair here while feeding. Some scattered treasure dropped by victims includes a random assortment of coins (11 sp, 8 gp) and a copper lantern (worth 35 gp).

Three **piercers** live on the ceiling and ambush any creatures that enter the cavern. Until they attack, they are indistinguishable from the normal stalactites due to their False Appearance trait. Since they fall on average 20 feet, each incurs 7 (2d6) piercing damage per attack. Each fights to the death.

AREA 45 – CAVERN OF THE MYSTICAL STONE

This antechamber is about 15 feet in diameter with a low, 8-foot-high ceiling. Along the opposite wall is the resting place for a large rough chunk of rock, about 3 feet in diameter, that softly glows pale yellow. The jagged gray rock has smooth, flat, flakes that glisten gold.

The stone rests permanently in its place and is not removable. The stone radiates strong conjuration magic. Although chips can easily be broken off the rock by hand, only one chip at a time may be broken away; until anything is done with it, the rest of the rock is impervious to breaking.

Once a chip is removed its glow begins to fade, and after 1 minute it becomes a normal piece of mica with no magical properties. Pieces of mica lose their magic qualities if removed from the room as well. The chip's magical properties are manifested only if it is consumed (or placed in the mouth) by any character before the flake loses its glow. The magical effects are highly variable and each individual can only be affected once.

If any character places a chip within his or her mouth, randomly determine its effect according to the following table:

D20	Effect
1	Immediately *teleports* the character and his gear to the webbed cave (area 42).
2	Immediately blinds the character for 1d6 hours of game time.
3	Increases Strength score permanently by 1 point.
4	Increases Charisma score permanently by 1 point.
5	Increases Wisdom score permanently by 1 point.
6	Increases Intelligence score permanently by 1 point.
7	Increases Dexterity score permanently by 1 point.
8	Lowers Strength score permanently by 1 point.
9	Lowers Charisma score permanently by 1 point.
10	Lowers Intelligence score permanently by 1 point.
11	Increases hit point maximum permanently by 1 point.
12	Causes *invisibility* for 1d6 hours (per the spell).
13	Forces a DC 13 Constitution saving throw; failure means the character gains the poisoned condition for 1d6 hours.
14	Creates a 500 gp pearl in the character's hand.
15	Grants a permanent +1 magic enchantment to any single weapon (randomly determined) carried by the character.
16	Heals all the character's lost hit points (if any).
17	Causes idiocy for 1d4 hours (as per the *bestow curse* spell; each round the target must succeed on a DC 13 Wisdom saving throw or waste its action).
18	Grants a one-time bonus of 1d6 temporary hit points to the character (these are the first ones lost the next time damage is taken).
19	Grants a *curse*: the character sleeps for 72 hours straight each month, beginning one day before and ending one day after each new moon. (This effect can only be removed by a *remove curse* spell.)
20	Has no effect.

AREA 46 – SUNKEN CAVERN

The rough passage gradually slopes down, becoming slightly cooler and more humid as you proceed. At the end of the corridor is a roughly circular 20-foot-diameter cavern. The walls here are wet with moisture, and glisten from reflected light.

This cavern appears to be empty. However, it is the lair of a deadly predator, a **carrion crawler**. This beast resides in a natural chimney located in the northern nook of the cavern. The ceiling here is about 12 feet high and the chimney is about 5 feet in diameter. It extends about 15 feet up and to the left before ending. Yet there is plenty of room for the bulk of the creature to hide. The carrion crawler dangles from the chimney while it attacks, using its Spider Climb trait to hang on. It uses its move action to retreat into the chimney for protection, which grants three-quarters cover. It fights until reduced to 10 hit points or less before retreating inside the chimney.

Should the characters cut open the crawler's gullet they are rewarded by finding three small gemstones that could not be digested and have not yet passed through its system. Each gem is a small yellow topaz worth 100 gp.

AREA 47 – CAVERN

This cavern is about 40 feet wide and 15 feet deep. On the southern wall is a tan-yellow flowstone formation, nearly 15 feet wide, that appears to be a frozen waterfall.

Although the formation on the southern wall is interesting, this cavern is empty.

AREA 48 – ARENA CAVERN

An unlocked solid wooden door provides access to this most unusual cavern.

After passing through a door and down a short 30-foot passage, you are greeted by an interesting cavern about 40 feet by 50 feet in size. This cavern, although unfinished, is designed as a small theatre or arena. The center portion of the room is sunken about 15 feet below the floor level, and the sides slope downward from the surrounding walls to form a small amphitheater. Some rock finishing was initiated to create terraced seating, but there is much work yet to be done.

The ceiling here is vaulted, approximately 35 feet overhead. The air here is noticeably drier. Even the slightest sound here is pleasantly amplified due to the natural rock shape of the cavern.

This area is dusty and empty.

AREA 49 – PHOSPHORESCENT CAVE

DM Note: There are six locations labeled area 49. Five of them are irregular caverns as depicted on the map. The final room (just south of area 38) is partially finished. Adjust the read-aloud text as appropriate.

This medium-sized cavern is irregularly-shaped and presents an eerie sight to explorers. A soft purple phosphorescent glow bathes the entire area independent of any other illumination. The floor is clear of rocky debris or other refuse.

The strange light is caused by the widespread growth of a light purplish mold. The mold grows on the ceiling, walls and even parts of the floor, and requires a successful DC 10 Wisdom (Perception) check to discover. The mold itself is harmless, which can be determined with a successful DC 12 Intelligence (Nature) check.

A **gelatinous cube** wanders these caverns and the associated passages constantly seeking prey. Strangely it always moves in a clockwise direction. The troglodytes to the north have piled rocks about 3 feet high in several

locations, which seems to prevent the cube from changing direction. These rock piles are indicated on the map. The Dungeon Master has two options to determine the location of the gelatinous cube when the characters enter one of the caverns labeled 49. Each time the characters enter an area 49, the DM could just roll a d6, with a 1 indicating the cube is present. Alternatively, the first time the characters explore one of the area 49's he can randomly determine (again with a 1d6) which cavern the cube is in. Then every hour of game time that passes, the gelatinous cube is moved to the next area 49 in a clockwise fashion.

When the cube detects the characters using its blindsight, it stops and remains motionless. If motionless, its Transparent trait requires a successful DC 15 Wisdom (Perception) check to spot. It hopes to engulf one or more creatures, using an action if needed. Note that while in a 10-foot-wide corridor, the cube fills most of the space. Most inhabitants on this level are aware of the cube and avoid it. Therefore, it is quite hungry and fights to the death.

Inside the cube are several bones (from a humanoid, and several bats), a battered small metal helm, 23 ep, 5 gp, and a *potion of healing* in a metal flask.

AREA 50 – WATER PIT

This room contains the 8-foot-deep pool of water into which any unwary adventurers are precipitated from the trap on the upper level. (See the special description of the trap in area 36.)

Slick with moisture, this natural cavern is about 40 feet wide and 50 feet long. Several natural, irregular niches and cracks line the west wall. To the north, the cavern extends although it is occupied by a pool of clear water.

This cavern is generally empty but the source of fresh clean water tends to attract dungeon denizens. There is double the chance for a wandering encounter here. The pool is about 20 feet across and is filled by a cold spring.

As described in area 36, the water is extremely cold. Anyone entering the water, whether dumped from above or to retrieve items in the pool, must brave the dangerous cold. A creature spending multiple rounds in the water must make a DC 13 Constitution saving throw each round beyond the first, taking 2 (1d4) cold damage on a failure. A character that suffers cold damage this way must spend a full hour recovering from its chilly effects. While under these effects, all attacks are at disadvantage.

At the bottom of the pool is an ivory scroll tube engraved with demonic visages in a variety of expressions. The scroll tube can be located with a successful DC 15 Wisdom (Perception) check, if a character enters the water and spends a few rounds (and several dives) searching the bottom. The tube was not waterproof, so the magic scroll once held inside is now ruined. But the ivory tube itself would fetch 125 gp.

AREA 51 – SIDE CAVERN

A locked iron door blocks access to this cavern. The key is hidden in area 5, although the lock can be picked with thieves' tools and a successful DC 20 Dexterity check. A *glyph of warding* has been placed on the door, triggered when opened. Its faint outline can be detected with a successful DC 17 Intelligence (Investigation) check. The *glyph* casts a *conjure minor elementals* spell that summons four **magma mephits** on the opposite side of the door. When the chamber is entered, continue:

This cavern extends about 50 feet to an opposite wall, and is about 20 feet wide. The cavern bends and continues to the north, but your attention is focused on a quartet of small hovering creatures composed of oozing magma. With a cackling laugh, they scatter to the ceiling, at least 15 feet overhead.

Zelligar placed the *glyph* on this door to protect this important location. The magma mephits are under command to attack. They remain out of reach near the ceiling, and in the first round, two cast *heat metal* on armored foes, while the other two use their fire breath. The next round, they reverse tactics. They fight to the death; if reduced to 8 or fewer hit points, a mephit flies down to engage in melee, so to be in range to use its Death Burst trait. If not defeated, the mephits remain in this cavern for 1 hour before being dispelled. Fleeing and returning later is a suitable option!

The cavern is mostly nondescript, save for the eastern wall. Although worthless, the rock here has diagonal streaks of blue mineral.

When the characters enter the middle of the chamber and can view the northern "dog-leg" of the room, continue with the following read-aloud:

Situated along the northern wall is white marble archway about 10 feet wide and 10 feet high. The marble is engraved with strange runes along the top, and arcane symbols up and down its support columns. Several stone steps have been carved into the floor leading up to this bizarre construction.

Zelligar was fascinated with *teleportation* portals after discovering one nearby in the wilderness (see area 11 in chapter 10). His ultimate goal was to construct a portal that could transport an army for tactical advantages, but he started on a much smaller scale, with the rooms on the upper level (areas 15 and 16) and this functioning portal. This portal, if activated, only leads to one destination: Zelligar's prepared tomb, hidden in the solid rock 80 feet to the east of this lower level chamber (see chapter 7 for details).

The runes on the top of the arch can be deciphered with a *comprehend languages* spell, or a successful DC 22 Intelligence (Arcana) check. The passage reads, "Sel Dourts knows the way." This is an obscure reference to a famous author and his most famous character, the ranger Aulfors. If the word "Aulfors" is spoken in any language while standing under the arch, the portal is activated and any characters standing underneath are *teleported* a short distance to the Gallery of Statues (see chapter 7).

AREA 52 – RAISED CAVERN

This room, off the southeast corner of the grand cavern, is accessible by climbing four upward steps.

This room has a short ceiling, being only 5 feet high. The cavern is about 30 feet wide and 40 feet deep. The floor is covered with refuse and the chamber smells of rot and offal.

This cavern is the lair of a strange magical monstrosity called a **thoul** (see appendix B). These creatures were created via some twisted breeding and/or magical experiment and represent a cross between a hobgoblin, a troll, and a ghoul (although not considered undead). Zelligar either created this one, or somehow acquired it for some nefarious purpose. It escaped its servitude years ago when its master did not return, and due to its ability to regenerate has survived on the lower level consuming rats, bats, and the occasional humanoid.

Due to the low ceiling and the refuse, this cavern is considered difficult terrain. All attacks made with weapons that don't have the Light property occur at disadvantage. The thoul uses this to its advantage, attempting to attack with surprise, relying on its darkvision and Keen Smell trait. If it succeeds in paralyzing a target, it switches to another target during its next turn. Cornered, the thoul fights like a trapped animal, to the death.

The thoul has created a sleeping area in the southern nook of the cavern. Piles of smelly linens, burlap, hemp, and other bits of cloth serve as its bed. Nearby is a small recess in the rock wall, covered with another rock. It requires a successful DC 13 Wisdom (Perception) check to locate. The recess is filled with shiny baubles the thoul has collected over the years, including a pewter belt buckle set with a tiny ruby (worth 15 gp), a silver cup (worth 45 gp), a necklace of crude pieces of smooth, shiny obsidian (worth 225 gp), and a worthless chunk of pyrite.

AREA 53 – GRAND CAVERN OF THE BATS

This majestic cave is the largest in the complex, and is impressive due to its size and volume, for the ceiling is about 60 feet above. The primary access is a main corridor which slopes downward into this cavern, easily detected by all characters. This route provides access along the south wall. A secondary entrance/exit is via a secret door to the west, which requires a successful DC 20 Wisdom (Perception) check to discover on each side. By placing the appropriate force to a particular location, the rock face can be pushed to reveal this route. Meanwhile steps to the southeast lead up to area 52. Optionally, the cave has a concealed door that leads to a passage heading northeast to the Caves of Chaos (chapter 11), or another location of the DM's design.

The passage slopes down to a grand chamber. The ceiling and walls of this massive cavern can't be penetrated by your feeble light source, so it must be at least 100 feet in all directions. A sort of fluffy and dusty guano covers the floor of the grand cavern.

If fully explored, this chamber is nearly 200 feet east to west and 80 feet north to south, with an irregular ceiling averaging 60 feet high. A southwestern arm of the room leads to an alcove of rock pillars of unusual and irregular shape. The pillars run from floor to ceiling to form a very meager catacomb.

When it is daytime outside, a small opening in the ceiling just off a midway point of the north wall reveals daylight. If the DM has not been meticulously charting time as night vs. day, there will be a 60% chance of daylight being visible at the time the characters enter the room. Without daylight, it requires a successful DC 25 Wisdom (Perception) check to discover this opening. The opening is little more than a crack and can only be used by Tiny-sized creatures. It is used by the many thousands of bats which live on the ceiling of the cavern by day and which venture out at sunset each day for feeding.

The bats are nocturnal by nature, but the particular species living in this cavern is very easily agitated. Any party of characters entering the cavern with torches or other bright sources of light (including unshielded lanterns) have a base 5% chance per light source per 10 minutes of disturbing the bats and causing them to swarm. In addition, any noise above subdued conversation adds another 10% to the chance of disturbing the bats, assuming of course that they are present in the cave when the party enters. For example, a party with four torches would have a 20% chance of disturbing the bats and causing them to swarm, or 30% if they are arguing in addition.

If the bats are disturbed, first a few begin squeaking and flying around. After a few moments, more and more swirl about until it becomes a giant churning mass, equivalent to four **swarms of bats**. The swarming bats squeak and squawk, flying madly about. They fill the grand cavern and overflow into adjacent areas and corridors, but those flying out of the cavern soon return. If the characters leave the grand cavern and remove their light sources with them, the swarms of bats slowly cease their activity and return to their inverted perches, although this takes about 30 minutes. If the characters stay in the room, extinguish their lights, and lie silently on the floor for the same period of time, the bats eventually return to their dormant state.

AREA 54 – TREASURE CAVE

This secret room, itself opening to a corridor shielded by secret doors on either end, was designed as the hiding place for the valuables in the stronghold. It requires a successful DC 20 Wisdom (Perception) check to find any of these three secret doors.

Behind the concealed door and down a twisting 60-foot-long passage is an oval cavern. This chamber is dry, about 15 feet wide and 35 feet long. The floor is dusty, and a scattering of gold coins are strewn about. Three large ironbound oak chests, each sporting a massive padlock, are pushed up against the wall. Two full-color statues of human guards, adorned in mail and wielding longswords, stand silent vigil, positioned between the chests.

The two statues are **living wax statues**. They animate and attack if any of the chests are disturbed. The constructs fight until destroyed.

The coins on the floor are real, and tally to 22 gp. The chests are each locked, and the keys have long been lost. Each can be opened with thieves' tools and a successful DC 16 Dexterity check. The chests can also be smashed (each has AC 15 and 20 hit points). The chests once were overflowing with riches but fighting wars and building underground complexes tend to drain the coffers. Still, the chests contain:

Chest #1. 1,222 cp, and 886 sp.

Chest #2. Three small sacks each holding 150 gp.

Chest #3. A gold crown set with emeralds (worth 425 gp), a matching gold scepter set with malachite (worth 175 gp), and a red silk pillow sewn with gold thread (worth 40 gp). As a set, these items can fetch 750 gp, but they are the stolen property of a nearby kingdom, and possession or selling them could lead to further adventures.

AREA 55 – EXIT CAVE

The stench of this cavern is obvious long before the characters arrive here. The rotting door was scavenged from another part of the complex and is merely propped into place. This huge chamber serves as the living area for tribe of troglodytes that inhabit the complex.

This massive cavern is at least 40 feet wide and stretches too far back for your light to penetrate. A thick, musty stench assaults your nostrils as you observe numerous reptilian humanoids scramble about and flee in the opposite direction.

The ceiling is about 35 feet high, and several wide stalagmites occupy the floor as indicated on the map. The stench from such a large number of troglodytes living here is overpowering. Each round the characters are in the chamber they need to make a DC 12 Constitution saving throw at advantage or gain the poisoned condition for 1 hour. On a failed save, the character can attempt a new saving throw (this one without advantage) to become immune to the effects of the stench.

Although most of the warriors are elsewhere, there still are three male and 16 female **troglodytes**, along with 11 noncombatant young, living here. While the rest of the tribe attempts to flee out the one-way secret door, the three males and 2d4 females engage the characters; they fight to the death to protect the others.

Rock nests are scattered among the stalagmites along with bits of debris and organic mud and rotting plant material. Although trinkets and odd items (bones, sticks, dead insects, dried algae wafers, and the like) are present, no valuables are found. In the northern reach of the chamber is a mound of moist mud covered with more rotting plant matter. Buried in the mud are 19 troglodyte eggs.

This large cavern is otherwise unremarkable, except for the fact that a secret one-way passage out of the stronghold is hidden in the northeast corner of the cave. This secret exit is triggered by pushing on a loose rock within the wall, at which time the opening appears in the wall, leading to the outside. The opening allows access for only 1 minute, at which time it closes once more, and can't be triggered for another 24 hours. The secret exit is but a one-way access, and allows only egress from the stronghold, never entrance. There is no way to trigger the door from the outside, and even if this were possible, a permanent magic spell upon the exit totally prevents movement into the complex via the opening.

Development. If characters take advantage of this exit, they find themselves on a rock ledge about 3 feet wide and 20 feet long. If they use ropes to scale down, they can rappel without too much difficulty to a location some 40 feet below. Here, the drop is less steep and a descent can be made through the trees and vegetation toward the valley below. Otherwise, this climb requires a successful DC 15 Strength (Athletics) check. If the characters stand on the ledge and observe the view, they notice that they are on the north face of the massive outcropping which houses the stronghold, whereas the other entrance is on the south face. Because of the wilderness which surrounds the entire area, it may take some effort to return to civilization.

AREA 56 – CAVERN OF THE STATUE

The male troglodytes that are loyal to the shaman (see below) lair in this chamber.

This cavern is roughly 30 feet wide and approximately 60 feet long. In the southern end of this cavern is a solitary stone figure, roughly sculpted from the same black stone of the cavern walls and firmly anchored to the floor. The figure, obviously a human male—although lacking any finished detail—stands some 5 feet high, with both arms slightly outstretched, pointing to the jagged rock outcropping which divides the two corridors to the north-northeast. The statue is covered with mud, offal, and dried dung.

Seven male **troglodytes** spend most of their time here. Here they hone their combat abilities, wielding clubs (1d4 + 2 bludgeoning damage), and occasionally employing several nets to capture bats in area 53 to supplement the tribe's diet. They don't hesitate to employ the nets to restrain targets, and restrained targets are the subject of club attacks in following rounds.

If the characters approach from the east, one troglodyte flees to area 55 to warn the rest of the tribe. If the characters approach from the south, one of the guards in the side chamber (see below) notices them, and summons the shaman to attack from behind. If the characters approach from the north, one troglodyte flees to warn the shaman in the side chamber.

The statue was carved from a stalagmite, and thus can't be toppled or moved.

Pit Trap. Just outside this cavern, in the corridor which leads eastward, is a large covered pit at the intersection of three corridors. A successful DC 15 Wisdom (Perception) check is required to locate the pit. If the characters are in combat or hastily moving down this corridor, use their passive Wisdom (Perception) scores instead. The pit is about 12 feet across and 10 feet deep. A fall into this pit inflicts 3 (1d6) bludgeoning damage.

Side Chamber. A **troglodyte shaman** (see appendix B) and his two personal **troglodyte** guards reside in this chamber. The back wall has a crude stone block altar. On the altar is a copper bowl (worth 7 gp) holding several animal teeth and dried blood, and a carved wooden idol of a many-legged reptile beast (worthless). Crude cave paintings, depicting monstrous lizard-like creatures savaging humanoids, cover the walls in haphazard fashion.

The troglodyte guards can avoid triggering the trap by hugging the walls, a fact observed with a successful DC 14 passive Wisdom (Perception) check. They hasten to join the battle in area 56, while the shaman hangs back behind the pit, hoping to catch the characters unaware. The shaman can cast *entangle* and *acid splash* on targets in area 56. He reserves *poison spray* and *inflict wounds* for melee combat. All troglodytes fight to the death.

The tribe's treasure is in a shallow hole behind the altar covered with mud. It includes a leather sack holding 103 gp, an electrum fish with tiny sapphire eyes (worth 220 gp), a silver candelabra (worth 65 gp), and three black dragon scales, each about 6 inches in diameter.

Access to the Upper Level. In this roughly 15-foot-diameter chamber is a route to and from the upper level. In the ceiling is a 3-foot-diameter opening that leads to area 19; it is about 40 feet off the floor. Climbing the walls is possible, but such a feat requires a successful DC 20 Strength (Athletics) check. Failure results in a fall, the distance determine by how poor the check was. If the check failed by 5 or less, the climber falls 10 feet and suffers 3 (1d6) bludgeoning damage. If the roll fails by 6 to 12, the climber falls 20 feet and suffers 7 (2d6) bludgeoning damage. If the climber fails by 12 or more, he falls the full 40 feet and suffers 14 (4d6) bludgeoning damage. If using a rope attached to something sturdy in area 19, the climb check DC is reduced to 15 and the check is made at advantage.

CHAPTER SEVEN
Additional Encounters
The Caverns of Quasqueton

THE LONELY TOWER

The Lonely Tower is referenced in the background for *B1: In Search of the Unknown*, "A single tower was constructed above ground for lookout purposes, even though there was little to see other than a hilly forested wilderness for miles around." The Lonely Tower is situated on the rocky outcropping, above and to the west of the main entrance. An overgrown meandering trail leads to the exterior entrance to the tower (area 2), but it requires a successful DC 15 Wisdom (Survival) check to discover. The tower can also be entered via the trapdoor located in area 20 (upper level) of Quasqueton. A band of kobolds, with an unusual leader, inhabit the tower these days.

GENERAL FEATURES

Description. The tower is 55 feet tall with a circular base 35 feet in diameter. The tower is constructed of large black stone blocks with a base that is wider than the upper parts. The peaked roof is constructed of wood timbers, but many of these have collapsed exposing the upper levels to the elements.

Light. The interior of the tower is generally unlit, unless the room description details otherwise.

Walls. The interior walls are relatively smoothly hewn and finished, typically in generally good repair. Climbing a standard interior wall requires a successful DC 15 Strength (Athletics) check. The exterior surfaces of the tower are somewhat smoother and more difficult to scale. Climbing an exterior tower surface requires a successful DC 20 Strength (Athletics) check.

Floors. The floors in areas 1 and 3 are stone. The floors in areas 4 through 6 are wooden. The floor in area 4 is in good condition, but the floors in areas 5 and 6 are damaged and rotten in places. Each of these areas sports gaping holes leading to the floor below.

Arrow Slits. Area 5 has six arrow slits placed equidistant around the circumference of the level. A Small-sized creature can squeeze through these to enter or exit the tower, and this is the typical route used by the winged kobolds that reside on this level. The arrow slits provide three-quarters cover.

Ceilings. Ceiling heights are depicted on the map.

Wandering Monsters. There are no wandering monsters in the Lonely Tower.

THE LONELY TOWER

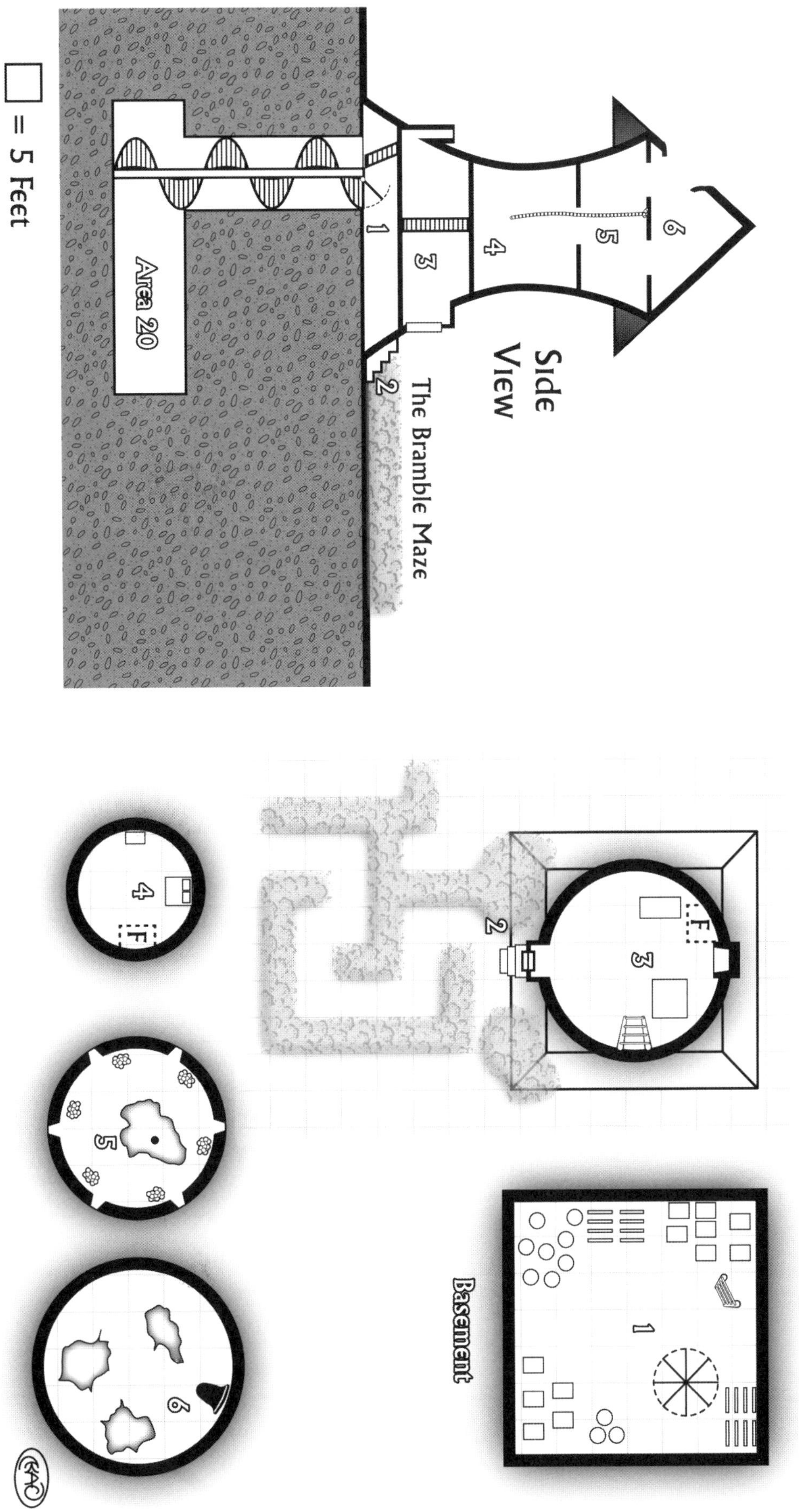

Area 20

□ = 5 Feet

The Bramble Maze

Side View

1
2
3
4
5
6

4
F

5

6

2
3
F

Basement

1

ENCOUNTER AREAS

AREA 1 – BASEMENT

This is a square chamber, perhaps 35 feet across, with a low 5-foot-high stone ceiling. The air here is stale and smells faintly of animal waste and rotting grain. A secured wooden trapdoor is situated on the floor, and a rickety wooden ladder leaning against a nearby wall leads to another closed wooden trapdoor on the ceiling. Numerous wooden crates, boxes, and casks are piled and stacked throughout the chamber.

Indeed, the lower level of the tower is used as a storeroom. The casks contain stale water, although one is half full of poor quality honey ale, and one small (5 gallon) sealed cask holds salt. The crates and boxes contain preserved foodstuffs and mundane equipment (candles, torches, burlap, etc.). There are two piles of rotting wooden timbers, each about 6 feet long.

The trapdoor in the floor is barred on this side and leads to a shaft with a metal spiral staircase that winds its way down to area 20 of the first level of Quasqueton. The door in the ceiling is not barred and leads to the lower level of the tower (area 3).

This chamber is inhabited by numerous rats, both normal and the giant variety. The equivalent of a **swarm of rats** and an additional seven **giant rats** are here. These rats are maintained as allies to the tribe by a unique kobold with a special affinity to rats. Called the Rat Master, he is actually a kobold wererat. Although accepted by the mundane kobolds, he is shunned nevertheless and spends all of his time in the basement with his rat allies. He is loyal to the tribe and commands his rats to attack any intruders entering the tower. The Rat Master has the statistics of a **wererat** with the following changes, which decrease his challenge rating to 1 (200 XP):

- His size is Small.
- He has 18 (4d6 + 4) hit points.
- He can speak Draconic.
- He has the additional traits Sunlight Sensitivity and Pack Tactics (as a kobold).

The Rat Master prefers to hang back and use the crates as half cover, while he commands the rats to overwhelm opposition. He snipes at the characters with his hand crossbow, and can spend an action to tip a heavy crate on a target within 5 feet; DC 12 Dexterity saving throw to avoid, or suffer 7 (2d6) bludgeoning damage.

Under the small cask of salt, located with a successful DC 14 Wisdom (Perception) check, is a hollow cavity in the floor. Inside the cavity is a stained leather pouch holding 13 gp, 17 pieces of worthless (although colorful) multi-colored glass shards, three pieces of blue quartz (each worth 15 gp), and six gold links of a chain (each worth 10 gp). It requires a successful DC 14 Intelligence (Investigation) check to discern the valuable quartz pieces from the worthless glass shards.

Developments. If the kobolds from area 20 (Quasqueton) warn the Rat Master, the kobolds in the tower are on alert. If there is time, the kobolds in area 3 (outside the tower) are in this chamber waiting to combat intruders. One is positioned at the top of the ladder in area 3, waiting to spend an action to tip the ladder if a character attempts to scale it.

AREA 2 – OUTSIDE THE TOWER

A hidden path located near the entrance to Quasqueton winds its way up the rocky outcropping to the Lonely Tower.

It takes patience and focus to follow the faint traces of the path as it winds up the black rocky slope. Ahead is a squat tower, perhaps 60 feet tall, with a wide base, thin mid-section, and a wide top. A wooden roof, collapsed in locations, is perched on top like a wizard's pointy hat.

The path is blocked by briar growth.

The kobolds that now lair inside the tower have collected piles of brambles and arranged them in front of the tower's single door. A successful DC 10 Intelligence (Nature) check reveals the brambles are not growing naturally. Actually, they form a rough path that twists and turns. Entering a bramble space is considered difficult terrain and causes 3 (1d6) piercing damage.

A short flight of stone steps lead to a weather-beaten wooden door. The door is locked but can be bashed down relatively easily with a DC 16 Strength check, although this takes an action and alerts the occupants in area 3. Alternatively, the lock can be picked with thieves' tools and a successful DC 15 Dexterity check. Assuming the kobolds in the tower are on alert, a target attempting to unlock the door is subject to dropped rock attacks from the arrow slits above. These have advantage to hit while the target is busy picking the lock.

Hiding behind the bramble walls are six **kobolds** armed with longspears (10 feet long, 2 [1d8 - 2] piercing damage). While the characters approach, they attack with spear thrusts and hoot and holler to alert the occupants of the tower. Two rounds later, four **winged kobolds** (from area 5) exit the arrow slits and begin an aerial assault on any targets. Each carries two rocks for dropping, but once they run out of these "bombs," they gladly swoop down to attack with daggers. These kobolds seek the glory of their mistress (see area 6), and fight to the death.

Each kobold carries 2d6 sp.

AREA 3 – LOWER LEVEL

The lower level of the tower is a circular room about 25 feet in diameter with a stone floor. The wooden beams of the ceiling are 10 feet overhead. On the back wall is a small fireplace complete with dying embers. Several battered tables are placed in the chamber and a wooden ladder provides access to an opening in the ceiling that likely leads to an upper level. The dark room smells faintly of animal.

The majority of the kobolds live on this level. Scattered about the chamber are piles of straw and cloth that serve as beds. Although 23 of these are present, only 11 **kobolds** are present in this chamber. Six are stationed as guards outside the tower (area 2) and another six are away hunting (but could return at any time while the characters explore the tower to present another challenge).

If on alert, these kobolds have flipped the tables (facing the door) and use them as half cover, pelting the intruders with sling stones. They fight to the death, fearing the retribution of the mistress if they fail to defeat foes.

Each kobold carries 2d6 sp. Hidden in pot near the fireplace is a cache of 123 cp. A loose flagstone along the southwest wall can be located with a successful DC 18 Wisdom (Perception) check. Behind the loose stone is an unlocked metal box. The box holds 44 ep, three zircon gemstones (each worth 50 gp), and a gold bracelet set with onyx (worth 235 gp).

Development. If half of the kobolds are defeated, one runs over to the trapdoor in the floor and stomps on it three times. This is signal for the Rat Master to release his pets. In the following round the door opens and 1d3 giant rats plus numerous normal rats enter the chamber. The giant rats can attack, but it takes 3 rounds for enough normal rats to pour into the chamber to form a swarm. Meanwhile, the kobold sorcerer in area 4 kicks down the ladder and starts lobbing spells from above targeting characters attempting to get to the upper levels.

AREA 4 – MIDDLE LEVEL

This level can be reached via a ladder up from area 3.

This circular room is about 15 feet in diameter. The ceiling is about 15 feet overhead, and sports a jagged opening. A thick rope disappears through the opening, its end dangling in this chamber. A wooden bench is pushed against the northern wall, covered with stained silk sheets and mangy animal pelts. A small table is next to the west wall.

The rope is attached to a rafter in area 5 and can be climbed with a successful DC 15 Strength (Athletics) check. The table contains various small clay pots and glass jars holding a variety of alchemical ingredients (powdered bone, grave dirt, sulfur, etc.). The silk sheets and animal pelts on the bench are worthless.

The former leader of this tribe, a **kobold sorcerer** (see appendix B), lives in this chamber with his three mates, large female **kobolds**. Each female kobold has two flasks of oil in addition to a dagger. The kobold sorcerer prefers to wield spells, and starts off casting *mage armor* and *blade ward* to protect himself. If alerted, he has already cast these spells before he confronts the characters. He uses *shatter* on the ladder while a character is scaling it to reach this room. Then he prefers to use *fire bolt* or *burning hands* (with the Empowered Spell Metamagic option to spend sorcery points on damage dice re-rolls if needed) on targets doused with oil from the female kobolds. The female kobolds fight to the death to protect the sorcerer. If reduced to 5 hit points or less, the kobold sorcerer attempts to flee down the shaft to area 3 and then out the door, if possible.

Each of the mates wears a piece of jewelry. These include a plain electrum nose ring (worth 65 gp), a gold anklet (worth 90 gp), and a gaudy copper bracer set with tiny emeralds (worth 225 gp). The kobold sorcerer carries 11 gp in a pouch and wears a necklace of jagged jade pieces (worth 300 gp). On the table are a variety of valuable items, if the time is spent to go through all the worthless bits. These include two flasks of acid, three flasks of oil, a scratched magnifying glass, and a scale with three small golden counterweights (each worth 15 gp).

Development. Combat in this chamber automatically alerts the winged kobolds in area 5. Two of them drop rocks through the opening attempting to hit the characters while they battle the sorcerer and his mates. These attacks are at disadvantage due to the restricted size of the opening and the ensuing battle. If a character attempts to climb the rope, a winged kobold uses an action to cut the rope with a dagger.

AREA 5 – UPPER LEVEL

The circular upper level is about 20 feet in diameter with a 10-foot-high ceiling. The ceiling, also composed of rotting timbers, sports numerous gaps and holes revealing another level above. Natural light spills into this chamber from six arrow slits placed equidistant in the stone exterior walls. Near each arrow slit is a pile of rubble and rocks. Several piles of rags, burlap, cloth, and animal pelts are scattered about the chamber.

This level was once an archer post to defend the tower. Each pile of rubble contains 5-10 rocks suitable for use as ranged attacks. The seven piles of cloth and such contain worthless scraps that constitute a bedding area for the occupants of this chamber. If searched, each pile contains a bit of treasure:

1. 6 cp and 13 sp

2. an empty silver hip flask (worth 35 gp)

3. six gold buttons (each worth 3 gp)

4. a large yellow topaz (500 gp)

5. a scrimshaw dolphin (worth 25 gp)

6. four moss agates (each worth 10 gp)

7. 4 gp and 1 pp

Now, this chamber serves as the lair for seven **winged kobolds**. These creatures are favored by the dragon mistress, and thus spend most of their time leisurely sleeping or resting here. They are quick to defend the tribe, as described in areas 2 and 4. Any remaining winged kobolds grab a rock or two before taking wing to drop them, if combat occurs here. If outnumbered, they retreat to the area 6 and defend their mistress to the death.

AREA 6 – THE LOFT

Special Note: There is no direct access to this level as the occupant can fly.

The top of the tower is about 25 feet in diameter with a peaked wooded roof. The roof has collapsed in places and has gaping holes due to general neglect and disrepair. Patchy natural light bathes this otherwise glooming abode. The floor is comprised of rotting wooden timbers, with three large holes. A large metal bell, once mounted above, is upside-down and pushed against a wall.

The floor is uneven and dangerous, considered difficult terrain. If more than 150 pounds of weight approaches one of the holes, there is a 40% chance the floor collapses. Grant the victim a DC 12 Dexterity saving throw to grab onto the floor, or fall into area 5 below, suffering 3 (1d6) bludgeoning damage.

The loft serves as the lair of a cunning **harpy** worshipped by the weak-minded kobolds. The harpy wears a *minor dragon mask* (red) (see appendix A), and a vest and a cape of dragon scales which grant her AC 13. She rules the other kobolds as a cruel deity and they live in fear. The use of her Luring Song, and the occasional breath attack, is all they needed to be swayed to awe, although the kobold sorcerer suspects the deception. The harpy sleeps most of the daylight hours in the bell, and leaves the tower at night to explore. She has grown lazy and demands food and treasure from her minions.

The harpy can always be found here, possibly with a few winged kobolds from area 5, if they fled here. If threatened, she commands two of them to flip the bell into the center of the floor. If successful, the bell tumbles through the floor to area 5. Any targets within range need to make a successful DC 13 Dexterity saving throw to only suffer 3 (1d6) bludgeoning damage. Failure indicates 7 (2d6) bludgeoning damage and a potential fall to the floor below. Meanwhile, the harpy unleashes her breath weapon with her first action, and then follows it up with her Luring Song. She commands victims enthralled by her song to move about the room, risking falling through one of the gaps, although the victim is immediately granted another saving throw to resist this bad decision. The harpy fights to the death protecting her lair.

The bell is propped up against the wall with a pile of rubble. Hidden in the rubble is the harpy's treasure hoard. Three sacks contain a mess of coins (544 cp, 344 sp, 21 ep, 124 gp, and 4 pp). Mixed in with the coins are several gems, including seven tiger eyes (worth 10 gp each), three bloodstones (worth 50 gp each), and a piece of amber with an oak leaf inside it (worth 250 gp). Also in the rubble is a bent silver tiara (worth 115 gp) and a metal potion flask with an azurite stopper (worth 25 gp) holding a *potion of greater healing*. Finally, a successful DC 14 Wisdom (Perception) check reveals a tiny soot-covered figurine of a raven. This is a *figurine of wondrous power* (silver raven).

ZELLIGAR'S SANCTUARY

Zelligar was a very powerful wizard and spared no expense when designing Quasqueton, often with the use of magic in addition to mundane mining practices. But he still craved more isolation to pursue his arcane discipline. Thus, he created his private sanctuary, a series of several chambers about 80 feet east of the lower level of the Quasqueton. He built a pair of teleporters for the ease of travel to and from his secret redoubt.

The only route to this sub-level is by use of the teleporter in area 51. Although to activate that portal it requires a password, the return trip does not require any such method. Even though he created a tomb here, he disliked labeling this place his tomb, preferring the term "sanctuary." Complete with a statue gallery, arcane laboratory, and a cozy library, this hideaway was truly a sanctuary.

GENERAL FEATURES

Light. The interior of the sanctuary is unlit, unless the room description details otherwise.

Walls. The interior walls are smoothly hewn and finished. Most of these chambers were carved via magic, which can be discerned with a DC 15 Intelligence (Arcana) check. Climbing a standard interior wall requires a successful DC 20 Dexterity (Acrobatics) check, due to the lack of handholds derived from traditional mining.

Floors/Ceilings. The floors of these chambers are smooth and lack flagstones. The floors are quite dusty, and typically covered with rocky debris in places. The ceiling in area 1 is 25 feet high, although less so at the east end due to the raised platforms. Area 4 has a 25-foot-high ceiling as well. The ceiling height in the other chambers is a uniform 15 feet.

Wandering Monsters. There are no wandering monsters in Zelligar's Sanctuary.

ENCOUNTER AREAS

AREA 1 – THE GALLERY OF STATUES

Stepping through the portal, your vision fades and you feel a magical pressure that causes your ears to pop. Your body is gently tugged, seemingly from the inside, and a moment later you stand on a raised platform in inky darkness.

The teleportation snuffs out any traditional light sources (but not magical light). Once the characters have a moment to adjust and apply a light source, continue:

You stand at the west end of a rectangular hallway, 25 feet wide and at least 40 feet long. Numerous statues occupy the dusty floor of the hall in a variety of poses and postures. At the far end of the hall are three raised steps, with each level displaying yet more statues. There do not appear to be any exits from this chamber.

A few stone steps lead to the west wall (behind the characters when they arrive), which is the teleporter. When active, it appears as a shimmering silvery surface that is pliable to the touch. One minute after someone uses the teleporter, the wall returns to normal and can't be used for 1 hour. White marble blocks of an archway inscribed with arcane symbols, similar to the arch in area 51, are set into the wall here. Although the characters are likely unaware of this, after recharging for an hour, the teleporter can be used without a command word to return to area 51.

Zelligar was obsessed with himself and adored looking at statues depicting various wizardly and sometimes even mundane activities. He spent hours in the hall admiring himself and some of his great accomplishments etched in stone for all those to share. A successful DC 8 Intelligence (Investigation) check reveals that the statues are all the same male human figure. He is tall (about 6 foot 5 inches), with gaunt features, but these are often concealed under voluminous robes. He sports an angu-

ROGAHN'S TOMB

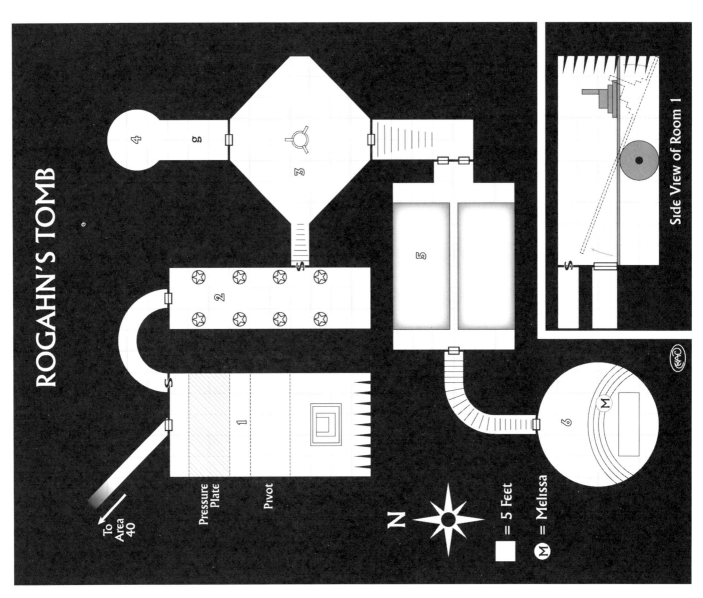

To Area 40

Pressure Plate

Pivot

Side View of Room 1

= 5 Feet

M = Melissa

ZELLIGAR'S SANCTUARY

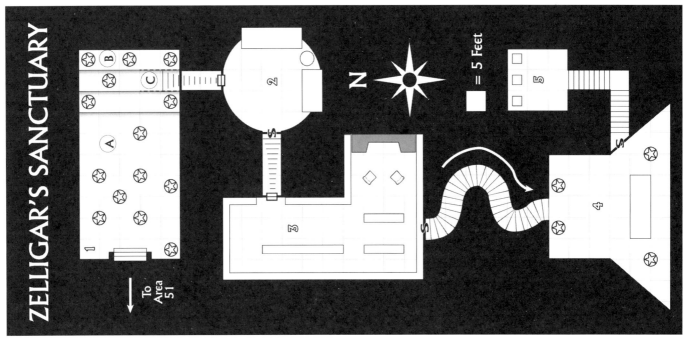

To Area 51

= 5 Feet

lar nose, sunken cheeks, and a protruding chin. About half the statues are adorned in a clichéd pointy wizard's hat. Close examination of any statue base reveals two engraved initials, a stylistic attached "JR," with a successful DC 20 Wisdom (Perception) check. This is a sculptor's insignia, a famous gnome artist Jolof Rims. Although well paid for his artistic efforts, the sculptor was little more than a slave to the wizard, unable to enjoy his lavish commissions. Below is a sample of the statue poses, although the DM is encouraged to create more as needed:

- Zelligar standing proud with his arms folded

- Zelligar having a pensive thought, with his fingers stroking his chin

- Zelligar crouching, arms outstretched, casting a spell

- Zelligar reading from a great tome cradled in one hand

- Zelligar standing with a ball of fire dancing on the fingertips of an outstretched arm

- Zelligar raising both arms over his head while uttering a dreaded incantation

This room contains 17 statues. Fourteen of them are all normal with no other function other than aesthetic appeal. The remaining three are detailed below, with the corresponding letter codes depicted on the map.

A. The Actual Zelligar. This statue appears similar to the others, its pose is one of being awestruck, but with a wry smile. But a successful DC 20 Wisdom (Perception) check reveals no engraved initials near its base. That is because this statue is Zelligar. On that fateful day decades ago, Zelligar was turned to stone by the gorgon ally of the barbarian hordes. But Zelligar was always one step ahead, and years before had cast a *greater contingency* (see appendix A) spell on himself to trigger a *teleport* spell should he ever become incapacitated. Since the petrification condition includes incapacitation, he was *teleported* to the chamber he was most familiar with: the gallery of statues. Ironically, the stony form of Zelligar now hides in plain sight among numerous other statues of himself. Should the petrification effect be removed (by a *greater restoration* spell, or perhaps the *elixir of stone to flesh* from the Stone Hovel (see area 13 in chapter 10), Zelligar is an aging CE male human **archmage**. He will be befuddled for some time until he pieces together what has happened. His fate and role in the campaign are left the devices of the DM.

B. Wizard Golem. This statue depicts Zelligar with a staff in one hand and a wand in the other. He is tense, as if poised to attack. This statue is a **wizard golem** (see appendix B) placed here to guard this chamber and the way deeper into the sanctuary. The golem is undetectable due to its False Appearance trait—until the statue hiding the secret door is investigated. The wizard golem begins by casting *magic missile* first and then resorts to *fire bolt*. Unless a successful DC 15 Wisdom (Perception) check is made, the source of the first attack goes unnoticed. The golem fights until destroyed. If the golem is sundered, a heart shaped ruby (worth 500 gp) can be found in the rubble.

C. Secret Door. This statue of Zelligar depicts him pointing with a crooked finger (to the west wall) while cradling an open book in his other hand. A successful DC 15 Wisdom (Perception) check reveals the statue's gaze is fixed to the left. This statue conceals a secret door, which can be located with a DC 20 Wisdom (Perception) check. A character gets advantage on this check if he attempts to swivel the base counterclockwise or notices the gaze to the left. If the statue is turned counterclockwise, following an audible click, the statue can be flipped with a successful DC 12 Strength check to reveal its base as a hatch. Investigating this statue triggers the wizard golem (statue B) to attack. A 5-foot-wide flight of steps leads down to area 2.

AREA 2 – ZELLIGAR'S SECRET LABORATORY

A short flight of steps leads to this locked iron door. The key is long lost, or might be the brass key found in area 31 on the first level of Quasqueton (see chapter 6). The door can be destroyed (AC 20, 35 hit points), bashed with a successful DC 25 Strength check, or the lock picked with thieves' tools and a successful DC 22 Dexterity check. A *glyph of warding* is triggered if the door is opened without the key. The *glyph* can be detected with a successful DC 17 Intelligence (Investigation) check. If triggered, the *glyph* releases a *polymorph* spell and the target needs to make a successful DC 17 Wisdom saving throw or be transmogrified into a **toad** for 1 hour.

When the door is opened, continue:

The iron door reveals a darkened circular chamber perhaps 25 feet in diameter. The ceiling is dome-shaped, and three fancy unlit black lanterns suspended from black chain are strategically placed about. A stone bench resides along the east wall, and another along the south wall. A metal brazier rests between the two benches. Above each bench are dusty wooden cabinets set into the stone wall.

This is Zelligar's laboratory. The lanterns are enchanted with *continual flame* and can be activated with two audible claps, or deactivated with two more claps. Each lantern is worth 100 gp. The stone benches sport surfaces pitted and scorched from acid and explosions. The doors conceal storage cabinets that are stocked with an array of bottles, flasks, and assorted vessels. Most of these are full. Consult area 8 on the first level of Quasqueton for a suitable list of what these vessels may contain. If searched for 5 minutes, for each successful DC 15 Intelligence (Investigation) check, a valuable item from the list below is located, with the number in parentheses indicating the total number that can be found.

D6	Contents
1	Alchemist's fire (4)
2	Antitoxin (2)
3	Poison, basic (2)
4	*Potion of healing* (3)
5	Powdered gemstones worth 200 gp (1)
6	Oil (5)

A successful DC 15 Wisdom (Perception) check reveals a small glass vial with a gilded gold stopper inside one of the cabinets. Inside the bottle is the form of a scantily clad female human soundlessly shouting and pounding on the glass. This is an *illusion*. If the bottle is broken or opened, it releases a trapped **bearded devil** in a puff of black smoke. The bearded devil attacks in the following round. It fights to the death but returns to its plane if defeated, or when 10 rounds have passed.

The brazier is soot-covered, hiding fanciful designs of demons conducting despicable acts on its brass surface. It would fetch 75 gp to the right buyer. It contains several inches of ashes. Hidden in the ashes are three small rubies (each worth 250 gp), that are very warm to the touch. These can be used to warm liquids.

The west wall is heavily scorched from magical blasts. It conceals a secret door that can be located with a successful DC 18 Wisdom (Perception) check. The door opens inward to reveal a short flight of steps going down.

AREA 3 – ZELLIGAR'S HIDDEN LIBRARY

The door opens to reveal a dimly lit chamber with a low ceiling and a floor covered with thick, soft carpet. The walls are covered with bookshelves from floor to ceiling, and one more 20-foot-long free-standing bookcase occupies the center of the room. The room stretches about 50 feet to the south, where two wooden tables are situated. The room turns to the east, another 20 feet or so. This nook is dominated by a roaring fireplace, the source of the illumination, and a pair of plush chairs.

Zelligar spent countless hours here studying arcane lore and researching esoteric topics. This was his sanctuary within his sanctuary, and he often slept here in one of the chairs. The light that emits from the fireplace is an *illusion* although it does give off slight heat. A pair of unlit electrum lanterns (each worth 125 gp) rest on the fireplace mantle. Most of the bookshelves are filled with tomes, librams, and manuals. These books cover a wide range of topics including history, science, nature, geography, and mathematics. All told, 1,112 books are stored here, and most remain in usable condition. The average book is worth 1 to 3 gp, although a few notable books could fetch as much as 20 gp on the open market. There are four noteworthy books here, should the characters search for at least an hour and make the required skill check indicated:

- With a successful DC 22 Intelligence (Investigation) check, the characters locate one of Zelligar's minor spellbooks. The book is covered with silver dragon hide and contains eight 1st-level spells, six 2nd-level spells, two 3rd-level spells, and a 4th-level spell. Randomly determine the spells or pick them as needed. Also, scribbled in the margins of the book are the command words for Zelligar's *staff of stone* (hidden in area 4), although these take another hour of study and a successful DC 20 Intelligence (Investigation) check to locate.

- With a successful DC 20 Intelligence (Investigation) check, the characters find a *manual of golems* that details the creation of bone golems (see appendix B). It takes 45 days and 25,000 gp to craft a bone golem using this manual as a guide.

- With a successful DC 18 Intelligence (Investigation) check, the characters find a book titled "How to Find Secret Doors." The book is fake and attached to the bookcase; if pulled forward, the bookcase slides to the left to reveal a staircase going down (to area 4).

- With a successful DC 18 Intelligence (Investigation) check, the characters find a map of the lower level of Quasqueton, and Zelligar's Sanctuary (save for area 5), along with complex mathematical calculations regarding angles. This was Zelligar's backup plan to escape the sanctuary should the teleporter in area 1 ever malfunction. He could use the *passwall* ability (there are just enough charges to complete the tunnel) on his *staff of stone* to tunnel his way back to Quasqueton. The characters can use this map and the *staff of stone* to escape the sanctuary, if they desire.

The fireplace contains a secret compartment behind a flagstone. It can be located with a DC 20 Wisdom (Perception) check. Inside is an ivory scroll tube set with onyx (worth 215 gp) holding three *spell scrolls* (*fly, gaseous form,* and *phantom steed*), along with a *ring of protection*. The scroll has a trick opening triggered by sliding the onyx studs in the right configuration, which requires three consecutive successful DC 15 Intelligence checks to open. Failure on one means the character must start over. Next to the scroll tube is a pouch holding 25 pp.

AREA 4 – ZELLIGAR'S TOMB

A steep sloping passage with stone steps leads to this sunken chamber. The stairs are trapped. The fifth step is a pressure plate that can be discovered only with a DC 22 Wisdom (Perception) check, although tapping on the steps with a sword, spear shaft, or 10-foot pole grants advantage on this check due to the hollow sound generated.

The following round, all steps flatten, and any characters on the steps must make a successful DC 14 Dexterity saving throw, or slide down the meandering passage, taking 3 (1d6) bludgeoning damage and being deposited in area 4, prone. Success on this saving throw means the target has grabbed hold of the wall or the door, but traversing the corridor still requires a successful DC 10 Dexterity saving throw. Failure on this save results in a controlled slide to area 4 and being prone, but no damage is suffered. At the entrance to area 4 are two statues of warriors, each holding a greataxe aloft. The following round after the trap is triggered, these greataxes chop down to the floor. Any targets spilled into the room must make a successful DC 15 Dexterity saving throw, or suffer 8 (1d12 + 2) slashing damage. Prone targets make this saving throw at disadvantage, and a critical failure indicates both greataxes hit!

Once both traps have been dealt with, continue:

This chamber has stale air, and a thick layer dust covers the stone floor. The chamber is 25 feet wide, but increases to nearly 50 feet with curved walls. The ceiling is at least 20 feet high. Two 7-foot-tall statues of warriors holding greataxes flank the entrance. At the far end of the room is a massive sealed stone sarcophagus about 15 feet long, with a plain, unadorned surface. Flanking this sarcophagus are a pair of 15-foot-tall stone statues, each of a helmed warrior holding a shield and longsword.

This chamber was designed to be Zelligar's final resting place, although the archmage had full intentions of avoiding that fate for many more years. The two statues flanking the door are part of the trap as described above, but otherwise considered normal statues. The two larger statues were crafted to be stone golems, but Zelligar never got around to enchanting them. Each weighs in excess of 3,000 pounds, and would be worth 20,000 gp if they could somehow be removed from this chamber.

There is a secret door located on the east wall, but its located 18 feet off the ground. It can only be located if the wall at that height is examined and with a successful DC 20 Wisdom (Perception) check. The door is activated by pressing a pressure plate concealed on the ceiling, which causes the door to slide to the right. Beyond is a passage to area 5. Zelligar was a sporting individual, and left potential tomb raiders a cunning clue on the eastern statue. Concealed on the blade of the sword, written in Infernal, is the phrase "Look up!" The blade is pointing towards the door's location. The phrase can only be found with a successful DC 22 Wisdom (Perception) check.

The sarcophagus is sealed tight, and functions much like

AREA 5 – TREASURY

The corridor is bathed in soft light and the faint scent of sulfur tingles your nostrils. The stone steps descend for 10 feet and then turn north, at which point you are greeted by a fabulous sight. The steps continue for 10 more feet before the passage opens up into a bright hall at least 40 feet wide and at least twice as far back. The floor gleams and almost twinkles from a polished golden surface.

But your attention quickly turns to the massive draconic form that wakes with a shake, sending dust flying. The crimson creature sports a sinuous neck, spiral horns, and fiery eyes just coming into focus. The beast stretches its bulk and unfurls its powerful wings. A massive black iron collar is affixed to its neck. A thick black chain leads from the collar to a stout ring sunk into the floor.

The chamber was reserved for Zelligar's considerable wealth. The light is from a few *continual flame* spells placed on several of the gold floor tiles. The scene is something of a practical joke. The red dragon is nothing but a *programmed illusion*, as are the apparent dimensions of the room. To keep the players on edge, ask them to immediately roll for initiative and proceed right to combat. Any character can spend an action to disbelieve the *illusion* with a successful DC 17 Intelligence (Investigation) check. Otherwise, it takes physical interaction with the *illusion* to discern it is indeed fake. At the end of the round, the red dragon unleashes its terrible fiery breath weapon. Ask for a DC 17 Dexterity saving throw from each character. Those that fail are incapacitated until the end of their next turn. Those that succeed can discern the red dragon for what it truly is, an *illusion*.

The chamber actually is only 15 feet wide by 15 feet deep, with three large ironbound oaken chests along the far wall. Each chest is closed and locked with a massive padlock. The keys are long lost, but sundering the padlock with a heavy object (AC 18, 10 hit points) or picking with thieves' tools and a successful DC 18 Dexterity check can open each chest. However, every chest is empty.

The golden floor is real, however it's not yet finished. The first 5-foot-by-15-foot section of the floor is clad in the gold tiles, each 1 foot square. Therefore, there are 75 tiles, each worth 50 gp. It is a time-consuming process to remove the tiles; each takes about 10 minutes to extract from the floor. So, with over 12 hours of labor, the characters can have their reward!

a puzzle box, if one is to open it. It requires pushing and sliding a series of stone tiles four times. Each correct maneuver requires a successful DC 18 Intelligence (Investigation) check. Each failure triggers a trap, releasing a mote of fire (fire damage) or a magic blast (force damage) that causes 5 (1d10) hit points of damage of the requisite type. There is a 50% chance of either effect.

If a persistent character manages to open the lid, it triggers a *magic mouth* spell that booms, "WHO DARES TO DISTURB MY ETERNAL REST. PREPARE TO FACE MY FULL WRATH!" Inside is a **zombie** wrapped in cloth strips, as to appear as a mummy. The zombie rises with a dreadful moan, and begins to attack. The zombie has maximum (33) hit points, but is unarmed so it resorts to slam attacks. Next to the zombie is Zelligar's *staff of stone* (see appendix A).

ROGAHN'S TOMB

Rogahn was good at two things in his life: swinging a sword and spending money. When Quasqueton was under construction, he insisted on a tomb for his final resting place, and he spared no expense. But he didn't simply want a chamber where his remains would lie. Instead, he demanded a series of rooms that would test potential grave robbers and adventurers. Based on his reputation, he knew they would come.

GENERAL FEATURES

Light. The interior of the tomb is unlit, unless the room description details otherwise.

Walls. The interior walls are smoothly hewn and finished. Most of these chambers were carved using traditional mining techniques. Climbing a standard interior wall requires a successful DC 15 Strength (Athletics) check, due to numerous handholds derived from traditional mining.

Floors/Ceilings. The floors of these chambers are smooth and lack flagstones. The floors are quite dusty, and typically covered with rocky debris in places. Ceiling heights are noted in the individual room descriptions.

Wandering Monsters. There are no wandering monsters in Rogahn's Tomb, although Melissa's ghost (see area 6) could be encountered in any chamber at the DM's discretion.

ENCOUNTER AREAS

AREA 1 – THE TEST OF BALANCE

The hewn steps descend to a stone door. Beyond is a large hall, about 25 feet wide and perhaps 50 feet long, bathed in soft illumination from several flickering torches. The ceiling is 15 feet overhead and the floor is smooth, polished stone, although covered with a thick layer of dust. At the far end of the room is a massive black stone throne, nearly 10 feet wide with a flared back almost as high. Mounted on the top of the throne is a dragon skull. On the back wall are numerous weapons mounted for display. Swords of various sizes, spears, polearms, and a variety of axes are all represented.

The torches (there are six of them) are all enchanted with *continual flame* spells. The stone throne is massive and weighs in excess of 5,000 pounds. The dragon skull belonged to a silver dragon, and two fire opals (each worth 1,000 gp) are set in the eye sockets. The weapons mounted along the back wall are all normal and include the following: seven swords (three long, two short, a scimitar, and a greatsword), nine spears, three halberds, two tridents, two greataxes, and five battleaxes with various blade shapes.

This chamber is a cunning trap designed to test the ingenuity of the characters. Following 5 feet of normal floor, the next 10-foot section (wall to wall) is a pressure plate that can be detected with a successful DC 21 Wisdom (Perception) check. The dust doesn't make it any easier to find! The trap can be disarmed with thieves' tools and a successful DC 22 Dexterity check. If triggered by placing more than 50 pounds on the pressure plate, a catch is released. The smooth, polished floor actually is a sub-floor about 10 feet above the real floor (see the side view map of this chamber for clarity). The middle of the sub-floor is balanced on a stone cylinder. Once the catch is released, the weight of the massive throne shifts the sub-floor like a teeter. Meanwhile, several of the mounted weapons spring out perpendicular to the wall. The polished floor, now sloped, likely sends victims sliding toward the far wall, and into the sharp weapons.

Anyone in the room when the trap is triggered must make a successful DC 13 Dexterity saving throw, or lose balance and be sent tumbling to the far wall, taking 7 (2d6) bludgeoning damage. Success indicates the target grabbed onto the door, or perhaps a nearby wall. Targets that fail their save must make a successful DC 16 Dexterity saving throw to grab onto the throne and halt their sliding. Failure indicates an introduction to the pointy end of several weapons mounted on the wall, for another 10 (3d6) damage, half of which is piercing and half of which is slashing damage.

There is a secret door concealed along the northern wall, but it is located about 10 feet off the floor. Assuming the trap has been triggered, this puts the sub-floor at just about the right elevation to easily search and pass through this door. It can be found with a successful DC 17 Wisdom (Perception) check and leads to area 2.

AREA 2 – THE TEST OF BATTLE

The door opens to reveal another long hall running north to south. This one is only 15 feet wide, but appears to be 50 feet long. The hall is bathed in the flickering illumination of several torches. Four pairs of statues line the walls of this hall, each depicting a human-oid warrior and each is armed with a different weapon. At the far end of the hall is a decorative mural.

Rogahn designed this chamber to test would-be tomb raiders in battle. The torches (there are four of them) are all enchanted with *continual flame* spells. The statues are all normal stone, but the weapons held by each are real weapons that can be removed. Further, six of these weapons have been animated with instructions to attack anyone who enters the chamber more than 5 feet. Two are longswords and are treated as **flying swords**. The other four weapons vary; use the statistics for a flying sword but apply the following changes:

Spear. AC 13, 14 (4d6) hit points, 4 (1d6 + 1) piercing damage.

Pike. AC 15, 14 (4d6) hit points, 6 (1d10 + 1) piercing damage.

Greataxe. AC 16, 17 (5d6) hit points, 7 (1d12 + 1) slashing damage.

Greatclub. AC 14, 21 (6d6) hit points, Strength 14, +4 to hit, 6 (1d8 + 2) bludgeoning damage.

The last two statues do not hold weapons aloft. Instead each holds a flask of oil in one hand and a torch outstretched in the other. Both torches are pointing toward the east wall, where the secret door is located. Each flask of oil is real and can be removed from the statue's grasp easily. One of these flasks would come in handy in area 3.

The secret door on the east wall can be located with a successful DC 15 Wisdom (Perception) check. Opening it is a bit tricky though as it requires both arms of the nearby statues to be pulled down at the same time. This can be discovered via trial and error, or with a successful DC 15 Intelligence (Investigation) check. A short flight of steps beyond leads to area 3.

The mural is composed of fancy tiles and depicts Rogahn battling a horde of barbarians on a grassy knoll. Many dead are at his feet. With a successful DC 15 Wisdom (Perception) check, several gems can be found decorating the mural. These can be easily pried out, yielding 10 gems (each worth 50 gp).

AREA 3 – THE TEST OF STRENGTH

A short flight of stone steps deposits you at an octagonal chamber perhaps 40 feet across. The ceiling is flat, about 15 feet high. In the center of this plain room is a stone wheel, on its side with three handle-like spokes. To the north is a massive stone door, much like a slab. A similar stone slab is positioned along the southern side of the chamber.

This chamber leads to the rest of the tomb. But the characters need to use their strength to proceed further. The stone slabs each weigh about 1,200 pounds, and are set in grooves. These portals can't be opened short of magic, such as a *stone shape*, or a *knock* spell. But turning the wheel in the center of the room can open one door at a time. A successful DC 15 Wisdom (Perception) check reveals a faint passage engraved on the top of the wheel: "Work smarter, not harder." This is a clue to use oil to lubricate the wheel to make it easier to turn.

If turned clockwise, the south door opens. If turned counterclockwise, the north door opens. To turn the wheel, a successful DC 24 Strength check is needed. But due to the massive weight of the stone wheel, this check is made at disadvantage. Additional characters using Help actions or applying oil to the stone wheel will grant advantage to the Strength check.

AREA 4 – TREASURY

The room beyond the northern stone slab is Rogahn's personal treasury.

The stone slab reveals a 10-foot-wide corridor that leads to a circular chamber about 15 feet in diameter. The center of the room is occupied by several racks holding a chain shirt and suits of studded leather, scale mail, and plate armor. Hanging on the walls on various pegs are an array of weapons.

Rogahn spent his wealth freely, so the only real "treasure" he had left was martial in function. Although the room appears unguarded, that would not be the case. Inscribed on the floor is a faint *glyph of warding* that can be detected with a successful DC 17 Intelligence (Investigation) check. It is triggered by anyone passing more than 5 feet down the corridor. The *glyph* casts a *conjure minor elemental* spell which summons two **fire snakes** to the corridor. They fight to the death, but return to the elemental plane of fire in 1 hour if not defeated.

After dealing with the fire snakes, the circular chamber can be investigated. All the items stored here are valuable. If the chamber is entered, the suit of plate armor animates to defend Rogahn's treasury. The **animated armor** spends its first action retrieving the *+1 longsword* from the wall and uses it to attack in addition to its slam. The animated armor fights until destroyed.

The following suits of armor are located on racks:

- **Plate armor.** This is the animated armor. When defeated, it is rendered a useless pile of metal.
- **Chain shirt.** This is human-sized *elven chain*.
- **Scale mail.** This is a human-sized suit of *+2 scale mail*.
- **Studded leather armor.** This human-sized suit of leather armor is studded with pewter and silver rivets and is worth 500 gp.

The following weapons hang on the walls:

- *+1 longsword* without a scabbard
- Silver shortsword with a ruby set on the pommel (worth 475 gp)
- *+1 halberd*
- Dark ash longbow with silver filigree (worth 245 gp)
- Wooden sword set with serrated shark teeth (worth 65 gp)
- Curved ceremonial dagger in an ivory and leather scabbard (worth 155 gp)
- War pick with a golden head (useless in combat, but worth 125 gp)

AREA 5 – THE TEST OF BATTLE AND BALANCE

The double doors open to a wide chamber, about 30 feet across and 40 feet long. The ceiling is but 10 feet high, but aside from a 5-foot-wide ledge, the floor is 10 feet below. Each of these recessed areas contains 10 skeletons wearing scraps of chain mail and wielding battered longswords. A 2-foot-wide walkway bisects the lower areas. At the opposite end of the room is another 5-foot-wide ledge and a single door centered on the wall. Standing guard at the door is a massive humanoid skeletal creature with four arms. Its eyes glow red, as it hefts a pair of halberds and approaches along the walkway. The skeleton horde below shambles in anticipation of battle.

Rogahn devised this challenge to test not only the skills in battle, but also balance and problem-solving. Often slaves or prisoners were sent to their doom in this chamber to fine-tune the guardians, but also for punishment and sometimes even for sport.

The large skeletal creature is a **bone golem** (see appendix B) with orders to defend the door and defeat all combatants who enter this chamber. It deftly walks out onto the walkway, waiting for a combatant. If targets hang back to employ ranged attacks, it charges and attempts to use Shove actions to knock targets onto the floor below. It wields two halberds (+4 to hit, 1d10 + 2 slashing damage). It often uses one of its actions on a special Sweeping Trip attack with the shaft of a halberd (see below). If a target is tripped on the walkway, he falls to the floor below, prone, taking 3 (1d6) bludgeoning damage and then needs to contend with the skeletons there. Any creature subject to a critical hit while on the walkway is automatically knocked off.

Sweeping Trip: *Melee Weapon Attack*: +4 to hit, reach 5 ft., one target. *Hit:* 4 (1d4 +2) bludgeoning damage and the target must make a DC 12 Dexterity saving throw or fall prone.

The floor below is strewn with bones and bits of armor and broken weapons, all useless. On each side of the room are 10 **skeletons**. Each wields a rusty longsword (+2 to hit, 4 [1d8] slashing damage). The skeletons can't get out of the pits without assistance. While waiting for prey to fall to them, the skeletons clamber up the walls (with aid from others) and attempt to grab, pull, or otherwise distract a character in combat with the bone golem. Unless the character makes a successful DC 10 Dexterity saving throw, all attacks, Dexterity skill checks, and Dexterity saving throws are at disadvantage until the end of the character's next turn.

If the bone golem is defeated (or knocked into the pit), the characters can safely exit the chamber. Although if they return, the bone golem will be ready to defend the opposite end of the room.

AREA 6 – ROGAHN'S TOMB

A curved corridor with stone steps descends deeper into the bowels of the dungeon. A nondescript stone door reveals a circular chamber 30 feet in diameter. The domed ceiling above stretches for 25 feet at its peak. At the opposite end of the chamber are three short steps that lead to a dais. Situated on the dais is a stone sarcophagus about 15 feet long and 4 feet high. Its stone surface is plain. Sprawled on the steps are the skeletal remains on a humanoid still wearing the tattered shreds of a fancy dress. The stale air smells faintly of perfume.

This chamber was designed to be Rogahn's tomb and final resting place. But instead, it played host to a terrible tragedy decades ago which still haunts it today. The walls and floor are plain. The sarcophagus is sealed, and a successful DC 15 Strength check is required to slide the lid off. Inside is the skeletal remains of a human in rotting clothes, but successful DC 15 Intelligence (Investigation) check reveals this body is unlikely to be Rogahn. Instead, it appears to be an adolescent male human.

The skeleton on the steps was Melissa, Rogahn's true love. The dagger plunged into her back is still in place. Under the skeleton is the dried caked stain of her blood. One of her bony hands still clutches a vial that once contained a virulent poison. A successful DC 15 Intelligence (Investigation) check reveals this fact following examination of the vial. Melissa was faithful to Rogahn in life, and still is decades after her cruel death. Even after months passed, and her true love did not return, her hope never faltered. Rogahn's advisor, Marevak, always had eyes for Melissa, but even when it was obvious Rogahn was dead, she refused his advances. Marevak went so far as to place a slave body in this tomb and he cast *silent image* on it to appear as Rogahn. He hoped it would provide closure for his beloved Melissa, and she would fall into his arms. But his plan failed, as Melissa threatened to quaff poison to join her lover in lieu of showing affection to Marevak. Outraged, the elf never gave her a chance as he plunged a dagger in her back. If he could not have her, no one would. Marevak left her body in the tomb and sealed the chambers before fleeing Quasqueton.

Murdered, betrayed, and apart from her one true love, Melissa's soul could find no peace. She soon arose as a **ghost**, and is bound to Rogahn's tomb for all eternity. Melissa now appears as an ethereal version of herself decades ago. She has a slight build and a freckled face. She once had long red hair with sparkling green eyes, but now she is a shimmering incorporeal form, still adorned in a fine dress. She speaks with a soft, lilting voice and the scent of perfume accompanies her. She has a constant itch on her back (caused by a dagger) that she can never quite seem to reach. She avoids the characters unless they disturb the sarcophagus, at which point she steps out of the wall and cautiously approaches. She is very inquisitive and forlorn, but doesn't quite understand that decades have passed since her death. While talking, she asks if someone can scratch this itch she can't seem to reach. Above all else, she dearly misses Rogahn.

She has finally come to grips with the death of her beloved hero Rogahn. She is aware that Marevak betrayed and murdered her. She longs to be reunited with Rogahn, but seems to be cursed in this undead state. She begs the characters for help, although she is unsure what needs to be done to be reunited with Rogahn in death. There are two ways Melissa's soul can be released to rejoin Rogahn, but they require her to possess a character. The first is to bring her to Rogahn's actual body, but that will be difficult since he was slain in a foreign land and was buried by his followers in an unnamed cairn. Clearly that is beyond the scope of this adventure. The other way is to bring Marevak to justice. Marevak is currently the advisor to the castellan of the Keep (see appendix B and area 26 in chapter 9). If confronted by the ghost of Melissa, Marevak succumbs to his guilt and pleads for mercy. Melissa swiftly slaughters him with an embrace laced with her Withering Touch. When he dies, she leaves the character and with a smile departs to be with Rogahn.

Awarding Experience. If the characters release Melissa's soul from its prison, divide 1,100 XP between them. As an additional reward the character that was possessed by Melissa receives a Blessing of Protection (+1 to AC and saving throws), although that character always faintly smells of fine perfume.

CHAPTER EIGHT
Keying the Dungeon of Quasqueton

The original version of module *B1: In Search of the Unknown* was simply a description of the encounter areas, and it was the Dungeon Master's job to assign monsters and treasure to the various rooms of the caverns. We have gone through all the trouble to stock the dungeon with monsters and treasures suitable for fifth edition Dungeons & Dragons. But if you would prefer to customize the adventure for your own fifth edition use, please consider the following guidelines and tables.

Once the Dungeon Master has read the entire module over one or more times and has gained a working familiarity with it, he or she is ready to key it. In doing so, the DM will take the basic descriptive framework and add his or her own ideas as to how and where the various monsters and treasures are located. The result will be a dungeon with his or her own indelible stamp, a bit different from all others—different even among those designed by others using the same descriptive outline.

With over 50 rooms and chambers noted on the two level maps by numbers (and several other unmarked open areas), there is plenty of space to explore even though this dungeon is actually quite small compared to most. With 15 to 25 randomly determined treasures (plus a few items of value that are part of the basic furnishings) and 16 to 20 monsters to place, the DM is offered a real choice in setting up the dungeon, for it is he or she who will decide on which areas are forbidding with danger or rich with reward.

The monsters (number keyed 1 to 30) and treasures should be placed with care and consideration. In many cases there should be a reason or rationale why a monster is located where it is and what it is doing. Just as there is a logical explanation behind the entire setting or scenario, so too should there be a similar thought behind what is to be found within the dungeon. Of course, in some cases, the unexpected or the inexplicable will be the exception as not everything should follow the normal order of things or it is too predictable for the players.

As mentioned previously elsewhere, not every room or chamber will have a monster, a treasure, or both. As a matter of fact, quite a number of places will simply be empty, while others may hold a monster with no treasure, or, rarely, a treasure without a monster guarding it. In the latter instance, the unguarded treasure will likely be well-hidden (as indeed any treasure can be) or concealed to make the room appear empty. Finally, in some instances, a room may contain a monster (being in its lair) as well as a treasure it is guarding, either wittingly (if it is its trove) or unwittingly (if its appearance there was only coincidental). In such a case, it will be necessary to defeat (either by killing or driving away) the monster or monsters before any attempt to discover or garner the treasure is attempted.

Once the DM has decided on where to place the various monsters and treasures (either randomly or with design purpose), he or she keys both the maps and the descriptive copy within this book by using codes (numbers or letters) for treasures and monsters, or simply jotting notes on a map. On the two game maps, these marks (preferably done in colored pencil for readability and possible erasure) of what type and number of monsters are there ("orcs" or "trogs," for instance) and where treasures are hidden will serve as a quick reference that makes running the adventure easier. The DM then refers to the descriptions of each room or chamber within the body of this book, and fills in the blanks following the proper sections corresponding to the marked map with the pertinent details. Additional side notes may include: what monster is located there (if any), where it hides (if it does so), what treasure is located within the room (if any), where it is located, and how it is hidden or protected (if it is). Any remaining space should be reserved for further notes, especially listing of the effects caused by subsequent player adventuring: monsters scared away to new locations, creatures slain, treasures removed, equipment abandoned, etc. Of course, notes on the map can likewise be made as desired.

Once the dungeon has been keyed, it is ready for exploration by the players. Good luck, and have fun! Follow these guidelines when setting up your own dungeon from scratch, and you should be successful.

MONSTER LIST

The monsters occupying the area to be explored are an assortment of creatures, some of which are descendants of former inhabitants (kobolds and goblins), and some of which have moved into the dungeon recently for unknown purpose. For continuity, the DM might want to draft a few notes on why these recent inhabitants have arrived.

The monsters (keeping in mind that the term refers to any encounter, no matter what the creature type) can be encountered in two ways: either in their "lair" (the particular room or chamber where they live, as keyed by the Dungeon Master), or as "wandering monsters." The latter encounters are more irregular, uncertain, and unpredictable as adventurers happen to meet the monsters on a random basis while exploring.

The monster table below is keyed by number for easy reference, and shows the monsters which will be shown on the game map as being in their "lair." The wandering monster lists appear within the descriptive copy of the module and are given prior to the information on each of the two levels of the dungeon—one being for the upper level, and the other for the lower level.

Monsters are shown on the list with pertinent details given (consult the full descriptions within the Monster Manual or appendix B for further information on each type), thus allowing them to be employed by the DM when encountered without additional dice rolling (except for the initial roll to determine number appearing). Important: although there are 30 listings, the Dungeon Master should use only 16 to 20 of them in the dungeon, placing some on each of the two levels in the rooms and chambers desired. The remainder will go unused. If you desire to randomly determine the monster encountered, roll 1d30 and consult the following table for the result. Should the result indicate a sub-table, roll the appropriate die on that table to get more detailed information on the monster and number encounter. If you don't have a d30, roll 1d20 plus 1d12, ignoring any result greater than 30.

5E MONSTER TABLE FOR BI

D30	# App	Monster	Statistics/Notes
1	1	Thoul (see appendix B)	AC 14; hp 30; Spd 30 ft.; **Traits** Keen Smell, Regeneration; **Actions** Multiattack, Claws (+5 melee, 1d6 + 3 slashing damage plus paralyzation); XP 200.
2	1	Gelatinous Cube	AC 6; hp 84; Spd 15 ft.; **Traits** Ooze Cube, Transparent; **Actions** Pseudopod (+4 melee, 3d6 acid damage); XP 450.
3	2-8	Skeletons	AC 13; hp 13; Spd 30 ft.; **Traits** NA; **Actions** Shortsword (+4 melee, 1d6 + 2 piercing damage); XP 50.
4	2-7	Troglodytes	AC 11; hp 13; Spd 30 ft.; **Traits** Chameleon Skin, Stench, Sunlight Sensitivity; **Actions** Multiattack, Bite (+4 melee, 1d4 + 2 piercing damage), Claw (+4 melee, 1d4 + 2 piercing damage); XP 50.
5	3-10	Female Troglodytes	AC 11; hp 13; Spd 30 ft.; **Traits** Chameleon Skin, Stench, Sunlight Sensitivity; **Actions** Multiattack, Bite (+4 melee, 1d4 + 2 piercing damage), Claw (+4 melee, 1d4 + 2 piercing damage); XP 50.
6	1-12	Kobolds	See Sub-Table A.
7	1-2	Ghouls	AC 12; hp 22; Spd 30 ft.; **Traits** NA; **Actions** Bite (+2 melee, 2d6 + 2 piercing damage), Claws (+4 melee, 2d4 + 2 slashing damage plus paralyzation); XP 200.
8	1	Carrion Crawler	AC 13; hp 51; Spd 30 ft., climb 30 ft.; **Traits** Keen Smell, Spider Climb; **Actions** Multiattack, Bite (+4 melee, 2d4 + 2 piercing damage), Tentacles (+8 melee, 1d4 + 2 poison damage plus poison); XP 450.
9	2-7	Skeletons	AC 13; hp 13; Spd 30 ft.; **Traits** NA; **Actions** Shortsword (+4 melee, 1d6 + 2 piercing damage); XP 50.
10	3-12	Giant Rats	AC 12; hp 7; Spd 30 ft.; **Traits** Keen Smell, Pack Tactics; **Actions** Bite (+4 melee, 1d4 + 2 piercing damage); XP 25.

11	1-2	Giant Spiders	AC 14; hp 26; Spd 30 ft., climb 30 ft.; **Traits** Spider Climb, Web Sense, Web Walker; **Actions** Bite (+5 melee, 1d8 + 3 piercing damage plus poison), Web (+5 ranged, restrain); XP 200.
12	2-4	Giant Wolf Spiders	AC 13; hp 11; Spd 40 ft., climb 20 ft.; **Traits** Spider Climb, Web Sense, Web Walker; **Actions** Bite (+3 melee, 1d6 + 1 piercing damage plus poison); XP 50.
13	2-7	Gnomes (see appendix B)	AC 14; hp 9; Spd 25 ft.; **Traits** Gnome Cunning, Innate Spellcasting; **Actions** Shortsword (+4 melee, 1d6 + 2 piercing damage), Light Crossbow (+4 ranged, 1d8 + 2 piercing damage), Alchemist's Fire (+4 ranged, 1d4 fire damage plus ignite); XP 25.
14	2-5	Giant Centipedes	AC 13; hp 4; Spd 30 ft., climb 30 ft.; **Traits** NA; **Actions** Bite (+4 melee, 1d4 + 2 piercing damage plus poison); XP 50.
15	1-4	Animated Objects	See Sub-Table B.
16	1-6	Fungi/Slimes/Molds	See Sub-Table C.
17	1	Rust Monster	AC 14; hp 27; Spd 40 ft.; **Traits** Iron Scent, Rust Metal; **Actions** Bite (+3 melee, 1d8 + 1 piercing damage), Antennae (rust); XP 100.
18	1-4	Swarms of Bats	AC 12; hp 22; Spd 0 ft., fly 30 ft.; **Traits** Echolocation, Keen Hearing, Swarm; **Actions** Bites (+4 melee, 2d4 piercing damage or 1d4 piercing damage if reduced to half hp); XP 50.
19	2-9	Stirges	AC 14; hp 2; Spd 10 ft., fly 40 ft.; **Traits** NA; **Actions** Blood Drain (+5 melee, 1d4 + 3 piercing damage plus attach); XP 25.
20	2-7	Giant Fire Beetles	AC 13; hp 4; Spd 30 ft.; **Traits** Illumination; **Actions** Bite (+1 melee, 1d6 - 1 slashing damage); XP 10.
21	1-4	Mephits	See Sub-Table D.
22	2-5	Zombies	AC 8; hp 22; Spd 20 ft.; **Traits** Undead Fortitude; **Actions** Slam (+3 melee, 1d6 + 1 bludgeoning damage); XP 50.
23	1-5	NPCs	See Sub-Table E.
24	2-5	Orcs	AC 13; hp 15; Spd 30 ft.; **Traits** Aggressive; **Actions** Greataxe (+5 melee, 1d12 + 3 slashing damage); XP 100.
25	1	Troglodyte Shaman (see appendix B)	AC 12; hp 22; Spd 30 ft.; **Traits** Chameleon Skin, Spellcasting, Stench, Sunlight Sensitivity; **Actions** Multiattack, Bite (+3 melee, 1d4 + 1 piercing damage), Bone Cudgel (+3 melee, 1d6 + 1 bludgeoning damage); XP 200.
26	1-4	Barbarian Warriors (see appendix B)	AC 13; hp 15; Spd 30 ft.; **Traits** Rage; **Actions** Spear (+5 melee, 1d8 + 3 piercing damage); XP 50.
27	2-5	Piercers	AC 15; hp 22; Spd 5 ft., climb 5 ft.; **Traits** False Appearance, Spider Climb; **Actions** Drop (+3 melee, 1d6 piercing damage for each 10-foot drop); XP 100.
28	1	Mimic	AC 12; hp 58; Spd 15 ft.; **Traits** Adhesive, False Appearance, Grappler, Shapechanger; **Actions** Bite (+5 melee, 1d8 + 3 piercing damage plus 1d8 acid damage), Pseudopod (+5 melee, 1d8 + 3 bludgeoning damage); XP 450.
29	2-7	Goblins	AC 15; hp 7; Spd 30 ft.; **Traits** Nimble Escape; **Actions** Scimitar (+4 melee, 1d6 + 2 slashing damage), Shortbow (+4 ranged, 1d6 + 2 piercing damage); XP 50.
30	1	Water Weird	AC 13; hp 58; Spd 0 ft., swim 60 ft.; **Traits** Invisible in Water, Water Bound; **Actions** Constrict (+5 melee, 3d6 + 3 bludgeoning damage plus grapple and suffocate); XP 700.

SUB-TABLE A: KOBOLDS

D6	# App	Monster	Statistics/Notes
1	2-8	Kobolds	AC 12; hp 5; Spd 30 ft.; **Traits** Pack Tactics, Sunlight Sensitivity; **Actions** Dagger (+4 melee, 1d4 + 2 piercing damage), Sling (+4 ranged, 1d4 + 2 bludgeoning damage); XP 25.
2	1-6	Kobolds	AC 12; hp 5; Spd 30 ft.; **Traits** Pack Tactics, Sunlight Sensitivity; **Actions** Club (+4 melee, 1d4 + 2 bludgeoning damage), Sling (+4 ranged, 1d4 + 2 bludgeoning damage); XP 25.
3	3-12	Female Kobolds	AC 12; hp 5; Spd 30 ft.; **Traits** Pack Tactics, Sunlight Sensitivity; **Actions** Dagger (+4 melee, 1d4 + 2 piercing damage); XP 25.
4	2-4	Elite Kobolds (see appendix B)	AC 13; hp 9; Spd 30 ft.; **Traits** Pack Tactics, Sunlight Sensitivity; **Actions** Shortsword (+4 melee, 1d6 + 2 piercing damage); XP 50.
5	1	Kobold Chieftain (see appendix B)	AC 14; hp 22; Spd 30 ft.; **Traits** Pack Tactics, Sunlight Sensitivity; **Actions** Longsword (+4 melee, 1d8 + 2 slashing damage); XP 200.
6	2-4	Winged Kobolds	AC 13; hp 7; Spd 30 ft., fly 30 ft.; **Traits** Pack Tactics, Sunlight Sensitivity; **Actions** Dagger (+5 melee, 1d4 + 3 piercing damage), Dropped Rock (+5 ranged, 1d6 + 3 bludgeoning damage); XP 50.

SUB-TABLE B: ANIMATED OBJECTS

D6	# App	Monster	Statistics/Notes
1	1-2	Living Stone Statues (see appendix B)	AC 15; hp 23; Spd 20 ft.; **Traits** False Appearance; **Actions** Multiattack, Stone Longsword (+4 melee, 1d8 + 2 slashing damage); XP 50.
2	1-4	Living Wax Statues (see appendix B)	AC 11; hp 9; Spd 30 ft.; **Traits** False Appearance; **Actions** Longsword (+2 melee, 1d8 slashing damage); XP 25.
3	1	Iron Cobra (see appendix B)	AC 18; hp 9; Spd 30 ft.; **Traits** Fire Absorption, Magic Resistance; **Actions** Bite (+5 melee, 1d4 + 3 piercing damage plus poison); XP 100.
4	1-3	Animated Weapons	AC 17; hp 17; Spd 0 ft., fly 50 ft. (hover); **Traits** Antimagic Susceptibility, False Appearance; **Actions** By Weapon (+3 melee, damage by weapon type); XP 50.
5	1	Broom of Animated Attack (see appendix B)	AC 15; hp 17; Spd 0 ft., fly 50 ft. (hover); **Traits** Antimagic Susceptibility, False Appearance; **Actions** Multiattack, Broomstick (+5 melee, 1d4 + 3 bludgeoning damage); **Reactions** Animated Attack; XP 50.
6	1-2	Rugs of Smothering	AC 12; hp 33; Spd 10 ft.; **Traits** Antimagic Susceptibility, Damage Transfer, False Appearance; **Actions** Smother (+5 melee, grapple plus suffocate); XP 450.

SUB-TABLE C: FUNGI/SLIMES/MOLDS

D4	# App	Monster	Statistics/Notes
1	1-6	Shriekers	AC 5; hp 13; Spd 0 ft.; **Traits** False Appearance; **Reactions** Shriek; XP 10.
2	1-4	Violet Fungi	AC 5; hp 18; Spd 5 ft.; **Traits** False Appearance; **Actions** Multiattack, Rotting Touch (+2 melee, 1d8 necrotic damage); XP 50.
3	1	Green Slime	See Dungeon Master's Guide p. 105.
4	1	Yellow Mold	See Dungeon Master's Guide p. 105.

SUB-TABLE D: MEPHITS

D4	# App	Monster	Statistics/Notes
1	1-2	Dust Mephits	AC 12; hp 17; Spd 30 ft., fly 30 ft.; **Traits** Death Burst (Blind), Innate Spellcasting; **Actions** Claws (+4 melee, 1d4 + 2 slashing damage), Blinding Breath; XP 100.
2	1-4	Magma Mephits	AC 11; hp 22; Spd 30 ft., fly 30 ft.; **Traits** Death Burst (Lava), False Appearance, Innate Spellcasting; **Actions** Claws (+3 melee, 1d4 + 1 slashing damage plus 1d4 fire damage), Fire Breath; XP 100.
3	2-4	Mud Mephits	AC 11; hp 27; Spd 20 ft., fly 20 ft. swim 20 ft.; **Traits** Death Burst (Sticky Mud), False Appearance; **Actions** Fists (+3 melee, 1d6 + 1 bludgeoning damage), Mud Breath; XP 50.
4	2-4	Smoke Mephits	AC 12; hp 22; Spd 30 ft., fly 30 ft.; **Traits** Death Burst (Smoke Cloud), Innate Spellcasting; **Actions** Claws (+4 melee, 1d4 + 2 slashing damage), Cinder Breath; XP 50.

SUB-TABLE E: NPCS

D4	# App	Monster	Statistics/Notes
1	1-3	Gnome Tricksters (see appendix B)	AC 16; hp 18; Spd 25 ft.; **Traits** Gnome Cunning, Innate Spellcasting, Spellcasting; **Actions** Dagger (+5 melee, 1d4 + 3 piercing damage), Dagger (+5 ranged, 1d4 + 3 piercing damage); XP 200.
2	1-2	Half-Ogres	AC 12; hp 30; Spd 30 ft.; **Traits** NA; **Actions** Battleaxe (+5 melee, 2d8 + 3 slashing damage, or 2d10 + 3 slashing damage if used two-handed), Javelin (+5 ranged, 2d6 + 3 piercing damage); XP 200.
3	1	Berserker	AC 13; hp 67; Spd 30 ft.; **Traits** Reckless; **Actions** Greataxe (+5 melee, 1d12 + 3 slashing damage); XP 450.
4	2-5	Acolytes	AC 10; hp 9; Spd 30 ft.; **Traits** Spellcasting; **Actions** Club (+2 melee, 1d4 bludgeoning damage); XP 50.

TREASURE LIST

Listed below are 21 different treasures organized on a table. To randomly determine what treasure is found in a given encounter area, roll 4d6 and consult the table. The dice cast will result in a bell curve distribution. That is, the numbers 12 to 16 will be the most common results with results 4 to 11 and 17 to 24 being much more rare. As such, common treasures (coins and gems) are more likely to occur, while expensive art objects and magic items will be rarer.

Also note there are several sub-tables you will be prompted to roll on for more specific details of the treasure. For example, if you roll a 10 ("coin hoard"), you are prompted to roll again on Sub-Table A (1d6). If you roll a 2 on this sub-table, it indicates the coin hoard contains copper (6d6), silver (4d6) and gold coins (2d6). The number in parentheses indicates the number of each coin type. In this example, 25 cp, 16 sp, and 4 gp might be the contents of the hoard. This method to determine random treasure is more complicated than the original system in module B1. But it allows for more flexibility, and is an homage to the old table/sub-table systems often employed by Mr. Gygax himself.

Considering their very nature, treasures, in most instances, should be concealed or hidden cleverly. The Dungeon Master should use his or her imagination in devising ways to hide items from discovery. Some suggestions for treasure location might be: inside an ordinary item in plain view, within a secret compartment in a container, disguised to appear as something else, under or behind a loose stone in the floor or wall, under a heap of trash or dung, or similarly hidden. The appropriate skill check (likely Wisdom (Perception)) and Difficulty Class (DC) should be added to the encounter description. For 1st- to 3rd-level characters, DCs typically range from 10 to 15. Occasionally a treasure may be easily noticed, but this should be the exception rather than the rule.

In some instances, valuable treasure will be protected by locks, traps, or protective magic. The deadlier protections are reserved for more experienced adventurers, so any such devices will be uncommon in dungeons designed for beginning players, such as this one. The DM should feel free to create an occasional protection which may confuse or delay characters attempting to find a particular treasure, however.

Special Note: The tables herein can be used to generate hundreds of different treasure results. However, only between 15 to 25 of them should actually be placed in the dungeon by the DM. The remainder should go unused. When treasures are chosen and placed, a good assortment of items should be represented: some very valuable, some worthless, most in between. The DM is responsible to ensure the monsters encountered possess or guard the appropriate treasure. Consult the Dungeon Master's Guide (chapter 7, pp. 136-139) for information on how to design treasure values appropriate to challenge ratings.

5E TREASURE TABLE FOR B1

4D6	# App	Treasure	Notes
4	1	Art object	Average value 750 gp.
5	1-2	Gems	Value 500 gp each.
6	1	Art object	Average value 250 gp.
7	1-2	Art objects	Average value 100 gp.
8	1-4	Art objects	Average value 50 gp.
9	2-8	Art objects	Average value 25 gp.
10	1	Coin hoard	See Sub-Table A.
11	3-12	Gems	Value 50 gp each.
12	20-70	Electrum coins	
13	400-2,400	Copper coins	
14	300-1,800	Silver coins	
15	20-120	Gold coins	
16	4-16	Gems	Value 10 gp each.
17	1-6	Gems	Value 100 gp each.
18	1-3	*Potions*	See Sub-Table B.
19	1-2	*Spell scrolls*	See Sub-Table C.
20	1	*Driftglobe*	
21	1	*+1 shield*	
22	1	*+1 weapon*	See Sub-Table D.
23	1	*Bag of holding*	
24	1	*Boots of elvenkind*	

SUB-TABLE A: COIN HOARD

D6	Coin Distribution
1	Copper (8d6 x 100), silver (3d6 x 100)
2	Copper (6d6), silver (4d6), gold (2d6)
3	Silver (10d10), gold (5d10)
4	Copper (2d6 x 100), silver (1d6 x 100), gold (2d6 x 10)
5	Silver (1d6 x 100), electrum (1d6 x 10), gold (1d4 x 100)
6	Gold (6d6), platinum (2d6)

SUB-TABLE B: POTIONS

D6	Potion
1	*Healing*
2	*Climbing*
3	*Water breathing*
4	*Resistance*
5	*Animal friendship*
6	*Greater healing* (counts as two potions)

SUB-TABLE C: SPELL SCROLLS

D8	Scroll (determine spell randomly)
1	Wizard-cantrip
2	Cleric-cantrip
3	Wizard-1st level
4	Wizard-2nd level
5	Cleric-1st level
6	Cleric-2nd level
7	Wizard-3rd level
8	2 *spell scrolls* (roll twice more on this table and ignore any 8's)

SUB-TABLE D: +1 WEAPONS

D6	Weapon
1	Dagger
2	Arrows (4d6)
3	Crossbow bolts (2d6)
4	Spear
5	Mace
6	Sword (Roll 1d4: 1-shortsword, 2-rapier, 3-longsword, 4-greatsword)

CHAPTER NINE
The Keep on the Borderlands

The Realm of mankind is narrow and constricted. Always the forces of Chaos press upon its borders, seeking to enslave its populace, rape its riches, and steal its treasures. If it were not for a stout few, many in the Realm would indeed fall prey to the evil which surrounds them. Yet, there are always certain exceptional and brave members of humanity, as well as similar individuals among its allies: the dwarves, elves, and halflings, who rise above the common level and join battle to stave off the darkness which would otherwise overwhelm the land. Bold adventurers from the Realm set off for the Borderlands to seek their fortune. It is these adventurers who, provided they survive the challenge, carry the battle to the enemy. Such adventurers meet the forces of Chaos in a testing ground where only the fittest return to relate the tale. Here, these individuals will become skilled in their profession, be it fighter or wizard, cleric or rogue. They will be tried in the fire of combat, those who return, hardened and more fit. True, some few who do survive the process will turn from Law and good and serve the masters of Chaos, but most will remain faithful and ready to fight chaos wherever it threatens to infect the Realm.

You are indeed members of that exceptional class, adventurers who have journeyed to the Keep on the Borderlands in search of fame and fortune. Of course you are inexperienced, but you have your skills and a heart that cries out for adventure. You have it in you to become great, but you must gain experience and knowledge and greater skill. There is much to learn, and you are willing and eager to be about it! Each of you has come with everything which could possibly be given you to help. Now you must fend for yourselves; your fate is in your hands, for better or worse.

Ahead, up the winding road, atop a sheer-walled mount of stone, looms the great Keep. Here, at one of civilization's strongholds between good lands and bad, you will base yourselves and equip for forays against the wicked monsters who lurk in the wilds. Somewhere nearby, amidst the dark forests and tangled fens, are the Caves of Chaos where fell creatures lie in wait. All this you know, but before you dare adventure into such regions you must become acquainted with the other members of your group, for each life will depend upon the ability of the others to cooperate against the common foe. Now, before you enter the grim fortress, is the time for introductions and an exchange of information, for fate seems to have decreed that you are to become an adventurous band who must pass through many harrowing experiences together on the path which leads towards greatness.

START

Read the following when the characters approach the Keep for the first time:

You have traveled for many days, leaving the Realm and entering into the wilder area of the Borderlands. Farms and towns have become less frequent and travelers few. The road has climbed higher as you enter the forested and mountainous country.

You now move up a narrow, rocky track. A sheer wall of natural stone is on your left, the path falling away to a steep cliff on the right. There is a small widening ahead, where the main gate to the Keep resides. The blue-clad men-at-arms who guard the entrance shout at you to give your names and state your business. All along the wall you see curious faces peering down at you, eager to welcome new champions of Law, but ready with crossbow and halberd to give another sort of welcome to enemies.

DM Note: Have each player identify his or her character's name and profession. Have them answer in their own words why they seek entrance to the place. If the answer sounds unnatural, assume the role of the corporal of the watch (see area 3), and begin to cross-examine the speaker. Now is the time to make the players realize that whatever they say, as speech or relating their actions, will be noted by you, as Dungeon Master, and acted upon accordingly in whatever role is appropriate to the situation. A courteous and full reply might well win a friend amongst the soldiers who might be of aid sometime. Rudeness and discourtesy may bring suspicion and enemies to trouble the course of things within the otherwise safe base area. When you are satisfied that the scene is played out, have the group enter.

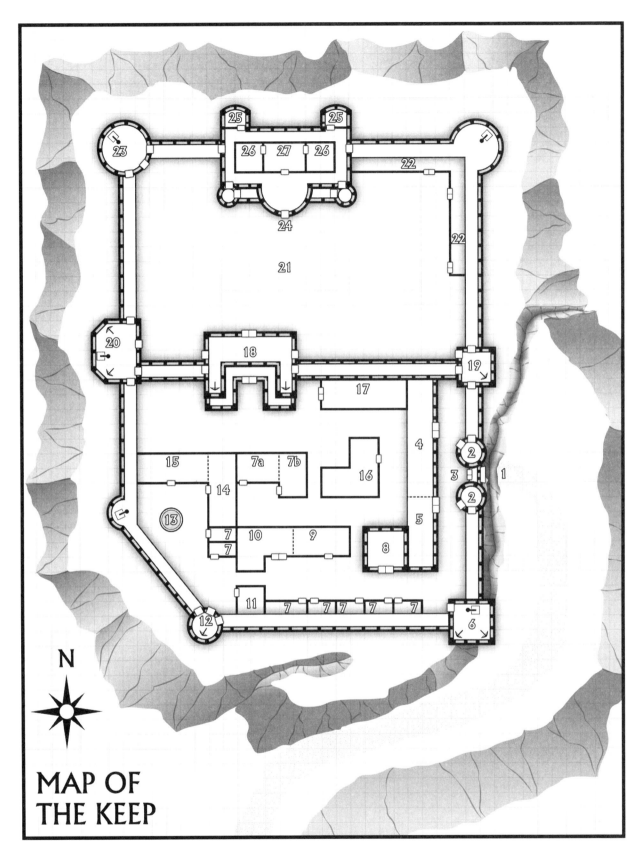

N

MAP OF
THE KEEP

 Battlements

 Door
Double Door

 Ballista
Catapult

 = 10 Feet

NOTES ABOUT THE KEEP

I. This whole place is well-organized for security and for defense. In time of need, many civilians will arm themselves and help man the walls, while noncombatants bring ammunition, food, and water to the walls and help the wounded. Sentries are alert. A group of guards patrols the walls regularly and the commander checks every half hour to hour. It is very unlikely that persons can enter or leave without being seen, unless magic is used. You can have magical traps placed in key areas to shout "ALARM!" whenever an invisible creature passes within 10 feet or so!

Within the Keep itself, the townspeople are generally law-abiding and honest. Boorishness and ill manners are frowned upon. If any member of a party should be caught in a criminal act, the alarm will be sounded instantly. Citizens will try to prevent the escape of any lawbreakers (without sacrificing their lives) until the guard arrives in 1-2 minutes. If met with resistance, the guard will not hesitate to use force, even killing if they must. Those offenders taken prisoner will be locked in the dungeons under the Keep and punished for their crimes.

II. Floor plans might be useful. Note that most areas have two or more stories, and there is furniture in the rooms not shown. Also left out are details of heating, light, and descriptive touches such as color, rafters, decoration, etc. If you have time, floor plans and detailing of each area might be very helpful, exceptionally so in places frequented by the adventurers.

III. Information regarding the Caves of Chaos from inhabitants of the Keep might be gained by player characters. You may give one rumor (at random, using a d20) to each player as starting information. Other rumors may be keyed to other persons in the Keep. For example: "Talking with the Taverner (area 15) might reveal either rumor #18 or #19; he will give the true rumor if his reaction is good." Do not give out all the rumors. You may add whatever false rumors you wish, but adding to the amount of true information is not recommended.

---

indicates a light catapult. Each requires two crewmen to operate, and takes two actions to load, two actions to aim, and one action to fire. There is ammunition for six catapult shots per machine.

LIGHT CATAPULT

Large object

AC: 15

Hit Points: 75

Damage Immunities: poison, psychic

Stone: *Ranged Weapon Attack:* +6 to hit, range 240/480 ft. (can't hit targets within 60 feet of the light catapult), all targets in a 10-foot diameter location. *Hit:* 27 (5d10) bludgeoning damage.

---

indicates a ballista, a huge heavy crossbow manned by two men. Each ballista has 12 missiles stored nearby. Before it can be fired, it must be loaded and then aimed. It takes one action to load the weapon, one action to aim it, and one action to fire it.

BALLISTA

Large object

AC: 15

Hit Points: 50

Damage Immunities: poison, psychic

Bolt: *Ranged Weapon Attack:* +6 to hit, range 120/480 ft., one target. *Hit:* 16 (3d10) piercing damage.

RUMOR TABLE

"F" denotes a false rumor

D20	Rumor
1	A merchant, imprisoned in the caves, will reward his rescuers.
2	(F) A powerful wizard will destroy all cave invaders.
3	Tribes of different creatures live in different caves.
4	An ogre sometimes helps the cave dwellers.
5	A magic wand was lost in the caves area.
6	(F) All of the cave entrances are trapped.
7	If you get lost, beware the eater of men!
8	Altars are very dangerous.
9	(F) A fair maiden is imprisoned within the caves.
10	(F) "Bree-yark" is goblin-language for "We surrender!"
11	Beware of treachery from within the party.
12	The big dog-men live very high in the caves.
13	There are hordes of tiny dragon-men in the lower caves.
14	(F) Piles of magic armor are hoarded in the southern caves.
15	(F) The bugbears in the caves are afraid of dwarves!
16	Lizard-men live in the marshes.
17	An elf once disappeared across the marshes.
18	Beware the Mad Hermit of the north lands.
19	(F) Nobody has ever returned from an expedition to the caves.
20	There is more than one tribe of orcs within the caves.

IV. Entrance to the Inner Bailey can be gained if the adventurers perform a heroic act on behalf of the Keep, if they bring back an exceptional trophy or valuable prisoners, or if they contribute a valuable magic item or 1,000 or more gold pieces to the place. They will be invited to a feast and revel, and then closely watched and carefully questioned. If the Castellan (see area 27) likes the looks of the group, and his assistants agree, he will ask them to perform a special mission that is suitable to their ability, but difficult. Use the area map (see chapter 10) or the Caves of Chaos (chapter 11) to find a suitable goal. On the other hand, if they are rude or behave badly, he will simply retire early, ending the revel, and they will never be aided or invited back. If they try to steal or are threatening, the group will be attacked and killed immediately (if this can be managed, of course).

Groups sent on a mission will be *blessed* and given up to 100 gp each for any needed supplies. If they succeed, they will be given passes to the Inner Bailey and can ask the Castellan for aid if there is a major foe to overcome in the caves. He will send a minimum of one corporal of the guard (see areas 20 and 23) and three archers in plate armor (see area 23), or at maximum the Sergeant of the Guard (see area 18), a corporal of the guard, and a dozen guards (see area 18).

V. After the normal possibilities of this module are exhausted, you might wish to continue to center the action of your campaign around the Keep by making it the base for further adventures which you may devise. For example (assuming that the group has done good service for the Castellan), have a large force of bandits move into the area, and then appoint the group to command an expedition of Keep troops, mercenaries, and so on to drive them away. Or the party might become "traders" operating out of the Keep, hoping to find adventures as they travel in the surrounding area. See pages 106-112 in the Dungeon Master's Guide for details on wilderness exploration, and chapter 10 for details of the lands surrounding the Keep.

AREAS OF THE KEEP

AREA 1 – MAIN GATE

Two towers, 30 feet high with battlements, flank a 20-foot-high gatehouse. All have slits for bow and crossbow fire. A deep crevice in front of the place is spanned by a drawbridge, usually in the raised position. There is a portcullis at the entry and large gates at the far end of the passage. The passage is about 10 feet wide and high, the ceiling above is pierced with murder holes, and the walls to either side adorned with slits for archery. It is obvious that the building is constructed of great blocks of the hardest granite, undoubtedly common throughout the entire fortress.

Two **guards** approach when the drawbridge is lowered and the portcullis raised. Each is clad in plate armor (AC 18, speed 20 ft.) and carries a halberd (1d10 + 1 slashing damage). They require that persons entering the Keep put their weapons away, before escorting them through the short tunnel into area 3.

AREA 2 – FLANKING TOWERS

Atop each tower are four **guards** armed with heavy crossbows (range 100/400 ft., 1d10 + 1 piercing damage), cocked and ready to fire. Each is clad in chain mail (AC 16), wearing a longsword (1d8 + 1 slashing damage, or 1d10 + 1 slashing damage if used two-handed) and a dagger (1d4 + 1 piercing damage), and has a shield (AC 18 when picked up) nearby.

Inside each tower are 12 other **guards**, four being "on-duty" wearing armor and armed as the guards on the tower tops. The other eight in the tower are resting, and it takes 10 minutes for these men to ready themselves for battle. They are exactly like the others, except instead of heavy crossbows, they carry longbows (range 150/600 ft., 1d8 + 1 piercing damage).

The three floors of these towers contain supplies of bolts and arrows, spears, rocks, and several barrels of oil (all for hurling down on attackers). There will also be pallets for sleeping, pegs with clothing belonging to the soldiers, and some small tables, stools, and benches.

Each guard has 1d6 cp and 1d4 sp on his person.

AREA 3 – ENTRY YARD

This narrow place is paved. All entrants, save those of the garrison, are required to dismount and stable their animals in the common stable (area 4). The **corporal of the watch** (see appendix B) is stationed here. The corporal has the keys to the common warehouse (area 5). He is rather grouchy, with a low Charisma of 6, but he admires outspoken, brave fighters and is easily taken in by a pretty girl. Beside him is a **commoner**, wearing robes (a scribe) who records the name of each person who enters or leaves, and flanking each man is another **guard** in plate armor (AC 18, speed 20 ft.) armed with a halberd (1d10 + 1 slashing damage).

Development. When dismounted, lackeys from the common stable arrive to take the mounts or mules. Any goods which are not carried by the adventurers are stored in the common warehouse. Another lackey then escorts travelers to the Traveler's Inn (area 14).

AREA 4 – COMMON STABLE

This long building is about 15 feet high, with a 3-foot parapet atop its flat roof, so that it can be used in defense of the gate. The gateside wall is pierced for archery. There are always 1d4 + 4 lackeys (**commoners**) inside tending to horses and gear. Each is unarmored (AC 10) but can fight with various available weapons (pitchforks and the like; 1d8 piercing damage).

There are various **riding horses** (2d4) and **draft horses** (2d8) here, as well as 1d4 **mules**.

AREA 5 – COMMON WAREHOUSE

Visiting merchants and other travelers who have quantities of goods are required to keep their materials here until they are either sold to the persons at the Keep or taken elsewhere. The building is the same layout as the common stable (area 4) with respect to height, parapet, etc. Its double doors are chained and padlocked, and the corporal of the watch (see area 3) must be called to gain entry, as he has the keys. Otherwise the chains and padlock need to be sundered (AC 19, 15 hit points)—a task that likely takes a few loud rounds to complete. Otherwise, the padlock can be picked with thieves' tools and a successful DC 20 Dexterity check.

Inside are two wagons, a cart, and many boxes, barrels, and bales. These contain various food items, cloth, arrows, bolts, salt, and two tuns of wine. The average value per wagon-load is 100 gp.

AREA 6 – BAILIFF'S TOWER

The whole tower is 40 feet high, with a 5-foot-tall battlement atop it. All walls are pierced for archery.

The superintendent of the fortress—or **bailiff of the outer bailey** (see appendix B)—lives here. A grizzled veteran of many campaigns, the balding man sports a black-gray beard. He and the scribe, a human male **commoner**, share an office on the lower floor. The bailiff's longbow and a quiver stocked with 20 arrows (three of which are magic *+1 arrows*) hang on the office wall, ready for use. The scribe has a bejeweled inkpot (worth 100 gp), but it is dirty and ink-covered, appearing worthless despite being on his table in plain sight. A successful DC 15 Intelligence check reveals the inkpot is valuable.

The bailiff has 3d6 gp with him always, and the scribe has 2d6 sp and 1d4 gp in his purse.

Their living quarters are on the second story. The usual furnishings of bed, chest, armoire, table and chair, plus a rug, are located in each room. Hidden in the bailiff's old boots in the armoire is a stash of 50 gp in a worn pouch, which requires a successful DC 13 Wisdom (Perception) check to locate. Hanging on his wall is another quiver filled with 20 arrows.

The third floor is a storage area stocked with barrels (fresh water), boxes (mundane objects), and crates (non-perishable foodstuffs).

The fourth story serves as a barracks for 12 **guards**. Six are clad in leather armor and shield (AC 14) and armed with halberds (1d10 + 1 slashing damage) and handaxes (range 20/60 ft., 1d6 + 1 slashing damage). The other six have chain mail (AC 16), light crossbows (range 80/320 ft., 1d8 + 1 piercing damage), and longswords (1d8 + 1 slashing damage, or 1d10 + 1 slashing damage if used two-handed). These guards serve as the escort of the bailiff from time to time.

Each guard carries 2d6 cp and 1d6 sp.

Their room contains pallets, pegs with cloaks and other clothing, two long tables with benches, a supply of 180 crossbow bolts, and several dozen large rocks.

AREA 7 – PRIVATE APARTMENTS

Special quarters are available for well-to-do families, rich merchants, guild masters, and the like. The five small apartments along the south wall are occupied by families of persons dwelling within the Outer Bailey of the Keep. The two large ones (area 7a and area 7b, respectively) currently house a jewel merchant and a priest.

a. Jewel Merchant. The jewel merchant, Lhodis, and his wife are human **commoners**. They are awaiting a caravan back to more civilized lands. They employ a pair of guards (use **corporal of the watch** statistics from appendix B) that are each wearing chain mail and carrying a shield (AC 18), wielding a longsword (+4 to hit, 1d8 + 2 slashing damage) and dagger (+4 to hit, 1d4 + 2 piercing damage). Each guard commands a huge **mastiff** (AC 13 from leather barding, 16 [3d8 + 3] hit points) trained to kill.

All persons here carry 3d6 sp each. The merchant has a locked iron box with 100 gp and 200 pp inside. The merchant has the key hidden in his left boot, or the lock can be picked with thieves' tools and a successful DC 22 Dexterity check. Secreted in his belt are 10 gems (worth 100 gp each). His wife wears a jeweled bracelet, necklace, and earrings (worth 600 gp, 1,200 gp, and 300 gp, respectively)—each of which is available for sale as per gems (see Development, below).

The four are lodged in the eastern portion of the building, with the merchant and his wife being on the upper floor most of the time. The apartment is well-furnished, but there is nothing of particular interest or value, except for the coins, gems, and jewelry noted.

Development. The merchant buys gems at 60% to 90% (1d4 x 10 + 50%) of value. He sells at 110% to 140% (1d4 x 10 + 100%) of value.

b. Priest. The western portion houses the jovial priest (an **adept**; see appendix B) who is taking advantage of his stopover at the Keep to discuss theology with learned folk and to convert others. Everyone speaks well of him, although the two **acolytes** with him are avoided, as they never speak. The priest says they must follow vows of silence until they attain priestly standing. His well-appointed chambers are comfortably furnished and guests are always welcomed with a cozy fire and plenty of ale or wine. The priest is a very fine companion and an excellent listener. He does not press his religious beliefs upon any unwilling person. He is outspoken in his hatred of evil, and if approached by a party of adventurers seeking the Caves of Chaos, he seeks to accompany them. He has *+1 plate armor* and a *+1 shield* (AC 22) and wields a *+1 mace* (+3 to hit, 1d6 + 1 bludgeoning damage). He has a Dexterity of 15 (+2), a Constitution of 16 (+2), and 19 (3d8 + 6) hit points. He carries two *spell scrolls*: *hold person* and *silence*. The acolytes have chain mail and shields (AC 18, speed 20 ft.) and wield maces (1d6 bludgeoning damage).

Each cleric carries 4d6 sp, and each wears a gold chain worth 100 gp. The priest also has a bloodstone gem worth 500 gp. A small sack hidden in the priest's chair requires a successful DC 15 Wisdom (Perception) check to locate should the chamber be searched. It contains 30 each of copper, silver, electrum, gold, and platinum pieces, plus a jeweled clasp worth 300 gp. This hidden stash is for bribes for subversion or to use to gain freedom if necessary.

Development. All these clerics are chaotic and evil, being in the Keep to spy and defeat those seeking to gain experience by challenging the monsters in the Caves of Chaos. Once in the caves, the priest uses spells such as *inflict wounds* or *command* as needed to hinder and harm adventurers. Betrayal always occurs during a crucial encounter with monsters.

AREA 8 – SMITHY AND ARMORER

This building is about 20 feet high, with the usual 5-foot parapet above and walls pierced for defense. The lower floor is occupied by a forge, bellows, and smith tools such as hammers, chisels, and tongs. At this location, horses and mules are shod, weapons forged, armor repaired, and similar work done.

The smith, a bulky human named Ghor, is a retired human **guard** (Constitution 17, 13 [2d8 + 4] hit points, and proficiency with smith's tools) and an armorer. He uses a hammer (1d4 + 1 bludgeoning damage) as a weapon and wears a thick leather apron, equivalent to leather armor (AC 12). Ghor has two smith human apprentices (**commoners**). If need be these apprentices utilize weapons in the shop to defend themselves.

There are two longswords, one mace, a suit of man-sized chain mail, and 11 finished spears in the shop. In the second story are rooms where the smith, his family, and his assistants live. The rooms have normal furnishings, but a jar hidden in the smith's bedroom holds 27 ep. Locating the hidden jar requires a successful DC 13 Wisdom (Perception) check. The smith carries 1d4 gp and each apprentice has 2d6 sp.

AREA 9 – PROVISIONER

This low building contains a shop that sells typical equipment used by adventurers during wilderness and dungeon exploration. He does not sell weapons other than a few spears, daggers, arrows, and bolts. He has several shields (seven), but does not sell armor or mounts. He directs any persons interested in such items to the trader next door. Availability of any particular item is at the discretion of the DM, and prices are standard from the Player's Handbook. He buys equipment from adventurers at 50% of the listed price, provided items are in usable condition.

The provisioner is a human **commoner**, but in time of need he has leather armor and shield (AC 13) and defends the walls or otherwise fights with a spear (1d6 piercing damage) to protect his family and the Keep. His wife and two children (also **commoners**) live in a small apartment in the place.

He carries 1d6 gp. He has a strongbox concealed under his bed that contains 30 cp, 16 ep, and 100 gp.

AREA 10 – TRADER

This place deals in all armor, weapons, and large quantities of goods such as salt, spices, cloth, rare woods, etc. Prices are as per the Players Handbook, with availability and quantity determined by the DM. The trader purchases similar items from adventurers at 50% of listed cost as long as the condition is suitable (but see Development, below).

The trader, Khalidd, is a human **commoner**, as are his two grown sons. All have leather armor and shields (AC 13), plus halberds (1d10 slashing damage) and shortswords (1d6 piercing damage) for use when necessary.

Each carries 2d6 gp in his purse. Hidden under the floorboards of their small apartment are 1,110 sp and 500 gp. The key floorboard is difficult to locate, requiring a successful DC 20 Wisdom (Perception) check to find.

Development. The trader is very interested in obtaining furs. He pays the full listed value for any fur as he is confident he can still turn a tidy profit.

AREA 11 – LOAN BANK

The banker is a retired **corporal of the watch** (see appendix B) with a longsword (1d8 + 2 slashing damage, or 1d10 + 2 slashing damage if used two-handed) handy, and plate armor and a shield stored in his apartment above. He carries 12 gp and 6 pp with him. There is a scrawny old clerk (a **fledgling mage**; see appendix B) in the place as well, who typically handles transactions. A hired mercenary (**guard**) wearing plate armor (AC 18, speed 20 ft.) and armed with a battleaxe (1d8 + 1 slashing damage) and a heavy crossbow (range 100/400 ft., 1d10 + 1 piercing damage) is on guard inside the door.

Here anyone can change money or gems for a 10% fee. The banker can also keep a person's wealth stored safely at no charge if it is left for at least 1 month. Otherwise there is a 10% fee. Loans at an interest rate of 10% per month can be obtained for up to 5 gp with no security deposit; over 5 gp requires some item of at least twice the value of the loan. A sign on the shop states clearly that this place is under direct protection of the Keep, and there is always a **guard** in chain mail (AC 16) with a longbow (range 150/600 ft., 1d8 + 1 piercing damage) and a longsword (1d8 + 1 slashing damage, or 1d10 + 1 slashing damage if used two-handed) watching the place from tower (area 12).

Displayed for sale are the following items. A successful DC 15 Intelligence check reveals the accurate value of a given item.

1 carved ivory tusk — price 50 gp
1 silver cup — price 20 gp
1 crystal decanter — price 45 gp (actual value 10 gp)
1 jade ring — price 250 gp (actual value 400 gp)
1 dagger with jeweled scabbard — price 600 gp
1 fur-trimmed cape — price 75 gp
3 blank vellum books — price 20 gp each
1 gold & silver belt — price 90 gp
1 set of thieves' tools — price 100 gp (actual value 35 gp)
1 iron box with secret lock — price 50 gp

The strong room of the place is in the cellar. It is protected by a locked iron door (AC 19, 22 hit points) which leads to a small vault. The door lock can be picked with thieves' tools and a successful DC 24 Dexterity check. The vault has 12 small compartments, each protected by a lock (DC 20 Dexterity check with thieves' tools to unlock) with hidden poison needle traps. Each needle trap can be detected with a successful DC 18 Wisdom (Perception) check. The trap can be disabled with a successful DC 16 Dexterity check. If triggered, a poison needle causes 1 piercing damage and the victim must make a successful DC 15 Constitution saving throw or suffer an additional 11 (2d10) poison damage and gain the poisoned condition for 1 hour. The banker has the keys to all of these locks. These compartments hold the following items:

#1 is empty.
#2 has 277 gp and one 500 gp gem.
#3 has a gold altar service set (worth 6,000 gp).
#4 is empty.
#5 is **trapped** with a sleeping gas. The trap can be detected with a successful DC 20 Wisdom (Perception) check and disabled with a DC 16 Dexterity check and thieves' tools. If triggered, all targets within 10 feet are required to make a DC 14 Constitution saving throw or suffer 9 (2d8) poison damage and gain the poisoned condition for the next 2 hours.
#6 has 1,000 each of copper, silver, electrum, gold, and platinum pieces.
#7 contains four pit vipers (**poisonous snakes**).
#8 has 18 10 gp gems, 25 50 gp gems, 11 100 gp gems, four 500 gp gems, and three 1,000 gp gems.
#9 is **trapped** with spring-loaded arrows. The trap can be detected with a successful DC 17 Wisdom (Perception) check and disabled with a DC 15 Dexterity check and thieves' tools. If triggered, four arrows each make a ranged attack with a +6 bonus at a random target within a 10-foot area in front of the compartment. On a hit, each arrow inflicts 3 (1d6) piercing damage.
#10 has an alabaster and gold statue (worth 3,000 gp) in a rare wood and silk case (worth 600 gp).
#11 is empty.
#12 has a sack with 91 ep and 58 pp.

Empty compartments indicate funds out on loan. **Bold-faced** numbers are those belonging to the banker.

AREA 12 – WATCH TOWER

This 45-foot-tall tower has all of the usual defensive devices. It houses six **guards** in chain mail (AC 16) with longbows (range 150/600 ft., 1d8 + 1 piercing damage) and longswords (1d8 + 1 slashing damage, or 1d10 + 1 slashing damage if used two-handed), and six other **guards** in leather armor, carrying shields (AC 14) and halberds (1d10 + 1 slashing damage). The **captain of the watch** (see appendix B)**,** a grizzled human named Mebros, is stationed here.

The captain lives on the first floor, with the usual furnishings. Mebros has a silver flagon and tankard (worth 750 gp), and he is known to carry quite a bit of money with him (8 sp, 11 gp, 20 pp). The guards have only a small amount of coins (2d6 sp each).

The second and third floors are barracks for the guards, adorned with sturdy bunks and chests for personal effects. The upper story holds a supply of 200 arrows, many rocks (ammunition for the light catapults), a few wheelbarrows, two barrels of oil, and 24 spears.

AREA 13 – FOUNTAIN SQUARE

There is a large, gushing fountain in the center of the square. On holidays, local farmers and tradesmen set up small booths to sell their goods in this place.

AREA 14 – TRAVELER'S INN

This long, low structure is 18 feet high. It has five small private rooms and a large common sleeping room for a full dozen. Private rooms cost 1 gp per night, but sleeping in the common room is only 1 sp per night. Servants and the like always sleep in the stables (area 4), of course.

The innkeeper and his family (wife and three sons) live in a small loft above the inn. They are all human **commoners** with no fighting ability or martial equipment.

AREA 15 – TAVERN

The Stretching Goat is the favorite of visitors and inhabitants of the Keep alike. The food is excellent, the drinks generous and of high quality. The place is always active, with 4-16 (4d4) patrons at any time of day or night. Consult the sidebar for a list of fare available.

ALE 1 ep/mug

SMALL BEER 1 sp/flagon

WINE 1 ep/glass

HONEY MEAD 1 gp/flagon

BARK TEA 1 sp/mug

BREAD 1 cp/slice

PUDDING 1 sp/bowl

VEGETABLE SOUP 1 sp/bowl

VENISON STEW 1 ep/bowl

ROAST FOWL 1 gp/plate

ROAST JOINT 2 gp/plate

HOT MEAT PIE 1 ep/pie

GOAT CHEESE 1 sp/wedge

FRUIT 1 sp/plate

The barkeep is a male human **commoner** named Bumbo Wickman. When talking to a good customer and drinking to his health, he sometimes talks about the lands around the Keep (one drink per story, but only half of which may be true; select an appropriate rumor). He is known to dislike small beer and love honey mead.

There is a 50% chance that 2-5 (1d4 + 1) of the patrons will be mercenary men-at-arms looking for work (**guards**). Each has leather armor and a shield (AC 14), a shortsword (1d6 + 1 piercing damage), and a dagger (1d4 + 1 piercing damage). All other desired equipment must be purchased by the employer, including at a minimum ranged weapons, and dungeon exploration gear. It is always necessary to buy mercenaries a drink before discussing terms of employment. Wages for duty include all gear purchased, room and board, and 1 sp per day of service. If no gear is purchased, the cost rises to 1 gp per day. Note that a mere spear or minor equipment is considered as no gear.

There is also a 10% chance that each of the following persons are in the tavern at any given time:

- Corporal of the watch (see area 3)

- Captain of the watch (see area 12)

- Bailiff of the outer bailey (see area 6)

- Priest (see area 7b)

- 2-4 guards (see area 12)

- Sergeant of the Guard (see area 18)

- NPC (Choose one of the pre-generated characters or hirelings from appendix C, with complete equipment for adventuring. An NPC is 75% likely to join an expedition if offered 25% of the treasure gained, but there is a 1 in 6 chance the NPC is of chaotic evil alignment.)

The taverner is a human **commoner** as are his son and the pot boy, but in time of need they don leather armor, carry shields (AC 13), and bear spears (1d6 piercing damage) against attackers. The place is also served by his wife and daughter, a serving wench, and a scullion—all non-combatants.

The cellar is where drink and food are stored and prepared, along with simple rooms for the servants. The family sleeps in the small loft over the tavern, which is well furnished.

The taverner and his son each have 2d6 gp in their purses, the wife 1d6 gp, and all others have 2d6 cp. Hidden in an old crock under empty flour bags in the back room are 82 cp and 29 sp. A successful DC 15 Wisdom (Perception) check is required to locate this coin stash.

AREA 16 – GUILD HOUSE

When members of any guild (merchants, craft, artisans, etc.) arrive at the Keep, they are offered the hospitality of this two-story building. This is a fee collection and administrative post, and the staff is careful to observe and record what traffic passes through the Keep. Any trader who passes through must pay guild dues of 5% of the value of his merchandise, but he then gains the protection of the Guild House, assuming he is not already a regular member. Craftsmen and artisans must gain Guild permission to enter or leave the land, paying a fee of 2d6 gp either way, depending on the value of their trade.

The lower floor contains the Guild Master's and his two clerks' quarters and an office, all sparsely furnished. They are all human **commoners**, but each has chain mail (AC 16, speed 20 ft.), a light crossbow (range 80/320 ft., 1d8 piercing damage), and a shortsword (1d6 piercing damage) kept in a closet for quick use. There are two noncombatant servants that have quarters in the cellar. The upper floor is divided into two private rooms and a dormitory for guests. The Guild Master is very influential, and his favor or dislike is reflected in the treatment of persons by fortress personnel. Four **guards** with leather armor and shields (AC 14), armed with spears and shortswords (1d6 + 1 piercing damage), are on duty at all times, two on the first floor plus two above. They are fanatical Guildsmen who obey any order from the Master without question. Guests of the Guild are welcome to eat here, but drinking to excess is frowned upon.

The Guild Master has a gold ring worth 50 gp, and 2d6 gp in his purse. Each clerk carries a purse with 1d4 each of cp, sp, and gp. A strongbox under the Guild Master's bed is easy to locate and holds 712 gp.

AREA 17 – CHAPEL

The spiritual center of the Keep is opposite the Guild House. This building has a peaked roof two stories tall. The interior is one large room, with an altar located at the eastern end, complete with a colored glass window (worth 350 gp intact) above it. The stained glass window is 20 feet high and 8 feet wide. An offering box is fastened securely atop a heavy pedestal in the southeast corner; it contains 1d100 cp and 1d100 sp at any time of the day. It is emptied each evening by the Curate, who deposits the coins with the banker (see area 11). A small stairway in the northwest corner, behind the bare wooden pews, leads to the cellar, where the Curate and his three assistants have their quarters.

The Curate—a male human **priest,** with an 18 Wisdom (+4)—named Xyneg is the most influential person in the Keep except for the Castellan (see area 26). He wears *+1 plate armor,* carries a shield, and always wears a *ring of protection* (AC 22, speed 20 ft.). He wields either a *+1 mace* (+3 to hit, 1d6 + 1 bludgeoning damage) or a *staff of the python.* He rarely wears his armor (unless the Keep is threatened), but is never without his ring (AC 11) and magical staff.

The Curate only uses healing magic on a member of his congregation, such as an officer of the Guard or a shopkeeper.

Spellcasting: The curate is a 5th-level spellcaster. His spellcasting ability is Wisdom (spell save DC 14, +6 to hit with spell attacks). He normally has the following cleric spells prepared:

- Cantrips (at will): *guidance, light, mending, resistance*
- 1st level (4 slots): *bless, cure wounds, detect magic*
- 2nd level (3 slots): *augury, hold person, zone of truth*
- 3rd level (2 slots): *mass healing word, remove curse, tongues*

His three **acolytes** have plate armor and shields (AC 20, speed 20 ft.) and carry maces (1d6 bludgeoning damage). They are typically clothed in simple robes (AC 10), but will arm for battle on command of the Curate. They prepare the following spells each day:

- Cantrips (at will): *light, spare the dying, thaumaturgy*
- 1st level (3 slots): *bless, cure wounds, detect poison and disease*

All of the clerics' armor and weapons are stored in the Curate's locked room in the Chapel cellar, which has normal, but sparse, furnishings. The Chapel also owns a *potion of gaseous form*, three *potions of healing*, a *potion of mind reading*, and several *spell scrolls*: *cure wounds* (x3), *hold person*, and *lesser restoration*. All of these magic items are hidden in a secret compartment underneath the offering box pedestal. The door of the compartment can only be found with a successful DC 20 Wisdom (Perception) check that requires removing the pedestal. The door has two locks in it, each which require thieves' tools and separate DC 17 Dexterity checks to pick. The Curate and the Castellan have the only sets of keys to these locks.

Development. If questioned closely by a friend, the Curate might (50% of the time) reveal his distrust of the priest (see area 7b) who visits the Keep regularly. The acolytes, however, think very highly of the priest, and will say so to any who ask about him.

AREA 18 – INNER GATEHOUSE

This stone structure is itself like a small fort. The southern portion is only about 15 feet high, plus battlement, while the rear part is some 30 feet tall, plus battlement. There are arrow slits (which provide three-quarters cover) in the southern section of course, and along the walls of the 20-foot-wide, 10-foot-high passage through to the north. This passage slopes upwards towards the inner courtyard. The heavy gates are double bound with iron and spiked. There are six **guards** on duty at all times (two inside the gateway, two on the lower battlement, two on the upper), plus one officer on call (see below). No visitor is allowed beyond this point except by invitation, unless he or she has special permits.

The first floor of the place is the main armory. There are dozens of shields and of each sort of weapon. Two small rooms with sparse furnishings are quarters for the Sergeant and Captain of the Guard. The second story on the north houses the guards stationed here.

The Captain of the Guard is a male human **veteran** with *+1 plate armor* and a *+1 shield* (AC 22). He has a *+2 longsword* (+7 to hit, 1d8 + 5 slashing damage) and a *+1 spear* (+6 to hit, range 20/60 ft., 1d6 + 4 piercing damage). This man is very kind, friendly, and an excellent leader. He sometimes moves about in the Outer Bailey disguised as a mercenary. He has 15 gp and a 150 gp gem in the pommel of his dagger.

The Sergeant of the Guard is a male human (use the **corporal of the watch** statistics from appendix B) named Evoe. He wears chain mail and a *ring of protection*, and carries a *+1 shield* (AC 20). This very strong fellow (Strength 17 [+3]) is a hard fighter and loves to drink and brawl. He wields a *+1 longsword* (+6 to hit, 1d8 + 4 slashing damage) and a *+1 dagger* (+6 to hit, 1d4 + 4 piercing damage). He carries 1d6 each of sp, ep, and gp. He also has a *potion of healing* in a chest in his room, under a spare cape.

There are 24 **guards** quartered here. Each has chain mail and shield (AC 18), longsword (1d8 + 1 slashing damage), dagger (1d4 + 1 piercing damage), and handaxe (range 20/60 ft., 1d6 + 1 slashing damage). Eight are light crossbowmen (range 80/320 ft., 1d8 + 1 piercing damage), eight are longbowmen (range 150/600 ft., 1d8 + 1 piercing damage), and eight have halberds (1d10 + 1 slashing damage). Two from each group are on duty at any given time; the rest take 5 minutes to don armor and arm themselves. Each guard has 2d6 sp.

AREA 19 – SMALL TOWER

This typical tower houses eight **guards** who are all armored in chain mail (AC 16) and carry light crossbows (range 80/320 ft., 1d8 + 1 piercing damage) and shortswords (1d6 + 1 piercing damage). Shields are stored below, so in hand-to-hand combat they are AC 18. Two are on duty atop the tower at all times. The other six are in the chamber below. The base of the tower is solid except for the small stair up.

AREA 20 – GUARD TOWER

This 50-foot-high structure houses 24 **guards** (see area 18, above). Their commander is a **corporal of the guard** (see appendix B).

There are supplies of food, weapons, and oil on the upper floor. The rest of the building is barracks for the guards and a room for the leader.

AREA 21 – INNER BAILEY

This entire area is grass-covered. The troops drill here, and there are practice fields plus jousting areas. During the daylight hours there are always a dozen or more soldiers engaged in weapons practice.

AREA 22 – CAVALRY STABLES

There are 30 **warhorses** and 1d4 **riding horses** kept within this stable. They are tended by two human **commoners** and watched by two human **guards**.

AREA 23 – GREAT TOWER

This 60-foot-high structure houses 24 **guards**. Eight are armed with light crossbows (range 80/320 ft., 1d8 + 1 piercing damage) and spears, eight with longbows (range 150/600 ft., 1d8 + 1 piercing damage) and longswords (1d8 + 1 slashing damage, or 1d10 + 1 slashing damage if used two-handed), and eight with halberds (1d10 + 1 slashing damage). Their leader is another **corporal of the guard** (see appendix B), but he lacks a magic dagger, wields a greatsword (2d6 + 2 slashing damage), and has no shield (AC 18).

The corporal carries 1d6 each of sp, ep, and gp. Each guard carries 2d6 sp.

AREA 24 – THE KEEP FORTRESS

This place has many tiers and is solidly built to withstand attack. The lowest level consists of a 15-foot-high front section. The round flanking towers are 60 feet high, while the main building is 30 feet high. All sections have battlements. The door is solid iron. Inside are a great hall, an armory for the cavalry, and several side chambers for small dinners or meetings. The cellars below have vast stores of provisions, quarters for a score of servants, a cistern, and a dungeon area with four stout cells.

The Castellan lives in area 27, but he and his assistants are in the lower part of this building during the day, tending to business and holding audience. There are always eight **guards** in plate armor (AC 18, speed 20 ft.) with light crossbows (range 80/320 ft., 1d8 + 1 piercing damage) and longswords (1d8 + 1 slashing damage, or 1d10 + 1 slashing damage if used two-handed) on duty on the wall, and the same number with plate armor and shield (AC 20, speed 20 ft.) wielding longswords (1d8 + 1 slashing damage) stationed inside.

The whole lower floor is well decorated, and the furniture is heavy and upholstered.

Second Floor. There are rooms here for up to 36 cavalrymen, plus two chambers for special guests. There are 12 heavy cavalrymen (**guards** with Wisdom 12 [+1] and the Animal Handling [+3] skill), each with plate armor and shield (AC 20, speed 20 ft.), a longsword (1d8 + 1 slashing damage), and a dagger (1d4 + 1 piercing damage). There are also 18 medium cavalrymen (**guards** with Wisdom 12 [+1] and the Animal Handling [+3] skill) in chain mail (AC 16), each with a light crossbow (range 80/320 ft., 1d8 + 1 piercing damage) and a handaxe (range 20/60 ft., 1d6 + 1 slashing damage), quartered here.

Their rooms are sparsely furnished with only a cot, chair, and armoire for each. Two couriers (**guards**), with leather armor (AC 12) and shortswords (1d6 + 1 piercing damage), are currently quartered in one side chamber.

AREA 25 – TOWER

Each tower is 40 feet high with battlements, and pierced with arrow slits (that provide three-quarters cover) to protect the east and west corners of the building. The fortress men-at-arms are housed in these structures and in the towers indicated by area 26.

AREA 26 – CENTRAL TOWERS

These structures rise 20 feet above the roof of the fortress, with a 5-foot battlement on their roofs. The two upper stories house 12 **guards** each. Six of these guards wear plate armor (AC 18, speed 20 ft.) with light crossbows (range 80/320 ft., 1d8 + 1 piercing damage) and shortswords (1d6 + 1 piercing damage), and six wear plate armor and carry shields (AC 20, speed 20 ft.) with longswords (1d8 + 1 slashing damage) who are off-duty. It takes 10 minutes for them to don armor and get ready for battle. In the two lower floors are the Castellan's assistants.

Scribe. This individual is a NG male human **adept** (see appendix B; no magic amulet) wearing plate armor and carrying a shield (AC 20). He carries a *spell scroll* of *hold person* and has the following cleric spells prepared:

- Cantrips (at will): *light, mending, resistance*
- 1st level (3 slots): *detect evil and good, detect magic, detect poison and disease, purify food and drink*

The scribe's chamber is austere, and there is nothing of value within except a gold holy symbol worth 150 gp. He has 48 gp in his purse.

MAREVAK THE ADVISOR

Marevak is 380 years old, and decades ago served as the advisor to Roghan and Zelligar (see chapter 6). Once it became clear that those two powerful figures were defeated and would not be returning Marevak attempted to seize control of their stronghold, Quasqueton. He could not overcome the numerous humanoid servants that fell into violence over its control. Marevak fled with a few belongings and returned to his distant homeland to recruit allies, intent on reclaiming the stronghold—but he could find none willing to support him.

Eventually, he wandered the Realm before returning to the Keep, further plotting to re-establish control over Quasqueton. Despite his questionable ethics, following the mysterious disappearance of the Castellen's former advisor, Marevak quickly proved his worth as an advisor. He seems to have an uncanny ability to understand others' motives, thanks to his natural insight plus the occasional *detect thoughts* spell. For decades he has bided his time (more like procrastinated due to his posh lifestyle), still desiring to control Quasqueton.

Marevak can be used in a variety of roles in a campaign. He can be a benefactor of sorts, hiring (or encouraging) characters to explore the ruins of Quasqueton to recover important items for him. Or, he can be a foil and work against the characters to conceal the true location of the stronghold. In this case, he can manipulate others and plant false rumors leading the characters away from the stronghold, and to the clutches of the humanoids that inhabit the Caves of Chaos.

Advisor. Marevak, Advisor to the Castellen (see appendix B), is a tall gangly elf. He typically wears voluminous robes (AC 13), but has a *+1 chain shirt* and a shortbow (with 10 *+1 arrows*) for use if needed. See the sidebar for additional information on this NPC.

The advisor's chamber contains fancy furniture with tapestries and carpets all about the room. One tapestry is valuable (worth 500 gp). He wears a jeweled pendant worth 1,000 gp and carries 10 gp and 6 pp in his purse.

AREA 27 – CASTELLAN'S CHAMBER

This portion of the fortress is 10 feet above the main roof and has battlements. Inside is the private room of the commander of the whole Keep, the Castellan Ferec. His chamber is lavishly furnished, with a silver mirror (worth 300 gp) on the wall, a malachite bowl (worth 750 gp) on a table, and a fox robe (worth 1,200 gp) in his armoire. He has a small silver case (worth 450 gp) which contains 40 pp and 12 gems (each worth 100 gp). There is a *+1 spear* on the wall by the door.

The Castellan is a **knight** with a Dexterity of 16 (+3), and he wears *+1 plate armor* and a *ring of protection* while carrying a *+1 shield* (AC 23). He wields a *+2 longsword* (+7 to hit, 1d8 + 5 slashing damage) and a *+1 dagger* (+6 to hit, 1d4 + 4 piercing damage). He wears *boots* and a *cloak of elvenkind*, and carries a *potion of levitation* (see appendix A) and a *potion of healing* with him at all times. His chain of office is silver with gems (worth 1,800 gp), and he carries 10 each of ep, gp, and pp, plus a gem worth 500 gp. He is a very clever fellow, but at times he can be too hasty in his decisions. His bravery and honesty are absolute. If a guest asks him any question, he will do his best to answer, providing it does not compromise the security of the Keep.

CHAPTER TEN
Adventures Outside the Keep

fter the group establishes itself at the Keep and obtains equipment, they should either follow clues gained in conversation with residents of the Keep or set out exploring on their own (or both). Naturally, they will be trying to locate the Caverns of Quasqueton or the Caves of Chaos, depending on which rumors and information they have gathered. However, this searching takes some traveling, and in the meantime they might well run into more than they can handle. Refer to the Wilderness Map when the characters set out to explore the region.

The "Realm" is to the west, off the map. The road branches, one path to the Keep on the Borderlands, the other leading off into the forsaken wilderness beyond the ken of Law. Note that most features are described below. Inspection of the map will also show that there are several set encounter areas. These are detailed below in the section appropriate to the setting. The Cave of the Unknown's area is actually the long-lost Caverns of Quasqueton (see chapter 6). Alternatively, the DM can use the Cave of the Unknown as the setting of a dungeon of their own design. Likewise, the bullywugs' reed maze in the Fell Fens is left for the DM to design. For details on the Caves of Chaos, see chapter 11. The Caves and the Caverns are designed for characters of levels 1 to 3, and the author recommends the Fell Fens be more challenging—perhaps suitable for characters of levels 3 to 5.

Each square of the map equals 100 yards, so 17.6 squares equals 1 mile. A typical party of characters can move 2 miles per hour while moving slowly, and 3 miles per hour at normal pace. Moving through the forest or the fens is considered difficult terrain, and thus at half speed. To thoroughly search a given square (to locate an established encounter area, for example) takes 1 hour per square.

Also take note of what provisions characters have and how they are being transported. They should bring enough food and water with them. If not, they need to forage for food and water or return to the Keep to restock their supplies. The region is considered to have abundant food and clean water sources, so a DC 10 Wisdom (Survival) check is required to forage. Also keep in mind potential effects of weather and becoming lost; all this is detailed in the Dungeon Master's Guide (pp. 109-112).

If you are not prepared to let the characters move off the map, then have a wandering NPC, a friendly talking magpie, or some other "helper" guide them back to the detailed adventure site.

RANDOM WILDERNESS ENCOUNTERS

Characters exploring the Borderlands around the Keep are likely to have encounters with wandering monsters. The region is wild, untamed, and infrequently patrolled by the Keep guards. Such encounters can occur as frequently as the DM desires, perhaps a 1 in 10 chance per 6 hours of travel. Caution: too many encounters can wear down the characters, force them to expend valuable resources, or require more frequent rests. They could also distract the characters from their true adventuring goals such as the Caverns of Quasqueton or the Caves of Chaos. Depending on the terrain, roll 1d6 or select an encounter from the table below. Each encounter is briefly described following the table. Be sure to adjust the encounter's difficulty based on the number and level of the characters. For guidelines on how to effectively present a random encounter, see chapter 3 of the Dungeon Master's Guide.

Camping Outdoors Overnight. When the party is camped outdoors, generally creatures will not bother them provided they have an active fire. That is, unless they are within 6 squares of a numbered encounter area. For each square they are within the 6-square range of a numbered encounter area, there is a 1 in 6 chance that the monsters from that area investigate. For example, at 6 squares away there is a 1 in 6 chance, at 5 there is a 2 in 6, at 4 there is a 3 in 6, at 3 there is a 4 in 6, at 2 there is a 5 in 6, and at 1 square there is an automatic encounter. Organized parties should post at least one guard in shifts throughout the night. However, if the party posts no guards, the monsters automatically surprise the party assuming they were sleeping and unaware

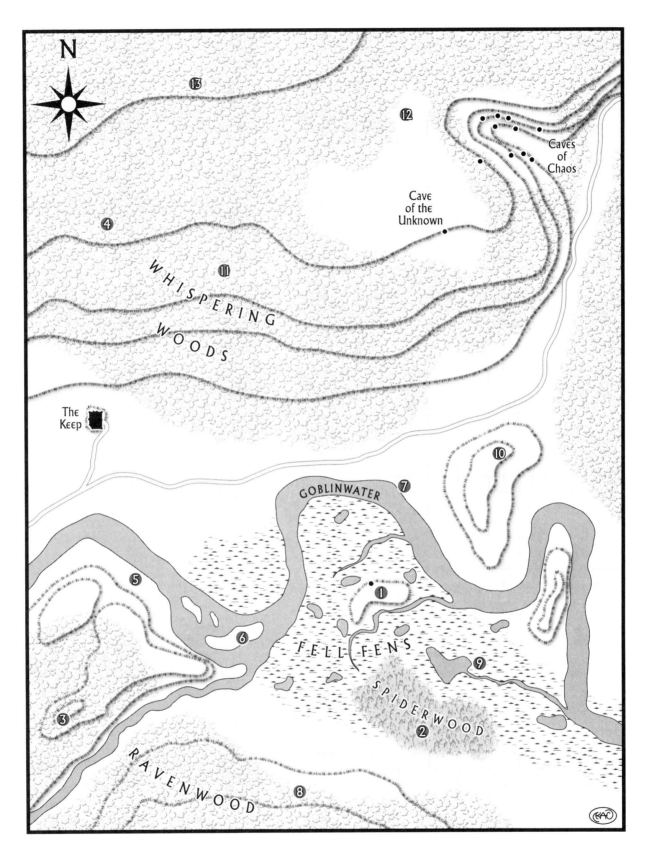

WILDERNESS MAP

☐ = 100 Yards

 Forest

Tamarack Stand

 Contour Line

Fens

 River

Road

 Water

D6	Fell Fens	Goblinwater River	Open/Road	Ravenwood	Spiderwood	Whispering Woods
1	Lizardfolk	Humanoid Band	Caravan	Bandits	Giant Wolf Spiders	Brown Bear
2	Giant Frogs	Bullywug Flyriders	Patrol	Swarm of Ravens	Giant Wolf Spiders	Giant Boar
3	Giant Lizards	Nixies	Bandits	Stirges	Giant Crab Spiders	Druid
4	Giant Constrictor Snake	Giant Water Spider	Al-mi'raj	Humanoid Band	Swarm of Spiders	Humanoid Band
5	Bullywug Patrol	Giant Pike	Humanoid Band	Elk/Deer	Needle Blights	Humanoid Band
6	Bullywug Flyriders	Stirges	Ankheg	Faerie Dragon	Ettercap	Ogre

AL-MI'RAJ

Some time ago, an enterprising merchant using the trade road was transporting several al-mi'raj (blink bunnies) in magic-proof cages to a distant market for sale. The caravan was attacked by goblins and in the ensuing mayhem, several blink bunnies escaped. The local predators had a difficult time preying on the teleporting fey, so the population has flourished. Now packs of 1d8 + 7 al-mi'raj (see appendix B) are often observed near the road grazing on tender leaves and other low growth. The blink bunnies often flee, but are aggressive if cornered. Recently, traveling nobles using the Keep as a base have conducted hunts targeting the elusive blink bunnies. A captured blink bunny could sell for as much as 500 gp if sold in a faraway city.

ANKHEG

While traveling through the open terrain or along the road, the characters stumble into an ambush set by a solitary **ankheg**. The predator has tunneled underneath a well-used path and lies in wait just under the earth, with its antennae sticking out. Using its Tremorsense, it bursts free from the earth attacking with surprise unless a character makes a DC 15 passive Perception check. The ankheg first attacks with its bite, attempting to grapple a target. If that fails, it unleashes its acid spray attack. If reduced to 12 or fewer hit points, it retreats down its burrow. The partially collapsed burrow meanders for several hundred yards, but the only thing the characters find is a recently shed exoskeleton.

BANDITS

This wandering group of 1d6 + 3 **bandits** hails from the nearby bandit hideout at Raven Rock (area 3). These human bandits are armed with scimitars and longbows (range 150/600 ft., 1d8 + 1 piercing damage). They are either setting up an ambush along the road or moving to or from the road back to their lair. If traveling, this group is complacent and if the characters are stealthy this band could be avoided, or even ambushed. Each bandit carries 2d6 sp and 1d6 gp.

BROWN BEAR

This local predator has a lair in a nearby underground hollow, but is currently prowling about gorging itself prior to hibernation. The **brown bear** is quite aggressive and likely picks up the characters' scent via its Keen Smell trait. It eventually attacks with reckless abandon, and due to its size likely gives away its approach if the characters are cautious. If reduced to less than 10 hit points, it flees back to its cave to lick its wounds.

BULLYWUG FLYRIDERS

A group of 1d3 + 1 **gripfoot bullywugs**, mounted in crude wicker saddles astride **giant horseflies** (see appendix B for both), flies overhead. Each flyrider has two large rocks tethered to the belly of the giant horsefly. In the first two rounds of combat, they release the rocks—assuming each can manage to untie the knot with a DC 12 Dexterity check. A falling rock is a ranged attack at +5 to hit and causes 9 (2d6 + 2) bludgeoning damage. After the rocks have been dropped, either the giant horseflies move in to attack or the gripfoot bullywugs fire their shortbows (range 80/320 ft., 1d6 + 3 piercing damage), although they can only attack every other round since they need to hold on for dear life. If two riders (or mounts) are defeated, the remaining flee back to their lair in the Fell Fens (area 9).

BULLYWUG PATROL

This wandering patrol contains 2d4 **bullywugs** led by an **elite bullywug** (see appendix B). They attempt to use the swamp or water to their advantage depending on the encounter setting. These frogfolk attempt to use their Standing Leap trait to maneuver in combat. If the elite bullywug is defeated the others flee, eventually making their way back to their lair (area 9). There is a 40% chance this patrol has two **giant frogs** led on 20-foot-long leashes. If so, in the first round of combat the handlers spend an action releasing the giant frogs and giving orders to attack. Each bullywugs carries 1d8 gp and various worthless effects (such as dried flies in a pouch, or pungent moss clumps).

CARAVAN

The caravan is traveling along the road, and consists of 1d4 + 2 wagons, each pulled by two **draft horses**, tended by 1-2 drovers (**commoners**), typically human, but possibly halfling or dwarven. Each wagon is guarded by 1d4 **guards** wearing chain mail (AC 16) and wielding spears (1d6 + 1 piercing damage) and shortbows (range 80/320 ft., 1d6 + 1 piercing damage); 1d3 merchants (**commoners**) are also present, typically riding in the wagons. Roll 1d6 to determine what goods are being transported.

D6	Goods	Value
1	Herbs, spices, tea	250 gp
2	Weapons (spears, bows, arrows)	600 gp
3	Wine	200 gp
4	Lumber	150 gp
5	Furs, pelts, hides	975 gp
6	Cloth, silk	750 gp

The guards each carry 2d10 sp, while merchants have 2d6 ep and 3d6 gp.

Development. There is a 20% chance that the caravan has already been sacked by a roaming band of humanoids or nearby bandits. In this case, all drovers, guards, and merchants have been killed, all the horses have been driven away, and all trade goods are gone.

DRUID

This strange fellow wanders the region, and refers to himself as the bee man. Before the characters encounter him, a successful DC 12 Wisdom (Perception) check reveals an increase in bee activity and buzzing in the area. The bee man is a crouched, aging human **druid** that wears dirty brown robes and carries a staff with a beehive attached to the end. An absentminded fool, the bee man knows more about bees and flower pollination than is healthy, and his skin is pockmarked with old bee stings. He is kindly, and offers to trade honeycombs or honey for mundane items, like rope, a new robe, or something to carry more honey in. If the characters are especially nice to him, he has four doses of royal honey, each of which heals 1d4 + 1 hit points if consumed. He is only willing to trade three of these, and only for important items (to him).

saving throw, or become ensnared and suspended upside down about 7 feet off the ground. The target is restrained until freed. The web snare can be burst with a successful DC 15 Strength check, or the web can be cut with 5 points of slashing damage. An **ettercap** that set the snares lairs in a nearby dead white oak tree. It arrives in 3 rounds to empty and reset its traps. If the characters resist being incapacitated, two **giant wolf spiders** are called to aid the ettercap. If the characters make a successful DC 15 Wisdom (Survival) check, the ettercaps tracks can be followed back to its lair. The partially hollowed tree trunk hides an assortment of coins (11 cp, 21 sp, and 6 gp) plus an electrum whistle (worth 65 gp) and an empty silver flask (worth 110 gp).

FAERIE DRAGON

The Ravenwood is the home of a capricious young **faerie dragon** named Flitiloneous ("Flit" for short). Flit has a bright orange scaly hide with deep red highlights and bright blue wings, although she typically uses Superior Invisibility to remain hidden. She spends some time (hours) observing the characters and eventually learns their names. While setting up camp or at some other time, she speaks to the characters via Limited Telepathy at first, and then maybe actual speech. She claims to be a helpful forest spirit, and if the characters bestow upon her gifts of sweetness (honey, candy, or even raw sugar) she rewards them with information of the area. For example, she knows the location of the bandits at Raven Rock (area 3), or the kobold camp (area 8) to the southeast. The DM is encouraged to roleplay Flit as an inquisitive toddler that might show up (or disappear) on a whim.

ELK/DEER

There is a 70% chance the characters encounter a herd of 4d4 **deer**, or a 30% chance of encountering a pack of 1d3 + 2 **elk**. These cautious herbivores give the characters a wide berth, preferring to Dash if approached within 150 feet. But if the characters could take one down with a ranged weapon, the fresh meat is a welcome addition to trail rations and stale bread.

ETTERCAP

While traveling along a faint forest trail, the characters encounter a series of four web snare traps designed to immobilize potential prey. Each web snare can be located with a successful DC 15 Wisdom (Perception) check. Failure to avoid them triggers one or more, requiring a Medium or smaller creature to make a DC 14 Dexterity

GIANT BOAR

The Whispering Woods are famous for an abundant population of boar, and often nobles from afar journey to the Keep to get outfitted for an extended hunt. This **giant boar** has a broken tusk which has recently become infected, making the beast even more aggressive. It attempts to charge a target, and then appears to flee into the understory of the forest, only to return for another charge a round or two later. Enraged by the infection, it fights to the death.

GIANT CONSTRICTOR SNAKE

This mottled brown-green **giant constrictor snake** is curled about the branches of a nearby tree limb. Its coloration grants it advantage on its Dexterity (Stealth) check to hide itself. If unnoticed and acting with surprise, it drops the lower part of its body to constrict a passing character. Once it has a target grappled, it recoils to the upper part of the tree, nearly 15 feet off the ground, and continues to constrict the target until it stops resisting. If left alone, the giant constrictor snake casually consumes its meal.

GIANT CRAB SPIDERS

While traveling through the dark Spiderwood, the characters stumble into a natural pit covered with forest debris. Unless the lead character makes a successful DC 15 Wisdom (Perception) check, he falls into a wide, shallow pit about 5 feet deep. The pit is full of leaves, so no damage is suffered, but it is 25 feet in diameter and considered to be difficult terrain. The pit is the lair for 1d6 + 2 **giant crab spiders** (see appendix B) that scuttle from leafy cover (consider it half cover) to attack. In the pit is a long-dead orc, desiccated from blood loss. Although his armor is ruined, his discarded scimitar is intact and nearby, and a pouch in his left boot still holds 7 gp. There is also a recently killed silver fox with an undamaged pelt. If removed with a sharp instrument and a DC 14 Dexterity check, the pelt would fetch 125 gp.

GIANT FROGS

While passing through a particularly wet area of the fens, a pack of 1d4 + 3 **giant frogs** attack the characters, seeking a fresh meal. The giant frogs are partially submerged, which grants them advantage on Dexterity (Stealth) checks to avoid detection. The giant frogs focus attacks on Small targets, seeking to swallow them whole. A few of the giant frogs display crude tactics, such as using Standing Leap to maneuver to advantageous locations in combat.

GIANT LIZARDS

As the characters push through the fens, 1d4 **giant lizards** attack from nearby fallen trees, or dry hummocks. If reduced to less than 8 hit points, a giant lizard seeks to flee. One of the giant lizards has a leather pouch (holding three 50 gp pearls) still in its gullet.

GIANT PIKE

A **giant pike** (see appendix B) attacks the characters as they cross the river, or if they wander too close to the river's marshy margin. This aggressive fish is nearly 10 feet long, and prefers to ambush prey from a weed bed using its Underwater Camouflage trait. It literally leaps out of the water (taking a round or two to flop its way back into the river) or launches itself at a boat to get prey. If it employs the latter tactic, characters in the boat need to make a successful DC 12 Dexterity saving throw, or fall into the water. If standing up in the boat, this saving throw attempt is at disadvantage.

GIANT WATER SPIDER

A **giant water spider** (see appendix B) attacks the characters while they cross the river or travel along the banks. With surprise, the giant arachnid bursts from the water and attacks a random target, attempting to envenom it. Even if the characters are on a raft or in a boat it still attacks, climbing on the vessel if need be. If successful, it attempts to drag the paralyzed victim into the water to feast at leisure.

GIANT WOLF SPIDERS

As the characters enter a clearing in the forest, four **giant wolf spiders** ambush from stick- and leaf-covered "trapdoors" concealing passage to soft earthen tunnels. Prior to the ambush, characters can notice the trapdoors with a DC 20 Wisdom (Perception) check, or a DC 15 Intelligence (Nature) check. If reduced to 3 hit points or less, a giant wolf spider retreats to its tunnel to hide. Each tunnel contains a random amount of treasure as indicated below:

- A crystal vial holding a *potion of climbing*.

- An assortment of coins (83 cp, 12 sp, 29 gp, 2 pp).

- Three small pieces of amber (worth 25 gp each) and a piece of jade (worth 15 gp).

- A thin gold chain (worth 85 gp) and crudely carved obsidian cat figurine (worth 55 gp).

HUMANOID BAND

The borderlands around the Keep are wild and host numerous wandering bands of humanoids. Some of these are looking for established tribes (such as those in the Caves of Chaos), while others are just preying on weak travelers and the like. Each time this encounter is indicated, randomly determine what type and how many humanoids are present.

Goblins. This band consists of 3d6 **goblins** lead by a **goblin boss**. The band has 1d4 + 1 **wolves** as pets. This group is looking for the tribe rumored to live in the Caves of Chaos, hoping to join them. Each goblin carries 1d6 sp, and the goblin boss has 11 gp, a gold nose ring (worth 75 gp), and a *potion of speed* which he uses in combat.

Orcs. This roaming band of 2d4 + 2 **orcs** has traveled down from the mountains to attack travelers. So far, they have only run into well-armed patrols and had a skirmish with adventurers, losing over half their numbers. Their orog leader was killed a few days ago, and they don't have much of an appetite for combat, fleeing if half their numbers are defeated. Each orc carries 2d6 sp and 1d4 gp.

Gnolls. This stealthy group of 1d4 + 2 **gnoll** hunters lead 1d4 **hyenas** by leashes, searching for slaves that can be easily captured and sold. In addition to typical weapons, these brutes have nets (see Player's Handbook, p. 148) and clubs (1d4 + 2 bludgeoning damage) to subdue victims. This group has been successful the past few months, selling slaves to other humanoid bands, and a local group of evil clerics inhabiting the Caves of Chaos. They are aware of the gnoll tribe at the Caves, but prefer the roaming life of hunters. Each gnoll carries 2d6 ep and 3d6 gp, and one of the hyenas wears a gem-studded leather collar (worth 125 gp).

LIZARDFOLK

The lizardfolk that live in the Fell Fens (area 1) have fallen on hard times due to the recent arrival of an aggressive tribe of bullywugs. This small patrol of three male **lizardfolk** is hunting for food and protecting what remains of their tribe. They flee if one of their numbers is defeated, taking a meandering route back to their mound. Each lizardfolk carries a random trinket such as a leather throng of animal teeth, or a few (1d4) freshwater pearls (each worth 10 gp). The group also has a field-dressed deer carcass.

NEEDLE BLIGHTS

Many foul creatures roam the Spiderwood, including various blights created by fell magic an age ago. As they pass through, a needle blight detects the characters and releases its pollen to encourage other needle blights to close in for a blood meal. About an hour later, 1d4 + 2

needle blights attack the characters from several different directions. The needle blights fight to the death.

NIXIES

A small tribe of nixies inhabit the Goblinwater near the large island (area 6). The tribe normally keep to themselves, but this band of 10 **nixies** is actively patrolling the river seeking a missing headstrong nixie named Elendiria. The nixies are convinced that she has been captured by the bullywugs and is a prisoner in their reed maze lair (area 9). They are correct, and they beg the characters to assist them. The bullywugs are too aggressive and well-equipped for the nixies to contend with. The nixies offer to perform a task for the characters, and can sweeten the offer with a cache of freshwater pearls (15 pearls, each worth 50 gp). The nixies are willing to give the characters five pearls in advance and the remaining if they return Elendiria safely. If all else fails, the nixies resort to using *charm person* to get the characters to help.

A FAVOR

If the characters are having an encounter near the Goblinwater that goes against them, feel free to have the nixie patrol arrive to save them. In return for aiding the characters, the nixies ask that they investigate the bullywugs' reed maze (area 9) to return Elendiria to her tribe.

OGRE

This **ogre** recently lost its lair to an aggressive manticore, and now wanders in search of another suitable cave to call home. At the DM's option, it could be still wounded (42 hit points), but regardless, it is in a foul mood. It has affixed several of the manticore's tail spikes to its greatclub, which now inflicts an additional 3 (1d6) piercing damage on a hit. He carries a dirty burlap sack with 221 sp, 45 gp, a haunch of rotting meat, and a dented copper lantern (worth 20 gp).

PATROL

The Keep occasionally sends out patrols along the road to assist travelers, but too infrequently to curb the predations by lawless bandits and marauding humanoids. The patrol consists of six human **guards** wearing plate armor

(AC 18, speed 20 ft.) armed with longswords (1d8 + 1 slashing damage, or 1d10 + 1 slashing damage if used two-handed) and longbows (range 150/600 ft., 1d8 + 1 piercing damage). They are led by a **corporal of the guard** (see appendix B). They are cordial to the characters, understanding that the presence of adventurers in the region does make their task easier. There is a 50% chance a given patrol has a rumor regarding the wilderness or the Caves of Chaos. Each guard carries 1d6 sp, and the corporal carries 2d6 sp and 1d8 gp.

STIRGES

The characters are attacked by a flight of 3d4 + 3 hungry **stirges**. This encounter likely occurs near dusk, when the stirges are most active. When a stirge drains 10 hit points of blood, it detaches on its own accord, and flies away to digest its meal.

SWARM OF RAVENS

While traveling, the characters come across the site of a recent battle between a band of goblins and Keep guards. The remaining bodies have been dead for at least a day and have attracted the attention of two **swarms of ravens**. The ravens pick away at the bodies, with numerous more in several nearby trees. If the scavengers are left alone they ignore the characters, but if the characters desire to investigate the scene the ravens become aggressive and attack. There are nine goblin bodies wearing bloodstained leather armor and four human guard bodies still adorned in Keep uniforms, although they are tattered and ruined. Despite the heavy losses, a successful DC 15 Intelligence (Investigation) check reveals the goblins won, and several guards fled the scene to the north. All useful items have been removed from the bodies, although a pack of unspoiled rations that was missed can be located. One of the guards has a small ruby (worth 50 gp) concealed in his left boot that requires a successful DC 15 Wisdom (Perception) check to locate.

SWARM OF SPIDERS

While traveling through the Spiderwood, the characters happen upon a clearing with three size Medium bodies in web cocoons suspended from tree limbs. All three contain the remains of Keep guards, still wearing chain mail and carrying longswords, longbows, and daggers. Each guard carries 2d6 sp. One of the cocoons (determine randomly) contains the recently hatched egg clutch of a giant spider. When disturbed, a **swarm of spiders** bursts out and attacks with surprise.

LOCATIONS OF THE REGION

The wild areas surrounding the Keep can be classified into six different terrain types. Each terrain has its own unique characteristics as described below. The random encounter charts detailed above vary based on the terrain. Following each description, one or more suggested set encounter areas are described, keyed to the DM's Wilderness Map. The DM is encouraged to create more set encounter areas or move the locations around to suit his needs.

FELL FENS

Located primarily to the south of the Goblinwater River, this low land is wet with a very spongy ground. For most of the day, a low fog enshrouds this fen and the area always seems to have thick, humid air. A fetid smell permeates the land. Vegetation is stunted with low trees, emergent water plants, and mossy ground cover. A few natural hills are present here, and tend to be dryer and covered with larger trees. The landscape is dotted with numerous shallow ponds, teeming with aquatic life and occasionally attracting larger predators. Snakes, lizards, and turtles, some monstrous in size, all dwell here.

Suggested Encounters. The following encounter areas are suggested for this landscape:

- A dwindling tribe of lizardfolk inhabits a mound located in the central part of the fens (area 1).

- An aggressive tribe of bullywugs has recently arrived at the fens, and live on a hill protected by the Goblinwater to the north, and a maze cut into the reeds to the south (area 9).

GOBLINWATER RIVER

Must locals just refer to this as the Goblinwater. Its name is derived from the large numbers of goblins in the region, not regarding the purity of the water. The river moves swiftly from the west to the east, and ranges in depth from about 5 feet to more than 25 feet in places. The few islands are little more than sandbars. There is only one well known natural ford (near area 7), but that provides access to the Fell Fens which is typically avoided at all costs.

Suggested Encounters. The following encounter areas are suggested for this landscape:

- There is a ford cloaked by magic used by the bandits of Raven Rock (area 5).

- A small tribe of nixies call the Goblinwater their home, and reside in an underwater cave system on the southern side of the large island (area 6).

- Near the locally known ford is the underwater lair of a voracious giant water spider (area 7).

OPEN/ROAD

A poorly maintained road runs from the west to east before turning north and cutting through the wild forested land. Travelers along this road best have a hired guard, or be able to swing a sword as bandits and humanoids roam the region looking to pick off easy targets. All caravans that use the trade route often are accompanied by at least 10 armed guards. The Keep sends out occasional patrols of armed guards, but at nowhere near the frequency required to institute any law in the region. The open terrain is relatively flat and dry with a single rocky hill to the east.

Suggested Encounters. The following encounter areas are suggested for this landscape:

- The Castellan of the Keep recently hired a band of adventurers to track down the lair of a group of bandits attacking merchants coming to and from the Keep. Currently the band is camped on the eastern hill (area 10).

RAVENWOOD

The southern woodland consists of deciduous trees and sparse undergrowth growing on rocky soil and rolling hills. A much younger forest, trees include black and red oak, maple, and chestnut. The Ravenwood provides ample habitat for avian species of all types, but the numerous black-feathered ravens are by far the most commonly observed. Abundant mammals, such as deer, skunk, and squirrels live in this forest.

Suggested Encounters. The following encounter areas are suggested for this landscape:

- A group of bandits have set up a semi-permanent camp on the rocky slopes of Raven Rock (area 3).

- A recent arrival to the region, a large group of kobolds have set up temporary camp along the edge of the Ravenwood. They seek to settle in a defensible lair to plunder the region (area 8).

SPIDERWOOD

The Spiderwood is a small copse of conifer trees just south of the Fell Fens. The acidic soil from the fens is favorable to pine trees, evergreen shrubberies, white oak, and white-barked birch trees. The gloomy wood, its branches often adorned with wispy white webs, is host to spiders, both normal and monstrous, giant insects, and vermin, but little else. The locals avoid this dark wood at all costs. The arachnids that dwell here are attracted to a malevolent shrine secluded in a clearing among the evergreens.

Suggested Encounters. The following encounter area is suggested for this landscape:

- An altar dedicated to a forgotten spider god guarded by giant spiders is hidden in this dark wood (area 2).

WHISPERING WOODS

The Whispering Woods are named after the sound of the wind blowing through the trees of this expansive wood. Travelers claim to hear voices both malignant and benign among the whispering chants. Located to the north of the trade road and the Goblinwater, only the southern reaches of this forest is depicted on the Wilderness Map. The deciduous trees, typically red oak, several varieties of maple, and beech, extend for many miles to the north and west. Herds of deer, elk, and the occasional bear all roam the lush, often tangled undergrowth. A thriving population of wild boar often attracts game hunters to this ancient forest. Only the very edges are harvested for lumber, although abundant herb and berry growth makes foraging easy.

Suggested Encounters. The following encounter areas are suggested for this landscape:

- A Mad Hermit and his pet mountain lion lair in an ancient tree in the western part of the forest (area 4).

- Hidden in the trackless center of the forest is a long forgotten magic portal. Although it still functions, it would require high magic to activate—plus a local predator lives nearby (area 11).

- The Cave of the Unknown adorns the southern face of an arrowhead-shaped rocky protrusion in the eastern end of the woods. This could be the location of the Caverns of Quasqueton (see chapter 6). Alternatively, this could just be another cave system ripe for exploration.

- On the northern side of the rocky outcropping is a massive natural sinkhole. Its interior is host to thousands of bones and the very dead roam the area near the pit (area 12).

- Just off the trade road in the northeast corner of the depicted region is a natural ravine host to numerous cave openings. These are the Caves of Chaos, inhabited by various evil bands of humanoids that prey on travelers and each other (see chapter 11).

WILDERNESS SET ENCOUNTERS

AREA 1 – MOUND OF THE LIZARDFOLK

The streams and pools of the fens are the home of a tribe of exceptionally evil lizardfolk. Being nocturnal, this group is unknown to the residents of the Keep, and they will not bother individuals moving about in daylight unless they set foot on the mound, under which the muddy burrows and dens of the tribe are found. Recently the numbers of this tribe have dwindled following clashes with the aggressive bullywugs that lair in a nearby reed maze (area 9).

There are six male **lizardfolk** who defend the lair, coming out of the marked opening. If all these males are defeated, the remainder of the tribe hides in the lair. Each has only crude weapons: a heavy club, three javelins, and a spiked turtle shell shield. The largest male has a gold necklace (worth 1,100 gp).

In the lair is another male **lizardfolk**, three female lizardfolk (use the **lizardfolk** stat block, but with 16 [3d8 + 3] hit points each), and eight noncombatant young. The first character crawling into the lair always loses the initiative to the remaining lizardfolk, unless a torch or weapon is thrust well ahead of his or her body. The passage leading to the lair is but 4 feet high; while traveling through a character must spend an extra 1 foot for every foot of movement, and is at disadvantage on attack rolls and Dexterity saving throws. The lizardfolk don't suffer these penalties if they only employ bite attacks.

The common area is about 30 feet in diameter and contains the tribal nest, which holds six eggs. Hidden under the nest with the eggs are 112 cp, 186 sp, a gold ingot (worth 90 gp), a *potion of healing*, and a *potion of poison*.

AREA 2 – SPIDERS' LAIR

Concealed among the boughs of several ancient pine trees is a black stone altar inscribed with runes and pictograms of monstrous spiders raining terror on humans. The altar is cool to the touch, and dedicated to a forgotten foul spider god. Its surface is covered with dried bloodstains. The malevolence of the altar is soothing to arachnids and over the decades has attracted all manner of spiders—normal and monstrous—to this fell wood. Two giant black widow spiders (**giant spiders**) have spun their webs amongst the trees here. They attack any who approach the altar for a closer look.

Under a pile of leaves nearby is the skeleton of a victim, a hapless elf. Everything he bore has turned to rot and ruin, save a filthy shield which appears quite worthless. It is actually a *+1 shield*, and a successful DC 17 Intelligence (Investigation) check hints at a higher quality. In any case it requires a thorough cleaning and oiling to look presentable.

AREA 3 – RAIDER CAMP

A band of a dozen bandits has camped here on a rocky outcropping, called Raven Rock due to the large number of ravens that roost in the area. The band is close enough to be able to spy on the Keep, but far enough away so as to be unlikely to be discovered by patrols. The members of this group are:

- Dee Dee Raven, a female human **bandit captain** wearing a chain shirt (AC 15) and wielding two shortswords (1d6 + 3 piercing damage) and a shortbow (range 80/320 ft., 1d6 + 3 piercing damage). She is fond of black clothes and carries 18 sp and 10 gp.

- The Lieutenant is a male human **scout** wearing leather armor and carrying a shield (AC 15), a shortsword (1d6 + 2 piercing damage) and a spear (+2 to hit, range 20/60 ft., 1d6 piercing damage). He carries 13 sp and 3 gp.

- Ten male and female human **bandits** round out the band. Two wear leather armor and wield longbows (range 150/600 ft., 1d8 + 1 piercing damage) and daggers (1d4 + 1 piercing damage), while the remaining eight wear leather armor and carry shields (AC 14), and wield spears (+2 to hit, range 20/60 ft., 1d6 piercing damage) and daggers (+3 to hit, range 20/60 ft., 1d4 + 1 piercing damage). Each bandit carries 3d6 sp.

The camp contains bedrolls for all the bandits and a tent for Dee Dee. The bandits with longbows have extra quivers of 20 arrows. There is a cask of good quality wine (worth 15 gp) on a tree stump in the camp. Several game animals are hung from branches and can be eaten or taken along as they are cleaned.

AREA 4 – THE MAD HERMIT

For many years a solitary **Mad Hermit** (see appendix B) has haunted this area of the forest, becoming progressively wilder and crazier and more dangerous. Such is the range of his lunacy, he has long forgotten his own name or where his home once was located. His home now is in a huge hollow oak tree, the entrance to the hollow concealed by a thick bush which requires a successful DC 15 Wisdom (Perception) to locate. Inside is a mound of leaves and a couple of pieces of crude furniture. Even his cup and plate are handmade of wood and are of no value. There is a small chest buried under a few inches of dirt under the leaves of the Mad Hermit's "bed." A successful DC 18 Wisdom (Perception) check is required to locate the chest. In this container are 164 sp, 31 gp, and a *potion of invisibility*.

The Mad Hermit approaches the characters on friendly terms, claiming to be a holy man seeking goodness in nature. And perhaps he actually believes that at times, although a successful DC 14 Wisdom (Insight) check reveals his unstable behavior. He suddenly turns on the group when the opportunity presents itself, using his Sneak Attack trait, and calling his ferocious "pet" to his aid, a mountain lion. Treat the mountain lion as a **lion**, but add the Athletics (+5) skill and replace its Running Leap trait with the following trait:

Quick Reflexes: The mountain lion makes all initiative checks at advantage.

The mountain lion uses its Stealth to hide out of reach in the upper branches of a tree. It uses its Pounce trait while jumping from the tree, and if the target is surprised the mountain lion gets advantage on the initial attack. It stays on the ground for a few rounds before using the Disengage action to jump back into a tree preparing for another Pounce attack.

AREA 5 – THE HIDDEN FORD

The previous Castellan of the Keep was aware of this natural ford, which was maintained (and improved) by the Keep guards for years. But realizing it was a defensive liability, the Castellan had a powerful wizard place an enchantment on the ford to hide it from plain sight. Essentially this spell was a greater version of *hallucinatory terrain*, with an increased area of effect and a permanent duration. The river here is quite shallow (no more than 2 feet deep) and somewhat sluggish, affording an easy route to cross. But the spell grants the appearance of a deeper, swifter flow, similar to much of the river. The illusion can be interacted with, but those who know where to cross can do so easily despite appearances. A successful DC 17 Intelligence (Investigation) check reveals the illusion as a vague image superimposed on the actual shallow water.

The leader of the Raven Rock Bandits (see area 3) is aware of this enchantment, and uses it to great effect when preying on travelers moving along the road. There is a 20% chance during the day that a **bandit** is watching the ford concealed in a tree along the edge of the Ravenwood. If he observes anyone crossing, he reports it to his leader, and the camp goes on alert for the next day or two.

AREA 6 – THE GLIMMERGLASS NIXIES

A tribe of nixies inhabit an underwater cave system located about 25 feet underwater, just south of the large island. The nixies plant aquatic plant crops on the river bottom, herd fish, and grow freshwater oysters in extensive beds. Thirty-eight **nixies** (see appendix B) inhabit the various chambers of the cave system, well hidden by cultivated aquatic plants. It requires a successful DC 20 Wisdom (Perception) check to locate the cave entrance. Their tribe name is derived from the glass-like walls of some cave chambers. Only 15 of the nixies are trained for battle, wearing shell armor (AC 15) and wielding daggers and nets (see Player's Handbook p. 148). The remaining male and female fey tend to the aquatic plant fields or bivalve beds, plus gather additional resources from the bountiful river. Each nixie caries 1d4 freshwater pearls (each worth 25 gp).

The nixies occasionally lure air breathers to the edge of the river, and enchant them with a powerful *charm* that lasts for 1 year (although it can be voluntarily dispelled by a group of 10 nixies). The nixies cast *water breathing* once per day on these prisoners, and put them to work assisting with daily tasks of construction, harvesting, gathering or hunting. "Prisoners" is a misleading term, as the enchanted folks are cared for, fed, and well-respected by the tribe. Currently four of them are a part of the tribe (select appropriate NPCs from appendix C as needed). All the gear once owned by these NPCs that could be ruined due to long-term exposure to water is stored in a hidden cave on the large island.

Recently, a young headstrong nixie by the name of Elendiria was captured by bullywugs, and is scheduled to be sacrificed soon. The nixies fear for Elendiria but are too few and not well trained to oppose the warlike bullywugs. If the characters encounter the nixie patrol (see Random Wilderness Encounters, above) or somehow find the cave system, the fey beg for assistance. If the characters agree to help, the nixies would be glad to bestow upon them a pouch of freshwater pearls (15 pearls, each worth 25 gp). Alternatively, the nixies could be convinced to release one or two of their "prisoners."

AREA 7 – ARACHNIA'S LAIR

This area of the Goblinwater appears to be a good place to ford the river. The water here is mostly shallow, with a fairly sluggish flow and a sandy bottom. The water is typically about 3 feet deep or less, but there are a few pools of deeper water. If the characters cross here, they gain the attention of **Arachnia, a giant water spider** (see appendix B) with a voracious appetite and a glimmer of intelligence. Always on the hunt, she likely detects the characters entering the water due to her Water Sense trait. She attacks from the rear of the party, preferring to pick off a straggler to envenom and take back to her lair for casual consumption.

Just to the west the water deepens to nearly 20 feet, and located on the bottom amid a dense stand of aquatic plants is Arachnia's underwater lair. The 20-foot-diameter structure is constructed out of reed and cattail stems woven together like a web. The dome-like chamber is air-filled, with enough oxygen to sustain a Large-sized creature for 4 hours and a Medium-sized creature for 12 hours. Unless a character observes Arachinia returning to her lair, it is difficult to locate, requiring a successful DC 18 Wisdom (Perception) check. Strewn outside the lair are the bones of previous victims, picked clean by fish.

Poorly hidden under a rotting pile of aquatic plants are the following shiny objects collected by Arachnia over the years: a random assortment of coins (17 cp, 11 sp, 3 ep, and 7 gp), a single gold earring (worth 50 gp), and a silver ring set with three tiny emeralds (worth 225 gp). There is also a large hourglass with an electrum base, holding powdered ruby instead of sand. The hourglass is worth 775 gp, but the glass is fragile. If the glass is broken, the ruby powder alone is worth 275 gp. The final item is a *+1 dagger*, although it doesn't glow. A successful DC 20 Wisdom (Perception) check reveals a tiny sigil etched into the base of the blade. The sigil is a stylized "N" with three curved hash marks above, and two circles below. A successful DC 25 Intelligence (History) check (or examination by a sage) reveals the blade belonged to a halfling bard named Nimboltin. Further research by a sage (costing no less than 50 gp) reveals a command word for the blade, "pirssaepad." While holding the blade and uttering the command word, the dagger turns *invisible* for 1 hour. This ability can be used once per day.

AREA 8 – KOBOLD CAMP

This large group of 21 **kobolds** recently arrived in the region. The band is led by a brash **elite kobold** (see appendix B) named Torgo the Face Gouger, son of Torgo the Eye Gouger. They were banished from their tribe (located many miles to the south) by Torgo's father for aggressive actions with a nearby tribe of elves which resulted in swift retribution.

The camp is situated in a clearing, with a firepit in the center surrounded by bedrolls. Six kobolds armed with shortbows (range 80/320 ft., 1d6 + 2 piercing damage) are out hunting, but return in about an hour. Four kobolds are posted in trees to keep watch about 100 feet away in all four directions. However, there is a 50% chance each guard is asleep. If the characters are spotted by a guard, it attempts to alert the camp with a poorly imitated bird call, revealed as a ruse with a DC 11 Intelligence (Nature) check. The rest of the kobolds are eating, resting, or playing knucklebones. Torgo rests on a large flat rock covered with a wolf pelt (worth 55 gp).

Torgo has no armor but carries a shield (AC 14), has a Strength of 12 (+1), and attacks with a wicked hook-like weapon (+3 to hit, 1d8 + 1 piercing damage) in addition to a sling (+4 to hit, range 30/120 ft., 1d4 + 2 bludgeoning damage). He carries 22 gp in a pouch and wears a gaudy silver necklace (worth 185 gp). The other kobolds each carry 2d6 sp. A successful DC 15 Wisdom (Perception) check reveals a recently disturbed patch of soil located behind Torgo's rock. Buried here is a wooden chest that holds the kobolds' communal treasure: 122 cp, 344 sp, and 41 gp.

AREA 9 – REED MAZE OF THE BULLYWUGS

Deep in the Fell Fens, an aggressive band of bullywugs led by a mysterious shaman have settled down on a natural hillock surrounded by the Goblinwater on three sides. The bullywugs have hacked a maze through the tall reeds to defend the southern approach to their lair. The Dungeon Master is encouraged to design this encounter area, making it a suitable challenge for a party of characters level 3-5.

AREA 10 – ADVENTURER CAMP

Recently, the bandits of Raven Rock (see area 3) have stepped up attacks on travelers coming to and from the Keep. In response, the Castellan secretly hired a band of adventurers (called "Fortune's Five") to strike out into the wilderness, locate the bandit hideout, and bring them to justice. They are supported by several Keep guards. The group has established a camp on the hill overlooking the road, plotting their next move. The group includes:

- Eddis, a female human **spy**.

- M'Baddah, a male human **scout**.

- M'Whan, a male human fighter (use **thug** statistics), M'Baddah's son.

- Jerdren and Blorys, male human fighters (use **thug** statistics), brothers.

- Willow, male elf **scout**.

- Mead, male elf **fledgling mage** (see appendix B).

- Six male human **guards** wearing chain mail (AC 16) and carrying longswords (1d8 + 1 slashing damage, or 1d10 + 1 slashing damage if used two-handed) and longbows (range 150/600 ft., 1d8 + 1 piercing damage).

Mead has the following spells prepared:

- Cantrips (at will): *fire bolt, light, mage hand*

- 1st level (3 slots): *detect magic, mage armor, magic missile, shield, sleep*

After several clashes with bandits and humanoids, the group has already lost a few of its members. They are cautious, but fast-talking characters with a successful DC 13 Charisma (Persuasion) check can convince the leaders they are friends. They are willing to barter supplies (food, rope, weapons) for the like, or for information. Each of the leaders (Eddis, M'Baddah, or Jerdren) knows 1d4 rumors pertaining to the Keep or the wilderness. They would be most appreciative of any information the characters have, including established encounter areas, or the location of the bandit hideout.

Each named NPC carries 2d6 sp and 1d8 gp. The guards each have 2d6 sp. Eddis carries a sack with a minor amount of coins recovered while overcoming humanoids and bandits while in the wilds (87 sp and 13 gp).

AREA 11 – THE FORGOTTEN PORTAL

Deep in the Whispering Woods is hidden an ancient eldritch structure created during a bygone age. Steeped in powerful—but forgotten—enchantments is a strange portal of white marble which is warm to the touch. Overgrown with lush vegetation and vines, the 20-foot-wide, 20-foot-high arch is engraved with bizarre runes along the top, and arcane symbols up and down its support columns. There is little chance the characters locate this structure, unless they find the map in Quasqueton (see chapter 6, area 32), or somehow get the information out of the Mad Hermit (see area 4) during a moment of lucid conversation.

The origin and purpose of the portal is left to the DM to decide, as well as if it still functions, or how to go about activating it. The mysterious place is now the lair of a **decapus** (see appendix B). Its green and brown bulk blends in with the surrounding vegetation, so those investigating the portal are likely in for a surprise attack from one of its many tentacles. The monstrosity hangs from the archway out of reach so it can attack with nine of its tentacles. If it establishes a grapple, it attempts to reel the target in for bite attacks. The decapus is strangely attracted to the portal, and thus fights to the death.

At the base of the portal, under a loose covering of leaves, bones, and organic debris, are some random valuables from previous victims. These include 44 ep, three yellow topaz gems (each worth 100 gp), a bronze tiara set with tiny pearls (worth 215 gp), and a *wand of secrets*. The command word for the wand is long forgotten and needs to be researched by a sage (at a cost of at least 100 gp and 2 weeks of research time).

AREA 12 – THE PIT OF DEMISE

Assuming the Dungeon Master is using Quasqueton as the Cave of the Unknown, then located on the northeastern facing of the rock outcropping that contains the dungeon is a massive sinkhole about 200 feet in diameter. The sinkhole was once 350 feet deep, but following a decade of construction at Quasqueton (the mined tailings were placed in the sinkhole), it's barely 100 feet deep now. But rock tailings are not the only thing in the pit. The bones of thousands of humanoid slaves are intermingled with the rocks. This pit was used to dispose of slaves from Quasqueton that had outlived their usefulness. The slaves were often hurled in alive and left to slowly die, hence the name the pit of demise. For many decades, the evil has festered here and the dead are not so quiet. Now packs of undead roam the area, but strangely are tied to the pit.

If Quasqueton is not being used as the Cave of the Unknown, then the origin of this pit is left to the DM to flesh out.

If a random encounter is indicated within 6 squares of this location, use the following table to determine the undead encountered:

D8	Encounter
1-2	Zombies (2d4)
3-5	Skeletons (2d6)
6-7	Ghouls (1d4)
8	Will-o'-wisp (1)

Faint trails meander around the area, eventually depositing a traveler at the pit's edge. Long before the pit is reached, bleached bones and dead or dying vegetation reveal the evil stench of this place. These paths are used by the evil priests from the Caves of Chaos (see chapter 11, cave area K), to collect bodies to animate, or even to collect already-created undead. Good-aligned characters should feel at unease here, and in the pit proper, undead have the Turn Resistance trait:

Turn Resistance: The undead has advantage on saving throws against any effect that turns undead.

The following undead inhabit the pit of demise. The DM should not throw all of these combatants at the characters at once. Instead, use waves of undead as progressively harder challenges if they insist on penetrating deeper into the recesses of the pit.

51 **skeletons** (groups of 2d6)

27 **zombies** (groups of 1d8)

11 **ghouls** (groups of 1d4)

4 **ogre zombies** (1 at a time)

2 **ogre skeletons** (see appendix B) (1 at a time)

If the characters insist on searching the interior of the pit, for each 10 minutes of searching, a character can find one object on the table below. But for every 10 minutes spent searching, the characters will encounter a wandering group of undead as described above.

D12	Item Found
1-4	Random coins (1d6 sp and 1d4 gp)
5-7	Broken weapon
8-9	Usable weapon or mundane item
10-11	Minor art object (worth 1d6 x 10 gp)
12	Art object (worth 1d4 x 100 gp)

AREA 13 – THE STONE HOVEL

Set deep in the Whispering Woods is a small stone hut with a solitary wooden door and a thatched roof. A path meanders through an overgrown herb garden leading to the door. A successful DC 17 Wisdom (Perception) check reveals several broken pieces of statues hidden in the undergrowth. Concealed in the garden are four **awakened vampiric shrubs** (see appendix B) that attack targets seeking entrance to the hovel. The door is unlocked (unlatched, actually).

This stone hut belongs to a reclusive **medusa** known as the Stone Witch. Her real name is Cynnia, and generally she keeps to herself, preferring to avoid contact with the locals. She is content to grow herbs and vegetables, brew potions, and conduct research. A few weeks ago, she was captured by the high priest in the Caves of Chaos and is currently held prisoner there (see chapter 11, area 64).

The interior of the hut contains one circular room, about 35 feet in diameter with a 15-foot-high ceiling. Two small circular windows are each covered with an animal pelt. The wooden rafters of the ceiling are adorned with hanging herbs, mushrooms, and salted meats for drying. A successful DC 15 Intelligence (Nature) check reveals a few bunches of herbs are quite valuable (worth 20 gp each). Furniture includes an overturned table, a broken chair, a wooden bench, and a bed covered with furs (including a red fox pelt worth 75 gp and a black bear pelt worth 115 gp). Hiding in the furs of the bed is a large blind black **cat** (named Truffle), Cynnia's pet. Unless calmed down with a successful DC 15 Wisdom (Animal Handling) check, the cat makes a dash for the door or through a pelt-covered window. If offered food, this check is attempted at advantage. If the characters cast *speak with animals*, Truffle relates that many feedings ago, his mistress was attacked in her home by several humanoids, but he sensed not all were living. Indeed, the evil priests had several zombies with them. She was captured and taken away.

The benchtop is covered with smashed clay pots, spilled pastes, residues, and evaporated fluids. On the opposite side of the room is a cold hearth with pots and pans stacked nearby. A single large cast-iron pot is positioned over the ashes. The pot contains the residue of a charred stew long since overcooked. On a peg near the hearth is a leather sack still holding several rare mushrooms considered a delicacy (worth 12 gp). A successful DC 12 Intelligence (Investigation) check reveals the place was recently ransacked.

A successful DC 18 Wisdom (Perception) check reveals a loose flagstone in the hearth. Behind it is a small cavity that contains a wooden rack holding six small clay pots. Four of these are *elixirs of stone to flesh* (see appendix A), while the two remaining pots each hold a *potion of animal friendship.*

CHAPTER ELEVEN
The Caves of Chaos

There are woods overlays and rough contour lines shown on the cave area map. These are only for surface movement references, and once your characters are underground you should ignore these markings.

START

DM Note: When the characters discover the ravine area, read the following description. Add whatever you feel is appropriate to the description of what they see, but be careful not to give any information away or mislead them. Additional information on how you should handle the whole area is detailed in the General Features section, below.

The forest you have been passing through has been getting denser, more tangled, and gloomier than before. The thick, twisted tree trunks, unnaturally misshapen limbs, writhing roots, clutching and grasping thorns, and briars all seem to warn and ward you off, but you have forced and hacked your way through regardless.

Now the strange growth has suddenly ended. Your band has stepped out of the thicket into a ravine-like area. A flock of ravens rise croaking from the ground, the beat of their wings and their cries magnified by the terrain to sound loud and horrible. Dark streaked rock mingles with the earthen walls of the canyon that rise rather steeply to either side, to a height of about 100 feet or so. Clumps of trees grow here and there, both on the floor of the ravine and up the sloping walls of the canyon. The opening you stand in is about 200 feet wide. The ravine runs at least 400 feet to the western end, where it rises in a steep slope. Here and there, at varying heights on all sides of the ravine, you can see the black mouths of cave-like openings in the rock walls. The sunlight is dim, the air dank, there is an oppressive feeling here, as if something evil is watching and waiting to pounce upon you.

There are bare, dead trees here and there, and upon one a vulture perches and gazes hungrily at you. Amongst the litter of rubble, boulders, and dead wood scattered about on the ravine floor, you can see bits of gleaming ivory and white—likely the bones and skulls of men, animals, and other things....

You know that you have certainly discovered the Caves of Chaos.

GENERAL FEATURES

Woods. The small groves and copses are thick growths, tangled and forbidding. You may, at your option, have characters encounter occasional monsters herein. Encounters with natural predators, stirges, or humanoids (kobolds, orcs, etc.) from the caves nearby, or the like, are appropriate. Movement through these wooded areas is considered difficult terrain, and characters must move in single file. Trees on the map average about 50 feet high, and can be climbed with a successful DC 15 Strength (Athletics) check. Even though not shown, there are single trees, shrubs, and bushes elsewhere.

Underground. The caves, passages, and rooms of the complex are on different levels. Passages slope upwards and downwards between the contours, even where stairways are not depicted. Areas are roofed by at least 5 feet of solid rock and often much more.

Interior. Except where noted otherwise, all underground areas are natural or cut from living rock. Unless specified in the encounter area key, assume all ceilings are 10 feet high. All surfaces are rough with small ledges, minor cracks, small holes, etc. Unless otherwise noted, assume climbing an interior wall requires a successful DC 10 Strength (Athletics) check.

Doors. Unless noted otherwise, doors in the caves are wooden and bound with iron. They can be smashed down with a successful DC 14 Strength check. Wooden doors are AC 15 and have 18 hit points.

AN EVOLVING ENCOUNTER AREA

Consider the following topics while running exploratory forays into the caves.

Ransoming Prisoners. Organized humanoid tribes can optionally take characters prisoner, instead of outright slaughter. If this occurs, all characters are bound while one is released to return to the Keep in order to bring a ransom back to free the captives. Set the ran-

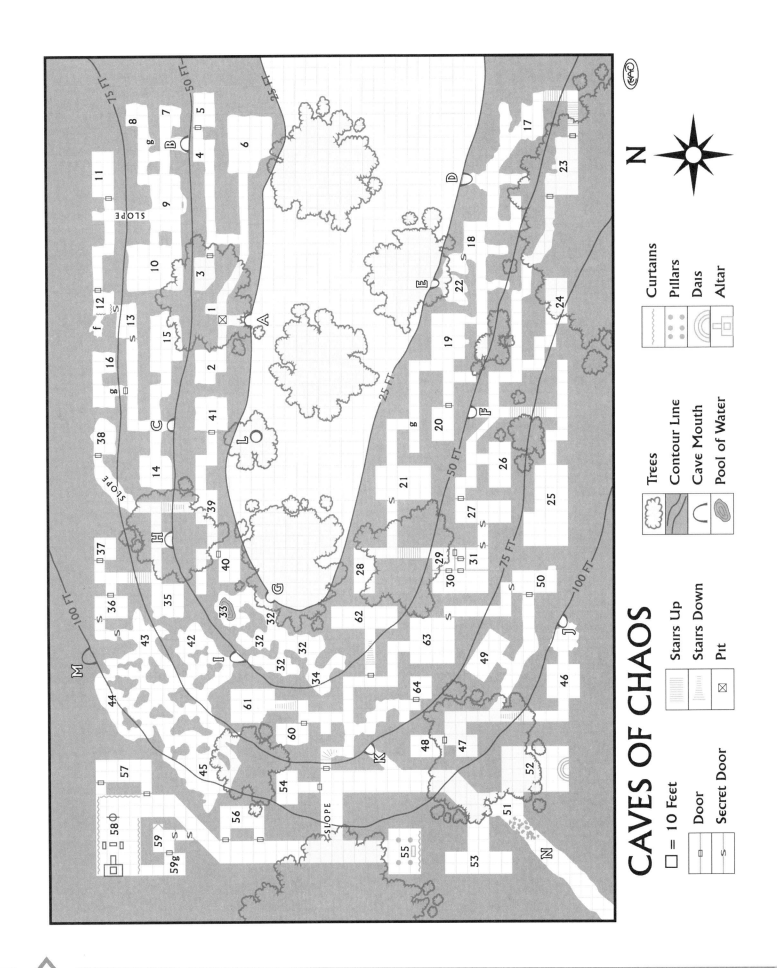

CAVES OF CHAOS

☐ = 10 Feet

Legend		
Door	Stairs Up	Trees
Secret Door	Stairs Down	Contour Line
	Pit	Cave Mouth
		Pool of Water
		Curtains
		Pillars
		Dais
		Altar

N

som sum low, perhaps 10 to 100 gold pieces (or a magic item which the ransoming monsters would find useful) per prisoner. If the ransom is paid, allow the characters to go free. Then, without telling the players, assume that this success brought fame to the capturing monsters, so their numbers increase by 2d6 additional members after a week. In this case, the tribe will also be very careful to watch for a return of the adventurers seeking revenge for their humiliating captivity. The period of extra alertness will last for 1d4 weeks, while the increase in numbers is permanent.

Tribal Alliances and Warfare. You might allow characters to somehow become aware that there is a constant fighting going on between the goblins and hobgoblins on one side and the orcs, sometimes with gnoll allies, on the other. Meanwhile, the kobolds hope to be forgotten by all, and the bugbears pick off any stragglers who happen by. With this knowledge, the characters might be able to set tribes to fighting one another, and then the adventurers can take advantage of the weakened state of the feuding humanoids. Be careful to handle this whole thing properly; it is a device you may use to aid players who are few in number but with a high level of playing skill. It will make it too easy if there are many players, or if players do not actually use wits instead of force when the opportunity presents itself.

Monsters Learn from Experience. Allow intelligent monsters (even those with only low intelligence) to learn from experience. If characters employ alchemist's fire against them, allow the monsters to employ similar tactics assuming they can obtain the needed supplies. If characters are always sneaking up on them, have the monsters set warning devices to alert them of intruders. If characters run from overwhelming numbers, have the monsters set up a ruse by causing a few to shout and make noise as if there were many coming, thus hopefully frightening off the intruders. This method of handling monsters is basic to becoming a good DM. Apply the principle wherever and whenever you have reason.

Emptied Areas. When monsters are cleared out of an area, the area is deserted for 1d4 weeks. If no further intrusion is made into the area, however, the surviving former inhabitants return or else some other monster eventually moves in. For instance, a wandering thoul might move into the minotaur's cave complex (cave area I), bringing with him whatever treasure he has.

A. KOBOLD LAIR

There is a 2 in 6 chance that as the group enters this cave-like tunnel, eight **kobolds** ambush from above. Since the kobolds are hiding in the trees, the characters need to succeed at a contested Wisdom (Perception) check against the kobolds' Dexterity (Stealth) check (which is +2). Failure indicates the kobolds have surprise. Four kobolds rappel from the trees using ropes and wielding javelins (+0 to hit, range 30/120 ft., 1d6 piercing damage), while the other four remain in the branches (which grant half cover) and fire sling stones below.

Each kobold carries 1d8 sp in addition to its weapons.

The entrance is an 8-foot-high cave partially obscured with vegetation. Located 30 feet inside the entrance is a pit trap at the intersection. The pit can be noticed with a successful DC 17 Wisdom (Perception) check, but if the characters are cautious and probing ahead, grant them advantage on this check. The weight of a few giant rats is not enough to trigger the trap; it takes at least 50 pounds of weight on the cover to trigger it. The pit is 10 feet deep, and those falling in suffer 3 (1d6) bludgeoning damage. The pit lid closes on the next round, and characters trapped within cannot escape without aid from the outside. The noise of the pit activating attracts the guards from area 1 and the 2d6 giant rats from area 2.

A character can skirt around the edges of the pit without falling in with a successful DC 10 Dexterity (Acrobatics) check. The kobolds use wooden planks (stored in area 1) for crossing the pit.

DM Note: Kobold losses are not to be replaced, although injured kobolds heal wounds naturally in a day. If the attackers hurl flaming oil or alchemist's fire at the kobolds, they retreat if possible, fearing fire damage. Should they have the opportunity to find any flasks of oil or alchemist's fire, the kobolds employ this tactic against the characters!

AREA 1 – GUARD ROOM

This 10-foot-by-10-foot alcove appears to be a guard post. Several grimy pallets and a few personal effects are strewn about the floor.

Stationed at this area are six **kobold** guards armed with spears (+0 to hit, range 20/60 ft., 1d6 piercing damage) and daggers. If they don't respond to the pit trap being triggered, they are here playing knucklebones and resting. At any time, at least two are alert and spying down the entrance corridor and thus are alerted to any loud noises (such as the pit trap being triggered) or any lights. They throw their spears the first round but switch to daggers in melee.

Each kobold carries 1d6 sp.

Developments. One kobold attempts to flee to warn the rest of the tribe. First he proceeds to area 6, and then on to area 4. After 2 rounds, 2d4 kobolds from area 6 arrive each round until all 17 males have been summoned. A few fall back to the intersection and attack with ranged weapons with half cover. The elite kobolds from area 4 arrive 4 rounds later.

AREA 2 – GIANT RATS

The organic rotting stench of this chamber is apparent before you enter. This 30-foot-by-20-foot room is littered with knee-deep refuse, garbage, and bits of debris. Something inhabits this mess as you occasionally catch a glance of brown fur tunneling through the waste.

This chamber serves as a garbage pit for the kobolds. The floor of this chamber is considered difficult terrain. Although the footing is somewhat stable, feel free to call for an occasional DC 10 Dexterity (Acrobatics) check if a character tries to run or perform some kind of delicate maneuver while in the chamber. Failure of this check results in the character falling prone. The waste is composed of bits of wood, cloth, rotting food, dung, and rotting vegetation. There is nothing of value in the mess, but if a character spends more than 30 minutes rummaging through the mess, he is required to make a DC 11 Constitution check, or become infected with sewer plague (see Dungeon Master's Guide, p. 257).

The stench has attracted a pack of 18 **giant rats**, which have become pets of the kobolds, living off their discarded scraps of food and other waste. These vermin carry a disease, and each bite delivered has a 1 in 20 chance of inflicting a disease, unless the target succeeds at a DC 11 Constitution saving throw. Failure indicates the target has contracted sewer plague. The giant rats greedily attack any characters that enter the chamber.

One of the fellows is an oversized **giant rat pack leader** (see appendix B) that hangs near the back. Its unusual size can be discovered with a DC 13 passive Perception check. If the pack leader is defeated, the rest of the giant rats flee, although they could be encountered in other locations of this cave system at the DM's discretion.

The pack leader wears a thin silver chain set with 5 small citrines (worth 400 gp). The silver chain itself is worth 50 gp, while each gem is worth 50 gp.

Development. The giant rats are trained to rush to the sound of the pit trap being triggered in the hallway. 2d4 giant rats arrive at the pit the round after it is triggered.

AREA 3 – FOOD STORAGE ROOM

The door to this room is always is locked. The key is carried by the kobold chieftain (see area 5). The lock is simple, and can be picked with thieves' tools and a successful DC 13 Dexterity check.

This 30-foot-by-20-foot room appears to be a storeroom. Sacks, crates, and barrels are all stacked and piled throughout the chamber. A large cask is pushed into one far corner of the room, and several large pieces of dried salted meat haunches hang from the ceiling.

The kobolds use this room to store various foodstuffs. Most is edible, but of poor quality. The sacks contain damp, moldy grain, the crates overripe vegetables, and the barrels stale water. One crate contains human jerky

and the hanging salted meats are from humans and other humanoid victims. The large cask is half full of thin and vinegary wine.

AREA 4 – GUARD ROOM

This 20-foot-square room contains a battered round table and four flimsy chairs. Scattered about the walls are several dirty sleeping pallets. A stained cloth hammock in is affixed to the wall in one corner.

This chamber is a guard room occupied by three **elite kobolds** (see appendix B). These kobolds wear chain mail (AC 16, speed 20 ft.), and wield shortbows (+4 to hit, range 80/320 ft., 1d6 + 2 piercing damage) and handaxes (+2 to hit, 1d6 slashing damage). If they detect characters approaching down the hallway, they use the corner of the room as half cover and fire arrows down the corridor. They fight to the death, to protect the chieftain in area 5.

In addition to their weapons and armor, each elite kobold carries a purse with 2d6 gp.

AREA 5 – KOBOLD CHIEFTAIN'S ROOM

This 20-foot-by-30-foot chamber is cluttered with heaping piles of cloth and battered, broken items of furniture. A dilapidated bed is pushed against the far wall, covered with grimy, stained sheets. Lounging on the bed is a well-muscled red-scaled draconic humanoid enjoying the company of several female draconic companions.

This is the lair of the **kobold chieftain** (see appendix B), a powerful brute that wears chain mail (AC 16) and wields a battleaxe two-handed (1d10 + 2 slashing damage). He has the key to the storage room (area 3) and a large black opal on a great golden chain about his neck (worth 1,200 gp). He brazenly engages the characters in combat with useless axe sweeps and flair, trying to impress his harem.

The chieftain is attended by five scantily-clad female **kobolds**. Each one aggressively defends the chieftain to the death, with hisses of displeasure. Each female also carries 1d6 gp.

The heaped cloth and furniture are worthless. Hidden in an old blanket hanging on the wall are 50 gp and a small iron key (to the chest) sewn into the hem. If not examined carefully, this requires a successful DC 15 Wisdom (Perception) check to discover. A locked chest is poorly hidden under a pile of stained, torn clothes. It can be unlocked with thieves' tools and a successful DC 15 Dex-

terity check, or smashed open (AC 14, 8 hit points). The chest holds a small hoard of coins, including 203 cp, 61 sp, and 22 ep.

AREA 6 – COMMON CHAMBER

This 50-foot-by-40-foot chamber smells heavily of animal musk. This room is the squalid living area for dozens of draconic humanoids. The floor is covered with straw nests, cloth piles, scraps, and broken mundane items.

The rest of the kobold tribe lives here. There are 17 male **kobolds** and 23 female **kobolds**. There are also eight noncombatant young kobolds which huddle in fear at the back of the cave. The kobolds fight until half their numbers have been eliminated. At this point, they surrender or attempt to flee the cave system.

Male kobolds have 1d6 sp each, while females carry 1d4 silver pieces each. The young kobolds have nothing. Amidst the litter of cloth, bits, and scraps of odds-and-ends there is a piece of silk worth 150 gp, but this requires a successful DC 17 Wisdom (Perception) check to locate among the numerous worthless bits of cloth and other debris.

Development. These kobolds defend the cave if invaded. They likely respond to the guards in area 1 or area 4, and can be organized into waves so as not to overwhelm the characters. In this case only the males respond to summons, while the females remain here to protect the lair and the young.

B. ORC LAIR

When the party enters this cave, continue with the following read-aloud text:

Twenty feet into this cave is an east/west intersection. The north wall is decorated with humanoid heads and skulls in various stages of decay, placed in niches which checker the wall at various heights to the left and right. Sounds of activity can be heard from the west, but all is quiet to the east.

Area g. This narrowing area is a guard post occupied by a single **orc** watcher; there is a small window-like opening from which he can observe the entrance to the lair. A piece of gray canvas behind gives the impression that the guard's head is another of the ghastly trophies which decorate the north wall. If adventurers enter, he quickly ducks down, slipping a goblin head into the place his own was, and alerts the orcs at area 8. A successful DC 12 passive Perception check reveals this action.

DM Note: Orc losses cannot be replaced, but after an

initial attack by adventurers, the males at area 10 move four of their number into area 9. These orcs are armed with light crossbows (+3 to hit, range 80/320 ft., 1d8 + 1 piercing damage) from area f, and lay an ambush for intruders. If the orc chief is slain, all surviving orcs from this locale seek refuge with the orc tribe at cave area C, taking everything of value (and several items without value) with them. Cave area B will thereafter be deserted.

AREA 7 – GUARD ROOM

This 20-foot-square cavern has rough-hewn walls. Several straw pallets line the floor, while pegs crudely adorn the walls, holding shabby clothing.

Four **orcs** guard this chamber. If the characters are using a light source, or make considerable noise at the intersection, these guards respond by rushing down the corridor. They are armed with two spears each, one for throwing (+5 to hit, range 20/60 ft., 1d6 + 3 piercing damage) and one for melee wielded in two hands (+5 to hit, 1d8 + 3 piercing damage). They fight to the death, being cut off from the rest of the tribe.

Each orc carries 1d8 ep. There is nothing of value in their chamber, as the pallets and clothing is all ruined and worthless.

Development. When these orcs engage the characters, they raise an alarm. If the guard in area g or the guards in area 8 have not been alerted yet, each responds in 2 rounds, attacking from the rear.

AREA 8 – GUARD ROOM

This 20-foot-square cavern has rough-hewn walls. Several straw pallets line the floor, while pegs crudely adorn the walls, holding shabby clothing.

This room is similar to area 7, although there is an extra pallet for the guard stationed at area g. The four **orcs** here are also armed with two spears (+5 to hit, range 20/60 ft., 1d6 + 3 piercing damage, or 1d8 + 3 piercing damage if used two-handed to make a melee attack).

Each orc carries 1d8 ep in a pouch.

Development. Depending on how the battle is going between the invaders and the orcs in area 7, these orcs either use the southern passage to flank, or set an ambush in area 9.

AREA 9 – BANQUET AREA

This great hall is 30 feet wide by 50 feet long. Two passages exit the opposite wall, while another passage on the north wall slopes up and away from the chamber. A great fireplace is situated along the south wall, dimly glowing with burning embers. In the center of the room are several large tables and chairs, with one huge chair positioned at the head of the largest table.

This chamber is used by the orcs as a banquet area, although it is likely empty when the characters arrive. The orc chief often "holds court" from the large chair in this chamber.

Development. The orc guards from area 8 might be here waiting to ambush interlopers into their lair. If that's the case, the tables are flipped over to form defensive walls, which provide half cover. If a battle breaks out here the male orcs from area 10 arrive, four per round, to join the fray.

AREA 10 – COMMON ROOM

This large chamber is 40 feet by 50 feet with a slightly higher ceiling. Numerous sleeping pallets and an assortment of worn tables and chairs are randomly placed about the chamber.

The majority of the orcs live in this common chamber. There are 12 male **orcs** in addition to 18 female **orcs** and nine noncombatant young orcs. Most likely the males respond to intruders in area 9. The females only fight if cornered or the young are threatened, using bits of furniture or other items as improvised clubs.

The males are armed with two spears (+5 to hit, range 20/60 ft., 1d6 + 3 piercing damage, or 1d8 + 3 piercing damage if used two-handed to make a melee attack) and have 2d6 sp each. The female and young orcs have nothing of worth. The few furnishings in the room are likewise of no value.

AREA 11 – STORAGE CHAMBER

The door to this chamber is locked (the orc chief has the only key). The lock can be picked with thieves' tools and a successful DC 16 Dexterity check or the door can be smashed down. Smashing the door down alerts nearby orcs.

This 20-foot-by-40-foot chamber is a storage room. Numerous sacks, crates, and casks are neatly stacked or piled along the walls. In addition, several shields hang on the east wall, along with numerous spears propped up in the corner. A pair of battleaxes rest on one of the crates.

Amidst the stacks and heaps of supplies here (similar to

the contents of area 3 in the kobold lair) are the following weapons and armor. There are three functional shields hanging on the wall, and 17 serviceable spears nearby. The two battleaxes are in excellent condition. A small crate in the far northeast corner contains a long-forgotten heavy crossbow with a broken drawstring and 60 bolts. There is nothing else of value in the place.

AREA 12 – ORC LEADER'S ROOM

The door opens to reveal a 20-foot-by-20-foot chamber covered with a mangy carpet. Several dirty, stained tapestries hang on the far walls, and a battered table and assortment of mismatched chairs occupy the room. At the opposite end is a sturdy cot on which rests a massive humanoid with porcine features. At his feet are strewn an assortment of grimy pillows occupied by a pair of muscular female humanoids.

The **orc chief** (see appendix B) wears chain mail, hefts a *+1 shield*, and wields a *black mace* (see appendix A) with deadly skill. His two female **orc** consorts conceal daggers (+5 to hit, range 20/60 ft., 1d4 + 3 piercing damage). The consorts fight to the death but the chief might attempt to flee (see Development, below).

Although the furniture here is functional, it is of no great value. The tapestries were once valuable, but now are ruined. One of these covers the entrance to the small cave to the west (area f). Another tapestry covers the south wall which conceals a secret door. This secret door can be located with a successful DC 15 Wisdom (Perception) check, or automatically if a character witnesses the orc chief use the door. Springing the catch to unlock the secret door is tricky, and requires two successful DC 14 Dexterity checks, or two characters working together.

The orc chief has 31 gp, a key to the lock for the chest in area f, a key to the area 11 door, and a gold ring set with a large aquamarine (worth 700 gp). Each female orc carries 2d6 gp on her person.

Development. If hard-pressed and reduced to 10 hit points or less, the orc chief wiggles behind the tapestries on the south wall and spends an action opening the secret door to the south. Although embarrassed, he goes to his rival tribe to beg for mercy and an alliance.

Area f. This alcove is used by the orc chief to store arms and treasure. There are two complete suits of chain mail here, one man-sized and the other dwarf-sized. Four longswords, five light crossbows with 40 bolts, and a locked iron chest are also present. The chest lock can be picked with thieves' tools and a successful DC 20 Dexterity check. Alternatively, the iron chest can be smashed open (AC 19, 10 hit points, resistant to piercing and slashing damage). The chest holds 205 cp, 286 sp, 81 gp, and 13 pp. A small niche in the back wall, with a boulder

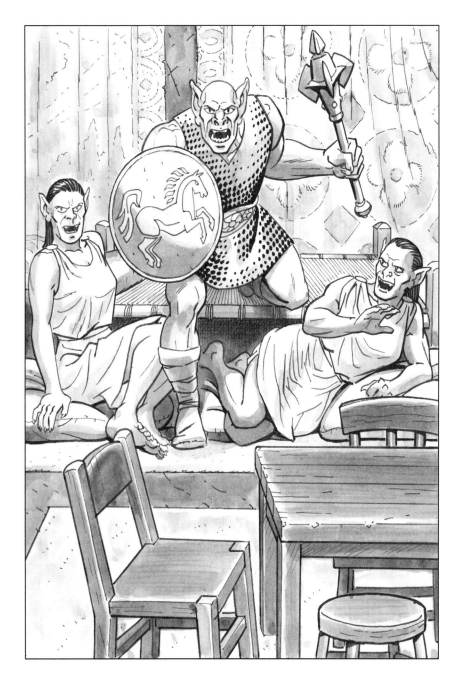

in front covering it, requires a successful DC 18 Wisdom (Perception) check to locate. It hides a *potion of healing* and a *spell scroll* of *fireball*.

C. ORC LAIR

Similar to the orcs at cave area B, these monsters inhabit cave areas 13 to 16. These orcs, however, do not rely upon a continual watch being kept; instead, they have a series of nearly invisible tripwires running across the entry passage, about 11 feet from the entrance. The tripwires can be detected with a successful DC 15 Wisdom (Perception) check. If triggered, a heavy weighted net suspended from the ceiling drops upon intruders, ensnaring all creatures in a 10-foot-by-10-foot area. Ensnared creatures are required to make a DC 12 Strength check, or be knocked prone by the weight of the net. A creature can use an action to escape or free another creature with a successful DC 10 Strength check. The numerous metal pieces tied to the net automatically alert the orcs in area 14, who arrive in 1 round.

DM Note: Orc losses cannot be replaced. If this tribe is attacked, and the characters retreat, the orcs from area 15 guard the entrance, ready for a second assault. If the orc chief is slain, the survivors seek safety in cave area B, if possible. Otherwise, they flee the caves entirely, carrying as much of their goods away.

AREA 13 – FORGOTTEN ROOM

Only the two orc leaders (from this area and from cave area B) know of this place. They secretly meet here on occasion to plan co-operative ventures or discuss tribal problems. Although the separate tribes are not exactly friendly, both leaders are aware of the fact that there is strength in numbers.

Finding the secret door at the end of the corridor is quite easy, as it only requires a successful DC 10 Wisdom (Perception) check. The stone door pivots inward, with a gentle push following the triggering of a release near the floor.

A small table and two chairs are in the middle of the hidden room, which is 20 feet by 30 feet. There is a wooden chest to one side of the table, and two shields are hung on the south wall.

The chest is unlocked and holds a longbow, a quiver of 20 arrows, two longswords, and two daggers, all in good condition. In the southeast corner of the room is an old wooden bucket filled with stagnant black water. Under-

neath the bucket are 20 sp, 10 gp, and two small pouches, each holding one gem (each worth 50 gp; one is a bloodstone, the other is a moonstone).

Nesting under these small pouches are two **giant centipedes**. A character disturbing the pouches must succeed in a Wisdom (Perception) contest against the giant centipedes' Dexterity (Stealth) check or be surprised. The giant centipedes, if disturbed, fight to the death.

AREA 14 – COMMON CHAMBER

This 30-foot-by-30-foot room is a mess of sleeping pallets, broken furniture, piles of cloth, and general refuse.

The jumbled mess of items is wooden furniture, flea-infested clothing, rotting straw, and food debris. All of it is worthless.

Most of the orc tribe inhabits this chamber. Nine male **orcs** armed with shields (AC 15) and longswords (1d8 + 3 slashing damage) reside here. In addition, eight unarmed female **orcs** and three noncombatant young orcs are present. The female orcs seek to flee and refuse to fight.

Each male orc carries 1d20 sp, in addition to its weapon and shield. Each female orc carries 1d4 cp.

Development. The male orcs rush to the entrance if they hear the net falling, arriving in 1 round.

AREA 15 – COMMON HALL

General meetings are held here, and food is likewise cooked and eaten here by the orc tribe.

This 50-foot-by-30-foot chamber appears to be used as a gathering place and mess hall. Several large tables surrounded by numerous chairs in various states of repair, condition, and type occupy the room. Along the back wall is a firepit with glowing embers and several large pots and cooking implements.

Several orcs dwell in this chamber due to lack of space in area 14. These include six male **orcs** armed with shields (AC 15) and longswords (1d8 + 3 slashing damage). Two of these orcs also have light crossbows (+3 to hit, range 80/320 ft., 1d8 + 1 piercing damage), and gladly hang back using a table for half cover while shooting recklessly into a melee. Four unarmed female **orcs** are also present, but these cower at the rear of the room, or flee if possible.

Each male orc carries 1d20 sp in addition to its weapon and shield. Each female orc carries 1d4 cp.

Development. The male orcs here also rush to the entrance if they hear the noise of the net falling, but it takes them 3 rounds to arrive.

AREA 16 – LEADER'S ROOM

Area g. A guard is always posted just inside the door, and he cannot be surprised. The **orc** wears chain mail (AC 16), wields a greataxe, and has 22 hit points. He carries 2d6 sp and 1d4 gp. He immediately shouts an alarm if any intruders attempt to enter.

Behind him to the west are stacks of barrels, boxes, and sacks. These are extra supplies for the tribe and the foodstuffs are not quite up to human standards. None of the other items here have value, except one small wine barrel that contains a good quality wine (worth 55 gp), although it weighs 40 pounds. The area to the east is a comfortable living area for the chief of this tribe.

This 20-foot-square chamber is comfortable with a stained but plush carpet on the floor. Along the back wall is a sturdy wooden bed, a small table holding a tarnished copper bowl, and a mismatched chest of drawers.

The **orc chief** (see appendix B) here is a very large specimen who wears plate armor and carries a shield (AC 20). He wields a longsword (+6 to hit, 1d8 + 4 slashing damage), and a *+1 handaxe* (+7 to hit, range 20/60 ft., 1d6 + 5 slashing damage) is on his belt. On his first turn, he throws the axe at a fighter-type and attacks with his longsword. His female **orc** mate wields a morningstar (1d8 + 3 piercing damage). Both fight to the death.

The orc chief's belt is made of silver, with a gold buckle (worth 160 gp), and his longsword has a 100 gp piece of jade set in its pommel. In his purse are 5 sp, 17 ep, and 8 gp. His mate has an ivory bracelet (worth 100 gp).

The area is well-furnished compared to the rest of the caves. The small chest of drawers contains a sack with 50 pp tied shut with a *rope of climbing*. The copper bowl on the small table is finely wrought and chased with silver. However, it is filled with garbage and very tarnished, so it appears to be worth a mere 10 sp. A successful DC 13 Intelligence check reveals its true value of 50 gp.

D. GOBLIN LAIR

The natural cave quickly turns into the worked stone tunnels typical of this whole complex. The corridor splits, continuing south, but also heading east and west.

The passageways here are very busy, and for every 30 feet explored by the characters, there is a 3 in 6 chance that they encounter a wandering group of goblins. This encounter only occurs once, but note that these goblins are in addition to those that inhabit the caves as described in the encounter areas.

The wandering group includes six **goblins** wielding scimitars. This group is patrolling, carrying messages, and moving supplies about the lair. Each carries 1d6 sp, and the group is also carrying 1d6 bags of relatively fresh foodstuffs, quite suitable for human consumption. When an encounter occurs, the entire bunch of goblins attack with zeal and cry out an alarm ("BREE-YARK!") at the same time.

DM Note: Goblin losses cannot be replaced. If the goblins are being soundly defeated by intruders, they attempt to hide or flee east. Those who flee go from area 17 to area 23 to inform the hobgoblins, and join forces with them. If this occurs, adjust encounters in cave area F accordingly.

AREA 17 – GUARD CHAMBER

The 20-foot-by-30-foot chamber has a small table, two worn benches, and a large keg in the far corner. Near the entrance is an open barrel full of spears ready for use.

The barrel holds 60 spears, while the keg is nearly full of stale but clean water. The table and benches are normal.

This room is a guard post inhabited by six **goblin** guards alertly watching both passages here for intruders of any sort, including hobgoblins from the south. Their alert status grants them advantage on all contests of Wisdom (Perception) checks against Dexterity (Stealth) checks. These goblins don't have shields (AC 13). Each goblin is armed with a spear (+1 to hit, range 20/60 ft., 1d6 - 1 piercing damage if thrown, or 1d8 - 1 piercing damage if used with two hands to make a melee attack), and they grab several more from the barrel for use to repel intruders. If the assault comes from the east, several goblins make their way down the corridor to use the western spur for half cover.

Each goblin carries 1d4 x 10 cp and 1d4 sp.

Development. If this guard post is attacked, these goblins shout "BREE-YARK!" each round, attempting to alert the other guards at area 18. The guards there hear the alarm with a successful DC 13 Wisdom (Perception) check made at advantage, and respond by joining the fray in 2 rounds. See area 18 for more details.

AREA 18 – GUARD CHAMBER

The 20-foot-by-30-foot chamber has a small table, two worn benches, and a large keg in the far corner. Near the entrance is an open barrel full of spears ready for use.

This barrel is also filled with 60 spears. The keg in the corner is only about half full. Hidden under the keg is a sack containing 250 gp. The sack is automatically found if the keg is moved, or it can be located with a successful DC 15 Wisdom (Perception) check.

This guard post is similar to area 17, except the six **goblins** here watch mainly to the east. These goblins lack shields (AC 13) and are armed with spears (+1 to hit, range 20/60 ft., 1d6 - 1 piercing damage if thrown, or 1d8 - 1 piercing damage if used with two hands to make a melee attack).

Developments. If there is a cry of "BREE-YARK" (similar to "Hey Rube!"), either from a wandering patrol of goblins, or from the goblins in area 17, two of these guards hold off attacking while the other four provide cover. One of these two tips over the keg to retrieve the sack of coins, while the other opens the secret door in the northwest corner of the room. In the following round the goblin with the sack rushes through the secret door, and tosses the sack with gold coins to the ogre in cave area E (see area 22) to ask him for help. The ogre gladly accepts the payment and enters the goblins' lair, moving to attack intruders in the next round.

AREA 19 – COMMON ROOM

This 30-foot-by-40-foot room is a cluttered mess. There are heaps of bedding, tables, stools, and benches all around the whole chamber. A natural recess in the southern wall serves as a crude fireplace.

The majority of the goblin tribe resides in this chamber. Food is prepared here in the oven, while eating and general meetings occur at the tables and benches. All furniture is functional but nondescript. The cluttered nature of the room is considered difficult terrain.

There are 10 male **goblins** armed with scimitars but not carrying shields (AC 13) here. These goblins fight to the death to protect the tribe, although one might use Stealth to attempt to slip out the western passage toward area 20 to gather reinforcements. Fourteen female goblins and six young goblins also dwell here. However, both the females and young are noncombatant and seek to flee out one of the exits.

Each male goblin has 1d6 sp while each female goblin carries 2d6 cp.

Development. If the characters have not encountered the wandering group of goblins by the time they enter this area, add those six additional males in this chamber.

AREA 20 – CHIEFTAIN'S ROOM

This 30-foot-by-20-foot chamber contains quite a bit of furniture, scaled for smaller humanoids. A low bench rests near a bed on the back wall. A small stand nearby holds a pewter bowl. Hanging on the north wall are several shortbows, with a few quivers hanging on pegs nearby.

This chamber serves as the lair for the **goblin boss**. He wears chain mail and carries a shield (AC 18, speed 20 ft.) and a scimitar. Three **goblin** guards, each with a chain shirt (AC 15) and a scimitar, are also present. These warriors are the best in the tribe and each has 11 hit points. If giving the time, the guards grab shortbows on the walls and use them in defense of the lair.

There are five female **goblins** also present, tending to the needs of the goblin boss. If hard-pressed, two of these females fight with daggers (1d4 + 2 piercing damage).

The goblin boss carries a purse with 18 gp and 2 pp. Each guard carries 1d6 sp and 8 ep.

Under the bed is a discarded silver cup (worth 90 gp) that can easily be found. The low bench near the bed has a secret drawer under the seat that requires a successful DC 14 Wisdom (Perception) check to discover. Inside is stored the goblin tribe's treasure: a folded tapestry with silver and gold threads (worth 900 gp). The pewter bowl (worth 12 sp) holds 321 cp and 273 sp.

AREA 21 – STORAGE CHAMBER

Area g. At this position in the intersection there are four **goblin** guards on duty armed with loaded light crossbows (1d8 + 2 piercing damage) and shortswords (1d6 + 2 piercing damage). When the characters reach the chamber, continue with the read-aloud:

This 50-foot-by-30-foot room is stacked and heaped with many bales, boxes, crates, barrels, and sacks.

The various containers hold cloth, food, beer, and wine, all of no special worth. The hard-working but not-too-bright goblins continually bring supplies of stolen and looted goods to this place. Yet, they do not realize that their large cousins, the hobgoblins at cave area F, use a secret door known only to them to steal the best of the foodstuffs and drink. The secret door can be discovered with a successful DC 17 Wisdom (Perception) check. The door can be opened from either side by pulling down a gray wooden handle disguised as part of the rock wall.

Development. If the adventurers stay in this chamber for more than 10 minutes searching, a party of four hobgoblins (see area 28) comes through the secret door. They are just as surprised as the characters, but quickly gather their wits and attack. Each carries 1d4 gp.

E. OGRE CAVE

A very large ogre makes his home in this small cave divided into two chambers. The ogre has grown wealthy by serving as a mercenary, generally on the side of the goblins (and their occasional allies, the hobgoblins) although he has been bought off by the orcs and gnolls from time to time. He rushes to aid the goblins when they toss him the sack of coins (as described in area 18). If a character offers him a bribe of 20 gp or more, one which he can actually see and feel, it requires a successful DC 18 Charisma (Persuasion) check for him to honor the bargain. Otherwise, he just takes the bribe (and the goblins' loot, too) and returns to his cave. However, if he honors the bargain but runs into the characters a second time, he attacks to kill.

AREA 22 – OGRE LAIR

A short passage opens into a roughly 20-foot-diameter chamber. Your nostrils are assaulted by a pungent, sour stench. In the southwestern corner of the chamber, a massive brown bear lies sprawled asleep. To the left is a passage heading deeper into the hillside.

A successful DC 12 Wisdom (Perception) check reveals that the bear is not real, nothing more than the skin of a huge bear which the ogre killed. The bearskin (worthless) is used as a bed, and is stuffed with leaves, heaped underneath for added comfort. The

ogre sits in the eastern portion of his lair, and noise likely brings him ready to do battle. He gets advantage on any contests of Wisdom (Perception) versus Dexterity (Stealth), due to his state of alertness. This huge ogre wears thick bearskins, equivalent to hide armor, and his unusually high (for an ogre) Dexterity of 12 (+1) grants him AC 13. He wields a massive wooden greatclub.

In the eastern chamber is a great leather bag, and the ogre often perches himself on it for safe keeping. In this bag are seven large sacks:

#1 has 287 sp.

#2 has a wheel of hard cheese.

#3 has 182 cp and 91 ep.

#4 has 289 gp.

#5 has a keg of fine brandy (worth 80 gp).

#6 has 303 cp.

#7 has 241 gp (actually lead coins with a wash of gold, so value of 1 cp each).

An additional stash of valuables is hidden under a heap of old bones in the southern portion of his cave. A successful DC 15 Wisdom (Perception) check is required to find this treasure. Intermixed with the bones are six *+1 arrows*, a *potion of invisibility*, and two *spell scrolls* inscribed with cleric spells: *cure wounds* and *hold person*.

F. HOBGOBLIN LAIR

Skulls are lined along the walls of the corridor. After a mere 20 feet, a stout oaken door blocks entrance into the caves. Several skulls are affixed to the oaken door to highlight a warning written in the Common tongue: "Come in! We'd like to have you for dinner!"

A large tribe of aggressive hobgoblins inhabits this cave. Seldom are these fierce creatures troubled by marauders, for the entrance to their lair is guarded by a stout, barred door at the back of the entry cave. The barred door can't be picked, so the characters need to resort to magic or bashing it down (AC 15, 20 hit points). Attempting to force it open requires a successful DC 15 Strength check, made at disadvantage. The noise of bashing or forcing the door alerts the guards in area 26. If a *knock* spell is used to open the door, the noise of the falling bar is still heard by the guards, but they have less time to react. In this case the intruders have 2 rounds before the guards arrive to investigate.

Careful inspection of the barred door with a successful DC 18 Wisdom (Perception) check reveals a secret mechanism. This mechanism allows a person outside the door to slide the bar back so the portal can be entered without making noise.

DM Note: As usual, hobgoblin losses cannot be replaced during the course of normal play, which is a period of only several days or weeks of action. The hobgoblins are fairly smart, well-organized, and alert. But if their captain is killed, the remainder of the tribe typically seeks to escape alive, unless their opponents are obviously weak and inferior. Survivors could reinforce the goblins at cave area D, unless their attackers are very dangerous and the hobgoblins believe that the whole Caves' area is in trouble.

AREA 23 – COMMON ROOM

This long hall is 20 feet wide, but 50 feet long. There are heaps of cloth and animal skins for beds, various odds and ends of furniture, and a small barrel.

Five male **hobgoblins** and eight female **hobgoblins** inhabit this common area. There are also three non-combatant young hobgoblins. The male hobgoblins are battle-ready, adorned in armor with weapons nearby, and actively watch the east door, which leads to the goblin lair (cave area D).

The heaps of animal skins and furniture are worthless. Seven longbows along with quivers full of arrows are also stored in the room. The barrel contains poor quality beer.

Each male hobgoblin carries 1d4 x 10 sp, while each female hobgoblin carries 2d6 sp.

AREA 24 – TORTURE CHAMBER/ PLAYROOM/FOOD STORAGE

This shadowy chamber is 20 feet wide by 40 feet long. Situated around a central firepit are two sturdy chairs and a table covered with a variety of metal torture implements. Chained to the far wall are several grimy forlorn humanoid prisoners adorned in tattered loincloths. Two burly ugly goblinoids with burnt orange skin guard the hapless prisoners.

Two **elite hobgoblins** (see appendix B) serve the tribe as guards and torturers. These two brutes enjoy their task of guarding the prisoners, and honing their crude skills in the art of torture. Luckily the tribe's efficiency at capturing prisoners keeps a steady supply of victims for their practice. With a gleeful growl, each attacks with his whip before the characters can close. They are then quick to switch to longswords for melee. They fight to the death and don't bother to call for help.

Each of these monsters has a purse with 1d6 each cp, sp, and ep. One also wears a silver armlet (worth 135 gp).

There are two chairs, and a small table near the central firepit. Various implements of torture (pokers, tongs, knives, screws, etc.) rest on the table.

Six prisoners are chained to the walls. The chains can be burst with a successful DC 24 Strength check, or the locks can picked with thieves' tools and a successful DC 20 Dexterity check. The keys to the prisoners' chains are hanging on the wall in the southwest corner. The prisoners are:

Prisoner #1. This poor fellow is a human male **commoner** named Lhodis. He is a portly, half-dead merchant (2 hit points remaining), scheduled to be eaten tonight in a special banquet. If he is rescued and returned to the Keep, the Guild pays a 100 gp reward, grants the rescuers honorary Guild status, and exempts them for 1 year from any fees, dues, taxes, and the like which the Guild would normally collect.

Prisoner #2. This **orc** (AC 11, due to no armor) gladly fights against the goblins and hobgoblins, if handed a weapon. But he is, of course, an orc and seeks to escape from the adventurers at first chance, possibly taking whatever he can with him. He heads to cave area B and alerts his fellows of the characters' actions.

Prisoner #3. This male human **guard** (AC 11, due to no armor) formerly served as a caravan guard for the merchant. If given weapons and armor, he agrees to serve his rescuers for 1 year provided they pay for his room and board.

Prisoner #4. A female human **commoner** named Laressa, the merchant's wife, who is also slated for the big feast tonight. She will personally reward her rescuers by giving them a *+1 dagger* she has in her room back at the Keep.

Prisoner #5. This crazy **gnoll** (AC 11, due to no armor) snatches up a weapon to attack his rescuers if he is freed. Due to his weakened condition his attack rolls are made at disadvantage.

Prisoner #6. Another human male **guard** (AC 11, due to no armor) who served the merchant as a caravan escort. He can join his rescuers if armed and armored, and receives room and board.

AREA 25 – COMMON CHAMBER

Approaching characters can hear the activity in area 25 about 30 feet before they arrive here.

This large chamber is 30 feet wide and 70 feet long. The room is busy with a flurry of activity as several burly orange-skinned humanoids rush about setting up tables, chairs, and cookware.

This large place is used for meals, meetings, and general revels of the hobgoblin tribe. There are many tables and benches set out now, as the place is being readied for the coming feast. Unless the characters make obvious noise or draw attention to themselves, they are granted surprise in the beginning of this encounter.

Nine **hobgoblins**—four males and five females—and nine noncombatant young hobgoblins are busy working here. The males lack their bows and all have stowed their shields along the back wall (AC 16), which would take an action to retrieve. The females use improvised weapons, such as cutlery (1d4 piercing damage), large pots or platters (1d4 bludgeoning damage), or flipped tables (1d6 bludgeoning damage). The young hobgoblins attempt to flee the chamber.

Male hobgoblins have 1d4 gp each, while female hobgoblins each carry 2d6 sp. The head table has a set of pewter dishes on it (worth 25 gp for the set).

AREA 26 – GUARD ROOM

This rough-hewn room is about 40 feet wide and 20 feet deep. Numerous piles of furs are scattered about as sleeping areas.

The guard room serves as the living quarters for six **hobgoblins**. Three of them have no shields (AC 16) and are armed with light crossbows (range 80/320 ft., 1d8 + 1 piercing damage) and maces (1d6 + 1 bludgeoning damage). These three hang back and shoot their crossbows first, before dropping them to close to melee range.

Each hobgoblin carries 1d4 each of cp, sp, and gp.

Development. If these guards hear the door being battered, or the bar falling at the entrance, all but one immediately rush to the entry, while the other runs to alert area 27. It takes 2 rounds for these guards to reach the entry, and the sixth returns with the other guards in the fourth round.

AREA 27 – ARMORY

A solid wooden door blocks entrance to this armory, although its generally unlocked.

This 20-foot-by-50-foot cavern is used as a storeroom. The walls are adorned with shields of various sizes and composition. Hanging from racks are suits of armor in variable condition. Several large chests are pushed against the far wall.

Three **hobgoblin** guards are on duty here at all times.

Each hobgoblin guard has 2d4 sp and 2d4 ep.

The secret door on the west wall can be discovered with a successful DC 18 Wisdom (Perception) check. If used by a hobgoblin to warn area 31 (see Development, below), in his haste he leaves it partially ajar, granting advantage on the check. Another DC 18 Wisdom (Perception) check is required to find the other secret door in the 20-foot corridor; this check is made at advantage, due to the likelihood of the door's presence. Both of these doors can be opened by releasing a concealed catch in the stone wall hidden behind gray canvas.

In the chamber are the following arms and armor. Shields are hanging on the wall, as are the suits of armor. The weapons are all stored in unlocked wooden chests. All equipment is in fine condition.

- 1 suit of man-sized plate armor
- 1 suit of dwarf-sized plate armor
- 3 suits of man-sized chain mail
- 2 suits of elf-sized chain mail
- 7 suits of man-sized leather armor
- 11 shields (metal, wood, leather-bound)
- 6 daggers
- 1 battleaxe
- 4 maces
- 3 longswords
- 2 shortbows
- 1 longbow
- 13 light crossbows
- 220 arrows (14 arrows have silvered heads)
- 180 crossbow bolts
- 51 spears
- 19 polearms (11 glaives and 8 halberds)
- 42 helmets of various sizes

Development. If a warning comes from area 26, two of these guards move to the door to wait in ambush, and the other passes through the secret doors, to area 31 to alert the captain.

AREA 28 – STOREROOM

This 20-foot-by-40-foot room appears to be storeroom. Numerous boxes, crates, sacks, and casks are randomly stacked about the chamber, some as high as the ceiling.

Goods stolen from the stupid goblins are kept here until needed above. The crates, boxes, and sacks contain various foodstuffs, most of it unfit for human consumption. The casks are full, but merely hold stale water.

There is a single **hobgoblin** guard on duty here at all times. He hides behind one of the stacks of crates, and likely can surprise the characters. On his first action, he attempts to tip over a heavy stack of crates on an unsuspecting victim (+4 to hit, 2d6 bludgeoning damage and the target must make a DC 11 Constitution saving throw or be stunned and knocked prone until the end of its next turn).

This lone guard has 2d8 ep.

Development. If the characters did not encounter the hobgoblin looting party in area 21, they are also here. These four hobgoblins are lounging around joking about the stupid goblins. Each hobgoblin is carrying 1d4 gp.

AREA 29 – GUARD ROOM

This 20-foot-square room has two doors. One is situated on the south wall, while the other is on the west wall. The room is sparsely furnished with two flimsy cots, a worn bench and stool, and a large wooden box.

Two **hobgoblins** armed with light crossbows (range 80/320 ft., 1d8 + 1 piercing damage) and longswords stand guard here. Also present are two female **hobgoblins**, who are likewise willing to fight. The males start by firing their crossbows before switching to longswords. The females are armed with shortswords (+3 to hit, 1d6 + 1 piercing damage).

The furniture is all nondescript and worthless. The large wooden storage box is filled with soiled, tattered clothes.

The male hobgoblins each carry 2d6 cp and sp, while the females have no treasure.

Development. If this chamber is assaulted, one female hobgoblin hastens to area 30, while the other rushes to area 31. After raising the alarm, they both return to fight.

AREA 30 – HOBGOBLIN CAPTAIN'S QUARTERS

The door opens to reveal a 50-foot-long, 20-foot-wide hall. The room is crowded with furniture such as a table, a bed, and several chairs. Cluttered piles of junk and broken furniture are also present.

The leader of the tribe, a great, ugly **hobgoblin captain** resides in this chamber. He has a Strength of 18 (+4) and a Charisma of 7 (-2), he wears plate armor and carries a shield (AC 20, speed 20 ft.), and he wields a longsword (+6 to hit, 1d8 + 4 slashing damage). With him are four large, longsword-wielding female **hobgoblins**. The hobgoblin captain begins the combat using his Leadership action, before wading into melee with his longsword. He and his female consorts fight to the death.

All the furniture in the room is worthless. In the southeast corner of the room is a fireplace with a stack of kindling nearby. There is a 10-foot-square closet that contains several crates of higher quality food, and a huge iron box. The box is full of mangy, worthless animal skins and pelts.

The hobgoblin captain carries a leather purse holding 31 gp and 5 pp. He also wears a silver and emerald studded belt (worth 600 gp). Each female hobgoblin carries 2d6 gp.

The iron box has a false bottom that can be found with a successful DC 15 Wisdom (Perception) check. The secret portion of the iron box holds 400 sp, 115 ep, 200 gp, and 25 pp, plus a piece of amber (worth 100 gp) and a *potion of poison*. Amidst the heap of kindling wood near the fireplace, there is concealed a *wand of paralysis*. Without the use of a *detect magic*, the wooden wand is difficult to discover, requiring a successful DC 22 Wisdom (Perception) check. Hidden along the shaft of the wand, among the stylistic engravings, is the command word "ffffiitss" written in Infernal. It can be discovered with close examination and a successful DC 15 Intelligence (Investigation) check.

AREA 31 – GUARD ROOM

This plain room is 20 feet on a side. There are two sleeping pallets, a stool, and a large barrel.

Four **hobgoblins** are stationed in this guardroom, alert and ready to respond to summons from areas 27, 29, or 30 as required. These brutes lack shields (AC 16) and wield greataxes (1d12 + 1 slashing damage).

The furnishings are all normal. The barrel is half full with water.

Each hobgoblin guard carries 2d6 cp, sp, and ep.

G. SHUNNED CAVERN

Even the normal inhabitants of this area, including the ogre, stay away from here, for the creatures that dwell herein are exceptionally dangerous. Any creature foolish enough to venture out at night becomes fair game.

On entering this cavern with ivy draped over the low entrance, your senses are assaulted by a horrible rotting stench.

AREA 32 – EMPTY GALLERY

There are four of these locations and each one shares a similar description, although each has a variable size.

This natural cavern is damp and the air is heavy. Bones and rotting corpses are spread here and there amidst a litter of dead leaves and old branches. The stench of death and decay is overpowering here.

The first time each character enters one of these chambers, they are required to make a successful DC 12 Constitution saving throw or become sickened by the stench. A sickened target gains the poisoned condition for the next hour. A successful saving throw grants immunity for the next hour.

If a careful search of the refuse and litter is attempted, characters find a random coin every minute. Roll 1d6 and consult the table to determine the coin type.

D6	Coin Type
1-2	Copper
3-4	Silver
5-6	Electrum

However, each minute of searching might attract the attention of one of the predators that lairs in these caves. Roll 1d6 and consult the table below to determine what creature (if any) arrives to investigate. The curious creature(s) arrive in 1d4 rounds.

D6	Encounter
1	Owlbear from area 34
2	Giant Rats (2d6)
3	Gray Ooze from area 33
4-6	No encounter

AREA 33 – SHALLOW POOL

This natural cavern is about 30 feet wide and 20 long. This cavern is very wet, and all the walls and floor glisten with condensation. Most of the cavern is occupied by a pool of clear water.

The pool is about 15 feet deep and fed by a natural spring. The water is cool and clean, inhabited by several blind cave fish that lazily swim about.

There are three **gray oozes** inhabiting this cave, although one might be encountered in area 32. One is always at the southern edge of the pool, and another is always on the ceiling in the southwestern portion of the cavern. Both are motionless and indistinguishable from the moist rock surfaces due to their False Appearance trait. Therefore, they likely attack with surprise.

There is a jewel-encrusted silver goblet (worth 1,300 gp) located at the bottom of the pool. The goblet can be located with a successful DC 20 Wisdom (Perception) check, made at advantage if the character enters the water and searches the bottom with a suitable light source.

Development. If the third gray ooze is encountered here, it hides on the ceiling to the left of the entrance.

AREA 34 – OWLBEAR'S DEN

This cavern is about 20 feet in diameter and although still humid, there is less condensation here. The chamber is covered with bones, branches, leaves, and other refuse on the floor. To the southeast is a passage.

An **owlbear** lairs here, and is generally avoided by the rest of the cavern inhabitants. The owlbear is an apex predator, and currently sleeps while digesting a meal of gnoll caught at dawn. The owlbear's Keen Sight and Smell means it likely detects the characters when they enter this area. In a few rounds, it rushes from its abode with a tremendous roar, attacking with claws and beak. If cornered in its lair, it fights to the death, but if the characters flee it does not pursue.

The creature has no treasure, but amidst the many sticks and bones it sleeps on is a bone scroll tube that can be found with a successful DC 18 Wisdom (Perception) check. Inside the tube is a *scroll of protection* (undead).

H. BUGBEAR LAIR

The group of bugbears is not numerous, but what it lacks in numbers, it makes up for in strength and cunning.

This cave entrance is wide, nearly 15 feet. Several crudely painted signs are posted near the entrance, each in a different tongue.

The signs beside the entrance cave are written in kobold, orcish, and goblin. Each says: "Safety, security and repose for all humanoids who enter. WELCOME! Come in and report to the first guard on the left for a hot meal and bed assignment."

DM Note: There are two **bugbears** out hunting, and not accounted for in the following description. They return with a human corpse and 83 gp the day after characters first enter the bugbear lair. They are placed on guard duty at area 35, if appropriate. See that area for their statistics. The bugbears defend the lair until all are dead, save the chief. He is no fool and seeks help from the minotaur in area 45.

AREA 35 – GUARD ROOM

The corridor ends at a 30-foot-by-30-foot chamber. Two cots are pushed against one wall, and at the back of the room is a battered metal gong suspended from a wooden frame. Several large hairy goblinoids lounge on stools near a smoky brazier which has skewers of meat toasting over the coals.

Three **bugbears** are stationed in this room. These guards lack shields (AC 14) and are armed with greatmaces (2d8 + 2 bludgeoning damage), but currently these are all resting along one wall. (A greatmace is a larger mace that does 1d8 bludgeoning damage and has the Heavy and Two-Handed properties.) When the characters arrive, the bugbears instead grab the skewers of meat, eating a chunk before offering the meat to the characters. Allow the characters to attempt a Wisdom (Insight) contest versus the bugbear's Charisma (Persuasion) check. If they fail this contest, the bugbears attack with the skewers with surprise (2d6 + 2 piercing damage).

The cots and stools are sturdy but nondescript. The gong is made of iron, attached to the frame via leather straps. The brazier is likewise composed of iron, with a damaged leg propped up with a rock.

Each bugbear carries 2d10 gp.

Development. If the battle goes against the bugbears (two are killed or incapacitated), the last one spends an action smiting the gong with his weapon to warn the rest of the tribe in the complex.

AREA 36 – CHIEFTAIN'S ROOM

The door to this chamber reveals a 30-foot-by-20-foot chamber.

The chief of the tribe is a tough, old **bugbear chief**. He wears chain mail and carries a shield (AC 18) and wields a morningstar. Hanging on a nearby wall is a *+1 handaxe* (+6 to hit, range 20/60 ft., 1d6 + 4 slashing damage). If the chief gets the chance, he grabs the axe and hurls it before closing to melee. The chief's female **bugbear** consort is armed with a mace (2d6 + 2 bludgeoning damage).

The furnishings of the room are battered and crude, but several pieces of silk are mixed up with the bedding. In all, six silk swatches can be found and if cleaned are valuable (each worth 20 gp). The secret door on the west wall can be located with a successful DC 20 Wisdom (Perception) check. Twisting a hook to the left of the door opens the rock portal, which pivots in the center. The characters get advantage on the check to locate the second secret door in the corridor beyond. This door also requires a successful DC 20 Wisdom (Perception) check, and functions in a similar manner.

The chief carries a pouch that contains a key, 29 pp, and three smoky gray pieces of quartz (each worth 50 gp). The female bugbear has gold earrings (worth 100 gp).

There is a gray chest stuck up on a ledge near the ceiling which can be located with a successful DC 15 Wisdom (Perception) check. The chest is heavy, and it requires a successful DC 18 Strength check to bring it down to the floor without rough handling. Two characters can work together on this task, granting advantage on the check. If this check fails, the two potions inside are smashed and become useless. It contains 1,462 sp, an alabaster statue set with ivory (worth 200 gp, but it weighs 30 pounds), and two *potions of healing*.

Development. The chief is well aware of the secret door on the west wall. If reduced to 15 hit points or less, the chief flees through the door (closing it behind him), leaving his consort behind to cover his retreat. The chief proceeds into the maze (cave area I), and seeks an alliance with the minotaur.

AREA 37 – SPOILS ROOM

The heavy door is locked, and the key is held by the chief (see area 36). Alternatively, the lock can be picked with thieves' tools and a successful DC 17 Dexterity check, or the door can be broken down with a successful DC 20 Strength check. Breaking down the door summons the guards from area 35, and the chief plus his mate from area 36, to investigate in 2 rounds.

Beyond the sturdy door is a 20-foot-square chamber. Various boxes, crates, and barrels are stacked about the room.

The various boxes and crates are full of high quality dried or salted foodstuffs. A pile of leather hides in a stack is pushed against the back wall. Sitting on one of the crates is a large metal tray—actually an upside-down *+1 shield*. The tray is being used to hold a heap of dried herbs (goblinnip, a variety of catnip, something these particular bugbears relish). The casks include three barrels of poor quality ale, a tun of watery wine, and a small keg of oil (about 20 flasks in capacity). If these items are sold at the Keep, the value is about 400 sp.

AREA 38 – COMMON ROOM

The passage gradually slopes up and turns to the east before ending at a typical wooden door. Beyond is a rough-hewn chamber perhaps 30 feet deep and 20 feet wide. Piles of bedding and discarded garments are strewn about the place. A soot-covered fireplace is situated on the back wall.

Ten adult **bugbears**—three males and seven females—and three noncombatant young bugbears inhabit this chamber. The males lack shields (AC 14) and wield morningstars, while the females wield javelins. Essentially being cornered, the adults fight to the death to protect the young.

The bedding and garments are worthless. Blackened by soot, there is a silver urn (worth 175 gp) near the fireplace, but is only discovered with a successful DC 16 Wisdom (Perception) check. Even if found, the cup is only recognized as valuable with a successful DC 12 Intelligence (Investigation) check.

Each male bugbear carries 2d6 sp and 2d6 gp.

AREA 39 – GUARD ROOM

At the bottom of a flight of rough steps is a 30-foot-by-20-foot room. Several bedrolls, along with a bench, a battered long table, and a water pail, adorn the chamber. Many sacks tied with thick cord lean against the wall.

Watching here are two male and three female **bugbears**. All are armed with javelins which are hurled before closing to melee. The males wield morningstars, while the females wield additional javelins. These bugbears tend to the slaves (in areas 40 and 41) as well as help to guard the entrance to their lair.

The furniture here is normal and the sacks contain ground meal. The keys for areas 40 and 41 hang from a metal peg on the wall opposite the stairs.

The male bugbears each carry 2d8 gp, while each female bugbear has 1d10 gp.

AREA 40 – SLAVE PEN

DM Note: Both corridors to the slave pens have sacks containing ground meal, small boxes of provisions, and barrels of watered wine along their lengths.

An iron door secured by a bar, chain, and heavy padlock blocks entrance to the chamber beyond.

The key to the padlock is in area 39, hanging on the wall. Otherwise the padlock needs to be picked with thieves' tools and a successful DC 20 Dexterity check. The lock can also be smashed with a heavy bludgeoning weapon (AC 19, 6 hit points, immunity to slashing and piercing damage). Once the lock is dealt with, the chain and bar can be easily removed.

The chamber beyond is a 30-foot-by-20-foot prison cell. Several prisoners are shackled to the walls. Keys to these padlocks are also on the ring in area 39, or they can be picked or smashed as per the door lock. These chains can be burst with a successful DC 24 Strength check. Near each slave is a litter of dirty, damp straw and a soiled wooden bucket.

The prisoners include:

- 3 **kobolds**
- 1 **goblin** (AC 12, due to no armor)
- 4 **orcs** (AC 11, due to no armor)
- 2 human **guards** (AC 11, due to no armor)

Developments. All the humanoids fight against the bugbears if given weapons; adjust their AC if they remain unarmored. However, at the first opportunity the humanoids flee for the wilderness. The human guards are from the same caravan as the guards from area 24. They agree to serve the characters as hirelings for 1 year, only requiring food and board. This assumes they are armed and armored as soon as possible.

DM Note: If any characters need to be replaced, or additional hirelings are needed to continually face the challenges of the Caves, consider replacing two of the kobolds and one of the orcs with a dwarf NPC and up to two elf NPCs. See appendix C for a list of suitable NPCs or design a few that would be helpful to the characters.

AREA 41 – SLAVE PEN

DM Note: Both corridors to the slave pens have sacks containing ground meal, small boxes of provisions, and barrels of watered wine along their lengths.

An iron door secured by a bar, chain, and heavy padlock blocks entrance to the chamber beyond.

The key to the padlock is in area 39, hanging on the wall. Otherwise the padlock needs to be picked with thieves' tools and a successful DC 20 Dexterity check. The lock can also be smashed with a heavy bludgeoning weapon (AC 19, 6 hit points, immunity to slashing and piercing damage). Once the lock is dealt with, the chain and bar can be easily removed.

This 30-foot-by-30-room serves as another prison for the bugbears. Several more prisoners are shackled to the walls of this room. Keys to these padlocks are also on the ring in area 39, or they can be picked or smashed as per the door lock. The chains can be burst with a successful DC 24 Strength check. Near each slave is a litter of dirty, damp straw and a soiled wooden bucket.

The prisoners include:

- 3 **hobgoblins** (AC 11, due to no armor)
- 2 **gnolls** (AC 11, due to no armor)
- 1 **bugbear** (rebel; AC 12, due to no armor)
- 1 male human **berserker** (AC 11, due to no armor)

The berserker is a huge wild man called Hebold with mighty muscles (Strength 19 [+4]), shaggy unkempt hair, and a tangled beard. Due to his enslavement, he is prone to fits of berserk fury. If armed, he must make a DC 10 Wisdom saving throw each round or fly into a bloodlust fury of battle against friend or foe.

Developments. If freed, these slaves attempt to flee, although they attack bugbears who are in the way of their escape. There are two exceptions: the rebel bugbear hates his fellows, and gladly takes up arms to fight against them or any of the other inhabitants of the whole area. He continues to do so for as long as the characters stay in the Caves. The berserker is a chaotic evil person; once he is armed, and after battle madness leaves him, he either kills the adventurers who freed him, so as to have all their treasure for himself, or else he steals whatever is most valuable and then sneaks off. He only pursues the latter option if he knows the characters are too strong for him.

I. CAVES OF THE MINOTAUR

This labyrinth houses a number of nasty things, but the worst is a fiendishly clever minotaur who abides herein. The minotaur is agreeable to help the bugbears against invaders at the cost of one human slave every 3 days of service. Of course, the slave is eaten in that period. The minotaur keeps only the choicest of treasures, tossing unwanted loot to whomever happens to find it at the mouth of the labyrinth. At the DM's option, the characters may find a few low-value coins, normal equipment, weapons, or armor at the entrance.

Immediately upon entering the cave, the characters feel slightly dizzy. This is the effects of a powerful enchantment which causes them to lose all sense of direction.

DM Note: About 30 feet past the cave mouth, a permanent spell of *directional confusion* (see appendix A) begins to function (DC 16 Wisdom saving throw). Assuming that the lead character misses their saving throw, start to misdirect the players by naming incorrect directions, i.e. southeast instead of northeast, east instead of west, etc. Don't worry about calling the same passage as a different direction should they travel over the same route twice—that's the effect of the magic on them. The navigator is allowed to make another saving throw attempt every 10 minutes to overcome the enchantment.

AREA 42 – STIRGE CAVE

As you approach the next cavern, you are greeted by excited animal-like squeals, squeaks, and leathery flapping sounds. The cavern has a low ceiling, perhaps 8 feet overhead, and is adorned with tiny stalactites. The chamber is approximately 25 feet in diameter and the floor is covered with foul-smelling refuse.

The sounds are generated by a flock of **stirges** that inhabit this cave. There are 13 of these bat-like creatures here. The minotaur enjoys catching and eating these tasty little morsels, so they tend to avoid its clutches. The result is a ravenously hungry flock as demonstrated by their ruckus as the characters approach. Thus they attack and fight to the death, craving their next blood meal. When a stirge drains 10 hit points of blood from a target, it detaches and flees the cavern to digest its meal.

The floor is covered with organic debris such as leaves, branches, and old clothing. Intermixed with stirge dung, it's a noxious mess. The stirges have no treasure.

AREA 43 – FIRE BEETLES

This rough-hewn chamber is little more than a four-way intersection. A trio of 3-foot-long black beetles scurries about the floor. Each beetle sports three glowing glands, two below the eyes and one at the abdomen, that pulse reddish illumination.

The three insects are **giant fire beetles**. Each is extremely hungry and hastens to attack.

The secret door to the north can be located with a successful DC 15 Wisdom (Perception) check. The stone door pushes open to the left, following the release of a catch near the floor. It leads to area 36.

The giant fire beetles lack treasure, but the glands can be harvested from a dead giant fire beetle with a successful DC 11 Dexterity check and a slashing weapon in about 1 minute. Each gland produces bright light in a 10-foot radius and dim light for another 10 feet. The glowing glands last 1d6 days.

AREA 44 – FIRE BEETLES

This oval chamber is about 20 feet by 30 feet. The floor is covered with sticks, leaves, rocky debris, and other refuse. Two 3-foot-long beetles with black carapaces and glowing glands mindlessly root through the refuse.

This chamber is occupied by two **giant fire beetles**. Eager for a fresh meal, they hasten to attack the characters.

The giant fire beetles lack treasure, but the glands can be harvested from a dead giant fire beetle with a successful DC 11 Dexterity check and a slashing weapon in about 1 minute. Each gland produces bright light in a 10-foot-radius and dim light for another 10 feet. The glowing glands last 1d6 days.

AREA 45 – THE MINOTAUR

This dark cavern is about 50 feet in diameter. The walls are rough-hewn and uneven. Scattered about the cavern are decorative piles of bones topped with mostly intact skulls. Likewise, bones and skull pieces adorn the walls in crude art-like designs.

This cavern is the lair of a vicious **minotaur**, avoided by the other tribes of the Caves in all cases. This huge monster has a *+1 spear* (+7 to hit, 1d8 + 5 piercing damage) and he wears a massive coat of chain mail (AC 16). His first attack is always a charge leading with his spear, but once he enters melee he switches between spear thrusts and gores at a whim. He fights to the death, but is not opposed to retreating to engage the characters in hit-and-run tactics throughout the maze. His Labyrinthine Recall trait grants him unerring knowledge of the maze, and the characters' only hope of escape is to leave this cave system, or find the secret route to area 36.

There is a secret chamber here that hides the minotaur's considerable wealth. The secret door requires a successful DC 20 Wisdom (Perception) check to locate. Even after locating it, the massive door requires the leverage of three characters working together to push open. Beyond is a 15-foot-by-10-foot rough-hewn chamber. The chamber contains the following items:

- A locked chest that requires thieves' tools and a successful DC 20 Dexterity check to unlock. The key is on a ring pierced through the minotaur's left ear. The chest is trapped with a poison needle trap. The trap can be detected with a successful DC 18 Wisdom (Perception) check. It can be removed with thieves' tools and a successful DC 18 Dexterity check. If triggered, the target takes 1 piercing damage and 11 (2d10) poison damage. The target must succeed on a DC 15 Constitution saving throw or become poisoned for 1 hour. The chest contains 310 ep and 930 gp.

- A driftwood *staff of healing* set with lapis lazuli.

- A man-sized suit of *+1 plate armor*. Optionally, this armor can be sized for an elf.

- A locked wooden coffer whose lock requires thieves' tools and a successful DC 17 Dexterity check to pick. The key is hidden in the minotaur's bedding, which requires a successful DC 22 Wisdom (Perception) check to discover. Alternatively, the coffer could be destroyed (AC 15, 6 hit points) in a vain effort to get to the contents. The coffer contains three potions in crystal vials: *gaseous form*, *growth*, *healing*. If the coffer is smashed open, all three vials shatter, and the potions become worthless.

- A locked iron chest that requires thieves' tools and a successful DC 18 Dexterity check to unlock. The key is also hidden

in the minotaur's bedding, which requires a successful DC 22 Wisdom (Perception) check to discover. The chest contains three pieces of jewelry: a silver diadem set with tiny rubies (worth 1,600 gp), a gold ring set with an emerald (worth 900 gp), and a string of black pearls (worth 600 gp).

J. GNOLL LAIR

The cave entrance opens directly into a 30-foot-diameter natural cavern with a 15-foot-high ceiling.

Characters accessing this entry cave with a light source automatically alert the occupants of area 46. These guards respond the following round ready for a fight. Otherwise, contest the characters' Dexterity (Stealth) check against the guards' Wisdom (Perception) check to determine if the guards are alerted.

Once the corridor toward area 46 is entered, it becomes obvious that the stone is worked smooth.

DM Note: Gnoll losses cannot be replaced. They are in a loose alliance with the orcs, so if there are surviving gnolls, they flee to the orc caves. As such, the orcs (either tribe) could flee to the gnolls as well. If the gnoll pack lord escapes, he hastens to depart the area.

AREA 46 – GUARD ROOM

This plain 30-foot-by-30-foot chamber is empty.

There are always four **gnolls** on duty guarding in this area. Two are armed with longbows and spears while two are armed with spears only. The bowmen hang back in the room and fire arrows into melee, while the spearmen hold attackers at bay.

Each gnoll carries 1d8 cp, 1d8 sp, and 1d8 ep.

Development. If the two spearmen falter, the bowmen flee to area 47 to gather reinforcements. If they succeed, one continues on to area 49 to rouse the gnolls in that chamber to take up arms and fight.

AREA 47 – GUARD ROOM

This chamber is 20 feet on a side with smooth walls and a 10-foot-high ceiling. Several animal hides and pelts hang on the walls.

Three male **gnoll** guards are quartered here and are ready to fight immediately. These gnolls are armed only with spears, but can use bite attacks if needed. In addition, five female **gnolls** keep these guards company. They attack as well, although unarmed and must rely on bite attacks.

There is a scattering of crude furniture in the place including a table, benches, and stools, along with heaps of bedding on the floor, and a barrel of fresh water in the southwest corner of the room.

The male gnolls have 1d6 gp each, while the females have 1d4 gp each. Of the numerous pelts on the walls, one is actually a sable cloak (worth 450 gp).

AREA 48 – LOCKED ROOM

The door to this room is locked. The gnoll pack lord (see area 50) has the key. Otherwise, the lock can be picked with a DC 15 Dexterity check using thieves' tools.

The door opens to reveal a 20-foot-wide room that stretches to 30 feet long. The chamber beyond is clearly a storeroom and an armory. Numerous crates are piled high and an array of armor and weapons hang on the walls.

This chamber is a storeroom and armory. The crates contain foodstuffs and mundane equipment (such as torches, rope, etc.). There are also three barrels. Two are empty (and once held water), but the third contains exceptionally fine ale. This barrel leaks and the sweet odor tempts characters to sample the drink. Characters that inspect this barrel are required to make a successful DC 10 Wisdom saving throw, or draw a healthy draught of the ale. If consumed, a character needs to make a successful DC 14 Constitution saving throw or become intoxicated for the next hour. During this time, impaired characters make all attack rolls at disadvantage.

Hanging on the walls are seven shields, and a suit of dwarf-sized chain mail is slumped in the corner of the room. The following weapons are lined up against another wall: 12 handaxes, three longbows, five quivers of arrows (20 in each), and a longsword in a leather scabbard. If removed from the scabbard, the blade glows soft yellow. The blade is magical, but is in fact a *cursed blade* (see appendix A).

AREA 49 – COMMON ROOM

This finished room is 50 feet wide and 25 feet long. The usual clutter of battered wooden furniture and heaps of animal skins is present. The pungent scent of body odor intermixed with an animal pen is nearly overwhelming.

This chamber serves as the common room for the gnoll tribe. The furniture and animal hides (used as beds) are worthless. Seventeen adult **gnolls**—six males and 11 females—and 18 noncombatant young gnolls are crammed into this living area. Cornered, the adults fight like animals to the death to protect the young.

Each male gnoll carries 1d6 sp and 1d6 ep. The females each carry 1d10 sp.

Development. If possible, one or more gnolls attempt to slip away during the chaos of battle. They proceed to area 50 to rouse the gnoll pack lord and his sons.

AREA 50 – GNOLL PACK LORD'S QUARTERS

The warm glow of a fireplace situated in the southeast corner of the room illuminates this chamber. It is about 40 feet wide by 20 feet long, occupied with battered and crude tables, benches, and several dilapidated beds covered with mangy animal pelts.

A **gnoll pack lord** serves as the leader of this tribe. He wears plate armor (AC 18), has a Strength of 18 (+4), and wields a glaive (+6 to hit, 1d10 + 4 slashing damage). Also present are his two **gnoll** sons, who wear chain mail (AC 16), and four female **gnolls**. All the gnolls are eager to engage in combat and fight to the death, although the pack lord might decide to flee (see Development, below), if both of his sons are defeated.

The furnishings are worthless. A large metal pot is hidden beneath a flagstone in the fireplace alcove. It takes a successful DC 15 Wisdom (Perception) check to locate the loose flagstone. Inside the pot are 200 cp, 157 sp, 76 ep, and 139 gp.

The pack lord has a pair of silver armbands (worth 50 gp each) and in his belt pouch there are 39 gp and the key to the door leading to area 48. His sons each have 1d10 sp, 1d10 ep, and 1d10 gp. Each female wears a silver neck chain (worth 30 gp) and has 2d6 ep in a pouch.

The secret door and passage to area 63 is unknown to all. A successful DC 24 Wisdom (Perception) check is required to find the door. The catch release needs to be triggered by pressing a series of knobs located 1 to 2 feet off the floor. Just inside the entrance is the skeleton of a human thief, his leg broken. He died here trying to escape through the secret door many years ago. His rotten leather armor and corroded weapons are valueless, but the purse on his belt holds 12 gems (each worth 50 gp), and the *boots of elvenkind* upon his bony feet are still in usable shape. The corridor leads to another blank wall, hiding a secret door. This one is easy to find on this side, requiring but a successful DC 13 Wisdom (Perception) check to locate. It is easily pushed open and leads at area 63.

Development. If you wish, allow the pack lord to escape enemies by climbing up the chimney of the fireplace in his area. A successful DC 15 Strength (Athletics) check is required to climb the chimney. If he escapes, he hastens to one of the orc lairs and joins forces with them.

THE EVIL OF THE CAVES OF CHAOS

These very caves are steeped in a forbidden evil older than history. If a *detect evil and good* spell is cast anywhere in this area, the entire cave system radiates faint evil with a purple glow.

Additionally, undead created in these unhallowed halls have the Turn Resistance trait.

Turn Resistance: The undead has advantage on saving throws against any effect that turns undead.

K. SHRINE OF EVIL CHAOS

A worn path wanders through a copse of obscenely twisted and oddly bloated trees, bestowing an eerie sense of unease. A faint, foul draft issues forth from the 20-foot-wide cave opening. Blood-red strata intertwine with bulging black veins of rock running through the hewn walls beyond the entrance. The wide corridor has a smooth, polished floor and all is deathly still. The stillness imparts a dim awareness of dread as your very footsteps echo in these vaulted halls.

A faint groaning sound and a shrill piping may be occasionally heard, with a successful DC 17 Wisdom (Perception) check.

Unless the characters take extreme care to muffle their sounds of movement, the continual noise brings a group of eight **zombie** guards to investigate within 1d4 minutes. These ghastly monsters are clad in filthy red and black striped uniforms. Each carries a cleaver-like battle-axe (1d10 + 1 slashing damage). These zombies wander the halls and are not tied to any particular location.

AREA 51 – BOULDER-FILLED PASSAGE

At this wide intersection, large rocks and boulders have been carefully placed to seal a corridor heading to the southwest.

At the DM's discretion, this route can be opened up with 20 man-hours of labor; this creates a safe passage large enough for a human to pass through into the area beyond. Otherwise, this area is impassible. The passage meanders for several hundred meters with many side passages and caves. One route leads to the Underdark, but the main passage eventually leads to the Cave of the Unknown about 600 meters to the southwest. (This can either be Quasqueton—see chapter 6, area 53—or an encounter site of the DM's own design.) Of course this route is not safe, and is prowled by many dangerous monsters. See chapter 12 for ideas on what these encounters could be.

AREA 52 – HALL OF SKELETONS

This finished chamber is 40 feet wide and 60 feet long. At the opposite end of the room is a dais with a stone throne-like chair set with four large red-faceted gems. Propped up against the east and west walls are six humanoid skeletons. They are clad in rags and worn chain mail armor, and bear battered shields and rusty scimitars.

These bony guards do not move, and any attempt to turn them immediately upon entering the chamber has no effect, as they are obviously not animated. However, as soon as intruders touch the dais or throne chair, these 12 **skeletons** animate from their positions on either wall of the chamber and attack. Although wearing chain mail and carrying shields (speed 20 ft.), these undead only have an effective AC 16 due to the state of disrepair of the equipment. They wield rusty scimitars (1d6 + 2 slashing damage). Since these undead guards were animated in the Caves, they have the Turn Resistance trait.

Once the skeletons are disposed of, the characters can pry the four garnets (each worth 500 gp) from the back of the stone throne. To remove each gem without damage, a character must succeed on a successful DC 12 Dexterity check with a sharp, pointed tool. Failure on this check results in damaging that particular gem, reducing its value to 100 gp.

AREA 53 – GUARD ROOM

This plain room is 60 feet wide but only 20 feet long. To the north and to the south silently stand a quartet of hulking decomposing humanoids, each adorned in dirty, red- and black-striped uniforms.

The guards are eight human **zombies** and although unarmed they are content to pummel opponents with their rotting fists. These undead were created in the Caves, so they have the Turn Resistance trait. These undead are under command not to attack anyone wearing temple garb (rusty-red robes with black cowls) or carrying an amulet unholy symbol. Otherwise they attack until destroyed.

There is no treasure here.

AREA 54 – ACOLYTES' CHAMBER

The occupants beyond this door are deep into prayer and chanting. If the characters listen at the door, a successful DC 14 Wisdom (Perception) check reveals the chanting.

The door opens to reveal a short 20-foot corridor that empties into a 30-foot-by-20-foot chamber. A pungent, almost acrid scent permeates your nostrils. In the center of the room is a plain metal brazier alit with a soft glow. Situated around the brazier are four prone figures on their knees, eyes closed, deep in the throes of a chant. Each wears rusty-red robes with a black cowl.

The figures are four CE human **acolytes**. Since they are deep in chant and prayer, they have disadvantage on Wisdom (Perception) checks to notice the characters. Furthermore, once they are roused, they are befuddled the first round of combat and lose their action. Under the robes each wears chain mail (AC 16, speed 20 ft.), and each has a mace (1d6 bludgeoning damage) at his belt.

Each acolyte has the following cleric spells prepared:

- *Cantrips (at will): light, resistance, sacred flame*
- *1st level: (3 slots): bane, command, inflict wounds*

One acolyte casts *bane* with his first available action, and maintains concentration while attacking on subsequent rounds. The other two cast *command* ("drop" or "halt"), or *inflict wounds*. These are followed up by *bane* or *sacred flame* as appropriate before simply resorting to blows from a mace.

Each acolyte carries a coin purse with 10 gp, and the leader wears an *amulet of protection from good* (see appendix A).

The room contains four hard pallets, the lit brazier, a wooden table with four matching stools, a cabinet for clothing, a water pail, a waste bucket, and a flagon full of wine and four cups. There is nothing of value amongst these items.

AREA 55 – CHAPEL OF EVIL CHAOS

This place is of red stone with the floor being a mosaic checkerboard of black and red. The south wall is covered by a huge tapestry which depicts a bleak landscape, barren trees, and unidentifiable—but horrible—black shapes in silhouette, holding aloft a struggling human. A gray sky is torn by wisps of purple clouds, and a bloody moon with a skull-like face on it leers down upon the scene.

Four black pillars support the domed ceiling some 25 feet overhead. Between these columns, just in front of the tapestry, is a stone altar of red-veined black rock, rough-hewn and stained brown with dried blood. Four tarnished bronze vessels rest upon this altar.

This evil shrine is empty. Characters are inevitably drawn to the bronze items on the altar. These include a shallow bowl, a pair of goblets, and a ewer. The vessels are of ancient design and the interior of each is bloodstained. These are obviously valuable objects (each cup is worth 1,000 gp, and the bowl and ewer are each worth 2,000 gp).

However, each of these objects are relics of evil, and if a *detect evil and good* spell is cast upon these items, they glow an ugly purple—even more intense than the surrounding chapel—and all good characters feel instant loathing from them. A character picking up one of these objects must make a DC 15 Wisdom saving throw. On a success, the character gets a "feeling of great evil" about the object, and he or she may voluntarily put it down. But if the saving throw fails, the character gradually falls under the influence of a demonic spell and over the next 7 days must attempt another DC 15 Wisdom saving throw with the DC increasing by 1 each day. If the character fails more saving throws than he succeeds, he becomes a servant of chaos and evil (alignment shifts to chaotic evil), returning to this chapel to replace the relics, and then staying as a guard forever after. During this time, any character possessing the vessels refuses to part with them, sell them, or even allow others to handle them. A *dispel evil and good* spell cast on the character during this 7-day period ends this effect. Otherwise, the character becomes a servant of evil forever.

Development. If someone attempts to destroy these relics, the great bell in area 58 sounds and the area's residents come running, beginning to arrive in 3 rounds. The first to arrive are the acolytes from area 54, followed by the wandering patrol of zombies a round later (if not already defeated). The next to arrive are the skeletons from area 52, and then the zombies from area 53 another 2 rounds after that.

AREA 56 – ADEPTS' CHAMBER

This 20-foot-by-40-foot room contains a table with four chairs, and four identical beds, stands, and chests.

There are four human **adepts** here, each clad in a black robe with a maroon-colored cowl. Their waists are circled with copper chains (worth 40 gp each) with skull-shaped clasps fashioned of bone. Each is engrossed in studying evil texts and scrolls. They prefer to cast spells, but if needed two engage opposition in melee while the other two hang back to toss offensive spells such as *command* ("flee" or "drop"), *necrotic bolt*, or *sacred flame*.

Each adept carries a purse with 20 gp and 5 pp.

All the furniture in the room is typical and nothing of value. The texts and scrolls are all evil in nature and also carry little value. However, if the characters opt to destroy these evil writings, grant them each a 50 XP bonus. On the table are copper dishes and vessels of exceptional craftsmanship (worth 175 gp as a set).

Development. If hard-pressed, and two of these adepts are defeated, at least one remaining evil cleric attempts to flee and warn their master by striking the great bell at area 58.

AREA 57 – HALL OF UNDEAD WARRIORS

This foreboding chamber is 20 feet by 50 feet. Standing a silent, unmoving vigil are four files of undead, two ranks of skeletons clad in pieces of tattered chain mail and two ranks of zombies also clad in chain mail. The skeletal warriors face the south, while the zombies face the north.

Each rank of undead is 10 strong. Therefore 20 **skeletons** and 20 **zombies** stand ready for battle in this chamber. The skeletons have an effective AC 14 from the armor scraps and each wields a shortsword. The zombies have better armor (AC 14) and each is armed with a spear (1d8 + 1 piercing damage). Since these undead were created in the temple, they all have the Turn Resistance trait. These guards remain unmoving, unless attacked or the great bell in area 58 is struck (see Development).

These undead lack any treasure.

Development. Upon striking of the great iron bell in the temple (area 58), the skeletons issue forth from the south door of this room and march into the temple to line the south wall, while the zombies plod out the north exit to line the north wall of the temple. If intruders enter area 57, are in the passage to the temple, or are within the temple itself, these undead warriors attack. Proper garments and/or amulets prevent attack, unless the evil priest commands the undead to do so.

AREA 58 – TEMPLE OF EVIL CHAOS

This huge area has an arched ceiling some 30 feet or more in height. The floor is of polished black stone which has swirling patterns of red veins through it. The west wall is of translucent red stone which is seemingly one piece, polished to mirror-like smoothness. The other walls are covered by draperies of deep purple with embroidered symbols and evil sayings, done in scarlet and gold and black thread. A great bell of black iron stands near the entrance point, with a pair of mallets beside its supports.

To the south are several long benches or pews. There are three stone altars to the west, the northernmost of pure black, the middle one of streaked red and black, the last of red with black flecks. At the western end of the temple area is a dais of black stone, with four lesser chairs on its lower tier and a great throne above. The chairs are of bone while the throne is composed of bleached ivory.

As soon as you enter this evil place, black candles in eight great candelabras on either side of the place become alight magically, shooting forth a disgusting red radiance. Shapeless forms of purple, yellow, and green begin to dance and sway on the western wall.

If a creature looks at the dancing forms for a moment, it must succeed on a DC 15 Wisdom saving throw or be mesmerized into chanting a hymn to chaotic evil. During this chanting, the target is considered incapacitated, although it can attempt a new saving throw at the end of each round to shake off the magical effect. The chanting likely alerts some of the temple occupants (see Development, below). Even if the characters examine this room in silence, the zombie guards that wander the temple arrive in 1d6 + 2 rounds as part of their normal patrol. In this case, one of the zombie guards attempts to strike the bell with a mallet (requiring an action) to alert the temple.

The walls behind the draperies and the ceiling are of dull black rock. The ivory throne is set with gold and adorned with gems of red and black (10 black stones each worth 100 gp, 10 red stones each worth 500 gp, and one large red stone worth 1,000 gp). The signs and sigils upon these seats are of pure chaos and evil.

Development. Should three or more voices be so raised from the mesmerizing chanting, the iron bell sounds automatically by magic, summoning the undead from area 57. But even one such chant alerts the guards of the head cleric (area 59), which arrive in 1 round. Regardless of how it occurs, if the bell is sounded the undead from area 57 file into this chamber.

AREA 59 – THE CHAMBERS OF THE EVIL PRIEST

This is a cozy 20-foot-by-20-foot room where the floor is covered by a thick, although dirty, carpet. There are lavish furnishings here, including three plush chairs and a fine wooden table.

Area g. This is the anteroom where special visitors are entertained by the chief cleric. Three **zombies** are on guard here. The zombies wear plate armor (AC 18, speed 10 ft.) and wield longswords two-handed (1d10 + 1 slashing damage). These zombies have the Turn Resistance trait. They stand unmoving unless they are summoned to the temple area (area 58), someone enters their area, or they are commanded by the evil priest. Combat here alerts the evil priest (see Developments, below).

None of the furnishings are of particular value except for a golden flagon and nine matching gold cups. The flagon is worth 500 gp, each of the nine cups is worth 100 gp.

When the characters move through the anteroom continue with the read-aloud:

This 20-foot-by-20-foot room is also furnished lavishly, with a red carpet, furniture of black wood with velvet upholstery of scarlet, and a large bed covered with silken black and red cushions and pillows. A demon idol leers from the wall to the north, directly over the bed. In the southeast corner of the room is an elaborate black and red fabric changing screen.

This room is the private chamber of the **evil priest**. He wears a black cape and cowl, with red robes over his armor. He prefers to avoid combat, relying on spells and his magic staff. He starts by tossing his staff on the ground; it transforms into a **giant constrictor snake** and he commands it to attack a fighter-type character. Then he casts spells as appropriate, such as *silence, command, hold person*, or *inflict wounds*. He uses his *spell scrolls* first, before resorting to spell slots. If he faces formidable opposition and is reduced to 7 hit points or less, he flees (see Developments).

The evil priest has a key to the cell at area 64, a gold ring with a black sapphire (worth 1,400 gp), and a purse with 51 pp in it. The demon idol hanging over the bed has two yellow topaz eyes (worth 100 gp each). But, if anyone other than the evil priest touches it, the heavy idol topples over upon the person. If the target fails a DC 11 Dexterity saving throw, the idol causes 7 (2d6) bludgeoning damage.

There is a secret door hidden in the recess of a wooden wardrobe that holds several red and black cloaks. It requires a successful DC 17 Wisdom (Perception) check to locate the door. However, this check is made with advantage if the evil priest flees via this exit. When the knob to open the secret door is pulled, 500 gp and 50 gems (blue quartz chunks, each worth 10 gp) spill into the room from a secret compartment in the top of the wardrobe.

Developments. If the characters engage in battle in the antechamber, the evil priest is alerted and awaiting them. If he has time, he casts defensive spells such as *sanctuary*, *aid*, or *shield of faith*, in that order.

If forced to flee, the evil priest darts behind the changing screen in the southeast corner, enters the wooden wardrobe there, and slips through a secret door in its back. He proceeds down a short passage and out into the corridor through another secret door. Hopefully spilling loot from the triggered secret door distracts pursuers who stop for the loot. The evil priest might either try to rally his forces, or else escape if most of his followers have

been defeated. When all else fails, he has a *potion of gaseous form* which he can use to escape through the boulder-filled corridor (area 51).

AREA 60 – GUEST CHAMBER

The door opens to reveal a comfortable 20-foot-by-30-foot chamber. There is a large wrought-iron bed, a worn table, and numerous chairs. Several tapestries cover the stone walls.

This lower room is for important guests of the temple. The furniture is all normal, and although the tapestries appear valuable, a successful DC 10 Intelligence check reveals they are moth-eaten and worthless. The tapestries depict evil cruelties and obscene rites. Beneath the velvet cloth on the table is a polished mirror (worth 5 gp).

AREA 61 – TORTURE CHAMBER

Chiseled stone steps lead down a corridor and deposit you into a 30-foot-wide, 40-foot-long chamber. The soft glow of embers emits from a fireplace at the opposite end of the room. There are various implements of torture here, both large and small, including a rack, iron maiden, tongs, pincers, and whips. Comfortable chairs are scattered along the walls, evidently so placed to allow visitors an enjoyable view of the proceedings.

The torturer lives in the forepart of the place, a hulking CE human **thug** with great strength. He wears chain mail (AC 16) under his black leather garments. He has a Strength of 18 (+4) and his weapon is a wickedly curved double-headed greataxe (+6 to hit, 1d12 + 4 slashing damage). Without hesitation he rushes to attack, although quick-thinking characters could attempt a DC 17 Charisma (Persuasion) check to deceive him and delay his attack. But they likely require at least one more successful check to truly convince the crazed torturer not to attack.

A successful DC 15 Wisdom (Perception) check reveals the torturer's treasure, hidden in his mattress. A concealed flap hides a pouch with 135 gp and a platinum bracelet (worth 700 gp).

AREA 62 – THE CRYPT

The door to this room is bolted shut from the outside. Although it can be easily removed, it's a clear warning something sinister resides beyond.

The door opens to reveal a stairway descending into darkness. The air here is stale with a lingering unnatural chill. At the base of the steps is a long hall of roughly hewn stone that runs north to south. The ceiling here is irregular and low, perhaps 7 feet high. Many stone sarcophagi line the floor in two rows.

This chamber is a tomb, holding the remains of previous servants of the Temple of Chaos. There are 12 stone sarcophagi here, each inscribed with Infernal runes and symbols (although harmless). Removing a lid requires a successful DC 15 Strength (Athletics) check, although a second character can assist with the check. Each contains the body of a long dead cleric, a servant of Chaos. None of these clerics were buried with any items of value.

The six sarcophagus the characters open contains a **wight**. The wight is aware of the characters shortly after they enter the tomb. If opened, the wight surprises the characters and attacks with its Life Drain action. If not opened in several minutes, the wight forces the lid off, although this takes 2 rounds, plenty of time for the characters to flee and potentially secure the door or prepare for battle. The wight wears chain mail (AC 16) and wields a longsword. The wight craves to extinguish the spark of life from any intruders that disturb its slumber. It pursues creatures into the caves above, but if the door is barred successfully (requiring a DC 14 Dexterity check if performed hastily), the wight remains trapped in this area.

There is a secret compartment in the wight's sarcophagus, requiring a successful DC 18 Wisdom (Perception) check to locate. The hidden compartment contains a *+2 shortsword*, a *scroll of protection* (undead), a *helm of opposite alignment* (see appendix A), and a silver dagger set with onyx into its pommel (worth 800 gp).

AREA 63 – STORAGE CHAMBER

This large plain chamber is 40 feet by 40 feet. Neat piles of crates, boxes, and barrels are present here. Several bulging sacks are propped up along one wall.

This is a storeroom, holding the supplies for the occupants of the temple. There is nothing of value as the barrels contain water, and the crates and boxes are full of mundane items and dried foodstuffs. The sacks are full of ground meal.

If the characters stay within this room for longer than 3 rounds, a **gelatinous cube** moves down the corridor into the room blocking the exit. Due to its Transparent trait, a successful DC 15 Wisdom (Perception) check is required to detect the creature. If a character was specifically watching the corridor, this check is made at advantage.

There is a secret door located in the southeastern corner of the room. It can be discovered with a successful DC 16 Wisdom (Perception) check. The release is a small pressure plate on the ceiling. The secret door leads to the gnoll pack lord's cave (area 50).

Inside the gelatinous cube are 1d12 each of cp, sp, ep, gp, and pp, as well as several bones, evidently parts of a victim not yet wholly digested. One of the "bones" is actually a *wand of enemy detection*. The wand can be discovered with a *detect magic* spell, or a successful DC 20 Wisdom (Perception) check. If the wand is not removed from the monster within 10 minutes, it will be ruined by digestive juices.

AREA 64 – CELL

The door is of iron, locked, and barred, but a window is set in the door. The evil priest (see area 59) has the key to the door, or the lock can be picked with thieves' tools and a successful DC 20 Dexterity check.

This 20-foot-by-20-foot cell is gloomy with thick, stale air. Several skeletons are chained to the walls, bony arms outstretched to the ceiling. There also appears to be a single living occupant chained to the back wall. She is scantily clad in torn robes, her shapely legs and pale arms exposed. A grimy burlap sack conceals her visage.

This is the place where prisoners are kept until tortured to death or sacrificed in the temple.

Those who enter and approach closer are in for a rude shock! The fair maiden in need of rescue is actually a **medusa** named Cynnia, recently taken by the evil priest's zombie guards. Not being above such things, the evil priest has plans for removing its snakes, blinding it, and then eventually sacrificing it at a special rite to a demon.

The medusa assumes the characters are temple clerics, and tries to convince them to remove the burlap sack. If they comply, she unleashes her Petrifying Gaze, although she spares one or two of the adventurers from her gaze. If they agree to free her from her bonds, she promises that she has magic able to turn their companions back to flesh again. She does, in fact, have a special *elixir of stone to flesh* (see appendix A), but it is hidden in her cottage in the wilderness (see area 13, chapter 10). However, her bargain is but a ploy, detected with a successful DC 15 Wisdom (Insight) check. She does not intend to simply give away the elixir, and instead attempts to petrify her rescuers, once free.

CHAPTER TWELVE
Additional Encounters
The Borderlands

L. XVART SHAFT

Most denizens of the Caves of Chaos have no idea this particular shaft—which leads to a series of dug-out chambers—even exists. Even fewer suspect it is inhabited by a degenerate band of diminutive humanoids called xvarts, who prey on the food and supplies of the other humanoids. At the base of a large tree is an opening barely a few feet across that leads to a shaft and the xvart lair. Xvarts appear in Volo's Guide to Monsters (pp. 199-200). If this resource is not available, kobolds or goblins can be substituted with relative ease.

In addition to those encountered in these chambers, there is a wandering band that "hunts" for food and supplies. These eight **xvarts** (see appendix B) are armed with spears, wielded two-handed (+1 to hit, 1d8 - 1 piercing damage), and slings, although they would rather avoid confrontation, preferring instead to pilfer supplies and flee. They carry dirty sacks full of foodstuffs and bones. If half are defeated, they flee, eventually making their way back to the shaft entrance. This is the easiest method to locate their lair. Otherwise, it requires a successful DC 17 Wisdom (Perception) check to find the opening. If the general area is searched for tracks with a successful DC 14 Wisdom (Survival) check, the Wisdom (Perception) check is made at advantage.

DM Note: Xvart losses are not replaced. The xvarts have long desired to live in one of the caves higher up off the canyon floor. If one of the nearby cave systems (likely A, B, C, or D; see chapter 11) are cleaned out by the characters, within a day, the xvarts could relocate, bringing along several of their osquip pets.

GENERAL FEATURES

AREA 1 – THE SHAFT

Hidden among the shrubbery at the base of a tree is a dark crack in the ground that appears to lead straight down, perhaps to another cave system. The air is stale, and numerous roots from the nearby tree can be seen poking from the walls of the shaft.

This is the entrance to the xvart lair. The shaft is about 35 feet deep. A fall causes 10 (3d6) bludgeoning damage plus an additional 3 (1d6) piercing damage from landing on the bone pile in area 2. Climbing down the shaft is easy, requiring a successful DC 8 Strength (Athletics) check, due to the numerous roots extruding from the soil and rock. One of the prominent roots is worn, as if it has been used often. This fact can be discerned with a successful DC 12 Intelligence (Investigation) check.

About 25 feet down the shaft, on the east wall, is a corridor concealed with a gray canvas. The concealed passage can be detected with a successful DC 10 Wisdom (Perception) check.

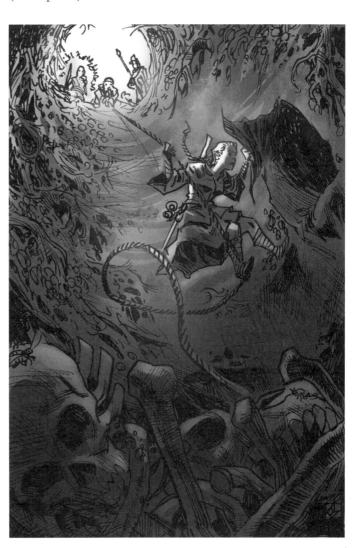

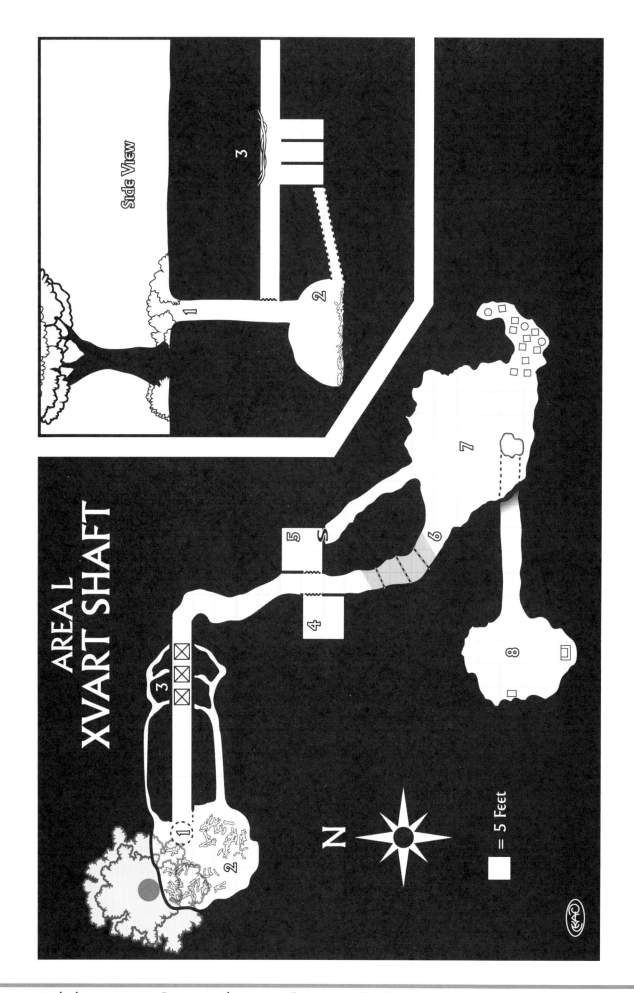

Side View

AREA L
XVART SHAFT

N

☐ = 5 Feet

AREA 2 – THE BONE PIT

The bottom of the shaft opens into a chamber perhaps 25 feet in diameter. The floor is covered with bleached bones and bone shards in a tangle at least a few feet deep. The air is heavy and stale, with a slight stench of animal waste.

The xvarts use this chamber to house their collection of bones and other refuse in a vain effort to impress their twisted degenerate god. The bones are mostly human-oid in origin, but numerous animal bones and the large bones of predators are also represented. The floor is considered difficult terrain.

The bone pit is the lair of six osquips (see appendix B), but usually only three are encountered in this chamber. The remaining can be found elsewhere in the xvart lair. The osquips are friendly to the xvarts and this tribe has learned to communicate with these vermin as they can with bats and rats. If a creature disturbs the bones, the osquips attack from under the pile using their Ambusher trait. The bone pile is not considered difficult terrain for the osquips. A typical tactic involves a bite attack and then fleeing into the bone pile, so it should be difficult for the characters to determine where the vermin are, or where attacks come from next. If two osquips are de-feated, the remaining one flees to area 3. Note that only six osquips are in the entire lair, so keep track of their numbers when they are defeated.

Persistent characters can find some random treasure if they search the bone pile. For each 10 minutes of search-ing with a successful DC 12 Wisdom (Perception) check, a character can find 3d4 random coins (75%), a small gem (15%, worth 50 gp) or a minor art object (10%, worth 1d6 x 10 gp).

AREA 3 – PIT TRAPS

This appears to be a normal corridor, but indeed it is trapped. There are three consecutive pit traps along the passageway. Each pit is covered with a thin piece of cloth covered with dirt and small rock debris. As little as 25 pounds of weight is required to trigger the trap. It requires a successful DC 13 Wisdom (Perception) check to spot the pit. A fall into the pit causes 3 (1d6) bludgeoning damage plus another 4 (1d8) piercing damage from the sharpened bones sunk into the floor of the pit. Climbing out of the pit requires a successful DC 12 Strength (Athletics) check.

The sound of one of these pits being triggered summons one or more **osquips** from area 2 via several small pas-sages as depicted on the map. Each of these passages is about 1 foot wide, but can be squeezed through by a Small

creature, or normally traversed by a Tiny creature. The os-quips attack using their Ambusher trait, and since the tun-nels link all three of the pits together, they can move about as needed when creatures fall into the pits. The osquips fight until reduced to less than 5 hit points, at which point they flee back to area 2.

Running along the ceiling above the pits is a root affixed at each end. The root blends into the dirt ceiling so it is only discovered with a successful DC 18 Wisdom (Perception) check. The xvarts use the root to climb hand over hand over the pit traps. The root can support 125 pounds. For every additional 10 pounds of weight, it has a 10% cumu-lative chance per round of breaking.

Development. If any of these pits are triggered, the guards in areas 4 and 5 are alerted and waiting for intrud-ers.

AREA 4 – GUARD ROOM

DM Note: The corridor is flanked by a pair of guard rooms. Each is concealed by a gray canvas that looks like the stone wall, especially when in a dimly lit corridor. It requires a successful DC 12 Wisdom (Perception) check to locate the room behind one of these canvases.

Beyond the canvas is a low chamber, perhaps 4 feet high and 10 feet square. Numerous roots dangle from the ceiling, some reaching the floor. A battered table covered with coins and knucklebones is the only furnishing.

Eight **xvarts** (see appendix B) are stationed (more like crammed) into this chamber. They pass the time by play-ing knucklebones and doing other immature xvart-things. Each is armed with a javelin (+1 to hit, 1d6 - 1 piercing damage) and a shortsword. They prefer to attack with javelins, and pull back after the initial assault. In the back rank, they flip over the table, and use it as half cover. Due to the low ceiling, creatures over 4 feet tall make all attacks at disadvantage in the chamber.

Each xvart carries 2d6 cp and 1d6 sp. A set of worn knucklebones and a smattering of coins (37 cp and 12 sp) cover the table.

Developments. If alerted from the pit traps in area 3, these guards are aware and ready to thrust javelins through the canvas if creatures pass by. Consider this as four attacks (two from each side) at disadvantage, since they can't see what they are stabbing at. If unaware of the characters, they are crowded around the table in a high stakes game of knucklebones and can be surprised.

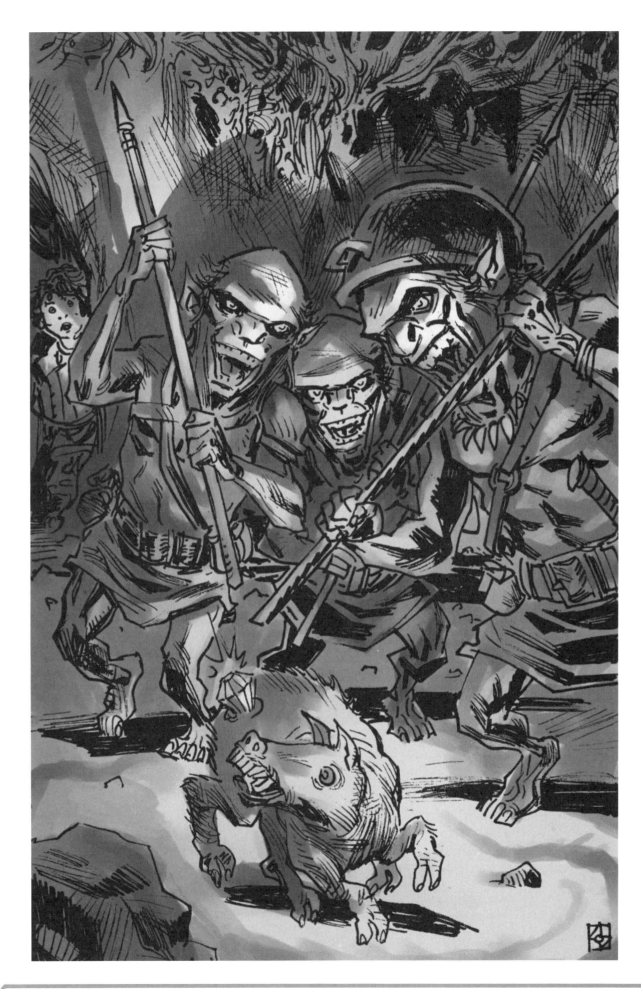

AREA 5 – GUARD ROOM

DM Note: The corridor is flanked by a pair of guard rooms. Each is concealed by a gray canvas that looks like the stone wall especially when in a dimly lit corridor. It requires a successful DC 12 Wisdom (Perception) check to locate the room behind one of these canvases.

Beyond the canvas is a low chamber, perhaps 4 feet high and 10 feet square. Numerous roots dangle from the ceiling, some reaching the floor. The room is empty of furnishings save for several small blue-skinned humanoids tormenting a hairless rodent-like creature with oversized teeth.

This guard room houses four **xvarts** (see appendix B) playing a game with an **osquip** (see appendix B). Using a rubber-like sticky substance (tree sap), they have affixed a gemstone to an osquip's back. The creature furiously tries to get it off, while the xvarts take turns trying to swat the gemstone off with a javelin. Whoever succeeds wins the game's pot. In this case, it is literally a pot that the winner wears triumphantly during the next game.

The xvarts are armed with javelins (+1 to hit, 1d6 - 1 piercing damage) and shortswords. The osquip is enraged at the recent abuse and slightly wounded (currently it has 19 hit points), so it attacks with advantage on the first 2 rounds. The xvarts hang back and let the osquip attack, before defending the lair to the death.

There is a secret door in the southeast corner of the room. It can be located with a successful DC 15 Wisdom (Perception) check. The door leads to a corridor which is an alternate route to and from area 7.

Each xvart carries 2d6 cp and 1d6 sp. The gemstone used to "play" with the osquip is a small deep green spinnel (worth 100 gp), but it requires a successful DC 15 Wisdom (Perception) check to locate after being tossed from the osquip's back during the creature's enraged assault.

Developments. If alerted from the pit traps in area 3, these guards are aware and ready to thrust javelins through the canvas if creatures pass by. Consider this as four attacks (two from each side) at disadvantage, since they can't see what they are stabbing at. If unaware of the characters, they are busy playing "whack an osquip" and can be surprised easily.

AREA 6 – TRAPPED CORRIDOR

This corridor is also trapped. A series of three thin tripwires covered with soot stretch from one wall to the next, a few inches off the ground. A successful DC 15 Wisdom (Perception) check is needed to notice the tripwires. The tripwires can be disabled with thieves' tools and a successful DC 15 Dexterity check. Without thieves' tools, a sharp weapon can be used to attempt the disable, but this check is at disadvantage. If triggered, the roof collapses in a 15-foot-long section of the corridor, potentially affecting three creatures. The rubble causes 10 (3d6) bludgeoning damage and each creature is restrained (escape DC 10) by the rubble. Success on a DC 13 Dexterity saving throws reduces the damage by half, and the creature is not restrained.

If the trap is triggered, the corridor is strewn with rubble, which is now considered difficult terrain. In addition, the members of the tribe in area 7 (and areas 4 and 5, if not aware already) are alerted to the presence of intruders.

AREA 7 – COMMON ROOM

The corridor ends in a cavern perhaps 40 feet in diameter with a ceiling about 8 feet high. Numerous sleeping pallets and an assortment of tables and chairs are scattered about the chamber.

This chamber serves as the main living quarters for the tribe. There are sleeping pallets for 31 xvarts here, but only 11 **xvarts** (see appendix B) are in this chamber when the characters arrive. The rest are in areas 4 and 5, or out "hunting." There are also 1d3 **osquips** (see appendix B) here, unless defeated in previous chambers. The xvarts defend the chamber to the last. If alerted from the collapsing roof trap, five xvarts exit down the passage to area 5, and double back around to attack the characters from the rear.

The furniture is all in poor condition, with most of it being gnawed on. In the rear of the chamber is a haphazard pile of crates. Most contain spoiled foodstuffs, but a few hold a random assortment of mundane goods (pots, blankets, clothes, and wood). There are also three casks among the crates, each about half full of stale water. Hanging from the ceiling are dried meats, including lizard, bat, and humanoid (mostly goblin and kobold) haunches. A 5-foot-wide shaft drops down 5 feet and leads to a sloping passage to the xvart speaker's private chamber (area 8).

Each xvart carries 2d6 sp.

Development. If it appears the intruders have the upper hand, one or two xvarts attempt to flee down the shaft to wake up the speaker and his guards in area 8.

AREA 8 – THE CHAMBER OF THE SPEAKER

DM Note: Unless alerted by xvarts fleeing from area 7, assume the occupants of this chamber are slumbering.

This cavern is perhaps 25 feet in diameter. Hanging from the ceiling are numerous wind chimes with decorative bones. Along the far wall is a large chest sporting a massive black iron padlock. To the south is great chair of random bone pieces lashed together with leather straps. Slumped on the throne is a gaunt blue-skinned humanoid with unkempt black hair. His eyes are shut, he snores loudly, and drool drips down to his stained tunic. His feet rest on a slumbering hairless rodent the size of pig with oversized incisors. At the foot of the throne are several grimy sacks overstuffed with leaves, occupied by several more slumbering blue-skinned humanoids.

The speaker of the tribe calls this chamber his home. He is tall (nearly 4 feet!) for a **xvart** (see appendix B) wears a chain shirt (AC 15), has 14 (4d6) hit points, has an Intelligence of 13 (+1), and he can speak Goblin in addition to Abyssal. He claims to be a chosen one of his degenerate god, who has granted him magical abilities. This is far from the truth, as instead he found a bone *wand of magic missiles*, and uses it to impress the other members of the tribe. The command word for the wand ("nobe") is etched into its surface, and it currently has 5 charges—he has used it twice today to dole out discipline. He uses the wand every single round, until he expends all 5 charges. If the wand's charges are depleted, it is automatically destroyed, releasing a blast of eldritch energy in a 10-foot diameter burst that causes 7 (2d6) necrotic damage.

Four more **xvarts** (each with 10 hit points; see appendix B), representing the finest guards in the tribe, serve as personal bodyguards; each wears studded leather armor (AC 14). The rodent being used as a footstool is a large, nasty **osquip** (30 hit points; see appendix B). The bodyguards fight to protect the speaker but give a wide berth to the crazed osquip. Meanwhile, the speaker hangs back using the bone chair as half cover to fire *magic missiles* at the intruders. The chair is relatively easy to destroy (AC 13, 5 hit points) due to its ramshackle construction.

The speaker wears a thick chain of gold (worth 220 gp), and has a gold earring studded with an emerald (worth 110 gp). Each guard carries 2d6 sp and 1d6 gp.

The large chest is locked. The key is hidden in the bone chair and requires a successful DC 18 Intelligence (Investigation) check to discover. Or the lock can be picked with thieves' tools and a successful DC 16 Dexterity check. Alternatively, the chest can be smashed open (AC 15, 10 hit points), but this enrages the occupant. Inside the chest are four large bulging sacks. Each holds rocks, but trapped in the chest is a **poisonous snake**. If the chest was smashed opened, the snake is agitated and gets advantage to attack rolls for the first 3 rounds.

The tribe's treasure is hidden behind a rock in the north wall. This cavity can be discovered with a successful DC 18 Wisdom (Perception) check. Inside the cavity are three large burlap sacks.

Sack #1. 556 cp and 13 gp.

Sack #2. 487 sp, 22 ep, and a silver crown with precious gemstones removed (but still worth 125 gp).

Sack #3. Three silver candlestick holders (each worth 15 gp), a cockatrice feather quill with a gold nib (worth 75 gp), an ivory statuette of a panther (worth 55 gp), an empty wine bottle with a gold filigree label (worth 24 gp), a collection of 17 smooth river pebbles in a pouch (worthless, although they appear to be valuable), 14 silvered arrowheads, a magnifying glass with an electrum handle (worth 45 gp), and three copper cups (each worth 5 gp).

M. THE VERMINOUS CAVES

This series of natural caverns is located high off the canyon floor to the northwest. The caves serve as a breeding ground for giant cave crickets. Although the giant cave crickets are generally not that dangerous, they make a suitable food source, and tend to attract larger predators and humanoid hunters.

While approaching the caves, creatures within 30 feet likely hear the distinctive chirping of the giant cave crickets. There is a 30% chance 1d6 **giant cave crickets** (see appendix B) are near the mouth of the cave or just outside of it, grazing on hardy lichens and other plant material. Likewise, the abundant giant cave crickets move around the cave system. Whenever a creature enters area 3, 5, or 6, there is a 50% chance that 1d6 giant cave crickets are present, grazing, in addition to what's noted in the area's descriptive text.

DM Note: It would be nearly impossible to wipe out the entire population of giant cave crickets in these caves. Every week that passes, 3d4 more giant cave crickets are added to the population. However, natural predation tends to keep the overall population in balance.

GENERAL FEATURES

AREA 1 – ENTRY CAVERN

The sound of droning chirping grows louder as you approach. A short walk from the entrance leads to a natural cavern perhaps 30 feet in diameter. The ceiling is at least 20 feet overhead. The floor is uneven and covered with rocky debris. Numerous pale white crickets the size of a large dog tarry about the chamber, idly grazing on bits of fungus and lichen growing on the walls. The vermin sport massive, oversized rear legs, but seem to ignore your presence.

This chamber is host to a sizable population of giant cave crickets. The vermin breed nearby (area 3), but roam throughout the caves to graze on organic matter growing on the rocky surfaces of the cave. The air here is moist and somewhat humid. Currently, 14 **giant cave crickets** (see appendix B) are here, but they ignore creatures that are not aggressive. They casually move out of the way if a creature approaches. Sudden movements, loud noises, or aggressive behavior incites the vermin to hop away, possibly incurring a swift kick en route. But a giant cave cricket seeks to escape back to area 3, instead of fighting.

The presence of an ample food source tends to attract predators. A **cave fisher** (see appendix B) is situated on a rock ledge along the west wall about 20 feet off the floor. Using its filament, it attacks a random creature that uses one of the two corridors leading to area 3, eager to add a different type of meat to its diet. It attempts to reel in a target to its ledge, to make short work of it via its claws. A few weeks ago, a trio of cave fishers was established in this cave, but they mistakenly attacked a roaming roper, which easily killed two of them before moving on (see area 5).

Climbing the wall to the cave fisher's ledge requires a successful DC 15 Strength (Athletics) check. Scattered about the ledge is an assortment of coins (37 sp, 8 gp) and numerous broken weapons (mostly spears and arrows), plus two damaged (but still usable) shields, among a tangle of bones and other debris. After a few minutes of searching, a silver dagger (worth 50 gp) in a leather scabbard can be located. A more diligent search through this mess with a successful DC 20 Wisdom (Perception) check reveals a single aquamarine (worth 500 gp).

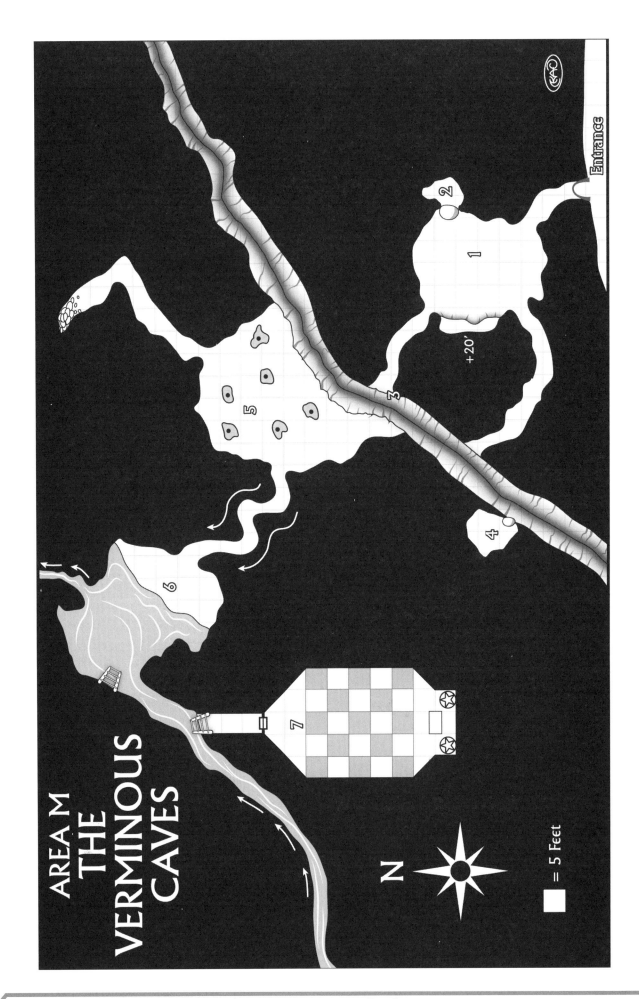

AREA M
THE
VERMINOUS
CAVES

Entrance

+20'

N

☐ = 5 Feet

AREA 2 – HIDDEN CHAMBER

DM Note: This hidden side chamber is concealed with a large rock so as to appear similar to a rock wall. It can be discovered with a successful DC 18 Wisdom (Perception) check, but moving the rock requires a successful DC 20 Strength (Athletics) check, although a second character can help with this check.

Pushing the rock aside reveals a small chamber perhaps 10 feet in diameter. About half of the chamber is stockpiled with numerous glass bottles; several are broken, but many are still intact.

This is the long forgotten hidden cache of bottled rum stashed here by a local band of bandits. The bandits were eventually brought to justice, but the stash has remained hidden for decades. A heavy coat of dust now covers all the bottles. Several bottles have broken, but 57 are still intact. Of these, 41 had poor seals, and the contents have since evaporated. These glass bottles, each holding about a gallon, are old and although fragile would likely fetch 4 gp each due to their age. More importantly, these bottles could be used as an air source in area 6 to discover and traverse the submerged passage. The remaining 16 bottles all contain fine quality aged rum. Each of these is worth 12 gp for the contents and the bottle.

AREA 3 – THE CREVASSE

A natural crevasse bisects the upper caves from the lower caves in this system. The crevasse runs from the northeast roughly to the southwest, and is about 15 to 20 feet wide at a given location. The crevasse is about 40 feet deep and it stretches for hundreds of feet in either direction. The bottom is dry, although covered with bat guano, and can be traversed easily.

There are two passages that lead to the crevasse. The northern passage leads to another cavern (area 5), that is about 10 feet lower than the current elevation. The southern passage just terminates at the crevasse. The crevasse can be climbed with a successful DC 10 Strength (Athletics) check on either side due to the numerous handholds.

Dozens of **giant cave crickets** (see appendix B) dwell in the crevasse, as it serves as a breeding ground. As the characters pass through the crevasse, they encounter 2d4 giant cave crickets, but these behave similarly to the ones in area 1. The crevasse is also home to several thousand bats. Any loud noise has a 25% to rouse a portion of the bat colony. This creates 1d3 **swarms of bats** that attack

creatures (and could also incite the giant cave crickets to attack while fleeing). Again, the bats simply want to escape the cave system, so the swarms disperse after 4 rounds.

The southern passage actually leads to a set of stone steps cunningly chiseled into the wall of the crevasse. These steps can be discovered with a DC 22 Wisdom (Perception) check, and can be used to safely get to the bottom of the crevasse without a skill check. These were crafted centuries ago when an evil priest was entombed nearby (area 4).

AREA 4 – SEALED TOMB

This rough natural chamber is concealed behind a massive rock. It requires a successful DC 20 Wisdom (Perception) check to locate, but also requires a successful DC 20 Strength (Athletics) check to move the rock. A second character can help with this check. The rock is engraved with a rune of chaos, signifying a slumbering evil. A successful DC 12 Intelligence (Arcana) or Intelligence (Religion) check reveals the meaning of the rune.

Pushing back the rock reveals a dusty natural cavern perhaps 10 feet in diameter. The air is stale and the stench of death permeates your nostrils most foul. Two piercing red pinpoints of light flicker, as a rotting corpse adorned in rusting chain mail and a tattered tabard steps into the light. With an unholy smile, the unliving humanoid hefts a black iron mace.

Several hundred years ago, an evil sect of priests arrived at the caves searching for the hidden temple of chaos. Led by their cruel master, fond of inflicting pain and torture on the under clergy in the name of his chaotic god, they spent weeks searching the area and caves to no avail. Finally the under priests grew weary of the cruel treatment and broken promises of finding the temple. They betrayed and slaughtered the priest, pushing him to his doom into this crevasse. Fearing retribution from beyond the grave (they were correct), the clergy hastily entombed the priest and placed a massive rock to seal his body in. Little did they know, the temple they sought was nearby (area 7).

The priest was never properly interred, and thus has risen as an undead monstrosity called a **coffer corpse** (see appendix B). The creature appears to be a zombie, and still wears its chain mail armor and carries its magical mace. It attacks a few times with the mace before discarding it in favor of strangling creatures to death. It fights until destroyed. If turned, it cowers in the back of its tomb.

Its armor is damaged, but still affords some protection. Its weapon is a *black mace* (see appendix A). Discarded in the tomb is an adamantine unholy symbol set with three tiny rubies (worth 250 gp, but only to an evil buyer). The rubies could be pried out and are worth 50 gp each.

AREA 5 – THE HATCHERY

This chamber is about 40 feet in diameter with a ceiling perhaps 20 feet overhead. The ceiling is covered with stalactites, some a few inches long to others a few feet long. The air here is moist and the walls glisten with condensation. Lichen, mold, and fungus adorn most surfaces. The floor is uneven, and several large stalagmite columns are scattered about, a few nearly reaching the ceiling. Several giant cave crickets mill about, grazing on the rocky surfaces.

Each time the characters enter this cavern 1d6 + 1 **giant cave crickets** (see appendix B) are present, but they scatter, quickly retreating to the crevasse for protection. But more return in a few minutes, attracted by the abundant fungal growth on the walls and ceiling.

A few weeks ago, a wandering roper deposited a clutch of eggs in this chamber, due to the warm, moist conditions, and the bountiful food sources in the form of both bats and giant cave crickets. Now the larval form of the roper, a clutch of piercers, inhabits the chamber while gorging on the giant cave crickets as they hone their skills at ambush. There are 14 **piercers** in this cavern, but at any given time, only a maximum of eight are hanging on the ceiling ready to attack. The others are slowly en route from the floor to the ceiling, a journey that takes a few hours. These use their False Appearance trait to hide from sight. Since the ceiling is about 20 feet high, a drop attack by one of these piercers causes 7 (2d6) piercing damage.

The northern passage meanders for nearly 100 feet before ending in a pile of rubble. If the DM desires to expand this portion of the adventure, this would make a fine location. The other passage slopes down to area 6.

Development. If the characters defeat the eight piercers and return through this cavern at least an hour later, 1d4 + 2 more piercers are on the ceiling ready to attack.

AREA 6 – PARTIALLY SUBMERGED CAVERN

The sloping passage descends with several twists and turns all the while becoming more humid. The passage terminates at a low cavern about 30 feet wide. Your light source reflects off the placid surface of the water that occupies most of the chamber. Only the sound of random drips from the ceiling can be heard.

The pool of water is cool, clear, and fed by an underground stream (as depicted on the map) plus a few springs. The water is shallow (less than 5 feet deep) near the ledge, but gradually deepens to about 20 feet as one moves to the northwest. Several large blind cave fish lazily swim about the water. When the characters first arrive, 1d3 **giant cave crickets** (see appendix B) are here, but they generally avoid this chamber due to the predator that lurks in the water.

The pool is inhabited by a **giant crayfish** (see appendix B). Currently it hides in the shallow water (getting advantage on its Dexterity (Stealth) check, since it is completely submerged). If any creatures (including giant cave crickets) wander within 5 feet of the edge of the pool, the giant crayfish attacks with surprise, bursting out of the water. Once the giant crayfish grabs a creature, it seeks to flee to the deep end of the pool to finish its meal.

At the deep end of the pool along the west wall is a metal ladder that extends about 5 feet above the water's surface. The ladder can be spotted with a successful DC 18 Wisdom (Perception) check from the shoreline, but anyone who enters the water or gets closer to the ladder makes this check at advantage. The ladder is affixed to the stone wall and descends 15 feet to a submerged 5-foot-high passage that leads to the southwest. Along this corridor are metal rungs set into the ceiling and walls to make passage easier. About 25 feet down the passage there is another ladder (easily found) that goes up about 30 feet. This ladder leads to a dry corridor and eventually to area 7. Meanwhile, the underground stream continues to the southwest. Note that characters desiring to traverse this submerged passage need to hold their breath (see Player's Handbook, p. 183) although the empty bottles in area 2 would be very useful as an air supply. A magical light source would also be helpful.

Over the years, some incidental treasure has been discarded by victims (mostly humanoids) preyed on by the giant crayfish. For every 10 minutes spent searching the bottom of the pool, one of the following valuables might be found, assuming a successful Wisdom (Perception) check (DC is listed below) is made:

- Wisdom (Perception) DC 13: A halberd with an ivory head and a shaft wrapped with gorgon hide (worth 475 gp, although if used as a weapon only causes 1d6 slashing damage).

- Wisdom (Perception) DC 15: A rotting sack with 225 sp and 15 gp.

- Wisdom (Perception) DC 20: A gold necklace (worth 315 gp).

- Wisdom (Perception) DC 22: A leather pouch containing five small aquamarine gems (each worth 75 gp).

AREA 7 – THE HIDDEN TEMPLE OF CHAOS

A short 15-foot-long corridor leads to a sealed iron door. There is no handle, just three ivory squares each depicting a different stylistic rune. The ivory squares are set into a rectangle and it appears they can be slid into different orders.

The temple was a series of tests to determine the worthiness of the worshippers. The method to open the door is one such test. Before play begins, the DM should randomly determine several orders (at least 10) for the symbols. Each order is the way to unlock and unseal the door. But due to the chaotic nature of the lock, the order resets after each unsuccessful attempt. The runes are depicted below.

If the incorrect order is set, the door pulses with blue energy and all creatures within 5 feet of the door suffer 1 force damage. Caution: This can get frustrating for the players real fast. It is recommended that after several attempts (say six to 10), if the characters don't by chance select the correct order, they should "get it right" anyway. But make them earn it. The door lock can't be picked (since there is no lock), but a *knock* spell would open the portal. The iron door can be also be destroyed (AC 20, 25 hit points).

Once they open the door, continue:

The door opens to a large hall that widens to 25 feet. The ceiling is plain and smooth and is 25 feet overhead. At the far end of the room, about 40 feet from where you stand, is a stone altar, its surface a swirling morass of colors and shapes from purple to blue to green. Beyond the altar on the back wall are detailed bas relief sculptures of two warrior maidens, armored, helmed, and holding thin swords. The 25-foot-by-25-foot section of the floor between the door and the altar is fashioned with alternating black and white 5-foot squares, similar to a chess board.

This is an ancient temple dedicated to a long forgotten god of chaos. The evil of this unholy place is what attracts the evil humanoids and other evil clergy to the Caves. The evil clergy in cave area K (chapter 11) have been searching for this temple, still rumored to be near, but complacency has rendered them ineffectual in actually finding it.

The chess board floor is another chaotic trap designed to test the faithful that would dare worship here. Cross the floor and survive, and you were deemed worthy. Although the characters might deduce that the white and black squares have some significance, they do not. Stepping on either color square triggers a random effect each round. Roll 1d6 and consult the table below. If damage is indicated without a type, then roll on the second table to determine the type of damage.

D6	Effect
1	2 (1d4) damage
2	5 (2d4) damage
3	7 (3d4) damage
4	2 (1d4) thunder damage and deafened for 1 minute
5	2 (1d4) cold damage and stunned for 1 minute
6	2 (1d4) radiant damage and blinded for 1 minute

D4	Damage Type
1	Fire
2	Force
3	Necrotic
4	Psychic

There is no way to disable this trap, although the characters can avoid touching the floor via magic, climbing the walls, or jumping as normal.

The altar is carved from some mysterious type of rock infused with chaos. It changes colors and patterns by the minute in random fashion. If the altar is touched without delivering a short prayer to a god of chaos, it has a random effect on the target. Roll 2d6 and consult the table below.

2D6	Altar Effect
2	Lose 1 attribute point permanently.
3	Teleport to the middle black square of chess board.
4	Cursed: disadvantage on all saving throws for 1 week.
5-6	Cursed: disadvantage on all attack rolls for 1 day.
7-8	7 (2d6) necrotic damage and disadvantage on all skill checks for 1 hour.
9-10	Gain insight: advantage on next attack, skill check, or saving throw.
11	Heal 7 (2d6) hit points.
12	Gain 7 (2d6) temporary hit points.

Also, touching the altar in this fashion animates the two warrior maiden **caryatid columns** (see appendix B) that guard the altar. They spend an action transforming and stepping out of the stone wall. They focus attacks on those who touch the altar or are near it. They attempt to maneuver targets back onto the trapped floor, using a shove attack in place of a sword attack if need be. This is the caryatid column's Strength (Athletics) check contested by the target's Strength (Athletics) or Dexterity (Acrobatics) check. If the caryatid column wins, the target is shoved 5 feet away. The caryatid columns fight until destroyed, but don't pursue targets out the door.

N. THE WAY DOWN

If the characters take the time and effort to open up the boulder-filled passage in cave area J (chapter 11, area 51), they can discover a 20-foot-wide passage carved into the rock that heads southwest. The passage eventually leads to the Cave of the Unknown, which can be Quasqueton (chapter 6, area 53) or an area designed by the DM. A side route leads off deeper into the Underdark, should the DM desire to expand the adventure.

There are several set encounter areas along this route as depicted on the map. It is likely the characters encounter a tribe of myconids that are being preyed on by an Underdark predator and have recently lost their sovereign. The myconids are cut off from their distant homeland by the predator and could use the characters' aid.

DM Note: There are wandering monsters in the main passage. For every 30 minutes the characters traverse these passages (or the route to the Underdark) there is a 1 in 6 chance for an encounter. If one occurs, roll on the table below to determine the creatures encountered and number appearing.

D6	Encounter
1	Myconid Sprouts (1d4 + 1)
2	Giant Rats (1d6 + 6)
3	Troglodytes (1d4 + 2)
4	Piercers (1d4 + 1)
5	Giant Spider (1)
6	Giant Fire Beetles (1d4 + 2)

GENERAL FEATURES

AREA 1 – GUARD POST

This passage guards the way to the Gloom Grove (area 2), recently settled by a wandering tribe of myconids (fungus men). The cavern beyond is moist, with a readily available supply of water via a small waterfall and stream, and a starter crop of fungus. But the newly established tribe has become cut off from its larger settlement in Underdark by a hook horror (see area 4). The horror frequents the grove to slaughter myconids, and recently defeated the tribe's sovereign. They have moved the remaining spore servants to this location to slow down the next attack.

Off the main passage is a side corridor perhaps 5 to 10 feet wide. The corridor is covered with fungus growing on the floor, the walls, and even stringy forms dangle from the ceiling.

Three **troglodyte spore servants** (see appendix B) hide in the fungus. If the corridor is entered, the spore servants seem to meld from the surrounding fungus and attack. Unarmed, they attack with reckless abandon using claw/claw/bite routines.

Development. During this battle, after a few rounds several myconid sprouts from area 2 arrive to observe. Once they determine the attack is not by the hook horror, they beckon the characters to follow them down the corridor, using their Rapport Spores action to communicate if needed.

AREA 2 – THE GLOOM GROVE

As you follow the corridor, the stench of organic rot increases, while the abundance of fungus on the ceiling and walls becomes more prolific. The corridor empties into a massive cavern with a vaulted ceiling. You are greeted by the twisted alien growth of fungus of a myriad of shapes and sizes. Some are a few inches high, while massive toadstools with tree-trunk-thick stems tower 10 feet high in scattered locations. The sound of crashing water betrays a nearby waterfall, likely feeding the gentle streams that zig-zag across the floor. Terraces to the north and east are covered with fungus, some of which appear to be cultivated in even rows. Several small fungus-like humanoids move about the fungus rows as if tending the growth.

This is the Gloom Grove, a natural cavern host to hundreds of types of fungi (as well as lichens, slimes, and molds). Recently settled by wandering myconids, although impressive, the growth is really just getting established. But the tribe has fallen on hard times, with frequent attacks by the hook horror and the recent death of their sovereign. Their numbers dwindle each week. All that remains are 26 **myconid sprouts** and eight **myconid adults**. These losses have disrupted the work, melding, and leadership of the tribe.

The myconids are not aggressive. They are no match for the hook horror, and see the characters as a means to an end. Several of the adults approach the characters and use their rapport spores to communicate. They explain their situation as best they can, and suggest the characters join in a meld with a circle of myconids. The melding is a form of relaxation, entertainment, and spiritual guidance. Depending on the results of the meld, the myconids might plea to the characters to defeat the hook horror.

If characters agree to participate in the meld, they sit in a circle and join hands with the myconids while spores are

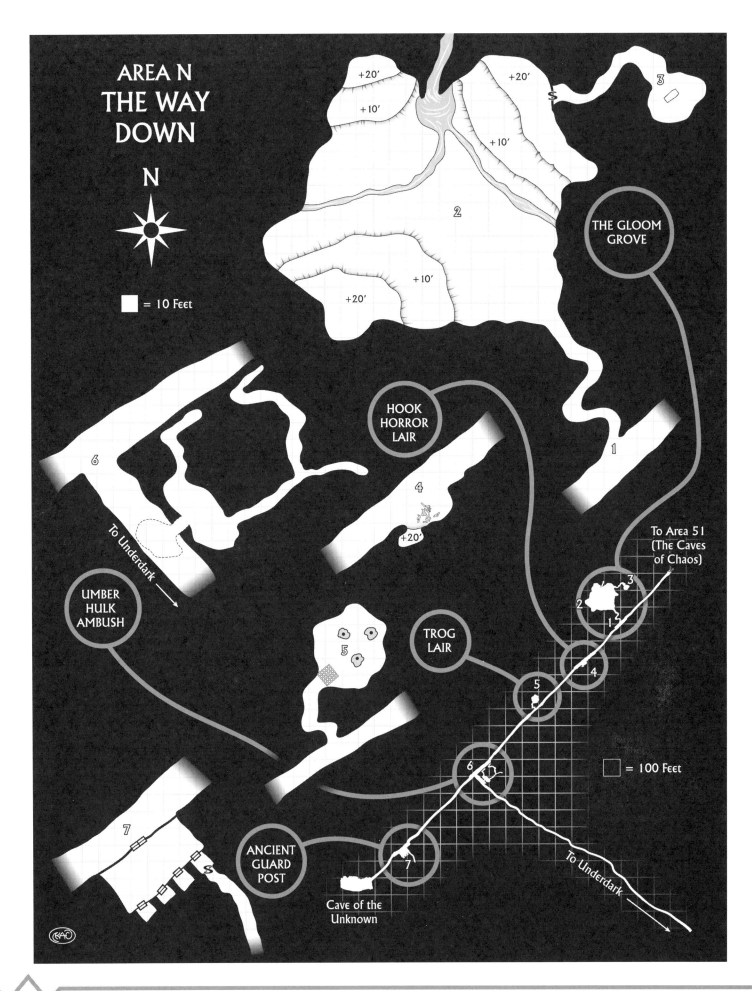

AREA N
THE WAY
DOWN

N

☐ = 10 Feet

+20'
+10'
+20'
+10'
+10'
2
+10'
+20'
+20'

S

3

THE GLOOM
GROVE

1

HOOK
HORROR
LAIR

4
+20'

6

To Underdark →

UMBER
HULK
AMBUSH

5

TROG
LAIR

To Area 51
(The Caves
of Chaos)

2
1
3

4

5

6

To Underdark

☐ = 100 Feet

7

S

ANCIENT
GUARD
POST

7

Cave of the
Unknown

released to pacify and communicate. Have each character make a DC 12 Constitution saving throw. Failure indicates a dream-like trance that lasts for 8 hours. During this time, characters get hints at campaign developments according to the DM's designs. These could include:

- Where the hook horror (or another powerful creature) lairs.

- How to get to another location, such as Quasqueton (chapter 6), the bandit lair at Raven Rock (chapter 10, area 3), the temple of evil chaos (chapter 11, area 58), the sealed tomb (cave area M, area 4), Zelligar's Sanctuary (chapter 7), or the nearby chamber of the crystal casket (area 3).

- Where a lost magic item can be found, such as the *black mace* in cave area M (area 4), the *+1 shield* in the spiders' lair (chapter 10, area 2), or the *elixirs of stone to flesh* in the stone hovel (chapter 10, area 13).

- A bit of lost knowledge, such as the name "Quasqueton," or a magic item command word.

Assuming the characters tolerate the melding, the myconids seem refreshed and energized. They lead the characters to the top eastern terrace of the cavern, and to the base of a large toadstool. At the base are the decaying remains of the sovereign. Near him are four fungal pots holding magic potions. These include two *potions of climbing*, a *potion of greater healing*, and a *potion of heroism*. These potions are bestowed upon the characters to aid in their quest. If a character makes a successful DC 15 Wisdom (Perception) check, he notices that the stone wall is a slightly different color in one section. This conceals the passage to area 3.

Development. If the hook horror is not defeated in the next 3 weeks, the entire myconid tribe is wiped out. If defeated, the tribe flourishes and expands to over 100 members in 6 months with a new sovereign. The myconids remain friendly with the characters, and could be a useful resource should they decide to explore the depths of the Underdark.

AREA 3 – HIDDEN CHAMBER

An ancient secret door blocks entrance to this cave. It can be detected with a successful DC 15 Wisdom (Perception) check. It is easily opened by placing pressure in the correct location.

The air in this chamber is somewhat drier and stale. The passage winds about, gradually sloping upward. After about 70 feet the corridor ends in a small natural cavern bathed in light. The chamber is about 25 feet in diameter with a 10-foot-high but uneven ceiling. The light emits from a dazzling sight: a crystal coffin resting on the floor. Although coated with dust, the contents are still visible. Resting on red silk pillows is a comely female elf wearing a pure

white gown. A platinum tiara is nestled into her flowing blonde hair, adorned with wildflowers. Her delicate facial features depict a peaceful smile.

Centuries ago, for long-forgotten reasons, this crystal casket was hidden in this chamber and sealed away from the prying eyes of greedy humans and humanoids. The casket itself is very valuable (worth 7,500 gp) and enchanted with a *continual flame* spell. However, the casket (empty) weighs nearly 200 pounds, and is in fact fragile (10 hit points).

An **iron cobra** (see appendix B) has been left to guard the crystal casket. Although the construct has maximum hit points (16) it is ancient and has not aged well. It makes all attacks at disadvantage due to rust damage. Likewise, although its poison bite is still deadly its effect is reduced. A successful bite only causes 7 (2d6) poison damage, and all saving throws against the poison are made at advantage.

The casket is locked and requires a *knock* spell or thieves' tools and a successful DC 20 Dexterity check to unlock. Although the casket appears to contain a slumbering elven princess (and it might), the DM is encouraged to determine the contents of the casket based on his campaign. Here are a few suggested ideas:

- The elven princess is an *illusion*. When the casket is opened poisonous gas is released in a 15-foot-diameter cloud. Those within the cloud must make a DC 16 Constitution saving throw, or suffer 14 (4d6) poison damage and is poisoned for 4 hours. A successful saving throw reduces the damage by half.

- The elven princess is real (her name is Ellespeth), cursed to an eternal slumber. The DM needs to determine how to break the curse, but it should be a quest onto itself. In this case the platinum tiara is also real (worth 1,750 gp).

- The elven princess is a **succubus** using its Shapechanger trait to appear as the elven princess Ellespeth. She tries to befriend the characters before betraying them at an optimal time and place.

- The elven princess is an *illusion* and opening the casket detonates a magical fire trap. The trap causes 21 (6d6) fire damage to everything in the entire chamber. Creatures that make a successful DC 14 Dexterity saving throw suffer half damage.

- The elven princess is real, but she has been dead for centuries. An *illusion* conceals her skeletal remains. Anyone opening the casket is *cursed* (disadvantage on all Dexterity skill checks and saving throws for 1 year plus 1 day).

- The elven princess is an *illusion* and opening the casket triggers a *glyph of warding* that casts a *conjure elemental* spell. This summons an **air elemental** which attacks until destroyed.

AREA 4 – HOOK HORROR LAIR

Characters traveling down the main passage might bypass this area altogether. However, the myconids (see area 2) can inform the characters of this location either via the melding process or by sending a guide (a myconid sprout) with them.

The main passage widens slightly along the southern wall. A pile of bleached bones, most of them broken, lies in a jumbled mess by the wall.

Only the pile of bones betrays the location of the hook horror's lair. But it does not reside at the corridor level. Instead, it has found a ledge, about 15 feet in diameter, located about 30 feet above the corridor. The bones are discarded once picked clean of all the meat and marrow. Climbing the wall is quite easy, requiring only a successful DC 15 Strength (Athletics) check. There is a 75% chance the **hook horror** is present on the ledge. Otherwise, it is out hunting the main corridor (and at the DM's discretion, could be encountered as a wandering monster).

If present, there is a good chance the hook horror detects the characters with its blindsight (60-foot range) and Keen Hearing. It has three large rocks in its lair which it can push off the ledge as an action, at targets climbing the wall: +3 to hit, 7 (2d6) bludgeoning damage on a hit, and the target must make a successful DC 15 Strength saving throw or lose their grip and fall (suffering standard falling damage based on height). The hook horror prefers to let creatures come to it, but if they flee or refuse to climb the wall, it climbs down the wall to pursue. If encountered in its lair, it fights to the death. If encountered outside of its lair, it fights until reduced to 15 or fewer hit points. At that point it retreats back to its ledge to lick its wounds.

On the ledge is a nest of burlap, cloth, and fungus. Hidden in the nest are the following items, all quite easily found: 111 sp, 34 gp, a small silver mirror with an electrum handle (worth 65 gp), a broken gold necklace (worth 75 gp), and seven random gems (2 x 10 gp, 2 x 25 gp, 2 x 50 gp, 100 gp).

AREA 5 – TROGLODYTE LAIR

A small 5-foot-wide passage leads north away from the main corridor. As you trek down the passage the fetid stench of the swamp becomes stronger and stronger. The passage ends in a cavern perhaps 40 feet across. Several large stalagmites, some as tall as a human, occupy the chamber.

This cavern is the lair for a band of seven **troglodytes**. They have rigged a net trap (covered with fine rocks to conceal it) at the entrance to the chamber. It requires a successful DC 20 Wisdom (Perception) check to discover the net trap before it is manually sprung. A pair of troglodytes behind a nearby stalagmite hoists the rope to set the trap. Any creatures in the 10-foot-by-10-foot section of the floor at the entrance must make a successful DC 15 Dexterity saving throw or become restrained by the net. The troglodytes continue to hoist the following round, suspending the net and restrained targets about 5 feet off the floor. After springing the trap, the other five troglodytes throw javelins (they each have three; +4 to hit, range 30/120 ft., 1d6 + 2 piercing damage) at random targets, including those in the net. The troglodytes hang back, using the stalagmites as half cover waiting for intruders to come to them. Once the two manning the net trap tie off the rope, they grab javelins and charge the net, leading with javelin thrusts at restrained targets. The troglodytes fight until five of them are disabled or defeated. The remaining troglodytes attempt to flee or surrender as appropriate.

This wandering band has accumulated a fair amount of wealth. In addition to the javelins, each troglodyte carries 2d6 gp. Hidden in a recess along the northern wall is a cavity covered with a rock, that requires a successful DC 18 Wisdom (Perception) check to find. Inside are two sacks; the first one contains 255 sp, while the second is actually a *bag of holding* that contains 1,345 sp, an ivory coffer (worth 125 gp) storing two clay vials (each holds two doses of *Keoghtom's ointment*), and a *ring of warmth*.

AREA 6 – UMBER HULK AMBUSH

DM Note: This is a very dangerous encounter for 1st- to 3rd-level characters. But the creature here involuntarily is guarding the route to the Underdark, and if the DM wishes to have the characters explore the dangers of the Underdark, he should consider reducing the challenge of this encounter appropriately. Perhaps the umber hulk is away hunting, or is wounded from a recent scruff with the hook horror.

An **umber hulk** has tunneled behind the main corridor in two spots, to within a few inches of the passage. Using its tremorsense, it waits for creatures to pass near the thin wall, at which point it bursts through with a shower of rocky debris. The next round it attacks with fury and creatures are likely to be affected by its Confusing Gaze.

The corridor splits just past the ambush site, continuing to the southwest (to area 7, plus eventually to the Cave of the Unknown). The passage heading to the southeast leads to the Underdark, and the DM is encouraged to expand the adventure in this direction, should he desire. The umber hulk has also tunneled under the corridor in this spur toward the route to Underdark. If it springs its ambush here, the attacked creature suffers 3 (1d6) bludgeoning damage from falling through the floor, and must make a successful DC 13 Constitution saving throw or be stunned for 1 round and land prone.

The passages and carved cavern comprise the umber hulk's lair. The floor is covered with rocky debris from the tunneling process so most of this area is considered difficult terrain. With a successful DC 15 Wisdom (Perception) check, the umber hulk's treasure can be found under a pile of loose rock debris tucked in a corner. It consists of 37 shards of blue quartz (each worth 25 gp), an iron scroll tube holding two *spell scrolls* (*fireball* and *flaming sphere*), and a *+1 spear head*. The spear head lacks a shaft. If a craftsman mounts the head on a suitable shaft, it becomes a functional *+1 spear*.

AREA 7 – ANCIENT GUARD POST

Along the southern wall is an iron door. It appears to be locked.

Zelligar and Rogahn (see chapter 6) insisted that a guard room be established in the main corridor, and they had a group of skeletons manning the post. (If the DM decides something other than Quasqueton comprises the Cave of the Unknown, then other suitable masters should be substituted here.) The room has been sealed for decades, but if the characters open the door, the skeletal guards are ready to attack. The door is locked, and can be picked with thieves' tools and a successful DC 15 Dexterity check. Otherwise, the door can be forced with a successful DC 22 Strength (Athletics) check, or destroyed with weapon blows (AC 19, 20 hit points). Both of these actions alert the skeletons, which prepare for battle.

Inside the room are 10 **skeletons**, each wearing damaged chain mail (AC 15) and wielding a pair of scimitars with Multiattack (+4 to hit, 1d6 + 2 slashing damage for each attack). The skeletons fight until destroyed. If the characters took more than 3 rounds to open the door, the skeletons burst out with surprise, spilling into the corridor to maneuver. Otherwise, they wait until a creature enters before attacking.

The chamber is about 40 feet wide by 25 feet deep. Aside from a cask full of warped (useless) arrows, a dozen broken shortbows, and a large whetstone, the chamber is empty. There are four lockable iron doors, each leading to a 5-foot-square cell. The keys are nowhere to be found, although all doors are currently unlocked. The northernmost cell has a secret door that can be located with a successful DC 23 Wisdom (Perception) check. Beyond the door is a corridor that winds for several hundred feet gradually climbing all the while. It eventually leads to the outside, although the exit is blocked by a massive rock that requires a successful DC 22 Strength (Athletics) check to move.

Aside from the weapons and armor, the skeletons carry no treasure.

APPENDIX A
New Magic Items & Spells

AMULET OF PROTECTION FROM GOOD

Wondrous item, uncommon (requires attunement)

This iron charm is affixed to a black leather cord. The disc-like amulet is shaped like a beastly maw with licking flames emitting from the mouth.

Once attuned to the device, the wearer is under the constant effects of a variant form of the *protection from good and evil* spell. Good-aligned creatures attack the bearer at disadvantage, and the wearer is immune to charm, fright, or possession by them.

BLACK MACE

Weapon (mace), uncommon

This magical mace is favored by evil priests or cultists. The weapon has a handle of ebonywood (or is stained black) and a black iron head. The wielder gains a +1 bonus to attack and damage rolls. Against good-aligned creatures, the wielder can re-roll any damage result of a 1, but must take the second roll.

BROWN BAG OF TRICKS

Wondrous item, uncommon

This ordinary bag, composed of brown cloth, functions exactly like a *bag of tricks* (see Dungeon Master's Guide, p. 154), but the animals pulled from this bag are all burrowing in nature.

D8	Creature
1	Armadillo (see appendix B)
2	Badger
3	Rat
4	Weasel
5	Giant Armadillo (see appendix B)
6	Giant Badger
7	Giant Rat
8	Giant Weasel

CURSED BLADE

Weapon (any sword), uncommon

When removed from its scabbard, this blade glows pale yellow, equivalent to dim light in a 10-foot radius. A character that wields this sword gains a +1 bonus to attack and damage rolls. However, the blade is cursed, which is revealed only in the heat of battle.

Curse. Despite the bonus to hit (and damage) all weapon attacks with a cursed blade are made at disadvantage. This can be revealed with the use of an *identify* spell. The cursed blade can't be willingly discarded until the character is the recipient of a *remove curse* spell or similar magic.

DRAGON MASK, MINOR

Wondrous item, rare (requires attunement)

This mask is covered with scales and depicts the typical features of a chromatic dragon. These masks are often adorned with bone horns, feathers, or even gems. Once attuned to a particular mask, the wearer gains damage resistance and a minor breath weapon; the type depends on the mask's color.

Breath Weapon (Recharge 6). The mask wearer can use an action to exhale a draconic breath weapon, causing 3d8 points of damage. The range is a 5-foot-by-30-foot line effect (for black and blue masks) or a 15-foot cone (for green, red, and white masks), and the damage type is determined by the mask's color. A target can attempt a DC 12 Dexterity saving throw to reduce the damage to half.

Color	Damage/Resistance Type
Black	Acid
Blue	Lightning
Green	Poison
Red	Fire
White	Cold

ELIXIR OF STONE TO FLESH

Potion, rare

This syrupy oil is typically stored in a clay or stone pot. If the oil is liberally applied (one dose is enough for a Medium-sized creature) to a creature that has been turned to stone (such as by the petrifying gaze of a medusa), the petrification effect ends, and the target is returned to flesh.

HELM OF OPPOSITE ALIGNMENT

Wondrous item, uncommon

This appears to be a typical metal cap or helm. It radiates a faint magical dweomer. If held and examined for more than a few moments, a creature must succeed on a DC 15 Wisdom saving throw, or place the helm on its head, triggering the curse.

Curse. Once a creature places the helm on its head, the curse takes effect immediately. The creature's alignment shifts to the radical opposite: good to evil, law to chaos, and neutral to an absolute commitment (LE, LG, CE, or CG). Unless a *remove curse* spell is cast within 10 minutes of placing the helm on its head, only a *wish* spell can break the enchantment, allowing the helm to be removed and returning the creature's alignment to its original state.

POTION OF LEVITATION

Potion, rare

When you drink this potion, you gain the effects of the *levitate* spell for 10 minutes (no concentration required). The potion's light blue fluid is carbonated and seems to be light and airy.

STAFF OF STONE

Staff, rare (requires attunement by a druid, sorcerer, or wizard)

This staff is about 6 feet long, and appears to be fashioned from a thin stony stalactite which glistens with moisture and has a ball-like head composed of glittery mica. Although it appears heavy and unwieldy, it's actually dry, cool to the touch, and quite light.

Once attuned to the device, the staff can be wielded as a magic quarterstaff that grants a +1 bonus to attack and damage rolls.

The staff has 21 charges that can be used to power the spells listed below. The staff regains 1d6 + 1 charges weekly as long as it is in contact with a stony surface. If the last charge is expended, roll 1d20. On a 1, the staff regains 1d6 + 1 charges. On a 2-4, the staff becomes inert for 1 day and loses 1d6 + 1 charges. On a 20, the staff crumbles and becomes a worthless pile of rubble.

Spells. While holding this staff and using an action, 1 or more of its charges can be used to cast one of the following spells, using your spell save DC and spell attack bonus: *blade ward* (1 charge), *passwall* (5 charges), *stone shape* (4 charges), or *wall of stone* (5 charges).

NEW SPELLS

DIRECTIONAL CONFUSION

5th-level enchantment

Casting Time: 1 hour
Range: 120 feet
Components: V, S, M (a lodestone and a powdered gem worth 500 gp, which the spell consumes)
Duration: Until dispelled

This spell of confusion is typically placed on a small labyrinth or series of dungeon corridors, to assault and twist a creature's sense of direction. Each creature that enters the 120-foot radius sphere enchanted with this spell is required to make a Wisdom saving throw. Success indicates the creature is immune to the effects of this casting of the spell for 1 hour. Failure results in the loss of all sense of direction: right becomes confused with left, north and south become mixed up, etc. The DM should randomly determine which direction a creature goes despite its instructions, even if the random direction doesn't make sense—such is the enchantment.

After every 10 minutes spent in the area of effect, a creature can attempt another Wisdom saving throw.

FRIGHT

1st-level illusion

Casting Time: 1 action
Range: Touch
Components: V, S, M (a pinch of grave dirt)
Duration: Concentration, up to 1 minute

Your touch can project a horrid image. Make a melee spell attack against a creature. On a hit, the target must make a successful Wisdom saving throw, or drop whatever it is holding and become frightened for the duration of the spell.

When frightened, the creature must take the Dash action and move away from the caster by the safest available route on each of its turns, unless there is nowhere to move. If the creature ends its turn in a location where it doesn't have line of sight, it can attempt another Wisdom saving throw. On a successful saving throw the spell ends for that creature.

GREATER CONTINGENCY

8th-level evocation

Casting Time: 10 minutes
Range: Self
Components: V, S, M (a statuette of yourself in carved ivory or a precious metal and decorated with gems worth at least 5,000 gp)
Duration: 30 days

This spell functions exactly as a *contingency* spell, except (and as noted above) the contingent spell can be any spell of 7th level or lower with a casting time 1 action and that can target you.

NECROTIC BOLT

1st-level evocation

Casting Time: 1 action
Range: 120 feet
Components: V, S
Duration: 1 round

An inky bolt of darkness streaks toward a creature within range. Make a ranged spell attack against the target. On a hit, the target takes 3d6 necrotic damage and a brief wave of enervation sweeps over the target. The target makes its next attack at disadvantage, assuming it occurs before the end of your next turn.

APPENDIX B
New Monsters

ADEPT

Medium humanoid (human), chaotic evil

AC: 18 (plate)

Hit Points: 11 (2d8 + 2)

Speed: 20 ft.

STR	DEX	CON	INT	WIS	CHA
10 (+0)	10 (+0)	12 (+1)	10 (+0)	14 (+2)	11 (+0)

Skills: Medicine +4, Religion +2

Senses: passive Perception 12

Languages: Common and any one language

Challenge: 1 (200 XP)

Special Equipment: The adept wears an *amulet of protection from good* (see appendix A).

Spellcasting: The adept is a 2nd-level spellcaster. Its spellcasting ability is Wisdom (spell save DC 12, +4 to hit with spell attacks). It has the following cleric spells prepared (an asterisked spell is from appendix A):

- Cantrips (at will): *light, resistance, sacred flame*
- 1st level (3 slots): *command, fright,* *inflict wounds, necrotic bolt**

ACTIONS

Mace: *Melee Weapon Attack:* +2 to hit, reach 5 ft., one target. *Hit:* 3 (1d6) bludgeoning damage.

AL-MI'RAJ (BLINK BUNNY)

Small fey, neutral

AC: 15 (natural armor)

Hit Points: 7 (2d6)

Speed: 40 ft., burrow 5 ft.

STR	DEX	CON	INT	WIS	CHA
6 (-2)	18 (+4)	11 (+0)	2 (-4)	14 (+2)	12 (+1)

Skills: Perception +4

Condition Immunities: charmed

Senses: darkvision 60 ft., passive Perception 14

Languages: -

Challenge: 1/4 (50 XP)

Keen Hearing: The al-mi'raj has advantage on all Wisdom (Perception) checks that rely on hearing.

ACTIONS

Horn: *Melee Weapon Attack:* +6 to hit, reach 5 ft., one target. *Hit:* 6 (1d4 + 4) piercing damage.

Teleport (Recharge 6): The al-mi'raj magically teleports itself to a location it is familiar with within 100 feet.

Covered with plush yellow fur, this hare-like creature is about 2 feet long. Its rodent-like head has oversized floppy ears, and a spiraled black horn, nearly as long as its body, protrudes from its brow.

ARACHNIA, GIANT WATER SPIDER

Large beast, unaligned

AC: 16 (natural armor)

Hit Points: 45 (6d10 + 12)

Speed: 40 ft., climb 40 ft., swim 20 ft.

STR	DEX	CON	INT	WIS	CHA
14 (+2)	18 (+4)	14 (+2)	7 (-2)	11 (+0)	4 (-3)

Skills: Stealth +8

Senses: blindsight 10 ft., darkvision 60 ft., passive Perception 13

Languages: -

Challenge: 2 (450 XP)

Hold Breath: Arachnia can hold her breath for 30 minutes using an air bubble affixed to the underside of her abdomen.

Spider Climb: Arachnia can climb difficult surfaces, including upside down on ceilings, without needing to make an ability check.

Water Sense: While in contact with water, Arachnia knows the exact location of any other creature in contact with the water within 100 feet.

Web Walker: Arachnia ignores movement restrictions caused by webbing.

ACTIONS

Bite: *Melee Weapon Attack:* +6 to hit, reach 5 ft., one creature. *Hit:* 11 (2d6 + 4) piercing damage, and the target must make a DC 12 Constitution saving throw, taking 10 (3d6) poison damage and becoming poisoned for 1 hour on a failed save. The target is paralyzed while poisoned in this way. Every 10 minutes, the target can attempt another saving throw to remove the poisoned condition.

ARMADILLO

Tiny beast, unaligned

AC: 14 (natural armor)

Hit Points: 3 (1d4 + 1)

Speed: 30 ft., burrow 10 ft.

STR	DEX	CON	INT	WIS	CHA
7 (-2)	12 (+1)	13 (+1)	2 (-4)	10 (+0)	6 (-2)

Senses: darkvision 30 ft., passive Perception 10

Languages: -

Challenge: 0 (0 XP)

Keen Smell: The armadillo has advantage on Wisdom (Perception) checks that rely on smell.

ACTIONS

Claws: *Melee Weapon Attack:* +0 to hit, reach 5 ft., one target. *Hit:* 1 slashing damage.

An armadillo is a small (2-foot-long) burrowing mammal with reticulated armor plates covering most of its gray body.

AWAKENED VAMPIRIC SHRUB

Small plant, unaligned

AC: 10

Hit Points: 14 (4d6)

Speed: 10 ft.

STR	DEX	CON	INT	WIS	CHA
3 (-4)	10 (+0)	11 (+0)	10 (+0)	10 (+0)	6 (-2)

Damage Vulnerabilities: fire

Damage Resistances: piercing

Senses: passive Perception 10

Languages: understands Common but can't speak

Challenge: 1/8 (25 XP)

ACTIONS

Tendril: *Melee Weapon Attack:* +2 to hit, reach 10 ft., one creature. *Hit:* The target is grappled (escape DC 12). While grappled, the target is restrained and subject to Blood Drain.

Blood Drain: At the start of each of the shrub's turns, it drains 5 (1d6 + 2) hit points from a grappled target. The shrub gains temporary hit points equal to the damage inflicted.

The dark green stems of this plant are crawling vines that occur among other plant growth. Tiny rose-like flowers are white, until it feeds. As it drains blood, the flowers turn crimson.

BAILIFF OF THE OUTER BAILEY

Medium humanoid (human), neutral

AC: 19 (*+1 plate*)

Hit Points: 26 (4d8 + 8)

Speed: 20 ft.

STR	DEX	CON	INT	WIS	CHA
14 (+2)	12 (+1)	15 (+2)	10 (+0)	11 (+0)	11 (+0)

Skills: Perception +2

Senses: passive Perception 12

Languages: Common and any one language

Challenge: 1/2 (100 XP)

ACTIONS

+1 Longsword: *Melee Weapon Attack:* +5 to hit, reach 5 ft., one target. *Hit:* 7 (1d8 + 3) slashing damage, or 8 (1d10 + 3) slashing damage if used with two hands.

Longbow: *Ranged Weapon Attack:* +3 to hit, range 150/600 ft., one target. *Hit:* 5 (1d8 + 1) piercing damage.

BARBARIAN WARRIOR

Medium humanoid (human), any chaotic alignment

AC: 13 (hide armor)

Hit Points: 15 (2d8 + 6)

Speed: 30 ft.

STR	DEX	CON	INT	WIS	CHA
16 (+3)	12 (+1)	16 (+3)	7 (-2)	10 (+0)	9 (-1)

Senses: passive Perception 10

Languages: Common

Challenge: 1/4 (50 XP)

Rage: Once per day, a barbarian warrior can enter a rage that lasts for 1 minute. While raging, a barbarian warrior has advantage on Strength checks and Strength saving throws, +2 damage on melee weapon attacks using Strength, and resistance to bludgeoning, piercing, and slashing damage.

ACTIONS

Spear: *Melee or Ranged Weapon Attack:* +5 to hit, reach 5 ft. or range 20/60 ft., one target. *Hit:* 6 (1d6 + 3) piercing damage, or 7 (1d8 + 3) piercing damage if used with two hands to make a melee attack.

A hulking brute of a warrior, adorned with layers of hide armor and leather, he hefts a spear. His bloodshot eyes and aggressive posture reveal his intent.

BONE GOLEM

Medium construct, unaligned

AC: 17 (natural armor)

Hit Points: 38 (7d8 + 7)

Speed: 30 ft.

STR	DEX	CON	INT	WIS	CHA
14 (+2)	10 (+0)	12 (+1)	1 (-5)	10 (+0)	1 (-5)

Damage Resistances: piercing, slashing

Damage Immunities: cold, fire, lightning, poison, psychic

Condition Immunities: blinded, charmed, deafened, exhaustion, frightened, paralyzed, petrified, poisoned

Senses: blindsight 60 ft., darkvision 60 ft., passive Perception 10

Languages: -

Challenge: 2 (450 XP)

ACTIONS

Multiattack: The golem makes four attacks if wielding weapons one-handed, or two attacks if wielding weapons two-handed.

Longsword: *Melee Weapon Attack:* +4 to hit, reach 5 ft., one target. *Hit:* 6 (1d8 + 2) slashing damage, or 7 (1d10 + 2) slashing damage if used with two hands.

Cobbled together with ill-fitting bones of various sizes and shapes, this bone-like humanoid moves with swift grace that belies its bony structure. It sports four mismatched arms, each wielding a battered longsword.

BROOM OF ANIMATED ATTACK

Small construct, unaligned

AC: 15 (natural armor)

Hit Points: 17 (5d6)

Speed: 0 ft., fly 50 ft. (hover)

STR	DEX	CON	INT	WIS	CHA
10 (+0)	17 (+3)	10 (+0)	1 (-5)	5 (-3)	1 (-5)

Damage Immunities: poison, psychic

Condition Immunities: blinded, charmed, deafened, exhaustion, frightened, paralyzed, petrified, poisoned, prone

Senses: blindsight 30 ft. (blind beyond this radius), passive Perception 7

Languages: -

Challenge: 1/4 (50 XP)

Antimagic Susceptibility: The broom is incapacitated while in the area of an *antimagic field*. If targeted by *dispel magic*, the broom must succeed on a Constitution saving throw against the caster's spell save DC or fall unconscious for 1 minute.

Constructed Nature: The broom doesn't require air, food, drink, or sleep.

The magic that animates the broom is dispelled when the construct drops to 0 hit points. A broom reduced to 0 hit points becomes inanimate and is too damaged to be of much use or value to anyone.

False Appearance: While the broom remains motionless and isn't flying, it is indistinguishable from a normal broom.

Flying Broom: Some brooms of animated attack allow their creators to ride them, in which case they behave like typical *brooms of flying*. A broom of animated attack, however, can carry only half the weight that a *broom of flying* can (see chapter 7, "Treasure," of the Dungeon Master's Guide).

ACTIONS

Multiattack: The broom makes two melee attacks.

Broomstick: *Melee Weapon Attack:* +5 to *hit,* reach 5 ft., one target. Hit: 5 (1d4 + 3) bludgeoning damage.

REACTIONS

Animated Attack: If the broom is motionless and a creature grabs hold of it, the broom makes a Dexterity check contested by the creature's Strength check. If the broom wins the contest, it flies out of the creature's grasp and makes a melee attack against it with advantage on the attack roll.

CAPTAIN OF THE WATCH

Medium humanoid (human), neutral

AC: 18 (plate)

Hit Points: 39 (6d8 + 12)

Speed: 30 ft.

STR	DEX	CON	INT	WIS	CHA
15 (+2)	12 (+1)	13 (+1)	10 (+0)	11 (+0)	11 (+0)

Skills: Perception +2

Senses: passive Perception 12

Languages: Common and any one language

Challenge: 1 (200 XP)

ACTIONS

Multiattack: The captain makes two longsword attacks. If it has a dagger drawn, it can also make a dagger attack.

+2 Longsword: *Melee Weapon Attack:* +6 to hit, reach 5 ft., one target. *Hit:* 8 (1d8 + 4) slashing damage.

+1 Dagger: *Melee or Ranged Weapon Attack:* +5 to hit, reach 5 ft. or range 20/60 ft., one target. *Hit:* 5 (1d4 + 3) piercing damage.

CARYATID COLUMN

Medium construct, unaligned

AC: 15 (natural armor)

Hit Points: 22 (4d8 + 4)

Speed: 20 ft.

STR	DEX	CON	INT	WIS	CHA
16 (+3)	12 (+1)	13 (+1)	3 (-4)	11 (+0)	8 (-1)

Damage Resistances: bludgeoning, piercing, and slashing from nonmagical attacks

Damage Immunities: poison, psychic

Condition Immunities: blinded, charmed, deafened, frightened, paralyzed, petrified, poisoned

Senses: darkvision 120 ft., passive Perception 10

Languages: -

Challenge: 1 (200 XP)

False Appearance: While the caryatid column remains motionless, it is indistinguishable from an inanimate statue.

Innate Resistance: A caryatid column makes all saving throws at advantage.

Stony Body: Any manufactured weapon that hits a caryatid column has a base 25% chance of breaking, rendering it useless. For every "plus" of a magic weapon, this chance is reduced by 5%. Therefore, a *+4 longsword* would only have a 5% chance of breaking on each hit.

ACTIONS

Longsword: *Melee Weapon Attack:* +5 to hit, reach 5 ft., one target. *Hit:* 7 (1d8 + 3) slashing damage, or 8 (1d10 + 3) slashing damage if used with two hands.

The stony column transforms into a fleshy female humanoid with fair, porcelain-like skin. With surprising agility, the feminine form advances, brandishing a previously hidden slim sword. Although its large eyes are emotionless, grim determination is etched on her smooth facial features.

CAVE FISHER

Medium monstrosity, unaligned

AC: 16 (natural armor)

Hit Points: 58 (9d8 + 18)

Speed: 20 ft., climb 20 ft.

STR	DEX	CON	INT	WIS	CHA
16 (+3)	13 (+1)	14 (+2)	3 (-4)	10 (+0)	3 (-4)

Skills: Perception +2, Stealth +5

Senses: blindsight 60 ft., passive Perception 12

Languages: -

Challenge: 3 (700 XP)

Adhesive Filament: The cave fisher can use its action to extend a sticky filament up to 60 feet, and the filament adheres to anything that touches it. A creature adhered to the filament is grappled by the cave fisher (escape DC 13), and ability checks made to escape this grapple have disadvantage. The filament can be attacked (AC 15; 5 hit points; immunity to poison and psychic damage), but a weapon that fails to sever it becomes stuck to it, requiring an action and a successful DC 13 Strength check to pull free. Destroying the filament deals no damage to the cave fisher, which can extrude a replacement filament on its next turn.

Flammable Blood: If the cave fisher drops to half its hit points or fewer, it gains vulnerability to fire damage.

Spider Climb: The cave fisher can climb difficult surfaces, including upside down on ceilings, without needing to make an ability check.

ACTIONS

Multiattack: The cave fisher makes two attacks with its claws.

Claw: *Melee Weapon Attack:* +5 to hit, reach 5 ft., one target. *Hit:* 10 (2d6 + 3) slashing damage.

Filament: One creature grappled by the cave fisher's adhesive filament must make a DC 13 Strength saving throw, provided that the target weighs 200 pounds or less. On a failure, the target is pulled into an unoccupied space within 5 feet of the cave fisher, and the cave fisher makes a claw attack against it as a bonus action. Reeling up the target releases anyone else who was attached to the filament. Until the grapple ends on the target, the cave fisher can't extrude another filament.

COFFER CORPSE

Medium undead, lawful evil

AC: 15 (damaged chain mail)

Hit Points: 22 (4d8 + 4)

Speed: 30 ft.

STR	DEX	CON	INT	WIS	CHA
14 (+2)	11 (+0)	12 (+1)	6 (-2)	8 (-1)	5 (-3)

Damage Vulnerabilities: bludgeoning from magical attacks

Damage Immunities: poison; bludgeoning, piercing, and slashing damage from nonmagical attacks

Condition Immunities: exhaustion, poisoned

Senses: darkvision 60 ft., passive Perception 9

Languages: understands Common but can't speak

Challenge: 1 (200 XP)

Special Equipment: The coffer corpse wields a *black mace*, a magic mace that grants a +1 bonus to attack and damage rolls made with it (included in its attack). See appendix A for the item's other properties.

Turn Resistance: The coffer corpse has advantage on saving throws against any affect that turns undead.

ACTIONS

Black Mace: *Melee Weapon Attack:* +5 to hit, reach 5 ft., one target. *Hit:* 6 (1d6 + 3) bludgeoning damage.

Choke: *Melee Weapon Attack:* +4 to hit, reach 5 ft., one creature. *Hit:* 5 (1d6 + 2) bludgeoning damage, and the coffer corpse locks its hands around the throat of the target. The target is grappled (escape DC 12), and begins to suffocate. Until this grapple ends, the target is restrained, and the coffer corpse can't choke another target. In addition, at the start of each of the coffer corpse's turns, the grappled target takes 5 (1d6 + 2) bludgeoning damage.

REACTIONS

Feign Death: When a coffer corpse suffers 15 hit points of damage (from any source, even nonmagical), it falls to the ground, apparently destroyed. If grappling a target, it does not release the target. On its next turn, the coffer corpse stands up as a bonus action and resumes its attack. All creatures within 60 feet of the coffer corpse that can see it must make a successful DC 13 Wisdom saving throw or gain the frightened condition for the next 1 minute, and must flee if possible.

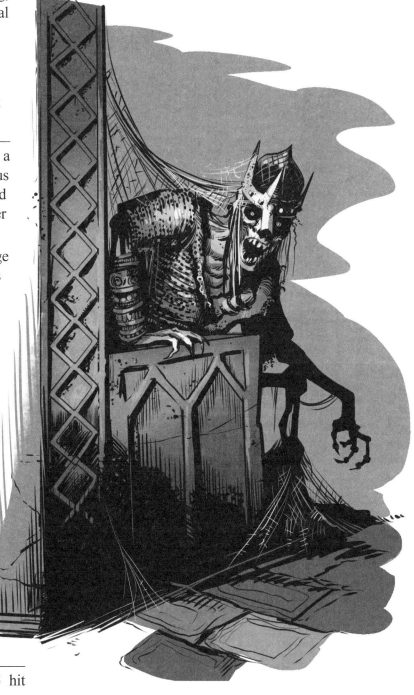

CORPORAL OF THE GUARD

Medium humanoid (human), neutral

AC: 20 (plate, shield)

Hit Points: 13 (2d8 + 4)

Speed: 20 ft.

STR	DEX	CON	INT	WIS	CHA
14 (+2)	12 (+1)	14 (+2)	10 (+0)	11 (+1)	10 (+0)

Skills: Perception +2

Senses: passive Perception 12

Languages: Common and any one language

Challenge: 1/4 (50 XP)

ACTIONS

Longsword: *Melee Weapon Attack:* +4 to hit, reach 5 ft., one target. *Hit:* 6 (1d8 + 2) slashing damage.

+1 Dagger: *Melee or Ranged Weapon Attack:* +5 to hit, reach 5 ft. or range 20/60 ft., one target. *Hit:* 5 (1d4 + 3) piercing damage.

CORPORAL OF THE WATCH

Medium humanoid (human), neutral

AC: 20 (plate, shield)

Hit Points: 19 (3d8 + 6)

Speed: 30 ft.

STR	DEX	CON	INT	WIS	CHA
15 (+2)	12 (+1)	14 (+2)	10 (+0)	11 (+0)	10 (+0)

Skills: Perception +2

Senses: passive Perception 12

Languages: Common and any one language

Challenge: 1/4 (50 XP)

ACTIONS

+1 Longsword: *Melee Weapon Attack:* +5 to hit, reach 5 ft., one target. *Hit:* 7 (1d8 + 3) slashing damage.

DECAPUS

Large monstrosity, chaotic evil

AC: 15 (natural armor)

Hit Points: 37 (5d10 + 10)

Speed: 10 ft., climb 30 ft.

STR	DEX	CON	INT	WIS	CHA
12 (+1)	11 (+0)	15 (+2)	6 (-2)	11 (+0)	7 (-2)

Skills: Athletics +3

Senses: darkvision 60 ft., passive Perception 10

Languages: -

Challenge: 3 (700 XP)

ACTIONS

Multiattack: The decapus makes nine tentacle attacks when suspended from above, or six tentacle attacks when on the ground. It also uses Reel and makes one bite attack.

Tentacle: *Melee Weapon Attack:* +3 to hit, reach 10 ft., one target. *Hit:* 4 (1d6 + 1) bludgeoning damage, and the target is grappled (escape DC 11). Until this grapple ends, the target is restrained.

Bite: *Melee Weapon Attack:* +3 to hit, reach 0 ft. (target must be grappled), one target. *Hit:* 8 (2d6 + 1) piercing damage.

Reel: The decapus pulls each creature grappled by it up to 10 feet straight toward it.

This horrid creature has a hairy bloated globular body that appears to be all mouth. Its broad maw is lined with wicked yellow teeth and a foul stench issues from within. Sprouting from its sickly green body are 10 tentacles covered with spiny suckers, used to hold it aloft.

ELITE BULLYWUG

Medium humanoid (bullywug), neutral evil

AC: 12 (hide armor)

Hit Points: 26 (4d8 + 8)

Speed: 20 ft., swim 30 ft.

STR	DEX	CON	INT	WIS	CHA
16 (+3)	11 (+0)	15 (+2)	8 (-1)	10 (+0)	6 (-2)

Skills: Athletics +5, Stealth +2

Senses: passive Perception 10

Languages: Bullywug, understands Common

Challenge: 1/2 (100 XP)

Amphibious: The bullywug can breathe air and water.

Speak with Frogs and Toads: The bullywug can communicate simple concepts to frogs and toads when it speaks in Bullywug.

Standing Leap: The bullywug's long jump is up to 25 feet and its high jump is up to 15 feet, with or without a running start.

Swamp Camouflage: The bullywug has advantage on Dexterity (Stealth) checks made to hide in swampy terrain.

ACTIONS

Multiattack: The bullywug makes two melee attacks: one with its bite and one with its spear.

Bite: *Melee Weapon Attack:* +5 to hit, reach 5 ft., one target. *Hit:* 6 (1d6 + 3) bludgeoning damage.

Spear: *Melee or Ranged Weapon Attack:* +5 to hit, reach 5 ft. or range 20/60 ft., one target. *Hit:* 6 (1d6 + 3) piercing damage, or 7 (1d8 + 3) piercing damage if used with two hands to make a melee attack.

This humanoid is bloated and toad-like with a wide maw full of piercing teeth. Its skin is gray-green and pockmarked with warty protrusions.

ELITE HOBGOBLIN

Medium humanoid (goblinoid), lawful evil

AC: 16 (chain mail)

Hit Points: 19 (3d8 + 6)

Speed: 30 ft.

STR	DEX	CON	INT	WIS	CHA
14 (+2)	12 (+1)	14 (+2)	10 (+0)	10 (+0)	9 (-1)

Senses: darkvision 60 ft., passive Perception 10

Languages: Common, Goblin

Challenge: 1 (200 XP)

Martial Advantage: Once per turn, the hobgoblin can deal an extra 7 (2d6) damage to a creature it hits with a weapon attack if that creature is within 5 feet of an ally of the hobgoblin that isn't incapacitated.

ACTIONS

Longsword: *Melee Weapon Attack:* +4 to hit, reach 5 ft., one target. *Hit:* 6 (1d8 + 2) slashing damage.

Whip: *Melee Weapon Attack:* +3 to hit, reach 15 ft., one target. *Hit:* The target is grappled (escape DC 12) and must succeed on an opposed Strength check, or become knocked prone and stunned until the end of its next turn.

ELITE KOBOLD

Small humanoid (kobold), lawful evil

AC: 13 (leather armor)

Hit Points: 9 (2d6 + 2)

Speed: 30 ft.

STR	DEX	CON	INT	WIS	CHA
10 (+0)	15 (+2)	12 (+1)	8 (-1)	7 (-2)	8 (-1)

Senses: darkvision 60 ft., passive Perception 8

Languages: Common, Draconic

Challenge: 1/4 (50 XP)

Pack Tactics: The kobold has advantage on an attack roll against a creature if at least one of the kobold's allies is within 5 feet of the creature and the ally isn't incapacitated.

Sunlight Sensitivity: While in sunlight, the kobold has disadvantage on attack rolls, as well as on Wisdom (Perception) checks that rely on sight.

ACTIONS

Shortsword: *Melee Weapon Attack:* +4 to hit, reach 5 ft., one target. *Hit:* 5 (1d6 + 2) piercing damage.

EVIL PRIEST

Medium humanoid (human), chaotic evil

AC: 22 (*+1 plate, +1 shield*)

Hit Points: 22 (4d8 + 4)

Speed: 20 ft.

STR	DEX	CON	INT	WIS	CHA
10 (+0)	10 (+0)	12 (+1)	10 (+0)	17 (+3)	14 (+2)

Skills: Medicine +2, Religion +5

Senses: passive Perception 13

Languages: Common, Infernal

Challenge: 2 (450 XP)

Special Equipment: The priest wears an *amulet of protection from good* (see appendix A) and carries a *staff of the python*, a *potion of gaseous form*, and *spell scrolls* of *detect magic*, *hold person*, and *silence*.

Spellcasting: The priest is a 4th-level spellcaster. Its spellcasting ability is Wisdom (spell save DC 13, +5 to hit with spell attacks). It has the following cleric spells prepared:

- Cantrips (at will): *guidance, light, resistance, sacred flame*
- 1st level (4 slots): *command, inflict wounds, sanctuary, shield of faith*
- 2nd level (3 slots): *aid, hold person, silence*

ACTIONS

Mace: *Melee Weapon Attack:* +2 to hit, reach 5 ft., one target. *Hit:* 3 (1d6) bludgeoning damage.

FLEDGLING MAGE

Medium humanoid (human), neutral

AC: 10

Hit Points: 9 (2d8)

Speed: 30 ft.

STR	DEX	CON	INT	WIS	CHA
7 (-2)	10 (+0)	10 (+0)	16 (+3)	13 (+1)	11 (+0)

Skills: Arcana +5

Senses: passive Perception 11

Languages: Common, Draconic

Challenge: 1/2 (100 XP)

Spellcasting: The mage is a 2nd-level spellcaster. Its spellcasting ability is Intelligence (spell save DC 13, +5 to hit with spell attacks). It has the following wizard spells prepared:

- Cantrips (at will): *friends, light, prestidigitation*
- 1st level (3 slots): *detect magic, illusory script, shield, silent image, sleep*

ACTIONS

Dagger: *Melee or Ranged Weapon Attack:* +2 to hit, reach 5 ft. or range 20/60 ft., one target. *Hit:* 2 (1d4) piercing damage.

GIANT ARMADILLO

Medium beast, unaligned

AC: 16 (natural armor)

Hit Points: 22 (3d8 + 9)

Speed: 20 ft., burrow 10 ft.

STR	DEX	CON	INT	WIS	CHA
13 (+1)	11 (+0)	16 (+3)	2 (-4)	10 (+0)	6 (-2)

Senses: darkvision 30 ft., passive Perception 10

Languages: -

Challenge: 1/4 (50 XP)

Keen Smell: The armadillo has advantage on Wisdom (Perception) checks that rely on smell.

ACTIONS

Claws: *Melee Weapon Attack:* +3 to hit, reach 5 ft., one target. *Hit:* 4 (1d6 + 1) slashing damage.

This mammal has gray skin covered with armored plates. Its body is about 5 feet long not including its whip-like tail. It sports a pointed snout and stout claws.

GIANT CAVE CRICKET

Small beast, unaligned

AC: 15 (natural armor)

Hit Points: 13 (2d6 + 6)

Speed: 20 ft.

STR	DEX	CON	INT	WIS	CHA
14 (+2)	12 (+1)	16 (+3)	2 (-4)	10 (+0)	2 (-4)

Skills: Athletics +4

Senses: darkvision 60 ft., passive Perception 10

Languages: -

Challenge: 1/8 (25 XP)

Hop: The cave cricket can use its powerful legs to hop up to 20 feet vertically or horizontally without provoking opportunity attacks. All Strength (Athletics) checks regarding jumping are made with advantage.

ACTIONS

Slam: *Melee Weapon Attack:* +4 to hit, reach 5 ft., one target. *Hit:* 4 (1d4 + 2) bludgeoning damage.

REACTIONS

Kick: When the cave cricket hops it can kick a target within 5 feet. *Melee Weapon Attack:* +4 to hit, reach 5 feet, one target. *Hit:* 7 (2d4 + 2) bludgeoning damage.

These monstrous insects have a 4-foot-long chitinous body with pale white to flat gray coloration. They have oversized rear legs, the source of their noisy chirping.

GIANT CRAB SPIDER

Small beast, unaligned

AC: 14

Hit Points: 7 (2d6)

Speed: 40 ft., climb 40 ft.

STR	DEX	CON	INT	WIS	CHA
11 (+0)	18 (+4)	11 (+0)	3 (-4)	12 (+1)	4 (-3)

Skills: Perception +3, Stealth +8

Senses: blindsight 10 ft., darkvision 60 ft., passive Perception 13

Languages: -

Challenge: 1/4 (50 XP)

Spider Climb: The spider can climb difficult surfaces, including upside down on ceilings, without needing to make an ability check.

Web Sense: While in contact with a web, the spider knows the exact location of any other creature in contact with the same web.

Web Walker: The spider ignores movement restrictions caused by webbing.

ACTIONS

Bite: *Melee Weapon Attack:* +6 to hit, reach 5 ft., one target. *Hit:* 2 (1d4) piercing damage, and the target must make a DC 10 Constitution saving throw, taking 3 (1d6) poison damage on a failed save, or half as much damage on a successful one. If the poison damage reduces the target to 0 hit points, the target is stable but poisoned for 1 hour, even after regaining hit points, and is paralyzed while poisoned in this way.

A giant crab spider has an abdomen about 1 to 2 feet in diameter, although flattened to hide in a rocky crevasse or wooden deadfall. It has coarse brown fur and spindly legs about 2 feet long.

GIANT CRAYFISH

Large beast, unaligned

AC: 15 (natural armor)

Hit Points: 45 (7d10 + 7)

Speed: 30 ft., swim 30 ft.

STR	DEX	CON	INT	WIS	CHA
15 (+2)	13 (+1)	13 (+1)	1 (-5)	9 (-1)	3 (-4)

Skills: Stealth +3

Senses: blindsight 30 ft., passive Perception 9

Languages: -

Challenge: 2 (450 XP)

Amphibious: The giant crayfish can breathe air and water.

ACTIONS

Multiattack: The giant crayfish makes two claw attacks.

Claw: *Melee Weapon Attack:* +4 to hit, reach 5 ft., one target. *Hit:* 7 (1d10 + 2) bludgeoning damage, and the target is grappled (escape DC 12). The crayfish has two claws, each of which can grapple only one target.

GIANT PIKE

Large beast, unaligned

AC: 15 (natural armor)

Hit Points: 26 (4d10 + 4)

Speed: swim 40 ft.

STR	DEX	CON	INT	WIS	CHA
15 (+2)	15 (+2)	12 (+1)	1 (-5)	10 (+0)	2 (-4)

Skills: Stealth +4

Senses: passive Perception 10

Languages: -

Challenge: 1 (200 XP)

Ambusher: The pike has advantage on attack rolls against any creature it has surprised.

Underwater Camouflage: The pike has advantage on Dexterity (Stealth) checks made to hide in underwater terrain assuming it has cover (such as from weeds).

Water Breathing: The pike can breathe only underwater.

ACTIONS

Bite: *Melee Weapon Attack:* +4 to hit, reach 5 ft., one target. *Hit:* 15 (3d8 + 2) piercing damage.

A giant pike is nearly 12 feet long, with a slender body. Its slivery sides are marked with black-green vertical bars and its oversized mouth is lined with sharp teeth.

GIANT RAT PACK LEADER

Small beast, unaligned

AC: 13

Hit Points: 18 (4d6 + 4)

Speed: 30 ft.

STR	DEX	CON	INT	WIS	CHA
9 (-1)	16 (+3)	12 (+1)	2 (-4)	10 (+0)	4 (-3)

Senses: darkvision 60 ft., passive Perception 10

Languages: -

Challenge: 1/4 (50 XP)

Keen Smell: The rat has advantage on Wisdom (Perception) checks that rely on smell.

Pack Tactics: The rat has advantage on an attack roll against a creature if at least one of the rat's allies is within 5 feet of the creature and the ally isn't incapacitated.

ACTIONS

Multiattack: The rat makes two bite attacks.

Bite: *Melee Weapon Attack:* +5 to hit, reach 5 ft., one target. *Hit:* 5 (1d4 + 3) piercing damage.

GIANT WATER SPIDER

Large beast, unaligned

AC: 14 (natural armor)

Hit Points: 32 (5d10 + 5)

Speed: 40 ft., climb 40 ft., swim 20 ft.

STR	DEX	CON	INT	WIS	CHA
14 (+2)	16 (+3)	12 (+1)	2 (-4)	11 (+0)	4 (-3)

Skills: Stealth +7

Senses: blindsight 10 ft., darkvision 60 ft., passive Perception 10

Languages: -

Challenge: 1 (200 XP)

Hold Breath: The spider can hold its breath for 30 minutes using an air bubble affixed to the underside of its abdomen.

Spider Climb: The spider can climb difficult surfaces, including upside down on ceilings, without needing to make an ability check.

Water Sense: While in contact with water, the spider knows the exact location of any other creature in contact with the water within 100 feet.

Web Walker: The spider ignores movement restrictions caused by webbing.

ACTIONS

Bite: *Melee Weapon Attack*: +5 to hit, reach 5 ft., one target. *Hit:* 7 (1d8 + 3) piercing damage, and the target must make a DC 11 Constitution saving throw, becoming poisoned for 1 hour on a failed save. The target is paralyzed while poisoned in this way.

A giant water spider has an abdomen about 6 feet in diameter, and gangly legs. It has coarse gray-green fur is often adorned with bits of algae and weeds. An oval air bubble is affixed underneath its abdomen.

GNOME

Small humanoid (gnome), chaotic neutral

AC: 14 (studded leather)

Hit Points: 9 (2d6 + 2)

Speed: 25 ft.

STR	DEX	CON	INT	WIS	CHA
10 (+0)	14 (+2)	12 (+1)	10 (+0)	12 (+1)	10 (+0)

Special Equipment: The gnome carries one flask of alchemist's fire and a pouch with 2d4 gp.

Skills: Stealth +4

Senses: darkvision 60 ft., passive Perception 11

Languages: Common, Gnomish, small beasts

Challenge: 1/8 (25 XP)

Gnome Cunning: The gnome has advantage on Dexterity, Wisdom, and Charisma saving throws against magic.

Innate Spellcasting (At Will): The gnome can innately cast *minor illusion* (spell save DC 10), requiring no material components. Its spellcasting ability is Intelligence.

ACTIONS

Shortsword: *Melee Weapon Attack:* +4 to hit, reach 5 ft., one target. *Hit:* 5 (1d6 + 2) piercing damage.

Light Crossbow: *Ranged Weapon Attack:* +4 to hit, range 80/320 ft., one target. *Hit:* 6 (1d8 + 2) piercing damage.

Alchemist's Fire: *Ranged Weapon Attack:* +4 to hit, range 20 ft., one target. *Hit:* The target takes 2 (1d4) fire damage at the start of each of its turns. The target can use an action to make a DC 10 Dexterity check to extinguish the flames.

This 3-foot-tall stocky humanoid wears leather armor studded with steel rivets. It has greasy black hair and leathery facial features. A crossbow is slung over its back, and a pair of shortswords dangle from its belt.

GNOME TRICKSTER

Small humanoid (gnome), chaotic neutral

AC: 16 (*mage armor*)

Hit Points: 18 (4d6 + 4)

Speed: 25 ft.

STR	DEX	CON	INT	WIS	CHA
10 (+0)	16 (+3)	12 (+1)	14 (+2)	12 (+1)	10 (+0)

Skills: Arcana +4, Stealth +5

Senses: darkvision 60 ft., passive Perception 11

Languages: Common, Gnomish, small beasts

Challenge: 1 (200 XP)

Special Equipment: See sidebar.

Gnome Cunning: The gnome has advantage on Dexterity, Wisdom, and Charisma saving throws against magic.

Innate Spellcasting (At Will): The gnome can innately cast *minor illusion* (with both sound and image; spell save DC 12), requiring no material components. Its innate spellcasting ability is Intelligence.

Spellcasting: See sidebar.

ACTIONS

Dagger: *Melee or Ranged Weapon Attack:* +5 to hit, reach 5 ft. or range 20/60 ft., one target. *Hit:* 5 (1d4 + 3) piercing damage.

This 3-foot-tall stocky humanoid is covered with folds and folds of dark blue robes. His ruddy cheeks flank a prominent nose among a scraggily black beard.

THE GNOME TRICKSTER TRIPLETS

MOTH-GAR

Special Equipment: Moth-gar has a *potion of healing*.

Spellcasting: Moth-gar is a 4th-level spellcaster. His spellcasting ability is Intelligence (spell save DC 12, +4 to hit with spell attacks). He has the following wizard spells prepared:

- Cantrips (at will): *blade ward, dancing lights, mage hand, shocking grasp, true strike*
- 1st level (3 slots; one used for *mage armor*): *chromatic orb, disguise self, mage armor, Tasha's hideous laughter*
- 2nd level (3 slots): *hold person, misty step*

HOTH-GAR

Special Equipment: Hoth-gar has a *wand of wonder*.

Spellcasting: Hoth-gar is a 4th-level spellcaster. His spellcasting ability is Intelligence (spell save DC 12, +4 to hit with spell attacks). He has the following wizard spells prepared:

- Cantrips (at will): *acid splash, dancing lights, mage hand, poison spray, true strike*
- 1st level (3 slots; one used for *mage armor*): *color spray, mage armor, ray of sickness*
- 2nd level (3 slots): *blur, Melf's acid arrow, misty step*

ROTH-GAR

Special Equipment: Roth-gar has a *brown bag of tricks* (see appendix A) and a diary.

Spellcasting: Roth-gar is a 4th-level spellcaster. His spellcasting ability is Intelligence (spell save DC 12, +4 to hit with spell attacks). He has the following wizard spells prepared:

- Cantrips (at will): *dancing lights, friends, mage hand, ray of frost, true strike*
- 1st level (3 slots; one used for *mage armor*): *charm person, disguise self, mage armor, sleep*
- 2nd level (3 slots): *mirror image, ray of enfeeblement*

GRIPFOOT BULLYWUG

Small humanoid (bullywug), neutral evil

AC: 13

Hit Points: 10 (3d6)

Speed: 30 ft., swim 40 ft.

STR	DEX	CON	INT	WIS	CHA
10 (+0)	16 (+3)	11 (+0)	8 (-1)	10 (+0)	8 (-1)

Skills: Stealth +5

Senses: passive Perception 10

Languages: Bullywug

Challenge: 1/4 (50 XP)

Amphibious: The bullywug can breathe air and water.

Speak with Frogs and Toads: The bullywug can communicate simple concepts to frogs and toads when it speaks in Bullywug.

Spider Climb: The bullywug has suction-like feet pads and can climb difficult surfaces, including upside down on ceilings, without needing to make an ability check.

Standing Leap: The bullywug's long jump is up to 20 feet and its high jump is up to 10 feet, with or without a running start.

Swamp Camouflage: The bullywug has advantage on Dexterity (Stealth) checks made to hide in swampy terrain.

ACTIONS

Bite: *Melee Weapon Attack:* +5 to hit, reach 5 ft., one target. *Hit:* 5 (1d4 + 3) bludgeoning damage.

Blowgun: *Ranged Weapon Attack:* +5 to hit, range 25/100 ft., one target. *Hit:* 1 piercing damage, and the target must succeed on a DC 11 Constitution saving throw or take an additional 4 (1d8) poison damage and be poisoned for 1 hour.

This frog-like humanoid is much smaller than a typical bullywug, and has bright green glistening skin with dark blotches.

IRON COBRA

Medium construct, unaligned

AC: 18 (natural armor)

Hit Points: 9 (2d8)

Speed: 30 ft.

STR	DEX	CON	INT	WIS	CHA
10 (+0)	16 (+3)	11 (+0)	1 (-5)	14 (+2)	1 (-5)

Skills: Perception +4

Damage Resistances: bludgeoning, piercing, and slashing from nonmagical attacks

Damage Immunities: fire, poison, psychic

Condition Immunities: blinded, charmed, deafened, frightened, paralyzed, petrified, poisoned

Senses: blindsight 60 ft. (blind beyond this radius), passive Perception 14

Languages: -

Challenge: 1/2 (100 XP)

Fire Absorption: Whenever the iron cobra is subjected to fire damage, it takes no damage and instead regains a number of hit points equal to the fire damage dealt.

Magic Resistance: The iron cobra has advantage on saving throws against spells and other magical effects.

ACTIONS

Bite: *Melee Weapon Attack*: +5 to hit, reach 5 ft., one target. *Hit:* 5 (1d4 + 3) piercing damage, and the target must make a DC 11 Constitution saving throw, taking 14 (4d6) poison damage on a failed save, or half as much damage on a successful one.

A metallic serpentine form coils aggressively from the shadowy recess of the niche. Its hollow eye sockets glow pale green, as its hinged jaw swings open in anticipation of the strike.

KOBOLD CHIEFTAIN

Small humanoid (kobold), lawful evil

AC: 14 (studded leather)

Hit Points: 22 (4d6 + 8)

Speed: 30 ft.

STR	DEX	CON	INT	WIS	CHA
14 (+2)	14 (+2)	14 (+2)	8 (-1)	11 (+0)	8 (-1)

Senses: darkvision 60 ft., passive Perception 10

Languages: Common, Draconic

Challenge: 1 (200 XP)

Pack Tactics: The kobold has advantage on an attack roll against a creature if at least one of the kobold's allies is within 5 feet of the creature and the ally isn't incapacitated.

Sunlight Sensitivity: While in sunlight, the kobold has disadvantage on attack rolls, as well as on Wisdom (Perception) checks that rely on sight.

ACTIONS

Longsword: *Melee Weapon Attack:* +4 to hit, reach 5 ft., one target. *Hit:* 6 (1d8 + 2) slashing damage, or 7 (1d10 + 2) slashing damage if used with two hands.

KOBOLD SORCERER

Small humanoid (kobold), lawful evil

AC: 12 (15 with *mage armor*)

Hit Points: 22 (5d6 + 5)

Speed: 30 ft.

STR	DEX	CON	INT	WIS	CHA
7 (-2)	15 (+2)	12 (+1)	10 (+0)	9 (-1)	16 (+3)

Skills: Arcana +2, Deception +5

Senses: darkvision 60 ft., passive Perception 9

Languages: Common, Draconic

Challenge: 1 (200 XP)

Pack Tactics: The kobold has advantage on an attack roll against a creature if at least one of the kobold's allies is within 5 feet of the creature and the ally isn't incapacitated.

Spellcasting: The kobold is a 3rd-level spellcaster. Its spellcasting ability is Charisma (spell save DC 13, +5 to hit with spell attacks). It has the following sorcerer spells prepared:

- Cantrips (at will): *blade ward, fire bolt, poison spray, shocking grasp*
- 1st level (4 slots): *burning hands, mage armor, magic missile*
- 2nd level (2 slots): *shatter*

Sorcery Points: The kobold has 3 sorcery points. It can spend 1 or more sorcery points as a bonus action to gain one of the following benefits:

- *Empowered Spell:* When it rolls damage for a spell, the kobold can spend 1 sorcery point to reroll up to three damage dice. It must use the new rolls. It can use Empowered Spell even if it has already used a different Metamagic option during the casting of the spell.
- *Heightened Spell:* When it casts a spell that forces a creature to make a saving throw to resist the spell's effects, the kobold can spend 3 sorcery points to give one target of the spell disadvantage on its first saving throw against the spell.

Sunlight Sensitivity: While in sunlight, the kobold has disadvantage on attack rolls, as well as on Wisdom (Perception) checks that rely on sight.

ACTIONS

Dagger: *Melee or Ranged Weapon Attack*: +4 to hit, reach 5 ft. or range 20/60 ft., one target. *Hit:* 4 (1d4 + 2) piercing damage.

LIVING STONE STATUE

Medium construct, unaligned

AC: 15 (natural armor)

Hit Points: 22 (5d8)

Speed: 20 ft.

STR	DEX	CON	INT	WIS	CHA
14 (+2)	10 (+0)	11 (+0)	1 (-5)	5 (-3)	1 (-5)

Damage Resistances: piercing, slashing

Damage Immunities: poison, psychic

Condition Immunities: blinded, charmed, deafened, frightened, paralyzed, petrified, poisoned

Senses: blindsight 60 ft. (blind beyond this radius), passive Perception 7

Languages: -

Challenge: 1/2 (100 XP)

False Appearance: While the statue remains motionless, it is indistinguishable from an inanimate statue.

ACTIONS

Multiattack: The statue makes two longsword attacks.

Stone Longsword: *Melee Weapon Attack:* +4 to hit, reach 5 ft., one target. *Hit:* 6 (1d8 + 2) slashing damage, or 7 (1d10 + 2) slashing damage if used with two hands.

This finely chiseled stone statue depicts a typical human guardsman. An ornately carved breastplate, a helm with visor, and a stony sword complete the design. Its eyes flicker with pale orange radiance as it awkwardly shuffles to advance.

LIVING WAX STATUE

Medium construct, unaligned

AC: 11 (natural armor)

Hit Points: 9 (2d8)

Speed: 30 ft.

STR	DEX	CON	INT	WIS	CHA
10 (+0)	10 (+0)	11 (+0)	1 (-5)	5 (-3)	1 (-5)

Damage Resistances: piercing, slashing

Damage Immunities: poison, psychic

Condition Immunities: blinded, charmed, deafened, frightened, paralyzed, petrified, poisoned

Senses: blindsight 60 ft. (blind beyond this radius), passive Perception 7

Languages: -

Challenge: 1/4 (50 XP)

False Appearance: While the statue remains motionless, it is indistinguishable from a normal wax sculpture.

ACTIONS

Longsword: *Melee Weapon Attack:* +2 to hit, reach 5 ft., one target. *Hit:* 4 (1d8) slashing damage, or 5 (1d10) slashing damage if used with two hands.

This lifelike wax sculpture of a humanoid begins to move with a stiff gait. It wields an actual longsword.

MAD HERMIT

Medium humanoid (human), chaotic evil

AC: 15 (leather armor, *ring of protection*)

Hit Points: 27 (5d8 + 5)

Speed: 30 ft.

STR	DEX	CON	INT	WIS	CHA
12 (+1)	17 (+3)	12 (+1)	10 (+0)	12 (+1)	7 (-2)

Skills: Deception +2, Perception +3, Sleight of Hand +5, Stealth +7

Senses: passive Perception 13

Languages: Common, Draconic, Thieves' Cant

Challenge: 1/2 (100 XP)

Special Equipment: The Mad Hermit wears a *ring of protection*.

Cunning Action: On each of his turns, the Mad Hermit can use a bonus action to take the Dash, Disengage, or Hide action.

Sneak Attack (1/Turn): The Mad Hermit deals an extra 7 (2d6) damage when he hits a target with a weapon attack and has advantage on the attack roll, or when the target is within 5 feet of an ally of the Mad Hermit that isn't incapacitated and the Mad Hermit doesn't have disadvantage on the attack roll.

ACTIONS

+1 Dagger: *Melee or Ranged Weapon Attack:* +6 to hit, reach 5 ft. or range 20/60 ft., one target. *Hit:* 6 (1d4 + 4) piercing damage.

MAREVAK, ADVISOR TO THE CASTELLAN

Medium humanoid (elf), chaotic evil

AC: 16 (*+1 chain shirt*)

Hit Points: 22 (5d8)

Speed: 30 ft.

STR	DEX	CON	INT	WIS	CHA
12 (+1)	16 (+3)	11 (+0)	16 (+3)	14 (+2)	13 (+1)

Skills: Arcana +5, History +5, Insight +4, Perception +4

Damage Resistances: fire

Senses: darkvision 60 ft., passive Perception 14

Languages: Common, Elvish

Challenge: 2 (450 XP)

Special Equipment: Marevak has a *ring of resistance* (fire), 10 *+1 arrows*, and his spellbook.

Fey Ancestry: Marevak has advantage on saving throws against being charmed, and magic can't put him to sleep.

Spellcasting: Marevak is a 3rd-level spellcaster. His spellcasting ability is Intelligence (spell save DC 13, +5 to hit with spell attacks). He has the following wizard spells prepared:

- Cantrips (at will): *dancing lights, fire bolt, prestidigitation*
- 1st level (4 slots): *charm person, comprehend languages, detect magic, sleep*
- 2nd level (2 slots): *detect thoughts, web*

ACTIONS

Dagger: *Melee or Ranged Weapon Attack*: +5 to hit, reach 5 ft. or range 20/60 ft., one target. *Hit:* 5 (1d4 + 3) piercing damage.

Shortbow: *Ranged Weapon Attack*: +5 to hit, range 80/320 ft., one target. *Hit:* 6 (1d6 + 3) piercing damage.

NIXIE

Small fey, chaotic good

AC: 13

Hit Points: 7 (2d6)

Speed: 20 ft., swim 40 ft.

STR	DEX	CON	INT	WIS	CHA
7 (-2)	17 (+3)	10 (+0)	13 (+1)	14 (+2)	18 (+4)

Skills: Animal Handling +4, Persuasion +6

Senses: passive Perception 12

Languages: Common, Sylvan

Challenge: 1/4 (50 XP)

Amphibious: The nixie can breathe air and water.

Innate Spellcasting: The nixie's spellcasting ability is Charisma (spell save DC 14, +6 to hit with spell attacks). The nixie can innately cast the following spells, requiring no material components:

- 1/day each: *charm person* (requires 10 nixies to cast), *water breathing* (with a kiss)

ACTIONS

Dagger: *Melee or Ranged Weapon Attack:* +5 to hit, reach 5 ft. or range 20/60 ft., one target. *Hit:* 5 (1d4 + 3) piercing damage.

Summon Swarm of Fish (1/Day): The nixie can summon a swarm of harmless fish, which arrives in 1 round. As a bonus action the nixie can command the swarm to distract a target (forcing it to make all attack rolls at disadvantage) or to surround the nixie (providing half cover). The swarm dissipates after 10 rounds, or as soon as it suffers damage.

OGRE SKELETON

Large undead, lawful evil

AC: 12 (natural armor)

Hit Points: 60 (8d10 + 16)

Speed: 30 ft.

STR	DEX	CON	INT	WIS	CHA
18 (+4)	11 (+0)	14 (+2)	6 (-2)	8 (-1)	5 (-3)

Damage Vulnerabilities: bludgeoning

Damage Immunities: poison

Condition Immunities: exhaustion, poisoned

Senses: darkvision 60 ft., passive Perception 9

Languages: understands Common and Giant but can't speak

Challenge: 2 (450 XP)

ACTIONS

Greatclub: *Melee Weapon Attack*: +6 to hit, reach 5 ft., one target. *Hit:* 13 (2d8 + 4) bludgeoning damage.

ORC CHIEF

Medium humanoid (orc), chaotic evil

AC: 19 (chain mail, *+1 shield*)

Hit Points: 42 (5d8 + 20)

Speed: 30 ft.

STR	DEX	CON	INT	WIS	CHA
18 (+4)	12 (+1)	18 (+4)	10 (+0)	11 (+0)	14 (+2)

Senses: darkvision 60 ft., passive Perception 10

Languages: Common, Orc

Challenge: 2 (450 XP)

Aggressive: As a bonus action, the orc can move up to its speed toward a hostile creature that it can see.

Special Equipment: The orc wears chain mail and carries a *+1 shield*.

ACTIONS

Multiattack: The orc makes two melee attacks.

Mace: *Melee Weapon Attack*: +6 to hit, reach 5 ft., one target. *Hit:* 7 (1d6 + 4) bludgeoning damage.

OSQUIP

Small beast, unaligned

AC: 14 (natural armor)

Hit Points: 22 (4d6 + 8)

Speed: 30 ft., burrow 10 ft.

STR	DEX	CON	INT	WIS	CHA
10 (+0)	17 (+3)	14 (+2)	2 (-4)	10 (+0)	2 (-4)

Skills: Perception +2, Stealth +5

Senses: darkvision 60 ft., passive Perception 12

Languages: -

Challenge: 1 (200 XP)

Ambusher: The osquip has advantage on attack rolls against any creature it has surprised.

Tunneler: The osquip can use its powerful jaws to burrow through solid rock, albeit at a very slow pace. In 1 hour the osquip can burrow a 10-foot-long tunnel approximately 2 feet in diameter. This tunnel can be used by Tiny creatures or osquips without penalty, or by other Small creatures as difficult terrain.

ACTIONS

Bite: *Melee Weapon Attack*: +5 to hit, reach 5 ft., one target. *Hit:* 10 (2d6 + 3) piercing damage.

This nasty little beast appears to be a hairless, multi-legged rodent, about the size of a small dog. Its rubbery leather hide is pale yellow or pasty white, and it sports an oversized head complete with a protruding bony jaw.

THOUL

Medium monstrosity, chaotic evil

AC: 14 (natural armor)

Hit Points: 30 (4d8 + 12)

Speed: 30 ft.

STR	DEX	CON	INT	WIS	CHA
16 (+3)	12 (+1)	16 (+3)	6 (-2)	11 (+0)	7 (-2)

Saving Throws: Con +5

Skills: Perception +2

Senses: darkvision 60 ft., passive Perception 12

Languages: Giant, Goblin

Challenge: 1 (200 XP)

Keen Smell: The thoul has advantage on Wisdom (Perception) checks that rely on smell.

Regeneration: The thoul regenerates 5 hit points at the start of its turn. If the thoul takes acid or fire damage, this trait doesn't function at the start of the thoul's next turn. The thoul dies only if it starts its turn with 0 hit points and doesn't regenerate.

ACTIONS

Multiattack: A thoul makes two attacks: two with its claws or one with a weapon and one with its claws.

Claws: *Melee Weapon Attack:* +5 to hit, reach 5 ft., one target. *Hit:* 6 (1d6 + 3) slashing damage. If the target is a creature other than an elf or undead, it must succeed on a DC 10 Constitution saving throw or be paralyzed for 1 minute. The target can repeat the saving throw at the end of each of its turns, ending the effect on itself on a success.

Standing a full 6 and a half feet tall, this burly humanoid has pale orange skin and dark gray to black unkempt hair. Yellow eyes pierce out beneath a beetling brow, and its wide mouth is full of pointy, yellowed teeth. Its limber arms seem stretched, and its hands end in wicked black claws.

TROGLODYTE SHAMAN

Medium humanoid (troglodyte), chaotic evil

AC: 12 (natural armor)

Hit Points: 22 (5d8)

Speed: 30 ft.

STR	DEX	CON	INT	WIS	CHA
12 (+1)	10 (+0)	11 (+0)	10 (+0)	13 (+1)	8 (-1)

Skills: Stealth +2

Senses: darkvision 60 ft., passive Perception 11

Languages: Troglodyte

Challenge: 1 (200 XP)

Chameleon Skin: The troglodyte has advantage on Dexterity (Stealth) checks made to hide.

Stench: Any creature other than a troglodyte that starts its turn within 5 feet of the troglodyte must succeed on a DC 12 Constitution saving throw or be poisoned until the start of the creature's next turn. On a successful saving throw, the creature is immune to the stench of all troglodytes for 1 hour.

Spellcasting: The troglodyte is a 2nd-level spellcaster. Its spellcasting ability is Wisdom (spell save DC 11, +3 to hit with spell attacks). The troglodyte has the following spells prepared:

- Cantrips (at will): *acid splash, poison spray, resistance*
- 1st level (3 slots): *entangle, fog cloud, inflict wounds*

Sunlight Sensitivity: While in sunlight, the troglodyte has disadvantage on attack rolls, as well as on Wisdom (Perception) checks that rely on sight.

ACTIONS

Multiattack: The troglodyte makes two attacks: one with its weapon and one with its bite.

Bone Cudgel: *Melee Weapon Attack:* +3 to hit, reach 5 ft., one target. *Hit:* 4 (1d6 + 1) bludgeoning damage.

Bite: *Melee Weapon Attack:* +3 to hit, reach 5 ft., one target. *Hit:* 3 (1d4 + 1) piercing damage.

TROGLODYTE SPORE SERVANT

Medium plant, unaligned

AC: 11 (natural armor)

Hit Points: 13 (2d8 + 4)

Speed: 20 ft.

STR	DEX	CON	INT	WIS	CHA
14 (+2)	10 (+0)	14 (+2)	2 (-4)	6 (-2)	1 (-5)

Senses: blindsight 30 ft., passive Perception 8

Damage Immunities: poison

Condition Immunities: blinded, charmed, frightened, paralyzed, poisoned

Languages: -

Challenge: 1/4 (50 XP)

ACTIONS

Multiattack: The spore servant makes three attacks: one with its bite and two with its claws.

Bite: *Melee Weapon Attack:* +4 to hit, reach 5 ft., one target. *Hit:* 4 (1d4 + 2) piercing damage.

Claw: *Melee Weapon Attack:* +4 to hit, reach 5 ft., one target. *Hit:* 4 (1d4 + 2) slashing damage.

WIZARD GOLEM
Medium construct, unaligned

AC: 15 (natural armor)

Hit Points: 27 (6d8)

Speed: 20 ft.

STR	DEX	CON	INT	WIS	CHA
10 (+0)	10 (+0)	11 (+0)	1 (-5)	5 (-3)	8 (-1)

Damage Resistances: piercing, slashing

Damage Immunities: poison, psychic

Condition Immunities: blinded, charmed, deafened, frightened, paralyzed, petrified, poisoned

Senses: blindsight 60 ft. (blind beyond this radius), passive Perception 7

Languages: -

Challenge: 1 (200 XP)

False Appearance: While the golem remains motionless, it is indistinguishable from an inanimate statue.

Innate Spellcasting: The golem's spellcasting ability is Charisma (spell save DC 9, +1 to hit with spell attacks). The golem can innately cast the following spells, requiring no material components:

- At will: *fire bolt*
- 2/day: *magic missile*

Magic Resistance: The golem has advantage on saving throws against spells and other magical effects.

ACTIONS

Slam: *Melee Weapon Attack:* +2 to hit, reach 5 ft., one target. *Hit:* 3 (1d6) bludgeoning damage.

XVART
Small humanoid (xvart), chaotic evil

AC: 13 (leather armor)

Hit Points: 7 (2d6)

Speed: 30 ft.

STR	DEX	CON	INT	WIS	CHA
8 (-1)	14 (+2)	10 (+0)	8 (-1)	7 (-2)	7 (-2)

Skills: Stealth +4

Senses: darkvision 30 ft., passive Perception 8

Languages: Abyssal

Challenge: 1/8 (25 XP)

Low Cunning: The xvart can take the Disengage action as a bonus action on each of its turns.

Overbearing Pack: The xvart has advantage on Strength (Athletics) checks to shove a creature if at least one of the xvart's allies is within 5 feet of the target and the ally isn't incapacitated.

Raxivort's Tongue: The xvart can communicate with ordinary bats and rats, as well as giant bats and giant rats.

ACTIONS

Shortsword: *Melee Weapon Attack:* +4 to hit, reach 5 ft., one target. *Hit:* 5 (1d6 + 2) piercing damage.

Sling: *Ranged Weapon Attack:* +4 to hit, range 30/120 ft., one target. *Hit:* 4 (1d4 + 2) bludgeoning damage.

APPENDIX C
Characters, Hirelings, and Followers

This appendix contains an array of 1st-level characters that can be used in a variety of ways. They can be used as player characters (PCs) with minimum preparation so players and Dungeon Masters can get right to the action of playing. They can also be used as nonplayer characters (NPCs) to fill out an adventuring party that needs a particular role, or just extra numbers. They may take the form of hirelings (who serve for pay) or followers (who serve out of respect and loyalty). They can also be used as NPCs encountered during the course of play, perhaps in the Keep, in the wilderness borderlands, or as prisoners in the Caves of Chaos. In this case, the text of the adventure prompts the DM when to use of one of these for such a purpose. Finally, these could be used to replace player characters that fall during the trials and tribulations of adventuring.

PRE-GENERATED PCS

The pre-generated player characters available for download at www.goodman-games.com are fully designed and ready to play. Each has its own character sheet, suitable for printing. There are 12 pre-generated player characters to choose from, including a variety of races and classes to assemble a balanced party of adventurers. A typical balanced party of five characters would include two fighter-types, a cleric-type, an arcane spellcaster, and a rogue or bard. Before play, allow the player to adjust any of the nonessential game statistics (such as name, sex, personality, ideals, bonds, flaws) and record the contents of the designated backpack (see sidebar).

NPCS / HIRELINGS / FOLLOWERS

Players about to embark on an adventure might well wish to have additional assistance in the form of other fellow explorers. These NPCs can be party members who earn full shares of experience points and treasure, or they can be monsters, hirelings, or followers. For more on how to create and use NPCs in your game, see chapter 4 of the Dungeon Master's Guide.

Hirelings, although not always plentiful, are nonetheless easier to find than followers. They serve for a fee, as well as a cut of any treasure gained. Their exact price is to be determined by the DM, who then interacts with the players if any bargaining is necessary, taking the part of the NPC.

Followers are usually willing to serve a particular character out of admiration or respect without special regard for compensation. In any case, with only 1st-level characters, players cannot expect to attract followers until they have accomplished enough to gain a bit of reputation and notice; i.e., until they have gained a few levels. Thus, any NPC gained for an adventure has only a minimal chance of being a follower. Of course, this fact is not crucial to the immediate adventure, but may bear upon future considerations. Note that a follower will serve a character of lower level only under special circumstances.

Below are two tables summarizing the NPCs available in the region. There are 12 different NPCs, one for each of the 12 classes in the Player's Handbook.

Name	Mohag the Wanderer	Afton Barr	Farned of the Great Church	Sho-Rembo	Yor	Tassit
Sex	Male	Male	Male	Female	Female	Female
Race	Human	Half-Elf	Wood Elf	Lightfoot Halfling	Dragonborn	Human
Level (HD)	1 (d12)	1 (d8)	1 (d8)	1 (d8)	1 (d10)	1 (d8)
Class	Barbarian	Bard	Cleric	Druid	Fighter	Monk
Background	Outlander	Entertainer	Acolyte	Hermit	Folk Hero	Hermit
Alignment	N	CG	NG	N	CN	LN
AC	15	13	17	16	17	15
Initiative	+1	+2	+0	+3	+2	+2
Speed	30 ft.	30 ft.	35 ft.	25 ft.	30 ft.	30 ft.
Prof. Bonus	+2	+2	+2	+2	+2	+2
Hit Points	16	9	9	8	13	9
Strength	16 (+3)	11 (+0)	10 (+0)	8 (-1)	16 (+3)	14 (+2)
Dexterity	12 (+1)	15 (+2)	11 (+0)	16 (+3)	15 (+2)	15 (+2)
Constitution	18 (+4)	12 (+1)	12 (+1)	10 (+0)	16 (+3)	13 (+1)
Intelligence	7 (-2)	12 (+1)	13 (+1)	14 (+2)	11 (+0)	12 (+1)
Wisdom	8 (-1)	9 (-1)	17 (+3)	16 (+3)	12 (+1)	16 (+3)
Charisma	9 (-1)	18 (+4)	15 (+2)	12 (+1)	7 (-2)	12 (+1)
Skills	Athletics +5	Acrobatics +4	History +3	Medicine +5	Acrobatics +4	Acrobatics +4
	Nature +0	Deception +6	Insight +5	Nature +4	Animal Handling +3	Medicine +5
	Perception +1	Investigation +3	Religion +3	Religion +4	Perception +3	Religion +3
	Survival +1	Perception +1	Perception +5	Survival +5	Survival +3	Stealth +4
		Performance +6	Persuasion +4			
		Persuasion +6				
		Stealth +4				
Armor	Unarmored Defense	Leather	Half Plate	Leather	Half Plate	Unarmored Defense
			Shield	Wood Shield		
Weapons	Greataxe	Rapier	Mace	Scimitar	Longsword	Quarterstaff
	Longbow	Shortbow	Sling	Sling	Shortsword	Javelin
	Dagger	Dagger			Heavy Cross-bow	Unarmed Strike
Backpack	A	B	D	D	A	D

Name	Sir Glendor the Fourth	Krago of the Mountains	Estra Zo	Trebbelos	The Mystical One	Lappoy the Unexpected
Sex	Male	Male	Female	Male	Female	Male
Race	Human	Mountain Dwarf	Forest Gnome	Tiefling	Human	High Elf
Level (HD)	1 (d10)	1 (d10)	1 (d8)	1 (d6)	1 (d8)	1 (d6)
Class	Paladin	Ranger	Rogue	Sorcerer	Warlock	Wizard
Background	Noble	Folk Hero	Urchin	Charlatan	Outlander	Sage
Alignment	LG	NG	CN	CG	CN	CG
AC	17	14	15	10	13	11
Initiative	+0	+2	+4	+0	+1	+1
Speed	30 ft.	25 ft.	25 ft.	30 ft.	30 ft.	30 ft.
Prof. Bonus	+2	+2	+2	+2	+2	+2
Hit Points	11	12	11	8	7	6
Strength	15 (+2)	15 (+2)	8 (-1)	10 (+0)	11 (+0)	12 (+1)
Dexterity	11 (+0)	15 (+2)	18 (+4)	11 (+0)	12 (+1)	12 (+1)
Constitution	13 (+1)	15 (+2)	16 (+3)	15 (+2)	8 (-1)	10 (+0)
Intelligence	10 (+0)	9 (-1)	12 (+1)	14 (+2)	12 (+1)	18 (+4)
Wisdom	14 (+2)	12 (+1)	11 (+0)	14 (+2)	17 (+3)	14 (+2)
Charisma	17 (+3)	11 (+0)	9 (-1)	17 (+3)	16 (+3)	11 (+0)
Skills	Athletics +4	Animal Handling +3	Acrobatics +6	Arcana +4	Arcana +3	Arcana +6
	History +2	Athletics +4	Insight +2	Deception +5	Athletics +2	History +6
	Medicine +4	Insight +3	Investigation +3	Intimidation +5	Deception +5	Investigation +6
	Persuasion +5	Perception +3	Perception +2	Sleight of Hand +2	Survival +5	Medicine +4
		Survival +3	Sleight of Hand +6			Perception +4
			Stealth +6			
Armor	Half Plate	Studded Leather	Leather	None	Studded Leather	None
	Shield					
Weapons	Longsword	Battleaxe	Shortsword	Quarterstaff	Spear	Longsword
	Flail	Handaxe	Shortsword	Light Crossbow	Shortbow	Shortbow
	Dagger	Blowgun	Shortbow		Dagger	
Backpack	A	A	B	C	C	C

AVAILABILITY OF NONPLAYER CHARACTERS

The number of NPCs available to a party of player characters is determined by consulting the table below, and by appropriate dice rolls as noted. The number of NPCs available depends upon the number of player characters in the party—the more player characters participating, the fewer NPCs available.

# of PCs	Chance of NPCs & # Available
2	100% chance of 1-4
3	75% chance of 1-3
4	50% chance of 1-2
5	25% chance of 1
6 or more	None

Once a party has determined that NPC(s) are willing to join their adventuring group (dependent upon the financial arrangements being finalized), the DM can randomly determine each NPC available (by rolling 1d12), or simply choosing one from the tables. Before play begins, be sure to outfit these NPCs with the listed armor, weapons, and backpack (see sidebar).

Nonplayer characters will carry no wealth other than 1d6 gold pieces for incidental expenses. In most cases, they carry their own weapons and/or armor as listed above. However, player characters may purchase additional equipment, arms, or armor for them to use while adventuring, either as a loan or an outright gift. These gifts can go a long way to earn the trust and loyalty of these NPCs.

Nonplayer characters may vary widely in personality. The DM plays their part to a great degree, although the players indicate what instructions or orders they are giving to the NPCs during the course of the adventure. The DM can choose any personality for an NPC, or select personality, ideals, bonds, and flaws from the Player's Handbook, or determine the various aspects by rolling for the categories of attitude, disposition, courage, and loyalty on the following tables. Players are never informed of the exact personalities of NPCs. It is up to them to discover their traits through interaction with the characters (as portrayed by the DM) and by observing them in the course of the adventure.

Alternatively, the DM can assign personality traits, ideals, bonds, and flaws to these NPCs to round out their personality and disposition. See chapter 4 in the Player's Handbook for more details.

NPC PERSONALITY

D6	Attitude
1	Helpful/cooperative
2	Helpful/cooperative
3	Helpful/cooperative
4	Apathetic/lazy
5	Unreliable
6	Obstinate/argumentative/domineering

D6	Disposition
1	Greedy/selfish
2	Normal
3	Normal
4	Normal
5	Normal
6	Unselfish

D6	Courage
1	Reckless/daring
2	Courageous
3	Normal
4	Normal
5	Hesitant
6	Cowardly

D6	Loyalty
1	Loyal
2	Loyal
3	Normal
4	Normal
5	Fickle
6	Fickle

BACKPACKS

The NPC tables and the pre-generated player characters list one of four backpacks (A, B, C or D). These are stocked equipment packs suitable for a type of character class. To speed preparation for play, instead of buying equipment, assign one of these packs to each player character or NPC as appropriate. If used for player characters, allow them an opportunity to swap out some equipment or even purchase a few items to round out adventuring gear.

Backpack A Barbarians, Fighters, Paladins, Rangers	Backpack B Bards, Rogues	Backpack C Sorcerers, Warlocks, Wizards	Backpack D Clerics, Druids, Monks
Hammer w/ 10 pitons	Candles (5)	Ink w/ 3 quills	Candles (10)
Torches (10)	Crowbar	Parchment (10 sheets)	Tinderbox
Tinderbox	Lantern w/ 3 oil flasks	Book (blank)	Blankets (2)
Rations (10 days)	Rations (5 days)	Glass bottles (2)	Bedroll
Waterskin (full)	Tinderbox	Candles (10)	Holy water (2 flasks)
Hempen rope (50 ft.)	Waterskin (full)	Tinderbox	Holy symbol / druidic focus
Bedroll	Chalk (4 pieces)	Mirror	Prayer book
Iron spikes (10)	Average lock w/ key	Component pouch	Waterskin (full)
Whetstone	Caltrops (20)	Arcane focus	Incense (4 blocks)
Sacks (2)	Bedroll	Rations (5 days)	Pouches (3)
Pouches (2)	Silk rope (50 ft.)	Bedroll	Rations (5 days)
Fishing tackle	Sacks (2)	Blanket	
		Waterskin (full)	
		Spellbook (Wizards)	

APPENDIX D
Cover and Map Gallery

In these last few pages, we present a full color gallery. Here are the original covers to B1 and B2, some of the most popular adventure modules TSR ever published. The authors are sure these images will bring back many fond memories to you fine readers! We have also included scans of the maps in their original shade of "TSR blue." On the pages that follow, you will find the covers of the second and sixth printings of B1: In Search of the Unknown, and the covers of the second and fourth printings of B2: The Keep on the Borderlands.

What is it like to work on a legend? Gary Gygax and Mike Carr made this book possible, but Chris Doyle and Tim Wadzinski actually made it happen. Chris (left) and Tim (right) are shown here at Gen Con 50 (August 2017 in Indianapolis, IN) at the What's New With Goodman Games seminar, where the cover art to this book was first announced. As you reach these final pages in the book, dear reader, we thank you for making this project possible. It's an honor to be able to continue to expand on the fundamental building blocks of the hobby originally established by Mr. Gygax and company!

DUNGEONS & DRAGONS®

Dungeon Module B1
In Search of the Unknown

by Mike Carr

This package (a cover folder with maps and descriptive booklet within) forms a complete module for use with BASIC DUNGEONS & DRAGONS®. It is especially designed as an instructional aid for beginning Dungeon Masters and players, specifically created to enable new Dungeon Masters to initiate play with a minimum of preparation. With only minor modifications, this module is also eminently suitable for use with ADVANCED DUNGEONS & DRAGONS® as well.

In addition to descriptive and situational material, this module also includes special informational sections giving: background history and legends, listings of possible monsters and treasures and how to place them, a list of adventuring characters, tips on various aspects of play for the Dungeon Master, and helpful advice for starting players.

If you enjoy this module, look for more releases in the D & D® family from TSR, The Game Wizards!

© 1979, TSR Games

TSR Games
POB 756
Lake Geneva, WI 53147

Special Instructional Module

9023

This item is only one of the many popular aids for DUNGEONS & DRAGONS® produced by TSR Hobbies, Inc. Other D & D accessory items currently available include:

Dungeon Geomorphs, Set One (Basic Dungeon)

Dungeon Geomorphs, Set Two (Caves & Caverns)

Dungeon Geomorphs, Set Three (Lower Dungeon)

Outdoor Geomorphs, Set One (Walled City)

Monster & Treasure Assortment, Set One (Levels One to Three)

Monster & Treasure Assortment, Set Two (Levels Four to Six)

Monster & Treasure Assortment, Set Three (Levels Seven to Nine)

D & D Character Record Sheets Pad

Dungeon Module B1 (In Search of the Unknown)

The entire selection of this series of Dungeon Modules for ADVANCED DUNGEONS & DRAGONS® is comprised of the following items:

Dungeon Module G1 (Steading of the Hill Giant Chief)

Dungeon Module G2 (Glacial Rift of the Frost Giant Jarl)

Dungeon Module G3 (Hall of the Fire Giant King)

Dungeon Module D1 (Descent into the Depths of the Earth)

Dungeon Module D2 (Shrine of the Kuo-Toa)

Dungeon Module D3 (Vault of the Drow)

Dungeon Module S1 (Tomb of Horrors)

Other releases of additional items relating to D & D are planned for the future.

TSR Hobbies publishes a complete line of fantasy, science fiction, and historical games and rules. A complete catalog on the entire selection of TSR items is available for $2.00 from TSR Hobbies, POB 756, Lake Geneva, WI 53147.

Dungeon Module B1
In Search of the Unknown
by Mike Carr

INTRODUCTORY MODULE FOR CHARACTER LEVELS 1-3

This package (a cover folder with maps and descriptive booklet within) forms a complete module for use with DUNGEONS & DRAGONS Basic Set. It is especially designed as an instructional aid for beginning Dungeon Masters and players, especially created to enable new Dungeon Masters to initiate play with a minimum of preparation.

In addition to descriptive and situational material, this module also includes special informational sections giving: background history and legends, listings of possible monsters and treasures and how to place them, a list of adventuring characters, tips on various aspects of play for the Dungeon Master, and helpful advice for starting players.

If you enjoy this module, look for more releases in the D&D family from TSR, The Game Wizards.

DUNGEONS & DRAGONS and D&D are registered trademarks owned by TSR Hobbies Inc.

Special
Instructional
Module

©1979, 1981 TSR Hobbies, Inc.
All Rights Reserved

TSR HOBBIES, INC.
POB 756
LAKE GENEVA, WI 53147

9023

This item is only one of the many popular playing aids for DUNGEONS & DRAGONS Fantasy Adventure Game produced by TSR Hobbies, Inc. Other playing aids for the D&D game system currently include:

> DUNGEONS & DRAGONS Basic Set (contains everything DMs and players need to get started, detailing char-
> acter creation, spells, and dungeon levels 1-3)

> DUNGEONS & DRAGONS Expert Set (designed to be used *with* the Basic Set, the Expert Set covers higher-level
> characters, deeper dungeon levels, and adventure in wilderness areas)

> Dungeon Module B1 (In search of the Unknown)

> Dungeon Module B2 (The Keep on the Boarderlands)

> Dungeon Module X1 (the Isle of Dread)

> Monster and Treasure Assortment, Sets One to Three: Levels One through Nine (makes the job of stocking dun-
> geon levels easy)

> Dungeon Geomorphs (allows the DM to create thousands of different dungeon levels by arranging the geo-
> morphs in different combinations)

> D&D Player Character Record Sheets (allows players to record all important information about their
> characters in an easy-to-use format)

Other releases of additional items relating to the D&D game system are planned for the future. TSR Hobbies publishes
a complete line of games, playing aids, and gaming accessories available from better hobby, game, and department
stores nationwide. If you desire a complete catalog write to: TSR Hobbies, Inc., POB 756, Lake Geneva, WI 53147.

116-F-9023

ISBN 0-935696-04-0

394-51572-2TSR0550

Dungeon Module B2
The Keep on the Borderlands

by Gary Gygax

INTRODUCTORY MODULE FOR CHARACTER LEVELS 1-3

This module includes a cover folder with maps and a complete description booklet to form a ready-made scenario for BASIC DUNGEON & DRAGONS®. It has been specially designed for use by beginning Dungeon Masters so that they may begin play with a minimum of preparations.

Within are many features to aid novice players and Dungeon Masters: legends, history and background information, a list of adventuring characters, tips on how to be an effective Dungeon Master, plus an interesting area for characters to base themselves in (the Keep) before setting out to explore the Caves of Chaos!

If you enjoy this module, look for more releases in the D&D® family from TSR, The Game Wizards.

© 1980 by TSR Hobbies, Inc.

TSR Hobbies, Inc.
POB 756
LAKE GENEVA, WI 53147

PRINTED IN U.S.A.

Special
Instructional
Module

9034

This item is only one of the many popular playing aids for DUNGEONS & DRAGONS produced by TSR Hobbies, Inc. Other playing aids for D&D currently available include:

Dungeon Module B1 (In Search of the Unknown), another beginning instructional module

Dungeon Geomorphs , Set One (Basic Dungeon)
Dungeon Geomorphs , Set Two (Caves & Caverns)
Dungeon Geomorphs , Set One (Lower Dungeon)

Outdoor Geomorphs, Set One (Walled City)

Monster & Treasure Assortment, Set One (Levels One to Three)
Monster & Treasure Assortment, Set Two (Levels Four to Six)
Monster & Treasure Assortment, Set Three (Levels Seven to Nine)

TSR also publishes the ADVANCED DUNGEONS & DRAGONS family of games and playing aids:

Players Handbook (everything the AD&D player needs to know)
Dungeon Masters Guide (essential reference work for DMs)
Monster Manual (over 350 monsters, profusely illustrated)

The World of Greyhawk (fantasy world setting approved for use with AD&D)

AD&D Dungeon Masters Screen (combat and saving throws reference)
Rogues Gallery (100's of pre-rolled chracters for AD&D)

AD&D Player Character Sheets
AD&D Permanent Character Folder and Adventure Record Sheets
AD&D Non-Player Character Sheets

Dungeon Module G1 (Steading of the Hill Giant Chief)
Dungeon Module G2 (Glacial Rift of the Frost Giant Jarl)
Dungeon Module G3 (Hall of the Fire Giant King)
Dungeon Module D1 (Descent into the Depths of the Earth)
Dungeon Module D2 (Shrine of the Kuo-Toa)
Dungeon Module D3 (Vault of the Drow)

Dungeon Module S1 (Tomb of Horrors)
Dungeon Module S2 (White Plume Mountain)
Dungeon Module S3 (Expedition to the Barrier Peaks)

Dungeon Module T1 (Village of Hommlet)
Dungeon Module C1 (Hidden Shrine of Tamoachan)

Other releases of additional items relating to D&D are planned for the future. TSR Hobbies pub-lishes a complete line of fantasy, science fiction and historical games and rules which are available from better hobby, game, and department stores nationwide. If you desire a complete catalog, write to: TSR Hobbies, POB 756 Lake Geneva, WI 53147.

ISBN 0-935696-47-4

Dungeon Module B2
The Keep on the Borderlands

by Gary Gygax

INTRODUCTORY MODULE FOR CHARACTER LEVELS 1-3

This module includes a cover folder with maps and a complete description booklet to form a ready-made scenario for DUNGEONS & DRAGONS® Basic Set. It has been specially designed for use by beginning Dungeon Masters so that they may begin play with a minimum of preperations.

Within are many features to aid novice players and Dungeon Masters: legends, history and background information, a list of adventuring characters, tips on how to be an effective Dungeon Master, plus and interesting area for characters to base themselves in (the Keep) before setting out to explore the Caves of Chaos!

If you enjoy this module, look for more releases in the D&D® family from TSR, the Game Wizards.

TSR Hobbies, Inc.
POB 756
LAKE GENEVA, WI 53147

PRINTED IN U.S.A.

Special
Instructional
Module

9034

This item is only one of the many popular playing aids for **DUNGEONS & DRAGONS** Fantasy Adventure Game produced by TSR Hobbies, Inc. Other playing aids currently available for use with the D&D games system include:

Dungeon Module B1 (In Search of the Unknown)
Dungeon Module B2 (The Keep on the Borderlands)

Dungeon Module X1 (The Isle of Dread)
**Monster and Treasure Assortment, Set One to Three: Levels One through Nine (makes the job of stocking dungeon
   levels easy)**

**Dungeon Geomorphs (allows the DM to create thousands of different dungeon levels by arranging them in different
   combinations)**

**D&D Player Character Record Sheets (allows players to record all important information about their characters in
   an easy-to-use format)**

Other releases of additional items relateing to D&D Adventure Games are planned for the future. TSR Hobbies publishes a complete line of fantasy and science fiction games and rules which are available from better hobby, game, and department stores nationwide. If you desire a complete catalog,write to: TSR Hobbies, Inc., POB 756 Lake Geneva, WI 53147.

ISBN 0-935696-47-4

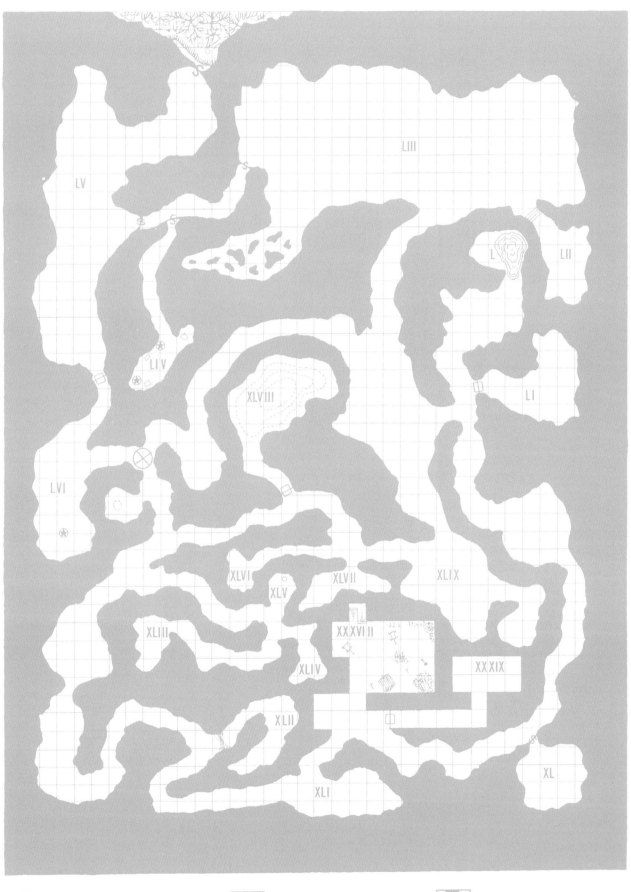

POOL

DEPRESSION

WEBS

DOOR

SECRET DOOR

FALSE DOOR

STAIRS, UP

STAIRS, DOWN

STATUE

PITS, COVERED

ENTRANCE

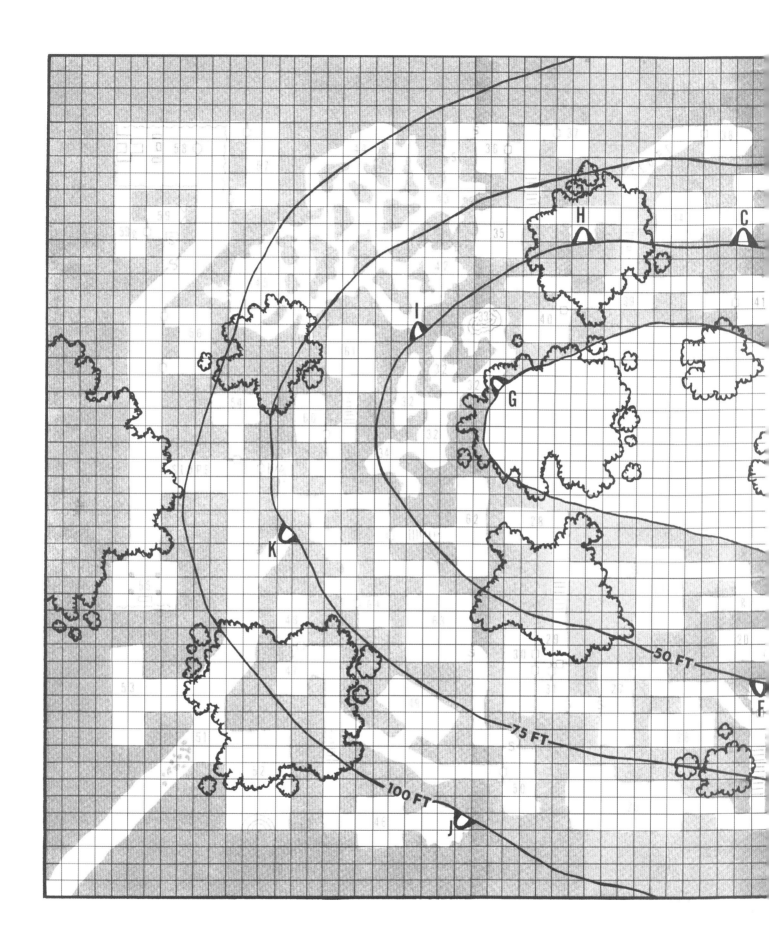

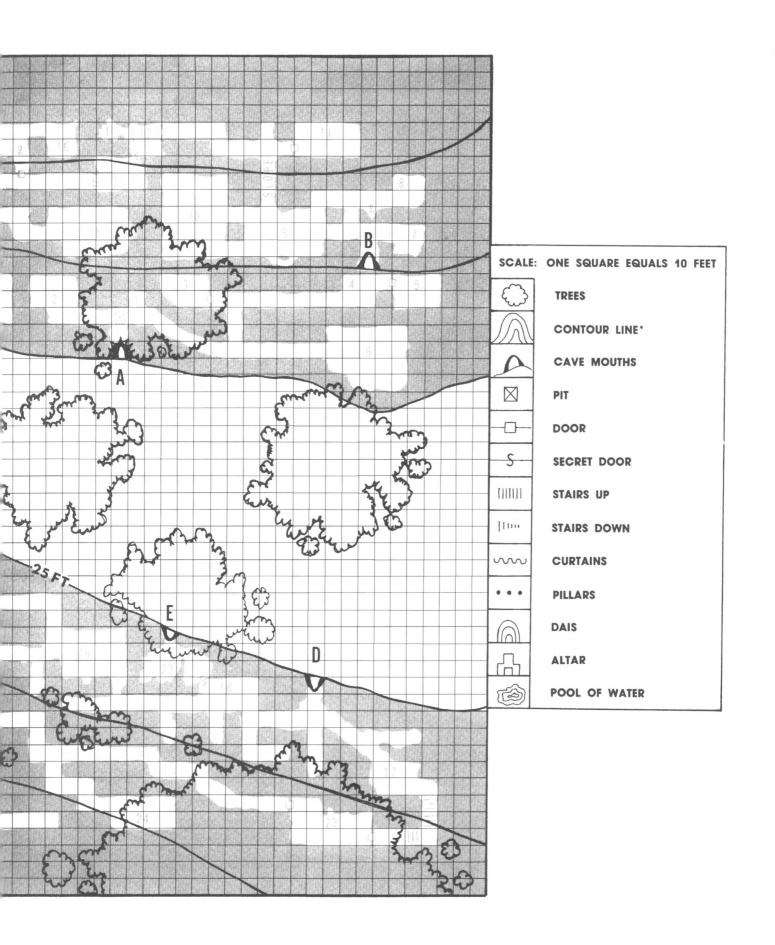

SCALE: ONE SQUARE EQUALS 10 FEET

	TREES
	CONTOUR LINE*
	CAVE MOUTHS
	PIT
	DOOR
S	SECRET DOOR
	STAIRS UP
	STAIRS DOWN
	CURTAINS
• • •	PILLARS
	DAIS
	ALTAR
	POOL OF WATER

25 FT

FIFTH EDITION FANTASY

Stand-alone, world-neutral adventure modules compatible with 5E. All print editions also include a code for free PDF edition. Look for them at your local game store or www.goodman-games.com!

FEF #4: War-Lock
Level 5 adventure

FEF #5: Into the Dragon's Maw
Level 12 adventure

FEF #6: Raiders of the Lost Oasis
Level 4 adventure

FEF #10: The Castle in the Sky
Level 5 adventure

FEF #11: The Archmage's Lost Hideaway
Level 7 adventure

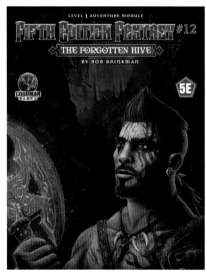

FEF #12: The Forgotten Hive
Level 1 adventure

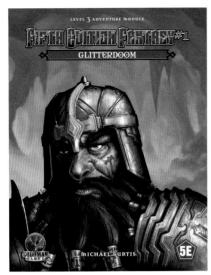

FEF #1: Glitterdoom
Level 3 adventure

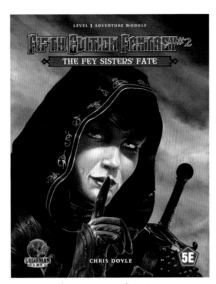

FEF #2: The Fey Sister's Fate
Level 1 adventure

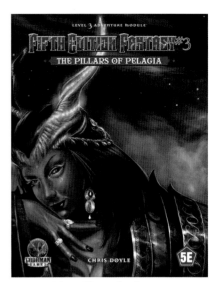

FEF #3: The Pillars of Pelagia
Level 3 adventure

FEF #7: Fantasy Encounters
A collection of short encounters

FEF #8: Eye of the Leviathan
Level 8 adventure

FEF #9: The Fallen Temple
Level 10 adventure

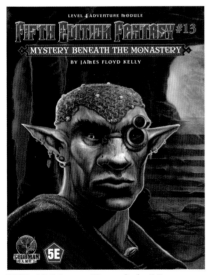

FEF #13: Mystery Beneath the Monastery
Level 4 adventure

www.goodman-games.com